821.808 Oxford

The Oxford book of
Victorian verse /
[1922?]

W9-DGP-295

3 1192 00123 6148

JAN 1 8 1982

APR 20 1986

DEC 1 4 1987

FEB 2 7 1988

EVANSTON PUBLIC LIBRARY
Evanston, Illinois
Each reader is responsible for all
books or other materials taken on his
card, and for any fines or fees charged
for overdues, damages, or loss.

The
Oxford Book
Of Victorian Verse

Oxford University Press, Ely House, London W. 1

GLASGOW NEW YORK TORONTO MELBOURNE WELLINGTON
CAPE TOWN SALISBURY IBADAN NAIROBI LUSAKA ADDIS ABABA
BOMBAY CALCUTTA MADRAS KARACHI LAHORE DACCA
KUALA LUMPUR HONG KONG TOKYO

FIRST PUBLISHED 1912
REPRINTED 1913, 1917, 1919, 1923
1924, 1935, 1948, 1955, 1962, 1965, 1968

The
Oxford Book
Of Victorian Verse

Chosen by

Arthur Quiller-Couch

821.08
Ox2v
cap.4

Oxford

At the Clarendon Press

EVANSTON PUBLIC LIBRARY
1703 ORRINGTON AVENUE
EVANSTON, ILLINOIS 60201

Bt1092840

The
Of Victorian Verse

PRINTED IN GREAT BRITAIN

TO

MY FUTURE FRIENDS AND PUPILS

AT

CAMBRIDGE

THIS PROPITIATORY WREATH

TO

MY FUTURE FRIENDS AND PUPILS

AT

CAMBRIDGE

THIS PROPITIATORY WREATH

PREFACE

TWELVE years ago when editing *The Oxford Book of English Verse*—to which the public has been kind beyond expectation—I was forced by exigencies of space to cut out many modern lyrics. The Delegates of the University Press now give me opportunity to make amends to conscience by repairing these omissions, and to include a number of beautiful poems written since 1900.

Within new limits I have followed my old rule of choosing what seems to me the best, and for that sole reason. It had been possible—indeed easy—to rule out all lyrics printed in the earlier selection and yet make a portly, presentable volume of Victorian Verse ; and some advisers have urged on me that the anthologist does his best service in recapturing fugitive, half-forgotten poems—frail things that by one chance or another cheated of their day have passed down to Limbo. I dare say he does ; and admit that in these hundred years innumerable poems have deserved better than fate allowed. Yet the most of them (I think) will be found on examination to miss being first-rate—

Nec vero hae sine sorte datae, sine judice, sedes.

At all events they must await another rescuer. The reader will allow me to pursue my old rule to the end ; and when he re-greets in this volume many a poem that adorned the former one, he will understand that by excluding these I should have condemned myself to anthologizing the second-rate and clearing the ground for an *Oxford Book of the Worst Poetry*—which, by the way, might be a not unentertaining work.

Of the difficulties that waylay a Victorian anthologist two are obvious. Where is he to begin ?—Where to end ? The first has proved less formidable than it looked, and the second scarcely formidable at all. Though Wordsworth happened to be the first Laureate of Queen Victoria's reign, no one will argue that he belongs to it. His valediction to the older bards, his glorious contemporaries, in his lines ' On the Death of James Hogg ' (written late in 1835), contained his own *Nunc dimittis*—

> Like clouds that rake the mountain-summits,
>   Or waves that own no curbing hand,
> How fast has brother followed brother
>   From sunshine to the sunless land !
>
> Yet I, whose lids from infant slumber
>   Were earliest raised, remain to hear
> A timid voice that asks in whispers—
>   ' Who next will drop and disappear ? '

Just there, with the breaking of that voice, comes the interval ; but with Landor left to launch us on a wave from the true deeps, which do not fail—' Tanagra ! think not I forget . . .' For the close : as we reckon Drummond of Hawthornden, Herrick, even Shirley, among the Elizabethans, and choose to forget how much of Shakespeare's best or of Ben Jonson's is later than Elizabeth, so I have thought it no insult to include any English poet, born in our time, under the great name 'Victorian'; a title the present misprision of which will no less surely go its way as a flippancy of fashion than it will be succeeded by fresh illustration of the habit, constant in fallen Man, of belittling his contemporaries in particular and the age next before his own in the gross. For my part, after many months spent in close study of Victorian verse—re-reading old favourites and eagerly making acquaintance with much that was new to me—I rise from the task in reverence and wonder not only at the mass (not easily sized) of poetry written with ardour in these less-than-a-hundred years, but at the amount of it which is excellent, and the height of some of that excellence; in some exultation too, as I step aside and—drawing difficult breath!—gaze after the stream of young runners with their torches.

All this is not to deny or extenuate the real difficulty of my task, which is less of a difficulty than an impossibility: since he who attempts on his contemporaries such assaying as these pages imply, attempts what no man can do. Yes, the business is not only laborious—as the late Mr. Palgrave confessed that his second *Golden Treasury* had cost him thrice the labour of his first, the most famous anthology in our language: it cannot be done. Yet it is so well worth doing !

> To find out what you cannot do,
> And then to go and do it;
> There lies the golden rule—

and there (if the reader will forgive the levity) lies a great part of the fun. My one doubt is that the attempt ought not to have taken for shield in this second book the name of a University which has ever with such lovely rightness chosen to await and teach perfection, ignoring clamours of the moment and the market. Yet, and though the judgements in this book be superseded, the pains spent on them may help to clear the ground and advance by so much the business of criticism, if not of poetry : and to that extent may be subsidiary to the great service Oxford is ever performing.

I must tender my thanks to all (a portentous list) who have helped me in various ways, and especially with permission to use copyright poems : to the Poet Laureate Mr. Alfred Austin, Mr. Lascelles Abercrombie, Mr. Percy Addleshaw, Mr. Douglas Ainslie, the Hon. Maurice Baring, Miss Barlow, Mr. George Barlow, the Dean of Norwich (H. C. Beeching), Mr. Hilaire Belloc, Mr. A. C. Benson, Mr. Laurence Binyon, Mr. Wilfrid Blunt, Mr. Gordon Bottomley, Mr. F. W. Bourdillon, Mr. Robert Bridges, Mr. Rupert Brooke ; to the Marquess of Crewe for a poem by the late Lord Houghton and one of his own ; to the Rev. A. S. Cripps, Mr. Francis Coutts, Mrs. Frances Cornford, Mr. Bliss Carman, Mr. Walter Crane, Lord Alfred Douglas, Professor Dowden, Mme Duclaux, Mr. William H. Davies, Mr. Austin Dobson, Mr. John Drinkwater, Miss M. Betham Edwards, ' Michael Field ', Mr. J. E. Flecker,

Miss Alice Furlong, Mr. Norman Gale, Mr. W. W. Gibson, Miss Louise Imogen Guiney, Mr. Edmund Gosse, Mr. Charles Granville, Mr. Thomas Hardy O.M., Mr. Maurice Hewlett, Mrs. Katharine Tynan Hinkson, Miss Emily Hickey, Mr. George Hookham (for a poem hitherto unpublished), Mr. Laurence Housman, Mr. W. D. Howells, 'Hugh Haliburton' (Mr. James Logie Robertson), Mr. James Joyce, Mr. Rudyard Kipling, Mr. Richard Le Gallienne, Mr. S. R. Lysaght; to the Hon. Emily Lawless, Mrs. Meynell (and again to her and to Mr. Wilfrid Meynell for the free selection made from the poems of Francis Thompson); to Sir Theophile Marzials, Miss Annie Matheson, Mr. John Masefield, Mr. Walter De La Mare, Mr. Compton Mackenzie, Mr. Harold Monro, Mr. T. Sturge Moore, Mr. Neil Munro, Mr. Ernest Myers (for himself and for his late brother, F. W. H. Myers); to Mr. Henry Newbolt (for his own poems published by Mr. John Murray, and, with Mr. Elkin Mathews, for several by the late Miss Mary Coleridge), Mr. Alfred Noyes, Miss Moira O'Neill, Sir Gilbert Parker, Mr. John Payne, Mr. J. S. Phillimore, Mr. Stephen Phillips, Mr. Eden Phillpotts, Mr. Walter Herries Pollock, Mr. Ezra Pound, Sir James Rennell Rodd, Canon Rawnsley, Mr. Ernest Radford, Mr. Ernest Rhys, Mr. T. W. Rolleston, Mr. G. W. Russell ('A. E.'), the Lady Margaret Sackville, Mr. George Santayana, Mrs. Clement Shorter (Dora Sigerson Shorter), Miss Elinor Sweetman, Mr. Douglas Sladen, Mr. Arthur Symons, Mrs. Rachel

Annand Taylor, Dr. Todhunter, Mr. Herbert Trench, Mr. Edward William Thompson, Mr. Wilfrid Thorley, Mr. William Watson, Mrs. Woods, Mr. Samuel Waddington, Dr. T. H. Warren, and Mr. W. B. Yeats; to Mrs. Allingham, to Mrs. Coventry Patmore, Mrs. Eugene Lee-Hamilton, Mrs. Cosmo Monkhouse; to Mr. Marriott Watson for the poems of Rosamund Marriott Watson; to the Lady Betty Balfour (for the late Earl of Lytton's), the Lady Victoria Buxton (for the Hon. Roden Noel's), Lady Leighton-Warren (for Lord de Tabley's), to Lord Rosslyn, to Miss Alexander, daughter of the late Archbishop of Armagh; to Mr. Stephen De Vere for those of Mr. Aubrey De Vere; to Miss Boyd of Penkill Castle for William Bell Scott's famous ballad; to Miss Harriett Jay for Robert Buchanan's poems, and to Mr. O. Locker-Lampson, M.P., for two by the late Frederick Locker-Lampson; to the families or executors of the late A. G. Butler, Lady Currie, Sir Lewis Morris, Sir Alfred Lyall (Lady Miller; Messrs. George Routledge & Sons consenting), George Meredith, Dr. George MacDonald, John Davidson, William Philpot, Walter C. Smith, George du Maurier, Oliver Madox Brown, Philip Bourke Marston, W. E. Henley, Robert Louis Stevenson, F. T. Palgrave, Father Hopkins, Henry Cust, Andrew Lang, E. C. Lefroy, William Sharp, John Addington Symonds (Mr. Horatio Brown), Amy Levy (Miss Clementina Black), Mathilde Blind (Mrs. Mond), H. D. Lowry, John M. Synge.

Last and by no means least in this section come the

names of Mr. Theodore Watts-Dunton and Mr. S. C. Cockerell, who have most handsomely given me *carte blanche* in dealing with Swinburne and Morris. These favours have been inestimable, and Mr. Watts-Dunton has added to his kindness by suffering me to anthologize his own poems.

My obligations to various publishers are almost too many to be recounted. I must thank Messrs. George Allen & Sons for the extracts from Ruskin and the author of *Ionica*; Messrs. George Bell & Sons for those from Thomas Ashe; Messrs. Blackwood & Sons for a poem by George Eliot, and for confirming permissions given by Mr. Neil Munro and Miss Moira O'Neill; Mr. Bertram Dobell for James Thomson, and Mr. David Nutt for W. E. Henley; Messrs. Chapman & Hall for much help, and specially for a poem by Herman Merivale. Messrs. Chatto & Windus have shown me unwearied kindness: they are the publishers of the poems by Swinburne, O'Shaughnessy, MacDonald, Bret Harte, the bulk of those by Stevenson, and others included in this volume. Messrs. Constable & Co. have confirmed the kindness of George Meredith's executors. To Messrs. Ellis & Elvey I owe the extracts from D. G. Rossetti; to Mr. A. C. Fifield those from Mr. W. H. Davies; to Messrs. Kegan Paul, Trench, Trübner & Co. those from Sir Edwin Arnold and Sir Lewis Morris; to Mr. John Murray for confirming Lord Crewe's permission; to the Walter Scott Publishing Company those from Joseph Skipsey. Messrs. Longmans, Green & Co. have allowed me to include Jean Ingelow and Andrew Lang; and Messrs. Macmillan & Co.'s

favours would alone make a long list. It includes the late
Lord Tennyson's ' Crossing the Bar ' (leave confirmed by
the present Lord Tennyson), and poems by Aubrey De
Vere, T. E. Brown, Christina Rossetti. Other poems by
Miss Rossetti are inserted by leave of the Society for Pro-
moting Christian Knowledge. Messrs. Macmillan again are
publishers of poems by Rudyard Kipling, Ernest Dowson,
Richard Garnett, and S. R. Lysaght. For the bulk of
Mr. Kipling's poems my obligation is to Messrs. Methuen
& Co., as for a lyric by Oscar Wilde, Stevenson's Alcaics,
and much friendly help given. Messrs. James MacLehose
& Sons grant me a poem by the late Dr. Smith ; Messrs.
George Routledge & Sons two by the late Lady Currie ;
Mr. Fisher Unwin has allowed me to use copyright poems
by the late Richard Middleton, Mathilde Blind, Amy
Levy, and has other claims on my gratitude. Messrs.
Smith, Elder & Co. have allowed me to print Browning's
Epilogue from *Asolando*. To Messrs. Maunsel & Co.,
Dublin, I owe leave to include poems by John M.
Synge and James Stephens ; to Messrs. Houghton,
Mifflin & Co. leave to include poems by Longfellow,
Whittier, Lowell, Bret Harte, T. B. Aldrich, and Julia
Ward Howe ; and some kind permissions have been
given by Messrs. Charles Scribner's Sons.

My especial helpers among publishers of recent verse
have been Mr. Elkin Mathews and Mr. John Lane ;
who—at first in conjunction, of late years separately—
have done so much to keep alive the fire of poetry in
England. The list of younger poets whose work bears

PREFACE

the imprint of one or another of these two would unduly swell this already plethoric preface. (They include such gifts as the poems of W. B. Rands, Lionel Johnson, Mary Coleridge, and Lascelles Abercrombie.) All readers of this book are their debtors and I am their most obliged one.

I must beg forgiveness of any one whose rights I have overlooked, and of a few whom, with the best will in the world and after repeated efforts, I have been unable to trace.

It has been a great pleasure to discuss this book in the making with friends; notably with Mr. Kenneth Grahame, Mr. George Hookham, and two whom I cannot name because of their near connexion with the Clarendon Press. But there are two others who have a peculiar share in any favour this not unlaborious task may earn among lovers of poetry—Mr. Bertram Dobell, veteran and prince of booksellers, and Sir Walter Raleigh, Professor of English Literature in the University whose name this book carries—once mine, and now to be exchanged (so fearfully, because of his example) for that other which once was his.

ARTHUR QUILLER-COUCH.

WALTER SAVAGE LANDOR

1.   Corinna, from Athens, to Tanagra

TANAGRA ! think not I forget
    Thy beautifully-storey'd streets ;
Be sure my memory bathes yet
    In clear Thermodon, and yet greets
The blythe and liberal shepherd boy,
Whose sunny bosom swells with joy
When we accept his matted rushes
Upheaved with sylvan fruit; away he bounds, and blushes.

I promise to bring back with me
    What thou with transport wilt receive,
The only proper gift for thee,
    Of which no mortal shall bereave
In later times thy mouldering walls,
Until the last old turret falls ;
A crown, a crown from Athens won,
A crown no god can wear, beside Latona's son.

There may be cities who refuse
    To their own child the honours due,
And look ungently on the Muse ;
    But ever shall those cities rue
The dry, unyielding, niggard breast,
Offering no nourishment, no rest,
    To that young head which soon shall rise
Disdainfully, in might and glory, to the skies.

Sweetly where cavern'd Dirce flows
    Do white-arm'd maidens chaunt my lay,
Flapping the while with laurel-rose
    The honey-gathering tribes away ;
And sweetly, sweetly, Attick tongues
Lisp your Corinna's early songs ;
To her with feet more graceful come
The verses that have dwelt in kindred breasts at home.

O let thy children lean aslant
    Against the tender mother's knee,
And gaze into her face, and want
    To know what magic there can be
In words that urge some eyes to dance,
While others as in holy trance
Look up to heaven ; be such my praise !
Why linger ? I must haste, or lose the Delphick bays.

2. *The Yacht*

THE vessel that rests here at last
    Had once stout ribs and topping mast,
And, whate'er wind there might prevail,
Was ready for a row or sail.
It now lies idle on its side,
Forgetful o'er the stream to glide.
And yet there have been days of yore,
When pretty maids their posies bore
To crown its prow, its deck to trim,
And freighted a whole world of whim.
A thousand stories it could tell,—
But it loves secrecy too well.—
Come closer, my sweet girl, pray do !
There may be still one left for you.

2

3.   *Ianthe*

IANTHE ! you are call'd to cross the sea !
        A path forbidden *me* !
Remember, while the Sun his blessing sheds
        Upon the mountain-heads,
How often we have watch'd him laying down
        His brow, and dropt our own
Against each other's, and how faint and short
        And sliding the support !
What will succeed it now ?   Mine is unblest,
        Ianthe ! nor will rest
But on the very thought that swells with pain.
        O bid me hope again !
O give me back what Earth, what (without you)
        Not Heaven itself can do—
One of the golden days that we have past ;
        And let it be my last !
Or else the gift would be, however sweet,
        Fragile and incomplete.

4.   *Her Name*

WELL I remember how you smiled
        To see me write your name upon
The soft sea-sand . . . ' *O, what a child !*
        You think you're writing upon stone ! '

I have since written what no tide
        Shall ever wash away ; what men
Unborn shall read o'er ocean wide
        And find Ianthe's name again.

3

5.   *The Gifts Return'd*

'YOU must give back,' her mother said,
    To a poor sobbing little maid,
'All the young man has given you,
Hard as it now may seem to do.'
  ''Tis done already, mother dear!'
Said the sweet girl, 'So, never fear.'
  Mother. Are you quite certain? Come, recount
(There was not much) the whole amount.
  Girl. The locket: the kid gloves.
  Mother.   Go on.
  Girl. Of the kid gloves I found but one.
  Mother. Never mind that. What else? Proceed.
You gave back all his trash?
  Girl.   Indeed.
  Mother. And was there nothing you would save?
  Girl. Everything I could give I gave.
  Mother. To the last tittle?
  Girl.   Even to that.
  Mother. Freely?
  Girl.   My heart went *pit-a-pat*
At giving up . . . ah me! ah me!
I cry so I can hardly see . . .
All the fond looks and words that past,
And all the kisses, to the last.

6.   *The Maid's Lament*

I LOVED him not; and yet now he is gone,
    I feel I am alone.
I check'd him while he spoke; yet, could he speak,
    Alas! I would not check.

4

For reasons not to love him once I sought,
    And wearied all my thought
To vex myself and him ; I now would give
    My love, could he but live
Who lately lived for me, and when he found
    'Twas vain, in holy ground
He hid his face amid the shades of death.
    I waste for him my breath
Who wasted his for me ; but mine returns,
    And this lorn bosom burns
With stifling heat, heaving it up in sleep,
    And waking me to weep
Tears that had melted his soft heart : for years
    Wept he as bitter tears.
' Merciful God ! ' such was his latest prayer,
    ' These may she never share ! '
Quieter is his breath, his breast more cold
    Than daisies in the mould,
Where children spell, athwart the churchyard gate,
    His name and life's brief date.
Pray for him, gentle souls, whoe'er you be,
    And, O, pray too for me !

7.   *The Dragon-fly*

LIFE (priest and poet say) is but a dream ;
    I wish no happier one than to be laid
      Beneath a cool syringa's scented shade,
Or wavy willow, by the running stream,
      Brimful of moral, where the dragon-fly,
      Wanders as careless and content as I.
Thanks for this fancy, insect king,
Of purple crest and filmy wing,

Who

Who with indifference givest up
The water-lily's golden cup,
To come again and overlook
What I am writing in my book.
Believe me, most who read the line
Will read with hornier eyes than thine ;
And yet their souls shall live for ever,
And thine drop dead into the river !
God pardon them, O insect king,
Who fancy so unjust a thing !

8.   *To Miss Arundell*

NATURE ! thou may'st fume and fret,
    There's but one white violet :
Scatter o'er the vernal ground
Faint resemblances around,
Nature ! I will tell thee yet
There's but one white violet.

9.   *Rose Aylmer*

AH, what avails the sceptred race !
    Ah, what the form divine !
What every virtue, every grace !
    Rose Aylmer, all were thine.

Rose Aylmer, whom these wakeful eyes
    May weep, but never see,
A night of memories and sighs
    I consecrate to thee.

10.   *On a Child*

CHILD of a day, thou knowest not
        The tears that overflow thine urn,
The gushing eyes that read thy lot,
        Nor, if thou knewest, couldst return !
And why the wish ! the pure and blest
        Watch like thy mother o'er thy sleep.
O peaceful night ! O envied rest !
        Thou wilt not ever see her weep.

11.   *To his Verse*

AWAY my verse ! and never fear,
        As men before such beauty do :
On you she will not look severe,
        She will not turn her eyes from you.
Some happier graces could I lend
        That in her memory you should live,
Some little blemishes might blend,
        For it would please her to forgive.

12.   *The Kiss*

THE maid I love ne'er thought of me
        Amid the scenes of gaiety ;
But when her heart or mine sank low,
Ah, then it was no longer so !
From the slant palm she rais'd her head,
And kiss'd the cheek whence youth had fled.
Angels ! some future day for this,
Give her as sweet and pure a kiss.

13.   *The Wall-flower*

THE place where soon I think to lie,
    In its old creviced nook hard-by
        Rears many a weed :
If parties bring you there, will you
Drop slily in a grain or two
        Of wall-flower seed ?

I shall not see it, and (too sure !)
I shall not ever hear that your
        Light step was there ;
But the rich odour some fine day
Will, what I cannot do, repay
        That little care.

14.   *On the Death of Southey*

NOT the last struggles of the Sun,
    Precipitated from his golden throne,
Hold darkling mortals in sublime suspense ;
    But the calm exod of a man
    Nearer, tho' far above, who ran
The race we run, when Heaven recalls him hence.

15.   *On his Own Death*

DEATH stands above me, whispering low
    I know not what into my ear :
Of his strange language all I know
    Is, there is not a word of fear.

8

16.   *His Epitaph*

LO! where the four mimosas blend their shade,
    In calm repose at last is Landor laid ;
For ere he slept he saw them planted here
    By her his soul had ever held most dear,
And he had lived enough when he had dried her tear.

17.   *Finis*

I STROVE with none, for none was worth my strife.
    Nature I loved and, next to Nature, Art :
I warm'd both hands before the fire of life ;
    It sinks, and I am ready to depart.

SAMUEL ROGERS

1763-1855

18.   *A Wish*

MINE be a cot beside the hill ;
    A bee-hive's hum shall soothe my ear ;
A willowy brook, that turns a mill,
    With many a fall shall linger near.

The swallow oft beneath my thatch
    Shall twitter from her clay-built nest ;
Oft shall the pilgrim lift the latch
    And share my meal, a welcome guest.

Around my ivied porch shall spring
    Each fragrant flower that drinks the dew ;
And Lucy at her wheel shall sing
    In russet gown and apron blue.

The village church among the trees,
    Where first our marriage vows were given,
With merry peals shall swell the breeze
    And point with taper spire to Heaven.

EBENEZER ELLIOT

1781-1849

19. *Plaint*

DARK, deep, and cold the current flows
    Unto the sea where no wind blows,
Seeking the land which no one knows.

O'er its sad gloom still comes and goes
The mingled wail of friends and foes,
Borne to the land which no one knows.

Why shrieks for help yon wretch, who goes
With millions, from a world of woes,
Unto the land which no one knows?

Though myriads go with him who goes,
Alone he goes where no wind blows,
Unto the land which no one knows.

For all must go where no wind blows,
And none can go for him who goes;
None, none return whence no one knows.

Yet why should he who shrieking goes
With millions, from a world of woes,
Reunion seek with it or those?

Alone with God, where no wind blows,
And Death, his shadow—doom'd, he goes:
That God is there the shadow shows.

O shoreless Deep, where no wind blows!
And thou, O Land which no one knows!
That God is All, His shadow shows.

WILLIAM STANLEY ROSCOE

1782-1841

20. *To Spring: On the Banks of the Cam*

O THOU that from the green vales of the West
Com'st in thy tender robes with bashful feet,
And to the gathering clouds
Liftest thy soft blue eye :

I woo thee, Spring !—tho' thy dishevell'd hair
In misty ringlets sweep thy snowy breast,
And thy young lips deplore
Stern Boreas' ruthless rage :

While morn is steep'd in dews, and the dank show'r
Drops from the green boughs of the budding trees ;
And the thrush tunes his song
Warbling with unripe throat :

Thro' the deep wood where spreads the sylvan oak
I follow thee, and see thy hands unfold
The love-sick primrose pale
And moist-eyed violet :

While in the central grove, at thy soft voice,
The Dryads start forth from their wintry cells,
And from their oozy waves
The Naiads lift their heads

In sedgy bonnets trimm'd with rushy leaves
And water-blossoms from the forest stream,
To pay their vows to thee,
Their thrice adorèd queen !

11   The

WILLIAM STANLEY ROSCOE

The stripling shepherd wand'ring thro' the wood
Startles the linnet from her downy nest,
Or wreathes his crook with flowers,
The sweetest of the fields.

From the grey branches of the ivied ash
The stock-dove pours her vernal elegy,
While further down the vale
Echoes the cuckoo's note.

Beneath this trellis'd arbour's antique roof,
When the wild laurel rustles in the breeze,
By Cam's slow murmuring stream
I waste the live-long day;

And bid thee, Spring, rule fair the infant year,
Till my loved Maid in russet stole approach:
O yield her to my arms,
Her red lips breathing love!

So shall the sweet May drink thy falling tears,
And on thy blue eyes pour a beam of joy;
And float thy azure locks
Upon the western wind.

So shall the nightingale rejoice thy woods,
And Hesper early light his dewy star;
And oft at eventide
Beneath the rising moon,

May lovers' whispers soothe thy list'ning ear,
And as they steal the soft impassion'd kiss,
Confess thy genial reign,
O love-inspiring Spring!

1784–1859

21. *The Nun*

IF you become a nun, dear,
    A friar I will be;
In any cell you run, dear,
    Pray look behind for me.
The roses all turn pale, too;
The doves all take the veil, too;
    The blind will see the show.
What! you become a nun, my dear?
    I'll not believe it, no!

If you become a nun, dear,
    The bishop Love will be;
The Cupids every one, dear,
    Will chant ' *We trust in thee* '.
The incense will go sighing,
The candles fall a-dying,
    The water turn to wine;
What! you go take the vows, my dear?
    You may—but they'll be mine!

22. *Jenny kiss'd Me*

JENNY kiss'd me when we met,
    Jumping from the chair she sat in;
Time, you thief, who love to get
    Sweets into your list, put that in!
Say I'm weary, say I'm sad,
    Say that health and wealth have miss'd me,
Say I'm growing old, but add,
        Jenny kiss'd me.

13

23.   *Abou Ben Adhem*

ABOU BEN ADHEM (may his tribe increase !)
Awoke one night from a deep dream of peace,
And saw, within the moonlight in his room,
Making it rich, and like a lily in bloom,
An angel writing in a book of gold :—
Exceeding peace had made Ben Adhem bold,
And to the presence in the room he said,
    'What writest thou ? '—The vision rais'd its head,
And with a look made of all sweet accord,
Answer'd, 'The names of those who love the Lord.'
    'And is mine one ? ' said Abou.   ' Nay, not so,'
Replied the angel.   Abou spoke more low,
But cheerly still ; and said, ' I pray thee, then,
Write me as one that loves his fellow men.'
    The angel wrote, and vanish'd.   The next night
It came again with a great wakening light,
And show'd the names whom love of God had blest,
And lo ! Ben Adhem's name led all the rest.

JOHN KENYON

1784-1856

24.   *Champagne Rosée*

LILY on liquid roses floating—
    So floats yon foam o'er pink champagne :
Fain would I join such pleasant boating,
        And prove that ruby main,
        And float away on wine !

Those seas are dangerous (greybeards swear)
    Whose sea-beach is the goblet's brim ;
And true it is they drown Old Care—
        But what care we for him,
        So we but float on wine ?

14

And true it is they cross in pain
　　Who sober cross the Stygian ferry :
But only make our Styx champagne,
　　And we shall cross right merry,
　　　　Floating away on wine !

Old Charon's self shall make him mellow,
　　Then gaily row his boat from shore ;
While we and every jovial fellow,
　　Hear unconcern'd the oar
　　　　That dips itself in wine !

BRYAN WALLER PROCTER

1787–1874

25.　　*Hermione*

THOU hast beauty bright and fair,
　　Manner noble, aspect free,
Eyes that are untouch'd by care ;
　　What then do we ask from thee ?
　　　　Hermione, Hermione !

Thou hast reason quick and strong,
　　Wit that envious men admire,
And a voice, itself a song !
　　What then can we still desire ?
　　　　Hermione, Hermione !

Something thou dost want, O queen !
　　(As the gold doth ask alloy,)
Tears—amidst thy laughter seen,
　　Pity—mingling with thy joy.
　　　　　　This is all we ask, from thee,
　　　　　　Hermione, Hermione !

15

26.   *For a Fountain*

REST! This little Fountain runs
     Thus for aye :—It never stays
For the look of summer suns,
     Nor the cold of winter days.
Whosoe'er shall wander near,
     When the Syrian heat is worst,
Let him hither come, nor fear
     Lest he may not slake his thirst :
He will find this little river
Running still, as bright as ever.
Let him drink, and onward hie,
Bearing but in thought, that I,
EROTAS, bade the Naiad fall,
And thank the great god Pan for all !

RICHARD HARRIS BARHAM

1788-1845

27.   *Last Lines*

AS I laye a-thynkynge, a-thynkynge, a-thynkynge,
     Merrie sang the Birde as she sat upon the spraye ;
       There came a noble Knyghte,
       With his hauberke shynynge brighte,
       And his gallant heart was lyghte,
         Free and gaye ;
As I laye a-thynkynge, he rode upon his waye.

As I laye a-thynkynge, a-thynkynge, a-thynkynge,
Sadly sang the Birde as she sat upon the tree !
       There seem'd a crimson plain,
       Where a gallant Knyghte lay slayne,

And a steed with broken rein
       Ran free,
As I laye a-thynkynge, most pitiful to see !

As I laye a-thynkynge, a-thynkynge, a-thynkynge,
Merrie sang the Birde as she sat upon the boughe ;
     A lovely Mayde came bye,
     And a gentil youth was nyghe,
     And he breathèd many a syghe
       And a vowe ;
As I laye a-thynkynge, her hearte was gladsome now.

As I laye a-thynkynge, a-thynkynge, a-thynkynge,
Sadly sang the Birde as she sat upon the thorne,
     No more a youth was there,
     But a Maiden rent her haire,
     And cried in sad despaire,
       'That I was borne ! '
As I laye a-thynkynge, she perishèd forlorne.

As I laye a-thynkynge, a-thynkynge, a-thynkynge,
Sweetly sang the Birde as she sat upon the briar ;
     There came a lovely Childe,
     And his face was meek and mild,
     Yet joyously he smiled
       On his sire ;
As I laye a-thynkynge, a Cherub mote admire.

But I laye a-thynkynge, a-thynkynge, a-thynkynge,
And sadly sang the Birde as it perch'd upon a bier ;
     That joyous smile was gone,
     And the face was white and wan,
     As the downe upon the Swan
       Doth appear,
As I laye a-thynkynge—O ! bitter flow'd the tear !

              As

As I laye a-thynkynge, the golden sun was sinking,
O merrie sang that Birde as it glitter'd on her breast
        With a thousand gorgeous dyes,
        While, soaring to the skies,
        'Mid the stars she seem'd to rise,
                As to her nest ;
As I laye a-thynkynge, her meaning was exprest :—
        ' Follow, follow me away,
        It boots not to delay,'—
        'Twas so she seem'd to saye,
            ' HERE IS REST ! '

SIR AUBREY DE VERE

1788–1846

28.   *The Right Use of Prayer*

THEREFORE, when thou wouldst pray, or dost thine
    alms,
  Blow not a trump before thee.   Hypocrites
  Do thus vaingloriously : the common streets
Boast of their largess, echoing their psalms.
On such the laud of men like unctuous balms
  Falls with sweet savour.   Impious Counterfeits !
  Prating of Heaven, for earth their bosom beats :
Grasping at weeds they lose immortal palms.

God needs not iteration nor vain cries ;
  That Man communion with his God might share
  Below, Christ gave the ordinance of prayer.
Vague ambages and witless ecstasies
  Avail not.   Ere a voice to prayer be given
  The heart should rise on wings of love to Heaven.

18

FITZ-GREENE HALLECK

1790–1867

29. On his Friend, Joseph Rodman Drake

GREEN be the turf above thee,
  Friend of my better days!
None knew thee but to love thee,
  None named thee but to praise.

JOHN KEBLE

1792–1866

30. *Balaam*

O FOR a sculptor's hand,
  That thou might'st take thy stand,
Thy wild hair floating on the eastern breeze,
  Thy tranc'd yet open gaze
  Fix'd on the desert haze,
As one who deep in heaven some airy pageant sees!

  In outline dim and vast
  Their fearful shadows cast
The giant forms of empires on their way
  To ruin: one by one
  They tower and they are gone,
Yet in the Prophet's soul the dreams of avarice stay.

  No sun or star so bright
  In all the world of light
That they should draw to Heaven his downward eye!
  He hears th' Almighty's word,
  He sees the angel's sword,
Yet low upon the earth his heart and treasure lie.

19   Lo!

Lo ! from yon argent field,
To him and us reveal'd,
One gentle Star glides down, on earth to dwell.
Chain'd as they are below
Our eyes may see it glow,
And as it mounts again, may track its brightness well.

To him it glared afar,
A token of wild war,
The banner of his Lord's victorious wrath :
But close to us it gleams,
Its soothing lustre streams
Around our home's green walls, and on our church-way
path.

We in the tents abide
Which he at distance eyed,
Like goodly cedars by the waters spread,
While seven red altar-fires
Rose up in wavy spires,
Where on the mount he watch'd his sorceries dark and
dread.

He watch'd till morning's ray
On lake and meadow lay,
And willow-shaded streams, that silent sweep
Around the banner'd lines,
Where by their several signs
The desert-wearied tribes in sight of Canaan sleep.

He watch'd till knowledge came
Upon his soul like flame,
Not of those magic fires at random caught :
But true prophetic light
Flash'd o'er him, high and bright,
Flash'd once, and died away, and left his darken'd thought.

And can he choose but fear,
   Who feels his God so near,
That when he fain would curse, his powerless tongue
   In blessing only moves ?—
   Alas ! the world he loves
Too close around his heart her tangling veil hath flung.

   Sceptre and Star divine,
   Who in Thine inmost shrine
Hast made us worshippers, O claim Thine own !
   More than Thy seers we know—
   O teach our love to grow
Up to Thy heavenly light, and reap what Thou hast sown.

31.   *November*

RED o'er the forest peers the setting sun ;
   The line of yellow light dies fast away
That crown'd the eastern copse ; and chill and dun
   Falls on the moor the brief November day.

Now the tired hunter winds a parting note,
   And Echo bids good-night from every glade ;
Yet wait awhile and see the calm leaves float
   Each to his rest beneath their parent shade.

How like decaying life they seem to glide
   And yet no second spring have they in store ;
But where they fall, forgotten to abide
   Is all their portion, and they ask no more.

Soon o'er their heads blithe April airs shall sing,
   A thousand wild-flowers round them shall unfold,
The green buds glisten in the dews of Spring,
   And all be vernal rapture as of old.

Unconscious

Unconscious they in waste oblivion lie,
     In all the world of busy life around
No thought of them—in all the bounteous sky
     No drop, for them, of kindly influence found.

Man's portion is to die and rise again :
     Yet he complains, while these unmurmuring part
With their sweet lives, as pure from sin and stain
     As his when Eden held his virgin heart.

JOHN CLARE

1793-1864

32.   *Graves of Infants*

INFANTS' gravemounds are steps of angels, where
     Earth's brightest gems of innocence repose.
God is their parent, so they need no tear ;
     He takes them to his bosom from earth's woes—
     A bud their lifetime and a flower their close.
Their spirits are the Iris of the skies,
     Needing no prayer ; a sunset's happy close.
Gone are the bright rays of their soft blue eyes ;
Flow'rs weep in dew-drops o'er them, and the gale gently
          sighs.

Their lives were nothing but a sunny shower,
     Melting on flowers as tears melt from the eye.
Each death
     Was toll'd on flowers as summer gales went by :
     They bow'd and trembled, yet they heaved no sigh ;
And the sun smiled to show the end was well.
     Infants have naught to weep for ere they die;
All prayers are needless, beads they need not tell ;
White flowers their mourners are, Nature their passing
          bell.

33.   *Song*

LOVE lives beyond the tomb
     And earth, which fades like dew:
  I love the fond,
The faithful, and the true.

  Love lives in sleep :
'Tis happiness of healthy dreams ;
  Eve's dews may weep,
But love delightful seems.

  'Tis seen in flowers,
And in the morning's pearly dew ;
  In earth's green bowers,
And in the heaven's eternal blue.

  'Tis heard in Spring ;
When light and sunbeams, warm and kind,
  On angel's wing
Bring love and music to the mind.

  And where 's the voice
So young, so beautiful, and sweet,
  As Nature's choice
Where Spring and lovers meet ?

  Love lives beyond the tomb
And earth, which fades like dew :
  I love the fond,
The faithful, and the true.

JOHN CLARE

34. *Written in Northampton County Asylum*

I AM! yet what I am who cares, or knows?
   My friends forsake me like a memory lost.
I am the self-consumer of my woes;
   They rise and vanish, an oblivious host,
Shadows of life, whose very soul is lost,
And yet I am—I live—though I am toss'd

Into the nothingness of scorn and noise,
   Into the living sea of waking dream,
Where there is neither sense of life, nor joys,
   But the huge shipwreck of my own esteem
And all that's dear.   Even those I loved the best
Are strange—nay, they are stranger than the rest.

I long for scenes where man has never trod—
   For scenes where woman never smiled or wept—
There to abide with my Creator, God,
   And sleep as I in childhood sweetly slept,
Full of high thoughts, unborn.   So let me lie,—
The grass below; above, the vaulted sky.

JOHN GIBSON LOCKHART

1794–1854

35. *Lines*

WHEN youthful faith hath fled,
   Of loving take thy leave;
Be constant to the dead—
   The dead cannot deceive.

Sweet modest flowers of Spring,
   How fleet your balmy day!
And Man's brief life can bring
   No secondary May:

JOHN GIBSON LOCKHART

No earthly burst again
  Of gladness out of gloom,
Fond hope and vision vain,
  Ungrateful to the tomb.

But 'tis an old belief
  That on some solemn shore
Beyond the sphere of grief
  Dear friends shall meet once more:

Beyond the sphere of Time
  And Sin and Fate's control,
Serene in endless prime
  Of body and of soul.

That creed I fain would keep,
  That hope I'll not forgo—
Eternal be the sleep
  Unless to waken so!

WILLIAM CULLEN BRYANT

1794-1878

36.   *The Forest Maid*

O FAIREST of the rural maids!
  Thy birth was in the forest shades;
And all the beauty of the place
Is in thy heart and on thy face.

The twilight of the trees and rocks
Is in the light shade of thy locks;
Thy step is as the wind that weaves
Its playful way among the leaves.

Thine

Thine eyes are springs, in whose serene
And silent waters heaven is seen;
Their lashes are the herbs that look
On their young figures in the brook.

The forest depths by foot unpress'd
Are not more sinless than thy breast;
The holy peace that fills the air
Of those calm solitudes is there.

37.   *Thanatopsis*

TO him who in the love of Nature holds
Communion with her visible forms, she speaks
A various language; for his gayer hours
She has a voice of gladness, and a smile
And eloquence of beauty, and she glides
Into his darker musings, with a mild
And healing sympathy, that steals away
Their sharpness, ere he is aware.   When thoughts
Of the last bitter hour come like a blight
Over thy spirit, and sad images
Of the stern agony, and shroud, and pall,
And breathless darkness, and the narrow house,
Make thee to shudder and grow sick at heart;—
Go forth, under the open sky, and list
To Nature's teachings, while from all around—
Earth and her waters, and the depths of air—
Comes a still voice—Yet a few days, and thee
The all-beholding sun shall see no more
In all his course; nor yet in the cold ground,
Where thy pale form was laid with many tears,

Nor in the embrace of ocean, shall exist
Thy image. Earth, that nourish'd thee, shall claim
Thy growth, to be resolved to earth again,
And, lost each human trace, surrendering up
Thine individual being, shalt thou go
To mix for ever with the elements,
To be a brother to the insensible rock,
And to the sluggish clod, which the rude swain
Turns with his share, and treads upon. The oak
Shall send his roots abroad, and pierce thy mould.

   Yet not to thine eternal resting-place
Shalt thou retire alone, nor couldst thou wish
Couch more magnificent. Thou shalt lie down
With patriarchs of the infant world—with kings,
The powerful of the earth—the wise, the good,
Fair forms, and hoary seers of ages past,
All in one mighty sepulchre. The hills
Rock-ribb'd and ancient as the sun,—the vales
Stretching in pensive quietness between;
The venerable woods; rivers that move
In majesty, and the complaining brooks
That make the meadows green; and, pour'd round all,
Old Ocean's grey and melancholy waste,—
Are but the solemn decorations all
Of the great tomb of man. The golden sun,
The planets, all the infinite host of heaven,
Are shining on the sad abodes of death,
Through the still lapse of ages. All that tread
The globe are but a handful to the tribes
That slumber in its bosom.—Take the wings
Of morning, pierce the Barcan wilderness,
Or lose thyself in the continuous woods
Where rolls the Oregon, and hears no sound

Save

Save his own dashings—yet the dead are there :
And millions in those solitudes, since first
The flight of years began, have laid them down
In their last sleep—the dead reign there alone.
So shalt thou rest : and what if thou withdraw
In silence from the living, and no friend
Take note of thy departure ?   All that breathe
Will share thy destiny.   The gay will laugh
When thou art gone, the solemn brood of care
Plod on, and each one as before will chase
His favourite phantom ; yet all these shall leave
Their mirth and their employments, and shall come
And make their bed with thee.   As the long train
Of ages glide away, the sons of men,
The youth in life's green spring, and he who goes
In the full strength of years, matron and maid,
The speechless babe, and the grey-headed man—
Shall one by one be gathered to thy side,
By those, who in their turn shall follow them.

So live, that when thy summons comes to join
The innumerable caravan, which moves
To that mysterious realm, where each shall take
His chamber in the silent halls of death,
Thou go not, like the quarry-slave at night,
Scourged to his dungeon ; but, sustain'd and soothed
By an unfaltering trust, approach thy grave,
Like one who wraps the drapery of his couch
About him, and lies down to pleasant dreams.

GEORGE DARLEY

1795-1846

38.   *Song*

IT is not Beauty I demand,
    A crystal brow, the moon's despair,
Nor the snow's daughter, a white hand,
    Nor mermaid's yellow pride of hair.

Tell me not of your starry eyes,
    Your lips that seem on roses fed,
Your breasts where Cupid tumbling lies,
    Nor sleeps for kissing of his bed.

A bloomy pair of vermeil cheeks,
    Like Hebe's in her ruddiest hours,
A breath that softer music speaks
    Than summer winds a-wooing flowers :

These are but gauds : nay, what are lips ?
    Coral beneath the ocean stream,
Whose brink when your adventurer sips
    Full oft he perisheth on them.

And what are cheeks but ensigns oft
    That wave hot youth to fields of blood ?
Did Helen's breast, though ne'er so soft,
    Do Greece or Ilium any good ?

Eyes can with baleful ardour burn ;
    Poison can breath that erst perfumed ;
There 's many a white hand holds an urn
    With lovers' hearts to dust consumed.

For crystal brows—there 's naught within ;
    They are but empty cells for pride ;
He who the Siren's hair would win
    Is mostly strangled in the tide.

Give

Give me, instead of beauty's bust,
    A tender heart, a loyal mind,
Which with temptation I could trust,
    Yet never link'd with error find.

One in whose gentle bosom I
    Could pour my secret heart of woes,
Like the care-burthen'd honey-fly
    That hides his murmurs in the rose.

My earthly comforter ! whose love
    So indefeasible might be,
That, when my spirit won above,
    Hers could not stay, for sympathy.

39.   *The Phoenix*

O BLEST unfabled Incense Tree,
    That burns in glorious Araby,
With red scent chalicing the air,
Till earth-life grow Elysian there !

Half buried to her flaming breast
In this bright tree, she makes her nest,
Hundred-sunn'd Phoenix ! when she must
Crumble at length to hoary dust !

Her gorgeous death-bed ! her rich pyre
Burnt up with aromatic fire !
Her urn, sight high from spoiler men !
Her birthplace when self-born again !

The mountainless green wilds among,
Here ends she her unechoing song !
With amber tears and odorous sighs
Mourn'd by the desert where she dies !

GEORGE DARLEY

Laid like the young fawn mossily
In sun-green vales of Araby,
I woke hard by the Phoenix tree
That with shadeless boughs flamed over me,
And upward call'd for a dumb cry
With moonbroad orbs of wonder I
Beheld the immortal Bird on high
Glassing the great sun in her eye.
Stedfast she gazed upon his fire,
—Still her destroyer and her sire !—
As if to his her soul of flame
Had flown already whence it came ;
Like those that sit and glare so still,
Intense with their death struggle, till
We touch, and curdle at their chill !—
But breathing yet while she doth burn,
  The deathless Daughter of the sun !
Slowly to crimson embers turn
  The beauties of the brightsome one.
O'er the broad nest her silver wings
Shook down their wasteful glitterings ;
Her brinded neck high-arch'd in air
Like a small rainbow faded there ;
But brighter glow'd her plumy crown
Mouldering to golden ashes down ;
With fume of sweet woods, to the skies,
Pure as a Saint's adoring sighs,
Warm as a prayer in Paradise,
Her life-breath rose in sacrifice !
The while with shrill triumphant tone
Sounding aloud, aloft, alone,
Ceaseless her joyful deathwail she
Sang to departing Araby !

O, fast

O, fast her amber blood doth flow
  From the heart-wounded Incense Tree,
Fast as earth's deep-embosom'd woe
  In silent rivulets to the sea !

Beauty may weep her fair first-born,
  Perchance in as resplendent tears,
Such golden dewdrops bow the corn
  When the stern sickleman appears :

But O ! such perfume to a bower
  Never allured sweet-seeking bee,
As to sip fast that nectarous shower
  A thirstier minstrel drew in me !

40.   *Love's Likeness*

O MARK yon Rose-tree ! When the West
  Breathes on her with too warm a zest,
    She turns her cheek away ;
Yet if one moment he refrain,
She turns her cheek to him again,
    And woos him still to stay !

Is she not like a maiden coy
Press'd by some amorous-breathing boy ?
    Tho' coy, she courts him too,
Winding away her slender form,
She will not have him woo so warm,
    And yet will have him woo !

41.   *The Lyre*

i

WHEREFORE, unlaurell'd Boy,
  Whom the contemptuous Muse will not inspire
With a sad kind of joy
  Still sing'st thou to thy solitary lyre ?

The melancholy winds
  Pour through unnumber'd reeds their idle woes,
And every Naiad finds
  A stream to weep her sorrow as it flows.

Her sighs unto the air
  The Wood-maid's native oak doth broadly tell.
And Echo's fond despair
  Intelligible rocks re-syllable.

Wherefore then should not I,
  Albeit no haughty Muse my heart inspire,
Fated of grief to die,
  Impart it to my solitary lyre ?

42.   *ii*

LISTEN to the Lyre !
  Listen to the knelling of its sweet-toned ditty !
Shrilly now as Pain resounds the various wire,
    Now as soft as Pity !
      Soft as Pity !

    Will the Dreamer know,
Who upon the melancholy harp loves weeping—
Dreamer, it is I that tell the tale of woe,
    Still while thou art sleeping,
      Thou art sleeping ?

Thrilling up the strings,
Down again to murmur of my own deep sorrow !
Raving o'er its bosom while the night-wind sings,
Silent all the morrow !
All the morrow !

The deceitful breeze
Sighing here to imitate my song doth glory,
Weetless of my woes ; it cannot tell thee these.
Listen to my story !
To my story !

I was once the flower,
The all-belovèd lily of this sweet, sweet valley ;
Every wooing Zephyr came to this green bower
Fain and fond to dally !
Fond to dally !

I could love but one ;
He had loved me ever, but the flood's green daughters
With their siren music drew the sweet youth down,
Down beneath the waters,
'Neath the waters !

In the roaring wave
Like a silly maiden did I plunge down after,
Where amid the billows I was shown my grave
With a hideous laughter !
Hideous laughter !

I was call'd above,
But I found no happiness in lone, lone Heaven ;
So because I would not, could not, cease to love,
Earthward I was driven,
I was driven !

34

GEORGE DARLEY

Like a wingèd dream
Here amid the bowers of my youth I hover,
Wailing o'er my sorrows to the deep, chill stream
    Where I lost my lover,
      Lost my lover !

In his oozy bed
Coffinless he slumbers, with the wild flood rolling :
Mermen are his ringers and his dirge is dread,
    Still for ever tolling !
      Ever tolling !

Hearken to the knell !
Hear it through the booming of the loud-voiced billows !
Hear it how it dingles like a clear death-bell,
    Underneath the willows,
      'Neath the willows !

In the desert hours,
Lyrist of thy visions, all my woes repeating,
With my tears for jewels do I fill the flowers,
    While the stars are fleeting,
      Stars are fleeting !

Thou wilt doubt the tale,
Wilt not still believe my woes.—Thy harp bear token !
See, its very bosom-strings with this deep wail,
    All, like mine, are broken !
      Mine are broken !

43.   *On the Death of a Recluse*

'MID roaring brooks and dark moss-vales,
   Where speechless Thought abides,
Still her sweet spirit dwells,
   That knew no world besides.

Her form the woodland still retains—
   Wound but a creeping flower,
Her very life-blood stains
   Thee, in a falling shower.

Touch but the stream, drink but the air,
   Her cheek, her breath is known ;
Ravish that red rose there,
   And she is all thine own.

44.   *Song*

SWEET in her green dell the flower of beauty slumbers,
   Lull'd by the faint breezes sighing through her hair ;
Sleeps she and hears not the melancholy numbers
   Breathed to my sad lute 'mid the lonely air.

Down from the high cliffs the rivulet is teeming
   To wind round the willow banks that lure him from
      above :
O that in tears, from my rocky prison streaming,
   I too could glide to the bower of my love !

Ah ! where the woodbines with sleepy arms have wound
    her,
  Opes she her eyelids at the dream of my lay,
Listening, like the dove, while the fountains echo round
    her,
  To her lost mate's call in the forests far away.

Come then, my bird ! For the peace thou ever bearest,
  Still Heaven's messenger of comfort to me—
Come—this fond bosom, O faithfullest and fairest,
  Bleeds with its death-wound, its wound of love for thee!

THOMAS CARLYLE

1795-1881

45.   *The Sower's Song*

NOW hands to seedsheet, boys !
  We step and we cast ; old Time 's on wing,
And would ye partake of Harvest's joys,
The corn must be sown in Spring.
    Fall gently and still, good corn,
    Lie warm in thy earthy bed ;
    And stand so yellow some morn,
    For beast and man must be fed.

Old Earth is a pleasure to see
In sunshiny cloak of red and green ;
The furrow lies fresh ; this Year will be
As Years that are past have been.
    Fall gently and still, good corn,
    Lie warm in thy earthy bed ;
    And stand so yellow some morn,
    For beast and man must be fed.

Old

Old Mother, receive this corn,
The son of Six Thousand golden sires :
All these on thy kindly breast were born ;
One more thy poor child requires.
    Fall gently and still, good corn,
    Lie warm in thy earthy bed ;
    And stand so yellow some morn,
    For beast and man must be fed.

Now steady and sure again,
And measure of stroke and step we keep ;
Thus up and thus down we cast our grain :
Sow well, and you gladly reap.
    Fall gently and still, good corn,
    Lie warm in thy earthy bed ;
    And stand so yellow some morn,
    For beast and man must be fed.

HARTLEY COLERIDGE

1796–1849

46.   *Song*

SHE is not fair to outward view
   As many maidens be ;
Her loveliness I never knew
   Until she smiled on me ;
O, then I saw her eye was bright,
A well of love, a spring of light !

But now her looks are coy and cold,
To mine they ne'er reply,
And yet I cease not to behold
   The love-light in her eye :
Her very frowns are fairer far
Than smiles of other maidens are.

47. *To a Lofty Beauty, from her Poor Kinsman*

FAIR maid, had I not heard thy baby cries,
　Nor seen thy girlish, sweet vicissitude,
　Thy mazy motions, striving to elude,
Yet wooing still a parent's watchful eyes,
Thy humours, many as the opal's dyes,
　And lovely all;—methinks thy scornful mood,
　And bearing high of stately womanhood,—
Thy brow, where Beauty sits to tyrannize
　O'er humble love, had made me sadly fear thee;
For never sure was seen a royal bride,
Whose gentleness gave grace to so much pride—
　My very thoughts would tremble to be near thee:
But when I see thee at thy father's side,
　Old times unqueen thee, and old loves endear thee.

48. *May, 1840*

A LOVELY morn, so still, so very still,
　It hardly seems a growing day of Spring,
　Though all the odorous buds are blossoming,
And the small matin birds were glad and shrill
Some hours ago; but now the woodland rill
　Murmurs along, the only vocal thing,
　Save when the wee wren flits with stealthy wing,
And cons by fits and bits her evening trill.
Lovers might sit on such a morn as this
　An hour together, looking at the sky,
Nor dare to break the silence with a kiss,
　Long listening for the signal of a sigh;
And the sweet Nun, diffused in voiceless prayer,
Feel her own soul through all the brooding air.

49.   *Ode to the Moon*

I

MOTHER of light ! how fairly dost thou go
      Over those hoary crests, divinely led !—
Art thou that huntress of the silver bow
Fabled of old ?   Or rather dost thou tread
Those cloudy summits thence to gaze below,
Like the wild Chamois from her Alpine snow,
Where hunter never climb'd,—secure from dread ?
How many antique fancies have I read
Of that mild presence !   and how many wrought !
          Wondrous and bright,
          Upon the silver light,
Chasing fair figures with the artist, Thought !

II

What art thou like ?   Sometimes I see thee ride
A far-bound galley on its perilous way,
Whilst breezy waves toss up their silvery spray ;—
          Sometimes behold thee glide,
Cluster'd by all thy family of stars,
Like a lone widow, through the welkin wide,
Whose pallid cheek the midnight sorrow mars ;—
Sometimes I watch thee on from steep to steep,
Timidly lighted by thy vestal torch,
Till in some Latmian cave I see thee creep,
To catch the young Endymion asleep,—
Leaving thy splendour at the jagged porch !

THOMAS HOOD

III

Oh, thou art beautiful, howe'er it be !
Huntress, or Dian, or whatever nam'd ;
And he the veriest Pagan, that first fram'd
A silver idol, and ne'er worshipp'd thee !
It is too late, or thou should'st have my knee ;
Too late now for the old Ephesian vows,
And not divine the crescent on thy brows !—
Yet, call thee nothing but the mere mild Moon,
      Behind those chestnut boughs,
Casting their dappled shadows at my feet ;
I will be grateful for that simple boon,
In many a thoughtful verse and anthem sweet,
And bless thy dainty face whene'er we meet.

IV

In nights far gone,—aye, far away and dead,—
Before Care-fretted with a lidless eye,—
I was thy wooer on my little bed,
Letting the early hours of rest go by,
To see thee flood the heaven with milky light,
And feed thy snow-white swans, before I slept ;
For thou wert then purveyor of my dreams,—
Thou wert the fairies' armourer, that kept
Their burnish'd helms, and crowns, and corslets bright,
      Their spears, and glittering mails ;
And ever thou didst spill in winding streams
Sparkles and midnight gleams,
For fishes to new gloss their argent scales !

V

Why sighs ?—why creeping tears ?—why clasped hands ?—
Is it to count the boy's expended dow'r ?

That

That fairies since have broke their gifted wands?
That young Delight, like any o'erblown flow'r,
Gave, one by one, its sweet leaves to the ground?—
Why then, fair Moon, for all thou mark'st no hour,
Thou art a sadder dial to old Time
     Than ever I have found
On sunny garden-plot, or moss-grown tow'r,
Motto'd with stern and melancholy rhyme.

VI

Why should I grieve for this?—O I must yearn,
Whilst Time, conspirator with Memory,
Keeps his cold ashes in an ancient urn,
Richly emboss'd with childhood's revelry,
With leaves and cluster'd fruits, and flowers eterne,—
(Eternal to the world, though not to me),
Ay there will those brave sports and blossoms be,
The deathless wreath, and undecay'd festoon,
     When I am hears'd within,—
Less than the pallid primrose to the Moon,
That now she watches through a vapour thin.

VII

So let it be! Before I liv'd to sigh,
Thou wert in Avon, and a thousand rills,
Beautiful Orb! and so, whene'er I lie
Trodden, thou wilt be gazing from thy hills.
Blest be thy loving light, where'er it spills,
And blessèd thy fair face, O Mother mild!
Still shine, the soul of rivers as they run,
Still lend thy lonely lamp to lovers fond,
And blend their plighted shadows into one :—
Still smile at even on the bedded child,
And close his eyelids with thy silver wand!

50. *Fair Ines*

O SAW ye not fair Ines?
　　She's gone into the West,
To dazzle when the sun is down,
　　And rob the world of rest:
She took our daylight with her,
　　The smiles that we love best,
With morning blushes on her cheek,
　　And pearls upon her breast.

O turn again, fair Ines,
　　Before the fall of night,
For fear the Moon should shine alone,
　　And stars unrivall'd bright;
And blessèd will the lover be
　　That walks beneath their light,
And breathes the love against thy cheek
　　I dare not even write!

Would I had been, fair Ines,
　　That gallant cavalier,
Who rode so gaily by thy side,
　　And whisper'd thee so near!
Were there no bonny dames at home,
　　Or no true lovers here,
That he should cross the seas to win
　　The dearest of the dear?

I saw thee, lovely Ines,
　　Descend along the shore,
With bands of noble gentlemen,
　　And banners waved before;
And gentle youth and maidens gay,
　　And snowy plumes they wore:
It would have been a beauteous dream,—
　　If it had been no more!

Alas,

Alas, alas! fair Ines!
　　She went away with song,
With Music waiting on her steps,
　　And shoutings of the throng;
But some were sad, and felt no mirth,
　　But only Music's wrong,
In sounds that sang Farewell, farewell,
　　To her you've loved so long.

Farewell, farewell, fair Ines!
　　That vessel never bore
So fair a lady on its deck,
　　Nor danced so light before,—
Alas for pleasure on the sea,
　　And sorrow on the shore!
The smile that bless'd one lover's heart
　　Has broken many more!

51. *Time of Roses*

IT was not in the Winter
　　Our loving lot was cast;
It was the time of roses—
　　We pluck'd them as we pass'd!

That churlish season never frown'd
　　On early lovers yet:
O no—the world was newly crown'd
　　With flowers when first we met!

'Twas twilight, and I bade you go,
　　But still you held me fast;
It was the time of roses—
　　We pluck'd them as we pass'd!

44

52.

The Death-bed

WE watch'd her breathing thro' the night,
   Her breathing soft and low,
As in her breast the wave of life
   Kept heaving to and fro.

So silently we seem'd to speak,
   So slowly moved about,
As we had lent her half our powers
   To eke her living out.

Our very hopes belied our fears,
   Our fears our hopes belied—
We thought her dying when she slept,
   And sleeping when she died.

For when the morn came dim and sad,
   And chill with early showers,
Her quiet eyelids closed—she had
   Another morn than ours.

53.

Ruth

SHE stood breast-high amid the corn,
   Clasp'd by the golden light of morn,
Like the sweetheart of the sun,
Who many a glowing kiss had won.

On her cheek an autumn flush,
Deeply ripen'd;—such a blush
In the midst of brown was born,
Like red poppies grown with corn.

Round

Round her eyes her tresses fell,
Which were blackest none could tell,
But long lashes veil'd a light,
That had else been all too bright.

And her hat, with shady brim,
Made her tressy forehead dim ;
Thus she stood amid the stooks,
Praising God with sweetest looks :—

Sure, I said, Heav'n did not mean,
Where I reap thou shouldst but glean :
Lay thy sheaf adown and come,
Share my harvest and my home.

54.   *The Bridge of Sighs*

O NE more Unfortunate,
    Weary of breath,
Rashly importunate,
    Gone to her death !

Take her up tenderly,
    Lift her with care ;
Fashion'd so slenderly,
    Young, and so fair !

Look at her garments
Clinging like cerements ;
Whilst the wave constantly
    Drips from her clothing ;
Take her up instantly,
    Loving, not loathing.

46

THOMAS HOOD

Touch her not scornfully ;
Think of her mournfully,
　Gently and humanly ;
Not of the stains of her,
All that remains of her
　Now is pure womanly.

Make no deep scrutiny
Into her mutiny
　Rash and undutiful :
Past all dishonour,
Death has left on her
　Only the beautiful.

Still, for all slips of hers,
　One of Eve's family—
Wipe those poor lips of hers
　Oozing so clammily.

Loop up her tresses
　Escaped from the comb,
Her fair auburn tresses ;
Whilst wonderment guesses
　Where was her home ?

Who was her father ?
　Who was her mother ?
Had she a sister ?
　Had she a brother ?
Or was there a dearer one
Still, and a nearer one
　Yet, than all other ?

Alas ! for the rarity
Of Christian charity
　Under the sun !
O, it was pitiful !
Near a whole city full,
　Home she had none.

Sisterly,

Sisterly, brotherly,
Fatherly, motherly
　　Feelings had changed :
Love, by harsh evidence,
Thrown from its eminence ;
Even God's providence
　　Seeming estranged.

Where the lamps quiver
So far in the river,
　　With many a light
From window and casement.
From garret to basement,
She stood, with amazement,
　　Houseless by night.

The bleak wind of March
　　Made her tremble and shiver ;
But not the dark arch,
Or the black flowing river :
Mad from life's history,
Glad to death's mystery
　　Swift to be hurl'd—
Anywhere, anywhere
　　Out of the world !

In she plunged boldly—
No matter how coldly
　　The rough river ran—
Over the brink of it,
Picture it—think of it,
　　Dissolute Man !
Lave in it, drink of it,
　　Then, if you can !

THOMAS HOOD

Take her up tenderly,
    Lift her with care ;
Fashion'd so slenderly,
    Young, and so fair !

Ere her limbs frigidly
Stiffen too rigidly,
    Decently, kindly,
Smooth and compose them ;
And her eyes, close them,
    Staring so blindly !

Dreadfully staring
    Thro' muddy impurity,
As when with the daring
Last look of despairing
    Fix'd on futurity.

Perishing gloomily,
Spurr'd by contumely,
Cold inhumanity,
Burning insanity,
    Into her rest.—
Cross her hands humbly
As if praying dumbly,
    Over her breast !

Owning her weakness,
    Her evil behaviour,
And leaving, with meekness,
    Her sins to her Saviour !

55. *The Song of the Shirt*

WITH fingers weary and worn,
    With eyelids heavy and red,
A Woman sat, in unwomanly rags,
    Plying her needle and thread—
        Stitch! stitch! stitch!
In poverty, hunger, and dirt,
And still with a voice of dolorous pitch
She sang the 'Song of the Shirt!'

'Work! work! work!
While the cock is crowing aloof!
    And work—work—work,
Till the stars shine through the roof!
It's O! to be a slave
    Along with the barbarous Turk,
Where woman has never a soul to save,
    If this is Christian work!

'Work—work—work
Till the brain begins to swim,
    Work—work—work
Till the eyes are heavy and dim!
Seam, and gusset, and band,
    Band, and gusset, and seam,
Till over the buttons I fall asleep,
    And sew them on in a dream!

'O, Men with Sisters dear!
    O, Men! with Mothers and Wives!
It is not linen you're wearing out,
    But human creatures' lives!
        Stitch—stitch—stitch,
    In poverty, hunger, and dirt,
Sewing at once, with a double thread,
    A Shroud as well as a Shirt.

50

'But why do I talk of Death?
  That Phantom of grisly bone,
I hardly fear his terrible shape,
  It seems so like my own—
  It seems so like my own,
  Because of the fasts I keep;
O God! that bread should be so dear,
  And flesh and blood so cheap!

'Work—work—work!
  My labour never flags;
And what are its wages? A bed of straw,
  A crust of bread—and rags.
That shatter'd roof,—and this naked floor—
  A table—a broken chair—
And a wall so blank, my shadow I thank
  For sometimes falling there!

'Work—work—work!
From weary chime to chime,
  Work—work—work—
As prisoners work for crime!
  Band, and gusset, and seam,
  Seam, and gusset, and band,
Till the heart is sick, and the brain benumb'd,
  As well as the weary hand.

'Work—work—work,
In the dull December light,
  And work—work—work,
When the weather is warm and bright—
While underneath the eaves
  The brooding swallows cling,
As if to show me their sunny backs
  And twit me with the spring.

51   'O, but

'O, but to breathe the breath
Of the cowslip and primrose sweet !—
  With the sky above my head,
And the grass beneath my feet ;
For only one short hour
  To feel as I used to feel,
Before I knew the woes of want
  And the walk that costs a meal !

'O, but for one short hour !
  A respite however brief !
No blessed leisure for Love or Hope,
  But only time for Grief !
A little weeping would ease my heart,
  But in their briny bed
My tears must stop, for every drop
  Hinders needle and thread !

' Seam, and gusset, and band,
Band, and gusset, and seam,
    Work, work, work,
Like the Engine that works by Steam !
A mere machine of iron and wood
    That toils for Mammon's sake—
Without a brain to ponder and craze
    Or a heart to feel—and break ! '

—With fingers weary and worn,
  With eyelids heavy and red,
A Woman sat, in unwomanly rags,
  Plying her needle and thread—
    Stitch ! stitch ! stitch !
  In poverty, hunger, and dirt,
And still with a voice of dolorous pitch,—
Would that its tone could reach the Rich !—
  She sang this ' Song of the Shirt ! '

THOMAS BABINGTON MACAULAY,
LORD MACAULAY

1800–1859

56.   *A Jacobite's Epitaph*

TO my true king I offer'd free from stain
    Courage and faith ; vain faith, and courage vain.
For him I threw lands, honours, wealth, away,
And one dear hope, that was more prized than they.
For him I languish'd in a foreign clime,
Grey-hair'd with sorrow in my manhood's prime ;
Heard on Lavernia Scargill's whispering trees,
And pined by Arno for my lovelier Tees ;
Beheld each night my home in fever'd sleep,
Each morning started from the dream to weep ;
Till God, who saw me tried too sorely, gave
The resting-place I ask'd, an early grave.
O thou, whom chance leads to this nameless stone,
From that proud country which was once mine own,
By those white cliffs I never more must see,
By that dear language which I spake like thee,
Forget all feuds, and shed one English tear
O'er English dust.   A broken heart lies here.

SIR HENRY TAYLOR

1800–1886

57.   *Elena's Song*

QUOTH tongue of neither maid nor wife
    To heart of neither wife nor maid—
Lead we not here a jolly life
    Betwixt the shine and shade ?

                            Quoth

53

Quoth heart of neither maid nor wife
  To tongue of neither wife nor maid—
Thou wagg'st, but I am worn with strife,
  And feel like flowers that fade.

58.   *Song*

THE bee to the heather,
  The lark to the sky,
The roe to the greenwood,
  And whither shall I ?

O, Alice ! Ah, Alice !
  So sweet to the bee
Are the moorland and heather
  By Cannock and Leigh !

O, Alice ! Ah, Alice !
  O'er Teddesley Park
The sunny sky scatters
  The notes of the lark !

O, Alice ! Ah, Alice !
  In Beaudesert glade
The roes toss their antlers
  For joy of the shade !—

But Alice, dear Alice !
  Glade, moorland, nor sky
Without you can content me—
  And whither shall I ?

Women Singing

59.

Thorbiorga sings :

BY Wellesbourne and Charlcote ford,
At break of day, I saw a sword.
Wessex warriors, rank by rank,
Rose on Avon's hither bank ;
Mercia's men in fair array
Look'd at them from Marraway ;
Close and closer ranged they soon,
And the battle join'd at noon.

By Wellesbourne and Charlcote Lea
I heard a sound as of the sea :
Thirty thousand rushing men,
Twenty thousand met by ten ;
Rang the shield and brake the shaft,
Tosty yell'd, Harcather laugh'd ;
Thoro' Avon's waters red
Chased by ten the twenty fled.

By Charlcote ford and Wellesbourne
I saw the moon's pale face forlorn.
River flow'd and rushes sigh'd,
Wounded warriors groan'd and died ;
Ella took his early rest,
The raven stood on his white breast ;
Hoarsely in the dead man's ear
Raven whisper'd, ' Friend, good cheer !
Ere the winter pinch the crow
He that slew thee shall lie low.'

Heidu

SIR HENRY TAYLOR

Heida sings :

> Love ye wisely, love ye well ;
> Challenge then the gates of Hell !
> Love and Truth can ride it out,
> Come bridal song or battle shout.

CAROLINE CLIVE

1801-1873

60.   *Conflict*

AS one whose country is distraught with war,
    Where each must guard his own with watchful hand,
Roams at the evening hour along the shore
    And fain would seek beyond a calmer land ;

So I, perplex'd on life's tumultuous way,
    Where evil pow'rs too oft my soul enslave,
Along thy ocean, Death, all pensive stray,
    And think of shores thy pensive billows lave.

And glad were I to hear the boatman's cry,
    Which to his shadowy bark my steps should call,
To woe and weakness heave my latest sigh,
    And cease to combat where so oft I fall :

Or, happier, where some victory cheer'd my breast,
    That hour to quit the anxious field would choose,
And seek th' eternal seal on virtue's rest,
    Oft won, oft lost, and O ! too dear to lose !

WILLIAM BARNES

1801-1886

61.   *Woodlands*

O SPREAD agen your leaves an' flow'rs,
    Luonesome woodlands! zunny woodlands!
Here undernēath the dewy show'rs
    O' warm-âir'd spring-time, zunny woodlands!
As when, in drong ar oben groun',
Wi' happy buoyish heart I voun'
The twitt'ren birds a-buildèn roun'
    Your high-bough'd hedges, zunny woodlands!

Ya gie'd me life, ya gie'd me jây,
    Luonesome woodlands! zunny woodlands!
Ya gie'd me health, as in my plây
    I rambled droo ye, zunny woodlands!
Ya gie'd me freedom var to rove
In âiry meäd ar shiady grove;
Ya gie'd me smilèn Fanny's love,
    The best ov al ō't, zunny woodlands!

My vust shill skylark whiver'd high,
    Luonesome woodlands! zunny woodlands!
To zing below your deep-blue sky
    An' white spring-clouds, O zunny woodlands!
An' boughs o' trees that oonce stood here,
Wer glossy green the happy year
That gie'd me oon I lov'd so dear,
    An' now ha lost, O zunny woodlands!

drong] lane.

57   O let

O let me rove agen unspied,
  Luonesome woodlands ! zunny woodlands !
Along your green-bough'd hedges' zide,
  As then I rambled, zunny woodlands !
An' where the missèn trees oonce stood,
Ar tongues oonce rung among the wood,
My memory shall miake em good,
  Though you've a-lost em, zunny woodlands !

62.   *The Oak-Tree*

THE girt woak tree that's in the dell !
  Ther's noo tree I da love so well ;
Var in thik tree, when I wer young,
I of'en climb'd an' of'en zwung,
An' pick'd the green-rin'd yacors, shed
In wrestlèn storm-winds vrom his head.
An' down below's the cloty brook
Wher I did vish wi' line an' hook,
An' beät, in plâysome dips an' zwims,
The foamy stream wi' white-skinn'd lims.
An' there my mother nimbly shot
Her knittèn-needles, as she zot
At evemen down below the wide
Woak's head, wi' fāther at her zide.
An' I've a-plây'd wi' many a buoy,
That's now a man an' gone awoy ;
  Zoo I da like noo tree so well
  'S the girt woak tree that's in the dell.

An' there, in liater years, I roved
Wi' thik poor mâid I fondly lov'd,—
The mâid too fiair to die so soon,—
When evemen twilight, ar the moon,
              cloty] water-lilied.
                    58

Drow'd light enough 'ithin the pliace
To show the smiles upon her fiace,
Wi' eyes so clear 's the glassy pool,
An' lips an' cheäks so soft as wool.
There han' in han', wi' bosoms warm,
Wi' love that burn'd but thought noo harm,
Below thik wide-bough'd tree we past
The happy hours that went too vast:
An' though she'll never be my wife,
She 's still my leäden star o' life.
She 's gone: an' she 've a-left to me
Her token o' the girt woak tree;
   Zoo I da love noo tree so well
    'S the girt woak tree that 's in the dell.

An' O! mid never ax nar hook
Be brote to spwile his stiately look;
Nar ever roun' his white-rin'd zides
Mid cattle rub ther hiary hides;
Nar pigs plow up his turf, but keep
His luonesome shiade var harmless sheep;
An' let en grow, an' let en spread,
An' let en live when I be dead.
But O! ef thä shou'd come an' vell
The girt woak tree that 's in the dell,
An' build his planks 'ithin the zide
O' zome girt ship to plow the tide,
Then, life ar death! I'd goo to sea,
A-sâilèn wi' the girt woak tree:
An' I upon thä planks wou'd stand,
An' die a-fightèn var the land,—
The land so dear,—the land so free,—
The land that bore the girt woak tree;
   Var I da love noo tree so well
    'S the girt woak tree that 's in the dell.

63.   *The Old House*

THE girt wold house o' mossy stuone,
   Up there upon the knap aluone,
Had oonce a bliazèn kitchèn vier,
That cook'd var poor-vo'ke an' a squier.
The very lāste ov all the riace
That liv'd the squier o' the pliace,
Died when my fāther wer a buoy,
An' all his kin be gone awoy
Var ever,—var 'e left noo son
To tiake the house o' mossy stuone.
An' zoo 'e got in other han's,
An' gramfer took en wi' the lan's :
An' there when he, poor man, wer dead,
My fāther liv'd an' I wer bred.
An' if I wer a squier, I
Should like to spend my life an' die
In thik wold house o' mossy stuone,
Up there upon the knap aluone.

Don't tell o' housen miade o' brick,
Wi' rockèn walls nine inches thick,
A-trigg'd together zide by zide
In streets, wi' fronts a stroddle wide,
Wi' yards a-sprinkled wi' a mop,
Too little var a vrog to hop ;
But let me live an' die where I
Can zee the groun', an' trees, an' sky.
The girt wold house o' mossy stuone
Had wings var either shiade ar zun :
Oone where the zun did glitter droo,
When vust 'e struck the marnèn dew ;
Oone fiaced the evemen sky, and oone
Push'd out a puorch to zweaty noon :

60

Zoo oone stood out to break the starm,
An' miade another lew an' warm.
There wer the copse wi' timber high,
Wher birds did build an' hiares did lie,
An' beds o' grēygles in the lew,
Did deck in Mây the groun' wi' blue.
An' there wer hills an' slopèn groun's,
That tha did ride down wi' the houn's;
An' droo the meäd did creep the brook
Wi' bushy bank an' rushy nook,
Wher perch did lie in shiady holes
Below the aller trees, an' shoals
O' gudgeon darted by, to hide
Therzelves in hollers by the zide.
An' there wer windèn lianes so deep,
Wi' mossy banks so high an' steep;
An' stuonèn steps, so smooth an' wide,
To stiles an' vootpāthes at the zide;
An' there, so big 's a little groun',
The giarden wer a-wall'd all roun';
An' up upon the wall wer bars
A-shiaped all out in wheels an' stars,
Var vo'kes to wā'k, an' look out droo
Vrom trees o' green to hills o' blue.
An' there wer wā'ks o' piavement, brode
Enough to miake a carriage-road,
Wher liadies farmerly did use
To wā'k wi' hoops an' high-heel shoes,
When yander holler woak wer sound,
Avore the walls wer ivy-bound,
Avore the elems met above
The road between 'em, wher tha drove
Ther coach all up ar down the road
A-comèn huome ar gwâin abrode.

greygles] bluebells.

The

The zummer âir o' theos green hill
'V a-heav'd in buzzoms now all still,
An' all ther hopes an' all ther tears
Be unknown things ov other years.
But if, in heaven, souls be free
To come back here ; ar there can be
An ethly pliace to miake 'em come
To zee it vrom a better huome,—
Then what 's a-tuold us mid be right,
That still, at dead o' tongueless night,
Ther gauzy shiapes da come an' trud
The vootwoys o' ther flesh an' blood ;
An' while the trees da stan' that grow'd
Var thāe, ar walls ar steps tha know'd
Da bide in pliace, tha'll always come
To look upon ther ethly huome.
Zoo I wou'd always let aluone
The girt wold house o' mossy stuone :
I wou'den pull a wing ō'n down,
To miake ther speechless shiades to frown ;
Var when our souls, zome other dae,
Be bodiless an' dumb lik' thāe,
How good to think that we mid vind
Zome thought vrom tha we left behind,
An' that zome love mid still unite
The hearts o' blood wi' souls o' light !
Zoo, if 'twer mine, I'd let aluone
The girt wold house o' mossy stuone.

64. *The Turnstile*

AH! sad wer we as we did peäce
   The wold church road, wi' downcast feäce,
The while the bells, that mwoan'd so deep
Above our child a-left asleep,
Wer now a-zingèn all alive
Wi' tother bells to meäke the vive.
But up at woone pleäce we come by,
'Twer hard to keep woone's two eyes dry;
On Steän-cliff road, 'ithin the drong,
Up where, as vo'k do pass along,
The turnèn-stile, a-païnted white,
Do sheen by day an' show by night.
Vor always there, as we did goo
To church, thik stile did let us drough,
Wi' spreadèn eärms that wheel'd to guide
Us each in turn to tother zide.
An' vu'st ov all the traïn he took
My wife, wi' winsome gaït an' look;
An' then zent on my little maïd,
A-skippèn onward, over-jay'd
To reach ageän the pleäce o' pride,
Her comely mother's left han' zide.
An' then, a-wheelèn roun', he took
On me, 'ithin his third white nook.
An' in the fourth, a-sheäkèn wild,
He zent us on our giddy child.
But eesterday he guided slow
My downcast Jenny, vull o' woe,
An' then my little maïd in black,
A-walkèn softly on her track;
An' after he'd a-turned ageän,
To let me goo along the leäne,
He had noo little buoy to vill
His last white eärms, an' they stood still.

65.   *The Wife a-lost*

SINCE I noo mwore do zee your feäce,
    Up steärs or down below,
I'll zit me in the lwonesome pleäce,
    Where flat-bough'd beech do grow;
Below the beeches' bough, my love,
    Where you did never come,
An' I don't look to meet ye now,
    As I do look at hwome.

Since you noo mwore be at my zide,
    In walks in zummer het,
I'll goo alwone where mist do ride,
    Droo trees a-drippèn wet;
Below the raïn-wet bough, my love,
    Where you did never come,
An' I don't grieve to miss ye now,
    As I do grieve at hwome.

Since now bezide my dinner-bwoard
    Your vaïce do never sound,
I'll eat the bit I can avword
    A-vield upon the ground;
Below the darksome bough, my love,
    Where you did never dine,
An' I don't grieve to miss ye now,
    As I at hwome do pine.

64

Since I do miss your vaïce an' feäce
  In prayer at eventide,
I'll pray wi' woone sad vaïce vor greäce
  To goo where you do bide ;
Above the tree an' bough, my love,
  Where you be gone avore,
An' be a-waïtèn vor me now,
  To come vor evermwore.

66. *Evening, and Maidens*

NOW the shiades o' the elems da stratch muore an
    muore,
Vrom the low-zinkèn zun in the west o' the sky ;
An' the mâidens da stan out in clusters avore
The doors, var to chatty an' zee vo'ke goo by.

An' ther cuombs be a-zet in ther bunches o' hiair,
An' ther curdles da hang roun' ther necks lily-white,
An' ther cheäks tha be ruosy, ther shoulders be biare,
Ther looks tha be merry, ther lims tha be light.

An' the times have a-been—but tha cānt be noo muore—
When I, too, had my jây under evemen's dim sky,
When my Fanny did stan' out wi' others avore
Her door, var to chatty an' zee vo'ke goo by.

An' up there, in the green, is her own honey-zuck,
That her brother trâin'd up roun' her winder ; an' there
Is the ruose an' the jessamy, where she did pluck
A flow'r var her buzom ar bud var her hiair.

curdles] curls.

An'

An' zoo smile, happy mâidens ! var every fiace,
As the zummers da come an' the years da roll by,
Wull soon sadden, ar goo vur awoy vrom the pliace,
Ar else, lik' my Fanny, wull wither an' die.

But when you be a-lost vrom the parish, some muore
Wull come on in y'ur pliazen to bloom an' to die ;
An' zoo zummer wull always have mâidens avore
Ther doors, var to chatty an' zee vo'ke goo by.

Var dã'ters ha' marnen when mothers ha' night,
An' there 's beauty alive when the fiairest is dead ;
As when oon sparklèn wiave da zink down vrom the light,
Another da come up an' catch it instead.

Zoo smile on, happy mâidens ! but I shall noo muore
Zee the mâid I da miss under evemen's dim sky ;
An' my heart is a-touch'd to zee you out avore
The doors, var to chatty and zee vo'ke goo by.

67.   *The Head-stone*

A S I wer readèn ov a stuone
  In Grenley church-yard all aluone,
A little mâid runn'd up wi' pride
To zee me there, an' push'd a-zide
A bunch o' bennits that did hide
    A vess her faether, as she zed,
    Put up above her mother's head,
        To tell how much 'e lov'd her.

vess] verse.

WILLIAM BARNES

The vess wer very good, but shart,
I stood an' larn'd en off by heart :—
'Mid God, dear Miary, gi'e me griace
To vind, lik' thee, a better pliace,
Wher I oonce muore mid zee thy fiace ;
  An' bring thy childern up to know
    His word, that thā mid come an' show
      Thy soul how much I lov'd thee.'

'Wher 's faether, then,' I zed, 'my chile ?'
'Dead, too,' she ānswer'd wi' a smile ;
'An' I an' brother Jim da bide
At Betty White's, o' t'other zide
O' road.' 'Mid He, my chile,' I cried,
  'That 's faether to the faetherless,
    Become thy faether now, an' bless,
      An' keep, an' leäd, an' love thee.'

Though she've a-lost, I thought, so much,
Still He don't let the thoughts ō't touch
Her litsome heart by day ar night ;
An' zoo, if we cood tiake it right,
Da show He'll miake his burdens light
  To weaker souls, an' that his smile
    Is sweet upon a harmless chile,
      When thā be dead that lov'd it.

JOHN HENRY, CARDINAL NEWMAN

1801-1890

68. *Rest*

THEY are at rest.
    We may not stir the heaven of their repose
By rude invoking voice, or prayer addrest
    In waywardness to those
Who in the mountain grots of Eden lie,
And hear the fourfold river as it murmurs by.

    They hear it sweep
In distance down the dark and savage vale ;
But they at rocky bed or current deep
    Shall never more grow pale.
They hear, and meekly muse, as fain to know
How long untired, unspent, that giant stream shall flow

    And soothing sounds
Blend with the neighb'ring waters as they glide ;
Posted along the haunted garden's bounds,
    Angelic forms abide,
Echoing, as words of watch, o'er lawn and grove,
The verses of that hymn which seraphs chant above.

69. *Chorus of the Elements*

MAN is permitted much
    To scan and learn
    In Nature's frame ;
    Till he wellnigh can tame
    Brute mischiefs, and can touch
    Invisible things, and turn
All warring ills to purposes of good.

Thus, as a god below,
He can control
And harmonize what seems amiss to flow
As sever'd from the whole
And dimly understood.

But o'er the elements
One Hand alone,
One Hand hath sway.
What influence day by day
In straiter belt prevents
The impious Ocean thrown
Alternate o'er the ever-sounding shore ?
Or who hath eye to trace
How the Plague came ?
Fore-run the doublings of the Tempest's race ?
Or the Air's weight and flame
On a set scale explore ?

Thus God hath will'd
That Man, when fully skill'd,
Still gropes in twilight dim ;
Encompass'd all his hours
By fearfull'st powers
Inflexible to him :
That so he may discern
His feebleness,
And e'en for Earth's success
To Him in wisdom turn,
Who holds for us the keys of either home,
—Earth, and the world to come.

1802–1839

70. *The Vicar*

SOME years ago, ere time and taste
   Had turn'd our parish topsy-turvy,
When Darnel Park was Darnel Waste,
   And roads as little known as scurvy,
The man who lost his way, between
   St. Mary's Hill and Sandy Thicket,
Was always shown across the green,
   And guided to the Parson's wicket.

Back flew the bolt of lissom lath ;
   Fair Margaret, in her tidy kirtle,
Led the lorn traveller up the path,
   Through clean-clipt rows of box and myrtle ;
And Don and Sancho, Tramp and Tray,
   Upon the parlour steps collected,
Wagg'd all their tails, and seem'd to say—
   ' Our master knows you—you're expected.'

Uprose the Reverend Dr. Brown,
   Uprose the Doctor's winsome marrow ;
The lady laid her knitting down,
   Her husband clasp'd his ponderous Barrow ;
Whate'er the stranger's caste or creed,
   Pundit or Papist, saint or sinner,
He found a stable for his steed,
   And welcome for himself, and dinner.

If, when he reach'd his journey's end,
   And warm'd himself in Court or College,
He had not gained an honest friend
   And twenty curious scraps of knowledge,—
If he departed as he came,
   With no new light on love or liquor,—
Good sooth, the traveller was to blame,
   And not the Vicarage, nor the Vicar.

His talk was like a spring, which runs
    With rapid change from rocks to roses :
It slipped from politics to puns,
    It passed from Mahomet to Moses ;
Beginning with the laws which keep
    The planets in their radiant courses,
And ending with some precept deep
    For dressing eels, or shoeing horses.

He was a shrewd and sound Divine,
    Of loud Dissent the mortal terror ;
And when, by dint of page and line,
    He 'stablish'd Truth, or startled Error,
The Baptist found him far too deep ;
    The Deist sigh'd with saving sorrow ;
And the lean Levite went to sleep,
    And dream'd of tasting pork to-morrow.

His sermons never said or show'd
    That Earth is foul, that Heaven is gracious,
Without refreshment on the road
    From Jerome or from Athanasius :
And sure a righteous zeal inspired
    The hand and head that penn'd and plann'd them,
For all who understood admired,
    And some who did not understand them.

He wrote, too, in a quiet way,
    Small treatises, and smaller verses,
And sage remarks on chalk and clay,
    And hints to noble Lords—and nurses ;
True histories of last year's ghost,
    Lines to a ringlet, or a turban,
And trifles for the *Morning Post*,
    And nothings for Sylvanus Urban.

He

He did not think all mischief fair,
    Although he had a knack of joking ;
He did not make himself a bear,
    Although he had a taste for smoking ;
And when religious sects ran mad,
    He held, in spite of all his learning,
That if a man's belief is bad,
    It will not be improved by burning.

And he was kind, and loved to sit
    In the low hut or garnish'd cottage,
And praise the farmer's homely wit,
    And share the widow's homelier pottage :
At his approach complaint grew mild ;
    And when his hand unbarr'd the shutter,
The clammy lips of fever smiled
    The welcome which they could not utter.

He always had a tale for me
    Of Julius Caesar, or of Venus ;
From him I learnt the rule of three,
    Cat's cradle, leap-frog, and *Quae genus* :
I used to singe his powder'd wig,
    To steal the staff he put such trust in,
And make the puppy dance a jig,
    When he began to quote Augustine.

Alack the change ! in vain I look
    For haunts in which my boyhood trifled,—
The level lawn, the trickling brook,
    The trees I climb'd, the beds I rifled :
The church is larger than before ;
    You reach it by a carriage entry ;
It holds three hundred people more,
    And pews are fitted up for gentry.

Sit in the Vicar's seat : you'll hear
  The doctrine of a gentle Johnian,
Whose hand is white, whose tone is clear,
  Whose phrase is very Ciceronian.
Where is the old man laid ?—look down,
  And construe on the slab before you,
' *Hic jacet Gvlielmvs Brown,*
  Vir nullâ non donandus lauru.'

71.   *Mater Desiderata*

I CANNOT guess her face or form ;
    But what to me is form or face ?
I do not ask the weary worm
    To give me back each buried grace
Of glistening eyes or trailing tresses.
    I only feel that she is here,
      And that we meet, and that we part ;
    And that I drink within mine ear,
      And that I clasp around my heart
Her sweet still voice and soft caresses.

Not in the waking thought by day,
  Nor in the sightless dream by night,
Do the mild tones and glances play
  Of her who was my cradle's light !
But in some twilight of calm weather
  She glides by fancy dimly wrought,
    A glittering cloud, a darkling beam,
  With all the quiet of a thought
    And all the passion of a dream
Link'd in a golden spell together.

73

72.   *The Mother*

FULL oft beside some gorgeous fane
    The youngling heifer bleeds and dies ;
Her life-blood issuing forth amain,
    While wreaths of incense climb the skies.

The mother wanders all around,
    Thro' shadowy grove and lightsome glade ;
Her footmarks on the yielding ground
    Will prove what anxious quest she made.

The stall where late her darling lay
    She visits oft with eager look ;
In restless movements wastes the day,
    And fills with cries each neighb'ring nook.

She roams along the willowy copse,
    Where purest waters softly gleam ;
But ne'er a leaf or blade she crops,
    Nor couches by the gliding stream.

No youthful kine, tho' fresh and fair,
    Her vainly searching eyes engage ;
No pleasant fields relieve her care,
    No murmuring streams her grief assuage.

73.   *Song*

HE came unlook'd for, undesir'd,
    A sun-rise in the northern sky :
More than the brightest dawn admir'd,
To shine and then for ever fly.

His love, conferr'd without a claim,
Perchance was like the fitful blaze,
Which lives to light a steadier flame,
And, while that strengthens, fast decays.

Glad fawn along the forest springing,
Gay birds that breeze-like stir the leaves,
Why hither haste, no message bringing
To solace one that deeply grieves ?

Thou star that dost the skies adorn
So brightly heralding the day,
Bring one more welcome than the morn,
Or still in night's dark prison stay.

GERALD GRIFFIN

1803–1840

74. *Eileen Aroon*

WHEN like the early rose,
    Eileen Aroon !
Beauty in childhood blows,
    Eileen Aroon !
When, like a diadem,
Buds blush around the stem,
Which is the fairest gem ?—
    Eileen Aroon !

Is it the laughing eye,
    Eileen Aroon !
Is it the timid sigh,
    Eileen Aroon !
Is it the tender tone,
Soft as the string'd harp's moan ?
O, it is truth alone,—
    Eileen Aroon !

When

When like the rising day,
        Eileen Aroon !
Love sends his early ray,
        Eileen Aroon !
What makes his dawning glow,
Changeless through joy or woe ?
Only the constant know :—
        Eileen Aroon !

I know a valley fair,
        Eileen Aroon !
I knew a cottage there,
        Eileen Aroon !
Far in that valley's shade
I knew a gentle maid,
Flower of a hazel glade,—
        Eileen Aroon !

Who in the song so sweet ?
        Eileen Aroon !
Who in the dance so fleet ?
        Eileen Aroon !
Dear were her charms to me,
Dearer her laughter free,
Dearest her constancy,—
        Eileen Aroon !

Were she no longer true,
        Eileen Aroon !
What should her lover do ?
        Eileen Aroon !
Fly with his broken chain
Far o'er the sounding main,
Never to love again,—
        Eileen Aroon !

Youth most with time decay,
        Eileen Aroon!
Beauty must fade away,
        Eileen Aroon!
Castles are sack'd in war,
Chieftains are scatter'd far
Truth is a fixèd star,—
        Eileen Aroon.

JAMES CLARENCE MANGAN

1803–1849

Dark Rosaleen

75.

O MY Dark Rosaleen,
   Do not sigh, do not weep!
The priests are on the ocean green,
  They march along the deep.
There 's wine from the royal Pope,
  Upon the ocean green;
And Spanish ale shall give you hope,
  My Dark Rosaleen!
  My own Rosaleen!
Shall glad your heart, shall give you hope,
Shall give you health, and help, and hope,
  My Dark Rosaleen!

Over hills, and thro' dales,
  Have I roam'd for your sake;
All yesterday I sail'd with sails
  On river and on lake.
The Erne, at its highest flood,
  I dash'd across unseen,
For there was lightning in my blood,
  My dark Rosaleen!

77

My

My own Rosaleen !
O, there was lightning in my blood,
Red lightning lighten'd thro' my blood,
    My Dark Rosaleen !

All day long, in unrest,
    To and fro do I move.
The very soul within my breast
    Is wasted for you, love !
The heart in my bosom faints
    To think of you, my Queen,
My life of life, my saint of saints,
    My Dark Rosaleen !
    My own Rosaleen !
To hear your sweet and sad complaints,
My life, my love, my saint of saints,
    My Dark Rosaleen !

Woe and pain, pain and woe,
    Are my lot, night and noon,
To see your bright face clouded so,
    Like to the mournful moon.
But yet will I rear your throne
    Again in golden sheen ;
'Tis you shall reign, shall reign alone,
    My Dark Rosaleen !
    My own Rosaleen !
'Tis you shall have the golden throne,
'Tis you shall reign, and reign alone,
    My Dark Rosaleen !

Over dews, over sands,
    Will I fly, for your weal :
Your holy delicate white hands
    Shall girdle me with steel.

JAMES CLARENCE MANGAN

At home, in your emerald bowers,
　From morning's dawn till e'en,
You'll pray for me, my flower of flowers,
　My Dark Rosaleen !
　My fond Rosaleen !
You'll think of me thro' daylight hours,
My virgin flower, my flower of flowers,
　My Dark Rosaleen !

I could scale the blue air,
　I could plough the high hills,
O, I could kneel all night in prayer,
　To heal your many ills !
And one beamy smile from you
　Would float like light between
My toils and me, my own, my true,
　My Dark Rosaleen !
　My fond Rosaleen !
Would give me life and soul anew,
A second life, a soul anew,
　My Dark Rosaleen !

O, the Erne shall run red,
　With redundance of blood,
The earth shall rock beneath our tread,
　And flames wrap hill and wood,
And gun-peal and slogan-cry
　Wake many a glen serene,
Ere you shall fade, ere you shall die,
　My Dark Rosaleen !
　My own Rosaleen !
The Judgement Hour must first be nigh,
Ere you can fade, ere you can die,
　My Dark Rosaleen !

76.   *The Fair Hills of Eiré, O*

TAKE a blessing from my heart to the land of my
     birth,
And the fair hills of Eiré, O !
And to all that yet survive of Eibhear's tribe on earth,
On the fair hills of Eiré, O !
In that land so delightful the wild thrush's lay,
Seems to pour a lament forth for Eiré's decay.
Alas, alas ! why pine I a thousand miles away
From the fair hills of Eiré, O !

The soil is rich and soft, the air is mild and bland,
Of the fair hills of Eiré, O !
Her barest rock is greener to me than this rude land ;
O the fair hills of Eiré, O !
Her woods are tall and straight, grove rising over grove ;
Trees flourish in her glens below and on her heights above;
Ah, in heart and in soul I shall ever, ever love
The fair hills of Eiré, O !

A noble tribe, moreover, are the now hapless Gael,
On the fair hills of Eiré, O !
A tribe in battle's hour unused to shrink or fail
On the fair hills of Eiré, O !
For this is my lament in bitterness outpour'd
To see them slain or scatter'd by the Saxon sword :
O woe of woes to see a foreign spoiler horde
On the fair hills of Eiré, O !

Broad and tall rise the *cruachs* in the golden morning glow
On the fair hills of Eiré, O !
O'er her smooth grass for ever sweet cream and honey flow,
On the fair hills of Eiré, O !

Oh, I long, I am pining, again to behold
The land that belongs to the brave Gael of old.
Far dearer to my heart than a gift of gems or gold
Are the fair hills of Eiré, O !

The dewdrops lie bright mid the grass and yellow corn
On the fair hills of Eiré, O !
The sweet-scented apples blush redly in the morn
On the fair hills of Eiré, O !
The water-cress and sorrel fill the vales below,
The streamlets are hush'd till the evening breezes blow,
While the waves of the Suir, noble river ! ever flow
Neath the fair hills of Eiré, O !

A fruitful clime is Eiré's, through valley, meadow, plain,
And the fair hills of Eiré, O !
The very bread of life is in the yellow grain
On the fair hills of Eiré, O !
Far dearer unto me than the tones music yields
Is the lowing of the kine and the calves in her fields,
In the sunlight that shone long ago on the shields
Of the Gaels, on the fair hills of Eiré, O !

77.   *The Karamanian Exile*

I SEE thee ever in my dreams,
  Karaman !
Thy hundred hills, thy thousand streams,
Karaman, O Karaman !
As when thy gold-bright morning gleams,
As when the deepening sunset seams
With lines of light thy hills and streams,
Karaman !

So

So thou loomest on my dreams,
Karaman!
On all my dreams, my homesick dreams,
Karaman, O Karaman!

The hot bright plains, the sun, the skies,
Karaman!
Seem death-black marble to mine eyes,
Karaman, O Karaman!
I turn from summer's blooms and dyes;
Yet in my dreams thou dost arise
In welcome glory to mine eyes,
Karaman!
In thee my life of life yet lies,
Karaman!
Thou still art holy in mine eyes,
Karaman, O Karaman!

Ere my fighting years were come,
Karaman!
Troops were few in Erzerome,
Karaman, O Karaman!
Their fiercest came from Erzerome,
They came from Ukhbar's palace dome,
They dragg'd me forth from thee, my home,
Karaman!
Thee, my own, my mountain home,
Karaman!
In life and death, my spirit's home,
Karaman, O Karaman!

O none of all my sisters ten,
Karaman!
Loved like me my fellow-men,
Karaman, O Karaman!

I was mild as milk till then,
I was soft as silk till then ;
Now my breast is as a den,
Karaman !
Foul with blood and bones of men,
Karaman !
With blood and bones of slaughter'd men,
Karaman, O Karaman !

My boyhood's feelings newly born,
Karaman !
Wither'd like young flowers uptorn,
Karaman, O Karaman !
And in their stead sprang weed and thorn ;
What once I loved now moves my scorn ;
My burning eyes are dried to horn,
Karaman !
I hate the blessèd light of morn,
Karaman !
It maddens me, the face of morn,
Karaman, O Karaman !

The Spahi wears a tyrant's chains,
Karaman !
But bondage worse than this remains,
Karaman, O Karaman !
His heart is black with million stains :
Thereon, as on Kaf's blasted plains,
Shall nevermore fall dews and rains,
Karaman !
Save poison-dews and bloody rains,
Karaman !
Hell's poison-dews and bloody rains,
Karaman, O Karaman !

But

But life at worst must end ere long,
Karaman !
Azrael avengeth every wrong,
Karaman, O Karaman !
Of late my thoughts rove more among
Thy fields ; o'ershadowing fancies throng
My mind, and texts of bodeful song,
Karaman !
Azrael is terrible and strong,
Karaman !
His lightning sword smites all ere long,
Karaman, O Karaman !

There's care to-night in Ukhbar's halls,
Karaman !
There's hope, too, for his trodden thralls,
Karaman, O Karaman !
What lights flash red along yon walls ?
Hark ! hark ! the muster-trumpet calls !
I see the sheen of spears and shawls,
Karaman !
The foe ! the foe !—they scale the walls,
Karaman !
To-night Muràd or Ukhbar falls,
Karaman, O Karaman !

78.   *The Three Khalandeers*

THE WAIL

*L*a' *laha, il Allah !*
   Here we meet, we three, at length,
Amrah, Osman, Perizad :
Shorn of all our grace and strength,
Poor, and old, and very sad.
We have lived, but live no more ;
Life has lost its gloss for us,
Since the days we spent of yore
Boating down the Bosphorus !
La' laha, il Allah !
The Bosphorus, the Bosphorus !
Old time brought home no loss for us ;
We felt full of health and heart
Upon the foamy Bosphorus !

La' laha, il Allah !
Days indeed ! A shepherd's tent
Served us then for house and fold ;
All to whom we gave or lent,
Paid us back a thousandfold.
Troublous years, by myriads wail'd,
Rarely had a cross for us,
Never, when we gaily sail'd
Singing down the Bosphorus.
La' laha, il Allah !
The Bosphorus, the Bosphorus !
There never came a cross for us,
While we daily, gaily sail'd
Adown the meadowy Bosphorus.

La'

JAMES CLARENCE MANGAN

La' laha, il Allah!
Blithe as birds we flew along,
Laugh'd and quaff'd and stared about;
Wine and roses, mirth and song,
Were what most we cared about.
Fame we left for quacks to seek,
Gold was dust and dross for us,
While we lived from week to week
Boating down the Bosphorus.
La' laha, il Allah!
The Bosphorus, the Bosphorus!
And gold was dust and dross for us,
While we lived from week to week
Boating down the Bosphorus.

La' laha, il Allah!
Friends we were, and would have shared
Purses, had we twenty full.
If we spent, or if we spared,
Still our funds were plentiful.
Save the hours we pass'd apart,
Time brought home no loss for us;
We felt full of hope and heart
While we clove the Bosphorus.
La' laha, il Allah!
The Bosphorus, the Bosphorus!
For life has lost its gloss for us
Since the days we spent of yore
Upon the pleasant Bosphorus!

La' laha, il Allah!
Ah! for youth's delirious hours,
Man pays well in after-days,
When quenched hopes and palsied powers
Mock his love-and-laughter days.
86

Thorns and thistles on our path
Took the place of moss for us,
Till false fortune's tempest-wrath
Drove us from the Bosphorus.
La' laha, il Allah !
The Bosphorus, the Bosphorus !
When thorns took place of moss for us,
Gone was all ! Our hearts were graves
Deep, deeper than the Bosphorus.

La' laha, il Allah !
Gone is all ! In one abyss
Lie health, youth, and merriment !
All we've learnt amounts to this :
Life's a sad experiment !
What it is we trebly feel
Pondering what it was for us,
When our shallop's bounding keel
Clove the joyous Bosphorus.
La' laha, il Allah !
The Bosphorus, the Bosphorus !
We wail for what life was for us,
When our shallop's bounding keel
Clove the joyous Bosphorus !

THE WARNING

La' laha, il Allah !
Pleasure tempts, yet man has none
Save himself t' accuse, if her
Temptings prove, when all is done,
Lures hung out by Lucifer.
Guard your fire in youth, O friends !
Manhood's is but phosphorus,
And bad luck attends and ends
Boatings down the Bosphorus !

La'

La' laha, il Allah !
The Bosphorus, the Bosphorus !
Youth's fire soon wanes to phosphorus,
And slight luck or grace attends
Your boaters down the Bosphorus !

79.   *Gone in the Wind*

SOLOMON, where is thy throne ?   It is gone in the
wind.
Babylon, where is thy might ?   It is gone in the wind.
Like the swift shadows of noon, like the dreams of the
blind,
Vanish the glories and pomps of the earth in the wind.

Man, canst thou build upon aught in the pride of thy
mind ?
Wisdom will teach thee that nothing can tarry behind :
Tho' there be thousand bright actions embalm'd and
enshrined,
Myriads and millions of brighter are snow in the wind.

Solomon, where is thy throne ?   It is gone in the wind.
Babylon, where is thy might ?   It is gone in the wind.
All that the genius of man hath achieved or design'd
Waits but its hour to be dealt with as dust by the wind.

Say what is pleasure ?   A phantom, a mask undefined :
Science ?   An almond whereof we can pierce but the rind :
Honour and affluence ?   Firmans that Fortune hath
sign'd,
Only to glitter and pass on the wings of the wind.

Solomon, where is thy throne ?   It is gone in the wind.
Babylon, where is thy might ?   It is gone in the wind.
Who is the fortunate ?   *He who in anguish hath pined !*
He shall rejoice when his relics are dust in the wind.

Mortal, be careful with what thy best hopes are entwined:
Woe to the miners for Truth, where the lampless have
    mined !
Woe to the seekers on earth for what none ever find !
They and their trust shall be scatter'd like leaves to the
    wind !

Solomon, where is thy throne ?   It is gone in the wind.
Babylon, where is thy might ?   It is gone in the wind.
Happy in death are they only whose hearts have consign'd
All earth's affections and longings and cares to the wind.

Pity thou, reader, the madness of poor humankind
Raving of knowledge—and Satan so busy to blind !
Raving of glory, like me ; for the garlands I bind,
Garlands of song, are but gather'd—and strewn in the wind.

Solomon, where is thy throne ?   It is gone in the wind
Babylon, where is thy might ?   It is gone in the wind.
I, Abul-Namez, must rest ; for my fire is declined,
And I hear voices from Hades like bells on the wind.

80.   *To Amine*

VEIL not thy mirror, sweet Amine,
    Till night shall also veil each star !
Thou seest a twofold marvel there :
The only face so fair as thine,
The only eyes that, near or far,
Can gaze on thine without despair.

81.   *Advice against Travel*

TRAVERSE not the globe for lore ! The sternest
But the surest teacher is the heart ;
Studying that and that alone, thou learnest
Best and soonest whence and what thou art.

Moor, Chinese, Egyptian, Russian, Roman,
Tread one common down-hill path of doom ;
Everywhere the names are man and woman,
Everywhere the old sad sins find room.

Evil angels tempt us in all places.
What but sands or snows hath earth to give ?
Dream not, friend, of deserts and oases ;
But look inwards, and begin to live !

82.   *The World: a Ghazel*

TÒ this khan, and from this khan
How many pilgrims came and went too !
In this khan, and by this khan
    What arts were spent, what hearts were rent too !
To this khan and from this khan
    (Which, for penance, man is sent to)
Many a van and caravan
    Crowded came, and shrouded went too.
Christian man and Mussulman,
    Guebre, heathen, Jew, and Gentoo,
To this khan, and from this khan,
    Weeping came, and sleeping went too.
A riddle this since time began,
    Which many a sage his mind hath bent to :
All came, all went ; but never man
    Knew whence they came, or where they went to !

83. *The Nameless One*

ROLL forth, my song, like the rushing river,
    That sweeps along to the mighty sea;
God will inspire me while I deliver
        My soul of thee!

Tell thou the world, when my bones lie whitening
    Amid the last homes of youth and eld,
That once there was one whose veins ran lightning
        No eye beheld.

Tell how his boyhood was one drear night-hour,
    How shone for him, through his griefs and gloom,
No star of all heaven sends to light our
        Path to the tomb.

Roll on, my song, and to after ages
    Tell how, disdaining all earth can give,
He would have taught men, from wisdom's pages,
        The way to live.

And tell how trampled, derided, hated,
    And worn by weakness, disease, and wrong,
He fled for shelter to God, who mated
        His soul with song.

—With song which alway, sublime or vapid,
    Flow'd like a rill in the morning beam,
Perchance not deep, but intense and rapid:
        A mountain stream.

Tell how this Nameless, condemn'd for years long
    To herd with demons from hell beneath,
Saw things that made him, with groans and tears, long
        For even death.

Go

Go on to tell how, with genius wasted,
  Betray'd in friendship, befool'd in love,
With spirit shipwreck'd, and young hopes blasted,
        He still, still strove ;

Till, spent with toil, dreeing death for others
  (And some whose hands should have wrought for him,
If children live not for sires and mothers),
        His mind grew dim ;

And he fell far through that pit abysmal,
  The gulf and grave of Maginn and Burns,
And pawn'd his soul for the devil's dismal
        Stock of returns.

But yet redeem'd it in days of darkness,
  And shapes and signs of the final wrath,
When death, in hideous and ghastly starkness,
        Stood on his path.

And tell how now, amid wreck and sorrow,
  And want, and sickness, and houseless nights,
He bides in calmness the silent morrow,
        That no ray lights.

And lives he still, then ? Yes ! Old and hoary
  At thirty-nine, from despair and woe,
He lives, enduring what future story
        Will never know.

Him grant a grave to, ye pitying noble,
  Deep in your bosoms : there let him dwell !
He, too, had tears for all souls in trouble,
        Here and in hell.

84.   *Mariners' Song*

TO sea, to sea ! The calm is o'er ;
      The wanton water leaps in sport,
And rattles down the pebbly shore ;
   The dolphin wheels, the sea-cows snort,
And unseen Mermaids' pearly song
Comes bubbling up, the weeds among.
   Fling broad the sail, dip deep the oar :
   To sea, to sea ! ᵗhe calm is o'er.

To sea, to sea ! our wide-wing'd bark
   Shall billowy cleave its sunny way,
And with its shadow, fleet and dark,
   Break the caved Tritons' azure day,
Like mighty eagle soaring light
O'er antelopes on Alpine height.
   The anchor heaves, the ship swings free,
   The sails swell full.   To sea, to sea !

85.   *Dirge*

THE swallow leaves her nest,
      The soul my weary breast ;
But therefore let the rain
      On my grave
Fall pure ; for why complain ?
Since both will come again
      O'er the wave.

The

The wind dead leaves and snow
Doth hurry to and fro ;
And, once, a day shall break
　O'er the wave,
When a storm of ghosts shall shake
The dead, until they wake
　In the grave.

86.　　　　　　　　*Dream-Pedlary*

IF there were dreams to sell,
　What would you buy ?
Some cost a passing bell ;
　Some a light sigh,
That shakes from Life's fresh crown
Only a rose-leaf down.
If there were dreams to sell,
Merry and sad to tell,
And the crier rang the bell,
　What would you buy ?

A cottage lone and still,
　With bowers nigh,
Shadowy, my woes to still,
　Until I die.
Such pearl from Life's fresh crown
Fain would I shake me down.
Were dreams to have at will,
This would best heal my ill,
　This would I buy.

87.   *Bridal Song to Amala*

By female voices

WE have bathed, where none have seen us,
    In the lake and in the fountain,
        Underneath the charmèd statue
Of the timid, bending Venus,
    When the water-nymphs were counting
In the waves the stars of night,
    And those maidens started at you,
Your limbs shone through so soft and bright.
        But no secrets dare we tell,
            For thy slaves unlace thee,
            And he, who shall embrace thee,
        Waits to try thy beauty's spell.

By male voices

We have crown'd thee queen of women,
    Since love's love, the rose, hath kept her
        Court within thy lips and blushes,
And thine eye, in beauty swimming,
    Kissing, we render'd up the sceptre,
At whose touch the startled soul
    Like an ocean bounds and gushes,
And spirits bend at thy control.
        But no secrets dare we tell,
            For thy slaves unlace thee,
            And he, who shall embrace thee,
        Is at hand, and so farewell!

88. *Wolfram's Song*

OLD Adam, the carrion crow,
   The old crow of Cairo ;
He sat in the shower, and let it flow
  Under his tail and over his crest ;
    And through every feather
    Leak'd the wet weather ;
  And the bough swung under his nest ;
  For his beak it was heavy with marrow.
    Is that the wind dying ? O no ;
    It 's only two devils, that blow
     Through a murderer's bones, to and fro,
      In the ghosts' moonshine.

Ho ! Eve, my grey carrion wife,
  When we have supped on kings' marrow,
Where shall we drink and make merry our life ?
  Our nest it is queen Cleopatra's skull,
    'Tis cloven and crack'd,
    And batter'd and hack'd,
  But with tears of blue eyes it is full :
  Let us drink then, my raven of Cairo !
    Is that the wind dying ? O no ;
    It 's only two devils, that blow
     Through a murderer's bones, to and fro,
      In the ghosts' moonshine.

EDWARD GEORGE EARLE BULWER-LYTTON,
LORD LYTTON

1803-1873

89.   *Absent yet Present*

AS the flight of a river
    That flows to the sea
My soul rushes ever
    In tumult to thee.

A twofold existence
    I am where thou art ;
My heart in the distance
    Beats close to thy heart.

Look up, I am near thee,
    I gaze on thy face ;
I see thee, I hear thee,
    I feel thine embrace.

As a magnet's control on
    The steel it draws to it,
Is the charm of thy soul on
    The thoughts that pursue it.

And absence but brightens
    The eyes that I miss,
And custom but heightens
    The spell of thy kiss.

It is not from duty,
    Though that may be owed,—
It is not from beauty,
    Though that be bestow'd ;

But

But all that I care for,
  And all that I know,
Is that, without wherefore,
  I worship thee so.

Through granite it breaketh
  A tree to the ray;
As a dreamer forsaketh
  The grief of the day,

My soul in its fever
  Escapes unto thee;
O dream to the griever!
  O light to the tree!

A twofold existence
  I am where thou art;
Hark, hear in the distance
  The beat of my heart!

90.   *Nydia's Song*

THE Wind and the Beam loved the Rose,
  And the Rose loved one:
For who recks the Wind where it blows?
  Or loves not the Sun?

None knew whence the humble Wind stole,
  Poor sport of the skies:
None dreamt that the Wind had a soul
  In its mournful sighs.

O happy Beam, how canst thou prove
    That bright love of thine ?
In thy light is the proof of thy love,
    Thou hast but to shine.

How its love can the Wind reveal ?
    Unwelcome its sigh :
Mute, mute to the Rose let it steal—
    Its proof is—to die !

CHARLES SWAIN

1803-1874

91. *The Field-Path*

TRIPPING down the field-path
    Early in the morn,
There I met my own love
    'Midst the golden corn ;
Autumn winds were blowing,
    As in frolic chase,
All her silken ringlets
    Backward from her face ;
Little time for speaking
    Had she, for the wind
Bonnet, scarf, or ribbon
    Ever swept behind.

Still some sweet improvement
    In her beauty shone ;
Every graceful movement
    Won me, one by one !
Little time for wooing
    Had we, for the wind

99   Still

CHARLES SWAIN

Still kept on undoing
    What we sought to bind . . .
Still I see the field-path :—
    Would that I could see
Her whose graceful beauty
    Lost is now to me !

RALPH WALDO EMERSON

1803-1882

Wood-notes

92.

WHOSO walks in solitude
    And inhabiteth the wood,
Choosing light, wave, rock and bird
Before the money-loving herd,
Into that forester shall pass,
From these companions, power and grace.
Clean shall he be, without, within,
From the old adhering sin ;
All ill dissolving in the light
Of his triumphant piercing sight :
Not vain, sour, nor frivolous ;
Nor mad, athirst, nor garrulous ;
Grave chaste, contented tho' retired,
And of all other men desired,
On him the light of star and moon
Shall fall with pure radiance down ;
All constellations of the sky
Shall shed their virtue thro' his eye.
Him Nature giveth for defence
His formidable innocence ;
The mountain sap, the shells, the sea,
All spheres, all stones, his helpers be ;

He shall meet the speeding year
Without wailing, without fear ;
He shall be happy in his love,
Like to like shall joyful prove ;
He shall be happy while he woos,
Muse-born, a daughter of the Muse.
But if with gold she bind her hair,
And deck her breast with diamond,
Take off thine eyes, thy heart forbear,
Tho' thou lie alone on the ground !

93.   *Fore-runners*

LONG I follow'd happy guides,
    I could never reach their sides ;
Their step is forth and, ere the day
Breaks, up their leaguer and away.
Keen my sense, my heart was young,
Right goodwill my sinews strung,
But no speed of mine avails
To hunt upon their shining trails.
On and away, their hasting feet
Make the morning proud and sweet ;
Flowers they strew,—I catch the scent ;
Or tone of silver instrument
Leaves on the wind melodious trace ;
Yet I could never see their face.
On eastern hills I see their smokes
Mix'd with mist by distant lochs.
I met many travellers,
Who the road had surely kept ;
They saw not my fine revellers—
These had cross'd them while they slept.

Some

Some had heard their fair report
In the country or the court:
Fleetest couriers alive
Never yet could once arrive,
As they went or they return'd,
At the house where these sojourn'd.
Sometimes their strong speed they slacken
Though they are not overtaken;
In sleep their jubilant troop is near—
I tuneful voices overhear,
It may be in wood or waste—
At unawares 'tis come and past.
Their near camp my spirit knows
By signs gracious as rainbows.
I thenceforward and long after
Listen for their harplike laughter,
And carry in my heart, for days,
Peace that hallows rudest ways.

94.   *Days*

DAUGHTERS of Time, the hypocritic Days,
  Muffled and dumb like barefoot dervishes
And marching single in an endless file,
Bring diadems and faggots in their hands.
To each they offer gifts after his will—
Bread, kingdoms, stars, and sky that holds them all.
I, in my pleachèd garden, watch'd the pomp,
Forgot my morning wishes, hastily
Took a few herbs and apples, and the Day
Turn'd and departed silent. I, too late,
Under her solemn fillet saw the scorn.

95.   *Give All to Love*

GIVE all to love ;
　　Obey thy heart ;
Friends, kindred, days,
Estate, good fame,
Plans, credit, and the Muse—
Nothing refuse.

'Tis a brave master ;
Let it have scope :
Follow it utterly,
Hope beyond hope :
High and more high
It dives into noon,
With wing unspent,
Untold intent ;
But it is a god,
Knows its own path,
And the outlets of the sky.

It was never for the mean ;
It requireth courage stout,
Souls above doubt,
Valour unbending :
Such 'twill reward ;—
They shall return
More than they were,
And ever ascending.

Leave all for love ;
Yet, hear me, yet,
One word more thy heart behoved,
One pulse more of firm endeavour—

103   Keep

Keep thee to-day,
To-morrow, for ever,
Free as an Arab
Of thy beloved.

Cling with life to the maid :
But when the surprise,
First vague shadow of surmise,
Flits across her bosom young,
Of a joy apart from thee,
Free be she, fancy-free ;
Nor thou detain her vesture's hem,
Nor the palest rose she flung
From her summer diadem.

Though thou loved her as thyself,
As a self of purer clay ;
Though her parting dims the day,
Stealing grace from all alive ;
Heartily know,
When half-gods go
The gods arrive.

96. *Brahma*

IF the red slayer think he slays,
    Or if the slain think he is slain,
They know not well the subtle ways
    I keep, and pass, and turn again.

Far or forgot to me is near ;
    Shadow and sunlight are the same ;
The vanish'd gods to me appear ;
    And one to me are shame and fame

RALPH WALDO EMERSON

They reckon ill who leave me out ;
  When me they fly, I am the wings ;
I am the doubter and the doubt,
  And I the hymn the Brahmin sings.

The strong gods pine for my abode,
  And pine in vain the sacred Seven ;
But thou, meek lover of the good !
  Find me, and turn thy back on heaven.

RICHARD HENRY HORNE

1803-1884

97.   *The Plough*

A LANDSCAPE IN BERKSHIRE

ABOVE yon sombre swell of land
    Thou see'st the dawn's grave orange hue,
With one pale streak like yellow sand,
    And over that a vein of blue.

The air is cold above the woods ;
  All silent is the earth and sky,
Except with his own lonely moods
  The blackbird holds a colloquy.

Over the broad hill creeps a beam,
  Like hope that gilds a good man's brow;
And now ascends the nostril-stream
  Of stalwart horses come to plough.

Ye rigid Ploughmen, bear in mind
  Your labour is for future hours :
Advance—spare not—nor look behind—
  Plough deep and straight with all your powers !

98.   *Solitude and the Lily*

The Lily :

I BEND above the moving stream,
  And see myself in my own dream,—
  Heaven passing, while I do not pass.
Something divine pertains to me,
Or I to it ;—reality
  Escapes me on this liquid glass.

Solitude :

The changeful clouds that float or poise on high,
Emblem earth's night and day of history ;
Renew'd for ever, evermore to die.
  Thy life-dream is thy fleeting loveliness ;
  But mine is concentrated consciousness,
  A life apart from pleasure or distress.
    The grandeur of the Whole
    Absorbs my soul,
  While my caves sigh o'er human littleness.

The Lily :

    Ah, Solitude,
    Of marble Silence fit abode !
I do prefer my fading face,
My loss of loveliness and grace,
  With cloud-dreams ever in my view ;
Also the hope that other eyes
May share my rapture in the skies,
  And, if illusion, feel it true.

CHARLES WHITEHEAD
1804-1862

99.
The Lamp

AS yonder lamp in my vacated room
   With arduous flame disputes the darksome night,
And can, with its involuntary light,
But lifeless things, that near it stand, illume ;
Yet all the while it doth itself consume,
   And, ere the sun begins its heavenly height
   With courier beams that meet the shepherd's sight,
There, whence its life arose, shall be its tomb—

So wastes my light away.   Perforce confined
   To common things, a limit to its sphere,
It shines on worthless trifles undesign'd
   With fainter ray each hour imprison'd here.
Alas ! to know that the consuming mind
   Shall leave its lamp cold, ere the sun appear.

ROBERT STEPHEN HAWKER
1804-1873

100.
The First Fathers

THEY rear'd their lodges in the wilderness,
   Or built them cells beside the shadowy sea,
And there they dwelt with angels, like a dream !
So they unroll'd the Volume of the Book
And fill'd the fields of the Evangelist
   With thoughts as sweet as flowers.

101. *The Song of the Western Men*

A GOOD sword and a trusty hand !
  A merry heart and true !
King James's men shall understand
  What Cornish lads can do.

And have they fix'd the where and when ?
  And shall Trelawny die ?
Here 's twenty thousand Cornish men
  Will know the reason why !

Out spake their Captain brave and bold,
  A merry wight was he :
' If London Tower were Michael's Hold,
  We'll set Trelawny free !

' We'll cross the Tamar, land to land,
  The Severn is no stay ;
With " One and All " and hand to hand,
  And who shall bid us nay ?

And when we come to London Wall,
  A pleasant sight to view,
Come forth, come forth, ye cowards all !
  Here 's men as good as you.

' Trelawny he 's in keep and hold,
  Trelawny he may die :
But here 's twenty thousand Cornish bold
  Will know the reason why.'
    And shall Trelawny die ?
    And shall Trelawny die ?
    Here 's twenty thousand Cornish men
    Will know the reason why !

102. *Death Song*

THERE lies a cold corpse upon the sands
    Down by the rolling sea ;
Close up the eyes and straighten the hands
    As a Christian man's should be.

Bury it deep, for the good of my soul,
    Six feet below the ground ;
Let the sexton come and the death-bell toll
    And good men stand around.

Lay it among the churchyard stones,
    Where the priest hath bless'd the clay :
I cannot leave the unburied bones,
    And I fain would go my way.

103. *King Arthur's Waes-hael*

WAES-HAEL for knight and dame !
    O merry be their dole !
Drink-hael ! in Jesu's name
    We fill the tawny bowl ;
But cover down the curving crest,
Mould of the Orient Lady's breast.

Waes-hael ! yet lift no lid :
    Drain ye the reeds for wine.
Drink-hael ! the milk was hid
    That soothed that Babe divine ;
Hush'd, as this hollow channel flows,
He drew the balsam from the rose.

            Waes-hael !

Waes-hael! thus glow'd the breast
  Where a God yearn'd to cling;
Drink-hael! so Jesu press'd
  Life from its mystic spring;
Then hush and bend in reverent sign,
And breathe the thrilling reeds for wine.

Waes-hael! in shadowy scene
  Lo! Christmas children we:
Drink-hael! behold we lean
  At a far Mother's knee;
To dream that thus her bosom smiled,
And learn the lip of Bethlehem's Child.

BENJAMIN DISRAELI, EARL OF
BEACONSFIELD

1804–1881

104.   *Wellington*

NOT only that thy puissant arm could bind
    The tyrant of a world, and, conquering Fate,
  Enfranchise Europe, do I deem thee great;
But that in all thy actions I do find
Exact propriety; no gusts of mind
  Fitful and wild, but that continuous state
  Of order'd impulse mariners await
In some benignant and enriching wind,—
  The breath ordain'd of Nature. Thy calm mien
Recalls old Rome as much as thy high deed;
  Duty thine only idol, and serene
When all are troubled; in the utmost need
  Prescient; thy country's servant ever seen,
Yet sovereign of thyself, whate'er may speed.

EDWARD WALSH

1805-1850

105.

Lament

WHEN the folk of my household
  Suppose I am sleeping,
On the cold sod that 's o'er you
  The lone watch I'm keeping.
My fondest! my fairest!
  We may now sleep together!
I've the cold earth's damp odour,
  And I'm worn from the weather.

Remember that lone night
  I last spent with you, Love,
Beneath the dark sloe-tree
  When the icy wind blew, Love.
High praise to thy Saviour
  No sin-stain had found you,
That your virginal glory
  Shines brightly around you!

The priests and the friars
  Are ceaselessly chiding
That I love a young maiden
  In life not abiding.
O! I'd shelter and shield you
  If wild storms were swelling—
And O, my wreck'd hope,
  That the cold earth 's your dwelling!

FRANCIS MAHONY

106. *The Bells of Shandon*

WITH deep affection,
  And recollection,
I often think of
  Those Shandon bells,
Whose sounds so wild would,
In the days of childhood,
Fling around my cradle
  Their magic spells :
On this I ponder
Where'er I wander,
And thus grow fonder,
  Sweet Cork, of thee ;
With thy bells of Shandon,
That sound so grand on
The pleasant waters
  Of the River Lee.

I've heard bells chiming
Full many a clime in,
Tolling sublime in
  Cathedral shrine,
While at a glib rate
Brass tongues would vibrate—
But all their music
  Spoke naught like thine ;

FRANCIS MAHONY

For memory, dwelling
On each proud swelling
Of the belfry knelling
   Its bold notes free,
Made the bells of Shandon
Sound far more grand on
The pleasant waters
   Of the River Lee.

I've heard bells tolling
Old Adrian's Mole in,
Their thunder rolling
   From the Vatican,
And cymbals glorious
Swinging uproarious
In the gorgeous turrets
   Of Notre Dame ;
But thy sounds were sweeter
Than the dome of Peter
Flings o'er the Tiber,
   Pealing solemnly—
O, the bells of Shandon
Sound far more grand on
The pleasant waters
   Of the River Lee.

There 's a bell in Moscow,
While on tower and kiosk O
In Saint Sophia
   The Turkman gets,
And loud in air
Calls men to prayer
From the tapering summits
   Of tall minarets.

Such

Such empty phantom
I freely grant them ;
But there 's an anthem
   More dear to me,—
'Tis the bells of Shandon,
That sound so grand on
The pleasant waters
   Of the River Lee.

THOMAS WADE

1805-1875

107.   *The True Martyr*

THE Martyr worthiest of the bleeding name
   Is he whose life a bloodless part fulfils ;
  Whom racks nor tortures tear, nor poniard kills,
Nor heat of bigots' sacrificial flame :
But whose great soul can to herself proclaim
   The fulness of the everlasting ills
     Wherewith all pain'd Creation writhes and thrills,
And yet pursue unblench'd her solemn aim :

Who works, all knowing work's futility,
   Creates, all conscious of ubiquitous death,
And hopes, believes, adores, while Destiny
   Points from Life's steep to all her graves beneath :
     Whose thought 'mid scorching woes is found apart,
     Perfect amid the flames, like Cranmer's heart.

ELIZABETH BARRETT BROWNING

1806-1861

108.   *Farewells from Paradise*

River-spirits.

HARK ! the flow of the four rivers—
       Hark the flow !
How the silence round you shivers,
While our voices through it go,
    Cold and clear.

A softer voice.

Think a little, while ye hear,
    Of the banks
Where the willows and the deer
Crowd in intermingled ranks,
As if all would drink at once
Where the living water runs !—
Of the fishes' golden edges
Flashing in and out the sedges ;
Of the swans on silver thrones,
Floating down the winding streams
With impassive eyes turned shoreward
And a chant of undertones,—
And the lotus leaning forward
To help them into dreams.
    Fare ye well, farewell !
The river-sounds, no longer audible,
    Expire at Eden's door.

                         Each

Each footstep of your treading
Treads out some murmur which ye heard before.
Farewell ! the streams of Eden
Ye shall hear nevermore !

Bird-spirit.

I am the nearest nightingale
That singeth in Eden after you ;
And I am singing loud and true,
And sweet,—I do not fail.
I sit upon a cypress bough,
Close to the gate, and I fling my song
Over the gate and through the mail
Of the warden angels marshall'd strong,—
   Over the gate and after you !
And the warden angels let it pass,
Because the poor brown bird, alas,
   Sings in the garden, sweet and true.
And I build my song of high pure notes,
   Note over note, height over height,
   Till I strike the arch of the Infinite,
And I bridge abysmal agonies
With strong, clear calms of harmonies,—
And something abides, and something floats,
In the song which I sing after you.
   Fare ye well, farewell !
The creature-sounds, no longer audible,
   Expire at Eden's door.
   Each footstep of your treading
Treads out some cadence which ye heard before.
   Farewell ! the birds of Eden
   Ye shall hear nevermore !

109.   *Cowper's Grave*

IT is a place where poets crown'd may feel the heart's
    decaying;
It is a place where happy saints may weep amid their
    praying.
Yet let the grief and humbleness, as low as silence,
    languish:
Earth surely now may give her calm to whom she gave
    her anguish.

O poets, from a maniac's tongue was poured the deathless
    singing!
O Christians, at your Cross of hope, a hopeless hand was
    clinging!
O men, this man in brotherhood your weary paths
    beguiling,
Groan'd inly while he taught you peace, and died while
    ye were smiling!

And now, what time ye all may read through dimming
    tears his story,
How discord on the music fell, and darkness on the glory,
And how when, one by one, sweet sounds and wandering
    lights departed,
He wore no less a loving face because so broken-hearted,

He shall be strong to sanctify the poet's high vocation,
And bow the meekest Christian down in meeker adoration;
Nor ever shall he be, in praise, by wise or good forsaken,
Named softly as the household name of one whom God
    hath taken.

With

With quiet sadness and no gloom I learn to think upon
 him,—
With meekness that is gratefulness to God whose heaven
 hath won him,
Who suffer'd once the madness-cloud to His own love to
 blind him,
But gently led the blind along where breath and bird
 could find him ;

And wrought within his shatter'd brain such quick poetic
 senses
As hills have language for, and stars, harmonious in-
 fluences.
The pulse of dew upon the grass kept his within its
 number,
And silent shadows from the trees refresh'd him like
 a slumber.

Wild timid hares were drawn from woods to share his
 home-caresses,
Uplooking to his human eyes with sylvan tendernesses.
The very world, by God's constraint, from falsehood's
 ways removing,
Its women and its men became, beside him, true and
 loving.

And though, in blindness, he remain'd unconscious of
 that guiding,
And things provided came without the sweet sense of
 providing,
He testified this solemn truth, while frenzy desolated,
—Nor man nor nature satisfy whom only God created.

Like a sick child that knoweth not his mother while she
    blesses
And drops upon his burning brow the coolness of her
    kisses,—
That turns his fevered eyes around—'My mother!
    where's my mother?'—
As if such tender words and deeds could come from any
    other!—

The fever gone, with leaps of heart he sees her bending
    o'er him,
Her face all pale from watchful love, the unweary love
    she bore him!—
Thus, woke the poet from the dream his life's long fever
    gave him,
Beneath those deep pathetic Eyes, which closed in death
    to save him.

Thus? oh, not *thus!* no type of earth can image that
    awaking,
Wherein he scarcely heard the chant of seraphs, round
    him breaking,
Or felt the new immortal throb of soul from body parted,
But felt those eyes alone, and knew,—'*My Saviour! not
    deserted!*'

Deserted! Who hath dreamt that when the cross in
    darkness rested,
Upon the Victim's hidden face, no love was manifested?
What frantic hands outstretch'd have e'er the atoning
    drops averted?
What tears have wash'd them from the soul, that *one*
    should be deserted?

Deserted!

Deserted ! God could separate from his own essence
    rather ;
And Adam's sins have swept between the righteous Son
    and Father.
Yea, once, Immanuel's orphan'd cry his universe hath
    shaken—
It went up single, echoless, ' *My God, I am forsaken !* '

It went up from the Holy's lips amid his lost creation,
That, of the lost, no son should use those words of desola-
    tion !
That earth's worst frenzies, marring hope, should mar
    not hope's fruition,
And I, on Cowper's grave, should see his rapture in
    a vision.

110.   *Praise of Earth*

O EARTH,
    I count the praises thou art worth,
By thy waves that move aloud,
By thy hills against the cloud,
By thy valleys warm and green,
By the copses' elms between,
By their birds which, like a sprite
Scatter'd by a strong delight
Into fragments musical,
Stir and sing in every bush ;
By thy silver founts that fall,
As if to entice the stars at night
To thine heart ; by grass and rush,
And little weeds the children pull,
Mistook for flowers !

—O, beautiful
Art thou, Earth, albeit worse
Than in heaven is callèd good !
Good to us, that we may know
Meekly from thy good to go ;
While the holy crying Blood,
Puts its music kind and low
'Twixt such ears as are not dull,
   And thine ancient curse !

Praisèd be the mosses soft
In thy forest pathways oft,
And the thorns, which make us think
Of the thornless river-brink
   Where the ransom'd tread ;
Praisèd be thy sunny gleams,
And the storm, that worketh dreams
   Of calm unfinishèd ;
Praisèd be thine active days,
And thy night-time's solemn need,
When in God's dear book we read
   No night shall be therein ;
Praisèd be thy dwellings warm
By household faggot's cheerful blaze,
Where, to hear of pardon'd sin,
Pauseth oft the merry din,
Save the babe's upon the arm,
Who croweth to the crackling wood;
Yea,—and, better understood,
Praisèd be thy dwellings cold,
Hid beneath the churchyard mould,
Where the bodies of the saints,
Separate from earthly taints,
Lie asleep, in blessing bound,
Waiting for the trumpet's sound

To

To free them into blessing ;—none
Weeping more beneath the sun,
Though dangerous words of human love
Be graven very near, above.

Earth, we Christians praise thee thus,
Even for the change that comes,
With a grief, from thee to us !
For thy cradles and thy tombs,
For the pleasant corn and wine,
And summer-heat ; and also for
The frost upon the sycamore,
    And hail upon the vine !

111.   *Confessions*

FACE to face in my chamber, my silent chamber,
    I saw her :
God and she and I only, . . . there, I sate down to draw her
Soul through the clefts of confession. . . . Speak, I am
            holding thee fast,
As the angels of resurrection shall do it at the last.
        ' My cup is blood-red
        With my sin,' she said,
    ' And I pour it out to the bitter lees,
As if the angels of judgement stood over me strong at
            the last,
        Or as thou wert as these ! '

When God smote his hands together, and struck out thy
            soul as a spark
Into the organized glory of things, from deeps of the
            dark,—

Say, didst thou shine, didst thou burn, didst thou honour
      the power in the form,
As the star does at night, or the fire-fly, or even the little
      ground-worm ?
     ' I have sinn'd,' she said,
     ' For my seed-light shed
  Has smoulder'd away from his first decrees !
The cypress praiseth the fire-fly, the ground-leaf praiseth
      the worm,—
    I am viler than these ! '

When God on that sin had pity, and did not trample
      thee straight
With his wild rains beating and drenching thy light
      found inadequate ;
When He only sent thee the north-winds, a little searching
      and chill,
To quicken thy flame . . . didst thou kindle and flash to
      the heights of his will ?
     ' I have sinn'd,' she said,
     ' Unquicken'd, unspread
  My fire dropt down, and I wept on my knees !
I only said of his winds of the north as I shrank from
      their chill, . . .
    What delight is in these ? '

When God on that sin had pity, and did not meet it as
      such,
But temper'd the wind to thy uses, and soften'd the
      world to thy touch,
At least thou wast moved in thy soul, though unable to
      prove it afar,
Thou couldst carry thy light like a jewel, not giving it
      out like a star ?

                                                   ' I

'I have sinn'd,' she said,
    'And not merited
  The gift He gives, by the grace He sees !
The mine-cave praiseth the jewel, the hillside praiseth
        the star ;
    I am viler than these.'

Then I cried aloud in my passion, . . . Unthankful and
        impotent creature,
To throw up thy scorn unto God through the rents in
        thy beggarly nature !
If He, the all-giving and loving, is served so unduly, what
        then
Hast thou done to the weak and the false, and the chang-
        ing, . . . thy fellows of men ?
    'I have *loved*,' she said,
    (Words bowing her head
  As the wind the wet acacia-trees !)
'I saw God sitting above me,—but I . . . I sate among
        men,
    And I have loved these.'

Again with a lifted voice, like a choral trumpet that takes
The lowest note of a viol that trembles, and triumphing
        breaks
On the air with it solemn and clear,—'Behold ! I have
        sinned not in this !
Where I loved, I have loved much and well,—I have
        verily loved not amiss.
    Let the living,' she said,
    'Inquire of the Dead,
  In the house of the pale-fronted Images :
My own true dead will answer for me, that I have not
        loved amiss
    In my love for all these.

'The least touch of their hands in the morning, I keep
 it by day and by night;
Their least step on the stair, at the door, still throbs
 through me, if ever so light;
Their least gift, which they left to my childhood, far off,
 in the long-ago years,
Is now turned from a toy to a relic, and seen through
 the crystals of tears.
  Dig the snow,' she said,
  'For my churchyard bed,
 Yet I, as I sleep, shall not fear to freeze,
If one only of these my belovèds, shall love me with
 heart-warm tears,
  As I have loved these!

'If I anger'd any among them, from thenceforth my
 own life was sore;
If I fell by chance from their presence, I clung to their
 memory more.
Their tender I often felt holy, their bitter I sometimes
 call'd sweet;
And whenever their heart has refused me, I fell down
 straight at their feet.
  I have loved,' she said,—
  'Man is weak, God is dread,
 Yet the weak man dies with his spirit at ease,
Having pour'd such an unguent of love but once on the
 Saviour's feet,
  As I lavish'd for these.'

'Go,' I cried, 'thou hast chosen the Human, and left
 the Divine!
Then, at least, have the Human shared with thee their
 wild berry-wine?

        Have

Have they loved back thy love, and when strangers
    approach'd thee with blame,
Have they cover'd thy fault with their kisses, and loved
    thee the same ? '
      But she shrunk and said,
      ' God, over my head,
Must sweep in the wrath of His judgement-seas,
If *He* shall deal with me sinning, but only indeed the same
    And no gentler than these.'

112.   *The Mask*

I HAVE a smiling face, she said,
    I have a jest for all I meet,
I have a garland for my head
    And all its flowers are sweet,—
And so you call me gay, she said.

Grief taught to me this smile, she said,
    And Wrong did teach this jesting bold ;
These flowers were pluck'd from garden-bed
    While a death-chime was toll'd.
And what now will you say ?—she said.

Behind no prison-grate, she said,
    Which slurs the sunshine half a mile
Live captives so uncomforted
    As souls behind a smile.
God's pity let us pray, she said.

ELIZABETH BARRETT BROWNING

I know my face is bright, she said,—
  Such brightness dying suns diffuse;
I bear upon my forehead shed
  The sign of what I lose,—
The ending of my day, she said.

If I dared leave this smile, she said,
  And take a moan upon my mouth,
And tie a cypress round my head,
  And let my tears run smooth,—
It were the happier way, she said.

And since that must not be, she said,
  I fain your bitter world would leave.
How calmly, calmly, smile the Dead,
  Who do not, therefore, grieve!
The yea of Heaven is yea, she said.

But in your bitter world, she said,
  Face-joy 's a costly mask to wear.
'Tis bought with pangs long nourishèd,
  And rounded to despair.
Grief's earnest makes life's play, she said.

Ye weep for those who weep? she said—
  Ah fools! I bid you pass them by.
Go, weep for those whose hearts have bled
  What time their eyes were dry.
Whom sadder can I say? she said.

113. *Grief*

I TELL you, hopeless grief is passionless;
  That only men incredulous of despair,
    Half-taught in anguish, through the midnight air
Beat upward to God's throne in loud access
Of shrieking and reproach. Full desertness
  In souls as countries lieth silent-bare
  Under the blanching, vertical eye-glare
Of the absolute Heavens. Deep-hearted man, express
Grief for thy Dead in silence like to death—
  Most like a monumental statue set
In everlasting watch and moveless woe
Till itself crumble to the dust beneath.
  Touch it; the marble eyelids are not wet:
If it could weep, it could arise and go.

114. *Mystery*

WE sow the glebe, we reap the corn,
  We build the house where we may rest,
And then, at moments, suddenly,
We look up to the great wide sky,
Inquiring wherefore we were born . . .
  For earnest, or for jest?

The senses folding thick and dark
  About the stifled soul within,
We guess diviner things beyond,
And yearn to them with yearning fond;
We strike out blindly to a mark
  Believed in, but not seen.

ELIZABETH BARRETT BROWNING

We vibrate to the pant and thrill
  Wherewith Eternity has curled
In serpent-twine about God's seat;
While, freshening upward to his feet,
In gradual growth his full-leaved will
  Expands from world to world.

And, in the tumult and excess
  Of act and passion under sun,
We sometimes hear—oh, soft and far,
As silver star did touch with star,
The kiss of Peace and Righteousness
  Through all things that are done.

God keeps His holy mysteries
  Just on the outside of man's dream.
In diapason slow, we think
To hear their pinions rise and sink,
While they float pure beneath His eyes,
  Like swans adown a stream.

And, sometimes, horror chills our blood
  To be so near such mystic Things,
And we wrap round us, for defence,
Our purple manners, moods of sense—
As angels, from the face of God,
  Stand hidden in their wings.

And, sometimes, through life's heavy swound
  We grope for them!—with strangled breath
We stretch our hands abroad and try
To reach them in our agony,—
And widen, so, the broad life-wound
  Which soon is large enough for death.

115.   *A Musical Instrument*

WHAT was he doing, the great god Pan,
　　Down in the reeds by the river ?
Spreading ruin and scattering ban,
Splashing and paddling with hoofs of a goat,
And breaking the golden lilies afloat
　　With the dragon-fly on the river.

He tore out a reed, the great god Pan,
　　From the deep cool bed of the river ;
The limpid water turbidly ran,
And the broken lilies a-dying lay,
And the dragon-fly had fled away,
　　Ere he brought it out of the river.

High on the shore sat the great god Pan,
　　While turbidly flow'd the river ;
And hack'd and hew'd as a great god can
With his hard bleak steel at the patient reed,
Till there was not a sign of the leaf indeed
　　To prove it fresh from the river.

He cut it short, did the great god Pan
　　(How tall it stood in the river !),
Then drew the pith, like the heart of a man,
Steadily from the outside ring,
And notch'd the poor dry empty thing
　　In holes, as he sat by the river.

' This is the way,' laugh'd the great god Pan
　　(Laugh'd while he sat by the river),
' The only way, since gods began
To make sweet music, they could succeed.'
Then dropping his mouth to a hole in the reed,
　　He blew in power by the river.

Sweet, sweet, sweet, O Pan!
  Piercing sweet by the river!
Blinding sweet, O great god Pan!
The sun on the hill forgot to die,
And the lilies revived, and the dragon-fly
  Came back to dream on the river.

Yet half a beast is the great god Pan,
  To laugh as he sits by the river,
Making a poet out of a man:
The true gods sigh for the cost and pain—
For the reed which grows nevermore again
  As a reed with the reeds of the river.

Sonnets from the Portuguese

116.   i

UNLIKE are we, unlike, O princely Heart!
    Unlike our uses and our destinies.
  Our minist'ring two angels look surprise
On one another, as they strike athwart
Their wings in passing. Thou, bethink thee, art
  A guest for queens to social pageantries,
  With gages from a hundred brighter eyes
Than tears even can make mine, to play thy part
Of chief musician. What hast thou to do
  With looking from the lattice-lights at me—
A poor, tired, wandering singer, singing through
  The dark, and leaning up a cypress tree?
The chrism is on thine head—on mine the dew—
  And Death must dig the level where these agree.

131

117.   *ii*

WHAT can I give thee back, O liberal
      And princely giver, who hast brought the gold
   And purple of thine heart, unstained, untold,
And laid them on the outside of the wall
For such as I to take or leave withal,
      In unexpected largesse ?   Am I cold,
      Ungrateful, that for these most manifold
High gifts, I render nothing back at all ?
Not so ; not cold,—but very poor instead.
      Ask God who knows.   For frequent tears have run
The colours from my life, and left so dead
      And pale a stuff, it were not fitly done
To give the same as pillow to thy head.
      Go farther ! let it serve to trample on.

118.   *iii*

GO from me.   Yet I feel that I shall stand
      Henceforward in thy shadow.   Nevermore
   Alone upon the threshold of my door
Of individual life I shall command
The uses of my soul, nor lift my hand
      Serenely in the sunshine as before,
      Without the sense of that which I forbore—
Thy touch upon the palm.   The widest land
Doom takes to part us, leaves thy heart in mine
      With pulses that beat double.   What I do
And what I dream include thee, as the wine
      Must taste of its own grapes.   And when I sue
God for myself, He hears that name of thine,
      And sees within my eyes the tears of two.

132

119.   *iv*

IF thou must love me, let it be for naught
  Except for love's sake only. Do not say,
' I love her for her smile—her look—her way
Of speaking gently,—for a trick of thought
That falls in well with mine, and certes brought
  A sense of pleasant ease on such a day '—
For these things in themselves, Belovèd, may
Be changed, or change for thee—and love, so wrought,
May be unwrought so. Neither love me for
  Thine own dear pity's wiping my cheeks dry :
A creature might forget to weep, who bore
  Thy comfort long, and lose thy love thereby !
But love me for love's sake, that evermore
  Thou mayst love on, through love's eternity.

120.   *v*

WHEN our two souls stand up erect and strong,
  Face to face, silent, drawing nigh and nigher,
Until the lengthening wings break into fire
At either curving point,—what bitter wrong
Can the earth do us, that we should not long
  Be here contented ? Think ! In mounting higher,
  The angels would press on us, and aspire
To drop some golden orb of perfect song
Into our deep, dear silence. Let us stay
  Rather on earth, Belovèd—where the unfit
Contrarious moods of men recoil away
  And isolate pure spirits, and permit
A place to stand and love in for a day,
  With darkness and the death-hour rounding it.

121.   *Inclusions*

O, wilt thou have my hand, Dear, to lie along in
       thine ?
As a little stone in a running stream, it seems to lie and
    pine.
Now drop the poor pale hand, Dear, . . . unfit to plight
    with thine.

O, wilt thou have my cheek, Dear, drawn closer to thine
    own ?
My cheek is white, my cheek is worn, by many a tear run
    down.
Now leave a little space, Dear, . . . lest it should wet thine
    own.

O, must thou have my soul, Dear, commingled with thy
    soul ?—
Red grows the cheek, and warm the hand, . . . the part is
    in the whole !
Nor hands nor cheeks keep separate, when soul is join'd
    to soul.

122.   *My Kate*

SHE was not as pretty as women I know,
    And yet all your best made of sunshine and snow
Drop to shade, melt to naught in the long-trodden ways,
While she 's still remember'd on warm and cold days—
                                        My Kate.

Her air had a meaning, her movements a grace ;
You turn'd from the fairest to gaze on her face :
And when you had once seen her forehead and mouth,
You saw as distinctly her soul and her truth—
                                        My Kate.

134

Such a blue inner light from her eyelids outbroke,
You look'd at her silence and fancied she spoke :
When she did, so peculiar yet soft was the tone,
Tho' the loudest spoke also, you heard her alone—
                                My Kate.

I doubt if she said to you much that could act
As a thought or suggestion : she did not attract
In the sense of the brilliant or wise : I infer
'Twas her thinking of others, made you think of her—
                                My Kate.

She never found fault with you, never implied
Your wrong by her right ; and yet men at her side
Grew nobler, girls purer, as thro' the whole town
The children were gladder that pull'd at her gown—
                                My Kate.

None knelt at her feet confess'd lovers in thrall ;
They knelt more to God than they used,—that was all :
If you praised her as charming, some ask'd what you
    meant,
But the charm of her presence was felt when she went—
                                My Kate.

The weak and the gentle, the ribald and rude,
She took as she found them, and did them all good ;
It always was so with her—see what you have !
She has made the grass greener even here . . . with her
    grave—
                                My Kate.

My dear one !—when thou wast alive with the rest,
I held thee the sweetest and loved thee the best :
And now thou art dead, shall I not take thy part
As thy smiles used to do for thyself, my sweet Heart—
                                My Kate ?

123.   *The Best*

WHAT 'S the best thing in the world ?
    June-rose, by May-dew impearl'd ;
Sweet south-wind, that means no rain ;
Truth, not cruel to a friend ;
Pleasure, not in haste to end ;
Beauty, not self-deck'd and curl'd
Till its pride is over-plain ;
Light, that never makes you wink ;
Memory, that gives no pain ;
Love, when, *so*, you're loved again.
What 's the best thing in the world ?
—Something out of it, I think.

124.   *The North and the South*

ROME, MAY 1861

I

'NOW give us lands where the olives grow,'
    Cried the North to the South,
'Where the sun with a golden mouth can blow
Blue bubbles of grapes down a vineyard-row ! '
    Cried the North to the South.

'Now give us men from the sunless plain,'
    Cried the South to the North,
'By need of work in the snow and the rain,
Made strong, and brave by familiar pain ! '
    Cried the South to the North.

II

' Give lucider hills and intenser seas,'
   Said the North to the South,
' Since ever by symbols and bright degrees
Art, childlike, climbs to the dear Lord's knees,'
   Said the North to the South.

' Give strenuous souls for belief and prayer,'
   Said the South to the North,
' That stand in the dark on the lowest stair,
While affirming of God, " He is certainly there," '
   Said the South to the North.

III

' Yet O, for the skies that are softer and higher ! '
   Sigh'd the North to the South ;
' For the flowers that blaze, and the trees that aspire,
And the insects made of a song or a fire ! '
   Sigh'd the North to the South.

' And O, for a seer to discern the same ! '
   Sigh'd the South to the North ;
' For a poet's tongue of baptismal flame,
To call the tree or the flower by its name ! '
   Sigh'd the South to the North.

IV

The North sent therefore a man of men
   As a grace to the South ;
And thus to Rome came Andersen.
—' *Alas, but must you take him again ?* '
   Said the South to the North.

NATHANIEL PARKER WILLIS

125.   *Two Women*   1807—1867

THE shadows lay along Broadway,
　　'Twas near the twilight-tide—
And slowly there a lady fair
　　Was walking in her pride.
Alone walk'd she ; but, viewlessly,
　　Walk'd spirits at her side.

Peace charm'd the street beneath her feet,
　　And Honour charm'd the air ;
And all astir looked kind on her,
　　And call'd her good as fair—
For all God ever gave to her,
　　She kept with chary care.

She kept with care her beauties rare
　　From lovers warm and true—
For her heart was cold to all but gold,
　　And the rich came not to woo—
But honour'd well are charms to sell,
　　If priests the selling do.

Now walking there was one more fair—
　　A slight girl, lily-pale ;
And she had unseen company
　　To make the spirit quail—
'Twixt Want and Scorn she walk'd forlorn.
　　And nothing could avail.

138

No mercy now can clear her brow
   For this world's peace to pray ;
For, as love's wild prayer dissolved in air,
   Her woman's heart gave way !—
But the sin forgiven by Christ in Heaven
   By man is cursed alway !

HENRY WADSWORTH LONGFELLOW

1807—1882

126.   *The Slave's Dream*

BESIDE the ungather'd rice he lay,
   His sickle in his hand ;
His breast was bare, his matted hair
   Was buried in the sand.
Again, in the mist and shadow of sleep,
   He saw his Native Land.

Wide through the landscape of his dreams
   The lordly Niger flowed ;
Beneath the palm-trees on the plain
   Once more a king he strode ;
And heard the tinkling caravans
   Descend the mountain-road.

He saw once more his dark-eyed queen
   Among her children stand ;
They clasp'd his neck, they kiss'd his cheeks,
   They held him by the hand !—
A tear burst from the sleeper's lids
   And fell into the sand.

And

And then at furious speed he rode
   Along the Niger's bank ;
His bridle reins were golden chains,
   And, with a martial clank,
At each leap he could feel his scabbard of steel
   Smiting his stallion's flank.

Before him, like a blood-red flag,
   The bright flamingoes flew ;
From morn till night he follow'd their flight,
   O'er plains where the tamarind grew,
Till he saw the roofs of Caffre huts,
   And the ocean rose to view.

At night he heard the lion roar,
   And the hyena scream,
And the river-horse, as he crush'd the reeds
   Beside some hidden stream ;
And it pass'd, like a glorious roll of drums,
   Through the triumph of his dream.

The forests, with their myriad tongues,
   Shouted of Liberty ;
And the blast of the Desert cried aloud,
   With a voice so wild and free,
That he started in his sleep and smiled
   At their tempestuous glee.

He did not feel the driver's whip,
   Nor the burning heat of day;
For Death had illumined the Land of Sleep,
   And his lifeless body lay
A worn-out fetter, that the soul
   Had broken and thrown away !

127.   *To an Old Danish Song-Book*

WELCOME, my old friend,
  Welcome to a foreign fireside,
While the sullen gales of autumn
Shake the windows.

The ungrateful world
Has, it seems, dealt harshly with thee,
Since, beneath the skies of Denmark,
First I met thee.

There are marks of age,
There are thumb-marks on thy margin,
Made by hands that clasp'd thee rudely,
At the alehouse.

Soil'd and dull thou art;
Yellow are thy time-worn pages,
As the russet, rain-molested
Leaves of autumn.

Thou art stain'd with wine
Scatter'd from hilarious goblets,
As the leaves with the libations
Of Olympus.

Yet dost thou recall
Days departed, half-forgotten,
When in dreamy youth I wander'd
By the Baltic,—

When I paused to hear
The old ballad of King Christian
Shouted from suburban taverns
In the twilight.

Thou

Thou recallest bards,
Who, in solitary chambers,
And with hearts by passion wasted,
Wrote thy pages.

Thou recallest homes
Where thy songs of love and friendship
Made the gloomy Northern winter
Bright as summer.

Once some ancient Scald,
In his bleak, ancestral Iceland,
Chanted staves of these old ballads
To the Vikings.

Once in Elsinore,
At the court of old King Hamlet,
Yorick and his boon companions
Sang these ditties.

Once Prince Frederick's Guard
Sang them in their smoky barracks ;—
Suddenly the English cannon
Join'd the chorus !

Peasants in the field,
Sailors on the roaring ocean,
Students, tradesmen, pale mechanics,
All have sung them.

Thou hast been their friend ;
They, alas ! have left thee friendless !
Yet at least by one warm fireside
Art thou welcome.

And, as swallows build
In these wide, old-fashion'd chimneys,
So thy twittering songs shall nestle
In my bosom,—

Quiet, close, and warm,
Sheltered from all molestation,
And recalling by their voices
Youth and travel.

128. *The Galley of Count Arnaldos*

AH ! what pleasant visions haunt me
   As I gaze upon the sea !
All the old romantic legends,
   All my dreams, come back to me.

Sails of silk and ropes of sandal,
   Such as gleam in ancient lore ;
And the singing of the sailors,
   And the answer from the shore !

Most of all, the Spanish ballad
   Haunts me oft, and tarries long,
Of the noble Count Arnaldos
   And the sailor's mystic song.

Telling how the Count Arnaldos,
   With his hawk upon his hand,
Saw a fair and stately galley,
   Steering onward to the land ;—

How

How he heard the ancient helmsman
    Chant a song so wild and clear,
That the sailing sea-bird slowly
    Poised upon the mast to hear,

Till his soul was full of longing,
    And he cried, with impulse strong,—
' Helmsman ! for the love of heaven,
    Teach me, too, that wondrous song ! '

' Wouldst thou,'—so the helmsman answered,—
    ' Learn the secret of the sea ?
Only those who brave its dangers
    Comprehend its mystery ! '

129.   *Simon Danz*

SIMON DANZ has come home again
    From cruising about with his buccaneers ;
He has singed the beard of the King of Spain,
And carried away the Dean of Jaen
    And sold him in Algiers.

In his house by the Maese, with its roof of tiles,
    And weathercocks flying aloft in air,
There are silver tankards of antique styles,
Plunder of convent and castle, and piles
    Of carpets rich and rare.

In his tulip-garden there by the town,
    Overlooking the sluggish stream,
With his Moorish cap and dressing-gown,
The old sea-captain, hale and brown,
    Walks in a waking dream.

HENRY WADSWORTH LONGFELLOW

A smile in his gray mustachio lurks
  Whenever he thinks of the King of Spain,
And the listed tulips look like Turks,
And the silent gardener as he works
  Is changed to the Dean of Jaen.

The windmills on the outermost
  Verge of the landscape in the haze,
To him are towers on the Spanish coast,
With whisker'd sentinels at their post,
  Though this is the river Maese.

But when the winter rains begin,
  He sits and smokes by the blazing brands,
And old seafaring men come in,
Goat-bearded, gray, and with double chin,
  And rings upon their hands.

They sit there in the shadow and shine
  Of the flickering fire of the winter night;
Figures in colour and design
Like those of Rembrandt of the Rhine,
  Half darkness and half light.

And they talk of ventures lost or won,
  And their talk is ever and ever the same,
While they drink the red wine of Tarragon,
From the cellars of some Spanish Don,
  Or convent set on flame.

Restless at times with heavy strides
  He paces his parlour to and fro ;
He is like a ship that at anchor rides,
And swings with the rising and falling tides,
  And tugs at her anchor-tow.

Voice?

Voices mysterious far and near,
  Sound of the wind and sound of the sea,
Are calling and whispering in his ear,
' Simon Danz ! Why stayest thou here ?
  Come forth and follow me ! '

So he thinks he shall take to the sea again
  For one more cruise with his buccaneers,
To singe the beard of the King of Spain,
And capture another Dean of Jaen
  And sell him in Algiers.

130.   *The Flight into Egypt*

(FROM A MIRACLE PLAY)

(*Here shall* JOSEPH *come in, leading an ass, on which are
    seated* MARY *and the* CHILD.)

MARY.   Here will we rest us, under these
      O'erhanging branches of the trees,
Where robins chant their litanies
      And canticles of joy.
  Joseph.   My saddle-girths have given way
With trudging through the heat to-day ;
To you I think it is but play
      To ride and hold the boy.
  Mary.   Hark ! how the robins shout and sing,
As if to hail their infant King !
I will alight at yonder spring
      To wash his little coat.

Joseph. And I will hobble well the ass,
Lest, being loose upon the grass,
He should escape ; for, by the mass,
    He 's nimble as a goat.

(*Here* MARY *shall alight and go to the spring.*)
Mary. O Joseph ! I am much afraid,
For men are sleeping in the shade ;
I fear that we shall be waylaid,
    And robb'd and beaten sore !

(*Here a band of robbers shall be seen sleeping, two of whom
        shall rise and come forward.*)
Dumachus. Cock's soul ! deliver up your gold !
Joseph. I pray you, Sirs, let go your hold !
You see that I am weak and old,
    Of wealth I have no store.
Dumachus. Give up your money !
Titus.   Prithee cease.
Let these good people go in peace.
Dumachus. First let them pay for their release,
    And then go on their way.
Titus. These forty groats I give in fee,
If thou wilt only silent be.
Mary. May God be merciful to thee,
    Upon the Judgement Day !
Jesus. When thirty years shall have gone by,
I at Jerusalem shall die,
By Jewish hands exalted high
    On the accursèd tree.
Then on my right and my left side,
These thieves shall both be crucified,
And Titus thenceforth shall abide
    In paradise with me.

(*Here a great rumour of trumpets and horses, like the noise
of a king with his army, and the robbers shall take flight.*)

131.   *Autumn*

THOU comest, Autumn, heralded by the rain,
   With banners, by great gales incessant fann'd,
  Brighter than brightest silks of Samarcand,
  And stately oxen harness'd to thy wain ;
Thou standest, like imperial Charlemagne,
  Upon thy bridge of gold ; thy royal hand
  Outstretched with benedictions o'er the land,
  Blessing the farms through all thy vast domain.
Thy shield is the red harvest moon, suspended
  So long beneath the heaven's o'erhanging eaves ;
Thy steps are by the farmer's prayers attended ;
  Like flames upon an altar shine the sheaves ;
And, following thee, in thy ovation splendid,
  Thine almoner, the wind, scatters the golden leaves !

132.   *Chaucer*

AN old man in a lodge within a park ;
   The chamber walls depicted all around
  With portraitures of huntsman, hawk, and hound,
  And the hurt deer. He listeneth to the lark,
Whose song comes with the sunshine through the dark
  Of painted glass in leaden lattice bound ;
  He listeneth and he laugheth at the sound,
  Then writeth in a book like any clerk.
He is the poet of the dawn, who wrote
  The Canterbury Tales, and his old age
  Made beautiful with song ; and as I read
I hear the crowing cock, I hear the note
  Of lark and linnet, and from every page
  Rise odours of plough'd field or flowery mead.

1807–1886

133.   *i. Retirement*

A WRETCHED thing it were, to have our heart
   Like a throng'd highway or a populous street,
   Where every idle thought has leave to meet,
Pause, or pass on, as in an open mart ;
Or like a roadside pool, which no nice art
   Has guarded that the cattle may not beat
   And foul it with a multitude of feet,
Till of the heavens it can give back no part.
But keep thou thine a holy Solitude :
   For He, who would walk there, would walk alone ;
He who would drink there, must be first endued
   With single right to call that stream his own.
      Keep thou thine heart close fasten'd, unreveal'd,
      A fencèd garden and a fountain seal'd.

134.   *ii. Gibraltar*

E NGLAND, we love thee better than we know.—
   And this I learn'd when, after wand'rings long
   'Mid people of another stock and tongue,
I heard again thy martial music blow,
And saw thy gallant children to and fro
   Pace, keeping ward at one of those huge gates,
   Twin giants watching the Herculean Straits.
When first I came in sight of that brave show,
   It made the very heart within me dance,
   To think that thou thy proud foot shouldst advance
      Forward so far into the mighty sea.
Joy was it and exultation to behold
   Thine ancient standard's rich emblazonry,
   A glorious picture by the wind unroll'd.

1807-1892

135. *Memories*

A BEAUTIFUL and happy girl,
  With step as light as summer air,
Eyes glad with smiles, and brow of pearl,
Shadow'd by many a careless curl
    Of unconfined and flowing hair ;
A seeming child in everything,
    Save thoughtful brow and ripening charms,
As Nature wears the smile of Spring
    When sinking into Summer's arms.

A mind rejoicing in the light
    Which melted through its graceful bower,
Leaf after leaf, dew-moist and bright,
And stainless in its holy white,
    Unfolding like a morning flower :
A heart, which, like a fine-toned lute,
    With every breath of feeling woke,
And, even when the tongue was mute,
    From eye and lip in music spoke.

How thrills once more the lengthening chain
    Of memory, at the thought of thee !
Old hopes which long in dust have lain
Old dreams, come thronging back again,
    And boyhood lives again in me ;
I feel its glow upon my cheek,
    Its fulness of the heart is mine,
As when I lean'd to hear thee speak,
    Or raised my doubtful eye to thine.

I hear again thy low replies,
  I feel thy arm within my own,
And timidly again uprise
The fringèd lids of hazel eyes,
  With soft brown tresses overblown.
Ah ! memories of sweet summer eves,
  Of moonlit wave and willowy way,
Of stars and flowers, and dewy leaves,
  And smiles and tones more dear than they !

Ere this, thy quiet eye hath smiled
  My picture of thy youth to see,
When, half a woman, half a child,
Thy very artlessness beguiled,
  And folly's self seem'd wise in thee ;
I too can smile, when o'er that hour
  The lights of memory backward stream,
Yet feel the while that manhood's power
  Is vainer than my boyhood's dream.

Years have pass'd on, and left their trace
  Of graver care and deeper thought ;
And unto me the calm, cold face
Of manhood, and to thee the grace
  Of woman's pensive beauty brought.
More wide, perchance, for blame than praise,
  The school-boy's humble name has flown ;
Thine, in the green and quiet ways
  Of unobtrusive goodness known.

And wider yet in thought and deed
  Diverge our pathways, one in youth ;
Thine the Genevan's sternest creed,
While answers to my spirit's need
  The Derby dalesman's simple truth.

For

For thee, the priestly rite and prayer,
　　And holy day, and solemn psalm ;
For me, the silent reverence where
　　My brethren gather, slow and calm.

Yet hath thy spirit left on me
　　An impress Time has worn not out,
And something of myself in thee,
A shadow from the past, I see,
　　Ling'ring, even yet, thy way about ;
Not wholly can the heart unlearn
　　That lesson of its better hours,
Not yet has Time's dull footstep worn
　　To common dust that path of flowers.

Thus, while at times before our eyes
　　The shadows melt, and fall apart,
And, smiling through them, round us lies
The warm light of our morning skies,—
　　The Indian Summer of the heart !
In secret sympathies of mind,
　　In founts of feeling which retain
Their pure, fresh flow, we yet may find
　　Our early dreams not wholly vain !

136.　　　　　*My Playmate*

THE pines were dark on Ramoth hill,
　　Their song was soft and low ;
The blossoms in the sweet May wind
　　Were falling like the snow.

152

The blossoms drifted at our feet,
    The orchard birds sang clear ;
The sweetest and the saddest day
    It seem'd of all the year.

For, more to me than birds or flowers,
    My playmate left her home,
And took with her the laughing spring,
    The music and the bloom.

She kiss'd the lips of kith and kin,
    She laid her hand in mine :
What more could ask the bashful boy
    Who fed her father's kine ?

She left us in the bloom of May :
    The constant years told o'er
Their seasons with as sweet May morns,
    But she came back no more.

I walk, with noiseless feet, the round
    Of uneventful years ;
Still o'er and o'er I sow the spring
    And reap the autumn ears.

She lives where all the golden year
    Her summer roses blow ;
The dusky children of the sun
    Before her come and go.

There haply with her jewell'd hands
    She smooths her silken gown,—
No more the homespun lap wherein
    I shook the walnuts down.

The

The wild grapes wait us by the brook,
    The brown nuts on the hill,
And still the May-day flowers make sweet
    The woods of Follymill.

The lilies blossom in the pond,
    The bird builds in the tree,
The dark pines sing on Ramoth hill
    The slow song of the sea.

I wonder if she thinks of them,
    And how the old time seems,—
If ever the pines of Ramoth wood
    Are sounding in her dreams.

I see her face, I hear her voice;
    Does she remember mine?
And what to her is now the boy
    Who fed her father's kine?

What cares she that the orioles build
    For other eyes than ours,—
That other hands with nuts are fill'd,
    And other laps with flowers?

O playmate in the golden time!
    Our mossy seat is green,
Its fringing violets blossom yet,
    The old trees o'er it lean.

The winds so sweet with birch and fern
    A sweeter memory blow;
And there in spring the veeries sing
    The song of long ago.

And still the pines of Ramoth wood
   Are moaning like the sea,—
The moaning of the sea of change
   Between myself and thee !

137.   *The Henchman*

MY lady walks her morning round,
   My lady's page her fleet greyhound,
My lady's hair the fond winds stir,
And all the birds make songs for her.

Her thrushes sing in Rathburn bowers,
And Rathburn side is gay with flowers :
But ne'er like hers, in flower or bird,
Was beauty seen or music heard.

The distance of the stars is hers ;
The least of all her worshippers,
The dust beneath her dainty heel,
She knows not that I see or feel.

Oh, proud and calm !—she cannot know
Where'er she goes with her I go ;
Oh, cold and fair !—she cannot guess
I kneel to share her hound's caress !

Gay knights beside her hunt and hawk,
I rob their ears of her sweet talk ;
Her suitors come from east and west,
I steal her smiles from every guest.

Unheard of her, in loving words,
I greet her with the song of birds;
I reach her with her green-arm'd bowers,
I kiss her with the lips of flowers.

The hound and I are on her trail,
The wind and I uplift her veil;
As if the calm, cold moon she were,
And I the tide, I follow her.

As unrebuked as they, I share
The licence of the sun and air,
And in a common homage hide
My worship from her scorn and pride.

World-wide apart, and yet so near,
I breathe her charmèd atmosphere,
Wherein to her my service brings
The reverence due to holy things.

Her maiden pride, her haughty name,
My dumb devotion shall not shame;
The love that no return doth crave
To knightly levels lifts the slave.

No lance have I, in joust or fight,
To splinter in my lady's sight;
But, at her feet, how blest were I
For any need of hers to die!

138.   *Song of Slaves in the Desert*

WHERE are we going ? where are we going,
    Where are we going, Rubee ?
Lord of peoples, lord of lands,
Look across these shining sands,
Through the furnace of the noon.
Through the white light of the moon,
Strong the Ghiblee wind is blowing,
Strange and large the world is growing !
Speak and tell us where we are going,
    Where are we going, Rubee ?

Bornou land was rich and good,
Wells of water, fields of food,
Dourra fields, and bloom of bean,
And the palm-tree cool and green :
Bornou land we see no longer,
Here we thirst and here we hunger,
Here the Moor-man smites in anger :
    Where are we going, Rubee ?

When we went from Bornou land,
We were like the leaves and sand,
We were many, we are few ;
Life has one, and death has two :
Whiten'd bones our path are showing.
Thou All-seeing, thou All-knowing !
Hear us, tell us, where are we going,
    Where are we going, Rubee ?

Moons of marches from our eyes
Bornou land behind us lies ;
Stranger round us day by day
Bends the desert circle grey ;
Wild the waves of sand are flowing,
Hot the winds above them blowing,—
Lord of all things ! where are we going ?
   Where are we going, Rubee ?

We are weak, but Thou art strong ;
Short our lives, but Thine is long ;
We are blind, but Thou hast eyes ;
We are fools, but Thou art wise !
Thou, our morrow's pathway knowing
Through the strange world round us growing,
Hear us, tell us where are we going ?
   Where are we going, Rubee ?

139. *The Barefoot Boy*

BLESSINGS on thee, little man,
  Barefoot boy, with cheek of tan !
With thy turn'd-up pantaloons,
And thy merry whistled tunes ;
With thy red lip, redder still
Kiss'd by strawberries on the hill ;
With the sunshine on thy face,
Through thy torn brim's jaunty grace ;
From my heart I give thee joy,—
I was once a barefoot boy !
Prince thou art,—the grown-up man
Only is republican.

JOHN GREENLEAF WHITTIER

Let the million-dollar'd ride !
Barefoot, trudging at his side,
Thou hast more than he can buy
In the reach of ear and eye,—
Outward sunshine, inward joy :
Blessings on thee, barefoot boy !

O for boyhood's painless play,
Sleep that wakes in laughing day,
Health that mocks the doctor's rules,
Knowledge never learn'd of schools,
Of the wild bee's morning chase,
Of the wild-flower's time and place,
Flight of fowl and habitude
Of the tenants of the wood ;
How the tortoise bears his shell,
How the woodchuck digs his cell,
And the ground-mole sinks his well ;
How the robin feeds her young,
How the oriole's nest is hung ;
Where the whitest lilies blow,
Where the freshest berries grow,
Where the ground-nut trails its vine,
Where the wood-grape's clusters shine ;
Of the black wasp's cunning way,
Mason of his walls of clay,
And the architectural plans
Of grey hornet artisans !
For, eschewing books and tasks,
Nature answers all he asks ;
Hand in hand with her he walks,
Face to face with her he talks,
Part and parcel of her joy.—
Blessings on the barefoot boy !

O for

O for boyhood's time of June,
Crowding years in one brief moon,
When all things I heard or saw,
Me, their master, waited for.
I was rich in flowers and trees,
Humming-birds and honey-bees;
For my sport the squirrel play'd,
Plied the snouted mole his spade;
For my taste the blackberry cone
Purpled over hedge and stone;
Laugh'd the brook for my delight
Through the day and through the night,
Whispering at the garden wall,
Talk'd with me from fall to fall;
Mine the sand-rimm'd pickerel pond,
Mine the walnut slopes beyond,
Mine, on bending orchard trees,
Apples of Hesperides!
Still as my horizon grew,
Larger grew my riches too;
All the world I saw or knew
Seemed a complex Chinese toy,
Fashioned for a barefoot boy!

O for festal dainties spread,
Like my bowl of milk and bread;
Pewter spoon and bowl of wood,
On the door-stone, grey and rude!
O'er me, like a regal tent,
Cloudy-ribb'd, the sunset bent,
Purple-curtain'd, fringed with gold,
Loop'd in many a wind-swung fold;
While for music came the play
Of the pied frogs' orchestra;

160

And, to light the noisy choir,
Lit the fly his lamp of fire.
I was monarch : pomp and joy
Waited on the barefoot boy !

Cheerily, then, my little man,
Live and laugh, as boyhood can !
Though the flinty slopes be hard,
Stubble-speared the new-mown sward,
Every morn shall lead thee through
Fresh baptisms of the dew ;
Every evening from thy feet
Shall the cool wind kiss the heat :
All too soon these feet must hide
In the prison cells of pride,
Lose the freedom of the sod,
Like a colt's for work be shod,
Made to tread the mills of toil,
Up and down in ceaseless moil :
Happy if their track be found
Never on forbidden ground ;
Happy if they sink not in
Quick and treacherous sands of sin.
Ah ! that thou couldst know thy joy,
Ere it passes, barefoot boy !

140.   *The Friend's Burial*

MY thoughts are all in yonder town,
    Where, wept by many tears,
To-day my mother's friend lays down
    The burden of her years.

JOHN GREENLEAF WHITTIER

True as in life, no poor disguise
　Of death with her is seen,
And on her simple casket lies
　No wreath of bloom and green.

Oh, not for her the florist's art,
　The mocking weeds of woe ;
Dear memories in each mourner's heart
　Like heaven's white lilies blow.

And all about the softening air
　Of new-born sweetness tells,
And the ungather'd May-flowers wear
　The tints of ocean shells.

The old, assuring miracle
　Is fresh as heretofore ;
And earth takes up its parable
　Of life from death once more.

Here organ-swell and church-bell toll
　Methinks but discord were ;
The prayerful silence of the soul
　Is best befitting her.

No sound should break the quietude
　Alike of earth and sky ;
O wandering wind in Seabrook wood,
　Breathe but a half-heard sigh !

Sing softly, spring-bird, for her sake ;
　And thou not distant sea,
Lapse lightly, as if Jesus spake,
　And thou wert Galilee !

For all her quiet life flow'd on
   As meadow streamlets flow,
Where fresher green reveals alone
   The noiseless ways they go.

And if her life small leisure found
   For feasting ear and eye,
And Pleasure, on her daily round,
   She pass'd unpausing by,

Yet with her went a secret sense
   Of all things sweet and fair,
And Beauty's gracious providence
   Refresh'd her unaware.

She kept her line of rectitude
   With love's unconscious ease;
Her kindly instincts understood
   All gentle courtesies.

An inborn charm of graciousness
   Made sweet her smile and tone,
And glorified her farm-wife dress
   With beauty not its own.

The dear Lord's best interpreters
   Are humble human souls;
The Gospel of a life like hers
   Is more than books or scrolls.

From scheme and creed the light goes out,
   The saintly fact survives;
The blessèd Master none can doubt
   Reveal'd in holy lives.

141.   *All's Well*

THE clouds, which rise with thunder, slake
  Our thirsty souls with rain ;
The blow most dreaded falls to break
  From off our limbs a chain ;
And wrongs of man to man but make
  The love of God more plain.
As through the shadowy lens of even
The eye looks farthest into heaven
On gleams of star and depths of blue
The glaring sunshine never knew !

142.   *In Memory of James T. Fields*

AS a guest who may not stay
  Long and sad farewells to say
Glides with smiling face away,

Of the sweetness and the zest
Of thy happy life possess'd
Thou hast left us at thy best.

Keep for us, O friend, where'er
Thou art waiting, all that here
Made thy earthly presence dear ;

Something of thy pleasant past
On a ground of wonder cast,
In the stiller waters glass'd !

Keep the human heart of thee ;
Let the mortal only be
Clothed in immortality.

And when fall our feet as fell
Thine upon the asphodel,
Let thy old smile greet us well.

FREDERICK TENNYSON

1807–1898

143.   *Harvest Home*

COME, let us mount the breezy down
And hearken to the tumult blown
Up from the champaign and the town.

The harvest days are come again,
The vales are surging with the grain ;
The merry work goes on amain.

Pale streaks of cloud scarce veil the blue ;
Against the golden harvest hue
The Autumn trees look fresh and new.

Wrinkled brows relax with glee,
And aged eyes they laugh to see
The sickles follow o'er the lea.

I see the little kerchief'd maid
With dimpling cheek and bodice staid,
'Mid the stout striplings half afraid ;

I see the sire with bronzèd chest :
Mad babes amid the blithe unrest
Seem leaping from the mother's breast.

       The

FREDERICK TENNYSON

The mighty youth and supple child
Go forth, the yellow sheaves are piled ;
The toil is mirth, the mirth is wild. . .

Lusty Pleasures, hobnail'd Fun
Throng into the noonday sun
And 'mid the merry reapers run.

Draw the clear October out !
Another, and another bout !
Then back to labour with a shout !

The banded sheaves stand orderly
Against the purple Autumn sky
Like armies of Prosperity.

Hark ! thro' the middle of the town
From the sunny slopes run down
Bawling boys and reapers brown ;

Laughter flies from door to door,
To see fat Plenty with his store
Led a captive by the poor. . .

Right thro' the middle of the town,
With a great sheaf for a crown,
Onward he reels, a happy clown.

Faintly cheers the tailor thin,
And the smith with sooty chin
Lends his hammer to the din ;

And the master, blithe and boon,
Pours forth his boys that afternoon
And locks his desk an hour too soon.

Yet when the shadows eastward lean
O'er the smooth-shorn fallows clean,
And Silence sits where they have been,

Amid the gleaners I will stay,
While the shout and roundelay
Faint off, and daylight dies away.

—Dies away, and leaves me lone
With dim ghosts, of years agone,
Summers parted, glories flown ;

Till Day beneath the West is roll'd,
Till grey spire and tufted wold
Purple in the evening gold.

Memories, when old age is come,
Are stray ears that deck the gloom,
And echoes of the Harvest-home.

144.   *The Holy Tide*

THE days are sad, it is the Holy tide :
    The Winter morn is short, the Night is long ;
So let the lifeless Hours be glorified
    With deathless thoughts and echo'd in sweet song :
And through the sunset of this purple cup
    They will resume the roses of their prime,
And the old Dead will hear us and wake up,
    Pass with dim smiles and make our hearts sublime !

167   The

FREDERICK TENNYSON

The days are sad, it is the Holy tide :
    Be dusky mistletoes and hollies strown,
Sharp as the spear that pierced His sacred side,
    Red as the drops upon His thorny crown ;
No haggard Passion and no lawless Mirth
    Fright off the solemn Muse,—tell sweet old tales,
Sing songs as we sit brooding o'er the hearth,
    Till the lamp flickers, and the memory fails.

HELEN SELINA, LADY DUFFERIN

1807-1867

145.   *Lament of the Irish Emigrant*

I'M sittin' on the stile, Mary,
    Where we sat side by side
On a bright May mornin' long ago,
    When first you were my bride ;
The corn was springin' fresh and green,
    And the lark sang loud and high—
And the red was on your lip, Mary,
    And the love-light in your eye.

The place is little changed, Mary,
    The day is bright as then,
The lark's loud song is in my ear,
    And the corn is green again ;
But I miss the soft clasp of your hand,
    And your breath warm on my cheek,
And I still keep list'ning for the words
    You never more will speak.

'Tis but a step down yonder lane,
  And the little church stands near,
The church where we were wed, Mary,
  I see the spire from here.
But the graveyard lies between, Mary,
  And my step might break your rest—
For I've laid you, darling! down to sleep,
  With your baby on your breast.

I'm very lonely now, Mary,
  For the poor make no new friends,
But, O, they love the better still,
  The few our Father sends!
And you were all *I* had, Mary,
  My blessin' and my pride:
There's nothin' left to care for now,
  Since my poor Mary died.

Yours was the good, brave heart, Mary,
  That still kept hoping on,
When the trust in God had left my soul,
  And my arm's young strength was gone:
There was comfort ever on your lip,
  And the kind look on your brow—
I bless you, Mary, for that same,
  Though you cannot hear me now.

I thank you for the patient smile
  When your heart was fit to break,
When the hunger pain was gnawin' there,
  And you hid it, for my sake!
I bless you for the pleasant word,
  When your heart was sad and sore—
O, I'm thankful you are gone, Mary,
  Where grief can't reach you more!

I'm

I'm biddin' you a long farewell,
   My Mary—kind and true !
But I'll not forget you, darling !
   In the land I'm goin' to ;
They say there 's bread and work for all,
   And the sun shines always there—
But I'll not forget old Ireland,
   Were it fifty times as fair !

And often in those grand old woods
   I'll sit, and shut my eyes,
And my heart will travel back again
   To the place where Mary lies ;
And I'll think I see the little stile
   Where we sat side by side :
And the springin' corn, and the bright May morn,
   When first you were my bride.

CAROLINE ELIZABETH SARAH NORTON

1808-1876

146.   *Love Not*

LOVE not, love not, ye hapless sons of clay !
   Hope's gayest wreaths are made of earthly flow'rs—
Things that are made to fade and fall away,
   When they have blossom'd but a few short hours.
                   Love not, love not !

Love not, love not ! The thing you love may die—
   May perish from the gay and gladsome earth ;
The silent stars, the blue and smiling sky,
   Beam on its grave as once upon its birth.
                   Love not, love not !

CAROLINE ELIZABETH SARAH NORTON

Love not, love not! The thing you love may change,
 The rosy lip may cease to smile on you;
The kindly beaming eye grow cold and strange;
 The heart still warmly beat, yet not be true.
                                        Love not, love not!

Love not, love not! O warning vainly said
 In present years, as in the years gone by!
Love flings a halo round the dear one's head,
 Faultless, immortal—till they change or die!
                                        Love not, love not!

CHARLES TENNYSON TURNER

1808-1879

147.   *The Lattice at Sunrise*

AS on my bed at dawn I mused and pray'd,
  I saw my lattice pranckt upon the wall,
 The flitting birds and flaunting leaves withal—
A sunny phantom interlaced with shade.
'Thanks be to heaven!' in happy mood I said;
 'What sweeter aid my matins could befall
Than this fair glory from the East hath made?
 What holy sleights hath God, the Lord of all
To bid us feel and see! We are not free
 To say we see not, for the glory comes
Nightly and daily like a flowing sea;
 His lustre pierceth thro' the midnight glooms,
And, at prime hour, behold!—He follows me
 With golden shadows to my secret rooms!

148.   *Letty's Globe*

WHEN Letty had scarce pass'd her third glad year,
    And her young artless words began to flow,
One day we gave the child a colour'd sphere
    Of the wide earth, that she might mark and know,
By tint and outline, all its sea and land.
    She patted all the world; old empires peep'd
Between her baby fingers; her soft hand
    Was welcome at all frontiers. How she leap'd,
    And laugh'd and prattled in her world-wide bliss;
But when we turn'd her sweet unlearnèd eye
On our own isle, she raised a joyous cry—
'Oh! yes, I see it, Letty's home is there!'
    And while she hid all England with a kiss,
Bright over Europe fell her golden hair.

EDGAR ALLAN POE

1809-1849

149.   *To Helen*

HELEN, thy beauty is to me
    Like those Nicèan barks of yore
That gently, o'er a perfumed sea,
    The weary way-worn wanderer bore
    To his own native shore.

On desperate seas long wont to roam,
    Thy hyacinth hair, thy classic face,
Thy Naiad airs have brought me home
    To the glory that was Greece,
    And the grandeur that was Rome.

Lo, in yon brilliant window-niche
    How statue-like I see thee stand,
    The agate lamp within thy hand,
Ah ! Psyche, from the regions which
    Are holy land !

150.   *Annabel Lee*

IT was many and many a year ago,
    In a kingdom by the sea,
That a maiden there lived whom you may know
    By the name of Annabel Lee.
And this maiden she lived with no other thought
    Than to love and be loved by me.

I was a child and she was a child
    In this kingdom by the sea :
But we loved with a love that was more than love—
    I and my Annabel Lee,
With a love that the wingèd seraphs of heaven
    Coveted her and me.

And this was the reason that, long ago,
    In this kingdom by the sea,
A wind blew out of a cloud, chilling
    My beautiful Annabel Lee,
So that her high-born kinsman came
    And bore her away from me,
To shut her up in a sepulchre
    In this kingdom by the sea.

173   The

The angels, not half so happy in heaven,
    Went envying her and me—
Yes ! that was the reason (as all men know,
    In this kingdom by the sea)
That the wind came out of the cloud one night,
    Chilling and killing my Annabel Lee.

But our love it was stronger by far than the love
    Of those who were older than we—
    Of many far wiser than we—
And neither the angels in heaven above,
    Nor the demons down under the sea,
Can ever dissever my soul from the soul
    Of the beautiful Annabel Lee :

For the moon never beams without bringing me dreams
    Of the beautiful Annabel Lee ;
And the stars never rise, but I feel the bright eyes
    Of the beautiful Annabel Lee ;
And so, all the night-tide, I lie down by the side
Of my darling—my darling—my life and my bride,
    In the sepulchre there by the sea,
    In her tomb by the sounding sea.

151.   *For Annie*

THANK Heaven ! the crisis—
    The danger is past,
And the lingering illness
    Is over at last—
And the fever called ' Living '
    Is conquer'd at last.

Sadly, I know
　　I am shorn of my strength,
And no muscle I move
　　As I lie at full length :
But no matter—I feel
　　I am better at length.

And I rest so composedly
　　Now, in my bed,
That any beholder
　　Might fancy me dead—
Might start at beholding me,
　　Thinking me dead.

The moaning and groaning,
　　The sighing and sobbing,
Are quieted now,
　　With that horrible throbbing
At heart—ah, that horrible,
　　Horrible throbbing !

The sickness—the nausea—
　　The pitiless pain—
Have ceased, with the fever
　　That madden'd my brain—
With the fever called ' Living '
　　That burn'd in my brain.

And O ! of all tortures
　　That torture the worst
Has abated—the terrible
　　Torture of thirst

For

For the naphthaline river
    Of Passion accurst :
I have drunk of a water
    That quenches all thirst.

—Of a water that flows,
    With a lullaby sound,
From a spring but a very few
    Feet under ground—
From a cavern not very far
    Down under ground.

And ah ! let it never
    Be foolishly said
That my room it is gloomy,
    And narrow my bed ;
For man never slept
    In a different bed—
And, to *sleep*, you must slumber
    In just such a bed.

My tantalized spirit
    Here blandly reposes,
Forgetting, or never
    Regretting its roses—
Its old agitations
    Of myrtles and roses :

For now, while so quietly
    Lying, it fancies
A holier odour
    About it, of pansies—

A rosemary odour,
    Commingled with pansies—
With rue and the beautiful
    Puritan pansies.

And so it lies happily,
    Bathing in many
A dream of the truth
    And the beauty of Annie—
Drown'd in a bath
    Of the tresses of Annie.

She tenderly kiss'd me,
    She fondly caress'd,
And then I fell gently
    To sleep on her breast—
Deeply to sleep
    From the heaven of her breast

When the light was extinguish'd,
    She cover'd me warm,
And she pray'd to the angels
    To keep me from harm—
To the queen of the angels
    To shield me from harm.

And I lie so composedly,
    Now, in my bed
(Knowing her love),
    That you fancy me dead—
And I rest so contentedly,

177   Now

Now, in my bed
(With her love at my breast),
   That you fancy me dead—
That you shudder to look at me,
   Thinking me dead.

But my heart it is brighter
   Than all of the many
Stars in the sky,
   For it sparkles with Annie—
It glows with the light
   Of the love of my Annie—
With the thought of the light
   Of the eyes of my Annie.

152.
The Sleeper

AT midnight, in the month of June,
   I stand beneath the mystic moon.
An opiate vapour, dewy, dim,
Exhales from out her golden rim,
And, softly dripping, drop by drop,
Upon the quiet mountain top,
Steals drowsily and musically
Into the universal valley.
The rosemary nods upon the grave ;
The lily lolls upon the wave ;
Wrapping the fog about its breast,
The ruin moulders into rest ;
Looking like Lethe, see ! the lake
A conscious slumber seems to take,
And would not, for the world, awake.
All Beauty sleeps !—and lo ! where lies
Irene, with her Destinies !

EDGAR ALLAN POE

O lady bright ! can it be right—
This window open to the night ?
The wanton airs, from the tree-top,
Laughingly through the lattice drop—
The bodiless airs, a wizard rout,
Flit through thy chamber in and out,
And wave the curtain canopy
So fitfully—so fearfully—
Above the closed and fringèd lid
'Neath which thy slumb'ring soul lies hid,
That, o'er the floor and down the wall,
Like ghosts the shadows rise and fall !
Oh, lady dear, hast thou no fear ?
Why and what art thou dreaming here ?
Sure thou art come o'er far-off seas,
A wonder to these garden trees !
Strange is thy pallor ! strange thy dress,
Strange, above all, thy length of tress,
And this all solemn silentness !

The lady sleeps ! Oh, may her sleep,
Which is enduring, so be deep !
Heaven have her in its sacred keep !
This chamber changed for one more holy,
This bed for one more melancholy,
I pray to God that she may lie
For ever with unopen'd eye,
While the pale sheeted ghosts go by !

My love, she sleeps ! Oh, may her sleep
As it is lasting, so be deep !
Soft may the worms about her creep !
Far in the forest, dim and old,
For her may some tall vault unfold—
Some vault that oft has flung its black

And

And wingèd panels fluttering back,
Triumphant, o'er the crested palls,
Of her grand family funerals—
Some sepulchre, remote, alone,
Against whose portal she hath thrown,
In childhood, many an idle stone—
Some tomb from out whose sounding door
She ne'er shall force an echo more,
Thrilling to think, poor child of sin !
It was the dead who groan'd within.

153.   *To One in Paradise*

THOU wast all that to me, love,
    For which my soul did pine—
A green isle in the sea, love,
    A fountain and a shrine,
All wreathed with fairy fruits and flowers,
    And all the flowers were mine.

Now all my days are trances,
    And all my nightly dreams
Are where thy grey eye glances,
    And where thy footstep gleams—
In what ethereal dances,
    By what eternal streams !

154.   *The Haunted Palace*

IN the greenest of our valleys
    By good angels tenanted,
Once a fair and stately palace—
    Radiant palace—reared its head.

EDGAR ALLAN POE

In the monarch Thought's dominion—
  It stood there !
Never seraph spread a pinion
  Over fabric half so fair !

Banners yellow, glorious, golden,
  On its roof did float and flow,
(This—all this—was in the olden
  Time long ago,)
And every gentle air that dallied,
  In that sweet day,
Along the ramparts plumed and pallid,
  A wingèd odour went away.

Wanderers in that happy valley,
  Through two luminous windows, saw
Spirits moving musically,
  To a lute's well-tunèd law,
Round about a throne where, sitting
  (Porphyrogene !)
In state his glory well-befitting,
  The ruler of the realm was seen.

And all with pearl and ruby glowing
  Was the fair palace door,
Through which came flowing, flowing, flowing,
  And sparkling evermore,
A troop of Echoes, whose sweet duty
  Was but to sing,
In voices of surpassing beauty,
  The wit and wisdom of their king.

But evil things, in robes of sorrow,
  Assailed the monarch's high estate.

(Ah,

(Ah, let us mourn !—for never morrow
   Shall dawn upon him desolate !)
And round about his home the glory
   That blush'd and bloom'd,
Is but a dim-remember'd story
   Of the old time entomb'd.

And travellers, now, within that valley
   Through the red-litten windows see
Vast forms, that move fantastically
   To a discordant melody,
While, like a ghastly rapid river,
   Through the pale door
A hideous throng rush out for ever
   And laugh—but smile no more.

EDWARD FITZGERALD

1809-1883

155.   *Old Song*

'TIS a dull sight
   To see the year dying,
When winter winds
   Set the yellow wood sighing :
    Sighing, O sighing !

When such a time cometh
   I do retire
Into an old room
   Beside a bright fire :
    O, pile a bright fire !

EDWARD FITZGERALD

And there I sit
  Reading old things,
Of knights and lorn damsels,
  While the wind sings—
    O, drearily sings !

I never look out
  Nor attend to the blast ;
For all to be seen
  Is the leaves falling fast :
    Falling, falling !

But close at the hearth,
  Like a cricket, sit I,
Reading of summer
  And chivalry—
    Gallant chivalry !

Then with an old friend
  I talk of our youth—
How 'twas gladsome, but often
  Foolish, forsooth :
    But gladsome, gladsome !

Or, to get merry,
  We sing some old rhyme
That made the wood ring again
  In summer time—
    Sweet summer time !

Then go we smoking,
  Silent and snug :
Naught passes between us,
  Save a brown jug—
    Sometimes !

And

And sometimes a tear
  Will rise in each eye,
Seeing the two old friends
  So merrily—
    So merrily !

And ere to bed
  Go we, go we,
Down on the ashes
  We kneel on the knee,
    Praying together !

Thus, then, live I
  Till, 'mid all the gloom,
By Heaven ! the bold sun
  Is with me in the room
    Shining, shining !

Then the clouds part,
  Swallows soaring between ;
The spring is alive,
  And the meadows are green !

I jump up like mad,
  Break the old pipe in twain
And away to the meadows,
  The meadows again !

156.   *The Three Arrows*

PORCIA'S SONG

OF all the shafts to Cupid's bow,
  The first is tipp'd with fire ;
All bare their bosoms to the blow
  And call the wound Desire.

Love's second is a poison'd dart,
  And Jealousy is named :
Which carries poison to the heart
  Desire had first inflamed.

The last of Cupid's arrows all
  With heavy lead is set :
That vainly weeping lovers call
  Repentance, or Regret.

157.   *From Omar Khayyám*

I

A BOOK of Verses underneath the Bough,
  A Jug of Wine, a Loaf of Bread—and Thou
Beside me singing in the Wilderness—
O, Wilderness were Paradise enow !

Some for the Glories of This World ; and some
Sigh for the Prophet's Paradise to come ;
  Ah, take the Cash, and let the Credit go,
Nor heed the rumble of a distant Drum !

Look

Look to the blowing Rose about us—' Lo,
Laughing,' she says, ' into the world I blow,
    At once the silken tassel of my Purse
Tear, and its Treasure on the Garden throw.'

And those who husbanded the Golden grain
And those who flung it to the winds like Rain
    Alike to no such aureate Earth are turn'd
As, buried once, Men want dug up again.

II

Think, in this batter'd Caravanserai
Whose Portals are alternate Night and Day,
    How Sultán after Sultán with his Pomp
Abode his destined Hour, and went his way.

They say the Lion and the Lizard keep
The Courts where Jamshyd gloried and drank deep;
    And Bahram, that great Hunter—the wild Ass
Stamps o'er his Head, but cannot break his sleep.

I sometimes think that never blows so red
The Rose as where some buried Caesar bled ;
    That every Hyacinth the Garden wears
Dropt in her Lap from some once lovely Head.

And this reviving Herb whose tender Green
Fledges the River-Lip on which we lean—
    Ah, lean upon it lightly ! for who knows
From what once lovely Lip it springs unseen !

Ah, my Belovèd, fill the Cup that clears
To-day of past Regrets and Future Fears :
    To-morrow !—Why, To-morrow I may be
Myself with Yesterday's Sev'n thousand Years.

186

EDWARD FITZGERALD

For some we loved, the loveliest and the best
That from his Vintage rolling Time hath prest,
  Have drunk their Cup a Round or two before,
And one by one crept silently to rest.

And we, that now make merry in the Room
They left, and Summer dresses in new bloom,
  Ourselves must we beneath the Couch of Earth
Descend—ourselves to make a Couch—for whom ?

Ah, make the most of what we yet may spend,
Before we too into the Dust descend ;
  Dust unto dust, and under Dust to lie,
Sans Wine, sans Song, sans Singer, and—sans End !

III

Ah, with the Grape my fading Life provide,
And wash my Body whence the Life has died,
  And lay me, shrouded in the living Leaf,
By some not unfrequented Garden-side ! . . .

Yon rising Moon that looks for us again—
How oft hereafter will she wax and wane ;
  How oft hereafter rising look for us
Through this same Garden—and for *one* in vain !

And when like her, O Sáki, you shall pass
Among the Guests star-scatter'd on the Grass,
  And in your joyous errand reach the spot
Where I made One—turn down an empty Glass !

RICHARD MONCKTON MILNES,
LORD HOUGHTON

158.　　　*The Men of Old*

I KNOW not that the men of old
　　Were better than men now,
Of heart more kind, of hand more bold,
　　Of more ingenuous brow :
I heed not those who pine for force
　　A ghost of Time to raise,
As if they thus could check the course
　　Of these appointed days.

Still it is true, and over true,
　　That I delight to close
This book of life self-wise and new,
　　And let my thoughts repose
On all that humble happiness
　　The world has since forgone,
The daylight of contentedness
　　That on those faces shone.

With rights, tho' not too closely scann'd,
　　Enjoy'd as far as known ;
With will by no reverse unmann'd,
　　With pulse of even tone,
They from to-day and from to-night
　　Expected nothing more
Than yesterday and yesternight
　　Had proffer'd them before.

To them was Life a simple art
   Of duties to be done,
A game where each man took his part,
   A race where all must run ;
A battle whose great scheme and scope
   They little cared to know,
Content as men-at-arms to cope
   Each with his fronting foe.

Man now his Virtue's diadem
   Puts on and proudly wears :
Great thoughts, great feelings came to them
   Like instincts, unawares.
Blending their souls' sublimest needs
   With tasks of every day,
They went about their gravest deeds
   As noble boys at play.

ALFRED TENNYSON, LORD TENNYSON

1809-1892

159.   *The Lady of Shalott*

Part I

ON either side the river lie
   Long fields of barley and of rye,
That clothe the wold and meet the sky ;
And thro' the field the road runs by
      To many-tower'd Camelot;
And up and down the people go,
Gazing where the lilies blow
Round an island there below,
      The island of Shalott.

Willows

Willows whiten, aspens quiver,
Little breezes dusk and shiver
Thro' the wave that runs for ever
By the island in the river
   Flowing down to Camelot.
Four gray walls, and four gray towers,
Overlook a space of flowers,
And the silent isle imbowers
   The Lady of Shalott.

By the margin, willow-veil'd,
Slide the heavy barges trail'd
By slow horses ; and unhail'd
The shallop flitteth silken-sail'd
   Skimming down to Camelot :
But who hath seen her wave her hand ?
Or at the casement seen her stand ?
Or is she known in all the land,
   The Lady of Shalott ?

Only reapers, reaping early
In among the bearded barley,
Hear a song that echoes cheerly
From the river winding clearly,
   Down to tower'd Camelot :
And by the moon the reaper weary,
Piling sheaves in uplands airy,
Listening, whispers ' 'Tis the fairy
   Lady of Shalott.'

Part II

There she weaves by night and day
A magic web with colours gay.
She has heard a whisper say,
A curse is on her if she stay
      To look down to Camelot.
She knows not what the curse may be,
And so she weaveth steadily,
And little other care hath she,
      The Lady of Shalott.

And moving thro' a mirror clear
That hangs before her all the year,
Shadows of the world appear.
There she sees the highway near
      Winding down to Camelot:
There the river eddy whirls,
And there the surly village-churls,
And the red cloaks of market girls,
      Pass onward from Shalott.

Sometimes a troop of damsels glad,
An abbot on an ambling pad,
Sometimes a curly shepherd-lad,
Or long-hair'd page in crimson clad,
      Goes by to tower'd Camelot:
And sometimes thro' the mirror blue
The knights come riding two and two:
She hath no loyal knight and true,
      The Lady of Shalott.

But

But in her web she still delights
To weave the mirror's magic sights,
For often thro' the silent nights
A funeral, with plumes and lights,
      And music, went to Camelot:
Or when the moon was overhead,
Came two young lovers lately wed;
' I am half sick of shadows,' said
      The Lady of Shalott.

Part III

A bow-shot from her bower-eaves,
He rode between the barley-sheaves,
The sun came dazzling thro' the leaves,
And flamed upon the brazen greaves
      Of bold Sir Lancelot.
A red-cross knight for ever kneel'd
To a lady in his shield,
That sparkled on the yellow field,
      Beside remote Shalott.

The gemmy bridle glitter'd free,
Like to some branch of stars we see
Hung in the golden Galaxy:
The bridle bells rang merrily
      As he rode down to Camelot:
And from his blazon'd baldric slung
A mighty silver bugle hung,
And as he rode his armour rung,
      Beside remote Shalott.

LORD TENNYSON

All in the blue unclouded weather
Thick-jewell'd shone the saddle-leather,
The helmet and the helmet-feather
Burn'd like one burning flame together,
       As he rode down to Camelot.
As often thro' the purple night,
Below the starry clusters bright,
Some bearded meteor, trailing light,
       Moves over still Shalott.

His broad clear brow in sunlight glow'd ;
On burnish'd hooves his war-horse trode ;
From underneath his helmet flow'd
His coal-black curls as on he rode,
       As he rode down to Camelot.
From the bank and from the river
He flash'd into the crystal mirror,
' Tirra lirra,' by the river
       Sang Sir Lancelot.

She left the web, she left the loom,
She made three paces thro' the room,
She saw the water-lily bloom,
She saw the helmet and the plume,
       She look'd down to Camelot.
Out flew the web and floated wide ;
The mirror crack'd from side to side ;
' The curse is come upon me ! ' cried
       The Lady of Shalott.

PART IV

In the stormy east-wind straining,
The pale yellow woods were waning,
The broad stream in his banks complaining,
Heavily the low sky raining
      Over tower'd Camelot ;
Down she came and found a boat
Beneath a willow left afloat,
And round about the prow she wrote
      The Lady of Shalott.

And down the river's dim expanse—
Like some bold seër in a trance,
Seeing all his own mischance—
With a glassy countenance
      Did she look to Camelot.
And at the closing of the day
She loosed the chain, and down she lay ;
The broad stream bore her far away,
      The Lady of Shalott.

Lying, robed in snowy white
That loosely flew to left and right—
The leaves upon her falling light—
Thro' the noises of the night
      She floated down to Camelot :
And as the boat-head wound along
The willowy hills and fields among,
They heard her singing her last song,
      The Lady of Shalott.

—Heard a carol, mournful, holy,
Chanted loudly, chanted lowly,
Till her blood was frozen slowly,
And her eyes were darken'd wholly,
      Turn'd to tower'd Camelot ;
For ere she reach'd upon the tide
The first house by the water-side,
Singing in her song she died,
      The Lady of Shalott.

Under tower and balcony,
By garden-wall and gallery,
A gleaming shape she floated by,
Dead-pale between the houses high,
      Silent into Camelot.
Out upon the wharfs they came,
Knight and burgher, lord and dame,
And round the prow they read her name,
      The Lady of Shalott.

Who is this ? and what is here ?
And in the lighted palace near
Died the sound of royal cheer ;
And they cross'd themselves for fear,
      All the knights at Camelot :
But Lancelot mused a little space ;
He said, ' She has a lovely face ;
God in His mercy lend her grace,
      The Lady of Shalott.'

160.   *Mariana*

WITH blackest moss the flower-plots
    Were thickly crusted, one and all :
The rusted nails fell from the knots
    That held the pear to the gable-wall.
The broken sheds look'd sad and strange :
    Unlifted was the clinking latch ;
    Weeded and worn the ancient thatch
Upon the lonely moated grange.
      She only said, ' My life is dreary,
        He cometh not,' she said ;
      She said, ' I am aweary, aweary,
        I would that I were dead ! '

Her tears fell with the dews at even ;
    Her tears fell ere the dews were dried ;
She could not look on the sweet heaven,
    Either at morn or eventide.
After the flitting of the bats,
    When thickest dark did trance the sky,
    She drew her casement-curtain by,
And glanced athwart the glooming flats.
      She only said, ' The night is dreary,
        He cometh not,' she said ;
      She said, ' I am aweary, aweary,
        I would that I were dead ! '

Upon the middle of the night,
    Waking she heard the night-fowl crow :
The cock sung out an hour ere light :
    From the dark fen the oxen's low
Came to her : without hope of change,

In sleep she seem'd to walk forlorn,
  Till cold winds woke the gray-eyed morn
About the lonely moated grange.
    She only said, ' The day is dreary,
      He cometh not,' she said ;
    She said, ' I am aweary, aweary,
      I would that I were dead ! '

About a stone-cast from the wall
  A sluice with blacken'd waters slept,
And o'er it many, round and small,
  The cluster'd marish-mosses crept.
Hard by a poplar shook alway,
  All silver-green with gnarlèd bark :
  For leagues no other tree did mark
The level waste, the rounding gray.
    She only said, ' My life is dreary,
      He cometh not,' she said ;
    She said, ' I am aweary, aweary,
      I would that I were dead ! '

And ever when the moon was low,
  And the shrill winds were up and away
In the white curtain, to and fro,
  She saw the gusty shadow sway.
But when the moon was very low,
  And wild winds bound within their cell,
  The shadow of the poplar fell
Upon her bed, across her brow.
    She only said, ' The night is dreary,
      He cometh not,' she said ;
    She said, ' I am aweary, aweary,
      I would that I were dead ! '

All

All day within the dreamy house,
　　The doors upon their hinges creak'd;
The blue fly sung in the pane; the mouse
　　Behind the mouldering wainscot shriek'd,
Or from the crevice peer'd about.
　　Old faces glimmer'd thro' the doors,
　　Old footsteps trod the upper floors,
Old voices call'd her from without.
　　　　She only said, 'My life is dreary,
　　　　　He cometh not,' she said;
　　　　She said, 'I am aweary, aweary,
　　　　　I would that I were dead!'

The sparrow's chirrup on the roof,
　　The slow clock ticking, and the sound
Which to the wooing wind aloof
　　The poplar made, did all confound
Her sense; but most she loath'd the hour
　　When the thick-moted sunbeam lay
　　Athwart the chambers, and the day
Was sloping toward his western bower.
　　　　Then, said she, 'I am very dreary,
　　　　　He will not come,' she said;
　　　　She wept, 'I am aweary, aweary,
　　　　　O God, that I were dead!'

161.　　　　*Sir Galahad*

MY good blade carves the casques of men,
　　My tough lance thrusteth sure,
My strength is as the strength of ten,
　　Because my heart is pure.

LORD TENNYSON

The shattering trumpet shrilleth high,
  The hard brands shiver on the steel,
The splinter'd spear-shafts crack and fly,
  The horse and rider reel :
They reel, they roll in clanging lists,
  And when the tide of combat stands,
Perfume and flowers fall in showers,
  That lightly rain from ladies' hands.

How sweet are looks that ladies bend
  On whom their favours fall !
For them I battle till the end,
  To save from shame and thrall :
But all my heart is drawn above,
  My knees are bow'd in crypt and shrine :
I never felt the kiss of love,
  Nor maiden's hand in mine.
More bounteous aspects on me beam,
  Me mightier transports move and thrill ;
So keep I fair thro' faith and prayer
  A virgin heart in work and will.

When down the stormy crescent goes,
  A light before me swims,
Between dark stems the forest glows,
  I hear a noise of hymns :
Then by some secret shrine I ride ;
  I hear a voice, but none are there ;
The stalls are void, the doors are wide,
  The tapers burning fair.
Fair gleams the snowy altar-cloth,
  The silver vessels sparkle clean,
The shrill bell rings, the censer swings,
  And solemn chaunts resound between.

199   Sometimes

Sometimes on lonely mountain-meres
   I find a magic bark;
I leap on board: no helmsman steers:
   I float till all is dark.
A gentle sound, an awful light!
   Three angels bear the holy Grail:
With folded feet, in stoles of white,
   On sleeping wings they sail.
Ah, blessed vision! blood of God!
   My spirit beats her mortal bars,
As down dark tides the glory slides,
   And star-like mingles with the stars.

When on my goodly charger borne
   Thro' dreaming towns I go,
The cock crows ere the Christmas morn,
   The streets are dumb with snow.
The tempest crackles on the leads,
   And, ringing, springs from brand and mail;
But o'er the dark a glory spreads,
   And gilds the driving hail.
I leave the plain, I climb the height;
   No branchy thicket shelter yields;
But blessed forms in whistling storms
   Fly o'er waste fens and windy fields.

A maiden knight—to me is given
   Such hope, I know not fear;
I yearn to breathe the airs of heaven
   That often meet me here.
I muse on joy that will not cease,
   Pure spaces clothed in living beams,
Pure lilies of eternal peace,
   Whose odours haunt my dreams;

And, stricken by an angel's hand,
    This mortal armour that I wear,
This weight and size, this heart and eyes,
    Are touch'd, are turn'd to finest air.

The clouds are broken in the sky,
    And thro' the mountain-walls
A rolling organ-harmony
    Swells up, and shakes and falls.
Then move the trees, the copses nod,
    Wings flutter, voices hover clear:
' O just and faithful knight of God!
    Ride on! the prize is near.'
So pass I hostel, hall, and grange;
    By bridge and ford, by park and pale,
All-arm'd I ride, whate'er betide,
    Until I find the holy Grail.

162. *The Miller's Daughter*

IT is the miller's daughter,
    And she is grown so dear, so dear,
That I would be the jewel
    That trembles in her ear:
For hid in ringlets day and night,
I'd touch her neck so warm and white.

And I would be the girdle
    About her dainty dainty waist,
And her heart would beat against me,
    In sorrow and in rest:
And I should know if it beat right,
I'd clasp it round so close and tight.

And

And I would be the necklace,
 And all day long to fall and rise
Upon her balmy bosom,
 With her laughter or her sighs :
And I would lie so light, so light,
I scarce should be unclasp'd at night.

163.   *Edward Gray*

SWEET Emma Moreland of yonder town
  Met me walking on yonder way,
' And have you lost your heart ? ' she said ;
  ' And are you married yet, Edward Gray ? '

Sweet Emma Moreland spoke to me :
 Bitterly weeping I turn'd away :
' Sweet Emma Moreland, love no more
 Can touch the heart of Edward Gray.

' Ellen Adair she loved me well,
 Against her father's and mother's will :
To-day I sat for an hour and wept,
 By Ellen's grave, on the windy hill.

' Shy she was, and I thought her cold ;
 Thought her proud, and fled over the sea ;
Fill'd I was with folly and spite,
 When Ellen Adair was dying for me.

' Cruel, cruel the words I said !
 Cruelly came they back to-day :
" You're too slight and fickle," I said,
 " To trouble the heart of Edward Gray."

'There I put my face in the grass—
   Whisper'd, "Listen to my despair :
I repent me of all I did :
   Speak a little, Ellen Adair ! "

'Then I took a pencil, and wrote
   On the mossy stone, as I lay,
"Here lies the body of Ellen Adair ;
   And here the heart of Edward Gray ! "

'Love may come, and love may go,
   And fly, like a bird, from tree to tree :
But I will love no more, no more,
   Till Ellen Adair come back to me.

'Bitterly wept I over the stone :
   Bitterly weeping I turn'd away :
There lies the body of Ellen Adair !
   And there the heart of Edward Gray ! '

164.   *St. Agnes' Eve*

DEEP on the convent-roof the snows
      Are sparkling to the moon :
My breath to heaven like vapour goes :
      May my soul follow soon !
The shadows of the convent-towers
      Slant down the snowy sward,
Still creeping with the creeping hours
      That lead me to my Lord :

Make

Make Thou my spirit pure and clear
   As are the frosty skies,
Or this first snowdrop of the year
   That in my bosom lies.

As these white robes are soil'd and dark,
   To yonder shining ground ;
As this pale taper's earthly spark,
   To yonder argent round ;
So shows my soul before the Lamb,
   My spirit before Thee ;
So in mine earthly house I am,
   To that I hope to be.
Break up the heavens, O Lord ! and far,
   Thro' all yon starlight keen,
Draw me, thy bride, a glittering star,
   In raiment white and clean.

He lifts me to the golden doors ;
   The flashes come and go ;
All heaven bursts her starry floors,
   And strows her lights below,
And deepens on and up ! the gates
   Roll back, and far within
For me the Heavenly Bridegroom waits,
   To make me pure of sin.
The sabbaths of Eternity,
   One sabbath deep and wide—
A light upon the shining sea—
   The Bridegroom with his bride !

Songs from ‘ The Princess ’

165.   i

AS thro’ the land at eve we went,
    And pluck’d the ripen’d ears,
We fell out, my wife and I,
O we fell out, I know not why,
    And kiss’d again with tears.
And blessings on the falling out
    That all the more endears,
When we fall out with those we love
    And kiss again with tears !
For when we came where lies the child
    We lost in other years,
There above the little grave,
O there above the little grave,
    We kiss’d again with tears.

166.   ii

TEARS, idle tears, I know not what they mean,
    Tears from the depth of some divine despair
Rise in the heart, and gather to the eyes,
In looking on the happy Autumn-fields,
And thinking of the days that are no more.

    Fresh as the first beam glittering on a sail,
That brings our friends up from the underworld,
Sad as the last which reddens over one
That sinks with all we love below the verge ;
So sad, so fresh, the days that are no more.

Ah,

Ah, sad and strange as in dark summer dawns
The earliest pipe of half-awaken'd birds
To dying ears, when unto dying eyes
The casement slowly grows a glimmering square ;
So sad, so strange, the days that are no more.

Dear as remember'd kisses after death,
And sweet as those by hopeless fancy feign'd
On lips that are for others ; deep as love,
Deep as first love, and wild with all regret ;
O Death in Life, the days that are no more ! '

167.   *iii*

THE splendour falls on castle walls
    And snowy summits old in story :
The long light shakes across the lakes,
    And the wild cataract leaps in glory.
Blow, bugle, blow, set the wild echoes flying,
Blow, bugle ; answer, echoes, dying, dying, dying.

O hark, O hear ! how thin and clear,
    And thinner, clearer, farther going !
O sweet and far from cliff and scar
    The horns of Elfland faintly blowing !
Blow, let us hear the purple glens replying :
Blow, bugle ; answer, echoes, dying, dying, dying.

O love, they die in yon rich sky,
    They faint on hill or field or river :
Our echoes roll from soul to soul,
    And grow for ever and for ever.
Blow, bugle, blow, set the wild echoes flying,
And answer, echoes, answer, dying, dying, dying.

168. *iv*

THY voice is heard thro' rolling drums,
  That beat to battle where he stands ;
Thy face across his fancy comes,
  And gives the battle to his hands :
A moment, while the trumpets blow,
  He sees his brood about thy knee ;
The next, like fire he meets the foe,
  And strikes him dead for thine and thee.

169. *v*

NOW sleeps the crimson petal, now the white ;
  Nor waves the cypress in the palace walk ;
Nor winks the gold fin in the porphyry font :
The firefly wakens : waken thou with me.

Now droops the milk-white peacock like a ghost,
And like a ghost she glimmers on to me.

Now lies the Earth all Danaë to the stars,
And all thy heart lies open unto me.

Now slides the silent meteor on, and leaves
A shining furrow, as thy thoughts in me.

Now folds the lily all her sweetness up,
And slips into the bosom of the lake :
So fold thyself, my dearest, thou, and slip
Into my bosom and be lost in me.

170.   *Come down, O Maid*

COME down, O maid, from yonder mountain height :
    What pleasure lives in height (the shepherd sang),
In height and cold, the splendour of the hills ?
But cease to move so near the Heavens, and cease
To glide a sunbeam by the blasted Pine,
To sit a star upon the sparkling spire ;
And come, for Love is of the valley, come,
For Love is of the valley, come thou down
And find him ; by the happy threshold, he,
Or hand in hand with Plenty in the maize,
Or red with spirted purple of the vats,
Or foxlike in the vine ; nor cares to walk
With Death and Morning on the silver horns,
Nor wilt thou snare him in the white ravine,
Nor find him dropt upon the firths of ice,
That huddling slant in furrow-cloven falls
To roll the torrent out of dusky doors :
But follow ; let the torrent dance thee down
To find him in the valley ; let the wild
Lean-headed Eagles yelp alone, and leave
The monstrous ledges there to slope, and spill
Their thousand wreaths of dangling water-smoke,
That like a broken purpose waste in air :
So waste not thou ; but come ; for all the vales
Await thee ; azure pillars of the hearth
Arise to thee ; the children call, and I
Thy shepherd pipe, and sweet is every sound,
Sweeter thy voice, but every sound is sweet ;
Myriads of rivulets hurrying thro' the lawn,
The moan of doves in immemorial elms,
And murmuring of innumerable bees.

171. *Ode on the Death of the Duke of*
Wellington

I

BURY the Great Duke
    With an empire's lamentation,
Let us bury the Great Duke
   To the noise of the mourning of a mighty nation,
Mourning when their leaders fall,
Warriors carry the warrior's pall,
And sorrow darkens hamlet and hall.

II

Where shall we lay the man whom we deplore ?
Here, in streaming London's central roar.
Let the sound of those he wrought for,
And the feet of those he fought for,
Echo round his bones for evermore.

III

Lead out the pageant : sad and slow,
As fits an universal woe,
Let the long long procession go,
And let the sorrowing crowd about it grow,
And let the mournful martial music blow ;
The last great Englishman is low.

IV

Mourn, for to us he seems the last,
Remembering all his greatness in the Past.
No more in soldier fashion will he greet
With lifted hand the gazer in the street.

         O friends,

O friends, our chief state-oracle is mute :
Mourn for the man of long-enduring blood,
The statesman-warrior, moderate, resolute,
Whole in himself, a common good.
Mourn for the man of amplest influence,
Yet clearest of ambitious crime,
Our greatest yet with least pretence,
Great in council and great in war,
Foremost captain of his time,
Rich in saving common-sense,
And, as the greatest only are,
In his simplicity sublime.
O good grey head which all men knew,
O voice from which their omens all men drew,
O iron nerve to true occasion true,
O fall'n at length that tower of strength
Which stood four-square to all the winds that blew !
Such was he whom we deplore.
The long self-sacrifice of life is o'er.
The great World-victor's victor will be seen no more.

v

All is over and done :
Render thanks to the Giver,
England, for thy son.
Let the bell be toll'd.
Render thanks to the Giver,
And render him to the mould.
Under the cross of gold
That shines over city and river,
There he shall rest for ever
Among the wise and the bold.
Let the bell be toll'd :
And a reverent people behold

The towering car, the sable steeds :
Bright let it be with its blazon'd deeds,
Dark in its funeral fold.
Let the bell be toll'd :
And a deeper knell in the heart be knoll'd ;
And the sound of the sorrowing anthem roll'd
Thro' the dome of the golden cross ;
And the volleying cannon thunder his loss ;
He knew their voices of old.
For many a time in many a clime
His captain's-ear has heard them boom
Bellowing victory, bellowing doom :
When he with those deep voices wrought,
Guarding realms and kings from shame ;
With those deep voices our dead captain taught
The tyrant, and asserts his claim
In that dread sound to the great name,
Which he has worn so pure of blame,
In praise and in dispraise the same,
A man of well-attemper'd frame.
O civic muse, to such a name,
To such a name for ages long,
To such a name,
Preserve a broad approach of fame,
And ever-echoing avenues of song.

VI

Who is he that cometh, like an honour'd guest,
With banner and with music, with soldier and with priest,
With a nation weeping, and breaking on my rest ?
Mighty Seaman, this is he
Was great by land as thou by sea.
Thine island loves thee well, thou famous man,
The greatest sailor since our world began.

Now,

Now, to the roll of muffled drums,
To thee the greatest soldier comes ;
For this is he
Was great by land as thou by sea ;
His foes were thine ; he kept us free ;
O give him welcome, this is he
Worthy of our gorgeous rites,
And worthy to be laid by thee ;
For this is England's greatest son,
He that gain'd a hundred fights,
Nor ever lost an English gun ;
This is he that far away
Against the myriads of Assaye
Clash'd with his fiery few and won ;
And underneath another sun,
Warring on a later day,
Round affrighted Lisbon drew
The treble works, the vast designs
Of his labour'd rampart-lines,
Where he greatly stood at bay,
Whence he issued forth anew,
And ever great and greater grew,
Beating from the wasted vines
Back to France her banded swarms,
Back to France with countless blows,
Till o'er the hills her eagles flew
Past the Pyrenean pines,
Follow'd up in valley and glen
With blare of bugle, clamour of men,
Roll of cannon and clash of arms,
And England pouring on her foes.
Such a war had such a close.
Again their ravening eagle rose
In anger, wheel'd on Europe-shadowing wings,

And barking for the thrones of kings ;
Till one that sought but Duty's iron crown
On that loud sabbath shook the spoiler down ;
A day of onsets of despair !
Dash'd on every rocky square
Their surging charges foam'd themselves away ;
Last, the Prussian trumpet blew ;
Thro' the long-tormented air
Heaven flash'd a sudden jubilant ray,
And down we swept and charged and overthrew.
So great a soldier taught us there,
What long-enduring hearts could do
In that world's-earthquake, Waterloo !
Mighty Seaman, tender and true,
And pure as he from taint of craven guile,
O saviour of the silver-coasted isle,
O shaker of the Baltic and the Nile,
If aught of things that here befall
Touch a spirit among things divine,
If love of country move thee there at all,
Be glad, because his bones are laid by thine !
And thro' the centuries let a people's voice
In full acclaim,
A people's voice,
The proof and echo of all human fame,
A people's voice, when they rejoice
At civic revel and pomp and game,
Attest their great commander's claim
With honour, honour, honour, honour to him,
Eternal honour to his name.

VII

A people's voice ! we are a people yet.
Tho' all men else their nobler dreams forget,

Confused

Confused by brainless mobs and lawless Powers;
Thank Him who isled us here, and roughly set
His Briton in blown seas and storming showers,
We have a voice, with which to pay the debt
Of boundless love and reverence and regret
To those great men who fought, and kept it ours.
And keep it ours, O God, from brute control;
O Statesmen, guard us, guard the eye, the soul
Of Europe, keep our noble England whole,
And save the one true seed of freedom sown
Betwixt a people and their ancient throne,
That sober freedom out of which there springs
Our loyal passion for our temperate kings;
For, saving that, ye help to save mankind
Till public wrong be crumbled into dust,
And drill the raw world for the march of mind,
Till crowds at length be sane and crowns be just.
But wink no more in slothful overtrust.
Remember him who led your hosts;
He bad you guard the sacred coasts.
Your cannons moulder on the seaward wall;
His voice is silent in your council-hall
For ever; and whatever tempests lour
For ever silent; even if they broke
In thunder, silent; yet remember all
He spoke among you, and the Man who spoke;
Who never sold the truth to serve the hour,
Nor palter'd with Eternal God for power;
Who let the turbid streams of rumour flow
Thro' either babbling world of high and low;
Whose life was work, whose language rife
With rugged maxims hewn from life;
Who never spoke against a foe;
Whose eighty winters freeze with one rebuke

All great self-seekers trampling on the right :
Truth-teller was our England's Alfred named ;
Truth-lover was our English Duke ;
Whatever record leap to light
He never shall be shamed.

VIII

Lo, the leader in these glorious wars
Now to glorious burial slowly borne,
Follow'd by the brave of other lands,
He, on whom from both her open hands
Lavish Honour shower'd all her stars,
And affluent Fortune emptied all her horn.
Yea, let all good things await
Him who cares not to be great,
But as he saves or serves the state.
Not once or twice in our rough island-story,
The path of duty was the way to glory ;
He that walks it, only thirsting
For the right, and learns to deaden
Love of self, before his journey closes,
He shall find the stubborn thistle bursting
Into glossy purples, which outredden
All voluptuous garden-roses.
Not once or twice in our fair island-story,
The path of duty was the way to glory :
He, that ever following her commands,
On with toil of heart and knees and hands,
Thro' the long gorge to the far light has won
His path upward, and prevail'd,
Shall find the toppling crags of Duty scaled
Are close upon the shining table-lands
To which our God Himself is moon and sun.

Such

Such was he : his work is done,
But while the races of mankind endure,
Let his great example stand
Colossal, seen of every land,
And keep the soldier firm, the statesman pure :
Till in all lands and thro' all human story
The path of duty be the way to glory :
And let the land whose hearths he saved from shame
For many and many an age proclaim
At civic revel and pomp and game,
And when the long-illumined cities flame,
Their ever-loyal iron leader's fame,
With honour, honour, honour, honour to him,
Eternal honour to his name.

IX

Peace, his triumph will be sung
By some yet unmoulded tongue
Far on in summers that we shall not see :
Peace, it is a day of pain
For one about whose patriarchal knee
Late the little children clung :
O peace ! it is a day of pain
For one, upon whose hand and heart and brain
Once the weight and fate of Europe hung.
Ours the pain, be his the gain !
More than is of man's degree
Must be with us, watching here
At this, our great solemnity.
Whom we see not we revere,
We revere, and we refrain
From talk of battles loud and vain,
And brawling memories all too free

For such a wise humility
As befits a solemn fane :
We revere, and while we hear
The tides of Music's golden sea
Setting toward eternity,
Uplifted high in heart and hope are we,
Until we doubt not that for one so true
There must be other nobler work to do
Than when he fought at Waterloo,
And Victor he must ever be.
For tho' the Giant Ages heave the hill
And break the shore, and evermore
Make and break, and work their will ;
Tho' world on world in myriad myriads roll
Round us, each with different powers,
And other forms of life than ours,
What know we greater than the soul ?
On God and Godlike men we build our trust.
Hush, the Dead March wails in the people's ears :
The dark crowd moves, and there are sobs and tears :
The black earth yawns : the mortal disappears
Ashes to ashes, dust to dust ;
He is gone who seem'd so great.—
Gone ; but nothing can bereave him
Of the force he made his own
Being here, and we believe him
Something far advanced in State,
And that he wears a truer crown
Than any wreath that man can weave him.
Speak no more of his renown,
Lay your earthly fancies down,
And in the vast cathedral leave him.
God accept him, Christ receive him.

Three Songs from 'Maud'

172.

i

GO not, happy day,
   From the shining fields,
Go not, happy day,
   Till the maiden yields.
Rosy is the West,
   Rosy is the South,
Roses are her cheeks,
   And a rose her mouth.
When the happy Yes
   Falters from her lips,
Pass and blush the news
   O'er the blowing ships.
Over blowing seas,
   Over seas at rest,
Pass the happy news,
   Blush it thro' the West;
Till the red man dance
   By his red cedar tree,
And the red man's babe
   Leap, beyond the sea.
Blush from West to East,
   Blush from East to West,
Till the West is East,
   Blush it thro' the West.
Rosy is the West,
   Rosy is the South,
Roses are her cheeks,
   And a rose her mouth.

173.   *ii*

COME into the garden, Maud,
　　For the black bat, Night, has flown,
Come into the garden, Maud,
　　I am here at the gate alone ;
And the woodbine spices are wafted abroad,
　　And the musk of the roses blown.

For a breeze of morning moves,
　　And the planet of Love is on high,
Beginning to faint in the light that she loves
　　On a bed of daffodil sky,
To faint in the light of the sun she loves,
　　To faint in his light, and to die.

All night have the roses heard
　　The flute, violin, bassoon ;
All night has the casement jessamine stirr'd
　　To the dancers dancing in tune ;
Till a silence fell with the waking bird,
　　And a hush with the setting moon.

I said to the lily, ' There is but one
　　With whom she has heart to be gay.
When will the dancers leave her alone ?
　　She is weary of dance and play.'
Now half to the setting moon are gone,
　　And half to the rising day ;
Low on the sand and loud on the stone
　　The last wheel echoes away.

I said

I said to the rose, ' The brief night goes
    In babble and revel and wine.
O young lord-lover, what sighs are those
    For one that will never be thine ?
But mine, but mine,' so I sware to the rose,
    ' For ever and ever, mine.'

And the soul of the rose went into my blood,
    As the music clash'd in the hall ;
And long by the garden lake I stood,
    For I heard your rivulet fall
From the lake to the meadow and on to the wood,
    Our wood, that is dearer than all ;

From the meadow your walks have left so sweet
    That whenever a March-wind sighs
He sets the jewel-print of your feet
    In violets blue as your eyes,
To the woody hollows in which we meet
    And the valleys of Paradise.

The slender acacia would not shake
    One long milk-bloom on the tree ;
The white lake-blossom fell into the lake,
    As the pimpernel dozed on the lea ;
But the rose was awake all night for your sake,
    Knowing your promise to me ;
The lilies and roses were all awake,
    They sigh'd for the dawn and thee.

Queen rose of the rosebud garden of girls,
    Come hither, the dances are done,
In gloss of satin and glimmer of pearls,
    Queen lily and rose in one ;
Shine out, little head, sunning over with curls,
    To the flowers, and be their sun.

There has fallen a splendid tear
   From the passion-flower at the gate.
She is coming, my dove, my dear ;
   She is coming, my life, my fate ;
The red rose cries, ' She is near, she is near ; '
   And the white rose weeps, ' She is late ; '
The larkspur listens, ' I hear, I hear ; '
   And the lily whispers, ' I wait.'

She is coming, my own, my sweet ;
   Were it ever so airy a tread,
My heart would hear her and beat,
   Were it earth in an earthy bed ;
My dust would hear her and beat,
   Had I lain for a century dead ;
Would start and tremble under her feet,
   And blossom in purple and red.

174.   *iii*

O THAT 'twere possible
   After long grief and pain
To find the arms of my true love
Round me once again ! . . .

A shadow flits before me,
Not thou, but like to thee :
Ah, Christ ! that it were possible
For one short hour to see
The souls we loved, that they might tell us
What and where they be !

175. *The Daisy*

WRITTEN AT EDINBURGH

O LOVE, what hours were thine and mine,
  In lands of palm and southern pine;
 In lands of palm, of orange-blossom,
Of olive, aloe, and maize and vine.

What Roman strength Turbia show'd
In ruin, by the mountain road;
  How like a gem, beneath, the city
Of little Monaco, basking, glow'd.

How richly down the rocky dell
The torrent vineyard streaming fell
  To meet the sun and sunny waters,
That only heaved with a summer swell.

What slender campanili grew
By bays, the peacock's neck in hue;
  Where, here and there, on sandy beaches
A milky-bell'd amaryllis blew.

How young Columbus seem'd to rove,
Yet present in his natal grove,
  Now watching high on mountain cornice,
And steering, now, from a purple cove,

Now pacing mute by ocean's rim;
Till, in a narrow street and dim,
  I stay'd the wheels at Cogoletto,
And drank, and loyally drank to him.

Nor knew we well what pleased us most,
Not the clipt palm of which they boast;
   But distant colour, happy hamlet,
A moulder'd citadel on the coast,

Or tower, or high hill-convent, seen
A light amid its olives green;
   Or olive-hoary cape in ocean;
Or rosy blossom in hot ravine,

Where oleanders flush'd the bed
Of silent torrents, gravel-spread;
   And, crossing, oft we saw the glisten
Of ice, far up on a mountain head.

We loved that hall, tho' white and cold,
Those niched shapes of noble mould,
   A princely people's awful princes,
The grave, severe Genovese of old.

At Florence too what golden hours,
In those long galleries, were ours;
   What drives about the fresh Cascinè.
Or walks in Boboli's ducal bowers.

In bright vignettes, and each complete
Of tower or duomo, sunny-sweet,
   Or palace, how the city glitter'd,
Thro' cypress avenues, at our feet.

But when we crost the Lombard plain
Remember what a plague of rain;
   Of rain at Reggio, rain at Parma;
At Lodi, rain, Piacenza, rain.

And

And stern and sad (so rare the smiles
Of sunlight) look'd the Lombard piles ;
    Porch-pillars on the lion resting,
And sombre, old, colonnaded aisles.

O Milan, O the chanting quires,
The giant windows' blazon'd fires,
    The height, the space, the gloom, the glory !
A mount of marble, a hundred spires !

I climb'd the roofs at break of day ;
Sun-smitten Alps before me lay.
    I stood among the silent statues,
And statued pinnacles, mute as they.

How faintly-flush'd, how phantom-fair,
Was Monte Rosa, hanging there
    A thousand shadowy-pencill'd valleys
And snowy dells in a golden air.

Remember how we came at last
To Como ; shower and storm and blast
    Had blown the lake beyond his limit,
And all was flooded ; and how we past

From Como, when the light was grey,
And in my head, for half the day,
    The rich Virgilian rustic measure
Of Lari Maxume, all the way,

Like ballad-burthen music, kept,
As on The Lariano crept
    To that fair port below the castle
Of Queen Theodolind, where we slept ;

Or hardly slept, but watch'd awake
A cypress in the moonlight shake,
   The moonlight touching o'er a terrace
One tall Agavè above the lake.

What more ? we took our last adieu,
And up the snowy Splugen drew,
   But ere we reach'd the highest summit
I pluck'd a daisy, I gave it you.

It told of England then to me,
And now it tells of Italy.
   O love, we two shall go no longer
To lands of summer across the sea ;

So dear a life your arms enfold
Whose crying is a cry for gold :
   Yet here to-night in this dark city,
When ill and weary, alone and cold,

I found, tho' crush'd to hard and dry,
This nurseling of another sky
   Still in the little book you lent me,
And where you tenderly laid it by :

And I forgot the clouded Forth,
The gloom that saddens Heaven and Earth,
   The bitter east, the misty summer
And grey metropolis of the North.

Perchance, to lull the throbs of pain,
Perchance, to charm a vacant brain,
   Perchance, to dream you still beside me,
My fancy fled to the South again.

176.   In the Valley of Cauteretz

ALL along the valley, stream that flashest white,
　　Deepening thy voice with the deepening of the night,
All along the valley, where thy waters flow,
I walk'd with one I loved two and thirty years ago.
All along the valley while I walk'd to-day,
The two and thirty years were a mist that rolls away;
For all along the valley, down thy rocky bed
Thy living voice to me was as the voice of the dead,
And all along the valley, by rock and cave and tree,
The voice of the dead was a living voice to me.

177.   In the Garden at Swainston

NIGHTINGALES warbled without,
　　Within was weeping for thee:
Shadows of three dead men
　　Walk'd in the walks with me:
　　Shadows of three dead men, and thou wast one of the
　　　　three.

Nightingales sang in his woods:
　　The Master was far away:
Nightingales warbled and sang
　　Of a passion that lasts but a day;
　　Still in the house in his coffin the Prince of courtesy lay.

Two dead men have I known
　　In courtesy like to thee:
Two dead men have I loved
　　With a love that ever will be:
　　Three dead men have I loved, and thou art last of the
　　　　three.

178.   *Crossing the Bar*

SUNSET and evening star,
    And one clear call for me !
And may there be no moaning of the bar,
    When I put out to sea,

But such a tide as moving seems asleep,
    Too full for sound and foam,
When that which drew from out the boundless deep
    Turns again home.

Twilight and evening bell,
    And after that the dark !
And may there be no sadness of farewell,
    When I embark ;

For tho' from out our bourne of Time and Place
    The flood may bear me far,
I hope to see my Pilot face to face
    When I have crost the bar.

FRANCES ANNE KEMBLE

1809-1893

179.   *Dream Land*

WHEN in my dreams thy lovely face
    Smiles with unwonted tender grace,
Grudge not the precious seldom cheer :
I know full well, my lady dear,
    It is no boon of thine !

In thy sweet sanctu'ry of sleep,
If my sad sprite should kneeling weep,
Suffer its speechless worship there :
Thou know'st full well, my lady fair,
    It is no fault of mine !

180.   *Faith*

BETTER trust all, and be deceived,
    And weep that trust and that deceiving,
Than doubt one heart that, if believed,
    Had bless'd one's life with true believing.

O, in this mocking world too fast
    The doubting fiend o'ertakes our youth !
Better be cheated to the last
    Than lose the blessèd hope of truth.

OLIVER WENDELL HOLMES

181.   *The Last Leaf.*

I SAW him once before,
  As he pass'd by the door,
    And again
The pavement stones resound,
As he totters o'er the ground
    With his cane.

They say that in his prime,
Ere the pruning-knife of Time
    Cut him down,
Not a better man was found
By the Crier on his round
    Through the town.

But now he walks the streets,
And he looks at all he meets
    Sad and wan,
And he shakes his feeble head,
That it seems as if he said,
    ' They are gone.'

The mossy marbles rest
On the lips that he has prest
    In their bloom,
And the names he loved to hear
Have been carved for many a year
    On the tomb.

My

My grandmamma has said—
Poor old lady, she is dead
    Long ago—
That he had a Roman nose,
And his cheek was like a rose
    In the snow.

But now his nose is thin,
And it rests upon his chin
    Like a staff,
And a crook is in his back,
And a melancholy crack
    In his laugh.

I know it is a sin
For me to sit and grin
    At him here ;
But the old three-corner'd hat,
And the breeches, and all that,
    Are so queer !

And if I should live to be
The last leaf upon the tree
    In the spring,
Let them smile, as I do now,
At the old forsaken bough
    Where I cling.

OLIVER WENDELL HOLMES

182. *The Chambered Nautilus*

THIS is the ship of pearl, which, poets feign,
　　Sails the unshadow'd main,—
　　　The venturous bark that flings
On the sweet summer wind its purpled wings
In gulfs enchanted, where the Siren sings,
　　　And coral reefs lie bare,
Where the cold sea-maids rise to sun their streaming hair.

Its webs of living gauze no more unfurl;
　　Wreck'd is the ship of pearl!
　　　And every chamber'd cell,
Where its dim dreaming life was wont to dwell,
As the frail tenant shaped his growing shell,
　　　Before thee lies reveal'd,—
Its irised ceiling rent, its sunless crypt unseal'd!

Year after year beheld the silent toil
　　That spread his lustrous coil;
　　　Still, as the spiral grew,
He left the past year's dwelling for the new,
Stole with soft step its shining archway through,
　　　Built up its idle door,
Stretch'd in his last-found home, and knew the old no
　　more.

Thanks for the heavenly message brought by thee,
　　Child of the wandering sea,
　　　Cast from her lap, forlorn!
From thy dead lips a clearer note is born
Than ever Triton blew from wreathèd horn!
　　　While on mine ear it rings,
Through the deep caves of thought I hear a voice that
　　sings:—

　　　　　　　　　　Build

Build thee more stately mansions, O my soul,
    As the swift seasons roll!
    Leave thy low-vaulted past!
Let each new temple, nobler than the last,
Shut thee from heaven with a dome more vast,
    Till thou at length art free,
Leaving thine outgrown shell by life's unresting sea!

JOHN STUART BLACKIE

1809-1895

183.   *My Loves*

NAME the leaves on all the trees,
    Name the waves on all the seas,
Name the notes of all the groves,
Thus thou namest all my loves.

I do love the young, the old,
Maiden modest, virgin bold;
Tiny beauties and the tall—
Earth has room enough for all!

Which is better—who can say?—
Mary grave or Lucy gay?
She who half her charms conceals,
She who flashes while she feels?

Why should I my love confine?
Why should fair be mine or thine?
If I praise a tulip, why
Should I pass the primrose by?

Paris was a pedant fool
Meting beauty by the rule:
Pallas? Juno? Venus?—he
Should have chosen all the three!

SIR SAMUEL FERGUSON

1810–1886

184. *Cean Dubh Deelish*

PUT your head, darling, darling, darling,
　　Your darling black head my heart above ;
O mouth of honey, with thyme for fragrance,
　　Who, with heart in breast, could deny you love ?

O many and many a young girl for me is pining,
　　Letting her locks of gold to the cold wind free,
For me, the foremost of our gay young fellows ;
　　But I'd leave a hundred, pure love, for thee !

Then put your head, darling, darling, darling,
　　Your darling black head my heart above ;
O mouth of honey, with thyme for fragrance,
　　Who with heart in breast could deny you love ?

185. *The Fair Hills of Ireland*

A PLENTEOUS place is Ireland for hospitable cheer,
　　　　Uileacan dubh O !
Where the wholesome fruit is bursting from the yellow
　　　　barley ear ;
　　　　Uileacan dubh O !
There is honey in the trees where her misty vales expand,
And her forest paths in summer are by falling waters
　　　　fann'd,
There is dew at high noontide there, and springs i' the
　　　　yellow sand,
　　　　On the fair hills of holy Ireland.

233   Curl'd

Curl'd he is and ringleted, and plaited to the knee—
   Uileacan dubh O !
Each captain who comes sailing across the Irish Sea ;
   Uileacan dubh O !
And I will make my journey, if life and health but stand,
Unto that pleasant country, that fresh and fragrant strand,
And leave your boasted braveries, your wealth and high
   command,
   For the fair hills of holy Ireland.

Large and profitable are the stacks upon the ground,
   Uileacan dubh O !
The butter and the cream do wondrously abound ;
   Uileacan dubh O !
The cresses on the water and the sorrels are at hand,
And the cuckoo 's calling daily his note of music bland,
And the bold thrush sings so bravely his song i' the
   forests grand,
   On the fair hills of holy Ireland.

186.   *Cashel of Munster*

From the Irish

I'D wed you without herds, without money or rich array,
 And I'd wed you on a dewy morn at day-dawn gray;
My bitter woe it is, love, that we are not far away
In Cashel town, tho' the bare deal board were our
 marriage-bed this day !

O fair maid, remember the green hill-side,
Remember how I hunted about the valleys wide ;

Time now has worn me ; my locks are turn'd to gray ;
The year is scarce and I am poor—but send me not, love,
  away !

O deem not my blood is of base strain, my girl ;
O think not my birth was as the birth of a churl ;
Marry me and prove me, and say soon you will
That noble blood is written on my right side still.

My purse holds no red gold, no coin of the silver white ;
No herds are mine to drive through the long twilight ;
But the pretty girl that would take me, all bare tho' I be
  and lone,
O, I'd take her with me kindly to the county Tyrone !

O my girl, I can see 'tis in trouble you are ;
And O my girl, I see 'tis your people's reproach you bear !
—I am a girl in trouble for his sake with whom I fly,
And, O, may no other maiden know such reproach as I !

187. *The Welshmen of Tirawley*

SCORNEY BWEE, the Barretts' bailiff, lewd and lame,
 To lift the Lynott's taxes when he came,
Rudely drew a young maid to him !
Then the Lynotts rose and slew him,
And in Tubber-na-Scorney threw him—
   Small your blame,
   Sons of Lynott !
Sing the vengeance of the Welshmen of **Tirawley.**

      Then

Then the Barretts to the Lynotts gave a choice,
Saying, ' Hear, ye murderous brood, men and boys,
Choose ye now, without delay,
Will ye lose your eyesight, say,
Or your manhoods, here to-day ?
      Sad your choice,
      Sons of Lynott !
Sing the vengeance of the Welshmen of Tirawley.

Then the little boys of the Lynotts, weeping, said,
' Only leave us our eyesight in our head.'
But the bearded Lynotts then
Quickly answered back again,
' Take our eyes, but leave us men,
      Alive or dead,
      Sons of Wattin ! '
Sing the vengeance of the Welshmen of Tirawley.

So the Barretts with sewing-needles sharp and smooth,
Let the light out of the eyes of every youth,
And of every bearded man,
Of the broken Lynott clan ;
Then their darkened faces wan
      Turning south
      To the river—
Sing the vengeance of the Welshmen of Tirawley.

O'er the slippery stepping-stones of Clochan-na-n'all
They drove them, laughing loud at every fall,
As their wandering footsteps dark
Fail'd to reach the slippery mark,
And the swift stream swallow'd stark,
      One and all
      As they stumbled—
From the vengeance of the Welshmen of Tirawley.

Of all the blinded Lynotts one alone
Walk'd erect from stepping-stone to stone :
So back again they brought you,
And a second time they wrought you
With their needles ; but never got you
   Once to groan,
   Emon Lynott,
For the vengeance of the Welshmen of Tirawley.

But with prompt-projected footsteps sure as ever,
Emon Lynott again cross'd the river.
Though Duvowen was rising fast,
And the shaking stones o'ercast
By cold floods boiling past ;
   Yet you never,
   Emon Lynott,
Falter'd once before your foemen of Tirawley.

But, turning on Ballintubber bank, you stood,
And the Barretts thus bespoke o'er the flood—
' O, ye foolish sons of Wattin,
Small amends are these you've gotten,
For, while Scorna Boy lies rotten,
   I am good
   For vengeance ! '
Sing the vengeance of the Welshmen of Tirawley.

' For 'tis neither in eye nor eyesight that a man
Bears the fortunes of himself and his clan,
But in the manly mind,
These darken'd orbs behind,
That your needles could never find
   Though they ran
   Through my heart-strings ! '
Sing the vengeance of the Welshmen of Tirawley.

            ' But

' But, little your women's needles do I reck ;
For the night from heaven never fell so black,
But Tirawley, and abroad
From the Moy to Cuan-an-fod,
I could walk it every sod,
            Path and track,
            Ford and togher,
Seeking vengeance on you, Barretts of Tirawley !

' The night when Dathy O'Dowda broke your camp,
What Barrett among you was it held the lamp—
Showed the way to those two feet,
When through wintry wind and sleet,
I guided your blind retreat
            In the swamp
            Of Beäl-an-asa ?
O ye vengeance-destin'd ingrates of Tirawley ! '

So leaving loud-shriek-echoing Garranard,
The Lynott like a red dog hunted hard,
With his wife and children seven,
'Mong the beasts and fowls of heaven
In the hollows of Glen Nephin,
            Light-debarr'd,
            Made his dwelling,
Planning vengeance on the Barretts of Tirawley.

And ere the bright-orb'd year its course had run,
On his brown round-knotted knee he nursed a son,
A child of light, with eyes
As clear as are the skies
In summer, when sunrise
            Has begun ;
            So the Lynott
Nursed his vengeance on the Barretts of Tirawley.

And, as ever the bright boy grew in strength and size,
Made him perfect in each manly exercise,
The salmon in the flood,
The dun deer in the wood,
The eagle in the cloud
      To surprise
      On Ben Nephin,
Far above the foggy fields of Tirawley.

With the yellow-knotted spear-shaft, with the bow,
With the steel, prompt to deal shot and blow,
He taught him from year to year
And train'd him, without a peer,
For a perfect cavalier,
      Hoping so—
      Far his forethought—
For vengeance on the Barretts of Tirawley.

And, when mounted on his proud-bounding steed,
Emon Oge sat a cavalier indeed ;
Like the ear upon the wheat
When winds in Autumn beat
On the bending stems, his seat ;
      And the speed
      Of his courser
Was the wind from Barna-na-gee o'er Tirawley !

Now when fifteen sunny summers thus were spent,
(He perfected in all accomplishment)—
The Lynott said, ' My child,
We are over long exiled
From mankind in this wild—
      —Time we went
      Through the mountain
To the countries lying over-against Tirawley.'

So,

So, out over mountain-moors, and mosses brown,
And green steam-gathering vales, they journey'd down :
Till, shining like a star,
Through the dusky gleams afar,
The bailey of Castlebar,
    And the town
     Of MacWilliam
Rose bright before the wanderers of Tirawley.

' Look southward, my boy, and tell me as we go,
What see'st thou by the loch-head below ? '
' O, a stone-house strong and great,
And a horse-host at the gate,
And a captain in armour of plate—
     Grand the show !
     Great the glancing !
High the heroes of this land below Tirawley!

' And a beautiful Bantierna by his side,
Yellow gold on all her gown-sleeves wide ;
And in her hand a pearl
Of a young, little, fair-hair'd girl.'
Said the Lynott, ' It is the Earl !
     Let us ride
     To his presence.'
And before him came the exiles of Tirawley.

' God save thee, MacWilliam,' the Lynott thus began ;
' God save all here besides of this clan ;
For gossips dear to me
Are all in company—
For in these four bones ye see
     A kindly man
     Of the Britons—
Emon Lynott of Garranard of Tirawley.

' And hither, as kindly gossip-law allows,
I come to claim a scion of thy house
To foster ; for thy race,
Since William Conquer's days,
Have ever been wont to place,
   With some spouse
   Of a Briton,
A MacWilliam Oge, to foster in Tirawley.

' And, to show thee in what sort our youth are taught,
I have hither to thy home of valour brought
This one son of my age,
For a sample and a pledge
For the equal tutelage,
   In right thought,
   Word, and action,
Of whatever son ye give into Tirawley.'

When MacWilliam beheld the brave boy ride and run,
Saw the spear-shaft from his white shoulder spun—
With a sigh, and with a smile,
He said,—' I would give the spoil
Of a county, that Tibbot Moyle,
   My own son,
   Were accomplish'd
Like this branch of the kindly Britons of Tirawley.'

When the Lady MacWilliam she heard him speak,
And saw the ruddy roses on his cheek,
She said, ' I would give a purse
Of red gold to the nurse
That would rear my Tibbot no worse ;
   But I seek
   Hitherto vainly—
Heaven grant that I now have found her in Tirawley ! '

So they said to the Lynott, ' Here, take our bird !
And as pledge for the keeping of thy word,
Let this scion here remain
Till thou comest back again :
Meanwhile the fitting train
        Of a lord
        Shall attend thee
With the lordly heir of Connaught into Tirawley.'

So back to strong-throng-gathering Garranard,
Like a lord of the country with his guard,
Came the Lynott, before them all,
Once again over Clochan-na-n'all
Steady and striding, erect and tall,
        And his ward
        On his shoulders
To the wonder of the Welshmen of Tirawley.

Then a diligent foster-father you would deem
The Lynott, teaching Tibbot, by mead and stream,
To cast the spear, to ride,
To stem the rushing tide,
With what feats of body beside,
        Might beseem
        A MacWilliam,
Foster'd free among the Welshmen of Tirawley.

But the lesson of hell he taught him in heart and mind,
For to what desire soever he inclined,
Of anger, lust, or pride,
He had it gratified,
Till he ranged the circle wide
        Of a blind
        Self-indulgence,
Ere he came to youthful manhood in Tirawley.

Then, even as when a hunter slips a hound,
Lynott loosed him—God's leashes all unbound—
In the pride of power and station,
And the strength of youthful passion,
On the daughters of thy nation,
      All around,
      Wattin Barrett!
O! the vengeance of the Welshmen of Tirawley!

Bitter grief and burning anger, rage and shame,
Fill'd the houses of the Barretts where'er he came;
Till the young men of the Back,
Drew by night upon his track,
And slew him at Cornassack.
      Small your blame,
      Sons of Wattin!
Sing the vengeance of the Welshmen of Tirawley.

Said the Lynott, 'The day of my vengeance is drawing
    near,
The day for which, through many a long dark year,
I have toil'd through grief and sin—
Call ye now the Brehons in,
And let the plea begin
      Over the bier
      Of MacWilliam,
For an eric upon the Barretts of Tirawley!'

Then the Brehons to MacWilliam Burke decreed
An eric upon Clan Barrett for the deed;
And the Lynott's share of the fine,
As foster-father, was nine
Ploughlands and nine score kine;
      But no need
      Had the Lynott,
Neither care, for land or cattle in Tirawley.

                                        But

But rising, while all sat silent on the spot,
He said, ' The law says—doth it not ?—
If the foster-sire elect
His portion to reject,
He may then the right exact
   To applot
   The short eric.'
' 'Tis the law,' replied the Brehons of Tirawley.

Said the Lynott, ' I once before had a choice
Proposed me, wherein law had little voice ;
But now I choose, and say,
As lawfully I may,
I applot the mulct to-day ;
   So rejoice
   In your ploughlands
And your cattle which I renounce throughout Tirawley.

' And thus I applot the mulct : I divide
The land throughout Clan Barrett on every side
Equally, that no place
May be without the face
Of a foe of Wattin's race—
   That the pride
   Of the Barretts
May be humbled hence for ever throughout Tirawley.

' I adjudge a seat in every Barrett's hall
To MacWilliam : in every stable I give a stall
To MacWilliam : and, beside,
Whenever a Burke shall ride
Through Tirawley, I provide
   At his call
   Needful grooming,
Without charge from any Brughaidh of Tirawley.

' Thus lawfully I avenge me for the throes
Ye lawlessly caused me and caused those
Unhappy shame-faced ones
Who, their mothers expected once,
Would have been the sires of sons—
        O'er whose woes
        Often weeping,
I have groan'd in my exile from Tirawley.

' I demand not of you your manhoods ; but I take—
For the Burkes will take it—your Freedom ! for the sake
Of which all manhood 's given
And all good under heaven,
And, without which, better even
        You should make
        Yourselves barren,
Than see your children slaves throughout Tirawley !

' Neither take I your eyesight from you ; as you took
Mine and ours : I would have you daily look
On one another's eyes
When the strangers tyrannize
By your hearths, and blushes arise,
        That ye brook
        Without vengeance
The insults of troops of Tibbots throughout Tirawley !

' The vengeance I design'd, now is done,
And the days of me and mine nearly run—
For, for this, I have broken faith,
Teaching him who lies beneath
This pall, to merit death ;
        And my son
        To his father
Stands pledged for other teaching in Tirawley.'

Said

Said MacWilliam—' Father and son, hang them high ! '
And the Lynott they hang'd speedily ;
But across the salt water,
To Scotland, with the daughter
Of MacWilliam—well you got her !—
       Did you fly,
       Edmund Lindsay,
The gentlest of all the Welshmen of Tirawley !

'Tis thus the ancient Ollaves of Erin tell
How, through lewdness and revenge, it befell
That the sons of William Conquer
Came over the sons of Wattin,
Throughout all the bounds and borders
Of the lands of Auley Mac Fiachra ;
Till the Saxon Oliver Cromwell,
And his valiant, Bible-guided,
Free heretics of Clan London,
Coming in, in their succession,
Rooted out both Burke and Barrett,
And in their empty places
New stems of freedom planted,
With many a goodly sapling
Of manliness and virtue ;
Which while their children cherish,
Kindly Irish of the Irish,
Neither Saxons nor Italians,
May the mighty God of Freedom
       Speed them well,
       Never taking
Further vengeance on his people of **Tirawley**

1810–1888

188.   *The Private of the Buffs*

LAST night, among his fellow roughs,
    He jested, quaff'd, and swore;
A drunken private of the Buffs,
    Who never look'd before.
To-day, beneath the foeman's frown,
    He stands in Elgin's place,
Ambassador from Britain's crown
    And type of all her race.

Poor, reckless, rude, low-born, untaught,
    Bewilder'd, and alone,
A heart with English instinct fraught
    He yet can call his own.
Aye, tear his body limb from limb,
    Bring cord, or axe, or flame:
He only knows, that not through him
    Shall England come to shame.

Far Kentish hop-fields round him seem'd,
    Like dreams, to come and go;
Bright leagues of cherry-blossom gleam'd,
    One sheet of living snow;
The smoke above his father's door
    In grey soft eddyings hung:
Must he then watch it rise no more,
    Doom'd by himself, so young?

Yes, honour calls!—with strength like steel
    He put the vision by.
Let dusky Indians whine and kneel;
    An English lad must die.

247   And

And thus, with eyes that would not shrink,
　　With knee to man unbent,
Unfaltering on its dreadful brink,
　　To his red grave he went.

Vain, mightiest fleets of iron framed ;
　　Vain, those all-shattering guns ;
Unless proud England keep, untamed,
　　The strong heart of her sons.
So, let his name through Europe ring—
　　A man of mean estate,
Who died, as firm as Sparta's king,
　　Because his soul was great.

189.　　　　　*The Epicurean*

UPON an everlasting tide
　　Into the silent seas we go ;
But verdure laughs along the side,
　　And on the margin roses blow.

Nor life, nor death, nor aught they hold
　　Rate thou above their natural height :
Yet learn that all our eyes behold
　　Has value, if we mete it right.

Pluck then the flowers that line the stream,
　　Instead of fighting with its power :
But pluck as flowers, not gems, nor deem
　　That they will bloom beyond their hour.

Whate'er betides, from day to day
　　An even pulse and spirit keep ;
And like a child worn out with play,
　　When wearied with existence, sleep.

1811-1863

190. *The Ballad of Bouillabaisse*

A STREET there is in Paris famous,
    For which no rhyme our language yields,
Rue Neuve des Petits Champs its name is—
    The New Street of the Little Fields ;
And here's an inn, not rich and splendid,
    But still in comfortable case ;
The which in youth I oft attended,
    To eat a bowl of Bouillabaisse.

This Bouillabaisse a noble dish is—
    A sort of soup or broth, or brew,
Or hotchpotch, of all sorts of fishes,
    That Greenwich never could outdo ;
Green herbs, red peppers, mussels, saffern,
    Soles, onions, garlic, roach, and dace ;
All these you eat at Terré's tavern,
    In that one dish of Bouillabaisse.

Indeed, a rich and savoury stew 'tis ;
    And true philosophers, methinks,
Who love all sorts of natural beauties,
    Should love good victuals and good drinks.
And Cordelier or Benedictine
    Might gladly, sure, his lot embrace,
Nor find a fast-day too afflicting
    Which served him up a Bouillabaisse.

I wonder if the house still there is ?
    Yes, here the lamp is, as before ;
The smiling red-cheek'd écaillère is
    Still opening oysters at the door.

Is

Is Terré still alive and able ?
    I recollect his droll grimace ;
He'd come and smile before your table,
    And hope you liked your Bouillabaisse.

We enter—nothing 's changed or older.
    ' How 's Monsieur Terré, waiter, pray ? '
The waiter stares and shrugs his shoulder—
    ' Monsieur is dead this many a day.'
' It is the lot of saint and sinner,
    So honest Terré 's run his race ! '
' What will Monsieur require for dinner ? '
    ' Say, do you still cook Bouillabaisse ? '

' Oh, oui, Monsieur,' 's the waiter's answer ;
    ' Quel vin Monsieur désire-t-il ? '
' Tell me a good one.'—' That I can, Sir :
    The Chambertin with yellow seal.'
' So Terré 's gone,' I say, and sink in
    My old accustom'd corner-place ;
' He 's done with feasting and with drinking,
    With Burgundy and Bouillabaisse.'

My old accustom'd corner here is,
    The table still is in the nook ;
Ah ! vanish'd many a busy year is,
    This well-known chair since last I took.
When first I saw ye, *cari luoghi*,
    I'd scarce a beard upon my face,
And now a grizzled, grim old fogy,
    I sit and wait for Bouillabaisse.

Where are you, old companions trusty,
    Of early days, here met to dine ?
Come, waiter ! quick, a flagon crusty—
    I'll pledge them in the good old wine.

WILLIAM MAKEPEACE THACKERAY

The kind old voices and old faces
    My memory can quick retrace;
Around the board they take their places,
    And share the wine and Bouillabaisse.

There 's Jack has made a wondrous marriage;
    There 's laughing Tom is laughing yet;
There 's brave Augustus drives his carriage;
    There 's poor old Fred in the Gazette;
On James's head the grass is growing:
    Good Lord! the world has wagged apace
Since here we set the Claret flowing,
    And drank, and ate the Bouillabaisse.

Ah me! how quick the days are flitting!
    I mind me of a time that 's gone,
When here I'd sit, as now I'm sitting,
    In this same place—but not alone.
A fair young form was nestled near me,
    A dear, dear face looked fondly up,
And sweetly spoke and smiled to cheer me
    —There 's no one now to share my cup.

    .   .   .   .   .   .

I drink it as the Fates ordain it.
    Come, fill it, and have done with rhymes:
Fill up the lonely glass, and drain it
    In memory of dear old times.
Welcome the wine, whate'er the seal is;
    And sit you down and say your grace
With thankful heart, whate'er the meal is.
    —Here comes the smoking Bouillabaisse!

191.   *The King on the Tower*

FROM UHLAND

'Da liegen sie alle, die grauen Höhen.'

THE cold grey hills they bind me around,
    The darksome valleys lie sleeping below;
But the winds as they pass o'er all this ground,
    Bring me never a sound of woe !

Oh ! for all I have suffer'd and striven,
    Care has embitter'd my cup and my feast ;
But here is the night and the dark blue heaven,
    And my soul shall be at rest.

O golden legends writ in the skies !
    I turn towards you with longing soul,
And list to the awful harmonies
    Of the Spheres as on they roll.

My hair is grey and my sight nigh gone ;
    My sword it rusteth upon the wall ;
Right have I spoken, and right have I done :
    When shall I rest me once for all ?

O blessèd rest ! O royal night !
    Wherefore seemeth the time so long
Till I see yon stars in their fullest light,
    And list to their loudest song ?

HENRY ELLISON

1811-1880

192.   *Fall of the Year*

WHEN Grasshopper, chirping late,
    Easing thus his merry heart,
Not from cares but over-joy
Tells that Summer's out of date,
Yet thereat no fears annoy
His blithe spirit—not one smart
For lost moments, wishes ill—
As he sang so sings he still ;
In his life-dregs keeping holy
That joy-essence fresh and clear,
Free from taint of melancholy,
Which from Nature, when the Year
Saw his birthday young like him,
He received, a boon of Glory
Man might envy, whom a whim—
A mere nothing—can o'er-dim . . .

When the Redbreast whistles blithe,
Taking of sweet song his fill,
Tho' the other birds be still ;
And the lambs full-sized bleat strong,
Well-wool'd 'gainst the Winter's chill ;
When no more the reaping-scythe
Finds a cornstalk to cut down,
And the stubble field looks brown
Where the formless vapour shows
Objects indistinct and wrong ;
When the daylight shorter grows,
And owl's and bat's delight is long ;

When,

When, nigh eveless, Night draws on,
Waiting scarce for set of sun;
Like enchantress whose high spell
Works a sudden miracle . . .

When the peasant, weather-wise,
Shakes his grey head at the skies;
By his blazing cottage-flame
Mutters Winter's chilly name,
Lives o'er the past, in many a tale,
And prophesies, and quaffs his ale:
While in chimney-nook to sleep
Tirèd dog and urchin creep:

When the weather-signs are rife,
Telling of new Season's life;
And all creatures, instinct-wise,
Tho' taught not to philosophise,
Now prepare, each in his way,
To protract life's little day;
And thy own heart plainer still
Than falling leaf or faded hill,
Tells thee that the Summer 's flown
With all joys that thou hast known . . .

Then look thro' thy heart, and say
What the Summer in its day
Has ripen'd there of good and bright
That may glad thy after-sight.
Has it had its harvest-home?
Its Spring growth? its Summer bloom?
And, when bloom has pass'd away,
Has it had its seeding-day
Of well-ripen'd season'd thought
From Experience duly bought;
Of wise joys which in the mind
Seeds of better leave behind;

Joys by sorrow touch'd and tried,
And freed from earthly dross and pride;
Such as unreproved and free
Sweeten after-memory ?
Has the Summer left for thee
In the soul's high-granary
Produce not of hasty growth
But of well-maturèd worth ?
Fellow-creature Love and Peace,
With a mind and heart at ease,
And a love for everything
With which Man holds communing,
From the meanest worm that creeps
To the babe that cradled sleeps ?
Has the Summer left thy heart
That which passes show, the art
Like wise Nature to prepare
From the Past a Future fair ?
As the Earth within her breast,
When she seems at barren rest
Still prepares in her good time
Coming Springs, and from the slime
Of the brute soil moulds to life
Forms with grace and beauty rife ;
So within thy inmost soul
Striving t'wards a higher goal,
From this life's impediments,
And the body's downward bents,
Frame thou the wings to upward aims
As from the gross wood rise pure flames.
In thy spirit's fertile womb
Mould thou shapes not for the tomb :
There let Faith beget on Love
The angel thou shalt be Above !

ALFRED DOMETT

193.   *A Maori Girl's Song*

ALAS, and well-a-day ! they are talking of me still :
   By the tingling of my nostril, I fear they are talking
     ill :
Poor hapless I—poor little I ! So many mouths to fill—
   And all for this strange feeling—O, this sad, sweet pain !

O senseless heart—O simple ! to yearn so and to pine
For one so far above me, confess'd o'er all to shine ;
For one a hundred dote upon, who never can be mine—
   O, 'tis a foolish feeling, all this fond sweet pain !

When I was quite a child, not many moons ago—
A happy little maiden—O then it was not so ;
Like a sunny-dancing wavelet then I sparkled to and fro,
   And I never had this feeling—O, this sad, sweet pain !

I think it must be owing to the idle life I lead
In the dreamy house for ever that this new bosom-weed
Has sprouted up and spread its shoots till it troubles me
     indeed
   With a restless, weary feeling—such a sad, sweet pain !

So in the pleasant islet, O, no longer will I stay,
And the shadowy summer dwelling I will leave this very
     day ;
On Arapa I'll launch my skiff, and soon be borne away
   From all that feeds this feeling—O, this fond sweet
     pain !

I'll go and see dear Rima.   She'll welcome me, I know,
And a flaxen cloak, her gayest, o'er my weary shoulders
    throw,
With purfle red and points so free—O, quite a lovely show
    To charm away this feeling—O, this sad, sweet pain !

Two feathers I will borrow, and so gracefully I'll wear—
Two feathers soft and snowy for my long, black, lustrous
    hair :
Of the albatross's down they'll be—O, how charming
    they'll look there,
    All to chase away this feeling—O, this fond, sweet pain !

Then the lads will flock around me with flattering talk
    all day ;
And, with anxious little pinches, sly hints of love convey;
And I shall blush with happy pride to hear them, I dare
    say,
    And quite forget this feeling—O, this sad, sweet pain !

194.   *A Christmas Hymn, 1837*

IT was the calm and silent night !—
  Seven hundred years and fifty-three
Had Rome been growing up to might,
    And now was Queen of land and sea !
No sound was heard of clashing wars ;
  Peace brooded o'er the hush'd domain ;
Apollo, Pallas, Jove and Mars
    Held undisturb'd their ancient reign,
      In the solemn midnight,
        Centuries ago !

ALFRED DOMETT

'Twas in the calm and silent night!
   The senator of haughty Rome
Impatient urged his chariot's flight
   From lordly revel rolling home.
Triumphal arches gleaming swell
   His breast with thought of boundless sway.
What reck'd the Roman what befell
   A paltry province far away,
      In the solemn midnight,
        Centuries ago?

Within that province far away
   Went plodding home a weary boor:
A streak of light before him lay,
   Fall'n thro' a half-shut stable door
Across his path. He pass'd—for naught
   Told what was going on within:
How keen the stars! his only thought;
   The air how cold and calm and thin,
      In the solemn midnight
        Centuries ago!

O strange indifference!—low and high
   Drowsed over common joys and cares:
The earth was still—but knew not why;
   The world was listening—unawares;
How calm a moment may precede
   One that shall thrill the world for ever!
To that still moment none would heed
   Man's doom was link'd, no more to sever,
      In the solemn midnight
        Centuries ago.

ALFRED DOMETT

It is the calm and solemn night!
    A thousand bells ring out and throw
Their joyous peals abroad, and smite
    The darkness, charm'd and holy now!
The night that erst no name had worn,
    To it a happy name is given;
For in that stable lay new-born
    The peaceful Prince of Earth and Heaven,
      In the solemn midnight
      Centuries ago.

ROBERT BROWNING

1812-1889

195.   *The Wanderers*

OVER the sea our galleys went,
    With cleaving prows in order brave
To a speeding wind and a bounding wave—
    A gallant armament:
Each bark built out of a forest-tree
    Left leafy and rough as first it grew,
And nail'd all over the gaping sides,
Within and without, with black bull-hides,
Seethed in fat and suppled in flame,
To bear the playful billows' game;
So, each good ship was rude to see,
Rude and bare to the outward view,
But each upbore a stately tent
Where cedar pales in scented row
Kept out the flakes of the dancing brine,
And an awning droop'd the mast below,
In fold on fold of the purple fine,
That neither noontide nor star-shine
Nor moonlight cold which maketh mad,

Might

Might pierce the regal tenement.
When the sun dawn'd, O, gay and glad
We set the sail and plied the oar ;
But when the night-wind blew like breath,
For joy of one day's voyage more,
We sang together on the wide sea,
Like men at peace on a peaceful shore ;
Each sail was loosed to the wind so free,
Each helm made sure by the twilight star,
And in a sleep as calm as death,
We, the voyagers from afar,
 Lay stretch'd along, each weary crew
In a circle round its wondrous tent
Whence gleam'd soft light and curl'd rich scent,
 And with light and perfume, music too :
So the stars wheel'd round, and the darkness pass'd,
And at morn we started beside the mast,
And still each ship was sailing fast !

Now, one morn, land appear'd—a speck
Dim trembling betwixt sea and sky—
' Avoid it,' cried our pilot, ' check
 The shout, restrain the eager eye ! '
But the heaving sea was black behind
For many a night and many a day,
And land, though but a rock, drew nigh ;
So we broke the cedar pales away,
Let the purple awning flap in the wind,
 And a statue bright was on every deck !
We shouted, every man of us,
And steer'd right into the harbour thus,
With pomp and pæan glorious.

A hundred shapes of lucid stone !
  All day we built its shrine for each,
A shrine of rock for every one,
Nor paused till in the westering sun
  We sat together on the beach
To sing because our task was done ;
When lo ! what shouts and merry songs !
What laughter all the distance stirs !
A loaded raft with happy throngs
Of gentle islanders !
' Our isles are just at hand,' they cried,
  ' Like cloudlets faint in even sleeping ;
Our temple-gates are open'd wide,
  Our olive-groves thick shade are keeping
For these majestic forms '—they cried.
O, then we awoke with sudden start
From our deep dream, and knew, too late,
How bare the rock, how desolate,
Which had received our precious freight :
  Yet we call'd out—' Depart !
Our gifts, once given, must here abide :
  Our work is done ; we have no heart
To mar our work,'—we cried.

196.　　　　　*Pippa's Song*

THE year 's at the spring,
  And day 's at the morn ;
Morning 's at seven ;
The hill-side 's dew-pearl'd ;
The lark 's on the wing ;
The snail 's on the thorn ;
God 's in his heaven—
All 's right with the world !

197.   *Misconceptions*

THIS is a spray the Bird clung to,
   Making it blossom with pleasure,
Ere the high tree-top she sprung to,
   Fit for her nest and her treasure.
    O, what a hope beyond measure
Was the poor spray's, which the flying feet hung to,—
So to be singled out, built in, and sung to !

This is a heart the Queen leant on,
   Thrill'd in a minute erratic,
Ere the true bosom she bent on,
   Meet for love's regal dalmatic.
    O, what a fancy ecstatic
Was the poor heart's, ere the wanderer went on—
Love to be saved for it, proffer'd to, spent on !

198.   *The Laboratory*

[ANCIEN RÉGIME]

NOW that I, tying thy glass mask tightly,
   May gaze thro' these faint smokes curling whitely,
As thou pliest thy trade in this devil's-smithy—
Which is the poison to poison her, prithee ?

He is with her ; and they know that I know
Where they are, what they do : they believe my tears flow
While they laugh, laugh at me, at me fled to the drear
Empty church, to pray God in, for them !—I am here.

Grind away, moisten and mash up thy paste,
Pound at thy powder,—I am not in haste !
Better sit thus, and observe thy strange things,
Than go where men wait me and dance at the King's.

That in the mortar—you call it a gum?
Ah, the brave tree whence such gold oozings come!
And yonder soft phial, the exquisite blue,
Sure to taste sweetly,—is that poison too?

Had I but all of them, thee and thy treasures,
What a wild crowd of invisible pleasures!
To carry pure death in an earring, a casket,
A signet, a fan-mount, a filigree-basket!

Soon, at the King's, a mere lozenge to give
And Pauline should have just thirty minutes to live!
But to light a pastille, and Elise, with her head
And her breast and her arms and her hands, should drop
    dead!

Quick—is it finished? The colour's too grim!
Why not soft like the phial's, enticing and dim?
Let it brighten her drink, let her turn it and stir,
And try it and taste, ere she fix and prefer!

What a drop! She's not little, no minion like me—
That's why she ensnared him: this never will free
The soul from those masculine eyes,—say, 'no!'
To that pulse's magnificent come-and-go.

For only last night, as they whisper'd, I brought
My own eyes to bear on her so, that I thought
Could I keep them one half minute fix'd, she would fall,
Shrivell'd; she fell not; yet this does it all!

Not that I bid you spare her the pain!
Let death be felt and the proof remain;
Brand, burn up, bite into its grace—
He is sure to remember her dying face!

Is

Is it done ? Take my mask off ! Nay, be not morose,
It kills her, and this prevents seeing it close :
The delicate droplet, my whole fortune's fee—
If it hurts her, beside, can it ever hurt me ?

Now, take all my jewels, gorge gold to your fill,
You may kiss me, old man, on my mouth if you will !
But brush this dust off me, lest horror it brings
Ere I know it—next moment I dance at the King's !

199.   *Love Among the Ruins*

WHERE the quiet-colour'd end of evening smiles
    Miles and miles
On the solitary pastures where our sheep
    Half-asleep
Tinkle homeward thro' the twilight, stray or stop
    As they crop—
Was the site once of a city great and gay,
    (So they say)
Of our country's very capital, its prince
    Ages since
Held his court in, gathered councils, wielding far
    Peace or war.

Now—the country does not even boast a tree,
    As you see,
To distinguish slopes of verdure, certain rills
    From the hills
Intersect and give a name to, (else they run
    Into one)
Where the domed and daring palace shot its spires
    Up like fires
O'er the hundred-gated circuit of a wall
    Bounding all,
Made of marble, men might march on nor be prest,
    Twelve abreast.

And such plenty and perfection, see, of grass
　　Never was !
Such a carpet as, this summer-time, o'erspreads
　　And embeds
Every vestige of the city, guess'd alone,
　　Stock or stone—
Where a multitude of men breathed joy and woe
　　Long ago ;
Lust of glory prick'd their hearts up, dread of shame
　　Struck them tame ;
And that glory and that shame alike, the gold
　　Bought and sold.

Now,—the single little turret that remains
　　On the plains,
By the caper overrooted, by the gourd
　　Overscored,
While the patching houseleek's head of blossom winks
　　Through the chinks—
Marks the basement whence a tower in ancient time
　　Sprang sublime,
And a burning ring, all round, the chariots traced
　　As they raced,
And the monarch and his minions and his dames
　　View'd the games.

And I know, while thus the quiet-coloured eve
　　Smiles to leave
To their folding, all our many-tinkling fleece
　　In such peace,
And the slopes and rills in undistinguished grey
　　Melt away—

　　　　　　　　　　　　　　　　That

That a girl with eager eyes and yellow hair
    Waits me there
In the turret whence the charioteers caught soul
    For the goal,
When the king look'd, where she looks now, breathless,
      dumb
    Till I come.

But he looked upon the city, every side,
    Far and wide,
All the mountains topp'd with temples, all the glades'
    Colonnades,
All the causeys, bridges, aqueducts,—and then,
    All the men!
When I do come, she will speak not, she will stand,
    Either hand
On my shoulder, give her eyes the first embrace
    Of my face,
Ere we rush, ere we extinguish sight and speech
    Each on each.

In one year they sent a million fighters forth
    South and North,
And they built their gods a brazen pillar high
    As the sky,
Yet reserved a thousand chariots in full force—
    Gold, of course.
Oh, heart! oh, blood that freezes, blood that burns!
    Earth's returns
For whole centuries of folly, noise and sin!
    Shut them in,
With their triumphs and their glories and the rest.
    Love is best!

200.   *Love in a Life*

ROOM after room,
    I hunt the house through
We inhabit together.
Heart, fear nothing, for, heart, thou shalt find her,
Next time, herself !—not the trouble behind her
Left in the curtain, the couch's perfume !
As she brush'd it, the cornice-wreath blossom'd anew :
Yon looking-glass gleam'd at the wave of her feather.

Yet the day wears,
And door succeeds door ;
I try the fresh fortune—
Range the wide house from the wing to the centre.
Still the same chance ! she goes out as I enter.
Spend my whole day in the quest,—who cares ?
But 'tis twilight, you see,—with such suites to explore,
Such closets to search, such alcoves to importune !

201.   *Life in a Love*

ESCAPE me ?
    Never—
    Beloved !
While I am I, and you are you,
    So long as the world contains us both,
    Me the loving and you the loth,
While the one eludes, must the other pursue.
My life is a fault at last, I fear :
    It seems too much like a fate, indeed !
    Though I do my best I shall scarce succeed.
But what if I fail of my purpose here ?

It

It is but to keep the nerves at strain,
　To dry one's eyes and laugh at a fall,
And baffled, get up and begin again,—
　So the chace takes up one's life, that's all.
While, look but once from your farthest bound
　At me so deep in the dust and dark,
No sooner the old hope drops to ground
　Than a new one, straight to the self-same mark,
　　　I shape me—
　　　Ever
　　　Removed !

202.　　　　　　*In a Gondola*

THE moth's kiss, first !
　Kiss me as if you made believe
You were not sure, this eve,
How my face, your flower, had pursed
Its petals up ; so, here and there
You brush it, till I grow aware
Who wants me, and wide ope I burst.

The bee's kiss, now !
Kiss me as if you entered gay
My heart at some noonday,
A bud that dares not disallow
The claim, so all is render'd up,
And passively its shatter'd cup
Over your head to sleep I bow.

203.   *Parting at Morning*

R OUND the cape of a sudden came the sea,
    And the sun look'd over the mountain's rim :
And straight was a path of gold for him,
And the need of a world of men for me.

204.   *The Lost Mistress*

A LL 's over, then : does truth sound bitter
    As one at first believes ?
Hark, 'tis the sparrows' good-night twitter
    About your cottage eaves !

And the leaf-buds on the vine are woolly,
    I noticed that, to-day ;
One day more bursts them open fully
    —You know the red turns gray.

To-morrow we meet the same then, dearest ?
    May I take your hand in mine ?
Mere friends are we,—well, friends the merest
    Keep much that I resign :

For each glance of the eye so bright and black,
    Though I keep with heart's endeavour,—
Your voice, when you wish the snowdrops back,
    Tho' it stay in my soul for ever !—

Yet I will but say what mere friends say,
    Or only a thought stronger ;
I will hold your hand but as long as all may,
    Or so very little longer !

205. *The Last Ride together*

I SAID—Then, dearest, since 'tis so,
　Since now at length my fate I know,
Since nothing all my love avails,
Since all, my life seem'd meant for, fails,
　　Since this was written and needs must be—
My whole heart rises up to bless
Your name in pride and thankfulness !
Take back the hope you gave,—I claim
Only a memory of the same,
—And this beside, if you will not blame ;
　　Your leave for one more last ride with me.

My mistress bent that brow of hers,
Those deep dark eyes where pride demurs
When pity would be softening through,
Fix'd me a breathing-while or two
　　With life or death in the balance : right !
The blood replenish'd me again ;
My last thought was at least not vain :
I and my mistress, side by side
Shall be together, breathe and ride,
So, one day more am I deified.
　　Who knows but the world may end to-night ?

Hush ! if you saw some western cloud
All billowy-bosom'd, over-bow'd
By many benedictions—sun's
And moon's and evening-star's at once—
　　And so, you, looking and loving best,
Conscious grew, your passion drew
Cloud, sunset, moonrise, star-shine too,

ROBERT BROWNING

Down on you, near and yet more near,
Till flesh must fade for heaven was here !—
Thus leant she and linger'd—joy and fear !
  Thus lay she a moment on my breast.

Then we began to ride.   My soul
Smooth'd itself out, a long-cramp'd scroll
Freshening and fluttering in the wind.
Past hopes already lay behind.
  What need to strive with a life awry ?
Had I said that, had I done this,
So might I gain, so might I miss.
Might she have loved me ? just as well
She might have hated, who can tell !
Where had I been now if the worst befell ?
  And here we are riding, she and I.

Fail I alone, in words and deeds ?
Why, all men strive and who succeeds ?
We rode ; it seem'd my spirit flew,
Saw other regions, cities new,
  As the world rush'd by on either side.
I thought,—All labour, yet no less
Bear up beneath their unsuccess.
Look at the end of work, contrast
The petty done, the undone vast,
This present of theirs with the hopeful past !
  I hoped she would love me ; here we ride.

What hand and brain went ever pair'd ?
What heart alike conceived and dared ?
What act proved all its thought had been ?
What will but felt the fleshly screen ?
  We ride and I see her bosom heave.

There

There 's many a crown for who can reach.
Ten lines, a statesman's life in each !
The flag stuck on a heap of bones,
A soldier's doing ! what atones ?
They scratch his name on the Abbey-stones.
    My riding is better, by their leave.

What does it all mean, poet ? Well,
Your brains beat into rhythm, you tell
What we felt only ; you express'd
You hold things beautiful the best,
    And pace them in rhyme so, side by side.
'Tis something, nay 'tis much : but then,
Have you yourself what 's best for men ?
Are you—poor, sick, old ere your time—
Nearer one whit your own sublime
Than we who never have turn'd a rhyme ?
    Sing, riding 's a joy ! For me, I ride.

And you, great sculptor—so, you gave
A score of years to Art, her slave,
And that 's your Venus, whence we turn
To yonder girl that fords the burn !
    You acquiesce, and shall I repine ?
What, man of music, you grown gray
With notes and nothing else to say,
Is this your sole praise from a friend,
' Greatly his opera's strains intend,
But in music we know how fashions end ! '
    I gave my youth : but we ride, in fine.

Who knows what 's fit for us ? Had fate
Proposed bliss here should sublimate
My being—had I sign'd the bond—
Still one must lead some life beyond,
    Have a bliss to die with, dim-descried.

This foot once planted on the goal,
This glory-garland round my soul,
Could I descry such ? Try and test !
I sink back shuddering from the quest.
Earth being so good, would heaven seem best ?
   Now, heaven and she are beyond this ride.

And yet—she has not spoke so long !
What if heaven be that, fair and strong
At life's best, with our eyes upturn'd
Whither life's flower is first discern'd,
   We, fix'd so, ever should so abide ?
What if we still ride on, we two
With life for ever old yet new,
Changed not in kind but in degree,
The instant made eternity,—
And heaven just prove that I and she
   Ride, ride together, for ever ride ?

206.   *Lyric Love*

'THE RING AND THE BOOK'

O LYRIC Love, half-angel and half-bird
   And all a wonder and a wild desire,—
Boldest of hearts that ever braved the sun,
Took sanctuary within the holier blue,
And sang a kindred soul out to his face,—
Yet human at the red-ripe of the heart—
When the first summons from the darkling earth
Reach'd thee amid thy chambers, blanch'd their blue,
And bared them of the glory—to drop down,
To toil for man, to suffer or to die,—
This is the same voice : can thy soul know change ?

Hail

Hail then, and hearken from the realms of help !
Never may I commence my song, my due
To God who best taught song by gift of thee,
Except with bent head and beseeching hand—
That still, despite the distance and the dark,
What was, again may be ; some interchange
Of grace, some splendour once thy very thought,
Some benediction anciently thy smile :
—Never conclude, but raising hand and head
Thither where eyes, that cannot reach, yet yearn
For all hope, all sustainment, all reward,
Their utmost up and on,—so blessing back
In those thy realms of help, that heaven thy home,
Some whiteness which, I judge, thy face makes proud,
Some wanness where, I think, thy foot may fall !

207.   *Home-thoughts, from Abroad*

O   TO be in England
   , Now that April 's there,
And whoever wakes in England
Sees, some morning, unaware,
That the lowest boughs and the brushwood sheaf
Round the elm-tree bole are in tiny leaf,
While the chaffinch sings on the orchard bough
In England—now !

And after April, when May follows,
And the whitethroat builds, and all the swallows !
Hark, where my blossom'd pear-tree in the hedge
Leans to the field and scatters on the clover
Blossoms and dewdrops—at the bent spray's edge—
That 's the wise thrush ; he sings each song twice over,

274

Lest you should think he never could recapture
The first fine careless rapture !
And though the fields look rough with hoary dew,
All will be gay when noontide wakes anew
The buttercups, the little children's dower
—Far brighter than this gaudy melon-flower !

208.   Home-thoughts, from the Sea

NOBLY, nobly Cape Saint Vincent to the North-west
    died away ;
Sunset ran, one glorious blood-red, reeking into Cadiz
    Bay ;
Bluish 'mid the burning water, full in face Trafalgar lay ;
In the dimmest North-east distance dawn'd Gibraltar
    grand and gray ;
' Here and here did England help me : how can I help
    England ? '—say,
Whoso turns as I, this evening, turn to God to praise and
    pray,
While Jove's planet rises yonder, silent over Africa.

209.   Johannes Agricola in Meditation

THERE 'S heaven above, and night by night,
    I look right through its gorgeous roof ;
No suns and moons tho' e'er so bright
    Avail to stop me ; splendour-proof
I keep the broods of stars aloof :
For I intend to get to God,
    For 'tis to God I speed so fast,
For in God's breast, my own abode,

Those

Those shoals of dazzling glory, pass'd,
I lay my spirit down at last.
I lie where I have always lain,
   God smiles as He has always smiled;
Ere suns and moons could wax and wane,
   Ere stars were thundergirt, or piled
The heavens, God thought on me his child;
Ordained a life for me, array'd
   Its circumstances, every one
To the minutest; aye, God said
   This head this hand should rest upon
Thus, ere He fashion'd star or sun.
And having thus created me,
   Thus rooted me, He bade me grow,
Guiltless for ever, like a tree
   That buds and blooms, nor seeks to know
   The law by which it prospers so:
But sure that thought and word and deed
   All go to swell his love for me,
Me, made because that love had need
   Of something irrevocably
Pledged solely its content to be.
Yes, yes, a tree which must ascend,
   No poison-gourd foredoom'd to stoop!
I have God's warrant, could I blend
   All hideous sins, as in a cup,
To drink the mingled venoms up,
Secure my nature will convert
   The draught to blossoming gladness fast,
While sweet dews turn to the gourd's hurt,
   And bloat, and while they bloat it, blast,
As from the first its lot was cast.
For as I lie, smiled on, full fed
   By unexhausted power to bless,

I gaze below on Hell's fierce bed,
    And those its waves of flame oppress,
Swarming in ghastly wretchedness;
Whose life on earth aspired to be
    One altar-smoke, so pure !—to win
If not love like God's love to me,
    At least to keep his anger in ;
And all their striving turn'd to sin.
    Priest, doctor, hermit, monk grown white
With prayer, the broken-hearted nun,
    The martyr, the wan acolyte,
The incense-swinging child,—undone
Before God fashion'd star or sun !
God, whom I praise ; how could I praise,
    If such as I might understand,
Make out and reckon on His ways,
    And bargain for his love, and stand,
Paying a price, at his right hand ?

210.   *The Ancient Doctrine*

O GOOD gigantic smile o' the brown old earth,
    This autumn morning ! How he sets his bones
To bask i' the sun, and thrusts out knees and feet
For the ripple to run over in its mirth ;
    Listening the while, where on the heap of stones
The white breast of the sea-lark twitters sweet.

That is the doctrine, simple, ancient, true ;
    Such is life's trial, as old earth smiles and knows.
If you loved only what were worth your love,
Love were clear gain, and wholly well for you :
    Make the low nature better by your throes !
Give earth yourself, go up for gain above !

277

211.　　　　*Rabbi Ben Ezra*

GROW old along with me !
The best is yet to be,
The last of life, for which the first was made :
Our times are in His hand
Who saith ' A whole I planned,
Youth shows but half ; trust God : see all, nor be
　　afraid ! '

Not that, amassing flowers,
Youth sighed ' Which rose make ours,
Which lily leave and then as best recall ? '
Not that, admiring stars,
It yearned ' Nor Jove, nor Mars ;
Mine be some figured flame which blends, transcends
　　them all ! '

Not for such hopes and fears
Annulling youth's brief years,
Do I remonstrate : folly wide the mark !
Rather I prize the doubt
Low kinds exist without,
Finish'd and finite clods, untroubled by a spark.

Poor vaunt of life indeed,
Were man but form'd to feed
On joy, to solely seek and find and feast :
Such feasting ended, then
As sure an end to men ;
Irks care the crop-full bird ?　Frets doubt the maw-
　　cramm'd beast ?

Rejoice we are allied
To That which doth provide
And not partake, effect and not receive !
A spark disturbs our clod ;
Nearer we hold of God
Who gives, than of His tribes that take, I must believe.

Then, welcome each rebuff
That turns earth's smoothness rough,
Each sting that bids nor sit nor stand but go !
Be our joys three-parts pain !
Strive, and hold cheap the strain ;
Learn, nor account the pang ; dare, never grudge the
    throe !

For thence,—a paradox
Which comforts while it mocks,—
Shall life succeed in that it seems to fail :
What I aspired to be,
And was not, comforts me :
A brute I might have been, but would not sink i' the
    scale.

What is he but a brute
Whose flesh hath soul to suit,
Whose spirit works lest arms and legs want play ?
To man, propose this test—
Thy body at its best,
How far can that project thy soul on its lone way ?

Yet gifts should prove their use :
I own the Past profuse
Of power each side, perfection every turn :

Eyes,

Eyes, ears took in their dole,
Brain treasured up the whole;
Should not the heart beat once 'How good to live and
    learn?'

Not once beat 'Praise be Thine!
I see the whole design,
I, who saw Power, see now Love perfect too:
Perfect I call thy plan:
Thanks that I was a man!
Maker, remake, complete,—I trust what Thou shalt do!

For pleasant is this flesh;
Our soul in its rose-mesh
Pull'd ever to the earth, still yearns for rest:
Would we some prize might hold
To match those manifold
Possessions of the brute,—gain most, as we did best!

Let us not always say
'Spite of this flesh to-day
I strove, made head, gain'd ground upon the whole!'
As the bird wings and sings,
Let us cry 'All good things
Are ours, nor soul helps flesh more, now, than flesh helps
    soul!'

Therefore I summon age
To grant youth's heritage,
Life's struggle having so far reach'd its term:
Thence shall I pass, approved
A man, for aye removed
From the develop'd brute; a God though in the germ.

And I shall thereupon
Take rest, ere I be gone
Once more on my adventure brave and new :
Fearless and unperplex'd,
When I wage battle next,
What weapons to select, what armour to indue.

Youth ended, I shall try
My gain or loss thereby ;
Be the fire ashes, what survives is gold :
And I shall weigh the same,
Give life its praise or blame :
Young, all lay in dispute ; I shall know, being old.

For note, when evening shuts,
A certain moment cuts
The deed off, calls the glory from the grey :
A whisper from the west
Shoots—' Add this to the rest,
Take it and try its worth : here dies another day.'

So, still within this life,
Though lifted o'er its strife,
Let me discern, compare, pronounce at last,
' This rage was right i' the main,
That acquiescence vain :
The Future I may face now I have proved the Past.'

For more is not reserved
To man, with soul just nerved
To act to-morrow what he learns to-day :
Here, work enough to watch
The Master work, and catch
Hints of the proper craft, tricks of the tool's true play.

As

As it was better youth
Should strive, through acts uncouth,
Toward making, than repose on aught found made :
So better, age, exempt
From strife, should know, than tempt
Further.   Thou waitedst age ; wait death nor be afraid !

Enough now, if the Right
And Good and Infinite
Be named here, as thou call'st thy hand thine own,
With knowledge absolute,
Subject to no dispute
From fools that crowded youth, nor let thee feel alone.

Be there, for once and all,
Sever'd great minds from small,
Announced to each his station in the Past !
Was I, the world arraign'd,
Were they, my soul disdain'd,
Right ?   Let age speak the truth and give us peace at last !

Now, who shall arbitrate ?
Ten men love what I hate,
Shun what I follow, slight what I receive ;
Ten, who in ears and eyes
Match me : we all surmise,
They, this thing, and I, that : whom shall my soul
    believe ?

Not on the vulgar mass
Called ' work ', must sentence pass,
Things done, that took the eye and had the price ;
O'er which, from level stand,
The low world laid its hand,
Found straightway to its mind, could value in a trice :

But all the world's coarse thumb
And finger failed to plumb,
So passed in making up the main account;
All instincts immature,
All purposes unsure,
That weigh'd not as his work, yet swell'd the man's
      amount:

Thoughts hardly to be pack'd
Into a narrow act,
Fancies that broke through language and escaped;
All I could never be,
All, men ignored in me,—
This I was worth to God, whose wheel the pitcher shaped.

Aye, note that Potter's wheel,
That metaphor! and feel
Why time spins fast, why passive lies our clay,—
Thou, to whom fools propound,
When the wine makes its round,
'Since life fleets, all is change; the Past gone, seize
      to-day!'

Fool! All that is, at all,
Lasts ever, past recall;
Earth changes, but thy soul and God stand sure:
What enter'd into thee,
That was, is, and shall be.
Time's wheel runs back or stops; Potter and clay endure.

He fix'd thee mid this dance
Of plastic circumstance,
This Present, thou, forsooth, wouldst fain arrest:
Machinery just meant
To give thy soul its bent,
Try thee and turn thee forth, sufficiently impress'd.

What

What though the earlier grooves
Which ran the laughing loves
Around thy base, no longer pause and press ?
What though, about thy rim,
Skull-things in order grim
Grow out, in graver mood, obey the sterner stress ?

Look not thou down but up !
To uses of a cup,
The festal board, lamp's flash and trumpet's peal,
The new wine's foaming flow,
The Master's lips aglow !
Thou, heaven's consummate cup, what needst thou with
earth's wheel ?

But I need, now as then,
Thee, God, who mouldest men ;
And since, not even while the whirl was worst,
Did I—to the wheel of life
With shapes and colours rife,
Bound dizzily—mistake my end, to slake Thy thirst :

So, take and use thy work !
Amend what flaws may lurk,
What strain o' the stuff, what warpings past the aim !
My times be in thy hand !
Perfect the cup as plann'd !
Let age approve of youth, and death complete the same !

212. *Prospice*

FEAR death ?—to feel the fog in my throat,
  The mist in my face,
When the snows begin, and the blasts denote
  I am nearing the place,
The power of the night, the press of the storm,
  The post of the foe ;
Where he stands, the Arch Fear in a visible form,
  Yet the strong man must go :
For the journey is done and the summit attain'd,
  And the barriers fall,
Though a battle 's to fight ere the guerdon be gain'd,
  The reward of it all.
I was ever a fighter, so—one fight more,
  The best and the last !
I would hate that death bandaged my eyes and forbore,
  And bade me creep past.
No ! let me taste the whole of it, fare like my peers
  The heroes of old,
Bear the brunt, in a minute pay glad life's arrears
  Of pain, darkness and cold.
For sudden the worst turns the best to the brave,
  The black minute 's at end,
And the element's rage, the fiend-voices that rave,
  Shall dwindle, shall blend,
Shall change, shall become first a peace, then a joy,
  Then a light, then thy breast,
O thou soul of my soul ! I shall clasp thee again,
  And with God be the rest !

213.   *Epilogue*

AT the midnight, in the silence of the sleep-time,
    When you set your fancies free,
Will they pass to where—by death, fools think, im-
        prison'd—
Low he lies who once so loved you, whom you loved so,
            —Pity me ?

Oh to love so, be so loved, yet so mistaken !
    What had I on earth to do
With the slothful, with the mawkish, the unmanly ?
Like the aimless, helpless, hopeless, did I drivel,
            —Being—who ?

One who never turn'd his back but march'd breast
        forward,
    Never doubted clouds would break,
Never dream'd, though right were worsted, wrong would
        triumph,
Held we fall to rise, are baffled to fight better,
            Sleep to wake.

No, at noonday in the bustle of man's work-time
    Greet the unseen with a cheer !
Bid him forward, breast and back as either should be,
' Strive and thrive ! ' cry ' Speed,—fight on, fare ever,
            There as here ! '

1812-1890

214.   *The Witch's Ballad*

O, I hae come from far away,
    From a warm land far away,
A southern land across the sea,
With sailor-lads about the mast,
Merry and canny, and kind to me.

And I hae been to yon town
    To try my luck in yon town ;
Nort, and Mysie, Elspie too.
Right braw we were to pass the gate,
Wi' gowden clasps on girdles blue.

Mysie smiled wi' miminy mouth,
    Innocent mouth, miminy mouth ;
Elspie wore a scarlet gown,
Nort's grey eyes were unco' gleg,
My Castile comb was like a crown.

We walk'd abreast all up the street,
    Into the market up the street ;
Our hair with marigolds was wound,
Our bodices with love-knots laced,
Our merchandise with tansy bound.

Nort had chickens, I had cocks,
    Gamesome cocks, loud-crowing cocks ;
Mysie ducks, and Elspie drakes,—
For a wee groat or a pound ;
We lost nae time wi' gives and takes.

miminy] prim, demure   gleg] sharp, bright

—Lost

—Lost nae time, for well we knew,
  In our sleeves full well we knew,
When the gloaming came that night,
Duck nor drake, nor hen nor cock
Would be found by candle-light.

And when our chaffering all was done,
  All was paid for, sold and done,
We drew a glove on ilka hand,
We sweetly curtsied, each to each,
And deftly danced a saraband.

The market-lassies look'd and laugh'd,
  Left their gear, and look'd and laugh'd ;
They made as they would join the game,
But soon their mithers, wild and wud,
With whack and screech they stopp'd the same.

Sae loud the tongues o' randies grew,
  The flytin' and the skirlin' grew,
At all the windows in the place,
Wi' spoons or knives, wi' needle or awl,
Was thrust out every hand and face.

And down each stair they throng'd anon,
  Gentle, semple, throng'd anon ;
Souter and tailor, frowsy Nan,
The ancient widow young again,
Simpering behind her fan.

Without a choice, against their will,
  Doited, dazed, against their will,
The market lassie and her mither,
The farmer and his husbandman,
Hand in hand dance a' thegither.

wud] mad   randies] viragoes   flytin'] scolding
skirlin'] screeching   souter] cobbler   doited] mazed

288

Slow at first, but faster soon,
　　Still increasing, wild and fast,
Hoods and mantles, hats and hose,
Blindly doff'd and cast away,
Left them naked, heads and toes.

They would have torn us limb from limb,
　　Dainty limb from dainty limb ;
But never one of them could win
Across the line that I had drawn
With bleeding thumb a-widdershin.

But there was Jeff the provost's son,
　　Jeff the provost's only son ;
There was Father Auld himsel',
The Lombard frae the hostelry,
And the lawyer Peter Fell.

All goodly men we singled out,
　　Waled them well, and singled out.
And drew them by the left hand in ;
Mysie the priest, and Elspie won
The Lombard, Nort the lawyer carle,
I mysel' the provost's son.

Then, with cantrip kisses seven,
　　Three times round with kisses seven,
Warp'd and woven there spun we
Arms and legs and flaming hair,
Like a whirlwind on the sea.

Like a wind that sucks the sea,
　　Over and in and on the sea,
Good sooth it was a mad delight ;

　a-widdershin] the wrong way of the sun : or E. to W.
through N.　　waled] chose.　　cantrip] magic.

And every man of all the four
Shut his eyes and laugh'd outright.

Laugh'd as long as they had breath,
   Laugh'd while they had sense or breath ;
And close about us coil'd a mist
Of gnats and midges, wasps and flies,
Like the whirlwind shaft it rist.

Drawn up I was right off my feet,
   Into the mist and off my feet ;
And, dancing on each chimney-top,
I saw a thousand darling imps
Keeping time with skip and hop.

And on the provost's brave ridge-tile,
   On the provost's grand ridge-tile,
The Blackamoor first to master me
I saw, I saw that winsome smile,
The mouth that did my heart beguile,
And spoke the great Word over me,
In the land beyond the sea.

I call'd his name, I call'd aloud,
   Alas ! I call'd on him aloud ;
And then he fill'd his hand with stour,
And threw it towards me in the air ;
My mouse flew out, I lost my pow'r !

My lusty strength, my power were gone ;
   Power was gone, and all was gone.
He will not let me love him more !
Of bell and whip and horse's tail
He cares not if I find a store.

stour] dust.
290

But I am proud if he is fierce !
   I am as proud as he is fierce ;
I'll turn about and backward go,
If I meet again that Blackamoor,
And he'll help us then, for he shall know
I seek another paramour.

And we'll gang once more to yon town,
   Wi' better luck to yon town ;
We'll walk in silk and cramoisie,
And I shall wed the provost's son,
My lady of the town I'll be !

For I was born a crown'd king's child,
   Born and nursed a king's child,
King o' a land ayont the sea,
Where the Blackamoor kiss'd me first,
And taught me art and glamourie.

Each one in her wame shall hide
   Her hairy mouse, her wary mouse,
Fed on madwort, and agramie,—
Wear amber beads between her breasts,
And blind-worm's skin about her knee.

The Lombard shall be Elspie's man,
   Elspie's gowden husband-man ;
Nort shall take the lawyer's hand ;
The priest shall swear another vow :
We'll dance again the saraband !

cramoisie] crimson.   glamourie] wizardry.

WILLIAM JAMES LINTON

1812-1898

215.   *Faint Heart*

FAINT heart wins not lady fair :
   Victory smiles on those who dare,
There is but one way to woo—
Think thy Mistress willing too !
Leave her never chance to choose,
Hold her powerless to refuse.

If she answer thee with No,
Wilt thou bow and let her go ?—
When, most like, her 'No' is meant
But to make more sweet consent ;
So thy suit may longer be
For so much she liketh thee.

Never heed her pretty airs !
He 's no lover who despairs ;
He 's no warrior whom a frown
Drives from his beleaguer'd town ;
And no hunter he who stops
Till his stricken quarry drops.

Aim as certain not to miss ;
Take her as thou would'st a kiss !
Or ask once, and if in vain,
Ask her twice, and thrice again :
Sure of this when all is said,—
They lose most who are afraid.

WILLIAM EDMONDSTOUNE AYTOUN

1813-1865

216.   *Hermotimus*

VAINLY were the words of parting spoken ;
 Evermore must Charon turn from me.
Still my thread of life remains unbroken,
 And unbroken it must ever be !
  Only they may rest
  Whom the Fates' behest
From their mortal mansion setteth free.

I have seen the robes of Hermes glisten—
 Seen him wave afar his serpent wand ;
But to me the Herald would not listen
 When the dead swept by at his command.
  Not with that pale crew
  Durst I venture too :
Ever shut for me the quiet land !

Day and night before the dreary portal
 Phantom shapes, the guards of Hades, lie :
None of heavenly kind, nor yet of mortal,
 May unchallenged pass the warders by.
  None that path may go
  If he cannot show
His last passport to eternity.

Cruel was the spirit-power thou gavest !
 Fatal, O Apollo, was thy love !
Pythian, Archer, brightest God and bravest,
 Hear, O hear me from thy throne above !
  Let me not, I pray,
  Thus be cast away :
Plead for me, thy slave—O plead to Jove !

I have

WILLIAM EDMONDSTOUNE AYTOUN

I have heard thee with the Muses singing—
　　Heard that full melodious voice of thine
Silver-clear throughout the ether ringing—
　　Seen thy locks in golden clusters shine:
　　　　And thine eye, so bright
　　　　With its innate light,
　　Hath ere now been bent so low as mine.

Hast thou lost the wish, the will, to cherish
　　Those who trusted in thy godlike power ?
Hyacinthus did not wholly perish !
　　Still he lives the firstling of thy bower :
　　　　Still he feels thy rays,
　　　　Fondly meets thy gaze,
　　Tho' but now the spirit of a flower.

THOMAS OSBORNE DAVIS

1814-1845

217.　　　　　*O, the Marriage!*

O, THE marriage, the marriage !
　　With love and *mo bhuachaill* for me,
The ladies that ride in a carriage
　　Might envy my marriage to me :
For Eoghan is straight as a tower,
　　And tender and loving and true ;
He told me more love in an hour
　　Than the Squires of the county could do.
　　　　Then, O, the marriage . . .

mo bhuachaill] ' my boy ', pronounced mu vohill.

THOMAS OSBORNE DAVIS

His hair is a shower of soft gold,
    His eye is as clear as the day,
His conscience and vote were unsold
    When others were carried away :
His word is as good as an oath,
    And freely 'twas given to me ;
O, sure 'twill be happy for both
    The day of our marriage to see !
            Then O, the marriage . . .

His kinsmen are honest and kind,
    The neighbours think much of his skill ;
And Eoghan 's the lad to my mind,
    Tho' he owns neither castle nor mill.
But he has a tilloch of land,
    A horse, and a stocking of coin,
A foot for the dance, and a hand
    In the cause of his country to join.
            Then O, the marriage . . .

We meet in the market and fair—
    We meet in the morning and night—
He sits on the half of my chair,
    And my people are wild with delight.
Yet I long thro' the winter to skim
    (Tho' Eoghan longs more, I can see),
When I will be married to him,
    And he will be married to me !
            Then O, the marriage, the marriage !
                With love and mo bhuachaill for me,
            The ladies that ride in their carriage
                Might envy my marriage to me.

AUBREY DE VERE

1814–1902

218.   *Song*

SEEK not the tree of silkiest bark
    And balmiest bud,
To carve her name while yet 'tis dark
    Upon the wood !
The world is full of noble tasks
    And wreaths hard won ;
Each work demands strong hearts, strong hands,
    Till day is done.

Sing not that violet-veinèd skin,
    That cheek's pale roses,
The lily of that form wherein
    Her soul reposes !
Forth to the fight, true man ! true knight !
    The clash of arms
Shall more prevail than whisper'd tale
    To win her charms.

The warrior for the True, the Right,
    Fights in Love's name ;
The love that lures thee from the fight
    Lures thee to shame :
That love which lifts the heart, yet leaves
    The spirit free,—
That love, or none, is fit for one
    Man-shaped like thee.

219.   *The Sun-God*

I SAW the Master of the Sun.   He stood
    High in his luminous car, himself more bright ;
  An Archer of immeasurable might :
On his left shoulder hung his quiver'd load ;
Spurn'd by his steeds the eastern mountains glow'd ;
  Forward his eagle eye and bow of Light
He bent, and while both hands that arch embow'd,
  Shaft after shaft pursued the flying night.

No wings profaned that godlike form : around
  His neck high-held an ever-moving crowd
Of locks hung glistening : while such perfect sound
  Fell from his bowstring that th' ethereal dome
Thrill'd as a dew-drop ; and each passing cloud
  Expanded, whitening like the ocean foam.

220.   *Epitaph*

HE roam'd half-round the world of woe,
    Where toil and labour never cease ;
Then dropp'd one little span below
    In search of peace.

And now to him mild beams and showers,
    All that he needs to grace his tomb,
From loneliest regions at all hours,
    Unsought-for, come.

FREDERICK WILLIAM FABER

221. *The World Morose*

I

I HEARD the wild beasts in the woods complain;
Some slept, while others waken'd to sustain
Thro' night and day the sad monotonous round,
Half savage and half pitiful the sound.

The outcry rose to God thro' all the air,
The worship of distress, an animal prayer,
Loud vehement pleadings not unlike to those
Job utter'd in his agony of woes.

The very pauses, when they came, were rife
With sick'ning sounds of too-successful strife;
As when the clash of battle dies away,
The groans of night succeed the shrieks of day.

Man's scent the untamed creatures scarce can bear,
As if his tainted blood defiled the air;
In the vast woods they fret as in a cage,
Or fly in fear, or gnash their teeth with rage.

The beasts of burden linger on their way,
Like slaves who will not speak when they obey;
Their faces, when their looks to us they raise,
With something of reproachful patience gaze.

All creatures round us seem to disapprove;
Their eyes discomfort us with lack of love;
Our very rights, with signs like these alloy'd,
Not without sad misgivings are enjoy'd.

FREDERICK WILLIAM FABER

II

Mostly men's many-featured faces wear
Looks of fix'd gloom, or else of restless care ;
The very babes, that in their cradles lie,
Out of the depths of unknown troubles cry.

Labour itself is but a sorrowful song,
The protest of the weak against the strong ;
Over rough waters, and in obstinate fields,
And from dank mines, the same sad sound it yields.

Doth Earth send nothing up to Thee but moans,
Father ? Canst thou find melody in groans ?
O, can it be that Thou, the God of bliss,
Canst feed Thy glory on a world like this ?

Yet it is well with us. From these alarms
Like children scared we fly into Thine arms ;
And pressing sorrows put our pride to rout
With a swift faith which has not time to doubt.

We cannot herd in peace with wild beasts rude ;
We dare not live in Nature's solitude ;
In how few eyes of men can we behold
Enough of love to make us calm and bold ?

O, it is well with us ! With angry glance
Life glares at us, or looks at us askance :
Seek where we will—Father, we see it now !—
None love us, trust us, welcome us, but Thou.

1814-1888

222 *Night of Spring*

SLOW, horses, slow,
  As thro' the wood we go—
We would count the stars in heaven,
  Hear the grasses grow :

Watch the cloudlets few
Dappling the deep blue,
In our open palms outspread
Catch the blessèd dew.

Slow, horses, slow,
  As thro' the wood we go—
We would see fair Dian rise
  With her huntress bow :

We would hear the breeze
Ruffling the dim trees,
Hear its sweet love-ditty set
To endless harmonies.

Slow, horses, slow,
  As thro' the wood we go—
All the beauty of the night
  We would learn and know !

300

CHARLES MACKAY

1814-1889

223.   *The Holly Bough*

YE who have scorn'd each other,
   Or injured friend or brother,
 In this fast-fading year ;
Ye who, by word or deed,
Have made a kind heart bleed,
   Come gather here.

Let sinn'd-against and sinning
Forget their strife's beginning,
   And join in friendship now,
Be links no longer broken,
Be sweet forgiveness spoken
   Under the holly bough.

Ye who have loved each other,
Sister and friend and brother,
   In this fast-fading year ;
Mother and sire and child,
Young man and maiden mild,
   Come gather here ;

And let your hearts grow fonder,
As memory shall ponder
   Each past unbroken vow.
Old love and younger wooing
Are sweet in the renewing,
   Under the holly bough.

301   Ye

CHARLES MACKAY

Ye who have nourish'd sadness,
Estranged from hope and gladness,
    In this fast-fading year ;
Ye with o'erburthen'd mind,
Made aliens from your kind,
    Come gather here.

Let not the useless sorrow
Pursue you night and morrow ;
    If e'er you hoped, hope now—
Take heart, uncloud your faces,
And join in our embraces
    Under the holly bough.

JOHN CAMPBELL SHAIRP

1815-1885

224.   *The Bush Aboon Traquair*

WILL ye gang wi' me and fare
    To the bush aboon Traquair ?
Owre the high Minchmuir we 'll up and awa',
    This bonny simmer noon,
    While the sun shines fair aboon,
And the licht sklents saftly doun on holm and ha'.

' And what wad ye do there,
    At the bush aboon Traquair ?
A lang dreich road, ye had better let it be ;
    Save some old scrunts o' birk
    I' the hill-side that lirk
There 's nocht i' the world for man to see.'

holm] water-mead.   dreich] dry, tedious.

302

But the blythe lilt o' that air,
  ' The Bush aboon Traquair,'
I need nae mair, it 's eneuch for me ;
    Owre my cradle its sweet chime
    Cam sughin' frae auld time,
Sae, tide what may, I'll awa' and see.

  ' And what saw ye there,
   At the bush aboon Traquair ?
Or what did ye hear that was worth your heed ? '
    —I heard the cushies croon
    Thro' the gowden afternoon,
And the Quair burn singing down to the Vale o' Tweed.

  And birks saw I three or four
   Wi' grey moss bearded owre,
The last that are left o' the birken shaw,
    Whar mony a simmer e'en
    Fond lovers did convene,
They bonny bonny gloamings that are lang awa'.

  Fra mony a but and ben,
   By muirland, holm and glen,
They came ane hour to spen' on the greenwood sward ;
    But lang ha'e lad an' lass
    Been lying 'neath the grass,
The green green grass o' Traquair Kirkyard.

  They were blest beyond compare
   When they held their trysting there,
Amang thae greenest hills shone on by the sun ;
    And then they wan a rest,
    The lonest and the best,
I' Traquair Kirkyard when a' was done.

but and ben] cottage kitchen and parlour.

303   Now

Now the birks to dust may rot,
Name o' luvers be forgot,
Nae lads and lasses there ony mair convene;
But the blythe lilt o' yon air
Keps the bush aboon Traquair,
And the luve that ance was there, aye fresh and green.

PHILIP JAMES BAILEY

1816–1902

225.   *My Lady*

I LOVED her for that she was beautiful;
And that to me she seem'd to be all Nature,
And all varieties of things in one:
Would set at night in clouds of tears, and rise
All light and laughter in the morning; fear
No petty customs nor appearances;
But think what others only dream'd about;
And say what others did but think; and do
What others did but say; and glory in
What others dared but do: so pure withal
In soul; in heart and act such conscious yet
Such perfect innocence, she made round her
A halo of delight. 'Twas these which won me;—
And that she never school'd within her breast
One thought or feeling, but gave holiday
To all; and that she made all even mine
In the communion of Love: and we
Grew like each other, for we loved each other;
She, mild and generous as the air in Spring;
And I, like Earth all budding out with love.

HENRY DAVID THOREAU

226.   *The Great Adventure*

'TIS sweet to hear of heroes dead,
   To know them still alive;
But sweeter if we earn their bread,
   And in us they survive.

Ye skies, drop gently round my breast
   And be my corselet blue;
Ye earth, receive my lance in rest,
   My faithful charger you:

Ye stars my spear-heads in the sky,
   My arrow-tips ye are:
I see the routed foemen fly
   My bright spears fix'd [for war].

Give me an angel for a foe!
   Fix now the place and time!
And straight to meet him I will go
   Above the starry chime:

And with our clashing bucklers' clang
   The heavenly spheres shall ring,
While bright the northern lights shall **hang**
   Beside our tourneying.

And if she lose her champion true,
   Tell Heaven not to despair;
For I will be her champion new,
   Her fame I will repair

227 *Love*

Totus est Inermis Idem . . .

NO show of bolts and bars
　Can keep the foeman out,
Or 'scape his secret mine
Who enter'd with the doubt
That drew the line.
No warder at the gate
Can let the friendly in ;
But, like the sun, o'er all
He will the castle win,
And shine along the wall.

Implacable is Love—
Foes may be bought or teased
From their hostile intent,
But he goes unappeased
Who is on kindness bent.

DENIS FLORENCE MACCARTHY
1817-1882

228. *Lament*

YOUTH'S bright palace
　Is overthrown,
With its diamond sceptre
　And golden throne ;
　As a time-worn stone
Its turrets are humbled—
All hath crumbled
　But grief alone !

DENIS FLORENCE MACCARTHY

Whither, O whither
  Have fled away
The dreams and hopes
  Of my early day ?
  Ruin'd and grey
Are the towers I builded ;
And the beams that gilded—
  Ah, where are they ?

Once this world
  Was fresh and bright,
With its golden noon
  And its starry night :
  Glad and light,
By mountain and river,
Have I bless'd the Giver
  With hush'd delight.

Youth's illusions
  One by one
Have pass'd like clouds
  That the sun look'd on.
  While morning shone,
How purple their fringes !
How ashy their tinges
  When that was gone !

As fire-flies fade
  When the nights are damp—
As meteors are quench'd
  In a stagnant swamp—
  Thus Charlemagne's camp
Where the Paladins rally,
And the Diamond valley,
  And the Wonderful Lamp,

And

And all the wonders
  Of Ganges and Nile,
And Haroun's rambles,
  And Crusoe's isle,
  And Princes who smile
On the Genii's daughters
'Neath the Orient waters
  Full many a mile,

And all that the pen
  Of Fancy can write
Must vanish in manhood's
  Misty light;
  Squire and Knight,
And damosel's glances,
Sunny romances,
  So pure and bright!

These have vanish'd,
  And what remains?
Life's budding garlands
  Have turn'd to chains—
  Its beams and rains
Feed but docks and thistles,
And sorrow whistles
  O'er desert plains.

1817-1890

229.   *Hymn*

WHEN by the marbled lake I lie and listen
       To one sweet voice that sings to me alone,
Veil'd by green leaves whose silver faces glisten
    In breezy light down the blue summer blown,
                              I praise thee, God.

When her white ivory fingers twine and quiver,
    Twinkling thro' mine, and when her golden hair
Flows down her neck, like sunlight down a river,
    And half she is, and half she is not there,
                              I praise thee, God.

When I can look from my proud height above her,
    In her quaint faëry face, or o'er her bend,
And know I am her friend but not her lover,
    That she is not my lover but my friend,
                              I praise thee, God.

When I have heard the imprison'd echoes breaking
    From rolling clouds, like shouts of gods in fight,
Or armies calling armies, when awaking,
    They rise all breathless from too large delight,
                              I praise thee, God.

When I have seen the scarlet lightnings falling
    From cloudy battlements, like throneless kings ;
Have seen great angels that, to angels calling,
    Open and shut their gold and silver wings,
                              I praise thee, God.

When I have passed a nobler life in sorrow :
    Have seen rude masses grow to fulgent spheres ;
Seen how To-day is father of To-morrow,
    And how the Ages justify the Years,
                              I praise thee, God.

230. *The People's Petition*

O LORDS ! O rulers of the nation!
　　O softly clothed ! O richly fed !
O men of wealth and noble station !
Give us our daily bread.

For you we are content to toil,
For you our blood like rain is shed ;
Then lords and rulers of the soil,
Give us our daily bread.

Your silken robes, with endless care,
Still weave we ; still unclothed, unfed,
We make the raiment that ye wear :
Give us our daily bread.

In the red forge-light do we stand,
We early leave—late seek our bed,
Tempering the steel for your right hand :
Give us our daily bread.

We sow your fields, ye reap the fruit,
We live in misery and in dread :
Hear but our prayer, and we are mute—
Give us our daily bread.

Throughout old England's pleasant fields,
There is no spot where we may tread,
No house to us sweet shelter yields :
Give us our daily bread.

Fathers are we ; we see our sons,
We see our fair young daughters, dead :
Then hear us, O ye mighty ones !
Give us our daily bread.

'Tis vain—with cold, unfeeling eye
Ye gaze on us, unclothed, unfed,
'Tis vain—ye will not hear our cry,
Nor give us daily bread.

We turn from you, our lords by birth,
To Him who is our Lord above ;
We all are made of the same earth,
Are children of one Love.

Then, Father of this world of wonders,
Judge of the living and the dead,
Lord of the lightnings and the thunders,
Give us our daily bread !

231. *Renunciation*

WAKEFUL I lay all night and thought of God,
Of heaven, and of the crowns pale martyrs gain,
Of souls in high and purgatorial pain,
And the red path which murder'd seers have trod :
I heard the trumpets which the angels blow
I saw the cleaving sword, the measuring rod,
I watch'd the stream of sound continuous flow
Past the gold towers where seraphs make abode.

But now I let the aching splendour go,
I dare not call the crownèd angels peers
Henceforth. I am content to dwell below
Mid common joys, with humble smiles and tears
Delighted in the sun and breeze to grow,
A child of human hopes and human fears.

JOHN MASON NEALE

232.   *Jerusalem*

FOR thee, O dear dear Country !
   Mine eyes their vigils keep ;
For very love, beholding
   Thy happy name, they weep :
The mention of thy glory
   Is unction to the breast,
And medicine in sickness,
   And love, and life, and rest.

O come, O onely Mansion !
   O Paradise of Joy !
Where tears are ever banish'd,
   And smiles have no alloy ;
Beside thy living waters
   All plants are, great and small,
The cedar of the forest,
   The hyssop of the wall :
With jaspers glow thy bulwarks ;
   Thy streets with emeralds blaze ;
The sardius and the topaz
   Unite in thee their rays :
Thine ageless walls are bonded
   With amethyst unpriced :
Thy Saints build up its fabric,
   And the corner-stone is Christ.

The Cross is all thy splendour,
   The Crucified thy praise :
His laud and benediction
   Thy ransom'd people raise :

312

JOHN MASON NEALE

Jesus, the Gem of Beauty,
　　True God and Man, they sing :
The never-failing Garden,
　　The ever-golden Ring :
The Door, the Pledge, the Husband,
　　The Guardian of his Court :
The Day-star of Salvation,
　　The Porter and the Port.
Thou hast no shore, fair ocean !
　　Thou hast no time, bright day !
Dear fountain of refreshment
　　To pilgrims far away !

Upon the Rock of Ages
　　They raise thy holy tower :
Thine is the victor's laurel,
　　And thine the golden dower :
Thou feel'st in mystic rapture,
　　O Bride that know'st no guile,
The Prince's sweetest kisses,
　　The Prince's loveliest smile :
Unfading lilies, bracelets
　　Of living pearl thine own :
The Lamb is ever near thee,
　　The Bridegroom thine alone :
The Crown is He to guerdon,
　　The Buckler to protect,
And He Himself the Mansion,
　　And He the Architect.
The only art thou needest,
　　Thanksgiving for thy lot :
The only joy thou seekest,
　　The Life where Death is not.

And

And all thine endless leisure
　In sweetest accents sings,
The ill that was thy merit,—
　The wealth that is thy King's !

Jerusalem the golden,
　With milk and honey blest,
Beneath thy contemplation
　Sink heart and voice oppress'd :
I know not, O I know not,
　What social joys are there !
What radiancy of glory,
　What light beyond compare !

And when I fain would sing them
　My spirit fails and faints,
And vainly would it image
　The assembly of the Saints.

They stand, those halls of Syon,
　Conjubilant with song,
And bright with many an angel,
　And all the martyr throng :
The Prince is ever in them ;
　The daylight is serene :
The pastures of the Blessèd
　Are deck'd in glorious sheen.

There is the Throne of David,—
　And there, from care released,
The song of them that triumph,
　The shout of them that feast ;
And they who, with their Leader
　Have conquer'd in the fight,
For ever and for ever
　Are clad in robes of white !

JOHN MASON NEALE

O holy, placid harp-notes
    Of that eternal hymn !
O sacred, sweet refection,
    And peace of Seraphim !
O thirst, for ever ardent,
    Yet evermore content !
O true, peculiar vision
    Of God cunctipotent !
Ye know the many mansions
    For many a glorious name
And divers retributions
    That divers merits claim .
For midst the constellations
    That deck our earthly sky,
This star than that is brighter,—
    And so it is on high.

Jerusalem the glorious !
    The glory of the Elect !
O dear and future vision
    That eager hearts expect :
Even now by faith I see thee
    Even here thy walls discern :
To thee my thoughts are kindled,
    And strive and pant and yearn :
Jerusalem the onely,
    That look'st from heaven below,
In thee is all my glory ;
    In me is all my woe !
And though my body may not,
    My spirit seeks thee fain,
Till flesh and earth return me
    To earth and flesh again.

O none

O none can tell thy bulwarks,
  How gloriously they rise :
O none can tell thy capitals
  Of beautiful device :
Thy loveliness oppresses
  All human thought and heart :
And none, O peace, O Syon,
  Can sing thee as thou art.
New mansion of new people,
  Whom God's own love and light
Promote, increase, make holy,
  Identify, unite.
Thou City of the Angels !
  Thou City of the Lord !
Whose everlasting music
  Is the glorious decachord !
And there the band of Prophets
  United praise ascribes,
And there the twelvefold chorus
  Of Israel's ransom'd tribes :
The lily-beds of virgins,
  The roses' martyr-glow,
The cohort of the Fathers
  Who kept the faith below !
And there the Sole-Begotten
  Is Lord in regal state ;
He, Judah's mystic Lion,
  He, Lamb Immaculate.

O fields that know no sorrow !
  O state that fears no strife !
O princely bow'rs ! O land of flow'rs !
  O realm and home of Life !

THOMAS TOKE LYNCH

1818-1871

233.   *Reinforcements*

WHEN little boys with merry noise
    In the meadows shout and run ;
And little girls, sweet woman buds,
    Brightly open in the sun ;
I may not of the world despair,
    Our God despaireth not, I see ;
For blithesomer in Eden's air
    These lads and maidens could not be.

Why were they born, if Hope must die ?
    Wherefore this health, if Truth should fail ?
And why such Joy, if Misery
    Be conquering us and must prevail ?
Arouse ! our spirit may not droop !
    These young ones fresh from Heaven are ;
Our God hath sent another troop,
    And means to carry on the war.

EMILY BRONTË

1818-1848

234.   *Stanzas*

OFTEN rebuked, yet always back returning
    To those first feelings that were born with me,
And leaving busy chase of wealth and learning
    For idle dreams of things which cannot be :

To-day

To-day I will seek not the shadowy region;
　　Its unsustaining vastness waxes drear;
And visions rising, legion after legion,
　　Bring the unreal world too strangely near.

I'll walk, but not in old heroic traces,
　　And not in paths of high morality,
And not among the half-distinguish'd faces,
　　The clouded forms of long-past history.

I'll walk where my own nature would be leading:
　　It vexes me to choose another guide:
Where the grey flocks in ferny glens are feeding,
　　Where the wild wind blows on the mountain side.

235.　　　　*The Old Stoic*

RICHES I hold in light esteem,
　　And Love I laugh to scorn;
And lust of fame was but a dream
　　That vanish'd with the morn:

And, if I pray, the only prayer
　　That moves my lips for me
Is, ' Leave the heart that now I bear,
　　And give me liberty!'

Yea, as my swift days near their goal,
　　'Tis all that I implore:
In life and death a chainless soul,
　　With courage to endure.

EMILY BRONTË

236.   *The Prisoner*

STILL let my tyrants know, I am not doom'd to wear
   Year after year in gloom and desolate despair;
A messenger of Hope comes every night to me,
And offers for short life, eternal liberty.

He comes with Western winds, with evening's wandering
      airs,
With that clear dusk of heaven that brings the thickest stars:
Winds take a pensive tone, and stars a tender fire,
And visions rise, and change, that kill me with desire.

Desire for nothing known in my maturer years,
When Joy grew mad with awe, at counting future tears:
When, if my spirit's sky was full of flashes warm,
I knew not whence they came, from sun or thunder-storm.

But first, a hush of peace—a soundless calm descends;
The struggle of distress and fierce impatience ends.
Mute music soothes my breast—unutter'd harmony
That I could never dream, till Earth was lost to me.

Then dawns the Invisible; the Unseen its truth reveals;
My outward sense is gone, my inward essence feels;
Its wings are almost free—its home, its harbour found;
Measuring the gulf, it stoops, and dares the final bound.

O dreadful is the check—intense the agony—
When the ear begins to hear, and the eye begins to see;
When the pulse begins to throb—the brain to think again—
The soul to feel the flesh, and the flesh to feel the chain.

Yet I would lose no sting, would wish no torture less;
The more that anguish racks, the earlier it will bless;
And robed in fires of hell, or bright with heavenly shine,
If it but herald Death, the vision is divine.

237.   *My Lady's Grave*

THE linnet in the rocky dells,
    The moor-lark in the air,
The bee among the heather bells
    That hide my lady fair :

The wild deer browse above her breast ;
    The wild birds raise their brood ;
And they, her smiles of love caress'd,
    Have left her solitude !

I ween that when the grave's dark wall
    Did first her form retain,
They thought their hearts could ne'er recall
    The light of joy again.

They thought the tide of grief would flow
    Uncheck'd through future years ;
But where is all their anguish now ?
    And where are all their tears ?

Well, let them fight for honour's breath,
    Or pleasure's shade pursue—
The dweller in the land of death
    Is changed and careless too.

And if their eyes should watch and weep
    Till sorrow's source were dry,
She would not, in her tranquil sleep,
    Return a single sigh ?

Blow, west wind, by the lonely mound :
    And murmur, summer streams !
There is no need of other sound
    To soothe my lady's dreams.

238.   *Warning and Reply*

IN the earth—the earth—thou shalt be laid,
    A grey stone standing over thee ;
Black mould beneath thee spread,
    And black mould to cover thee.

' Well—there is rest there,
    So fast come thy prophecy :
The time when my sunny hair
    Shall with grass roots entwinèd be ! '

But cold—cold is that resting-place,
    Shut out from joy and liberty,
And all who lov'd thy living face
    Will shrink from it shudderingly.

' Not so.   Here the world is chill,
    And sworn friends fall from me ;
But there—they will own me still,
    And prize my memory.'

Farewell, then, all that love,
    All that deep sympathy ;
Sleep on : Heaven laughs above,
    Earth never misses thee.

Turf-sod and tombstone drear
    Part human company :
One heart breaks only—here,
    But that heart was worthy thee !

239.   *Last Lines*

NO coward soul is mine,
  No trembler in the world's storm-troubled sphere:
I see Heaven's glories shine,
And faith shines equal, arming me from fear.

O God within my breast,
Almighty, ever-present Deity !
  Life—that in me has rest,
As I—undying Life—have power in Thee !

Vain are the thousand creeds
That move men's hearts : unutterably vain ;
  Worthless as wither'd weeds,
Or idlest froth amid the boundless main,

To waken doubt in one
Holding so fast by thine infinity ;
  So surely anchor'd on
The steadfast rock of immortality.

With wide-embracing love
Thy Spirit animates eternal years,
  Pervades and broods above,
Changes, sustains, dissolves, creates, and rears.

Though earth and man were gone,
And suns and universes ceased to be,
  And Thou were left alone,
Every existence would exist in Thee.

There is not room for Death,
Nor atom that his might could render void :
  Thou—Thou art Being and Breath,
And what Thou art may never be destroy'd.

ERNEST CHARLES JONES

1819-1869

240.   *The Song of the Lower Classes*

WE plough and sow—we're so very, very low
     That we delve in the dirty clay,
Till we bless the plain with the golden grain,
     And the vale with the fragrant hay.
Our place we know—we're so very low,
     'Tis down at the landlord's feet :
We're not too low the bread to grow,
     But too low the bread to eat.

Down, down we go—we're so very, very low,
     To the hell of the deep-sunk mines,
But we gather the proudest gems that glow
     When the crown of a despot shines.
And, whenever he lacks, upon our backs
     Fresh loads he deigns to lay :
We're far too low to vote the tax,
     But not too low to pay.

We're low—we're low—mere rabble, we know,
     But at our plastic power,
The mould at the lordling's feet will grow
     Into palace and church and tower.
Then prostrate fall in the rich man's hall,
     And cringe at the rich man's door :
We're not too low to build the wall,
     But too low to tread the floor.

We're low—we're low—we're very, very low,
     Yet from our fingers glide
The silken flow—and the robes that glow
     Round the limbs of the sons of pride.

And

And what we get—and what we give—
    We know, and we know our share :
We're not too low the cloth to weave,
    But too low the cloth to wear !

We're low—we're low—we're very, very low,
    And yet when the trumpets ring,
The thrust of a poor man's arm will go
    Thro' the heart of the proudest king.
We're low—we're low—our place we know,
    We're only the rank and file,
We're not too low to kill the foe,
    But too low to touch the spoil.

ARTHUR HUGH CLOUGH

1819-1861

241.   *Qua cursum ventus*

AS ships, becalm'd at eve, that lay
    With canvas drooping, side by side,
Two towers of sail at dawn of day
    Are scarce, long leagues apart, descried ;

When fell the night, upsprung the breeze,
    And all the darkling hours they plied,
Nor dreamt but each the self-same seas
    By each was cleaving, side by side :

E'en so—but why the tale reveal
    Of those, whom year by year unchanged,
Brief absence join'd anew to feel,
    Astounded, soul from soul estranged ?

At dead of night their sails were fill'd,
    And onward each rejoicing steer'd—
Ah, neither blame, for neither will'd,
    Or wist, what first with dawn appear'd !

To veer, how vain ! On, onward strain,
    Brave barks ! In light, in darkness too,
Thro' winds and tides one compass guides,—
    To that, and your own selves, be true.

But O blithe breeze ! and O great seas,
    Though ne'er, that earliest parting past,
On your wide plain they join again,
    Together lead them home at last.

One port, methought, alike they sought,
    One purpose hold where'er they fare,—
O bounding breeze, O rushing seas,
    At last, at last, unite them there !

242.   *Where lies the Land?*

WHERE lies the land to which the ship would go ?
    Far, far ahead, is all her seamen know.
And where the land she travels from ? Away,
Far, far behind, is all that they can say.

On sunny noons upon the deck's smooth face,
Linked arm in arm, how pleasant here to pace !
Or, o'er the stern reclining, watch below
The foaming wake far widening as we go.

On stormy nights when wild north-westers rave,
How proud a thing to fight with wind and wave !
The dripping sailor on the reeling mast
Exults to bear, and scorns to wish it past.

Where lies the land to which the ship would go ?
Far, far ahead, is all her seamen know.
And where the land she travels from ? Away
Far, far behind, is all that they can say.

243.   *Isolation*

(FROM DIPSYCHUS)

WHERE are the great, whom thou wouldst wish to
            praise thee ?
Where are the pure, whom thou wouldst choose to love
      thee ?
Where are the brave, to stand supreme above thee,
Whose high commands would cheer, whose chiding raise
      thee ?
   Seek, seeker, in thyself ; submit to find
   In the stones, bread, and life in the blank mind

244.   *The Latest Decalogue*

THOU shalt have one God only ; who
      Would be at the expense of two ?

No graven images may be
Worshipp'd, except the currency :

Swear not at all ; for, for thy curse
Thine enemy is none the worse :

At church on Sunday to attend
Will serve to keep the world thy friend :

Honour thy parents ; that is, all
From whom advancement may befall :

Thou shalt not kill ; but need'st not strive
Officiously to keep alive :

Do not adultery commit ;
Advantage rarely comes of it :

Thou shalt not steal ; an empty feat,
When 'tis so lucrative to cheat :

Bear not false witness ; let the lie
Have time on its own wings to fly :

Thou shalt not covet, but tradition
Approves all forms of competition.

245.   *Say not the Struggle Naught*
availeth

SAY not the struggle naught availeth,
    The labour and the wounds are vain,
The enemy faints not, nor faileth,
    And as things have been they remain.

If hopes were dupes, fears may be liars ;
    It may be, in yon smoke conceal'd,
Your comrades chase e'en now the fliers,
    And, but for you, possess the field.

For while the tired waves, vainly breaking,
    Seem here no painful inch to gain,
Far back, through creeks and inlets making,
    Comes silent, flooding in, the main.

And not by eastern windows only,
    When daylight comes, comes in the light ;
In front the sun climbs slow, how slowly !
    But westward, look, the land is bright !

246. *Hey, Nonny !*

THE world goes up and the world goes down,
  And the sunshine follows the rain ;
And yesterday's sneer and yesterday's frown
  Can never come over again,
    Sweet wife ;
  No never come over again.

For woman is warm tho' man be cold,
  And the night will hallow the day !
Till the heart which at even was weary and old
  Can rise in the morning gay,
    Sweet wife ;
  To its work in the morning gay.

247. *The Old Song*

WHEN all the world is young, lad,
  And all the trees are green ;
And every goose a swan, lad,
  And every lass a queen ;
Then hey for boot and horse, lad,
  And round the world away !
Young blood must have its course, lad,
  And every dog his day.

When all the world is old, lad,
  And all the trees are brown ;
And all the sport is stale, lad,
  And all the wheels run down ;
Creep home, and take your place there
  The spent and maim'd among ;
God grant you find one face there
  You loved when all was young !

JULIA WARD HOWE

b. 1819

248. Battle Hymn of the American Republic

MINE eyes have seen the glory of the coming of the
        Lord :
He is trampling out the vintage where the grapes of
    wrath are stored ;
He hath loosed the fatal lightning of his terrible swift
    sword :
            His truth is marching on.

I have seen him in the watch-fires of a hundred circling
        camps ;
They have builded him an altar in the evening dews and
        damps ;
I can read his righteous sentence by the dim and flaring
    lamps :
            His day is marching on.

I have read a fiery gospel, writ in burnish'd rows of steel :
' As ye deal with my contemners, so with you my grace
    shall deal ;
Let the Hero, born of woman, crush the serpent with his
    heel !
            Since God is marching on.'

He

JULIA WARD HOWE

He has sounded forth the trumpet that shall never call
    retreat ;
He is sifting out the hearts of men before his Judgment
    Seat ;
O, be swift, my soul to answer Him, be jubilant my feet !
    Our God is marching on.

In the beauty of the lilies Christ was born, across the sea,
With a glory in his bosom that transfigures you and me :
As He died to make men holy, let us die to make men free,
    While God is marching on.

GEORGE ELIOT

1819-1880

249.　　*The Choir Invisible*

*Longum illud tempus quum non ero magis me movet quam hoc
exiguum.*—CICERO, *ad Att.* xii. 18.

O MAY I join the choir invisible
  Of those immortal dead who live again
In minds made better by their presence : live
In pulses stirred to generosity,
In deeds of daring rectitude, in scorn
For miserable aims that end with self,
In thoughts sublime that pierce the night like stars,
And with their mild persistence urge man's search
To vaster issues.
        So to live is heaven .
To make undying music in the world,
Breathing as beauteous order that controls
With growing sway the growing life of man.

GEORGE ELIOT

So we inherit that sweet purity
For which we struggled, failed, and agonized
With widening retrospect that bred despair.
Rebellious flesh that would not be subdued,
A vicious parent shaming still its child
Poor anxious penitence, is quick dissolved;
Its discords, quenched by meeting harmonies,
Die in the large and charitable air.
And all our rarer, better, truer self,
That sobb'd religiously in yearning song,
That watch'd to ease the burthen of the world,
Laboriously tracing what must be,
And what may yet be better—saw within
A worthier image for the sanctuary,
And shaped it forth before the multitude
Divinely human, raising worship so
To higher reverence more mix'd with love—
That better self shall live till human Time
Shall fold its eyelids, and the human sky
Be gather'd like a scroll within the tomb
Unread for ever.
              This is life to come,
Which martyr'd men have made more glorious
For us who strive to follow. May I reach
That purest heaven, be to other souls
The cup of strength in some great agony,
Enkindle generous ardour, feed pure love,
Beget the smiles that have no cruelty—
Be the sweet presence of a good diffused,
And in diffusion ever more intense.
So shall I join the choir invisible
Whose music is the gladness of the world.

JAMES RUSSELL LOWELL

1819-1891

250.   *The Courtin'*

G OD makes sech nights, all white an' still
        Fur 'z you can look or listen,
Moonshine an' snow on field an' hill,
    All silence an' all glisten.

Zekle crep' up quite unbeknown
    An' peeked in thru' the winder,
An' there sot Huldy all alone,
    'ith no one nigh to hender.

A fireplace fill'd the room's one side
    With half a cord o' wood in—
There warn't no stoves (till comfort died)
    To bake ye to a puddin'.

The wa'nut logs shot sparkles out
    Towards the pootiest, bless her !
An' leetle flames danced all about
    The chiny on the dresser.

Agin the chimbley crook-necks hung,
    An' in amongst 'em rusted
The ole queen's-arm thet gran'ther Young
    Fetched back from Concord busted.

The very room, coz she was in,
    Seemed warm from floor to ceilin',

332

An' she look'd full ez rosy agin
   Ez the apples she was peelin'.

'T was kin' o' kingdom-come to look
   On sech a blessèd cretur,
A dogrose blushin' to a brook
   Ain't modester nor sweeter.

He was six foot o' man, A 1,
   Clear grit an' human natur';
None could n't quicker pitch a ton
   Nor dror a furrer straighter.

He 'd spark'd it with full twenty gals,
   Hed squired 'em, danced 'em, druv 'em,
Fust this one, an' then thet, by spells—
   All is, he could n't love 'em.

But long o' her his veins 'ould run
   All crinkly like curl'd maple,
The side she bresh'd felt full o' sun
   Ez a south slope in Ap'il.

She thought no v'ice hed sech a swing
   Ez hisn in the choir ;
My ! when he made Ole Hunderd ring,
   She *knowed* the Lord was nigher !

An' she 'd blush scarlit, right in prayer,
   When her new meetin'-bunnet
Felt somehow thru' its crown a pair
   O' blue eyes sot upun it.

Thet

Thet night, I tell ye, she looked *some*
　　She seemed to 've gut a new soul,
For she felt sartin-sure he'd come,
　　Down to her very shoe-sole.

She heer'd a foot, an' know'd it tu,
　　A-raspin' on the scraper,—
All ways to once her feelins flew
　　Like sparks in burnt-up paper.

He kin' o' l'iter'd on the mat,
　　Some doubtfle o' the sekle,
His heart kep' goin' pity-pat,
　　But hern went pity Zekle.

An' yit she gin her cheer a jerk
　　Ez though she wish'd him furder,
An' on her apples kep' to work,
　　Parin' away like murder.

'You want to see my Pa, I s'pose ? '
　　' Wal . . . no . . . I come dasignin' '—
' To see my Ma ?　She 's sprinklin' clo'es
　　Agin to-morrer's i'nin'.'

To say why gals acts so or so,
　　Or don't, 'ould be presumin' ;
Mebby to mean *yes* an' say *no*
　　Comes nateral to women.

He stood a spell on one foot fust,
　　Then stood a spell on t' other,
An' on which one he felt the wust
　　He could n't ha' told ye nuther.

Says he, ' I 'd better call agin ' ;
  Says she, ' Think likely, Mister ' ;
Thet last word prick'd him like a pin.
  An' . . . Wal, he up an' kist her.

When Ma bimeby upon 'em slips,
  Huldy sot pale ez ashes,
All kin' o' smily roun' the lips
  An' teary roun' the lashes.

For she was jes' the quiet kind
  Whose naturs never vary,
Like streams that keep a summer mind
  Snow-hid in Jenooary.

The blood clost roun' her heart felt glued
  Too tight for all expressin',
Tell mother see how metters stood,
  An' gin 'em both her blessin'.

Then her red come back like the tide
  Down to the Bay o' Fundy,—
An' all I know is, they was cried
  In meetin' come nex' Sunday.

251.   *Auspex*

MY heart, I cannot still it,
    Nest that had song-birds in it ;
And when the last shall go,
The dreary days, to fill it,
Instead of lark or linnet,
Shall whirl dead leaves and snow.

Had

JAMES RUSSELL LOWELL

Had they been swallows only,
Without the passion stronger
That skyward longs and sings,—
Woe 's me, I shall be lonely
When I can feel no longer
The impatience of their wings !

A moment, sweet delusion,
Like birds the brown leaves hover ;
But it will not be long
Before their wild confusion
Fall wavering down to cover
The poet and his song.

WALT WHITMAN

1819-1892

252. *The Beasts*

I THINK I could turn and live with animals, they are
   so placid and self-contain'd ;
I stand and look at them long and long.
They do not sweat and whine about their condition ;
They do not lie awake in the dark and weep for their sins ;
They do not make me sick discussing their duty to God ;
Not one is dissatisfied—not one is demented with the
   mania of owning things ;
Not one kneels to another, nor to his kind that lived
   thousands of years ago ;
Not one is respectable or industrious over the whole earth.

253.   *On the Beach at Night*

I

ON the beach, at night,
   Stands a child, with her father,
Watching the east, the autumn sky.

Up through the darkness,
While ravening clouds, the burial clouds, in black masses
    spreading,
Lower, sullen and fast, athwart and down the sky,
Amid a transparent clear belt of ether yet left in the east,
Ascends, large and calm, the lord-star Jupiter ;
And nigh at hand, only a very little above,
Swim the delicate brothers, the Pleiades.

II

From the beach, the child, holding the hand of her father,
Those burial-clouds that lower, victorious, soon to devour
    all,
Watching, silently weeps.

Weep not, child,
Weep not, my darling,
With these kisses let me remove your tears ;
The ravening clouds shall not long be victorious,
They shall not long possess the sky—shall devour the
    stars only in apparition :
Jupiter shall emerge—be patient—watch again another
    night—the Pleiades shall emerge,
They are immortal—all those stars, both silvery and
    golden, shall shine out again,

The

The great stars and the little ones shall shine out again—
    they endure ;
The vast immortal suns, and the long-enduring pensive
    moons, shall again shine.

III

Then, dearest child, mournest thou only for Jupiter ?
Considerest thou alone the burial of the stars ?

Something there is
(With my lips soothing thee, adding, I whisper,
I give thee the first suggestion, the problem and indirec-
    tion,)
Something there is more immortal even than the stars,
(Many the burials, many the days and nights, passing
    away,)
Something that shall endure longer even than lustrous
    Jupiter,
Longer than sun, or any revolving satellite,
Or the radiant brothers, the Pleiades.

254.   *The Brown Bird*

I

OUT of the cradle endlessly rocking,
    Out of the mocking-bird's throat, the musical
    shuttle,
Out of the Ninth-month midnight,
Over the sterile sands, and the fields beyond, where the
    child, leaving his bed, wander'd alone, bare-headed,
    barefoot,
Down from the shower'd halo,

Up from the mystic play of shadows, twining and twisting
    as if they were alive,
Out from the patches of briers and blackberries,
From the memories of the bird that chanted to me,
From your memories, sad brother—from the fitful risings
    and fallings I heard,
From under that yellow half-moon, late-risen, and swollen
    as if with tears,
From those beginning notes of sickness and love, there in
    the transparent mist,
From the thousand responses of my heart, never to cease,
From the myriad thence-arousèd words,
From the word stronger and more delicious than any,
From such, as now they start, the scene revisiting
As a flock, twittering, rising, or overhead passing,
Borne hither—ere all eludes me, hurriedly,
A man—yet by these tears a little boy again,
Throwing myself on the sand, confronting the waves,
I, chanter of pains and joys, uniter of here and hereafter,
Taking all hints to use them—but swiftly leaping beyond
    them,
A reminiscence sing.

II

Once, Paumanok,
When the snows had melted—when the lilac-scent was
    in the air, and the Fifth-month grass was growing,
Up this sea-shore, in some briers,
Two guests from Alabama—two together,
And their nest, and four light-green eggs, spotted with
    brown,
And every day the he-bird, to and fro, near at hand,

And

And every day the she-bird, crouch'd on her nest, silent,
  with bright eyes,
And every day I, a curious boy, never too close, never
  disturbing them,
Cautiously peering, absorbing, translating!

III

Shine ! shine ! shine !
Pour down your warmth, great Sun !
While we bask—we two together.

Two together !
Winds blow South, or winds blow North,
Day come white, or night come black,
Home, or rivers and mountains from home,
Singing all time, minding no time,
While we two keep together.

IV

Till of a sudden,
May-be kill'd, unknown to her mate,
One forenoon the she-bird crouch'd not on the nest,
Nor return'd that afternoon, nor the next,
Nor ever appear'd again.

And thenceforward, all summer, in the sound of the sea,
And at night, under the full of the moon, in calmer
  weather,
Over the hoarse surging of the sea,
Or flitting from brier to brier by day,
I saw, I heard at intervals, the remaining one, the he-bird,
The solitary guest from Alabama.

V

Blow ! blow ! blow !
Blow up, sea-winds, along Paumanok's shore !
I wait and I wait, till you blow my mate to me.

VI

Yes, when the stars glisten'd,
All night long, on the prong of a moss-scallop'd stake,
Down, almost amid the slapping waves,
Sat the lone singer, wonderful, causing tears.

He call'd on his mate ;
He pour'd forth the meanings which I, of all men, know.

Yes, my brother, I know ;
The rest might not—but I have treasured every note ;
For once, and more than once, dimly, down to the beach
    gliding,
Silent, avoiding the moonbeams, blending myself with
    the shadows,
Recalling now the obscure shapes, the echoes, the sounds
    and sights after their sorts,
The white arms out in the breakers tirelessly tossing,
I, with bare feet, a child, the wind wafting my hair,
Listen'd long and long.

Listen'd, to keep, to sing—now translating the notes,
Following you, my brother.

341   *Soothe !*

WALT WHITMAN

Soothe ! soothe ! soothe !
Close on its wave soothes the wave behind,
And again another behind, embracing and lapping, every
     one close,
But my love soothes not me, not me.

Low hangs the moon—it rose late ;
O it is lagging—O I think it is heavy with love, with love.

O madly the sea pushes, pushes upon the land,
With love—with love.

O night ! do I not see my love fluttering out there among
     the breakers ?
What is that little black thing I see there in the white ?

Loud ! loud ! loud !
Loud I call to you, my love !
High and clear I shoot my voice over the waves ;
Surely you must know who is here, is here ;
You must know who I am, my love.

Low-hanging moon !
What is that dusky spot in your brown yellow ?
O it is the shape, the shape of my mate !
O moon, do not keep her from me any longer.

Land ! land ! O land !
Whichever way I turn, O I think you could give me my
     mate back again, if you only would ;
For I am almost sure I see her dimly whichever way I look.

O rising stars !
Perhaps the one I want so much will rise, will rise with
*   some of you.*
O throat ! O trembling throat !
Sound clearer through the atmosphere !
Pierce the woods, the earth ;
Somewhere listening to catch you, must be the one I want.

Shake out, carols !
Solitary here—the night's carols !
Carols of lonesome love ! Death's carols !
Carols under that lagging, yellow, waning moon !
O, under that moon, where she droops almost down into the
*   sea !*
O reckless, despairing carols !

But soft ! sink low ;
Soft ! let me just murmur ;
And do you wait a moment, you husky-noised sea ;
For somewhere I believe I heard my mate responding to me,
So faint—I must be still, be still to listen ;
But not altogether still, for then she might not come imme-
*   diately to me.*

Hither, my love !
Here I am ! Here !
With this just-sustain'd note I announce myself to you ;
This gentle call is for you, my love, for you.

Do not be decoy'd elsewhere .
That is the whistle of the wind—it is not my voice ;
That is the fluttering, the fluttering of the spray ;
Those are the shadows of leaves.

O darkness !

O darkness ! O in vain !
O I am very sick and sorrowful !

O brown halo in the sky, near the moon, drooping upon the
    sea !
O troubled reflection in the sea !
O throat ! O throbbing heart !
O all—and I singing uselessly, uselessly all the night !

Yet I murmur, murmur on.
O murmurs—you yourselves make me continue to sing, I know
    not why !

O past ! O life ! O songs of joy !
In the air—in the woods—over fields ;
Loved ! loved ! loved ! loved ! loved !
But my love no more, no more with me !
We two together no more !

VIII

The aria sinking ;
All else continuing—the stars shining,
The winds blowing—the notes of the bird continuous
    echoing,
With angry moans the fierce old mother incessantly
    moaning,
On the sands of Paumanok's shore, grey and rustling ;
The yellow half-moon enlarged, sagging down, drooping,
    the face of the sea almost touching ;
The boy ecstatic—with his bare feet the waves, with his
    hair the atmosphere dallying,
The love in the heart long pent, now loose, now at last
    tumultuously bursting,

344

The aria's meaning, the ears, the Soul, swiftly depositing,
The strange tears down the cheeks coursing,
The colloquy there—the trio—each uttering,
The undertone—the savage old mother, incessantly crying,
To the boy's Soul's questions sullenly timing—some
    drown'd secret hissing,
To the outsetting bard of love.

IX

Demon or bird ! (said the boy's soul,)
Is it indeed toward your mate you sing ? or is it mostly
    to me ?
For I, that was a child, my tongue's use sleeping,
Now I have heard you,
Now in a moment I know what I am for—I awake,
And already a thousand singers—a thousand songs, clearer,
    louder and more sorrowful than yours,
A thousand warbling echoes have started to life within me,
Never to die.
O you singer, solitary, singing by yourself—projecting
    me ;
O solitary me, listening—nevermore shall I cease per-
    petuating you ;
Never more shall I escape, never more the reverberations,
Never more the cries of unsatisfied love be absent from me,
Never again leave me to be the peaceful child I was
    before what there, in the night,
By the sea, under the yellow and sagging moon,
The messenger there aroused—the fire, the sweet hell
    within,
The unknown want, the destiny of me !

O give

O give me the clue! (it lurks in the night here some-
    where ;)
O if I am to have so much, let me have more!
O a word! O what is my destination? (I fear it is
    henceforth chaos ;)
O how joys, dreads, convolutions, human shapes, and all
    shapes, spring as from graves around me!
O phantoms! you cover all the land and all the sea!
O I cannot see in the dimness whether you smile or
    frown upon me ;
O vapour, a look, a word! O well-beloved!
O you dear women's and men's phantoms!

A word then, (for I will conquer it,)
The word final, superior to all,
Subtle, sent up—what is it ?—I listen ;
Are you whispering it, and have been all the time, you
    sea-waves ?
Is that it from your liquid rims and wet sands ?

x

Whereto answering, the sea,
Delaying not, hurrying not,
Whisper'd me through the night, and very plainly before
    daybreak,
Lisp'd to me the low and delicious word DEATH ;
And again Death—ever Death, Death, Death,
Hissing melodious, neither like the bird, nor like my
    aroused child's heart,
But edging near, as privately for me, rustling at my feet,
Creeping thence steadily up to my ears, and laving me
    softly all over,
Death, Death, Death, Death, Death.

346

Which I do not forget,
But fuse the song of my dusky demon and brother,
That he sang to me in the moonlight on Paumanok's grey
    beach,
With the thousand responsive songs, at random,
My own songs, awaked from that hour ;
And with them the key, the word up from the waves,
The word of the sweetest song, and all songs,
That **strong** and delicious word which, creeping to my
    feet,
The sea whisper'd me.

CHARLES DENT BELL

b. 1819

255.   *Solemn Rondeau*

BEFORE he pass'd from mortal view
   To where he sleeps beneath the yew
    He said ' Weep not : to thee I'll come,
    If spirits ever leave that home
Thro' whose dark gates I go from you.'

How firm his promise well I knew ;
So as he spake life sweeter grew,
    And flower'd again my heart in bloom,
    Before he pass'd.

Alas ! the sweet hope is not true ;
He may not tread the avenue
    That leadeth from the nether gloom ;
    Else would he come to this dear room,
I heard his vow,—God heard it too,
    Before he pass'd !

347

JOHN RUSKIN

256.   *Trust Thou Thy Love*

TRUST thou thy Love : if she be proud, is she not
   sweet ?
Trust thou thy Love : if she be mute, is she not pure ?
Lay thou thy soul full in her hands, low at her feet ;
Fail, Sun and Breath !—yet, for thy peace, She shall
   endure.

EBENEZER JONES

1820-1860

257.   *When the World is burning*

WHEN the world is burning,
   Fired within, yet turning
Round with face unscathed ;
Ere fierce flames, uprushing,
O'er all lands leap, crushing,
   Till earth fall, fire-swathed ;
Up amidst the meadows,
Gently through the shadows,
   Gentle flames will glide,
Small, and blue, and golden.
Though by bard beholden,
When in calm dreams folden,—
   Calm his dreams will bide.

Where the dance is sweeping,
Through the greensward peeping,
   Shall the soft lights start ;
Laughing maids, unstaying,

Deeming it trick-playing,
High their robes upswaying,
    O'er the lights shall dart ;
And the woodland haunter
Shall not cease to saunter
    When, far down some glade,
Of the great world's burning,
One soft flame upturning
Seems, to his discerning,
    Crocus in the shade.

258.   *The Hand*

LONE o'er the moors I stray'd ;
    With basely timid mind,
Because by some betray'd,
Denouncing human-kind ;
I heard the lonely wind,
And wickedly did mourn
I could not share its loneliness,
And all things human scorn.

And bitter were the tears
I cursèd as they fell ;
And bitterer the sneers
I strove not to repel :
With blindly mutter'd yell,
I cried unto mine heart,—
' Thou shalt beat the world in falsehood,
And stab it ere we part.'

My hand I backward drave
As one who seeks a knife ;

349   When

EBENEZER JONES

When startlingly did crave
To quell that hand's wild strife
Some other hand ; all rife
With kindness, clasp'd it hard
On mine, quick frequent claspings
That would not be debarr'd.

I dared not turn my gaze
To the creature of the hand ;
And no sound did it raise,
Its nature to disband
Of mystery ; vast, and grand,
The moors around me spread,
And I thought, some angel message
Perchance their God may have sped.

But it press'd another press,
So full of earnest prayer,
While o'er it fell a tress
Of cool, soft, human hair,
I fear'd not ;—I did dare
Turn round, 'twas Hannah there !
O ! to no one out of heaven
Could I what pass'd declare.

We wander'd o'er the moor
Through all that blessèd day ;
And we drank its waters pure,
And felt the world away ;
In many a dell we lay,
And we twined flower-crowns bright ;
And I fed her with moor-berries
And bless'd her glad eye-light.

And still that earnest pray-er
That saved me many stings,
Was oft a silent sayer
Of countless loving things ;—
I'll ring it all with rings,
Each ring a jewell'd band ;
For heaven shouldn't purchase
That little sister hand.

MENELLA BUTE SMEDLEY

1820-1877

259.   *Wind me a Summer Crown*

' WIND me a summer crown,' she said,
    ' And set it on my brows ;
For I must go, while I am young,
    Home to my Father's house.

' And make me ready for the day,
    And let me not be stay'd ;
I would not linger on the way
    As if I was afraid.

' O, will the golden courts of heaven,
    When I have paced them o'er,
Be lovely as the lily walks
    Which I must see no more ?

' And will the seraph hymns and harps,
    When they have fill'd my ear,
Be tender as my mother's voice,
    Which I must never hear ?

351   ' An

MENELLA BUTE SMEDLEY

' And shall I lie where sunsets drift,
  Or where the stars are born,
Or where the living tints are mixt
  To paint the clouds of morn ? '

Your mother's tones shall reach you still,
  Even sweeter than they were ;
And the false love that broke your heart
  Shall be forgotten there :

And not a star or flower is born
  The beauty of that shore ;
There is a face which you shall see
  And wish for nothing more.

FREDERICK LOCKER-LAMPSON

1821-1895

260.　　　*To My Grandmother*

(Suggested by a picture by Mr. Romney)

THIS relative of mine
  Was she seventy and nine
    When she died?
By the canvas may be seen
How she looked at seventeen,
    As a bride.

Beneath a summer tree
As she sits, her reverie
    Has a charm ;
Her ringlets are in taste,—
What an arm ! and what a waist
    For an arm !

FREDERICK LOCKER-LAMPSON

In bridal coronet,
Lace, ribbons, and *coquette*
  Falbala ;
Were Romney's limning true,
What a lucky dog were you,
  Grandpapa !

Her lips are sweet as love,—
They are parting ! Do they move ?
  Are they dumb ?—
Her eyes are blue, and beam
Beseechingly, and seem
  To say, ' Come.'

What funny fancy slips
From atween these cherry lips ?
  Whisper me,
Sweet deity, in paint,
What canon says I mayn't
  Marry thee ?

That good-for-nothing Time
Has a confidence sublime !
  When I first
Saw this lady, in my youth,
Her winters had, forsooth,
  Done their worst.

Her locks (as white as snow)
Once shamed the swarthy crow;
  By and by
That fowl's avenging sprite
Set his cloven foot for spite
  In her eye.

Her rounded form was lean,
And her silk was bombazine :—
　Well I wot,
With her needles would she sit,
And for hours would she knit,—
　Would she not ?

Ah, perishable clay !
Her charms had dropp'd away
　One by one.
But if she heaved a sigh
With a burthen, it was ' Thy
　Will be done '.

In travail, as in tears,
With the fardel of her years
　Overprest,—
In mercy was she borne
Where the weary ones and worn
　Are at rest.

I'm fain to meet you there,—
If as witching as you were,
　Grandmamma !
This nether world agrees
That the better it must please
　Grandpapa.

261. *At Her Window*

BEATING Heart! we come again
  Where my Love reposes:
This is Mabel's window-pane;
  These are Mabel's roses.

Is she nested? Does she kneel
  In the twilight stilly,
Lily clad from throat to heel,
  She, my virgin Lily?

Soon the wan, the wistful stars,
  Fading, will forsake her;
Elves of light, on beamy bars,
  Whisper then, and wake her.

Let this friendly pebble plead
  At her flowery grating;
If she hear me will she heed?
  Mabel, I am waiting!

Mabel will be deck'd anon,
  Zoned in bride's apparel;
Happy zone! O hark to yon
  Passion-shaken carol!

Sing thy song, thou trancèd thrush,
  Pipe thy best, thy clearest;—
Hush, her lattice moves, O hush—
  Dearest Mabel!—dearest . . .

262.   *Epitaph of Dionysia*

HERE doth Dionysia lie :
　　She whose little wanton foot
Tripping (ah, too carelessly !)
　　Touch'd this tomb and fell into 't.

Trip no more shall she, nor fall,
　　And her trippings were so few !
Summers only eight in all
　　Had the sweet child wander'd through.

But already life's few suns
　　Love's strong seeds had ripen'd warm,
All her ways were winning ones,
　　All her cunning was to charm.

And the fancy, in the flower
　　While the flesh was in the blood,
Childhood's dawning sex did dower
　　With warm gusts of womanhood.

O what joys by hope begun,
　　O what kisses kiss'd by thought,
What love-deeds by fancy done,
　　Death to endless dust hath wrought !

Had the Fates been kind as thou,
　　Who, till now, wast never cold,
Once Love's aptest scholar, now
　　Thou hadst been his teacher bold.

But if buried seeds upthrow
　　Fruits and flowers ; if flower and fruit
By their nature fitly show
　　What the seeds are whence they shoot ;

Dionysia, o'er this tomb,
   Where thy buried beauties be,
From their dust shall spring and bloom
   Loves and graces like to thee.

DORA GREENWELL

1821-1882

263.   *The Battle-Flag of Sigurd*[1]

I HAVE no folded flock to show,
   Tho' from my youth I have loved the sheep
And the lambs, as they stray'd in the valleys low
   Or clomb the upland pastures steep ;
   But none were given me to keep !
I stood on the hill when the dawn brake red ;
   Thro' the darkling glen the fire drew nigh ;
They came on swift with a stealthy tread ;
   I gave the earliest warning cry !
Then flash'd the falchion, the arrow flew ;
   I did not fight, nor yield, nor fly—
I held up the flag the whole day through—
   Wrap it round me when I die !

I have no garner'd sheaf to show ;
   Tho' oft with my shining sickle bared
I have wrought with the reapers, row by row,
   And join'd in the shout as they homeward fared :
   I was not by when the land was shared !
I stood at noon when the maidens dread
   Came forth ere the battle to choose the slain,
And at nightfall the raven's foot was red
   And the wolves were met on the dark'ning plain.

---

[1] The flag of Sigurd carried victory with it, but brought death
to its bearer.

            Then

Then hew'd the hanger, the sword smote sore,
  I held up the flag till the day went by ;
It was glued to my straining clasp with gore—
  Wrap it round me when I die !

I have no silken spoil to show,
  Nor torque of the beaten gold, no red
Rich broider'd mantle, wrung from the foe
  Or flung by chief as the banquet sped ;
  I have only watch'd, and toil'd, and bled !
I stand at eve on the vessel's prow,
  My heart is wounded, and I have striven
So long that my arm is weary now,
  And the flag I bear is stain'd and riven ;
The dark waves mutter, the night dews fall ;
  Twixt a sullen sea and a stormy sky
I hold up the flag in sight of all—
  Wrap it round me when I die !

264.   *The Man with Three Friends*

TO one full sound and silently
  That slept, there came a heavy cry,
' Awake, arise ! for thou hast slain
A man.' ' Yea, have I to mine own pain,'

He answer'd ; ' but of ill intent
  And malice am I, that naught forecast,
As is the babe innocent.

' From sudden anger our strife grew :
  I hated not, in times past,
Him whom unwittingly I slew.'

If it be thus indeed, thy case
   Is hard,' they said ; ' for thou must die,
Unless with the Judge thou canst find grace.
   Hast thou, in thine extremity,
Friends soothfast for thee to plead ? '

Then said he, ' I have friends three :
One [1] whom in word and will and deed
From my youth I have served, and loved before
   Mine own soul, and for him striven ;
   To him was all I got given ;
And the longer I lived, I have loved him more.

' And another [2] have I, whom (sooth to tell)
I love as I love my own heart well ;
And the third [3] I cannot now call
To mind that ever loved at all
He hath been of me, or in aught served ;
And yet, may be, he hath well deserved
That I should love him with the rest.

' Now will I first to the one loved best.'
Said the first, ' And art thou so sore bestead ?
   See, I have gain'd of cloth good store,
   So will I give thee three ells and more
(If more thou needest) when thou art dead,
   To wrap thee.   Now hie thee away from my door :
I have friends many, and little room.'

And the next made answer, weeping sore,
' We will go with thee to the place of doom :
   There must we leave thee evermore.'

[1] The World.   [2] Wife and Children.   [3] Christ.

        ' Alack ! '

' Alack ! ' said the man, ' and well-a-day ! '
But the third only answered, ' Yea ' ;
   And while the man spake, all to start soon,
   Knelt down and buckled on his shoon,
And said, ' By thee in the Judgement Hall
   I will stand and hear what the Judge decree ;
And if it be death, I will die with thee,
   Or for thee, as it may befall.'

WILLIAM PHILPOT

1833-1889

265.   *Maritae Suae*

OF all the flowers rising now,
   Thou only saw'st the head
Of that unopen'd drop of snow
   I placed beside thy bed.

In all the blooms that blow so fast,
   Thou hast no further part,
Save those, the hour I saw thee last,
   I laid above thy heart.

Two snowdrops for our boy and girl,
   A primrose blown for me,
Wreath'd with one often-play'd-with curl
   From each bright head for thee.

And so I graced thee for thy grave,
   And made these tokens fast
With that old silver heart I gave,
   My first gift—and my last.

1822-1888

266.   *The Forsaken Merman*

COME, dear children, let us away ;
    Down and away below.
Now my brothers call from the bay ;
Now the great winds shoreward blow ;
Now the salt tides seaward flow ;
Now the wild white horses play,
Champ and chafe and toss in the spray.
    Children dear, let us away.
        This way, this way !

Call her once before you go.
    Call once yet.
In a voice that she will know :
    ' Margaret ! Margaret ! '
Children's voices should be dear
(Call once more) to a mother's ear :
Children's voices, wild with pain.
Surely she will come again.
Call her once and come away.
        This way, this way !
' Mother dear, we cannot stay.'
The wild white horses foam and fret.
    Margaret ! Margaret !

Come, dear children, come away down.
        Call no more.
One last look at the white-wall'd town,
And the little grey church on the windy shore.
        Then come down.
She will not come though you call all day.
    Come away, come away.

Children

Children dear, was it yesterday
We heard the sweet bells over the bay ?
In the caverns where we lay,
Through the surf and through the swell,
The far-off sound of a silver bell ?
Sand-strewn caverns, cool and deep,
Where the winds are all asleep ;
Where the spent lights quiver and gleam ;
Where the salt weed sways in the stream ;
Where the sea-beasts, ranged all round,
Feed in the ooze of their pasture-ground ;
Where the sea-snakes coil and twine,
Dry their mail, and bask in the brine ;
Where great whales come sailing by,
Sail and sail, with unshut eye,
Round the world for ever and aye ?
When did music come this way ?
Children dear, was it yesterday ?

Children dear, was it yesterday
(Call yet once) that she went away ?
Once she sate with you and me,
On a red gold throne in the heart of the sea,
And the youngest sate on her knee.
She comb'd its bright hair, and she tended it well,
When down swung the sound of the far-off bell.
She sigh'd, she look'd up through the clear green sea.
She said, ' I must go, for my kinsfolk pray
In the little grey church on the shore to-day.
'Twill be Easter-time in the world—ah me !
And I lose my poor soul, Merman, here with thee.'
I said, ' Go up, dear heart, through the waves.
Say thy prayer, and come back to the kind sea-caves.'
She smiled, she went up through the surf in the bay.
Children dear, was it yesterday ?

Children dear, were we long alone ?
' The sea grows stormy, the little ones moan.
Long prayers,' I said, ' in the world they say.
Come,' I said, and we rose through the surf in the bay
We went up the beach, by the sandy down
Where the sea-stocks bloom, to the white-wall'd town.
Through the narrow paved streets, where all was still,
To the little grey church on the windy hill.
From the church came a murmur of folk at their prayers,
But we stood without in the cold-blowing airs.
We climb'd on the graves, on the stones worn with rains,
And we gazed up the aisle through the small leaded panes.
　She sate by the pillar ; we saw her clear :
　' Margaret, hist ! come quick, we are here.
　Dear heart,' I said, ' we are long alone.
　The sea grows stormy, the little ones moan.
But, ah ! she gave me never a look,
For her eyes were seal'd to the holy book.
Loud prays the priest ; shut stands the door.
　Come away, children, call no more.
　Come away, come down, call no more.

　　Down, down, down ;
　Down to the depths of the sea.
She sits at her wheel in the humming town,
　Singing most joyfully.
Hark what she sings : ' O joy, O joy,
For the humming street, and the child with its toy !
For the priest, and the bell, and the holy well :
　For the wheel where I spun,
　And the blessèd light of the sun ! '
　And so she sings her fill,
　Singing most joyfully,
　Till the shuttle falls from her hand,

　　　　　　　　　　　　　And

And the whizzing wheel stands still.
She steals to the window, and looks at the sand ;
And over the sand at the sea ;
And her eyes are set in a stare ;
And anon there breaks a sigh,
And anon there drops a tear,
From a sorrow-clouded eye,
And a heart sorrow-laden,
   A long, long sigh
For the cold strange eyes of a little Mermaiden,
And the gleam of her golden hair.

Come away, away, children !
Come children, come down !
The hoarse wind blows colder ;
Lights shine in the town.
She will start from her slumber
When gusts shake the door ;
She will hear the winds howling,
Will hear the waves roar.
We shall see, while above us
The waves roar and whirl,
A ceiling of amber,
A pavement of pearl.
Singing, ' Here came a mortal,
But faithless was she :
And alone dwell for ever
The kings of the sea.'

But, children, at midnight,
When soft the winds blow ;
When clear falls the moonlight :
When spring-tides are low :

When sweet airs come seaward
From heaths starr'd with broom ;
And high rocks throw mildly
On the blanch'd sands a gloom .
Up the still, glistening beaches,
Up the creeks we will hie ;
Over banks of bright seaweed
The ebb-tide leaves dry.
We will gaze, from the sand-hills,
At the white, sleeping town ;
At the church on the hill-side—
    And then come back down.
Singing, ' There dwells a loved one,
    But cruel is she.
She left lonely for ever
    The kings of the sea.'

267.   *The Song of Callicles*

THROUGH the black, rushing smoke-bursts,
    Thick breaks the red flame.
All Etna heaves fiercely
Her forest-clothed frame.

Not here, O Apollo !
Are haunts meet for thee.
But, where Helicon breaks down
In cliff to the sea.

Where the moon-silver'd inlets
Send far their light voice
Up the still vale of Thisbe,
O speed, and rejoice !

On

MATTHEW ARNOLD

On the sward at the cliff-top,
Lie strewn the white flocks ;
On the cliff-side, the pigeons
Roost deep in the rocks.

In the moonlight the shepherds,
Soft lull'd by the rills,
Lie wrapt in their blankets,
Asleep on the hills.

—What forms are these coming
So white through the gloom ?
What garments out-glistening
The gold-flower'd broom ?

What sweet-breathing Presence
Out-perfumes the thyme ?
What voices enrapture
The night's balmy prime ?—

'Tis Apollo comes leading
His choir, The Nine.
—The Leader is fairest,
But all are divine.

They are lost in the hollows.
They stream up again.
What seeks on this mountain
The glorified train ?—

They bathe on this mountain,
In the spring by their road.
Then on to Olympus,
Their endless abode.

—Whose praise do they mention ?
Of what is it told ?—
What will be for ever.
What was from of old.

First hymn they the Father
Of all things : and then,
The rest of Immortals,
The action of men.

The Day in his hotness,
The strife with the palm ;
The Night in her silence,
The Stars in their calm.

268.   *Cadmus and Harmonia*

FAR, far from here,
    The Adriatic breaks in a warm bay
Among the green Illyrian hills ; and there
The sunshine in the happy glens is fair,
And by the sea, and in the brakes.
The grass is cool, the sea-side air
Buoyant and fresh, the mountain flowers
As virginal and sweet as ours.
And there, they say, two bright and agèd snakes,
Who once were Cadmus and Harmonia,
Bask in the glens or on the warm sea-shore,
In breathless quiet, after all their ills.
Nor do they see their country, nor the place
Where the Sphinx lived among the frowning hills,
Nor the unhappy palace of their race,
Nor Thebes, nor the Ismenus, any more.

There

There those two live, far in the Illyrian brakes.
They had stay'd long enough to see,
In Thebes, the billow of calamity
Over their own dear children roll'd,
Curse upon curse, pang upon pang,
For years, they sitting helpless in their home,
A grey old man and woman ; yet of old
The Gods had to their marriage come,
And at the banquet all the Muses sang.

Therefore they did not end their days
In sight of blood ; but were rapt, far away,
To where the west wind plays,
And murmurs of the Adriatic come
To those untrodden mountain lawns; and there
Placed safely in changed forms, the Pair
Wholly forget their first sad life, and home,
And all that Theban woe, and stray
For ever through the glens, placid and dumb.

269.   *Dover Beach*

THE sea is calm to-night,
    The tide is full, the moon lies fair
Upon the Straits ;—on the French coast, the light
Gleams, and is gone ; the cliffs of England stand,
Glimmering and vast, out in the tranquil bay.
Come to the window, sweet is the night air !
Only, from the long line of spray
Where the ebb meets the moon-blanch'd sand,
Listen ! you hear the grating roar
Of pebbles which the waves suck back, and fling,

At their return, up the high strand,
Begin, and cease, and then again begin,
With tremulous cadence slow, and bring
The eternal note of sadness in.

Sophocles long ago
Heard it on the Aegaean, and it brought
Into his mind the turbid ebb and flow
Of human misery; we
Find also in the sound a thought,
Hearing it by this distant northern sea.

The sea of faith
Was once, too, at the full, and round earth's shore
Lay like the folds of a bright girdle furl'd ;
But now I only hear
Its melancholy, long, withdrawing roar,
Retreating to the breath
Of the night-wind down the vast edges drear
And naked shingles of the world.

Ah, love, let us be true
To one another ! for the world, which seems
To lie before us like a land of dreams,
So various, so beautiful, so new,
Hath really neither joy, nor love, nor light,
Nor certitude, nor peace, nor help for pain ;
And we are here as on a darkling plain
Swept with confused alarms of struggle and flight,
Where ignorant armies clash by night.

270.   *Isolation*

YES : in the sea of life enisled,
    With echoing straits between us thrown,
Dotting the shoreless watery wild,
    We mortal millions live alone.
The islands feel the enclasping flow,
And then their endless bounds they know.

But when the moon their hollows lights,
    And they are swept by balms of spring,
And in their glens, on starry nights,
    The nightingales divinely sing ;
And lovely notes, from shore to shore,
Across the sounds and channels pour ;

O then a longing like despair
    Is to their farthest caverns sent !
For surely once, they feel, we were
    Parts of a single continent.
Now round us spreads the watery plain—
O might our marges meet again !

Who order'd, that their longing's fire
    Should be, as soon as kindled, cool'd ?
Who renders vain their deep desire ?—
    A God, a God their severance rul'd ;
And bade betwixt their shores to be
The unplumb'd, salt, estranging sea.

271.   *Requiescat*

STREW on her roses, roses,
    And never a spray of yew.
In quiet she reposes :
    Ah ! would that I did too !

Her mirth the world required :
    She bathed it in smiles of glee.
But her heart was tired, tired,
    And now they let her be.

Her life was turning, turning,
    In mazes of heat and sound.
But for peace her soul was yearning
    And now peace laps her round.

Her cabin'd, ample Spirit,
    It flutter'd and fail'd for breath.
To-night it doth inherit
    The vasty hall of Death.

272.   *The Scholar-Gipsy*

GO, for they call you, Shepherd, from the hill ;
    Go, Shepherd, and untie the wattled cotes :
    No longer leave thy wistful flock unfed,
Nor let thy bawling fellows rack their throats,
    Nor the cropp'd grasses shoot another head.
        But when the fields are still,
And the tired men and dogs all gone to rest,
    And only the white sheep are sometimes seen
    Cross and recross the strips of moon-blanch'd green ;
Come, Shepherd, and again begin the quest.

                        371   Here,

Here, where the reaper was at work of late,
  In this high field's dark corner, where he leaves
    His coat, his basket, and his earthen cruise,
  And in the sun all morning binds the sheaves,
    Then here, at noon, comes back his stores to use;
      Here will I sit and wait,
  While to my ear from uplands far away
    The bleating of the folded flocks is borne,
    With distant cries of reapers in the corn—
  All the live murmur of a summer's day.

Screen'd is this nook o'er the high, half-reap'd field,
  And here till sundown, Shepherd, will I be.
    Through the thick corn the scarlet poppies peep,
  And round green roots and yellowing stalks I see
    Pale pink convolvulus in tendrils creep:
      And air-swept lindens yield
  Their scent, and rustle down their perfumed showers
    Of bloom on the bent grass where I am laid,
    And bower me from the August sun with shade;
  And the eye travels down to Oxford's towers:

And near me on the grass lies Glanvil's book—
  Come, let me read the oft-read tale again:
    The story of that Oxford scholar poor,
  Of pregnant parts and quick inventive brain,
    Who, tired of knocking at Preferment's door,
      One summer morn forsook
  His friends, and went to learn the Gipsy lore,
    And roam'd the world with that wild brotherhood,
    And came, as most men deem'd, to little good,
  But came to Oxford and his friends no more.

But once, years after, in the country lanes,
   Two scholars, whom at college erst he knew,
     Met him, and of his way of life inquired.
   Whereat he answer'd that the Gipsy crew,
     His mates, had arts to rule as they desired
       The workings of men's brains ;
   And they can bind them to what thoughts they will :
     ' And I,' he said, ' the secret of their art,
     When fully learn'd, will to the world impart :
   But it needs Heaven-sent moments for this skill ! '

This said, he left them, and return'd no more,
   But rumours hung about the country-side,
     That the lost Scholar long was seen to stray,
   Seen by rare glimpses, pensive and tongue-tied,
     In hat of antique shape, and cloak of grey,
       The same the Gipsies wore.
   Shepherds had met him on the Hurst in spring ;
     At some lone alehouse in the Berkshire moors,
     On the warm ingle-bench, the smock-frock'd boors
   Had found him seated at their entering,

But, 'mid their drink and clatter, he would fly :
   And I myself seem half to know thy looks,
     And put the shepherds, Wanderer, on thy trace ;
   And boys who in lone wheatfields scare the rooks
     I ask if thou hast passed their quiet place ;
       Or in my boat I lie
   Moor'd to the cool bank in the summer heats,
     'Mid wide grass meadows which the sunshine fills,
     And watch the warm green-muffled Cumnor hills,
   And wonder if thou haunt'st their shy retreats.

          For

For most, I know, thou lov'st retirèd ground.
 Thee, at the ferry, Oxford riders blithe,
  Returning home on summer nights, have met
Crossing the stripling Thames at Bablock-hithe,
 Trailing in the cool stream thy fingers wet,
  As the slow punt swings round :
And leaning backwards in a pensive dream,
 And fostering in thy lap a heap of flowers
 Pluck'd in shy fields and distant Wychwood bowers,
And thine eyes resting on the moonlit stream :

And then they land, and thou art seen no more.
 Maidens who from the distant hamlets come
  To dance around the Fyfield elm in May,
Oft through the darkening fields have seen thee roam,
 Or cross a stile into the public way.
  Oft thou hast given them store
Of flowers—the frail-leaf'd, white anemone—
 Dark bluebells drench'd with dews of summer eves,
 And purple orchises with spotted leaves—
But none has words she can report of thee.

And, above Godstow Bridge, when hay-time 's here
 In June, and many a scythe in sunshine flames,
  Men who through those wide fields of breezy grass
Where black-wing'd swallows haunt the glittering
    Thames,
 To bathe in the abandon'd lasher pass,
  Have often pass'd thee near
Sitting upon the river bank o'ergrown :
 Mark'd thine outlandish garb, thy figure spare,
 Thy dark vague eyes, and soft abstracted air ;
But, when they came from bathing, thou wert gone.

At some lone homestead in the Cumnor hills,
  Where at her open door the housewife darns,
    Thou hast been seen, or hanging on a gate
  To watch the threshers in the mossy barns.
    Children, who early range these slopes and late
      For cresses from the rills,
  Have known thee watching, all an April day,
    The springing pastures and the feeding kine,
    And mark'd thee, when the stars come out and shine,
  Through the long dewy grass move slow away.

In autumn, on the skirts of Bagley Wood,
  Where most the Gipsies by the turf-edged way
    Pitch their smoked tents, and every bush you see
  With scarlet patches tagg'd and shreds of gray,
    Above the forest-ground call'd Thessaly—
      The blackbird picking food
  Sees thee, nor stops his meal, nor fears at all ;
    So often has he known thee past him stray
    Rapt, twirling in thy hand a wither'd spray,
  And waiting for the spark from Heaven to fall.

And once, in winter, on the causeway chill
  Where home through flooded fields foot-travellers go,
    Have I not pass'd thee on the wooden bridge
  Wrapt in thy cloak and battling with the snow,
    Thy face towards Hinksey and its wintry ridge ?
      And thou hast climb'd the hill
  And gain'd the white brow of the Cumnor range ;
    Turn'd once to watch, while thick the snowflakes fall,
    The line of festal light in Christ Church hall—
  Then sought thy straw in some sequester'd grange.

But

But what—I dream ! Two hundred years are flown
  Since first thy story ran through Oxford halls,
    And the grave Glanvil did the tale inscribe
  That thou wert wander'd from the studious walls
    To learn strange arts, and join a Gipsy tribe :
      And thou from earth art gone
  Long since, and in some quiet churchyard laid ;
    Some country nook, where o'er thy unknown grave
    Tall grasses and white flowering nettles wave—
  Under a dark red-fruited yew-tree's shade.

—No, no, thou hast not felt the lapse of hours.
  For what wears out the life of mortal men ?
    'Tis that from change to change their being rolls :
  'Tis that repeated shocks, again, again,
    Exhaust the energy of strongest souls,
      And numb the elastic powers.
  Till having used our nerves with bliss and teen,
    And tired upon a thousand schemes our wit,
    To the just-pausing Genius we remit
  Our worn-out life, and are—what we have been.

Thou hast not lived, why shouldst thou perish, so ?
  Thou hadst *one* aim, *one* business, *one* desire :
    Else wert thou long since number'd with the dead—
  Else hadst thou spent, like other men, thy fire.
    The generations of thy peers are fled,
      And we ourselves shall go ;
  But thou possessest an immortal lot,
    And we imagine thee exempt from age
    And living as thou liv'st on Glanvil's page,
  Because thou hadst—what we, alas, have not !

For early didst thou leave the world, with powers
   Fresh, undiverted to the world without,
     Firm to their mark, not spent on other things ;
   Free from the sick fatigue, the languid doubt,
     Which much to have tried, in much been baffled,
       brings.
     O Life unlike to ours !
Who fluctuate idly without term or scope,
   Of whom each strives, nor knows for what he strives,
   And each half lives a hundred different lives ;
Who wait like thee, but not, like thee, in hope.

Thou waitest for the spark from Heaven : and we,
   Vague half-believers of our casual creeds,
     Who never deeply felt, nor clearly will'd,
   Whose insight never has borne fruit in deeds,
     Whose weak resolves never have been fulfill'd ;
     For whom each year we see
Breeds new beginnings, disappointments new ;
   Who hesitate and falter life away,
   And lose to-morrow the ground won to-day—
Ah, do not we, Wanderer, await it too ?

Yes, we await it, but it still delays,
   And then we suffer ; and amongst us One,
     Who most has suffer'd, takes dejectedly
His seat upon the intellectual throne ;
     And all his store of sad experience he
      Lays bare of wretched days ;
Tells us his misery's birth and growth and signs,
   And how the dying spark of hope was fed,
   And how the breast was soothed, and how the head,
And all his hourly varied anodynes.

Tennyson

This

This for our wisest : and we others pine,
    And wish the long unhappy dream would end,
      And waive all claim to bliss, and try to bear,
    With close-lipp'd Patience for our only friend,
      Sad Patience, too near neighbour to Despair :
        But none has hope like thine.
    Thou thro' the fields and thro' the woods dost stray,
      Roaming the country-side, a truant boy,
      Nursing thy project in unclouded joy,
And every doubt long blown by time away.

O born in days when wits were fresh and clear,
    And life ran gaily as the sparkling Thames ;
      Before this strange disease of modern life,
    With its sick hurry, its divided aims,
      Its heads o'ertaxed, its palsied hearts, was rife—
        Fly hence, our contact fear !
    Still fly, plunge deeper in the bowering wood !
      Averse, as Dido did with gesture stern
      From her false friend's approach in Hades turn,
Wave us away, and keep thy solitude.

Still nursing the unconquerable hope,
    Still clutching the inviolable shade,
      With a free onward impulse brushing through,
    By night, the silver'd branches of the glade—
      Far on the forest-skirts, where none pursue,
        On some mild pastoral slope
    Emerge, and resting on the moonlit pales,
      Freshen thy flowers, as in former years,
      With dew, or listen with enchanted ears,
From the dark dingles, to the nightingales

But fly our paths, our feverish contact fly :
  For strong the infection of our mental strife,
    Which, though it gives no bliss, yet spoils for rest ;
  And we should win thee from thy own fair life,
    Like us distracted, and like us unblest.
      Soon, soon thy cheer would die,
  Thy hopes grow timorous, and unfix'd thy powers,
    And thy clear aims be cross and shifting made :
  And then thy glad perennial youth would fade,
  Fade, and grow old at last, and die like ours.

Then fly our greetings, fly our speech and smiles !
  —As some grave Tyrian trader, from the sea,
    Descried at sunrise an emerging prow
  Lifting the cool-hair'd creepers stealthily,
    The fringes of a southward-facing brow
      Among the Ægean isles ;
  And saw the merry Grecian coaster come,
    Freighted with amber grapes, and Chian wine,
    Green bursting figs, and tunnies steep'd in brine ;
  And knew the intruders on his ancient home,

The young light-hearted Masters of the waves ;
  And snatch'd his rudder, and shook out more sail,
    And day and night held on indignantly
  O'er the blue Midland waters with the gale,
    Betwixt the Syrtes and soft Sicily,
      To where the Atlantic raves
  Outside the Western Straits, and unbent sails
    There, where down cloudy cliffs, through sheets of
      foam,
  Shy traffickers, the dark Iberians come ;
  And on the beach undid his corded bales.

273.   *Thyrsis*

A Monody, *to commemorate the author's friend,* Arthur
    Hugh Clough, *who died at Florence,* 1861

HOW changed is here each spot man makes or fills !
    In the two Hinkseys nothing keeps the same ;
  The village-street its haunted mansion lacks,
And from the sign is gone Sibylla's name,
    And from the roofs the twisted chimney-stacks ;
      Are ye too changed, ye hills ?
See, 'tis no foot of unfamiliar men
    To-night from Oxford up your pathway strays :
    Here came I often, often, in old days ;
Thyrsis and I ; we still had Thyrsis then.

Runs it not here, the track by Childsworth Farm,
  Up past the wood, to where the elm-tree crowns
    The hill behind whose ridge the sunset flames ?
The signal-elm, that looks on Ilsley Downs,
    The Vale, the three lone weirs, the youthful
          Thames ?—
        This winter-eve is warm,
  Humid the air ; leafless, yet soft as spring,
    The tender purple spray on copse and briers ;
    And that sweet City with her dreaming spires,
She needs not June for beauty's heightening,

Lovely all times she lies, lovely to-night !
 Only, methinks, some loss of habit's power
  Befalls me wandering through this upland dim ;
 Once pass'd I blindfold here, at any hour,
  Now seldom come I, since I came with him.
   That single elm-tree bright
 Against the west—I miss it ! is it gone ?
  We prized it dearly ; while it stood, we said,
  Our friend, the Scholar-Gipsy, was not dead ;
 While the tree lived, he in these fields lived on.

Too rare, too rare, grow now my visits here !
 But once I knew each field, each flower, each stick ;
  And with the country-folk acquaintance made
 By barn in threshing-time, by new-built rick.
  Here, too, our shepherd-pipes we first assay'd.
   Ah me ! this many a year
 My pipe is lost, my shepherd's-holiday !
  Needs must I lose them, needs with heavy heart
  Into the world and wave of men depart ;
 But Thyrsis of his own will went away.

It irk'd him to be here, he could not rest.
 He loved each simple joy the country yields,
  He loved his mates ; but yet he could not keep,
 For that a shadow lower'd on the fields,
  Here with the shepherds and the silly sheep.
   Some life of men unblest
 He knew, which made him droop, and fill'd his head.
  He went ; his piping took a troubled sound
  Of storms that rage outside our happy ground ;
 He could not wait their passing, he is dead !

So,

So, some tempestuous morn in early June,
   When the year's primal burst of bloom is o'er,
      Before the roses and the longest day—
   When garden-walks, and all the grassy floor,
      With blossoms, red and white, of fallen May,
         And chestnut-flowers are strewn—
   So have I heard the cuckoo's parting cry,
      From the wet field, through the vext garden-trees,
      Come with the volleying rain and tossing breeze :
   The bloom is gone, and with the bloom go I.

Too quick despairer, wherefore wilt thou go ?
   Soon will the high Midsummer pomps come on,
      Soon will the musk carnations break and swell,
   Soon shall we have gold-dusted snapdragon,
      Sweet-William with its homely cottage-smell,
         And stocks in fragrant blow ;
   Roses that down the alleys shine afar,
      And open, jasmine-muffled lattices,
      And groups under the dreaming garden-trees,
   And the full moon, and the white evening-star.

He hearkens not ! light comer, he is flown !
   What matters it ? next year he will return,
      And we shall have him in the sweet spring-days,
   With whitening hedges, and uncrumpling fern,
      And blue-bells trembling by the forest-ways,
         And scent of hay new-mown.
   But Thyrsis never more we swains shall see !
      See him come back, and cut a smoother reed,
      And blow a strain the world at last shall heed—
   For Time, not Corydon, hath conquer'd thee.

Alack, for Corydon no rival now !—
    But when Sicilian shepherds lost a mate,
        Some good survivor with his flute would go,
    Piping a ditty sad for Bion's fate,
        And cross the unpermitted ferry's flow,
            And relax Pluto's brow,
    And make leap up with joy the beauteous head
        Of Proserpine, among whose crownèd hair
        Are flowers, first open'd on Sicilian air,
    And flute his friend, like Orpheus, from the dead.

O easy access to the hearer's grace
    When Dorian shepherds sang to Proserpine !
        For she herself had trod Sicilian fields,
    She knew the Dorian water's gush divine,
        She knew each lily white which Enna yields,
            Each rose with blushing face ;
    She loved the Dorian pipe, the Dorian strain.
        But ah, of our poor Thames she never heard !
        Her foot the Cumnor cowslips never stirr'd !
    And we should tease her with our plaint in vain.

Well ! wind-dispers'd and vain the words will be,
    Yet, Thyrsis, let me give my grief its hour
        In the old haunt, and find our tree-topp'd hill !
    Who, if not I, for questing here hath power ?
        I know the wood which hides the daffodil,
            I know the Fyfield tree,
    I know what white, what purple fritillaries
        The grassy harvest of the river-fields,
        Above by Ensham, down by Sandford, yields,
    And what sedg'd brooks are Thames's tributaries ;

I know

I know these slopes ; who knows them if not I ?—
    But many a dingle on the loved hill-side,
        With thorns once studded, old, white-blossom'd trees,
    Where thick the cowslips grew, and, far descried,
        High tower'd the spikes of purple orchises,
          Hath since our day put by
    The coronals of that forgotten time.
        Down each green bank hath gone the ploughboy's
          team,
        And only in the hidden brookside gleam
    Primroses, orphans of the flowery prime.

Where is the girl, who, by the boatman's door,
    Above the locks, above the boating throng,
        Unmoor'd our skiff, when, through the Wytham flats
    Red loosestrife and blond meadow-sweet among,
        And darting swallows, and light water-gnats,
          We track'd the shy Thames shore ?
    Where are the mowers, who, as the tiny swell
        Of our boat passing heav'd the river-grass,
        Stood with suspended scythe to see us pass ?—
    They all are gone, and thou art gone as well.

Yes, thou art gone ! and round me too the night
    In ever-nearing circle weaves her shade.
        I see her veil draw soft across the day,
    I feel her slowly chilling breath invade
        The cheek grown thin, the brown hair sprent with
          grey ;
          I feel her finger light
    Laid pausefully upon life's headlong train ;
        The foot less prompt to meet the morning dew,
        The heart less bounding at emotion new,
    And hope, once crush'd, less quick to spring again.

And long the way appears, which seem'd so short
  To the unpractised eye of sanguine youth ;
    And high the mountain-tops, in cloudy air,
  The mountain-tops where is the throne of Truth,
    Tops in life's morning-sun so bright and bare !
      Unbreachable the fort
Of the long-batter'd world uplifts its wall.
  And strange and vain the earthly turmoil grows,
  And near and real the charm of thy repose,
And night as welcome as a friend would fall.

But hush ! the upland hath a sudden loss
  Of quiet ;—Look ! adown the dusk hill-side,
    A troop of Oxford hunters going home,
  As in old days, jovial and talking, ride !
    From hunting with the Berkshire hounds they
      come—
      Quick, let me fly, and cross
Into yon further field !—'Tis done ; and see,
  Back'd by the sunset, which doth glorify
  The orange and pale violet evening-sky,
Bare on its lonely ridge, the Tree ! the Tree !

I take the omen ! Eve lets down her veil,
  The white fog creeps from bush to bush about,
    The west unflushes, the high stars grow bright,
And in the scatter'd farms the lights come out.
    I cannot reach the Signal-Tree to-night,
      Yet, happy omen, hail !
Hear it from thy broad lucent Arno vale
  (For there thine earth-forgetting eyelids keep
  The morningless and unawakening sleep
Under the flowery oleanders pale),

Hear it, O Thyrsis, still our Tree is there !—
   Ah, vain ! These English fields, this upland dim,
     These brambles pale with mist engarlanded,
That lone, sky-pointing tree, are not for him.
    To a boon southern country he is fled,
      And now in happier air,
Wandering with the great Mother's train divine
    (And purer or more subtle soul than thee,
    I trow, the mighty Mother doth not see !)
Within a folding of the Apennine,

Thou hearest the immortal strains of old.
   Putting his sickle to the perilous grain
    In the hot cornfield of the Phrygian king,
For thee the Lityerses song again
    Young Daphnis with his silver voice doth sing ;
     Sings his Sicilian fold,
His sheep, his hapless love, his blinded eyes ;
    And how a call celestial round him rang
    And heavenward from the fountain-brink he sprang,
And all the marvel of the golden skies.

There thou art gone, and me thou leavest here
   Sole in these fields ; yet will I not despair ;
    Despair I will not, while I yet descry
'Neath the soft canopy of English air
    That lonely Tree against the western sky.
     Still, still these slopes, 'tis clear,
Our Gipsy-Scholar haunts, outliving thee !
    Fields where soft sheep from cages pull the hay,
    Woods with anemonies in flower till May,
Know him a wanderer still ; then why not me ?

A fugitive and gracious light he seeks,
  Shy to illumine ; and I seek it too.
    This does not come with houses or with gold,
  With place, with honour, and a flattering crew ;
      'Tis not in the world's market bought and sold.
      But the smooth-slipping weeks
  Drop by, and leave its seeker still untired ;
    Out of the heed of mortals he is gone,
    He wends unfollow'd, he must house alone ;
  Yet on he fares, by his own heart inspired.

Thou too, O Thyrsis ! on like quest wert bound,
  Thou wanderedst with me for a little hour :
    Men gave thee nothing; but this happy quest,
  If men esteem'd thee feeble, gave thee power,
      If men procured thee trouble, gave thee rest.
      And this rude Cumnor ground,
  Its fir-topped Hurst, its farms, its quiet fields,
    Here cam'st thou in thy jocund youthful time,
    Here was thine height of strength, thy golden prime ;
  And still the haunt beloved a virtue yields.

What though the music of thy rustic flute
  Kept not for long its happy country tone,
    Lost it too soon, and learnt a stormy note
  Of men contention-tost, of men who groan,
      Which task'd thy pipe too sore, and tired thy throat—
      It fail'd, and thou wast mute ;
  Yet hadst thou alway visions of our light,
    And long with men of care thou couldst not stay,
    And soon thy foot resumed its wandering way,
  Left human haunt, and on alone till night.

Too

Too rare, too rare, grow now my visits here !
  'Mid city-noise, not, as with thee of yore,
    Thyrsis, in reach of sheep-bells is my home !
  Then through the great town's harsh, heart-wearying
      roar,
    Let in thy voice a whisper often come,
      To chase fatigue and fear :
Why faintest thou ? I wander'd till I died.
  Roam on ! the light we sought is shining still.
  Dost thou ask proof ? Our Tree yet crowns the hill,
Our Scholar travels yet the loved hillside.

274.   *Austerity of Poetry*

THAT son of Italy who tried to blow,
  Ere Dante came, the trump of sacred song,
In his light youth amid a festal throng
Sate with his bride to see a public show.

Fair was the bride, and on her front did glow
Youth like a star ; and what to youth belong,
Gay raiment, sparkling gauds, elation strong.
A prop gave way ! crash fell a platform ! lo,

Mid struggling sufferers, hurt to death, she lay !
Shuddering they drew her garments off—and found
A robe of sackcloth next the smooth, white skin.

Such, poets, is your bride, the Muse ! young, gay,
Radiant, adorn'd outside ; a hidden ground
Of thought and of austerity within.

That son of Italy] Giacopone di Todi.

275. *Shakespeare*

OTHERS abide our question. Thou art free.
　　We ask and ask : Thou smilest and art still,
Out-topping knowledge. For the loftiest hill
That to the stars uncrowns his majesty,
Planting his steadfast footsteps in the sea,
Making the heaven of heavens his dwelling-place,
Spares but the cloudy border of his base
To the foil'd searching of mortality ;
And thou, who didst the stars and sunbeams know,
Self-school'd, self-scann'd, self-honour'd, self-secure,
Didst walk on earth unguess'd at. Better so !
All pains the immortal spirit must endure,
　　All weakness that impairs, all griefs that bow,
　　Find their sole voice in that victorious brow.

276. *From the Hymn of Empedocles*

IS it so small a thing
　　To have enjoy'd the sun,
To have lived light in the spring,
　　To have loved, to have thought, to have done ;
To have advanced true friends, and beat down baffling
　　　　foes ;

That we must feign a bliss
　　Of doubtful future date,
And while we dream on this
　　Lose all our present state,
And relegate to worlds yet distant our repose ?

Not

Not much, I know, you prize
What pleasures may be had,
Who look on life with eyes
Estranged, like mine, and sad :
And yet the village churl feels the truth more than you ;

Who 's loth to leave this life
Which to him little yields :
His hard-task'd sunburnt wife,
His often-labour'd fields ;
The boors with whom he talk'd, the country spots he knew

But thou, because thou hear'st
Men scoff at Heaven and Fate ·
Because the gods thou fear'st
Fail to make blest thy state,
Tremblest, and wilt not dare to trust the joys there are.

I say, Fear not ! life still
Leaves human effort scope.
But, since life teems with ill,
Nurse no extravagant hope.
Because thou must not dream, thou need'st not then
despair.

MATTHEW ARNOLD

277.   *The Last Word*

CREEP into thy narrow bed,
    Creep, and let no more be said !
Vain thy onset ! all stands fast ;
Thou thyself must break at last.

Let the long contention cease !
Geese are swans, and swans are geese.
Let them have it how they will !
Thou art tired ; best be still !

They out-talk'd thee, hiss'd thee, tore thee
Better men fared thus before thee ;
Fired their ringing shot and pass'd,
Hotly charged—and broke at last.

Charge once more, then, and be dumb !
Let the victors, when they come,
When the forts of folly fall,
Find thy body by the wall.

WILLIAM CALDWELL ROSCOE
1823-1859

278.   *Parting*

THRICE with her lips she touch'd my lips,
 Thrice with her hand my hand,
And three times thrice look'd t'wards the sea,
 But never to the land :
Then ' Sweet,' she said, ' no more delay,
For Heaven forbids a longer stay.'

I, with my passion in my heart,
 Could find no words to waste ;
But, striving often to depart,
 I strain'd her to my breast :
Her wet tears wash'd my weary cheek ;
I could have died, but could not speak.

The anchor swings, the sheet flies loose,
 And, bending to the breeze,
The tall ship never to return
 Flies thro' the foaming seas.
Cheerily ho ! the sailors cry—
My sweet love lessening in my eye.

O Love, turn towards the land thy sight !
 No more peruse the sea :
Our God, who severs thus our hearts,
 Shall surely care for thee :
For me, let waste-wide Ocean swing,
I too lie safe beneath his wing.

279. *Spiritual Love*

WHAT care I tho' beauty fading
  Die ere Time can turn his glass ?
What tho' locks the Graces braiding
  Perish like the summer grass ?
    Tho' thy charms should all decay,
    Think not my affections may !

For thy charms—tho' bright as morning—
  Captured not my idle heart ;
Love so grounded ends in scorning,
  Lacks the barb to hold the dart.
    My devotion more secure
    Woos thy spirit high and pure.

280. *The Poetic Land*

THE bubble of the silver-springing waves,
  Castalian music, and that flattering sound,
Low rustle of the loved Apollian leaves
  With which my youthful hair was to be crown'd,
Grow dimmer in my ears ; while Beauty grieves
  Over her votary less frequent found ;
And, not untouch'd by storms, my life-boat heaves
  Thro' the splash'd ocean-waters, outward bound.

And as the leaning mariner, his hand
  Clasp'd on his oar, strives trembling to reclaim
Some loved lost echo from the fleeting strand,
  So lean I back to the poetic land ;
    And in my heart a sound, a voice, a name
    Hangs, as above the lamp hangs the expiring flame.

WILLIAM BRIGHTY RANDS

1823-1880

281. *Praise and Love*

TELL me, Praise, and tell me, Love,
What you both are thinking of ?

' O, we think,' said Love, said Praise,
' Now of children and their ways.'

Give me of your cup to drink,
Praise, and tell me what you think.

' O, I think of crowns of gold
For the clever and the bold.'

Then I turn'd to Love, and said—
Love was glowing heavenly-red—

Give me of your cup to drink,
Love, and tell me what you think :

Let me taste your bitter-sweet ;
Who are those that kiss your feet ?

Love look'd up—I read her eyes,
They were stars and they were skies.

Clinging to her garment's hem,
Smiling as I look'd at them,

There were children scarr'd and halt,
Children weeping for a fault ;

394

Those who scarcely dared to raise
Doubtful eyes to smiling Praise.

Love look'd round, and Praise and Pride
Brought their glad ones to her side.

' Yea, these too ! ' she said, or sang ;
And the world with music rang.

282.   *The World : a Child's Song*

GREAT, wide, beautiful, wonderful World !
    With the wonderful water round you curl'd,
And the wonderful grass upon your breast—
World, you are beautifully drest.

The wonderful air is over me,
And the wonderful wind is shaking the tree ;
It walks on the water, and whirls the mills,
And talks to itself on the tops of the hills.

You friendly Earth ! how far do you go,
With the wheatfields that nod, and the rivers that flow
With cities and gardens and cliffs and isles,
And people upon you for thousands of miles ?

Ah, you are so great, and I am so small,
I tremble to think of you, World, at all !
And yet, when I said my prayers to-day,
A whisper inside me seem'd to say—

' You are more than the Earth, tho' you are such a dot :
You can love and think, and the Earth cannot ! '

283.   *The Thought*

INTO the skies, one summer's day,
    I sent a little Thought away;
Up to where, in the blue round,
The sun sat shining without sound.

Then my Thought came back to me.—
Little Thought, what did you see
In the regions whence you come?
And when I spoke, my Thought was dumb.

But she breathed of what was there,
In the pure bright upper air;
And, because my Thought so shone,
I knew she had been shone upon.

Next, by night a Thought I sent
Up into the firmament,
When the eager stars were out,
And the still moon shone about.

And my Thought went past the moon,
In between the stars, but soon
Held her breath and durst not stir,
For the fear that covered her;
Then she thought, in this demur:

'Dare I look beneath the shade,
Into where the worlds are made;
Where the suns and stars are wrought?
Shall I meet another Thought?

'Will that other Thought have wings?
Shall I meet strange, heavenly things?
Thought of Thoughts, and Light of Lights,
Breath of Breaths, and Night of Nights?'

Then my Thought began to hark
In the illuminated dark,
Till the silence, over, under,
Made her heart beat more than thunder.

And my Thought came trembling back,
But with something on her track,
And with something at her side ;
Nor till she has lived and died,
Lived and died, and lived again,
Will that awful thing seem plain.

284.   *The Flowers*

WHEN Love arose in heart and deed
    To wake the world to greater joy,
' What can she give me now ? ' said Greed,
    Who thought to win some costly toy.

He rose, he ran, he stoop'd, he clutch'd ;
    And soon the Flowers, that Love let fall,
In Greed's hot grasp were fray'd and smutch'd,
    And Greed said, ' Flowers ! Can this be all ? '

He flung them down and went his way,
    He cared no jot for thyme or rose ;
But boys and girls came out to play,
    And some took these and some took those—

Red, blue, and white, and green and gold ;
    And at their touch the dew return'd,
And all the bloom a thousandfold—
    So red, so ripe, the roses burn'd !

GEORGE HENRY BOKER

1823–1890

285. *Dirge for a Soldier*

CLOSE his eyes ; his work is done.
   What to him is friend or foeman,
Rise of moon or set of sun,
   Hand of man or kiss of woman ?

    Lay him low, lay him low,
    In the clover or the snow !
    What cares he ? He cannot know :
    Lay him low !

As man may, he fought his fight,
   Proved his truth by his endeavour :
Let him sleep in solemn night,
   Sleep for ever and for ever.

Fold him in his country's stars,
   Roll the drum and fire the volley !
What to him are all our wars ?
   What but death bemocking folly ?

Leave him to God's watching eye :
   Trust him to the hand that made him.
Mortal love weeps idly by :
   God alone has power to aid him.

    Lay him low, lay him low,
    In the clover or the snow !
    What cares he ? He cannot know :
    Lay him low !

1823-1892

286.   *An Invocation*

I NEVER prayed for Dryads, to haunt the woods again ;
  More welcome were the presence of hungering, thirst-
    ing men,
Whose doubts we could unravel, whose hopes we could
    fulfil,
Our wisdom tracing backward, the river to the rill ;
Were such beloved forerunners one summer day restored,
Then, then we might discover the Muse's mystic hoard.

Oh, dear divine Comatas, I would that thou and I
Beneath this broken sunlight this leisure day might lie ;
Where trees from distant forests, whose names were
    strange to thee,
Should bend their amorous branches within thy reach to
    be,
And flowers thine Hellas knew not, which art hath made
    more fair,
Should shed their shining petals upon thy fragrant hair.

Then thou shouldst calmly listen with ever-changing looks
To songs of younger minstrels and plots of modern books,
And wonder at the daring of poets later born,
Whose thoughts are unto thy thoughts as noon-tide is to
    morn ;
And little shouldst thou grudge them their greater
    strength of soul,
Thy partners in the torch-race, though nearer to the goal.

            As

As when ancestral portraits look gravely from the walls
Upon the youthful baron who treads their echoing halls;
And whilst he builds new turrets, the thrice ennobled heir
Would gladly wake his grandsire his home and feast to
　　share;
So from Ægean laurels that hide thine ancient urn
I fain would call thee hither, my sweeter lore to learn.

Or in thy cedarn prison thou waitest for the bee:
Ah, leave that simple honey, and take thy food from me!
My sun is stooping westward.　Entrancèd dreamer, haste:
There's fruitage in my garden, that I would have thee
　　taste.
Now lift the lid a moment: now, Dorian shepherd, speak:
Two minds shall flow together, the English and the Greek.

287.　　　　　　　*Anterôs*

NAIAD, hid beneath the bank
　　By the willowy river-side,
Where Narcissus gently sank,
　　Where unmarried Echo died,
Unto thy serene repose
Waft the stricken Anterôs.

Where the tranquil swan is borne,
　　Imaged in a watery glass,
Where the sprays of fresh pink thorn
　　Stoop to catch the boats that pass,
Where the earliest orchis grows,
Bury thou fair Anterôs.

Glide we by, with prow and oar :
  Ripple shadows off the wave,
And reflected on the shore
  Haply play about the grave.
Folds of summer-light enclose
All that once was Anterôs.

On a flickering wave we gaze,
  Not upon his answering eyes :
Flower and bird we scarce can praise,
  Having lost his sweet replies ;
Cold and mute the river flows
With our tears for Anterôs.

288. *Heraclitus*

THEY told me, Heraclitus, they told me you were
    dead,
They brought me bitter news to hear and bitter tears to
    shed.
I wept as I remember'd how often you and I
Had tired the sun with talking and sent him down the sky.

And now that thou art lying, my dear old Carian guest,
A handful of grey ashes, long, long ago at rest,
Still are thy pleasant voices, thy nightingales, awake ;
For Death, he taketh all away, but them he cannot take.

289. *Remember*

YOU come not, as aforetime, to the headstone every
    day,
And I, who died, I do not chide because, my friend, you
    play ;
Only, in playing, think of him who once was kind and dear,
And, if you see a beauteous thing, just say, he is not here.

COVENTRY PATMORE

1823-1896

290. *Woman*

A WOMAN is a foreign land,
　Of which, though there he settle young,
A man will ne'er quite understand
　The customs, politics and tongue,
The foolish hie them post-haste thro',
　See fashions odd and prospects fair,
Learn of the language *How d'ye do ?*
　And go and brag they have been there.
The most for leave to trade apply
　For once at Empire's seat, her heart,
Then get what knowledge ear and eye
　Glean chancewise in the life-long mart.
And certain others, few and fit,
　Attach them to the Court and see
The Country's best, its accent hit,
　And partly sound its Polity.

291. *Thoughts*

i. CONSTANCY

I VOW'D unvarying faith ; and she,
　To whom in full I pay that vow,
Rewards me with variety
　Which men who change can never know.

ii. SHAME

THE wrong is made and measured by
　The right's inverted dignity.
Change love to shame, as love is high
　So low in hell your bed shall be.

iii. ATTAINMENT

YOU love ? That's high as you shall go :
　For 'tis as true as Gospel text,
Not noble then is never so,
　Either in this world or the next.

iv. SENSUALITY

WHO pleasure follows pleasure slays ;
　God's wrath upon himself he wreaks ;
But all delights rejoice his days
　Who takes with thanks and never seeks.

v. COURTESY

LOVE'S perfect blossom only blows
　Where noble manners veil defect.
Angels may be familiar ; those
　Who err each other must respect.

292.　　　　*The Kiss*

' I SAW you take his kiss ! '　' 'Tis true.'
　' O modesty ! '　' 'Twas strictly kept :
He thought me asleep—at least, I knew
　He thought I thought he thought I slept.'

293.   *Departure*

IT was not like your great and gracious ways !
　Do you, that have naught other to lament,
Never, my Love, repent
Of how, that July afternoon,
You went,
With sudden, unintelligible phrase,
And frighten'd eye,
Upon your journey of so many days
Without a single kiss, or a good-bye ?
I knew, indeed, that you were parting soon ;
And so we sate, within the low sun's rays,
You whispering to me, for your voice was weak,
Your harrowing praise.
Well, it was well
To hear you such things speak,
And I could tell
What made your eyes a growing gloom of love,
As a warm South-wind sombres a March grove.
And it was like your great and gracious ways
To turn your talk on daily things, my Dear,
Lifting the luminous, pathetic lash
To let the laughter flash,
Whilst I drew near,
Because you spoke so low that I could scarcely hear.
But all at once to leave me at the last,
More at the wonder than the loss aghast,
With huddled, unintelligible phrase,
And frighten'd eye,
And go your journey of all days
With not one kiss, or a good-bye,
And the only loveless look the look with which you pass'd :
'Twas all unlike your great and gracious ways.

294.   *The Toys*

MY little Son, who look'd from thoughtful eyes
    And moved and spoke in quiet grown-up wise,
Having my law the seventh time disobey'd,
I struck him, and dismiss'd
With hard words and unkiss'd,
—His Mother, who was patient, being dead.
Then, fearing lest his grief should hinder sleep,
I visited his bed,
But found him slumbering deep,
With darken'd eyelids, and their lashes yet
From his late sobbing wet.
And I, with moan,
Kissing away his tears, left others of my own ;
For, on a table drawn beside his head,
He had put, within his reach,
A box of counters and a red-vein'd stone,
A piece of glass abraded by the beach,
And six or seven shells,
A bottle with bluebells,
And two French copper coins, ranged there with careful art.
To comfort his sad heart.
So when that night I pray'd
To God, I wept, and said :
Ah ! when at last we lie with trancèd breath,
Not vexing Thee in death,
And Thou rememberest of what toys
We made our joys,
How weakly understood
Thy great commanded good,
Then, fatherly not less
Than I whom Thou hast moulded from the clay,
Thou'lt leave Thy wrath, and say,
' I will be sorry for their childishness.'

295.   *A Farewell*

WITH all my will, but much against my heart,
    We two now part.
My Very Dear,
    Our solace is, the sad road lies so clear.
It needs no art,
With faint, averted feet
    And many a tear,
In our opposèd paths to persevere.
    Go thou to East, I West.
We will not say
There's any hope, it is so far away.
But, O, my Best!
When the one darling of our widowhead,
The nursling Grief,
Is dead,
And no dews blur our eyes
To see the peach-bloom come in evening skies,
Perchance we may,
Where now this night is day,
And even through faith of still averted feet,
Making full circle of our banishment,
Amazèd meet;
The bitter journey to the bourne so sweet
Seasoning the termless feast of our content
With tears of recognition never dry.

296.   *Magna Est Veritas*

HERE, in this little Bay,
        Full of tumultuous life and great repose,
Where, twice a day,
The purposeless, glad ocean comes and goes,
Under high cliffs, and far from the huge town,
I sit me down.
For want of me the world's course will not fail :
When all its work is done, the lie shall rot ;
The truth is great, and shall prevail,
When none cares whether it prevail or not.

297.   *The First Spousal*

TWICE thirty centuries and more ago,
        All in a heavenly Abyssinian vale,
Man first met woman ; and the ruddy snow
On many-ridgèd Abora turn'd pale,
And the song choked within the nightingale.
A mild white furnace in the thorough blast
Of purest spirit seem'd She as she pass'd ;
And of the Man enough that this be said,
He look'd her Head.
    Towards their bower
Together as they went,
With hearts conceiving torrents of content,
And linger'd prologue fit for Paradise,
He, gathering power
From dear persuasion of the dim-lit hour,
And doubted sanction of her sparkling eyes,
Thus supplicates her conjugal assent,

And

And thus she makes replies :
   ' Lo, Eve, the Day burns on the snowy height,
But here is mellow night ! '
   ' Here let us rest. The languor of the light
Is in my feet.
It is thy strength, my Love, that makes me weak ;
Thy strength it is that makes my weakness sweet.
What would thy kiss'd lips speak ? '
   ' See, what a world of roses I have spread
To make the bridal bed.
Come, Beauty's self and Love's, thus to thy throne b
    led ! '
   ' My Lord, my Wisdom, nay !
Does not yon love-delighted Planet run,
(Haply against her heart,)
A space apart
For ever from her strong-persuading Sun !
O say,
Shall we no voluntary bars
Set to our drift ? I, Sister of the Stars,
And Thou, my glorious, course-compelling Day ! '
   ' Yea, yea !
Was it an echo of her coming word
Which, ere she spake, I heard ?
Or through what strange distrust was I, her Head,
Not first this thing to have said ?
Alway
Speaks not within my breast
The uncompulsive, great and sweet behest
Of something bright,
Not named, not known, and yet more manifest
Than is the morn,
The sun being just at point then to be born ?
O Eve, take back thy " Nay ".

Trust me, Belovèd, ever in all to mean
Thy blissful service, sacrificial, keen ;
But bondless be that service, and let speak—'
   ' This other world of roses in my cheek,
Which hide them in thy breast, and deepening seek
That thou decree if they mean Yea or Nay.'
   ' Did e'er so sweet a word such sweet gainsay ! '
   ' And when I lean, Love, on you, thus, and smile
So that my Nay seems Yea,
You must the while
Thence be confirm'd that I deny you still.'
   ' I will, I will ! '
   ' And when my arms are round your neck, like this,
And I, as now,
Melt like a golden ingot in your kiss,
Then, more than ever, shall your splendid word
Be as Archangel Michael's severing sword !
Speak, speak !
Your might, Love, makes me weak,
Your might it is that makes my weakness sweet.'
   ' I vow, I vow ! '
   ' And are you happy, O my Hero and Lord ;
And is your joy complete ? '
   ' Yea, with my joyful heart my body rocks,
And joy comes down from Heaven in floods and shocks,
As from Mount Abora comes the avalanche.'
   ' My Law, my Light !
Then am I yours as your high mind may list.
No wile shall lure you, none can I resist ! '
   Thus the first Eve
With much enamour'd Adam did enact
Their mutual free contract
Of virgin spousals, blissful beyond flight
Of modern thought, with great intention staunch,

        Though

Though unobliged until that binding pact.
Whether She kept her word, or He the mind
To hold her, wavering, to his own restraint,
Answer, ye pleasures faint,
Ye fiery throes, and upturn'd eyeballs blind
Of sick-at-heart Mankind,
Whom nothing succour can,
Until a heaven-caress'd and happier Eve
Be join'd with some glad Saint
In like espousals, blessed upon Earth,
And she her Fruit forth bring ;
No numb, chill-hearted, shaken-witted thing,
'Plaining his little span,
But of proud virgin joy the appropriate birth,
The Son of God and Man.

298.   *Auras of Delight*

BEAUTIFUL habitations, auras of delight !
Who shall bewail the crags and bitter foam
And angry sword-blades flashing left and right
Which guard your glittering height,
That none thereby may come !
The vision which we have
Revere we so,
That yet we crave
To foot those fields of ne'er-profanèd snow ? . . .
And Him I thank, who can make live again,
The dust, but not the joy we once profane,
That I, of ye,
Beautiful habitations, auras of delight,
In childish years and since had sometime sense and sight,
But that ye vanish'd quite,

Even from memory,
Ere I could get my breath, and whisper ' See ! '
  But did for me
They altogether die,
Those trackless glories glimps'd in upper sky ?
Were they of chance, or vain,
Nor good at all again
For curb of heart or fret ?
Nay, though, by grace,
Lest haply I refuse God to His face,
Their likeness wholly I forget,
Ah ! yet,
Often in straits which else for me were ill,
I mind me still
I *did* respire the lonely auras sweet,
I *did* the blest abodes behold, and, at the mountains' feet,
Bathed in the holy Stream by Hermon's thymy hill.

SYDNEY DOBELL
1824-1874

299. *The Ballad of Keith of Ravelston*

THE murmur of the mourning ghost
  That keeps the shadowy kine,
' O, Keith of Ravelston,
  The sorrows of thy line ! '

Ravelston, Ravelston,
  The merry path that leads
Down the golden morning hill,
  And thro' the silver meads ;

Ravelston,

SYDNEY DOBELL

Ravelston, Ravelston,
  The stile beneath the tree,
The maid that kept her mother's kine,
  The song that sang she !

She sang her song, she kept her kine,
  She sat beneath the thorn,
When Andrew Keith of Ravelston
  Rode thro' the Monday morn.

His henchmen sing, his hawk-bells ring,
  His belted jewels shine ;
O, Keith of Ravelston,
  The sorrows of thy line !

Year after year, where Andrew came,
  Comes evening down the glade,
And still there sits a moonshine ghost
  Where sat the sunshine maid.

Her misty hair is faint and fair,
  She keeps the shadowy kine ;
O, Keith of Ravelston,
  The sorrows of thy line !

I lay my hand upon the stile,
  The stile is lone and cold,
The burnie that goes babbling by
  Says naught that can be told.

Yet, stranger ! here, from year to year,
  She keeps her shadowy kine ;
O, Keith of Ravelston,
  The sorrows of thy line !

Step out three steps, where Andrew stood—
   Why blanch thy cheeks for fear ?
The ancient stile is not alone,
   'Tis not the burn I hear !

She makes her immemorial moan,
   She keeps her shadowy kine ;
O, Keith of Ravelston,
   The sorrows of thy line !

300.   *Isabel*

MY heart's despair
   Looks for thee ere the firstling smoke hath curl'd
While the rapt earth is at her morning pray'r,
Ere yet she putteth on her workday air
And robes her for the world,
Isabel.

When the sun-burst is o'er
My lonely way about the world I take,
Doing and saying much, and feeling more,
And all things for thy sake,
Isabel.

But never once I dare
To see thine image till the day be new,
And lip hath sullied not the unbreathed air,
And waking eyes are few,
Isabel.

Then

Then that lost form appears
Which was a joy to few on earth but me :
In the young light I see thy guileless glee,
In the deep dews thy tears,
Isabel.

So with Promethean moan
In widowhood renew'd I learn to grieve ;
Blest with one only thought—that I alone
Can fade : that thou thro' years shalt still shine on
In beauty, as in beauty art thou gone,
Thou morn that knew no eve,
Isabel.

In beauty art thou gone ;
As some bright meteor gleams across the night,
Gazed on by all, but understood by none,
And dying by its own excess of light,
Isabel.

301.   *Return !*

RETURN, return ! all night my lamp is burning,
   All night, like it, my wide eyes watch and burn ;
Like it, I fade and pale, when day returning
Bears witness that the absent can return,
        Return, return.

Like it, I lessen with a lengthening sadness,
Like it, I burn to waste and waste to burn,
Like it, I spend the golden oil of gladness
To feed the sorrowy signal for return,
        Return, return.

Like it, like it, whene'er the east wind sings,
I bend and shake ; like it, I quake and yearn,
When Hope's late butterflies, with whispering wings,
Fly in out of the dark, to fall and burn—
    Burn in the watchfire of return,
        Return, return.

Like it, the very flame whereby I pine
Consumes me to its nature.   While I mourn
My soul becomes a better soul than mine,
And from its brightening beacon I discern
My starry love go forth from me, and shine
Across the seas a path for thy return,
        Return, return.

Return, return ! all night I see it burn,
All night it prays like me, and lifts a twin
Of palmèd praying hands that meet and yearn—
Yearn to the impleaded skies for thy return.
Day, like a golden fetter, locks them in,
And wans the light that withers, tho' it burn
    As warmly still for thy return ;
Still thro' the splendid load uplifts the thin
Pale, paler, palest patience that can learn
Naught but that votive sign for thy return—
That single suppliant sign for thy return,
        Return, return.

Return, return ! lest haply, love, or e'er
Thou touch the lamp the light have ceased to burn,
And thou, who thro' the window didst discern
The wonted flame, shalt reach the topmost stair
    To find no wide eyes watching there,
No wither'd welcome waiting thy return !

A passing

A passing ghost, a smoke-wreath in the air,
The flameless ashes, and the soulless urn,
Warm with the famish'd fire that lived to burn—
Burn out its lingering life for thy return,
Its last of lingering life for thy return,
Its last of lingering life to light thy late return,
   Return, return.

302.   *An Even-Song*

IN the spring twilight, in the colour'd twilight
 Whereto the latter primroses are stars,
And early nightingale
Letteth her love adown the tender wind,
That thro' the eglantine
In mixed delight the fragrant music bloweth
On to me,
Where in the twilight, in the colour'd twilight,
I sit beside the thorn upon the hill.
The mavis sings upon the old oak tree
Sweet and strong,
Strong and sweet,
Soft, sweet, and strong,
And with his voice interpreteth the silence
Of the dim vale when Philomel is mute !
The dew lies like a light upon the grass,
The cloud is as a swan upon the sky,
The mist is as a brideweed on the moon.
The shadows new and sweet
Like maids unwonted in the dues of joy
Play with the meadow flowers,
And give with fearful fancies more and less,
And come, and go, and flit

A brief emotion in the moving air,
And now are stirr'd to flight, and now are kind,
Unset, uncertain, as the cheek of Love.
As tho' amid the eve
Stood Spring with fluttering breast,
And like a butterfly upon a flower,
Spreading and closing with delight's excess,
A-sudden fann'd and shut her tinted wings.
In the spring twilight, in the colour'd twilight,
Ere Hesper, eldest child of Night, run forth
On mountain-top to see
If Day hath left the dale,
And hears, well-pleased, the dove
From ancient elm and high
In murmuring dreams still bid the sun good night,
And sound of lowing kine,
And echoes long and clear,
And herdsman's evening call,
And bells of penning folds,
Sweet and low ;
O maid, as fair as thou
Behold the young May moon !
O, happy, happy maid !
With love as young as she
In the spring twilight, in the colour'd twilight,
Meet, meet me, by the thorn upon the hill !

303.   *Eden-Gate*

THERE grew a lowly flower by Eden-gate
Among the thorns and thistles. High the palm
Branch'd o'er her, and imperial by her side
Upstood the sunburnt lily of the East.

1346 P   417   The

The goodly gate swung oft, with many gods
Going and coming, and the spice-winds blew
Music and murmurings, and paradise
Well'd over and enrich'd the outer wild.

Then the palm trembled fast-bound by the feet,
And the imperial Lily bow'd her down
With yearning, but they could not enter in.

The lowly flower she look'd up to the palm
And lily, and at eve was full of dews,
And hung her head and wept and said, ' Ah these
Are tall and fair, and shall I enter in ? '

There came an angel to the gate at even,
A weary angel, with dishevell'd hair ;
For he had wander'd far, and as he went,
The blossoms of his crown fell one by one
Thro' many nights, and seem'd a falling star.

He saw the lovely flower by Eden-gate,
And cried, ' Ah, pure and beautiful ! ' and turn'd
And stoop'd to her and wound her in his hair,
And in his golden hair she enter'd in.

Husband ! I was the weed at Eden-gate ;
I look'd up to the lily and the palm
Above me, and I wept and said, ' Ah these
Are tall and fair, and shall I enter in ? '

And one came by me to the gate at even,
And stoop'd to me and wound me in his hair
And in his golden hair I enter'd in.

304. *Sonnets. America*

i

MEN say, Columbia, we shall hear thy guns.
But in what tongue shall be thy battle-cry ?
Not that our sires did love in years gone by,
When all the Pilgrim Fathers were little sons
In merry homes of England ? Back, and see
Thy satchell'd ancestor ! Behold, he runs
To mine, and, clasp'd, they tread the equal lea
To the same village-school, where side by side
They spell ' Our Father '. Hard by, the twin-pride
Of that grey hall whose ancient oriel gleams
Thro' yon baronial pines, with looks of light
Our sister-mothers sit beneath one tree.
Meanwhile our Shakespeare wanders past and dreams
His Helena and Hermia. Shall we fight ?

ii

NOR force nor fraud shall sunder us ! O ye
Who north or south, on east or western land,
Native to noble sounds, say truth for truth,
Freedom for freedom, love for love, and God
For God ; Oh ye who in eternal youth
Speak with a living and creative flood
This universal English, and do stand
Its breathing book ; live worthy of that grand
Heroic utterance—parted, yet a whole,
Far, yet unsever'd,—children brave and free
Of the great Mother-tongue, and ye shall be
Lords of an Empire wide as Shakespeare's soul,
Sublime as Milton's immemorial theme,
And rich as Chaucer's speech, and fair as Spenser's dream.

WILLIAM ALLINGHAM

1824–1889

305.   *The Fairies*

UP the airy mountain,
     Down the rushy glen,
We daren't go a-hunting
     For fear of little men ;
Wee folk, good folk,
     Trooping all together ;
Green jacket, red cap,
     And white owl's feather !

Down along the rocky shore
     Some make their home,
They live on crispy pancakes
     Of yellow tide-foam ;
Some in the reeds
     Of the black mountain lake,
With frogs for their watch-dogs,
     All night awake.

High on the hill-top
     The old King sits ;
He is now so old and gray
     He's nigh lost his wits.
With a bridge of white mist
     Columbkill he crosses,
On his stately journeys
     From Slieveleague to Rosses ;
Or going up with music
     On cold starry nights
To sup with the Queen
     Of the gay Northern Lights.

They stole little Bridget
   For seven years long ;
When she came down again
   Her friends were all gone.
They took her lightly back,
   Between the night and morrow,
They thought that she was fast asleep,
   But she was dead with sorrow.
They have kept her ever since
   Deep within the lake,
On a bed of flag-leaves,
   Watching till she wake.

By the craggy hill-side,
   Through the mosses bare,
They have planted thorn-trees
   For pleasure here and there.
If any man so daring
   As dig them up in spite,
He shall find their sharpest thorns
   In his bed at night.

Up the airy mountain,
   Down the rushy glen,
We daren't go a-hunting
   For fear of little men ;
Wee folk, good folk,
   Trooping all together ;
Green jacket, red cap,
   And white owl's feather !

306.   *The Lover and Birds*

WITHIN a budding grove
    In April's ear sang every bird his best,
But not a song to pleasure my unrest
    Or touch the tears unwept of bitter love ;
Some spake, methought, with pity, some as if in jest :
        To every word
        Of every bird
    I listen'd, and replied as it behove.

    Scream'd Chaffinch, ' Sweet, sweet, sweet !
Pretty lovey, come and meet me here ! '
' Chaffinch,' quoth I, ' be dumb awhile, in fear
    Thy darling prove no better than a cheat,
And never come, or fly when wintry days appear.'
        Yet from a twig
        With voice so big,
    The little fowl his utterance did repeat.

    Then I, ' The man forlorn
Hears Earth send up a foolish noise aloft.'
—' And what'll *he* do ?   What'll *he* do ? ' scoff'd
    The Blackbird, standing in an ancient thorn,
Then spread his sooty wings and flitted to the croft
        With cackling laugh :
        Whom I, being half
    Enraged, call'd after, giving back his scorn.

    Worse mock'd the Thrush, ' Die ! die !
Oh, could he do it ? could he do it ? Nay !
Be quick ! be quick ! Here, here, here ! ' (went his lay)

'Take heed ! take heed !' then, 'Why ? why ? why ?
    why ? why ?
See-ee now ! see-ee now !' (he drawl'd) 'Back ! back !
    back ! R-r-r-run away !'
            O Thrush, be still !
            Or, at thy will,
    Seek some less sad interpreter than I.

'Air, air ! blue air and white !
Whither I flee, whither, O whither, O whither I flee !'
(Thus the Lark hurried, mounting from the lea)
    'Hills, countries, many waters glittering bright,
Whither I see, whither I see ! deeper, deeper, deeper,
        whither I see, see, see !'
            'Gay Lark,' I said,
            'The song that 's bred
    In happy nest may well to heaven make flight.'

'There 's something, something sad,
I half remember '—piped a broken strain.
Well sung, sweet Robin ! Robin sung again :
    'Spring's opening cheerily, cheerily ! be we glad !'
Which moved, I wist not why, me melancholy mad,
            Till now, grown meek,
            With wetted cheek,
    Most comforting and gentle thoughts I had.

307.   *A Memory*

FOUR ducks on a pond,
    A grass-bank beyond,
A blue sky of spring,
White clouds on the wing :
What a little thing
To remember for years—
To remember with tears !

308.   *That Holy Thing*

THEY all were looking for a king
   To slay their foes and lift them high :
Thou cam'st, a little baby thing
   That made a woman cry.

O Son of Man, to right my lot
   Naught but Thy presence can avail ;
Yet on the road Thy wheels are not,
   Nor on the sea Thy sail !

My how or when Thou wilt not heed,
   But come down thine own secret stair,
That Thou mayst answer all my need—
   Yea, every bygone prayer.

309.   *Dorcas*

IF I might guess, then guess I would
   That, mid the gather'd folk,
This gentle Dorcas one day stood,
   And heard when Jesus spoke.

She saw the woven seamless coat—
   Half envious, for his sake :
' Oh, happy hands,' she said, ' that wrought
   The honoured thing to make ! '

Her eyes with longing tears grow dim :
   She never can come nigh
To work one service poor for him
   For whom she glad would die !

But hark, he speaks ! O, precious word !
   And she has heard indeed !
' When did we see thee naked, Lord,
   And clothed thee in thy need ?

' The King shall answer, Inasmuch
   As to my brethren ye
Did it—even to the least of such—
   Ye did it unto me.'

Home, home she went, and plied the loom,
   And Jesus' poor array'd.
She died—they wept about the room,
   And showed the coats she made.

310

Mammon Marriage

THE croak of a raven hoar !
   A dog's howl, kennel-tied !
Loud shuts the carriage-door :
   The two are away on their ghastly ride
To Death's salt shore !

Where are the love and the grace ?
   The bridegroom is thirsty and cold !
The bride's skull sharpens her face !
   But the coachman is driving, jubilant, bold,
The devil's pace.

The horses shiver'd and shook
   Waiting gaunt and haggard
With sorry and evil look ;
   But swift as a drunken wind they stagger'd
'Longst Lethe brook.

Long

Long since, they ran no more ;
   Heavily pulling they died
On the sand of the hopeless shore
   Where never swell'd or sank a tide,
And the salt burns sore.

Flat their skeletons lie,
   White shadows on shining sand ;
The crusted reins go high
   To the crumbling coachman's bony hand
On his knees awry.

Side by side, jarring no more,
   Day and night side by side,
Each by a doorless door,
   Motionless sit the bridegroom and bride
On the Dead-Sea-shore.

311.   *Sonnet*

THIS infant world has taken long to make,
   Nor hast Thou done with it, but mak'st it yet,
   And wilt be working on when death has set
A new mound in some churchyard for my sake.
On flow the centuries without a break ;
   Uprise the mountains, ages without let ;
   The lichens suck ; the hard rock's breast they fret ;
Years more than past the young earth yet will take.
But in the dumbness of the rolling time
   No veil of silence shall encompass me—
   Thou wilt not once forget and let me be ;
Rather Thou wouldst some old chaotic prime
Invade, and, moved by tenderness sublime,
   Unfold a world that I, thy child, might see.

312.   *Song*

WHY do the houses stand
    When they that built them are gone ;
  When remaineth even of one
That lived there and loved and planned
Not a face, not an eye, not a hand,
    Only here and there a bone ?
Why do the houses stand
    When they who built them are gone ?
Oft in the moonlighted land
    When the day is overblown,
    With happy memorial moan
Sweet ghosts in a loving band
Roam through the houses that stand—
    For the builders are not gone.

WALTER C. SMITH

1824-1908

313.   *Glenaradale*

THERE is no fire of the crackling boughs
    On the hearth of our fathers,
There is no lowing of brown-eyed cows
    On the green meadows,
Nor do the maidens whisper vows
    In the still gloaming,
        Glenaradale.

Then

WALTER C. SMITH

There is no bleating of sheep on the hill
  Where the mists linger,
There is no sound of the low hand-mill
  Ground by the women,
And the smith's hammer is lying still
  By the brown anvil,
   Glenaradale.

Ah ! we must leave thee and go away
  Far from Ben Luibh,
Far from the graves where we hoped to lay
  Our bones with our fathers',
Far from the kirk where we used to pray
  Lowly together,
   Glenaradale.

We are not going for hunger of wealth,
  For the gold and silver,
We are not going to seek for health
  On the flat prairies,
Nor yet for the lack of fruitful tilth
  On thy green pastures,
   Glenaradale.

Content with the croft and the hill were we,
  As all our fathers,
Content with the fish in the lake to be
  Carefully netted,
And garments spun of the wool from thee,
  O black-faced wether
   Of Glenaradale !

No father here but would give a son
  For the old country,

WALTER C. SMITH

And his mother the sword would have girded on
    To fight her battles :
Many 's the battle that has been won
    By the brave tartans,
      Glenaradale.

But the big-horn'd stag and his hinds, we know,
    In the high corries,
And the salmon that swirls in the pool below
    Where the stream rushes
Are more than the hearts of men, and so
    We leave thy green valley,
      Glenaradale.

WILLIAM ALEXANDER
ARCHBISHOP OF ARMAGH
1824–1911

314.   *From ' A Vision of Oxford '*

METHOUGHT I met a Lady yester even ;
    A passionless grief, that had nor tear nor wail,
Sat on her pure proud face, that gleam'd to Heaven
    White as a moonlit sail.

She spake : ' On this pale brow are looks of youth,
    Yet angels listening on the argent floor
Know that these lips have been proclaiming truth
    Nine hundred years and more ;

' And Isis knows what time-grey towers rear'd up,
    Gardens and groves and cloister'd halls are mine ;
When quaff my sons from many a myrrhine cup
    Draughts of ambrosial wine.

' He

'He knows how night by night my lamps are lit,
　How day by day my bells are ringing clear,—
Mother of ancient lore and Attic wit
　　　And discipline severe.

'And I have led my children on steep mountains
　By fine attraction of my spirit brought
Up to the dark inexplicable fountains
　　　That are the springs of thought:

'Led them, where on the old poetic shore
　The flowers that change not with the changing moon
Breathe round young hearts, as breathes the sycamore
　　　About the bees in June.

'And I will bear them as on eagle's wings,
　To leave them bow'd before the sapphire Throne,
High o'er the haunts where dying Pleasure sings
　　　With sweet and swan-like tone.

'And I will lead the age's great expansions,
　Progressive circles t'ward thought's Sabbath rest,
And point beyond them to the many mansions
　　　Where Christ is with the blest.

315.　　　*The Birthday Crown*

IF aught of simple song have power to touch
　Your silent being, O ye country flowers,
　　　Twisted by tender hands
　　　Into a royal brede,

O hawthorn, tear thou not the soft white brow
Of the small queen upon her rustic throne;
    But breathe thy finest scent
      Of almond round about.

And thou, laburnum, and what other hue
Tinct deeper gives variety of gold,
    Inwoven lily, and vetch
      Bedropp'd with summer's blood,

I charge you wither not this long June day!
O, wither not until the sunset come,
    Until the sunset's shaft
      Slope through the chestnut tree;

Until she sit, high-gloried round about
With the great light above her mimic court—
    Her threads of sunny hair
      Girt sunnily by you!

What other crown that queen may wear one day,
What drops may touch her forehead not of balm,
    What thorns, what cruel thorns,
      I will not guess to-day.

Only, before she is discrown'd of you,
Ye dying flowers, and thou, O dying light,
    My prayer shall rise—' O Christ!
      Give her the unfading crown.

' The crown of blossoms worn by happy bride,
The thorny crown o'er pale and dying lips,
    I dare not choose for her—
      Give her the unfading crown!'

ADELAIDE ANNE PROCTER

1825-1864

316. *The Warrior to His Dead Bride*

IF in the fight my arm was strong
  And forced my foes to yield,
If conquering and unhurt I come
  Back from the battle-field—
It is because thy prayers have been
  My safeguard and my shield.

Thy heart, my love, still beats in Heaven
  With the same love divine
That made thee stoop to such a soul,
  So hard, so stern, as mine—
My eyes have learnt to weep, Beloved,
  Since last they look'd on thine.

I hear thee murmur words of peace,
  Thro' the dim midnight air ;
And a calm falls from the angel stars
  And soothes my great despair—
The heavens themselves look brighter, Love,
  Since thy sweet soul is there.

1825–1892

317.   *My Beautiful Lady*

I LOVE my Lady ; she is very fair ;
Her brow is wan and bound by simple hair ;
Her spirit sits aloft and high,
But glances from her tender eye
In sweetness droopingly.

As a young forest while the wind drives thro',
My life is stirr'd when she breaks on my view ;
Her beauty grants my will no choice
But silent awe, till she rejoice
My longing with her voice.

Her warbling voice, tho' ever low and mild,
Oft makes me feel as strong wine would a child ;
And tho' her hand be airy light
Of touch, it moves me with its might
As would a sudden fright.

A hawk high poised in air, whose nerved wing-tips
Tremble with might suppress'd before he dips,
In vigilance, scarce more intense
Than I, when her voice holds my sense
Contented in suspense.

Her mention of a thing, august or poor,
Makes it far nobler than it was before :
As, where the sun strikes, life will gush
And what is pale receive a flush,
Rich hues, a richer blush.

My

My Lady's name when I hear strangers use,
Not meaning her, to me seems lax misuse ;
    I love none but my Lady's name ;
    Maud, Grace, Rose, Marian, all the same
        Are harsh, or blank and tame.

My lady walks as I have watch'd a swan
Swim where a glory on the water shone :
    There ends of willow-branches ride
    Quivering in the flowing tide,
        By the deep river's side.

Fresh beauties, howsoe'er she moves, are stirr'd ;
As the sunn'd bosom of a humming-bird
    At each pant lifts some fiery hue,
    Fierce gold, bewildering green or blue—
        The same, yet ever new.

FRANCIS TURNER PALGRAVE

1825-1897

318.   *Eutopia*

THERE is a garden where lilies
    And roses are side by side ;
And all day between them in silence
    The silken butterflies glide.

I may not enter the garden,
    Tho' I know the road thereto ;
And morn by morn to the gateway
    I see the children go.

They bring back light on their faces;
But they cannot bring back to me
What the lilies say to the roses,
Or the songs of the butterflies be.

RICHARD DODDRIDGE BLACKMORE

1825-1900

319.   *Dominus Illuminatio Mea*

IN the hour of death, after this life's whim,
When the heart beats low, and the eyes grow dim,
And pain has exhausted every limb—
The lover of the Lord shall trust in Him.

When the will has forgotten the lifelong aim,
And the mind can only disgrace its fame,
And a man is uncertain of his own name—
The power of the Lord shall fill this frame.

When the last sigh is heaved, and the last tear shed,
And the coffin is waiting beside the bed,
And the widow and child forsake the dead—
The angel of the Lord shall lift this head.

For even the purest delight may pall,
And power must fail, and the pride must fall,
And the love of the dearest friends grow small—
But the glory of the Lord is all in all.

DINAH MARIA (MULOCK) CRAIK

1826–1887

320.   *Douglas*

'*Douglas, Douglas, tender and true*'

COULD ye come back to me, Douglas, Douglas,
  In the old likeness that I knew,
I would be so faithful, so loving, Douglas,
  Douglas, Douglas, tender and true!

Never a scornful word should grieve ye,
  I'd smile on ye sweet as the angels do:
Sweet as your smile on me shone ever,
  Douglas, Douglas, tender and true.

O, to call back the days that are not!
  My eyes were blinded, your words were few:
Do you know the truth now, up in heaven,
  Douglas, Douglas, tender and true?

I never was worthy of you, Douglas—
  Not half worthy the like of you:
Now all men beside seem to me like shadows—
  I love you, Douglas, tender and true.

Stretch out your hand to me, Douglas, Douglas,
  Drop forgiveness from heaven like dew;
As I lay my heart on your dead heart, Douglas,
  Douglas, Douglas, tender and true!

436

MORTIMER COLLINS

1827-1876

321.   *Queen and Slave*

O HAPPY life, whose love is found !
    O happy love, whose life is free !
O happy strings whose soft notes sound
     Athwart the sea !

The sea has mistress in the moon,
    The moon has lover in the sea :
They meet too late, they part too soon—
     And so do we.

I am adored, yet must obey ;
    I am a queen, and yet a slave.
It seems to me the self-same way
     With moon and wave.

O be it so ! O let it be !
    O may I always rule and serve,
And live the life whose love is free,
     And never swerve !

ROBERT BARNABAS BROUGH

1828-1860

322. *An Early Christian*

CHRISTIANS were on the earth ere Christ was born ;
  His laws, not yet a code, were follow'd still
By sightless Pagans in the dark forlorn,
  Groping toward the light, as blind men will :
Thousands of years ago men dared to die
Loving their enemies—and wonder'd why !

Who that has read in Homer's truthful page
  Of brave Achilles brooding o'er the corse
Of Hector sacrificed—less to his rage
  Than iron custom's law, without remorse
Claiming revenge for mild Patroclus slain—
Can doubt he wish'd great Hector lived again ?

Full half the tears he shed were Hector's due,
  Whose noble soul he had to Hades sent.
Why—was Patroclus gainer, if they knew ?
  Methinks I see Achilles in his tent
Beating his breast and twitching at his hair,
Wanting a few words only—the Lord's Prayer !

And more for his than Priam's sake I feel
  Rejoiced when I am told the good old man
Comes with his simple fatherly appeal
  For Hector's body—pointing out a plan
Of kindliness, atonement, and of peace,
That in Achilles' breast hate's strife may cease.

What joy he must have felt to see a way
   To turn him from revenge's irksome path ;
Like a worn seaman who descries the day
   After a night-watch 'mid the tempest's wrath.
Methinks I see him in his huge arms bear
Great Hector's body, with admiring care,

And, chuckling to evade the sentries dull,
   Convey it thro' the sleeping camp with glee,
With sense of lightness, new and wonderful,
   To grateful Priam's car. 'What can it be,'
—I hear him ask—' thus makes my bosom glow,
Showing such weakness to a fallen foe ? '

WALTER THORNBURY

1828-1878

323.   *The Court Historian*

LOWER EMPIRE. *Circa* A.D. 700

THE Monk Arnulphus uncork'd his ink
   That shone with a blood-red light
Just now as the sun began to sink ;
   His vellum was pumiced a silvery white :
' The Basileus '—for so he began—
' Is a royal sagacious Mars of a man,
   Than the very lion bolder ;
He has married the stately widow of Thrace—'
   ' Hush ! ' cried a voice at his shoulder.

439

His

His palette gleam'd with a burnish'd green,
    Bright as a dragon-fly's skin :
His gold-leaf shone like the robe of a queen,
    His azure glow'd as a cloud worn thin,
Deep as the blue of the king-whale's lair :
' The Porphyrogenita Zoë the fair
    Is about to wed with a Prince much older,
Of an unpropitious mien and look—'
    ' Hush ! ' cried a voice at his shoulder.

The red flowers trellis'd the parchment page,
    The birds leap'd up on the spray,
The yellow fruit sway'd and droop'd and swung,
    It was Autumn mixt up with May.
(O, but his cheek was shrivell'd and shrunk !)
' The child of the Basileus,' wrote the Monk,
    ' Is golden-hair'd—tender the Queen's arms fold her.
Her step-mother Zoë doth love her so—'
    ' Hush ! ' cried a voice at his shoulder.

The Kings and Martyrs and Saints and Priests
    All gather'd to guard the text :
There was Daniel snug in the lions' den
    Singing no whit perplex'd—
Brazen Samson with spear and helm—
' The Queen,' wrote the Monk, 'rules firm this realm,
    For the King gets older and older.
The Norseman Thorkill is brave and fair—'
    ' Hush ! ' cried a voice at his shoulder.

DANTE GABRIEL ROSSETTI

1828-1882

324. *The Blessed Damozel*

THE blessèd damozel lean'd out
  From the gold bar of Heaven;
Her eyes were deeper than the depth
  Of waters still'd at even;
She had three lilies in her hand,
  And the stars in her hair were seven.

Her robe, ungirt from clasp to hem,
  No wrought flowers did adorn,
But a white rose of Mary's gift,
  For service meetly worn;
Her hair that lay along her back
  Was yellow like ripe corn.

Herseem'd she scarce had been a day
  One of God's choristers;
The wonder was not yet quite gone
  From that still look of hers;
Albeit, to them she left, her day
  Had counted as ten years.

(To one, it is ten years of years.
  . . . Yet now, and in this place,
Surely she lean'd o'er me—her hair
  Fell all about my face. . . .
Nothing: the autumn-fall of leaves.
  The whole year sets apace.)

441   It

It was the rampart of God's house
 That she was standing on ;
By God built over the sheer depth
 The which is Space begun ;
So high, that looking downward thence
 She scarce could see the sun.

It lies in Heaven, across the flood
 Of ether, as a bridge.
Beneath, the tides of day and night
 With flame and darkness ridge
The void, as low as where this earth
 Spins like a fretful midge.

Around her, lovers, newly met
 'Mid deathless love's acclaims,
Spoke evermore among themselves
 Their heart-remember'd names ;
And the souls mounting up to God
 Went by her like thin flames.

And still she bow'd herself and stoop'd
 Out of the circling charm ;
Until her bosom must have made
 The bar she lean'd on warm,
And the lilies lay as if asleep
 Along her bended arm.

From the fix'd place of Heaven she saw
 Time like a pulse shake fierce
Through all the worlds. Her gaze still strove
 Within the gulf to pierce
Its path ; and now she spoke as when
 The stars sang in their spheres.

The sun was gone now ; the curl'd moon
    Was like a little feather
Fluttering far down the gulf ; and now
    She spoke through the still weather.
Her voice was like the voice the stars
    Had when they sang together.

(Ah sweet ! Even now, in that bird's song,
    Strove not her accents there,
Fain to be hearkened ? When those bells
    Possess'd the mid-day air,
Strove not her steps to reach my side
    Down all the echoing stair ?)

' I wish that he were come to me :
    For he will come,' she said.
' Have I not pray'd in Heaven ?—on earth,
    Lord, Lord, has he not pray'd ?
Are not two prayers a perfect strength ?
    And shall I feel afraid ?

' When round his head the aureole clings,
    And he is clothed in white,
I'll take his hand and go with him
    To the deep wells of light ;
As unto a stream we will step down,
    And bathe there in God's sight.

' We two will stand beside that shrine,
    Occult, withheld, untrod,
Whose lamps are stirred continually
    With prayer sent up to God ;
And see our old prayers, granted, melt
    Each like a little cloud.

' We

' We two will lie i' the shadow of
   That living mystic tree,
Within whose secret growth the Dove
   Is sometimes felt to be,
While every leaf that His plumes touch
   Saith His Name audibly.

' And I myself will teach to him,
   I myself, lying so,
The songs I sing here ; which his voice
   Shall pause in, hush'd and slow,
And find some knowledge at each pause,
   Or some new thing to know.'

(Alas ! We two, we two, thou say'st !
   Yea, one wast thou with me
That once of old. But shall God lift
   To endless unity
The soul whose likeness with thy soul
   Was but its love for thee ?)

' We two,' she said, ' will seek the groves
   Where the lady Mary is,
With her five handmaidens, whose names
   Are five sweet symphonies,
Cecily, Gertrude, Magdalen,
   Margaret and Rosalys.

' Circlewise sit they, with bound locks
   And foreheads garlanded ;
Into the fine cloth white like flame
   Weaving the golden thread,
To fashion the birth-robes for them
   Who are just born, being dead.

'He shall fear, haply, and be dumb :
　　Then will I lay my cheek
To his, and tell about our love,
　　Not once abash'd or weak :
And the dear Mother will approve
　　My pride, and let me speak.

' Herself shall bring us, hand in hand,
　　To Him round whom all souls
Kneel, the clear-ranged unnumbered heads
　　Bowed with their aureoles :
And angels meeting us shall sing
　　To their citherns and citoles.

' There will I ask of Christ the Lord
　　Thus much for him and me :—
Only to live as once on earth
　　With Love,—only to be,
As then awhile, for ever now
　　Together, I and he.'

She gazed and listen'd and then said,
　　Less sad of speech than mild,—
' All this is when he comes.'　She ceased.
　　The light thrill'd towards her, fill'd
With angels in strong level flight.
　　Her eyes prayed, and she smiled.

(I saw her smile.)　But soon their path
　　Was vague in distant spheres :
And then she cast her arms along
　　The golden barriers,
And laid her face between her hands,
　　And wept.　(I heard her tears.)

325.   *Soul's Beauty*

UNDER the arch of Life, where love and death,
    Terror and mystery, guard her shrine, I saw
  Beauty enthroned; and though her gaze struck awe,
I drew it in as simply as my breath.
Hers are the eyes which, over and beneath,
    The sky and sea bend on thee,—which can draw,
    By sea or sky or woman, to one law,
The allotted bondman of her palm and wreath.

This is that Lady Beauty, in whose praise
    Thy voice and hand shake still,—long known to thee
      By flying hair and fluttering hem,—the beat
      Following her daily of thy heart and feet,
    How passionately and irretrievably,
In what fond flight, how many ways and days!

326.   *Love sight*

WHEN do I see thee most, beloved one?
    When in the light the spirits of mine eyes
  Before thy face, their altar, solemnize
The worship of that love thro' thee made known?
Or when, in the dusk hours (we two alone),
    Close-kiss'd, and eloquent of still replies
    Thy twilight hidden glimmering visage lies,
And my soul only sees thy soul its own?

O love, my love! if I no more should see
Thyself, nor on the earth the shadow of thee,
    Nor image of thine eyes in any spring,—
How then should sound upon Life's darkening slope
The ground-whirl of the perish'd leaves of Hope,
    The wind of Death's imperishable wing?

327.   *The Choice*

I

EAT thou and drink ; to-morrow thou shalt die.
  Surely the earth, that 's wise being very old,
  Needs not our help. Then loose me, love, and hold
Thy sultry hair up from my face ; that I
May pour for thee this golden wine, brim-high,
  Till round the glass thy fingers glow like gold.
  We'll drown all hours : thy song, while hours are toll'd,
Shall leap, as fountains veil the changing sky.

Now kiss, and think that there are really those,
  My own high-bosom'd beauty, who increase
    Vain gold, vain lore, and yet might choose our way !
    Through many years they toil ; then on a day
  They die not,—for their life was death,—but cease ;
And round their narrow lips the mould falls close.

II

Watch thou and fear ; to-morrow thou shalt die.
  Or art thou sure thou shalt have time for death ?
  Is not the day which God's word promiseth
To come man knows not when ?   In yonder sky,
Now while we speak, the sun speeds forth : can I
  Or thou assure him of his goal ?   God's breath
  Even at this moment haply quickeneth
The air to a flame ; till spirits, always nigh
Though screened and hid, shall walk the daylight here.
  And dost thou prate of all that man shall do ?
    Canst thou, who hast but plagues, presume to be
    Glad in his gladness that comes after thee?
  Will *his* strength slay *thy* worm in Hell ?   Go to :
Cover thy countenance, and watch, and fear !

          Think

III

Think thou and act; to-morrow thou shalt die.
　Outstretch'd in the sun's warmth upon the shore,
　　Thou say'st : ' Man's measured path is all gone o'er :
Up all his years, steeply, with strain and sigh,
Man clomb until he touch'd the truth ; and I,
　　Even I, am he whom it was destined for.'
　How should this be ? Art thou then so much more
Than they who sow'd, that thou shouldst reap thereby ?

Nay, come up hither. From this wave-wash'd mound
　Unto the furthest flood-brim look with me ;
Then reach on with thy thought till it be drown'd.
　Miles and miles distant though the last line be,
And though thy soul sail leagues and leagues beyond,—
　Still, leagues beyond those leagues, there is more sea.

GERALD MASSEY

1828–1907

328.　　　*Young Love*

ALL glorious as the Rainbow's birth
　　She came in Spring-tide's golden hours,
When Heaven went hand-in-hand with Earth,
　And May was crown'd with buds and flowers.
The mounting devil at my heart
　Clomb faintlier, as my life did win
The charmèd heaven she wrought apart
　To wake its better Angel in.
With radiant mien she trod serene
　And pass'd me smiling by—
O, who that look'd could help but love ?
　Not I, sweet soul, not I !

Her budding breasts like fragrant fruit
 Of love were ripening to be press'd :
Her voice that shook my heart's red root
 Might not have broken a Babe's rest,—
More liquid than the running brooks,
 More vernal than the voice of Spring,
When Nightingales are in their nooks,
 And all the leafy thickets ring.
The love she coyly hid at heart
 Was shyly conscious in her eye ;
O, who that look'd could help but love ?
 Not I, sweet soul, not I !

GEORGE MEREDITH

1828-1909

329. *Love in the Valley*

U NDER yonder beech-tree single on the green-sward,
 Couch'd with her arms behind her golden head,
Knees and tresses folded to slip and ripple idly,
 Lies my young love sleeping in the shade.
Had I the heart to slide an arm beneath her,
 Press her parting lips as her waist I gather slow,
Waking in amazement she could not but embrace me :
 Then would she hold me and never let me go ?

   . . .

Shy as the squirrel and wayward as the swallow,
 Swift as the swallow along the river's light
Circleting the surface to meet his mirror'd winglets,
 Fleeter she seems in her stay than in her flight.
Shy as the squirrel that leaps among the pine-tops,
 Wayward as the swallow overhead at set of sun,
She whom I love is hard to catch and conquer,
 Hard, but O the glory of the winning were she won !

   . . .

When her mother tends her before the laughing mirror,
    Tying up her laces, looping up her hair,
Often she thinks, were this wild thing wedded,
    More love should I have, and much less care.
When her mother tends her before the lighted mirror,
    Loosening her laces, combing down her curls,
Often she thinks, were this wild thing wedded,
    I should miss but one for many boys and girls.

.   .   .

Heartless she is as the shadow in the meadows
    Flying to the hills on a blue and breezy noon.
No, she is athirst and drinking up her wonder :
    Earth to her is young as the slip of the new moon.
Deals she an unkindness, 'tis but her rapid measure,
    Even as in a dance ; and her smile can heal no less :
Like the swinging May-cloud that pelts the flowers with
        hailstones
    Off a sunny border, she was made to bruise and bless.

.   .   .

Lovely are the curves of the white owl sweeping
    Wavy in the dusk lit by one large star.
Lone on the fir-branch, his rattle-note unvaried,
    Brooding o'er the gloom, spins the brown evejar.
Darker grows the valley, more and more forgetting :
    So were it with me if forgetting could be will'd.
Tell the grassy hollow that holds the bubbling well-spring,
    Tell it to forget the source that keeps it fill'd.

.   .   .

Stepping down the hill with her fair companions,
    Arm in arm, all against the raying West,
Boldly she sings, to the merry tune she marches,
    Brave is her shape, and sweeter unpossess'd.

Sweeter, for she is what my heart first awaking
   Whisper'd the world was ; morning light is she.
Love that so desires would fain keep her changeless ;
   Fain would fling the net, and fain have her free.

      .   .   .

Happy happy time, when the white star hovers
   Low over dim fields fresh with bloomy dew,
Near the face of dawn, that draws athwart the darkness,
   Threading it with colour, like yewberries the yew.
Thicker crowd the shades as the grave East deepens
   Glowing, and with crimson a long cloud swells.
Maiden still the morn is ; and strange she is, and secret ;
   Strange her eyes ; her cheeks are cold as cold sea-shells.

      .   .   .

Sunrays, leaning on our southern hills and lighting
   Wild cloud-mountains that drag the hills along,
Oft ends the day of your shifting brilliant laughter
   Chill as a dull face frowning on a song.
Ay, but shows the South-west a ripple-feather'd bosom
   Blown to silver while the clouds are shaken and ascend
Scaling the mid-heavens as they stream, there comes a
     sunset
   Rich, deep like love in beauty without end.

      .   .   .

When at dawn she sighs, and like an infant to the window
   Turns grave eyes craving light, released from dreams,
Beautiful she looks, like a white water-lily
   Bursting out of bud in havens of the streams.
When from bed she rises clothed from neck to ankle
   In her long nightgown sweet as boughs of May,
Beautiful she looks, like a tall garden-lily
   Pure from the night, and splendid for the day.

      .   .   .

                     Mother

Mother of the dews, dark eye-lash'd twilight,
   Low-lidded twilight, o'er the valley's brim,
Rounding on thy breast sings the dew-delighted skylark,
   Clear as though the dewdrops had their voice in him.
Hidden where the rose-flush drinks the rayless planet,
   Fountain-full he pours the spraying fountain-showers.
Let me hear her laughter, I would have her ever
   Cool as dew in twilight, the lark above the flowers.

.   .   .

All the girls are out with their baskets for the primrose ;
   Up lanes, woods through, they troop in joyful bands.
My sweet leads : she knows not why, but now she loiters,
   Eyes the bent anemones, and hangs her hands.
Such a look will tell that the violets are peeping,
   Coming the rose : and unaware a cry
Springs in her bosom for odours and for colour,
   Covert and the nightingale ; she knows not why.

.   .   .

Kerchief'd head and chin she darts between her tulips,
   Streaming like a willow gray in arrowy rain :
Some bend beaten cheek to gravel, and their angel
   She will be ; she lifts them, and on she speeds again.
Black the driving raincloud breasts the iron gateway :
   She is forth to cheer a neighbour lacking mirth.
So when sky and grass met rolling dumb for thunder
   Saw I once a white dove, sole light of earth.

.   ○   .

Prim little scholars are the flowers of her garden,
   Train'd to stand in rows, and asking if they please.
I might love them well but for loving more the wild ones :
   O my wild ones ! they tell me more than these.

452

GEORGE MEREDITH

You, my wild one, you tell of honied field-rose,
    Violet, blushing eglantine in life ; and even as they,
They by the wayside are earnest of your goodness,
    You are of life's, on the banks that line the way.

Peering at her chamber the white crowns the red rose,
    Jasmine winds the porch with stars two and three.
Parted is the window ; she sleeps ; the starry jasmine
    Breathes a falling breath that carries thoughts of me.
Sweeter unpossess'd, have I said of her my sweetest ?
    Not while she sleeps : while she sleeps the jasmine
       breathes,
Luring her to love ; she sleeps ; the starry jasmine
    Bears me to her pillow under white rose-wreaths.

Yellow with birdfoot-trefoil are the grass-glades ;
    Yellow with cinquefoil of the dew-gray leaf ;
Yellow with stonecrop ; the moss-mounds are yellow ;
    Blue-neck'd the wheat sways, yellowing to the sheaf.
Green-yellow, bursts from the copse the laughing yaffle ;
    Sharp as a sickle is the edge of shade and shine :
Earth in her heart laughs looking at the heavens,
    Thinking of the harvest : I look and think of mine.

This I may know : her dressing and undressing
    Such a change of light shows as when the skies in sport
Shift from cloud to moonlight ; or edging over thunder
    Slips a ray of sun ; or sweeping into port
White sails furl ; or on the ocean borders
    White sails lean along the waves leaping green.
Visions of her shower before me, but from eyesight
    Guarded she would be like the sun were she seen.

                 Front

Front door and back of the moss'd old farmhouse
   Open with the morn, and in a breezy link
Freshly sparkles garden to stripe-shadow'd orchard,
   Green across a rill where on sand the minnows wink.
Busy in the grass the early sun of summer
   Swarms, and the blackbird's mellow fluting notes
Call my darling up with round and roguish challenge :
   Quaintest, richest carol of all the singing throats !

       .   .   .

Cool was the woodside ; cool as her white dairy
   Keeping sweet the cream-pan ; and there the boys
     from school,
Cricketing below, rush'd brown and red with sunshine ;
   O the dark translucence of the deep-eyed cool !
Spying from the farm, herself she fetch'd a pitcher
   Full of milk, and tilted for each in turn the beak.
Then a little fellow, mouth up and on tiptoe,
   Said, ' I will kiss you ' : she laugh'd and lean'd her
     cheek.

       .   .   .

Doves of the fir-wood walling high our red roof
   Through the long noon coo, crooning through the coo.
Loose droop the leaves, and down the sleepy roadway
   Sometimes pipes a chaffinch ; loose droops the blue.
Cows flap a slow tail knee-deep in the river,
   Breathless, given up to sun and gnat and fly.
Nowhere is she seen ; and if I see her nowhere,
   Lightning may come, straight rains and tiger sky.

       .   .   .

O the golden sheaf, the rustling treasure-armful !
   O the nutbrown tresses nodding interlaced !
O the treasure-tresses one another over
   Nodding ! O the girdle slack about the waist !

GEORGE MEREDITH

Slain are the poppies that shot their random scarlet
    Quick amid the wheat-ears : wound about the waist,
Gather'd, see these brides of Earth one blush of ripeness !
    O the nutbrown tresses nodding interlaced !

Large and smoky red the sun's cold disk drops,
    Clipp'd by naked hills, on violet shaded snow :
Eastward large and still lights up a bower of moonrise,
    Whence at her leisure steps the moon aglow.
Nightlong on black print-branches our beech-tree
    Gazes in this whiteness : nightlong could I.
Here may life on death or death on life be painted.
    Let me clasp her soul to know she cannot die !

Gossips count her faults ; they scour a narrow chamber
    Where there is no window, read not heaven or her.
' When she was a tiny,' one agèd woman quavers,
    Plucks at my heart and leads me by the ear.
Faults she had once as she learn'd to run and tumbled :
    Faults of feature some see, beauty not complete.
Yet, good gossips, beauty that makes holy
    Earth and air, may have faults from head to feet.

Hither she comes ; she comes to me ; she lingers,
    Deepens her brown eyebrows, while in new surprise
High rise the lashes in wonder of a stranger ;
    Yet am I the light and living of her eyes.
Something friends have told her fills her heart to brim-
      ming,
    Nets her in her blushes, and wounds her, and tames.—
Sure of her haven, O like a dove alighting,
    Arms up, she dropp'd : our souls were in our names.

Soon

Soon will she lie like a white frost sunrise.
 Yellow oats and brown wheat, barley pale as rye,
Long since your sheaves have yielded to the thresher,
 Felt the girdle loosen'd, seen the tresses fly.
Soon will she lie like a blood-red sunset.
 Swift with the to-morrow, green-wing'd Spring!
Sing from the South-west, bring her back the truants,
 Nightingale and swallow, song and dipping wing.

.   .   .

Soft new beech-leaves, up to beamy April
 Spreading bough on bough a primrose mountain, you
Lucid in the moon, raise lilies to the skyfields,
 Youngest green transfused in silver shining through:
Fairer than the lily, than the wild white cherry:
 Fair as in image my seraph love appears
Borne to me by dreams when dawn is at my eyelids:
 Fair as in the flesh she swims to me on tears.

.   .   .

Could I find a place to be alone with heaven,
 I would speak my heart out: heaven is my need.
Every woodland tree is flushing like the dogwood,
 Flashing like the whitebeam, swaying like the reed.
Flushing like the dogwood crimson in October;
 Streaming like the flag-reed South-west blown;
Flashing as in gusts the sudden-lighted whitebeam:
 All seem to know what is for heaven alone.

330. *Phoebus with Admetus*

WHEN by Zeus relenting the mandate was revoked,
 Sentencing to exile the bright Sun-God,
Mindful were the ploughmen of who the steer had yoked,
 Who: and what a track show'd the upturn'd sod!

GEORGE MEREDITH

Mindful were the shepherds, as now the noon severe
   Bent a burning eyebrow to brown evetide,
How the rustic flute drew the silver to the sphere,
   Sister of his own, till her rays fell wide.
         God ! of whom music
         And song and blood are pure,
         The day is never darken'd
         That had thee here obscure.

Chirping none, the scarlet cicalas crouch'd in ranks :
   Slack the thistle-head piled its down-silk gray :
Scarce the stony lizard suck'd hollows in his flanks :
   Thick on spots of umbrage our drowsed flocks lay.
Sudden bow'd the chestnuts beneath a wind unheard,
   Lengthen'd ran the grasses, the sky grew slate :
Then amid a swift flight of wing'd seed white as curd,
   Clear of limb a Youth smote the master's gate.
         God ! of whom music
         And song and blood are pure,
         The day is never darken'd
         That had thee here obscure.

Water, first of singers, o'er rocky mount and mead,
   First of earthly singers, the sun-loved rill,
Sang of him, and flooded the ripples on the reed,
   Seeking whom to waken and what ear fill.
Water, sweetest soother to kiss a wound and cool,
   Sweetest and divinest, the sky-born brook,
Chuckled, with a whimper, and made a mirror-pool
   Round the guest we welcomed, the strange hand shook.
         God ! of whom music
         And song and blood are pure,
         The day is never darken'd
         That had thee here obscure.

Many

Many swarms of wild bees descended on our fields :
   Stately stood the wheatstalk with head bent high :
Big of heart we labour'd at storing mighty yields,
   Wool and corn, and clusters to make men cry !
Hand-like rush'd the vintage ; we strung the bellied skins
   Plump, and at the sealing the Youth's voice rose :
Maidens clung in circle, on little fists their chins ;
   Gentle beasties through push'd a cold long nose.
          God ! of whom music
          And song and blood are pure,
          The day is never darken'd
          That had thee here obscure.

Foot to fire in snowtime we trimm'd the slender shaft :
   Often down the pit spied the lean wolf's teeth
Grin against his will, trapp'd by masterstrokes of craft ;
   Helpless in his froth-wrath as green logs seethe !
Safe the tender lambs tugg'd the teats, and winter sped
   Whirl'd before the crocus, the year's new gold.
Hung the hooky beak up aloft, the arrowhead
   Redden'd through his feathers for our dear fold.
          God ! of whom music
          And song and blood are pure,
          The day is never darken'd
          That had thee here obscure.

Tales we drank of giants at war with gods above :
   Rocks were they to look on, and earth climb'd air !
Tales of search for simples, and those who sought of love
   Ease because the creature was all too fair.
Pleasant ran our thinking that while our work was good,
   Sure as fruits for sweat would the praise come fast.

He that wrestl'ed stoutest and tamed the billow-brood
  Danced in rings with girls, like a sail-flapp'd mast.
      God ! of whom music
      And song and blood are pure,
      The day is never darken'd
      That had thee here obscure.

Lo, the herb of healing, when once the herb is known,
  Shines in shady woods bright as new-sprung flame,
Ere the string was tighten'd we heard the mellow tone,
  After he had taught how the sweet sounds came.
Stretch'd about his feet, labour done, 'twas as you see
  Red pomegranates tumble and burst hard rind.
So began contention to give delight and be
  Excellent in things aim'd to make life kind.
      God ! of whom music
      And song and blood are pure,
      The day is never darken'd
      That had thee here obscure.

You with shelly horns, rams ! and, promontory goats,
  You whose browsing beards dip in coldest dew !
Bulls, that walk the pastures in kingly-flashing coats !
  Laurel, ivy, vine, wreathed for feasts not few !
You that build the shade-roof, and you that court the rays,
  You that leap besprinkling the rock stream-rent :
He has been our fellow, the morning of our days ;
  Us he chose for housemates, and this way went.
      God ! of whom music
      And song and blood are pure,
      The day is never darken'd
      That had thee here obscure.

GEORGE MEREDITH

331. *Melampus*

WITH love exceeding a simple love of the things
    That glide in grasses and rubble of woody wreck ;
Or change their perch on a beat of quivering wings
    From branch to branch, only restful to pipe and peck ;
Or, bristled, curl at a touch their snouts in a ball ;
    Or cast their web between bramble and thorny hook ;
The good physician Melampus, loving them all,
    Among them walk'd, as a scholar who reads a book.

For him the woods were a home and gave him the key
    Of knowledge, thirst for their treasures in herbs and
      flowers.
The secrets held by the creatures nearer than we
    To earth he sought, and the link of their life with ours :
And where alike we are, unlike where, and the vein'd
    Division, vein'd parallel, of a blood that flows
In them, in us, from the source by man unattain'd
    Save marks he well what the mystical woods disclose.

And this he deem'd might be boon of love to a breast
    Embracing tenderly each little motive shape,
The prone, the flitting, who seek their food whither best
    Their wits direct, whither best from their foes escape :
For closer drawn to our mother's natural milk,
    As babes they learn where her motherly help is great :
They know the juice for the honey, juice for the silk,
    And, need they medical antidotes, find them straight.

Of earth and sun they are wise, they nourish their broods
    Weave, build, hive, burrow and battle, take joy and pain
Like swimmers varying billows : never in woods
    Runs white insanity fleeing itself : all sane
The woods revolve : as the tree its shadowing limns
    To some resemblance in motion, the rooted life
Restrains disorder : you hear the primitive hymns
    Of earth in woods issue wild of the web of strife.

Now sleeping once on a day of marvellous fire
    A brood of snakes he had cherish'd in grave regret
That death his people had dealt their dam and their sire,
    Through savage dread of them, crept to his neck, and
      set
Their tongues to lick him : the swift affectionate tongue
    Of each ran licking the slumberer : then his ears
A fork'd red tongue tickled shrewdly : sudden upsprung,
    He heard a voice piping : Aye, for he has no fears !

A bird said that, in the notes of birds, and the speech
    Of men, it seem'd : and another renew'd : He moves
To learn and not to pursue, he gathers to teach ;
    He feeds his young as do we, and as we love loves.
No fears have I of a man who goes with his head
    To earth, chance looking aloft at us, kind of hand :
I feel to him as to earth of whom we are fed ;
    I pipe him much for his good could he understand.

Melampus touch'd at his ears, laid finger on wrist :
    He was not dreaming, he sensibly felt and heard.
Above, through leaves, where the tree-twigs thick inter-
      twist,
    He spied the birds and the bill of the speaking bird.

His cushion mosses in shades of various green,
   The lump'd, the antler'd, he press'd, while the sunny
    snake
Slipp'd under : draughts he had drunk of clear Hippo-
    crene,
   It seem'd, and sat with a gift of the Gods awake.

Divinely thrill'd was the man, exultingly full,
   As quick well-waters that come of the heart of earth,
Ere yet they dart in a brook are one bubble-pool
   To light and sound, wedding both at the leap of birth.
The soul of light vivid shone, a stream within stream ;
   The soul of sound from a musical shell outflew ;
Where others hear but a hum and see but a beam,
   The tongue and eye of the fountain of life he knew.

He knew the Hours : they were round him, laden with
    seed
Of hours bestrewn upon vapour, and one by one
They wing'd as ripen'd in fruit the burden decreed
   For each to scatter ; they flush'd like the buds in sun,
Bequeathing seed to successive similar rings,
   Their sisters, bearers to men of what men have earn'd :
He knew them, talk'd with the yet unredden'd ; the
    stings,
   The sweets, they warm'd at their bosoms divined,
    discern'd.

Not unsolicited, sought by diligent feet,
   By riddling fingers expanded, oft watch'd in growth
With brooding deep as the noon-ray's quickening wheat,
   Ere touch'd, the pendulous flower of the plants of sloth,
The plants of rigidness, answer'd question and squeeze,
   Revealing wherefore it bloom'd uninviting, bent,
Yet making harmony breathe of life and disease,
   The deeper chord of a wonderful instrument.

So pass'd he luminous-eyed for earth and the fates
   We arm to bruise or caress us ; his ears were charged
With tones of love in a whirl of voluble hates,
   With music wrought of distraction his heart enlarged.
Celestial-shining, though mortal, singer, though mute,
   He drew the Master of harmonies, voiced or still'd,
To seek him ; heard at the silent medicine-root
   A song, beheld in fulfilment the unfulfill'd.

Him Phoebus, lending to darkness colour and form
   Of light's excess, many lessons and counsels gave ;
Show'd Wisdom lord of the human intricate swarm,
   And whence prophetic it looks on the hives that
      rave,
And how acquired, of the zeal of love to acquire,
   And where it stands, in the centre of life a sphere ;
And Measure, mood of the lyre, the rapturous lyre,
   He said was Wisdom, and struck him the notes to
      hear.

Sweet, sweet : 't was glory of vision, honey, the breeze
   In heat, the run of the river on root and stone,
All senses joined, as the sister Pierides
   Are one, uplifting their chorus, the Nine, his own.
In stately order, evolved of sound into sight,
   From sight to sound intershifting, the man descried
The growths of earth, his adored, like day out of night,
   Ascend in song, seeing nature and song allied.

And there vitality, there, there solely in song,
   Resides, where earth and her uses to men, their needs,
Their forceful cravings, the theme are : there is it
      strong,
   The Master said : and the studious eye that reads,

         (Yea,

(Yea, even as earth to the crown of Gods on the mount),
  In links divine with the lyrical tongue is bound.
Pursue thy craft : it is music drawn of a fount
  To spring perennial ; well-spring is common ground.

Melampus dwelt among men : physician and sage,
  He served them, loving them, healing them ; sick or
    maim'd
Or them that frenzied in some delirious rage
  Outran the measure, his juice of the woods reclaim'd.
He play'd on men, as his master, Phoebus, on strings
  Melodious : as the God did he drive and check,
Through love exceeding a simple love of the things
  That glide in grasses and rubble of woody wreck.

332.   *Lucifer in Starlight*

ON a starr'd night Prince Lucifer uprose.
  Tired of his dark dominion swung the fiend
  Above the rolling ball in cloud part screen'd,
Where sinners hugg'd their spectre of repose.
Poor prey to his hot fit of pride were those.
  And now upon his western wing he lean'd,
  Now his huge bulk o'er Afric's sands careen'd,
Now the black planet shadow'd Arctic snows.
Soaring through wider zones that prick'd his scars
  With memory of the old revolt from Awe,
He reach'd a middle height, and at the stars,
Which are the brain of heaven, he look'd, and sank.
Around the ancient track march'd, rank on rank,
  The army of unalterable law.

333.   *Dirge in Woods*

A WIND sways the pines,
        And below
Not a breath of wild air;
Still as the mosses that glow
On the flooring and over the lines
Of the roots here and there.
The pine-tree drops its dead;
They are quiet, as under the sea.
Overhead, overhead
Rushes life in a race,
As the clouds the clouds chase;
        And we go,
And we drop like the fruits of the tree,
        Even we,
        Even so.

ALEXANDER SMITH

1829-1867

334.   *Scorned*

THE callow young were huddling in the nests,
    The marigold was burning in the marsh
Like a thing dipt in sunset, when he came.

My blood went up to meet him on my face,
Glad as a child that hears its father's step
And runs to meet him at the open porch.

I gave him all my being, like a flower
That flings its perfume on a vagrant breeze—
A breeze that wanders on and heeds it not.

465   His

His scorn is lying on my heart like snow,
My eyes are weary, and I fain would sleep :
The quietest sleep is underneath the ground.

Are ye around me, friends ? I cannot see,
I cannot hear the voices that I love,
I lift my hands to you from out the night !

Methought I felt a tear upon my cheek.—
Weep not, my mother ! It is time to rest,
And I am very weary ; so, good-night !

335. *Barbara*

ON the Sabbath-day,
    Through the churchyard old and gray,
Over the crisp and yellow leaves I held my rustling way ;
And amid the words of mercy, falling on my soul like
    balms,
'Mid the gorgeous storms of music—in the mellow organ-
    calms,
'Mid the upward-streaming prayers, and the rich and
    solemn psalms,
    I stood careless, Barbara.

My heart was otherwhere,
    While the organ shook the air,
And the priest, with outspread hands, bless'd the people
    with a prayer ;
But when rising to go homeward, with a mild and saint-
    like shine

Gleam'd a face of airy beauty with its heavenly eyes on
    mine—
Gleam'd and vanish'd in a moment—O that face was
    surely thine
        Out of heaven, Barbara !

      O pallid, pallid face !
      O earnest eyes of grace !
When last I saw thee, dearest, it was in another place.
You came running forth to meet me with my love-gift
    on your wrist :
The flutter of a long white dress, then all was lost in
    mist—
A purple stain of agony was on the mouth I kiss'd,
        That wild morning, Barbara.

      I search'd, in my despair,
      Sunny noon and midnight air ;
I could not drive away the thought that you were lingering
    there.
O many and many a winter night I sat when you were
    gone,
My worn face buried in my hands, beside the fire alone—
Within the dripping churchyard, the rain plashing on
    your stone,
        You were sleeping, Barbara.

      'Mong angels, do you think
      Of the precious golden link
I clasp'd around your happy arm while sitting by yon
    brink ?
Or when that night of gliding dance, of laughter and
    guitars,

Was

Was emptied of its music, and we watch'd through lattice-
    bars
The silent midnight heaven moving o'er us with its stars,
      Till the day broke, Barbara ?

      In the years I've changed ;
      Wild and far my heart has ranged,
And many sins and errors now have been on me avenged ;
But to you I have been faithful whatsoever good I lack'd :
I loved you, and above my life still hangs that love intact—
Your love the trembling rainbow, I the reckless cataract.
      Still I love you, Barbara.

      Yet, Love, I am unblest ;
      With many doubts opprest,
I wander like the desert wind without a place of rest.
Could I but win you for an hour from off that starry
    shore,
The hunger of my soul were still'd ; for Death hath told
    you more
Than the melancholy world doth know—things deeper
    than all lore
      You could teach me, Barbara.

      In vain, in vain, in vain !
      You will never come again.
There droops upon the dreary hills a mournful fringe of
    rain ;
The gloaming closes slowly round, loud winds are in the
    tree,
Round selfish shores for ever moans the hurt and wounded
    sea ;
There is no rest upon the earth, peace is with Death and
    thee—
      Barbara !

HENRY KINGSLEY

1830-1876

336.   *Magdalen*

MAGDALEN at Michael's gate
   Tirlèd at the pin ;
On Joseph's thorn sang the blackbird,
   ' Let her in ! Let her in ! '

' Hast thou seen the wounds ? ' said Michael,
   ' Know'st thou thy sin ? '
' It is evening, evening,' sang the blackbird,
   ' Let her in ! Let her in ! '

' Yes, I have seen the wounds,
   And I know my sin.'
' She knows it well, well, well,' sung the blackbird,
   ' Let her in ! Let her in ! '

' Thou bringest no offerings,' said Michael.
   ' Nought save sin.'
And the blackbird sang, ' She is sorry, sorry, sorry,
   ' Let her in ! Let her in ! '

When he had sung himself to sleep,
   And night did begin,
One came and open'd Michael's gate,
   And Magdalen went in.

EMILY DICKINSON

1830-1886

337.   *Parting*

MY life closed twice before its close ;
    It yet remains to see
If Immortality unveil
    A third event to me

So huge, so hopeless to conceive,
    As these that twice befell.
Parting is all we know of heaven,
    And all we need of hell.

CHRISTINA GEORGINA ROSSETTI

1830-1894

338.   *Bride Song*

FROM ' THE PRINCE'S PROGRESS '

TOO late for love, too late for joy,
    Too late, too late !
You loiter'd on the road too long,
    You trifled at the gate :
The enchanted dove upon her branch
    Died without a mate ;
The enchanted princess in her tower
    Slept, died, behind the grate ;
Her heart was starving all this while
    You made it wait.

470

Ten years ago, five years ago,
    One year ago,
Even then you had arrived in time,
    Though somewhat slow ;
Then you had known her living face
    Which now you cannot know :
The frozen fountain would have leap'd,
    The buds gone on to blow,
The warm south wind would have awaked
    To melt the snow.

Is she fair now as she lies ?
    Once she was fair ;
Meet queen for any kingly king,
    With gold-dust on her hair.
Now there are poppies in her locks,
    White poppies she must wear ;
Must wear a veil to shroud her face
    And the want graven there :
Or is the hunger fed at length,
    Cast off the care ?

We never saw her with a smile
    Or with a frown ;
Her bed seem'd never soft to her,
    Though toss'd of down ;
She little heeded what she wore,
    Kirtle, or wreath, or gown ;
We think her white brows often ached
    Beneath her crown,
Till silvery hairs show'd in her locks
    That used to be so brown.

We

We never heard her speak in haste :
    Her tones were sweet,
And modulated just so much
    As it was meet :
Her heart sat silent through the noise
    And concourse of the street.
There was no hurry in her hands,
    No hurry in her feet ;
There was no bliss drew nigh to her,
    That she might run to greet.

You should have wept her yesterday,
    Wasting upon her bed :
But wherefore should you weep to-day
    That she is dead ?
Lo, we who love weep not to-day,
    But crown her royal head.
Let be these poppies that we strew,
    Your roses are too red :
Let be these poppies, not for you
    Cut down and spread.

339.   *A Birthday*

MY heart is like a singing bird
    Whose nest is in a water'd shoot ;
My heart is like an apple-tree
    Whose boughs are bent with thick-set fruit ;
My heart is like a rainbow shell
    That paddles in a halcyon sea ;
My heart is gladder than all these,
    Because my love is come to me.

Raise me a daïs of silk and down ;
    Hang it with vair and purple dyes ;
Carve it in doves and pomegranates,
    And peacocks with a hundred eyes ;
Work it in gold and silver grapes,
    In leaves and silver fleurs-de-lys ;
Because the birthday of my life
    Is come, my love is come to me.

340.   *Song*

WHEN I am dead, my dearest,
    Sing no sad songs for me ;
Plant thou no roses at my head,
    Nor shady cypress tree :
Be the green grass above me
    With showers and dewdrops wet ;
And if thou wilt, remember,
    And if thou wilt, forget.

I shall not see the shadows,
    I shall not feel the rain ;
I shall not hear the nightingale
    Sing on, as if in pain ;
And dreaming through the twilight
    That doth not rise nor set,
Haply I may remember,
    And haply may forget.

473

341.   *Twice*

I TOOK my heart in my hand
  (O my love, O my love),
I said : Let me fall or stand,
  Let me live or die,
But this once hear me speak
  (O my love, O my love)—
Yet a woman's words are weak :
  You should speak, not I.

You took my heart in your hand
  With a friendly smile,
With a critical eye you scann'd,
  Then set it down,
And said, ' It is still unripe,
  Better wait awhile ;
Wait while the skylarks pipe,
  Till the corn grows brown.'

As you set it down it broke—
  Broke, but I did not wince ;
I smiled at the speech you spoke,
  At your judgement I heard :
But I have not often smiled
  Since then, nor question'd since,
Nor cared for cornflowers wild,
  Nor sung with the singing bird.

I take my heart in my hand,
  O my God, O my God,

My broken heart in my hand :
    Thou hast seen, judge Thou.
My hope was written on sand,
    O my God, O my God :
Now let Thy judgement stand—
    Yea, judge me now.

This, contemn'd of a man,
    This, marr'd one heedless day,
This heart take Thou to scan
    Both within and without :
Refine with fire its gold,
    Purge Thou its dross away—
Yea, hold it in Thy hold,
    Whence none can pluck it out.

I take my heart in my hand—
    I shall not die, but live—
Before Thy face I stand ;
    I, for Thou callest such :
All that I have I bring,
    All that I am I give,
Smile Thou and I shall sing,
    But shall not question much.

342.   *Italia, Io Ti Saluto!*

TO come back from the sweet South, to the North
    Where I was born, bred, look to die ;
Come back to do my day's work in its day,
    Play out my play—
Amen, amen, say I.

To

To see no more the country half my own,
    Nor hear the half familiar speech,
Amen, I say ; I turn to that bleak North
        Whence I came forth—
    The South lies out of reach.

But when our swallows fly back to the South,
    To the sweet South, to the sweet South,
The tears may come again into my eyes
        On the old wise,
    And the sweet name to my mouth.

343.   *Uphill*

DOES the road wind uphill all the way ?
    Yes, to the very end.
Will the day's-journey take the whole long day ?
    From morn to night, my friend.

But is there for the night a resting-place ?
    A roof for when the slow, dark hours begin.
May not the darkness hide it from my face ?
    You cannot miss that inn.

Shall I meet other wayfarers at night ?
    Those who have gone before.
Then must I knock, or call when just in sight ?
    They will not keep you waiting at that door.

Shall I find comfort, travel-sore and weak ?
    Of labour you shall find the sum.
Will there be beds for me and all who seek ?
    Yea, beds for all who come.

344.   *Remember*

REMEMBER me when I am gone away,
   Gone far away into the silent land ;
  When you can no more hold me by the hand,
Nor I half turn to go, yet turning stay.
Remember me when no more day by day
   You tell me of our future that you plann'd :
   Only remember me ; you understand
It will be late to counsel then or pray.
Yet if you should forget me for a while
   And afterwards remember, do not grieve :
   For if the darkness and corruption leave
   A vestige of the thoughts that once I had,
Better by far you should forget and smile
   Than that you should remember and be sad.

345.   *Aloof*

THE irresponsive silence of the land,
   The irresponsive sounding of the sea,
  Speak both one message of one sense to me :—
Aloof, aloof, we stand aloof, so stand
Thou too aloof, bound with the flawless band
   Of inner solitude ; we bind not thee ;
   But who from thy self-chain shall set thee free ?
What heart shall touch thy heart ? What hand thy hand ?
And I am sometimes proud and sometimes meek,
   And sometimes I remember days of old
When fellowship seem'd not so far to seek,
   And all the world and I seem'd much less cold,
   And at the rainbow's foot lay surely gold,
And hope felt strong, and life itself not weak.

346.   *Rest*

O EARTH, lie heavily upon her eyes ;
    Seal her sweet eyes weary of watching, Earth ;
Lie close around her ; leave no room for mirth
With its harsh laughter, nor for sound of sighs.
She hath no questions, she hath no replies,
    Hush'd in and curtain'd with a blessèd dearth
    Of all that irk'd her from the hour of birth ;
With stillness that is almost Paradise.
Darkness more clear than noonday holdeth her,
    Silence more musical than any song ;
Even her very heart has ceased to stir :
Until the morning of Eternity
Her rest shall not begin nor end, but be ;
    And when she wakes she will not think it long.

347.   *Bride Song*

W HO is this that cometh up not alone
    From the fiery-flying-serpent wilderness,
Leaning upon her own Beloved One :
    Who is this ?

    Lo, the King of kings' daughter, a high princess,
Going home as bride to her Husband's Throne,
    Virgin queen in perfected loveliness.

Her eyes a dove's eyes and her voice a dove's moan,
    She shows like a full moon for heavenliness :
Eager saints and angels ask in Heaven's zone,
    Who is this ?

348.   *A Prayer*

CLOTHER of the lily, Feeder of the sparrow,
  Father of the fatherless, dear Lord,
Tho' Thou set me as a mark against Thine arrow,
  As a prey unto Thy sword,
As a plough'd-up field beneath Thy harrow,
  As a captive in Thy cord,
Let that cord be love ; and some day make my narrow
  Hallow'd bed according to Thy Word.   Amen.

349.   *Passing Away*

PASSING away, saith the World, passing away :
  Chances, beauty and youth sapp'd day by day :
Thy life never continueth in one stay.
Is the eye waxen dim, is the dark hair changing to gray
That hath won neither laurel nor bay ?
I shall clothe myself in Spring and bud in May :
Thou, root-stricken, shalt not rebuild thy decay
On my bosom for aye.
Then I answer'd : Yea.

Passing away, saith my Soul, passing away :
With its burden of fear and hope, of labour and play,
Hearken what the past doth witness and say :
Rust in thy gold, a moth is in thine array,
A canker is in thy bud, thy leaf must decay.
At midnight, at cockcrow, at morning, one certain day,
Lo, the Bridegroom shall come and shall not delay :
Watch thou and pray.
Then I answer'd : Yea.

Passing away, saith my God, passing away :
Winter passeth after the long delay :
New grapes on the vine, new figs on the tender spray,
Turtle calleth turtle in Heaven's May.
Though I tarry, wait for me, trust me, watch and pray.
Arise, come away ; night is past, and lo, it is day ;
My love, my sister, my spouse, thou shalt hear me say—
Then I answer'd : Yea.

350.   *Marvel of Marvels*

MARVEL of marvels, if I myself shall behold
    With mine own eyes my King in his city of gold ;
Where the least of lambs is spotless white in the fold,
Where the least and last of saints in spotless white is stoled,
Where the dimmest head beyond a moon is aureoled.
O saints, my belovèd, now mouldering to mould in the
    mould,
Shall I see you lift your heads, see your cerements
    unroll'd,
See with these very eyes ? who now in darkness and cold
Tremble for the midnight cry, the rapture, the tale
    untold,—
The Bridegroom cometh, cometh, his Bride to enfold !

Cold it is, my belovèd, since your funeral bell was toll'd :
Cold it is, O my King, how cold alone on the wold !

351. *Wisdom*

WISEST of sparrows that sparrow which sitteth alone
    Perch'd on the housetop, its own upper chamber,
    for nest ;
Wisest of swallows that swallow which timely has flown
    Over the turbulent sea to the land of its rest :
    Wisest of sparrows and swallows, if I were as wise !
Wisest of spirits that spirit which dwelleth apart
    Hid in the Presence of God for a chapel and nest,
Sending a wish and a will and a passionate heart
    Over the eddy of life to that Presence in rest :
    Seated alone and in peace till God bids it arise.

352. *Last Prayer*

BEFORE the beginning Thou hast foreknown the end,
    Before the birthday the death-bed was seen of Thee :
Cleanse what I cannot cleanse, mend what I cannot mend,
    O Lord All-Merciful, be merciful to me.

While the end is drawing near I know not mine end ;
    Birth I recall not, my death I cannot foresee :
O God, arise to defend, arise to befriend,
    O Lord All-Merciful, be merciful to me.

JEAN INGELOW

1820–1897

353. *The High Tide on the Coast of Lincolnshire, 1571*

THE old mayor climb'd the belfry tower,
  The ringers ran by two, by three;
' Pull, if ye never pull'd before;
  Good ringers, pull your best,' quoth he.
' Play uppe, play uppe, O Boston bells!
Ply all your changes, all your swells,
    Play uppe " The Brides of Enderby ".'

Men say it was a stolen tyde—
  The Lord that sent it, He knows all;
But in myne ears doth still abide
  The message that the bells let fall:
And there was naught of strange, beside
The flights of mews and peewits pied
    By millions crouch'd on the old sea wall.

I sat and spun within the doore,
  My thread brake off, I raised myne eyes;
The level sun, like ruddy ore,
  Lay sinking in the barren skies,
And dark against day's golden death
She moved where Lindis wandereth,
My sonne's fair wife, Elizabeth.

'Cusha! Cusha! Cusha!' calling,
Ere the early dews were falling,
Farre away I heard her song.
'Cusha! Cusha!' all along
Where the reedy Lindis floweth,
    Floweth, floweth;
From the meads where melick groweth
Faintly came her milking song—

'Cusha! Cusha! Cusha!' calling,
'For the dews will soone be falling;
Leave your meadow grasses mellow,
    Mellow, mellow;
Quit your cowslips, cowslips yellow;
Come uppe Whitefoot, come uppe Lightfoot,
Quit the stalks of parsley hollow,
    Hollow, hollow;
Come uppe Jetty, rise and follow,
From the clovers lift your head;
Come uppe Whitefoot, come uppe Lightfoot,
Come uppe Jetty, rise and follow,
Jetty, to the milking shed.'

If it be long, ay, long ago,
   When I beginne to think howe long,
Againe I hear the Lindis flow,
   Swift as an arrowe, sharp and strong;
And all the aire, it seemeth mee,
Bin full of floating bells (sayth shee),
That ring the tune of Enderby.

Alle fresh the level pasture lay,
   And not a shadowe mote be seene,
Save where full fyve good miles away
   The steeple tower'd from out the greene;

And

And lo ! the great bell farre and wide
Was heard in all the country side
That Saturday at eventide.

The swanherds where their sedges are
    Moved on in sunset's golden breath,
The shepherde lads I heard afarre,
    And my sonne's wife, Elizabeth ;
Till floating o'er the grassy sea
Came downe that kyndly message free,
The ' Brides of Mavis Enderby '.

Then some look'd uppe into the sky,
    And all along where Lindis flows
To where the goodly vessels lie,
    And where the lordly steeple shows.
They sayde, ' And why should this thing be ?
What danger lowers by land or sea ?
They ring the tune of Enderby !

' For evil news from Mablethorpe,
    Of pyrate galleys warping down ;
For shippes ashore beyond the scorpe,
    They have not spared to wake the towne ;
But while the west bin red to see,
And storms be none, and pyrates flee,
Why ring " The Brides of Enderby " ? '

I look'd without, and lo ! my sonne
    Came riding downe with might and main :
He raised a shout as he drew on,
    Till all the welkin rang again,
' Elizabeth ! Elizabeth ! '
(A sweeter woman ne'er drew breath
Than my sonne's wife, Elizabeth.)

' The olde sea wall (he cried) is downe,
　　The rising tide comes on apace,
And boats adrift in yonder towne
　　Go sailing uppe the market-place.'
He shook as one that looks on death :
　God save you, mother ! ' straight he saith ;
' Where is my wife, Elizabeth ? '

' Good sonne, where Lindis winds away,
　　With her two bairns I mark'd her long ;
And ere yon bells beganne to play
　　Afar I heard her milking song.'
He looked across the grassy lea,
To right, to left, ' Ho Enderby ! '
They rang ' The Brides of Enderby ! '

With that he cried and beat his breast ;
　　For, lo ! along the river's bed
A mighty eygre reared his crest,
　　And uppe the Lindis raging sped.
It swept with thunderous noises loud ;
Shaped like a curling snow-white cloud,
Or like a demon in a shroud.

And rearing Lindis backward press'd
　　Shook all her trembling bankes amaine ;
Then madly at the eygre's breast
　　Flung uppe her weltering walls again.
Then bankes came downe with ruin and rout—
Then beaten foam flew round about—
Then all the mighty floods were out.

So

So farre, so fast the eygre drave,
　　The heart had hardly time to beat,
Before a shallow seething wave
　　Sobbed in the grasses at oure feet :
The feet had hardly time to flee
Before it brake against the knee,
And all the world was in the sea.

Upon the roofe we sate that night,
　　The noise of bells went sweeping by ;
I mark'd the lofty beacon light
　　Stream from the church tower, red and high—
A lurid mark and dread to see ;
And awsome bells they were to mee,
That in the dark rang ' Enderby '.

They rang the sailor lads to guide
　　From roofe to roofe who fearless row'd ;
And I—my sonne was at my side,
　　And yet the ruddy beacon glow'd ;
And yet he moan'd beneath his breath,
' O come in life, or come in death !
O lost ! my love, Elizabeth.'

And didst thou visit him no more ?
　　Thou didst, thou didst, my daughter deare ;
The waters laid thee at his doore,
　　Ere yet the early dawn was clear.
Thy pretty bairns in fast embrace,
The lifted sun shone on thy face,
Downe drifted to thy dwelling-place.

That flow strew'd wrecks about the grass,
That ebbe swept out the flocks to sea ;
A fatal ebbe and flow, alas !
　　To manye more than myne and mee :

But each will mourn his own (she saith),
And sweeter woman ne'er drew breath
Than my sonne's wife, Elizabeth.

   I shall never hear her more
    By the reedy Lindis shore,
' Cusha ! Cusha ! Cusha ! ' calling,
Ere the early dews be falling ;
I shall never hear her song,
' Cusha ! Cusha ! ' all along
Where the sunny Lindis floweth,
     Goeth, floweth ;
From the meads where melick groweth,
When the water winding down,
Onward floweth to the town.

I shall never see her more
Where the reeds and rushes quiver,
     Shiver, quiver ;
Stand beside the sobbing river,
Sobbing, throbbing, in its falling
To the sandy lonesome shore ;
I shall never hear her calling,
Leave your meadow grasses mellow,
     Mellow, mellow ;
Quit your cowslips, cowslips yellow ;
Come uppe Whitefoot, come uppe Lightfoot ;
Quit your pipes of parsley hollow,
     Hollow, hollow ;
Come uppe Lightfoot, rise and follow ;
     Lightfoot, Whitefoot,
From your clovers lift the head ;
Come uppe Jetty, follow, follow,
Jetty, to the milking shed.

354.   *Apprenticed*

He sings :

COME out and hear the waters shoot, the owlet hoot,
  the owlet hoot ;
  Yon crescent moon, a golden boat, hangs dim behind
    the tree, O !
The dropping thorn makes white the grass, O sweetest
    lass, and sweetest lass ;
  Come out and smell the ricks of hay adown the croft
    with me, O !

She answers :

My granny nods before her wheel, and drops her reel,
    and drops her reel ;
  My father with his crony talks as gay as gay can be, O !
But all the milk is yet to skim, ere light wax dim, ere
    light wax dim ;
  How can I step adown the croft, my 'prentice lad, with
    thee, O ?

He replies :

And must ye bide, yet waiting 's long, and love is strong,
    and love is strong ;
  And O, had I but served the time that takes so long
    to flee, O !
And thou, my lass, by morning light wast all in white,
    wast all in white,
  And parson stood within the rails, a-marrying me and
    thee, O !

JEAN INGELOW

355. *For Exmoor*

FOR Exmoor—
   For Exmoor, where the red deer run, my weary
     heart doth cry :
She that will a rover wed, far her feet shall hie.
Narrow, narrow, shows the street, dull the narrow sky.
   —Buy my cherries, whiteheart cherries, good my masters,
     buy !

For Exmoor—
O he left me, left alone, aye to think and sigh—
' Lambs feed down yon sunny coombe, hind and yearling
     shy
Mid the shrouding vapours walk now like ghosts on high.'
   —Buy my cherries, blackheart cherries, lads and lasses,
     buy !

For Exmoor—
Dear my dear, why did ye so ? Evil day have I ;
Mark no more the antler'd stag, hear the curlew cry,
Milking at my father's gate while he leans anigh.
   —Buy my cherries, whiteheart, blackheart, golden girls,
     O buy !

THOMAS EDWARD BROWN

1830-1897

356. *Opifex*

AS I was carving images from clouds,
   And tinting them with soft ethereal dyes
Pressed from the pulp of dreams, one comes, and cries :—
' Forbear ! ' and all my heaven with gloom enshrouds.

                    ' Forbear !

' Forbear ! Thou hast no tools wherewith to essay
  The delicate waves of that elusive grain :
  Wouldst have due recompense of vulgar pain ?
The potter's wheel for thee, and some coarse clay !

' So work, if work thou must, O humbly skill'd !
  Thou hast not known the Master ; in thy soul
  His spirit moves not with a sweet control ;
Thou art outside, and art not of the guild.'

Thereat I rose, and from his presence pass'd,
  But, going, murmur'd :—' To the God above,
  Who holds my heart, and knows its store of love,
I turn from thee, thou proud iconoclast.'

Then on the shore God stoop'd to me, and said :—
  ' He spake the truth : even so the springs are set
  That move thy life, nor will they suffer let,
Nor change their scope ; else, living, thou wert dead.

' This is thy life : indulge its natural flow,
  And carve these forms. They yet may find a place
  On shelves for them reserved. In any case,
I bid thee carve them, knowing what I know.'

357. *Catherine Kinrade*

[A poor Manxwoman, mother of four base-born children,
sundry times (1713-1720) dragged through the sea for punishment
by order of Thomas Wilson, Bishop of Sodor and Man.]

NONE spake when Wilson stood before
    The throne—
And He that sat thereon
Spake not ; and all the presence-floor

Burnt deep with blushes, as the angels cast
Their faces downwards.   Then at last,
Awe-stricken, he was 'ware
How on the emerald stair
A woman sat, divinely clothed in white,
And at her knees four cherubs bright,
That laid
Their heads within her lap.   Then, trembling, he essay'd
To speak :—' Christ's mother, pity me ! '
Then answered she :—
' Sir, I am Catherine Kinrade.'
Even so—the poor dull brain,
Drench'd in unhallow'd fire,
It had no vigour to restrain—
God's image trodden in the mire
Of impious wrongs—whom last he saw
Gazing with animal awe
Before his harsh tribunal, proved unchaste,
Incorrigible, woman's form defaced
To uttermost ruin by no fault of hers—
So gave her to the torturers ;
And now—some vital spring adjusted,
Some faculty that rusted
Cleansed to legitimate use—
Some undeveloped action stirr'd, some juice
Of God's distilling dropt into the core
Of all her life—no more
In that dark grave entomb'd,
Her soul had bloom'd
To perfect woman—swift celestial growth
That mocks our temporal sloth—
To perfect woman—woman made to honour,
With all the glory of her youth upon her.
And from her lips and from her eyes there flow'd

A smile

A smile that lit all heaven ; the angels smiled ;
God smiled, if that were smile beneath the state that
 glow'd
Soft purple—and a voice :—' Be reconciled ! '
So to his side the children crept,
And Catherine kiss'd him, and he wept.
Then said a seraph :—' Lo ! he is forgiven.'
And for a space again there was no voice in Heaven.

358. *The Organist in Heaven*

[SAMUEL SEBASTIAN WESLEY]

WHEN Wesley died, the Angelic orders,
  To see him at the state,
Press'd so incontinent that the warders
  Forgot to shut the gate.
So I, that hitherto had follow'd
  As one with grief o'ercast,
Where for the doors a space was hollow'd,
  Crept in, and heard what pass'd.
And God said :—' Seeing thou hast given
  Thy life to my great sounds,
Choose thou through all the cirque of Heaven
  What most of bliss redounds.'
Then Wesley said :—' I hear the thunder
  Low growling from Thy seat—
Grant me that I may bind it under
  The trampling of my feet.'
And Wesley said :—' See, lightning quivers
  Upon the presence walls—
Lord, give me of it four great rivers,
  To be my manuals.'

And then I saw the thunder chidden
  As slave to his desire ;
And then I saw the space bestridden
  With four great bands of fire ;
And stage by stage, stop stop subtending,
  Each lever strong and true,
One shape inextricable blending,
  The awful organ grew.
Then certain angels clad the Master
  In very marvellous wise,
Till clouds of rose and alabaster
  Conceal'd him from mine eyes.
And likest to a dove soft brooding,
  The innocent figure ran ;
So breathed the breath of his preluding,
  And then the fugue began—
Began ; but, to his office turning,
  The porter swung his key ;
Wherefore, although my heart was yearning,
  I had to go ; but he
Play'd on ; and, as I downward clomb,
  I heard the mighty bars
Of thunder-gusts, that shook heaven's dome,
  And moved the balanced stars.

359.   *Salve !*

TO live within a cave—it is most good ;
  But, if God make a day,
    And some one come, and say,
' Lo ! I have gather'd faggots in the wood ! '
    E'en let him stay,
And light a fire, and fan a temporal mood !

So

So sit till morning ! when the light is grown
    That he the path can read,
    Then bid the man God-speed !
His morning is not thine : yet must thou own
They have a cheerful warmth—those ashes on the stone.

360.   *My Garden*

A GARDEN is a lovesome thing, God wot !
    Rose plot,
  Fringed pool,
Fern'd grot—
    The veriest school
    Of peace ; and yet the fool
Contends that God is not—
Not God ! in gardens ! when the eve is cool ?
    Nay, but I have a sign ;
    'Tis very sure God walks in mine.

361.   *Preparation*

HAST thou a cunning instrument of play,
    'Tis well ; but see thou keep it bright,
And tuned to primal chords, so that it may
Be ready day and night.
For when He comes thou know'st not, who shall say :—
' These virginals are apt ' ; and try a note,
And sit, and make sweet solace of delight,
That men shall stand to listen on the way,
And all the room with heavenly music float.

362.   *When Love meets Love*

WHEN love meets love, breast urged to breast,
      God interposes,
An unacknowledged guest,
And leaves a little child among our roses.

We love, God makes : in our sweet mirth
God spies occasion for a birth.
Then is it His, or is it ours ?
I know not—He is fond of flowers.

EDWARD ROBERT BULWER LYTTON
FIRST EARL OF LYTTON

1831-1892

363.   *The Chess-Board*

IRENE, do you yet remember
      Ere we were grown so sadly wise,
Those evenings in the bleak December,
Curtain'd warm from the snowy weather,
When you and I play'd chess together,
      Checkmated by each other's eyes ?
      Ah, still I see your soft white hand
Hovering warm o'er Queen and Knight,
      Brave Pawns in valiant battle stand :
The double Castles guard the wings :
The Bishop, bent on distant things,
Moves, sidling, through the fight,
      Our fingers touch ; our glances meet,
      And falter ; falls your golden hair
      Against my cheek ; your bosom sweet
Is heaving.   Down the field, your Queen
Rides slow her soldiery all between,
      And checks me unaware.

Ah me !

Ah me! the little battle's done,
Disperst is all its chivalry;
Full many a move, since then, have we
'Mid Life's perplexing chequers made,
And many a game with Fortune play'd,—
    What is it we have won?
    This, this at least—if this alone;—
That never, never, never more,
As in those old still nights of yore,
    (Ere we were grown so sadly wise)
    Can you and I shut out the skies,
Shut out the world, and wintry weather,
And, eyes exchanging warmth with eyes,
Play chess, as then we play'd, together!

364.   *Tempora Acta*

O FOR the times which were (if any
    Time be heroic) heroic indeed!
    When the men were few,
    And the deeds to do
Were mighty and many,
    And each man in his hand held a noble deed.
    Now the deeds are few,
        And the men are many,
        And each man has, at most, but a noble need.

365.   *The Last Wish*

SINCE all that I can ever do for thee
    Is to do nothing, this my prayer must be:
That thou mayst never guess nor ever see
The all-endured this nothing-done costs me.

496

JOSEPH SKIPSEY

1832-1903

366.   *The Violet and the Rose*

THE Violet invited my kiss,—
    I kiss'd it and call'd it my bride :
' Was ever one slighted like this ? '
    Sigh'd the Rose as it stood by my side.

My heart ever open to grief,
    To comfort the fair one I turn'd :
' Of fickle ones thou art the chief ! '
    Frown'd the Violet and pouted and mourn'd.

Then, to end all disputes I entwined
    The love-stricken blossoms in one ;
But that instant their beauty declined,
    And I wept for the deed I had done !

367.   *A Merry Bee*

A GOLDEN bee a-cometh
    O'er the mere, glassy mere,
And a merry tale he hummeth
    In my ear.

How he seized and kiss'd a blossom
    From its true thorny tree,
Pluck'd and placed in Annie's bosom,
    Hums the bee !

368.   *Dewdrop, Wind and Sun*

I

AH, be not vain ! In yon flower-bell
      As rare a pearl did I appear,
As ever grew in ocean shell,
      To dangle at a Helen's ear.

So was I till a cruel blast
      Arose and swept me to the ground,
When, in a jewel of the past,
      Earth but a drop of water found.

II

'Queen Pearl's our equal—nay,
      A fairer far am I,' May Dewdrop said,
As Sol at break of day
      Did kiss the sparkler on her grass-blade bed.

'None may my charms resist !'
      'None,' Sol still kissing answer'd, when alas !
The proud one turn'd to mist,
      And with her pride did into Lethe pass.

369.   *Mother Wept*

MOTHER wept, and father sigh'd ;
      With delight aglow
Cried the lad, ' To-morrow ', cried,
      ' To the pit I go.'

Up and down the place he sped,—
      Greeted old and young ;
Far and wide the tidings spread ;
      Clapt his hands and sung.

JOSEPH SKIPSEY

Came his cronies ; some to gaze
  Wrapp'd in wonder ; some
Free with counsel ; some with praise ;
  Some with envy dumb.

' May he ', many a gossip cried,
  ' Be from peril kept.'
Father hid his face and sigh'd,
  Mother turn'd and wept.

SIR EDWIN ARNOLD

1832-1904

370. *To a Pair of Egyptian Slippers*

TINY slippers of gold and green,
  Tied with a mouldering golden cord !
What pretty feet they must have been
  When Caesar Augustus was Egypt's lord !
Somebody graceful and fair you were !
  Not many girls could dance in these !
When did your shoemaker make you, dear,
  Such a nice pair of Egyptian ' threes ' ?

Where were you measured ? In Saïs, or On,
  Memphis, or Thebes, or Pelusium ?
Fitting them neatly your brown toes upon,
  Lacing them deftly with finger and thumb,
I seem to see you !—so long ago,
  Twenty-one centuries, less or more !
And here are your sandals : yet none of us know
  What name, or fortune, or face you bore.

Your

Your lips would have laugh'd, with a rosy scorn,
  If the merchant, or slave-girl, had mockingly said,
' The feet will pass, but the shoes they have worn
  Two thousand years onward Time's road shall tread,
And still be footgear as good as new ! '
  To think that calf-skin, gilded and stitch'd,
Should Rome and the Pharaohs outlive—and you
  Be gone, like a dream, from the world you bewitch'd !

Not that we mourn you ! 'Twere too absurd !
  You have been such a long while away !
Your dry spiced dust would not value one word
  Of the soft regrets that my verse could say.
Sorrow and Pleasure, and Love and Hate,
  If you ever felt them, have vaporized hence
To this odour—so subtle and delicate—
  Of myrrh, and cassia, and frankincense.

Of course they embalm'd you ! Yet not so sweet
  Were aloes and nard, as the youthful glow
Which Amenti stole when the small dark feet
  Wearied of treading our world below.
Look ! it was flood-time in valley of Nile,
  Or a very wet day in the Delta, dear !
When your slippers tripp'd lightly their latest mile—
  The mud on the soles renders that fact clear.

You knew Cleopatra, no doubt ! You saw
  Antony's galleys from Actium come.
But there ! if questions could answers draw
  From lips so many a long age dumb,
I would not teaze you with history,
  Nor vex your heart for the men that were ;
The one point to learn that would fascinate me
  Is, where and what are you to-day, my dear !

You died, believing in Horus and Pasht,
   Isis, Osiris, and priestly lore ;
And found, of course, such theories smash'd
   By actual fact on the heavenly shore.
What next did you do ? Did you transmigrate ?
   Have we seen you since, all modern and fresh ?
Your charming soul—so I calculate—
   Mislaid its mummy, and sought new flesh.

Were you she whom I met at dinner last week,
   With eyes and hair of the Ptolemy black,
Who still of this find in the Fayoum would speak,
   And to Pharaohs and scarabs still carry us back ?
A scent of lotus about her hung,
   And she had such a far-away wistful air
As of somebody born when the Earth was young ;
   And she wore of gilt slippers a lovely pair.

Perchance you were married ? These might have been
   Part of your *trousseau*—the wedding shoes ;
And you laid them aside with the garments green,
   And painted clay Gods which a bride would use ;
And, may be, to-day, by Nile's bright waters
   Damsels of Egypt in gowns of blue—
Great-great-great—very great—grand-daughters
   Owe their shapely insteps to you !

But vainly I beat at the bars of the Past,
   Little green slippers with golden strings !
For all you can tell is that leather will last
   When loves, and delightings, and beautiful things
Have vanish'd, forgotten—No ! not quite that !
   I catch some gleam of the grace you wore
When you finish'd with Life's daily pit-a-pat,
   And left your shoes at Death's bedroom door

        You

You were born in the Egypt which did not doubt ;
   You were never sad with our new-fashion'd sorrows :
You were sure, when your play-days on Earth ran out,
   Of play-times to come, as we of our morrows !
Oh, wise little Maid of the Delta ! I lay
   Your shoes in your mummy-chest back again,
And wish that one game we might merrily play
   At ' Hunt the Slippers '—to see it all plain.

ADAM LINDSAY GORDON

1833-1870

371. *Whisperings in Wattle-Boughs*

O, GAILY sings the bird ! and the wattle-boughs are
   stirr'd
   And rustled by the scented breath of spring ;
O, the dreary wistful longing ! O, the faces that are
    thronging !
   O, the voices that are vaguely whispering !

O, tell me, father mine, ere the good ship cross'd the
    brine,
   On the gangway one mute hand-grip we exchang'd,
Do you, past the grave, employ, for your stubborn, reckless
    boy,
   Those petitions that in life were ne'er estrang'd ?

O, tell me, sister dear, parting word and parting tear
   Never pass'd between us ;—let me bear the blame,
Are you living, girl, or dead ? bitter tears since then I've
    shed
   For the lips that lisp'd with mine a mother's name.

O, tell me, ancient friend, ever ready to defend
   In our boyhood, at the base of life's long hill,
Are you waking yet or sleeping ? have you left this vale
    of weeping ?
   Or do you, like your comrade, linger still ?

O, whisper, buried love, is there rest and peace above ?—
   There is little hope or comfort here below ;
On your sweet face lies the mould, and your bed is
    straight and cold—
   Near the harbour where the sea-tides ebb and flow.

All silent—they are dumb—and the breezes go and come
   With an apathy that mocks at man's distress ;
Laugh, scoffer, while you may ! I could bow me down
    and pray
   For an answer that might stay my bitterness.

O, harshly screams the bird ! and the wattle-bloom is
    stirr'd ;
   There 's a sullen, weird-like whisper in the bough :
' Aye, kneel, and pray, and weep, but HIS BELOVED SLEEP
   CAN NEVER BE DISTURB'D BY SUCH AS THOU ! '

372.   *The Sick Stockrider*

HOLD hard, Ned ! Lift me down once more, and
   lay me in the shade.
  Old man, you've had your work cut out to guide
Both horses, and to hold me in the saddle when I sway'd,
   All through the hot, slow, sleepy, silent ride.
The dawn at 'Moorabinda' was a mist-rack dull and dense,
   The sunrise was a sullen, sluggish lamp ;
I was dozing in the gateway at Arbuthnot's bound'ry
    fence,
   I was dreaming on the Limestone cattle camp.

     We

We cross'd the creek at Carricksford, and sharply through
    the haze,
  And suddenly the sun shot flaming forth;
To southward lay 'Katâwa', with the sandpeaks all ablaze,
  And the flush'd fields of Glen Lomond lay to north.
Now westward winds the bridle path that leads to Lindis-
    farm,
  And yonder looms the double-headed Bluff;
From the far side of the first hill, when the skies are clear
    and calm,
  You can see Sylvester's woolshed fair enough.
Five miles we used to call it from our homestead to the
    place
  Where the big tree spans the roadway like an arch;
'Twas here we ran the dingo down that gave us such
    a chase
  Eight years ago—or was it nine?—last March.

'Twas merry in the glowing morn, among the gleaming
    grass,
  To wander as we've wander'd many a mile,
And blow the cool tobacco cloud, and watch the white
    wreaths pass,
  Sitting loosely in the saddle all the while.
'Twas merry 'mid the blackwoods, when we spied the
    station roofs,
  To wheel the wild scrub cattle at the yard,
With a running fire of stockwhips and a fiery run of hoofs;
  O! the hardest day was never then too hard!

Aye! we had a glorious gallop after ' Starlight ' and his
    gang,
  When they bolted from Sylvester's on the flat;
How the sun-dried reed-beds crackled, how the flint-
    strewn ranges rang
    To the strokes of ' Mountaineer ' and ' Acrobat '.

Hard behind them in the timber, harder still across the
heath,
  Close beside them through the tea-tree scrub we dash'd;
And the golden-tinted fern leaves, how they rustled
underneath !
  And the honeysuckle osiers, how they crash'd !

We led the hunt throughout, Ned, on the chestnut and
the grey,
  And the troopers were three hundred yards behind,
While we emptied our six-shooters on the bushrangers
at bay,
  In the creek with stunted box-tree for a blind !
There you grappled with the leader, man to man and
horse to horse,
  And you roll'd together when the chestnut rear'd ;
He blazed away and miss'd you in that shallow water-
course—
  A narrow shave—his powder singed your beard !

In these hours when life is ebbing, how those days when
life was young
  Come back to us ; how clearly I recall
Even the yarns Jack Hall invented, and the songs Jem
Roper sung ;
  And where are now Jem Roper and Jack Hall ?

Aye ! nearly all our comrades of the old colonial school,
  Our ancient boon companions, Ned, are gone ;
Hard livers for the most part, somewhat reckless as a rule,
  It seems that you and I are left alone.

There was Hughes, who got in trouble through that
business with the cards,
  It matters little what became of him ;

But

But a steer ripp'd up MacPherson in the Cooraminta
    yards,
    And Sullivan was drown'd at Sink-or-swim ;
And Mostyn—poor Frank Mostyn—died at last a fearful
    wreck,
    In ' the horrors ', at the Upper Wandinong,
And Carisbrooke, the rider, at the Horsefall broke his neck,
    Faith ! the wonder was he saved his neck so long !
Ah ! those days and nights we squander'd at the Logans'
    in the glen—
    The Logans, man and wife, have long been dead.
Elsie's tallest girl seems taller than your little Elsie then ;
    And Ethel is a woman grown and wed.

I've had my share of pastime, and I've done my share
    of toil,
    And life is short—the longest life a span ;
I care not now to tarry for the corn or for the oil,
    Or the wine that maketh glad the heart of man.
For good undone and gifts misspent and resolutions vain,
    'Tis somewhat late to trouble.   This I know—
I should live the same life over, if I had to live again ;
    And the chances are I go where most men go.

The deep blue skies wax dusky, and the tall green trees
    grow dim,
    The sward beneath me seems to heave and fall ;
And sickly, smoky shadows through the sleepy sunlight
    swim,
    And on the very sun's face weave their pall.
Let me slumber in the hollow where the wattle blossoms
    wave,
    With never stone or rail to fence my bed ;
Should the sturdy station children pull the bush flowers
    on my grave,
    I may chance to hear them romping overhead.

ADAM LINDSAY GORDON

373.   *After the Quarrel*

H E never gave me a chance to speak,
    And he call'd her—worse than a dog—
The girl stood up with a crimson cheek,
    And I fell'd him there like a log.

I can feel the blow on my knuckles yet—
    He feels it more on his brow.
In a thousand years we shall all forget
    The things that trouble us now.

FRANCIS ROBERT ST. CLAIR ERSKINE

EARL OF ROSSLYN

1833-1890

374.   *Bed-time*

T IS bedtime ; say your hymn, and bid ' Good-night,
    God bless Mamma, Papa, and dear ones all,'
Your half-shut eyes beneath your eyelids fall,
Another minute you will shut them quite.
Yes, I will carry you, put out the light,
And tuck you up, although you are so tall !
What will you give me, Sleepy One, and call
My wages, if I settle you all right ?
I laid her golden curls upon my arm,
I drew her little feet within my hand,
Her rosy palms were joined in trustful bliss,
Her heart next mine beat gently, soft and warm ;
She nestled to me, and, by Love's command,
Paid me my precious wages- ' Baby's kiss.'

JOHN NICHOL

1833-1894

375.   *Good Night*

GOOD night, my love, good night !
  Farewell ! the breeze is sighing
  Along the harbour height ;
The fleecy clouds are flying
  Beneath Astarte's light.
My mariners are crying
  ' In favouring winds away !
And I, my love denying,
  Must cleave th' Aegean spray.
The song that the sea is singing
  On the bay is tender and bright :
The bark like a bird is springing
  And speeding from thy sight :
And a tune in my head is ringing
  That thrills my heart for flight
Across the waves—soon winging
Return to thee, and bringing
  Treasures for thy delight.
Good night, my love ! good night !

RICHARD WATSON DIXON

1833–1900

376.   *Song*

THE feathers of the willow
  Are half of them grown yellow
   Above the swelling stream ;
And ragged are the bushes,
And rusty now the rushes,
   And wild the clouded gleam.

The thistle now is older,
His stalks begin to moulder,
   His head is white as snow ;
The branches all are barer,
The linnet's song is rarer,
   The robin pipeth low.

377.   *Humanity*

THERE is a soul above the soul of each,
  A mightier soul, which yet to each belongs :
There is a sound made of all human speech,
  And numerous as the concourse of all songs :
And in that soul lives each, in each that soul,
  Tho' all the ages are its life-time vast ;
Each soul that dies in its most sacred whole
  Receiveth life that shall for ever last.

And thus for ever with a wider span
  Humanity o'erarches time and death ;
Man can elect the universal man
  And live in life that ends not with his breath ;
   And gather glory that increases still
    Till Time his glass with Death's last dust shall fill.

SIR LEWIS MORRIS

378. *Tolerance*

1833-1907

CALL no faith false which e'er has brought
     Relief to any laden life,
Cessation from the pain of thought,
Refreshment 'mid the dust of strife.

What though the thing to which they kneel
Be dumb and dead as wood or stone,
Though all the rapture which they feel
Be for the worshipper alone ?

They worship, they adore, they bow
Before the Ineffable Source, before
The hidden soul of good ; and thou,
With all thy wit, what dost thou more ?

Kneel with them, only if there come
Some zealot or sleek knave who strives
To mar the sanctities of home,
To tear asunder wedded lives ;

Or who by subtle wile has sought,
By shameful promise, shameful threat,
To turn the thinker from his thought,
To efface the eternal landmarks set

'Twixt faith and knowledge ; hold not peace
For such, but like a sudden flame
Let loose thy scorn on him, nor cease
Till thou hast cover'd him with shame.

SIR LEWIS MORRIS

379.　　*A Separation Deed*

WHEREAS we twain, who still are bound for life,
　　Who took each other for better and for worse,
Are now plunged deep in hate and bitter strife,
And all our former love is grown a curse ;
So that 'twere better, doubtless, we should be
In loneliness, so that we were apart,
Nor in each other's changed eyes looking, see
The cold reflection of an alien heart :
To this insensate parchment we reveal
Our joint despair, and seal it with our seal.

Forgetting the dear days not long ago,
When we walk'd slow by starlight through the corn :
Forgetting, since our hard fate wills it so,
All but our parted lives and souls forlorn ;
Forgetting the sweet fetters strong to bind
Which childish fingers forge, and baby smiles,
Our common pride to watch the growing mind,
Our common joy in childhood's simple wiles,
The common tears we shed, the kiss we gave,
Standing beside the open little grave ;

Forgetting these and more, if to forget
Be possible, as we would fain indeed.
And if the past be not too deeply set
In our two hearts, with roots that, touch'd, will bleed
Yet, could we cheat by any pretext fair
The world, if not ourselves—'twere so far well—
We would not put our bonds from us, and bare
To careless eyes the secrets of our hell ;
So this indenture witnesseth that we,
As follows here, do solemnly agree.

We

SIR LEWIS MORRIS

We will take each our own, and will abide
Separate from bed and board for all our life ;
Whatever chance of weal or woe betide,
Naught shall re-knit the husband and the wife.
Though one grow gradually poor and weak,
The other, lapt in luxury, will not heed ;
Though one, in mortal pain, the other seek,
The other may not answer to the need ;
We, who thro' long years did together rest
In wedlock, heart to heart, and breast to breast.

One shall the daughter take, and one the boy,—
Poor boy, who shall not hear his mother's name,
Nor feel her kiss ; poor girl, for whom the joy
Of her sire's smile is changed for sullen shame :
Brother and sister, who, if they should meet,
With faces strange, amid the careless crowd,
Will feel their hearts beat with no quicker beat,
Nor inward voice of kinship calling loud :
Two widow'd lives, whose fullness may not come ;
Two orphan lives, knowing but half of home.

We have not told the tale, nor will, indeed,
Of dissonance, whether cruel wrong or crime,
Or sum of petty injuries which breed
The hate of hell when multiplied by time,
Dishonour, falsehood, jealous fancies, blows,
Which in one moment wedded souls can sunder ;
But, since our yoke intolerable grows,
Therefore we set our seals and souls as under :
Witness the powers of Wrong and Hate and Death.
And this Indenture also witnesseth.

380.   *On a Thrush Singing in Autumn*

SWEET singer of the Spring, when the new world
  Was fill'd with song and bloom, and the fresh year
Tripp'd, like a lamb playful and void of fear,
Through daisied grass and young leaves scarce unfurl'd,
Where is thy liquid voice
That all day would rejoice ?
Where now thy sweet and homely call,
Which from grey dawn to evening's chilling fall
Would echo from thin copse and tassell'd brake,
For homely duty tuned and love's sweet sake ?

The spring-tide pass'd, high summer soon should come.
The woods grew thick, the meads a deeper hue ;
The pipy summer growths swell'd, lush and tall ;
The sharp scythes swept at daybreak through the dew.
Thou didst not heed at all,
Thy prodigal voice grew dumb ;
No more with song mightst thou beguile,
—She sitting on her speckled eggs the while—
Thy mate's long vigil as the slow days went,
Solacing her with lays of measureless content.

Nay, nay, thy voice was Duty's, nor would dare
Sing were Love fled, though still the world were fair ;
The summer wax'd and waned, the nights grew cold,
The sheep were thick within the wattled fold,
The woods began to moan,
Dumb wert thou and alone ;
Yet now, when leaves are sere, thy ancient note
Comes low and halting from thy doubtful throat.
Oh, lonely loveless voice ! what dost thou here
In the deep silence of the fading year ?

Thus do I read the answer of thy song :
' I sang when winds blew chilly all day long ;
I sang because hope came and joy was near,
I sang a little while, I made good cheer ;
In summer's cloudless day
My music died away ;
But now the hope and glory of the year
Are dead and gone, a little while I sing
Songs of regret for days no longer here,
And touched with presage of the far-off Spring.'

Is this the meaning of thy note, fair bird ?
Or do we read into thy simple brain
Echoes of thoughts which human hearts have stirred,
High-soaring joy and melancholy pain ?
Nay, nay, that lingering note
Belated from thy throat—
' Regret,' is what it sings, ' regret, regret !
The dear days pass, but are not wholly gone.
In praise of those I let my song go on ;
'Tis sweeter to remember than forget.'

381.   *Song*

LOVE took my life and thrill'd it
      Through all its strings,
Play'd round my mind and fill'd it
      With sound of wings :
But to my heart he never came
To touch it with his golden flame.

Therefore it is that singing
   I do rejoice,
Nor heed the slow years bringing
   A harsher voice :
Because the songs which he has sung
Still leave the untouch'd singer young.

But whom in fuller fashion
   The Master sways,
For him, swift wing'd with passion,
   Fleet the brief days :
Betimes the enforcèd accents come,
And leave him ever after dumb.

JAMES THOMSON

1834–1882

382.   *Gifts*

GIVE a man a horse he can ride,
   Give a man a boat he can sail ;
And his rank and wealth, his strength and health,
   On sea nor shore shall fail.

Give a man a pipe he can smoke,
   Give a man a book he can read :
And his home is bright with a calm delight,
   Though the room be poor indeed.

        Give

Give a man a girl he can love,
    As I, O my love, love thee ;
And his heart is great with the pulse of Fate,
    At home, on land, on sea.

383.   *The Bridge*

'O WHAT are you waiting for here, young man ?
    , What are you looking for over the bridge ? '
A little straw hat with the streaming blue ribbons
    Is soon to come dancing over the bridge.

Her heart beats the measure that keeps her feet dancing,
    Dancing along like a wave o' the sea ;
Her heart pours the sunshine with which her eyes glancing
    Light up strange faces in looking for me.

The strange faces brighten in meeting her glances ;
    The strangers all bless her, pure, lovely, and free :
She fancies she walks, but her walk skips and dances,
    Her heart makes such music in coming to me.

O, thousands and thousands of happy young maidens
    Are tripping this morning their sweethearts to see ;
But none whose heart beats to a sweeter love-cadence
    Than hers who will brighten the sunshine for me.

' O, what are you waiting for here, young man ?
    What are you looking for over the bridge ? '
A little straw hat with the streaming blue ribbons ;
—And here it comes dancing over the bridge !

Songs

i

384.

LIKE violets pale i' the Spring o' the year
Came my Love's sad eyes to my youth ;
Wan and dim with many a tear,
But the sweeter for that in sooth :
Wet and dim,
Tender and true,
Violet eyes
Of the sweetest blue.

Like pansies dark i' the June o' the year
Grow my Love's glad eyes to my prime ;
Rich with the purple splendour clear
Of their thoughtful bliss sublime :
Deep and dark,
Solemn and true,
Pansy eyes
Of the noblest blue.

ii

385.

MY love is the flaming Sword
To fight through the world ·
Thy love is the Shield to ward,
And the Armour of the Lord
And the Banner of Heaven unfurl'd.

386.   *iii*

LET my voice ring out and over the earth,
        Through all the grief and strife,
With a golden joy in a silver mirth :
        Thank God for Life !

Let my voice swell out through the great abyss
        To the azure dome above,
With a chord of faith in the harp of bliss :
        Thank God for Love !

Let my voice thrill out beneath and above,
        The whole world through :
O my Love and Life, O my Life and Love,
        Thank God for you !

387.   *The Vine*

THE wine of Love is music,
        And the feast of Love is song :
And when Love sits down to the banquet,
        Love sits long :

Sits long and arises drunken,
        But not with the feast and the wine ;
He reeleth with his own heart,
        That great, rich Vine.

388.   *Midsummer Courtship*

O HOW the nights are short,
        , These heavenly nights of June !
The long hot day amort
With toil, the time to court
        So stinted in its boon !

But three or four brief hours
  Between the afterglow
And dawnlight ; while the flowers
Are dreaming in their bowers,
  And birds their song forgo ;

And in the noon of night,
  As in the noon of day,
Flowers close on their delight,
Birds nestle from their flight,
  Deep stillness holdeth sway :

Only the nightingales
  Yet sing to moon and stars,
Although their full song fails ;
The corncrake never quails,
  But through the silence jars.

So few brief hours of peace ;
  And only one for us,
Alone, in toil's surcease,
To feed on love's increase :
  It is too cruel thus !

Did little Mother chide
  Because our sewing dropp'd
And we sat dreamy-eyed ?
Dear Mother, good betide,
  The scolding must be stopp'd.

Dear Mother, good and true,
  All-loving while you blame,
When spring brings skies of blue
And buds and flowers anew,
  I come in with my claim !

I claim

I claim my Love, my Own,
 Yet ever yours the while,
Under whose care hath grown
The sweetest blossom blown
 In all our flower-loved isle.

The Spring renews its youth
 And youth renews its Spring :
Love's wildest dreams are truth,
Magic is sober sooth ;
 Charm of the Magic Ring !

389.   *Art*

WHAT precious thing are you making fast
 In all these silken lines ?
And where and to whom will it go at last ?
 Such subtle knots and twines !

I am tying up all my love in this,
 With all its hopes and fears,
With all its anguish and all its bliss,
 And its hours as heavy as years.

I am going to send it afar, afar,
 To I know not where above ;
To that sphere beyond the highest star
 Where dwells the soul of my Love.

But in vain, in vain, would I make it fast
 With countless subtle twines ;
For ever its fire breaks out at last,
 And shrivels all the lines.

390.   *In the Room*

THE sun was down, and twilight grey
     Fill'd half the air ; but in the room,
Whose curtain had been drawn all day,
     The twilight was a dusky gloom :
Which seem'd at first as still as death,
     And void ; but was indeed all rife
With subtle thrills, the pulse and breath
     Of multitudinous lower life.

In their abrupt and headlong way
     Bewilder'd flies for light had dash'd
Against the curtain all the day,
     And now slept wintrily abash'd ;
And nimble mice slept, wearied out
     With such a double night's uproar ;
But solid beetles crawl'd about
     The chilly hearth and naked floor.

And so throughout the twilight hour
     That vaguely murmurous hush and rest
There brooded ; and beneath its power
     Life throbbing held its throbs supprest :
Until the thin-voiced mirror sigh'd,
     I am all blurr'd with dust and damp,
So long ago the clear day died,
     So long has gleamed nor fire nor lamp.

Whereon the curtain murmur'd back,
     Some change is on us, good or ill ;
Behind me and before is black
     As when those human things lie still :

But

But I have seen the darkness grow
   As grows the daylight every morn;
Have felt out there long shine and glow,
   In here long chilly dusk forlorn.

The cupboard grumbled with a groan,
   Each new day worse starvation brings:
Since *he* came here I have not known
   Or sweets or cates or wholesome things:
But now! a pinch of meal, a crust,
   Throughout the week is all I get.
I am so empty; it is just
   As when they said we were to let.

What is become, then, of our Man?
   The petulant old glass exclaim'd;
If all this time he slumber can,
   He really ought to be ashamed.
I wish we had our Girl again,
   So gay and busy, bright and fair:
The girls are better than these men,
   Who only for their dull selves care.

It is so many hours ago—
   The lamp and fire were both alight—
I saw him pacing to and fro,
   Perturbing restlessly the night.
His face was pale to give one fear,
   His eyes when lifted looked too bright;
He mutter'd; what, I could not hear:
   Bad words though; something was not right.

The table said, He wrote so long
   That I grew weary of his weight;
The pen kept up a cricket song,
   It ran and ran at such a rate:

And in the longer pauses he
    With both his folded arms downpress'd
And stared as one who does not see,
    Or sank his head upon his breast.

The fire-grate said, I am as cold
    As if I never had a blaze ;
The few dead cinders here I hold,
    I held unburn'd for days and days.
Last night he made them flare ; but still
    What good did all his writing do ?
Among my ashes curl and thrill
    Thin ghosts of all those papers too.

The table answer'd, Not quite all ;
    He saved and folded up one sheet,
And seal'd it fast, and let it fall ;
    And here it lies now white and neat.
Whereon the letter's whisper came,
    My writing is closed up too well ;
Outside there's not a single name,
    And who should read me I can't tell.

The mirror sneer'd with scornful spite,
    (That ancient crack which spoil'd her looks
Had marr'd her temper), Write and write !
    And read those stupid, worn-out books !
That's all he does,—read, write, and read,
    And smoke that nasty pipe which stinks :
He never takes the slightest heed
    How any of us feels or thinks.

But Lucy fifty times a day
    Would come and smile here in my face,
Adjust a tress that curl'd astray,
    Or tie a ribbon with more grace :

She

She look'd so young and fresh and fair,
   She blush'd with such a charming bloom,
It did one good to see her there,
   And brighten'd all things in the room.

She did not sit hours stark and dumb
   As pale as moonshine by the lamp ;
To lie in bed when day was come,
   And leave us curtain'd chill and damp.
She slept away the dreary dark,
   And rose to greet the pleasant morn ;
And sang as gaily as a lark
   While busy as the flies sun-born.

And how she loved us every one ;
   And dusted this and mended that,
With trills and laughs and freaks of fun,
   And tender scoldings in her chat !
And then her bird, that sang as shrill
   As she sang sweet ; her darling flowers
That grew there in the window-sill,
   Where she would sit at work for hours.

It was not much she ever wrote ;
   Her fingers had good work to do ;
Say, once a week a pretty note ;
   And very long it took her too.
And little more she read, I wis ;
   Just now and then a pictured sheet,
Besides those letters she would kiss
   And croon for hours, they were so sweet.

She had her friends too, blithe young girls,
   Who whisper'd, babbled, laugh'd, caress'd,
And romp'd and danced with dancing curls,
   And gave our life a joyous zest.

But with this dullard, glum and sour,
  Not one of all his fellow-men
Has ever pass'd a social hour ;
  We might be in some wild beast's den.

This long tirade aroused the bed,
  Who spoke in deep and ponderous bass,
Befitting that calm life he led,
  As if firm-rooted in his place :
In broad majestic bulk alone,
  As in thrice venerable age,
He stood at once the royal throne,
  The monarch, the experienced sage :

I know what is and what has been ;
  Not anything to me comes strange,
Who in so many years have seen
  And lived through every kind of change.
I know when men are good or bad,
  When well or ill, he slowly said ;
When sad or glad, when sane or mad,
  And when they sleep alive or dead.

At this last word of solemn lore
  A tremor circled through the gloom,
As if a crash upon the floor
  Had jarr'd and shaken all the room :
For nearly all the listening things
  Were old and worn, and knew what curse
Of violent change death often brings,
  From good to bad, from bad to worse ;

They get to know each other well,
  To feel at home and settled down ;
Death bursts among them like a shell,
  And strews them over all the town.

The

The bed went on, This man who lies
    Upon me now is stark and cold;
He will not any more arise,
    And do the things he did of old.

But we shall have short peace or rest;
    For soon up here will come a rout,
And nail him in a queer long chest,
    And carry him like luggage out.
They will be muffled all in black,
    And whisper much, and sigh and weep:
But he will never more come back,
    And some one else in me must sleep.

Thereon a little phial shrill'd,
    Here empty on the chair I lie:
I heard one say, as I was fill'd,
    With half of this a man would die.
The man there drank me with slow breath,
    And murmur'd, Thus ends barren strife:
O sweeter, thou cold wine of death,
    Than ever sweet warm wine of life!

One of my cousins long ago,
    A little thing, the mirror said,
Was carried to a couch to show,
    Whether a man was really dead.
Two great improvements marked the case:
    He did not blur her with his breath,
His many-wrinkled, twitching face
    Was smooth old ivory: verdict, Death.—

It lay, the lowest thing there, lull'd
    Sweet-sleep-like in corruption's truce;
The form whose purpose was annull'd,
    While all the other shapes meant use.

It lay, the *he* become now *it*,
  Unconscious of the deep disgrace,
Unanxious how its parts might flit
  Through what new forms in time and space.

It lay and preach'd, as dumb things do,
  More powerfully than tongues can prate ;
Though life be torture through and through,
  Man is but weak to plain of fate :
The drear path crawls on drearier still
  To wounded feet and hopeless breast ?
Well, he can lie down when he will,
  And straight all ends in endless rest.

And while the black night nothing saw,
  And till the cold morn came at last,
That old bed held the room in awe
  With tales of its experience vast.
It thrill'd the gloom ; it told such tales
  Of human sorrows and delights,
Of fever moans and infant wails,
  Of births and deaths and bridal nights.

391.   *William Blake*

HE came to the desert of London town
  Grey miles long ;
He wander'd up and he wander'd down,
  Singing a quiet song.

He came to the desert of London town,
  Mirk miles broad ;
He wander'd up and he wander'd down,
  Ever alone with God.

527   There

There were thousands and thousands of human kind
   In this desert of brick and stone :
But some were deaf and some were blind,
   And he was there alone.

At length the good hour came ; he died
   As he had lived, alone :
He was not miss'd from the desert wide,—
   Perhaps he was found at the Throne.

THE HON. RODEN BERKELEY
WRIOTHESLEY NOEL

1834-1894

392.   *A Lady to a Lover*

IF the sun low down in the West, my friend,
   Fill'd earth with fiery wine,
If a hand were on my breast, my friend,
And lips were laid on mine,
And we together
In summer weather
Lay in a leafy dell,
Could the weariness,
Or the long distress,
Or any fiends from hell,
Wipe out that hour of rest, my friend,
And the rapture all divine ?
Then if thy blade were buried deep
Within this heart of mine,
From the warm whiteness fierce would leap
My fiery blood like wine ;
Earth all about the West, my friend,
After orgies of rich wine,
Wan lying in the sun's decline,
And I in arms of thine, my friend,
In dying arms of thine !

The Swimmer

WHO would linger idle,
 Dallying would lie,
When wind and wave, a bridal
Celebrating, fly?
Let him plunge among them,
Who hath woo'd enough,
Flirted with them, sung them!
In the salt sea-trough
He may win them, onward
On a buoyant crest,
Far to seaward, sunward,
Ocean-borne to rest!
Wild wind will sing over him,
And the free foam cover him,
Swimming seaward, sunward,
On a blithe sea-breast!
 On a blithe sea-bosom
Swims another too,
Swims a live sea-blossom,
A grey-wing'd seamew!
Grape-green all the waves are,
By whose hurrying line
Half of ships and caves are
Buried under brine;
Supple, shifting ranges
Lucent at the crest,
With pearly surface-changes
Never laid to rest:
Now a dripping gunwale
Momently he sees,
Now a fuming funnel,
Or red flag in the breeze.

Arms

Arms flung open wide,
Lip the laughing sea :
For playfellow, for bride,
Claim her impetuously !

394. *The Water-Nymph and the Boy*

I FLUNG me round him,
I drew him under ;
I clung, I drown'd him,
My own white wonder ! . .

Father and mother,
Weeping and wild,
Came to the forest,
Calling the child,
Came from the palace,
Down to the pool,
Calling my darling,
My beautiful !
Under the water,
Cold and so pale !
Could it be love made
Beauty to fail ?

Ah me for mortals !
In a few moons,
If I had left him,
After some Junes
He would have faded,
Faded away,
He the young monarch, whom
All would obey,

530

Fairer than day ;
Alien to springtime,
Joyless and gray,
He would have faded,
Faded away,
Moving a mockery,
Scorn'd of the day !
Now I have taken him
All in his prime,
Saved from slow poisoning
Pitiless Time,
Fill'd with his happiness,
One with the prime,
Saved from the cruel
Dishonour of Time.
Laid him, my beautiful,
Laid him to rest,
Loving, adorable,
Softly to rest,
Here in my crystalline,
Here in my breast !

395. *Vale !*

O TENDER dove, sweet circling in the blue,
  Whom now a delicate cloud receives from view,
A cool, soft, delicate cloud, we name dim Death !
O pure white lamb-lily, inhaling breath
From spiritual ether among bowers
Of evergreen in the ever-living flowers
Yonder aloft upon the airy height,
Mine eyes may scarce arrive at thy still light !

Wandering

Wandering ever higher, O, farewell !
Wilt thou the dear God tell
We loved thee well,
While He would lend thee ? Why may we not follow ?
Do thou remember us in our dim hollow !
Farewell, love ! O, farewell, farewell, farewell !
We wave to thee, as when of old
Thou waved, and we waved, heart of gold !
Parting for a little while ?
And is all parting only for a while ?
O faint perfume from realms beyond the sky !
Waft of a low celestial melody !
O pure live water from our earthly well,
Whom Love changed to a heavenly oenomel,
The while he kiss'd the bowl with longing lip,
And drew the soul therein to fellowship !
Shimmer of white wings, ere ye vanish !
Glimmer of white robes, are ye banish,
With your full glory, mortal eyes
From paradise !
So far, so far,
Little star !
Unless thine own dear happiness it mar,
Remember us in our low dell,
Who love thee well !
Farewell !

396.   *The Old*

THEY are waiting on the shore
     For the bark to take them home :
They will toil and grieve no more ;
     The hour for release hath come.

All their long life lies behind
   Like a dimly blending dream :
There is nothing left to bind
   To the realms that only seem.

They are waiting for the boat ;
   There is nothing left to do :
What was near them grows remote,
   Happy silence falls like dew ;
Now the shadowy bark is come,
And the weary may go home.

By still water they would rest
   In the shadow of the tree :
After battle sleep is best,
   After noise, tranquillity.

GEORGE LOUIS PALMELLA BUSSON
DU MAURIER

1834-1896

397.   *Music*

(AFTER SULLY PRUDHOMME)

KINDLY watcher by my bed, lift no voice in prayer,
  Waste not any words on me when the hour is nigh,
Let a stream of melody but flow from some sweet player,
And meekly will I lay my head and fold my hands to die.

Sick am I of idle words, past all reconciling,
Words that weary and perplex and pander and conceal,
Wake the sounds that cannot lie, for all their sweet be-
   guiling ;
The language one need fathom not, but only hear and feel.

533   Let

Let them roll once more to me, and ripple in my hearing,
Like waves upon a lonely beach where no craft anchoreth :
That I may steep my soul therein, and craving naught,
    nor fearing,
Drift on through slumber to a dream, and through a
    dream to death.

WILLIAM MORRIS

1834-1896

398.   *Shameful Death*

THERE were four of us about that bed ;
    The mass-priest knelt at the side,
I and his mother stood at the head,
    Over his feet lay the bride ;
We were quite sure that he was dead,
    Though his eyes were open wide.

He did not die in the night,
    He did not die in the day,
But in the morning twilight
    His spirit pass'd away,
When neither sun nor moon was bright,
    And the trees were merely grey.

He was not slain with the sword,
    Knight's axe, or the knightly spear,
Yet spoke he never a word
    After he came in here ;
I cut away the cord
    From the neck of my brother dear.

He did not strike one blow,
 For the recreants came behind,
In the place where the hornbeams grow,
 A path right hard to find,
For the hornbeam boughs swing so,
 That the twilight makes it blind.

They lighted a great torch then,
 When his arms were pinion'd fast,
Sir John the Knight of the Fen,
 Sir Guy of the Dolorous Blast,
With knights threescore and ten,
 Hung brave Lord Hugh at last.

I am threescore and ten,
 And my hair is all turn'd grey,
But I met Sir John of the Fen,
 Long ago on a summer day,
And am glad to think of the moment when
 I took his life away.

I am threescore and ten,
 And my strength is mostly pass'd,
But long ago I and my men,
 When the sky was overcast,
And the smoke roll'd over the reeds of the fen,
 Slew Guy of the Dolorous Blast.

And now, knights all of you,
 I pray you pray for Sir Hugh,
A good knight and a true,
 And for Alice, his wife, pray too.

399.   *The Sailing of the Sword*

ACROSS the empty garden-beds,
　　When the Sword went out to sea,
I scarcely saw my sisters' heads
　　Bow'd each beside a tree.
I could not see the castle leads,
　　When the Sword went out to sea.

Alicia wore a scarlet gown,
　　When the Sword went out to sea,
But Ursula's was russet brown :
　　For the mist we could not see
The scarlet roofs of the good town,
　　When the Sword went out to sea.

Green holly in Alicia's hand,
　　When the Sword went out to sea,
With sere oak-leaves did Ursula stand ;
　　O ! yet alas for me !
I did but bear a peel'd white wand,
　　When the Sword went out to sea.

O, russet brown and scarlet bright,
　　When the Sword went out to sea,
My sisters wore ; I wore but white ;
　　Red, brown, and white, are three ;
Three damozels ; each had a knight,
　　When the Sword went out to sea.

536

Sir Robert shouted loud, and said,
  When the Sword went out to sea,
' Alicia, while I see thy head,
  What shall I bring for thee ? '
' O, my sweet Lord, a ruby red : '
  The Sword went out to sea.

Sir Miles said, while the sails hung down,
  When the Sword went out to sea,
' Oh, Ursula ! while I see the town,
  What shall I bring for thee ? '
' Dear knight, bring back a falcon brown : '
  The Sword went out to sea.

But my Roland, no word he said
  When the Sword went out to sea ;
But only turn'd away his head,—
  A quick shriek came from me :
' Come back, dear lord, to your white maid ! '—
  The Sword went out to sea.

The hot sun bit the garden-beds,
  When the Sword came back from sea ;
Beneath an apple-tree our heads
  Stretch'd out toward the sea ;
Grey gleam'd the thirsty castle-leads,
  When the Sword came back from sea.

Lord Robert brought a ruby red,
  When the Sword came back from sea ;
He kiss'd Alicia on the head :
  ' I am come back to thee ;
'Tis time, sweet love, that we were wed,
  Now the Sword is back from sea ! '

Sir

Sir Miles he bore a falcon brown,
   When the Sword came back from sea ;
His arms went round tall Ursula's gown,—
   ' What joy, O love, but thee ?
Let us be wed in the good town,
   Now the Sword is back from sea ! '

My heart grew sick, no more afraid,
   When the Sword came back from sea ;
Upon the deck a tall white maid
   Sat on Lord Roland's knee ;
His chin was press'd upon her head,
   When the Sword came back from sea !

400. *The Eve of Crecy*

GOLD on her head, and gold on her feet,
   And gold where the hems of her kirtle meet,
And a golden girdle round my sweet ;—
   Ah ! qu'elle est belle La Marguerite.

Margaret's maids are fair to see,
Freshly dress'd and pleasantly ;
Margaret's hair falls down to her knee ;—
   Ah ! qu'elle est belle La Marguerite.

If I were rich I would kiss her feet,
I would kiss the place where the gold hems meet,
And the golden girdle round my sweet—
   Ah ! qu'elle est belle La Marguerite.

Ah me ! I have never touch'd her hand,
When the arriere-ban goes through the land,
Six basnets under my pennon stand ;—
   Ah ! qu'elle est belle La Marguerite.

And many an one grins under his hood :
' Sir Lambert de Bois, with all his men good,
Has neither food nor firewood ; '—
 Ah ! qu'elle est belle La Marguerite.

If I were rich I would kiss her feet,
And the golden girdle of my sweet,
And thereabouts where the gold hems meet ;
 Ah ! qu'elle est belle La Marguerite.

Yet even now it is good to think,
While my few poor varlets grumble and drink
In my desolate hall, where the fires sink,—
 Ah ! qu'elle est belle La Marguerite.

Of Margaret sitting glorious there,
In glory of gold and glory of hair,
And glory of glorious face most fair ;—
 Ah ! qu'elle est belle La Marguerite.

Likewise to-night I make good cheer,
Because this battle draweth near :
For what have I to lose or fear ?—
 Ah ! qu'elle est belle La Marguerite.

For, look you, my horse is good to prance
A right fair measure in this war-dance,
Before the eyes of Philip of France ;—
 Ah ! qu'elle est belle La Marguerite.

And sometime it may hap, perdie,
While my new towers stand up three and three,
And my hall gets painted fair to see—
 Ah ! qu'elle est belle La Marguerite—

    That

That folks may say : ' Times change, by the rood !
For Lambert, banneret of the wood,
Has heaps of food and firewood ;—
    Ah ! qu'elle est belle La Marguerite ;—

' And wonderful eyes, too, under the hood
Of a damsel of right noble blood : '
St. Ives, for Lambert of the wood !—
    Ah ! qu'elle est belle La Marguerite.

401.   *The Judgement of God*

' SWERVE to the left, son Roger,' he said,
    ' When you catch his eyes through the helmet-slit,
Swerve to the left, then out at his head,
    And the Lord God give you joy of it ! '

The blue owls on my father's hood
    Were a little dimm'd as I turn'd away ;
This giving up of blood for blood
    Will finish here somehow to-day.

So—when I walk'd out from the tent,
    Their howling almost blinded me ;
Yet for all that I was not bent
    By any shame.   Hard by, the sea

Made a noise like the aspens where
    We did that wrong ; but now the place
Is very pleasant, and the air
    Blows cool on any passer's face.

And all the wrong is gather'd now
   Into the circle of these lists—
Yea, howl out, butchers ! tell me how
   His hands were cut off at the wrists ;

And how Lord Roger bore his face
   A league above his spear-point, high
Above the owls, to that strong place
   Among the waters—yea, yea, cry :

' What a brave champion we have got !
   Sir Oliver, the flower of all
The Hainault knights.' The day being hot,
   He sat beneath a broad white pall,

White linen over all his steel ;
   What a good knight he look'd ! his sword
Laid thwart his knees ; he liked to feel
   Its steadfast edge clear as his word.

And he look'd solemn : how his love
   Smiled whitely on him, sick with fear !
How all the ladies up above
   Twisted their pretty hands ! so near

The fighting was—Ellayne ! Ellayne !
   They cannot love like you can, who
Would burn your hands off, if that pain
   Could win a kiss—am I not true

To you for ever ? therefore I
   Do not fear death or anything ;
If I should limp home wounded, why,
   While I lay sick you would but sing,

And

And soothe me into quiet sleep.
   If they spat on the recreant knight,
Threw stones at him, and cursed him deep,
   Why then—what then? your hand would light

So gently on his drawn-up face,
   And you would kiss him, and in soft
Cool scented clothes would lap him, pace
   The quiet room and weep oft,—oft

Would turn and smile, and brush his cheek
   With your sweet chin and mouth; and in
The order'd garden you would seek
   The biggest roses—any sin.

And these say : ' No more now my knight,
   Or God's knight any longer '—you
Being than they so much more white,
   So much more pure and good and true,

Will cling to me for ever—There,
   Is not that wrong turn'd right at last
Through all these years, and I wash'd clean?
   Say, yea, Ellayne; the time is past,

Since on that Christmas-day last year
   Up to your feet the fire crept,
And the smoke through the brown leaves sere
   Blinded your dear eyes that you wept;

Was it not I that caught you then,
   And kiss'd you on the saddle-bow?
Did not the blue owl mark the men
   Whose spears stood like the corn a-row?

This Oliver is a right good knight,
   And must needs beat me, as I fear,
Unless I catch him in the fight,
   My father's crafty way—John, here !

Bring up the men from the south gate,
   To help me if I fall or win,
For even if I beat, their hate
   Will grow to more than this mere grin.

402.   *Summer Dawn*

PRAY but one prayer for me 'twixt thy closed lips,
   Think but one thought of me up in the stars.
The summer night waneth, the morning light slips
   Faint and gray 'twixt the leaves of the aspen, betwixt
      the cloud-bars,
That are patiently waiting there for the dawn :
   Patient and colourless, though Heaven's gold
Waits to float through them along with the sun.
Far out in the meadows, above the young corn,
   The heavy elms wait, and restless and cold
The uneasy wind rises ; the roses are dun ;
Through the long twilight they pray for the dawn
Round the lone house in the midst of the corn.
   Speak but one word to me over the corn,
   Over the tender, bow'd locks of the corn.

403.   *Love is Enough*

i

LOVE is enough : though the World be a-waning,
   And the woods have no voice but the voice of com-
     plaining,
  Though the sky be too dark for dim eyes to discover
The gold-cups and daisies fair blooming thereunder,
Though the hills be held shadows, and the sea a dark
     wonder,
  And this day draw a veil over all deeds pass'd over,
Yet their hands shall not tremble, their feet shall not
     falter ;
The void shall not weary, the fear shall not alter
  These lips and these eyes of the loved and the lover.

ii

LOVE is enough : ho ye who seek saving,
   Go no further ; come hither ! there have been who
     have found it,
And these know the House of Fulfilment of Craving ;
  These know the Cup with the roses around it ;
  These know the World's wound and the balm that
     hath bound it :
Cry out, the World heedeth not, ' Love, lead us home ! '

He leadeth, He hearkeneth, He cometh to you-ward ;
  Set your faces as steel to the fears that assemble
Round his goad for the faint, and his scourge for the
     froward :
  Lo his lips, how with tales of last kisses they tremble !
  Lo his eyes of all sorrow that may not dissemble !
Cry out, for he heedeth, ' O Love, lead us home ! '

O hearken the words of his voice of compassion :
  ' Come cling round about me, ye faithful who sicken
Of the weary unrest and the world's passing fashion !
    As the rain in mid-morning your troubles shall thicken,
    But surely within you some Godhead doth quicken,
As ye cry to me heeding and leading you home.

' Come—pain ye shall have, and be blind to the ending !
    Come—fear ye shall have, mid the sky's overcasting !
Come—change ye shall have, for far are ye wending !
    Come—no crown ye shall have for your thirst and your
        fasting,
    But the kiss'd lips of Love and fair life everlasting !
Cry out, for one heedeth, who leadeth you home ! '

Is he gone ? was he with us ?—ho ye who seek saving,
    Go no further ; come hither ! for have we not found it ?
Here is the House of Fulfilment of Craving ;
    Here is the Cup with the roses around it ;
    The World's wound well healed, and the balm that
        hath bound it :
Cry out ! for he heedeth, fair Love that led home.

404. *Inscription for an Old Bed*

THE wind 's on the wold
    And the night is a-cold,
And Thames runs chill
'Twixt mead and hill.
But kind and dear
Is the old house here
And my heart is warm
Midst winter's harm.
Rest then and rest,
And think of the best

'Twixt summer and spring,
When all birds sing
In the town of the tree,
And ye lie in me
And scarce dare move,
Lest the earth and its love
Should fade away
Ere the full of the day.
I am old and have seen
Many things that have been;
Both grief and peace
And wane and increase.
No tale I tell
Of ill or well,
But this I say:
Night treadeth on day,
And for worst or best
Right good is rest.

405. *The Message of the March Wind*

FAIR now is the spring-tide, now earth lies beholding
With the eyes of a lover, the face of the sun;
Long lasteth the daylight, and hope is enfolding
The green-growing acres with increase begun.

Now sweet, sweet it is thro' the land to be straying,
'Mid the birds and the blossoms and the beasts of the field;
Love mingles with love, and no evil is weighing
On thy heart or mine, where all sorrow is heal'd.

From township to township, o'er down and by tillage,
Far, far have we wander'd and long was the day;
But now cometh eve at the end of the village,
Where over the grey wall the church riseth grey.

There is wind in the twilight; in the white road
    before us
The straw from the ox-yard is blowing about;
The moon's rim is rising, a star glitters o'er us,
And the vane on the spire-top is swinging in doubt.

Down there dips the highway, toward the bridge crossing
    over
The brook that runs on to the Thames and the sea.
Draw closer, my sweet, we are lover and lover;
This eve art thou given to gladness and me.

Shall we be glad always? Come closer and hearken:
Three fields further on, as they told me down there,
When the young moon has set, if the March sky should
    darken,
We might see from the hill-top the great city's glare.

Hark, the wind in the elm-boughs! from London it
    bloweth,
And telleth of gold, and of hope and unrest;
Of power that helps not; of wisdom that knoweth,
But teacheth not aught of the worst and the best.

Of the rich men it telleth, and strange is the story
How they have and they hanker, and grip far and wide;
And they live and they die, and the earth and its glory
Has been but a burden they scarce might abide.

Hark! the March wind again of a people is telling;
Of the life that they live there, so haggard and grim,
That if we and our love amidst them had been dwelling,
My fondness had falter'd, thy beauty grown dim.

                                          This

This land we have loved in our love and our leisure,
For them hangs in heaven, high out of their reach ;
The wide hills o'er the sea-plain for them have no pleasure,
The grey homes of their fathers no story to teach.

The singers have sung and the builders have builded,
The painters have fashioned their tales of delight ;
For what and for whom hath the world's book been gilded,
When all is for these but the blackness of night ?

How long, and for what is their patience abiding ?
How long and how oft shall their story be told,
While the hope that none seeketh in darkness is hiding,
And in grief and in sorrow the world groweth old ?

Come back to the inn, love, and the lights and the fire,
And the fiddler's old tune and the shuffling of feet ;
For there in a while shall be rest and desire,
And there shall the morrow's uprising be sweet.

Yet, love, as we wend, the wind bloweth behind us,
And beareth the last tale it telleth to-night,
How here in the spring-tide the message shall find us ;
For the hope that none seeketh is coming to light.

Like the seed of midwinter, unheeded, unperish'd,
Like the autumn-sown wheat 'neath the snow lying green,
Like the love that o'ertook us, unawares and uncherish'd,
Like the babe 'neath thy girdle that groweth unseen ;

So the hope of the people now buddeth and groweth,
Rest fadeth before it, and blindness and fear ;
It biddeth us learn all the wisdom it knoweth ;
It hath found us and held us, and biddeth us hear :

For it beareth the message : ' Rise up on the morrow,
And go on thy ways toward the doubt and the strife ;
Join hope to our hope and blend sorrow with sorrow,
And seek for men's love in the short days of life.'

But lo, the old inn, and the lights, and the fire,
And the fiddler's old tune and the shuffling of feet ;
Soon for us shall be quiet and rest and desire,
And to-morrow's uprising to deeds shall be sweet.

JOHN LEICESTER WARREN
LORD DE TABLEY

1835-1895

406.   *Nuptial Song*

SIGH, heart, and break not ; rest, lark, and wake not !
   Day I hear coming to draw my Love away.
As mere-waves whisper, and clouds grow crisper,
    Ah, like a rose he will waken up with day !

In moon-light lonely, he is my Love only,
    I share with none when Luna rides in grey.
As dawn-beams quicken, my rivals thicken,
    The light and deed and turmoil of the day.

To watch my sleeper to me is sweeter,
    Than any waking words my Love can say ;
In dream he finds me and closer winds me !
    Let him rest by me a little more and stay.

Ah, mine eyes, close not : and, tho' he knows not,
    My lips, on his be tender while you may ;
Ere leaves are shaken, and ring-doves waken,
    And infant buds begin to scent new day.

       Fair

Fair Darkness, measure thine hours, as treasure
  Shed each one slowly from thine urn, I pray ;
Hoard in and cover each from my lover ;
  I cannot lose him yet ; dear night, delay !

Each moment dearer, true-love lie nearer,
  My hair shall blind thee lest thou see the ray ;
My locks encumber thine ears in slumber,
  Lest any bird dare give thee note of day.

He rests so calmly ; we lie so warmly ;
  Hand within hand, as children after play ;—
In shafted amber on roof and chamber
  Dawn enters ; my Love wakens ; here is day.

407.   *Ode*

SIRE of the rising day,
  Lord of the faded ray,
King of sweet ways of morn or daylight done.
Ruler of cloud and sleep,
Whose tread is on the deep,
Whose feet are red in glory like the sun.
Whose hand binds up the winds as in a sheaf,
Whose shadow makes them tremble like a leaf.

Lordship and Fear are thine,
Upon whose brow divine
The diadem of pale eternal fire
Burns over eyes that fear
No stain of earthly tear,
Nor soften for a yearning world's desire.
The treasure of strong thunder at thy hand
Waits like an eagle watching thy command.

Thee rosy beams enshroud ;
Rich airs and amber cloud
Reach the calm golden spaces of thy hall.
The floods awake with noise
Churning the deep, whose voice
Thou heedest not, altho' the storm-wind call
And break beneath the swollen vapour-bands,
In wild rains wearing at the sodden lands.

Can then our weak-wing'd prayer
Ascend and touch thee there,
Sailing between the gleaming gates of heaven ?
Can our wail climb and smite
Thy council-seat of light ?
Where for a garment is the moon-ray given
To clothe thy shoulders, and blue star-dust strown
Bickers about the borders of thy throne.

Ah, Lord, who may withstand
One reaching of thy hand,
Who from thy fury fence his house secure ?
What citadel is there,
In lifted hand or prayer,
If all the radiant heaven may not endure
The scathing of thine anger, keen to blight
The strong stars rolling in their fields of light ?

Arise and take thine ease,
For thou art Lord ; and these
Are but as sprinkled dust before thy power.
Art thou the less divine,
If they lift hands and whine,
Or less eternal since they crawl an hour ?
After a little pain to fold their hands,
And perish like the beasts that till'd their lands.

They

They dug their field and died,
Believed thee or denied ;
Cursed at thy name, or fed thy shrine with fume.
Loved somewhat, hated more,
Hoarded, grew stiff and sore,
Gat sturdy sons to labour in their room ;
Became as alien faces in their land ;
Died, worn and done with as a waste of sand.

Strong are alone the dead.
They need not bow the head,
Or reach one hand in ineffectual prayer.
Safe in their iron sleep
What wrong shall make them weep,
What sting of human anguish reach them there ?
They are gone safe beyond the strong one's reign,
Who shall decree against them any pain ?

Will they entreat in tears
The inexorable years
To sprinkle trouble gently on their head ?
Safe in their house of grass,
Eternity may pass,
And be to these an instant in its tread,
Calm as an autumn night, brief as the song
Of the wood dove. The dead alone are strong.

Love is not there, nor Hate,
Weak slaves of feebler Fate,
Their lord is nothing here, his reign is done.
Here side by side can lie
Glory and Infamy,
Hero and herdsman in red earth are one.
Their day is over : sad they silence keep,
Abash'd before the perfect crowning sleep.

552

408.   *Chorus from ' Medea '*

SWEET are the ways of death to weary feet,
    Calm are the shades of men.
The phantom fears no tyrant in his seat,
    The slave is master then.

Love is abolish'd ; well, that this is so ;
    We knew him best as Pain.
The gods are all cast out, and let them go !
    Who ever found them gain ?

Ready to hurt and slow to succour these ;
    So, while thou breathest, pray.
But in the sepulchre all flesh has peace ;
    Their hand is put away.

409.   *Fortune's Wheel*

I HAD a true-love, none so dear,
    And a friend both leal and tried.
I had a cask of good old beer,
    And a gallant horse to ride.

A little while did Fortune smile
    On him and her and me.
We sang along the road of life
    Like birds upon a tree.

My lady fell to shame and hell,
    And with her took my friend.
My cask ran sour, my horse went lame,—
    So alone in the cold I end.

410.   *The Two Old Kings*

IN ruling well what guerdon ?   Life runs low,
  As yonder lamp upon the hour-glass lies,
  Waning and wasted.   We are great and wise,
But Love is gone ; and Silence seems to grow
Along the misty road where we must go.
  From summits near the morning star's uprise
  Death comes, a shadow from the northern skies,
As, when all leaves are down, there comes the snow.

Brother and King, we hold our last carouse.
  One loving-cup we drain and then farewell.
    The night is spent : the crystal morning ray
Calls us, as soldiers laurell'd on our brows,
  To march undaunted while the clarions swell—
    Heroic hearts, upon our lonely way.

RICHARD GARNETT
1835-1906

411.   *Fading-Leaf and Fallen-Leaf*

SAID Fading-leaf to Fallen-leaf :—
  ' I toss alone on a forsaken tree,
It rocks and cracks with every gust that racks
  Its straining bulk ; say, how is it with thee ? '

Said Fallen-leaf to Fading-leaf :—
  ' A heavy foot went by, an hour ago ;
Crushed into clay I stain the way ;
  The loud wind calls me, and I cannot go.'

Said Fading-leaf to Fallen-leaf :—
   ' Death lessons Life, a ghost is ever wise ;
Teach me a way to live till May
   Laughs fair with fragrant lips and loving eyes.'

Said Fallen-leaf to Fading-leaf :—
   ' Hast loved fair eyes and lips of gentle breath ?
Fade then and fall—thou hast had all
   That Life can give : ask somewhat now of Death.'

412.   *The Fair Circassian*

FORTY Viziers saw I go
   Up to the Seraglio,
Burning, each and every man,
For the fair Circassian.

Ere the morn had disappear'd,
Every Vizier wore a beard ;
Ere the afternoon was born,
Every Vizier came back shorn.

' Let the man that woos to win
Woo with an unhairy chin : '
Thus she said, and as she bid
Each devoted Vizier did.

From the beards a cord she made,
Loop'd it to the balustrade,
Glided down and went away
To her own Circassia.

      When

When the Sultan heard, wax'd he
Somewhat wroth, and presently
In the noose themselves did lend
    Every Vizier did suspend.

Sages all, this rhyme who read,
Of your beards take prudent heed,
And beware the wily plans
    Of the fair Circassians.

413. *Epigram*

AMID all Triads let it be confest
    The Chase, the Feast, the Song compose the best ,
So aptly link'd a mutual aid to lend
To life's enjoyment, their concurrent end.
The chase provides what doth to feasts belong ;
The banquet prompts and animates the song ;
The song, resounding with a twofold grace,
Cheers the repast, and celebrates the chase.

414. *Nocturne*

KEEN winds of cloud and vaporous drift
    Disrobe yon star, as ghosts that lift
A snowy curtain from its place,
To scan a pillow'd beauty's face.

They see her slumbering splendours lie
Bedded on blue unfathom'd sky.
And swoon for love and deep delight,
And stillness falls on all the night.

RICHARD GARNETT

415.   *Sonnet—Age*

I WILL not rail or grieve when torpid eld
  Frosts the slow-journeying blood, for I shall see
  The lovelier leaves hang yellow on the tree,
The nimbler brooks in icy fetters held.
Methinks the aged eye that first beheld
  Pale Autumn in her waning pageantry,
  Then knew himself, dear Nature, child of thee,
Marking the common doom, that all compell'd.

No kindred we to her belovèd broods,
  If, dying these, we draw a selfish breath ;
But one path travel all their multitudes,
  And none dispute the solemn Voice that saith :
Sun to thy setting ; to your autumn, woods ;
  Stream to thy sea ; and man unto thy death.

SIR ALFRED COMYN LYALL
1835-1911

416.   *Studies at Delhi*

i. *The Hindu Ascetic*

HERE as I sit by the Jumna bank,
  Watching the flow of the sacred stream,
Pass me the legions, rank on rank,
  And the cannon roar, and the bayonets gleam.

Is it a god or a king that comes ?
  Both are evil, and both are strong ;
With women and worshipping, dancing and drums,
  Carry your gods and your kings along.

557

Fanciful

Fanciful shapes of a plastic earth,
    These are the visions that weary the eye;
These I may 'scape by a luckier birth,
    Musing, and fasting, and hoping to die.

When shall these phantoms flicker away
    Like the smoke of the guns on the wind-swept hill,
Like the sounds and colours of yesterday:
    And the soul have rest, and the air be still?

ii.   Badminton

Hardly a shot from the gate we storm'd,
    Under the Moree battlement's shade;
Close to the glacis our game was form'd,
    There had the fight been, and there we play'd.

Lightly the demoiselles titter'd and leapt,
    Merrily caper'd the players all;
North, was the garden where Nicholson slept,
    South, was the sweep of a batter'd wall.

Near me a Musalmán, civil and mild,
    Watch'd as the shuttlecocks rose and fell;
And he said, as he counted his beads and smiled,
    ' God smite their souls to the depths of hell.'

417.   *Primroses*

I

LATEST, earliest, of the year,
      Primroses that still were here,
Snugly nestling round the boles
Of the cut down chestnut poles,
When December's tottering tread
Rustled 'mong the deep leaves dead,
And with confident young faces
Peep'd from out the shelter'd places
When pale January lay
In its cradle day by day,
Dead or living, hard to say ;
Now that mid-March blows and blusters,
Out you steal in tufts and clusters,
Making leafless lane and wood
Vernal with your hardihood.
Other lovely things are rare,
You are prodigal as fair.
First you come by ones, and ones,
Lastly in battalions ;
Skirmish along hedge and bank,
Turn old Winter's wavering flank ;
Round his flying footsteps hover,
Seize on hollow, ridge, and cover,
Leave nor slope nor hill unharried,
Till, his snowy trenches carried,
O'er his sepulchre you laugh,
Winter's joyous epitaph.

This

ALFRED AUSTIN

II

This, too, be your glory great,
Primroses, you do not wait,
As the other flowers do,
For the Spring to smile on you;
But with coming are content,
Asking no encouragement.
Ere the hardy crocus cleaves
Sunny borders 'neath the eaves;
Ere the thrush his song rehearse,
Sweeter than all poets' verse;
Ere the early bleating lambs
Cling like shadows to their dams;
Ere the blackthorn breaks to white,
Snowy-hooded anchorite;
Out from every hedge you look,
You are bright by every brook,
Wearing for your sole defence
Fearlessness of innocence.
While the daffodils still waver,
Ere the jonquil gets its savour;
While the linnets yet but pair,
You are fledged, and everywhere.
Nought can daunt you, nought distress,
Neither cold nor sunlessness.
You, when Lent sleet flies apace,
Look the tempest in the face
As descend the flakes more slow,
From your eyelids shake the snow,
And, when all the clouds have flown,
Meet the sun's smile with your own.
Nothing ever makes you less
Gracious to ungraciousness.
March may bluster up and down,

Pettish April sulk and frown;
Closer to their skirts you cling,
Coaxing Winter to be Spring.

III

Then, when your sweet task is done,
And the wild-flowers, one by one,
Here, there, everywhere do blow,
Primroses, you haste to go,
Satisfied with what you bring,
Fading morning-stars of Spring.
You have brighten'd doubtful days,
You have sweeten'd long delays,
Fooling our enchanted reason
To miscalculate the season.
But when doubt and fear are fled,
When the kine leave wintry shed,
And 'mong grasses green and tall
Find their fodder, make their stall;
When the wintering swallow flies
Homeward back from southern skies,
To the dear old cottage thatch
Where it loves to build and hatch,
That its young may understand,
Nor forget, this English land;
When the cuckoo, mocking rover,
Laughs that April loves are over;
When the hawthorn, all ablow,
Mimics the defeated snow;
Then you give one last look round,
Stir the sleepers underground,
Call the campion to awake,
Tell the speedwell courage take,
Bid the eyebright have no fear,

Whisper

Whisper in the bluebell's ear
Time has come for it to flood
With its blue waves all the wood,
Mind the stitchwort of its pledge
To replace you in the hedge,
Bid the ladysmocks good-bye,
Close your bonnie lids and die ;
And, without one look of blame,
Go as gently as you came.

418.   *The Lover's Song*

WHEN Winter hoar no longer holds
    The young year in his gripe,
And bleating voices fill the folds,
    And blackbirds pair and pipe ;
Then coax the maiden where the sap
    Awakes the woodlands drear,
And pour sweet wildflowers in her lap,
    And sweet words in her ear.
For Springtime is the season, sure,
    Since Love's game first was play'd,
When tender thoughts began to lure
    The heart of April maid,
                    Of maid,
    The heart of April maid.

When June is wreath'd with wilding rose,
    And all the buds are blown,
And O, 'tis joy to dream and doze
    In meadows newly mown ;
Then take her where the graylings leap,
    And where the dabchick dives,
Or where the bees in clover reap
    The harvest for their hives.

For Summer is the season when,
   If you but know the way,
The maid that 's kiss'd will kiss again,
   Then pelt you with the hay,
               The hay,
   Then pelt you with the hay.

When sickles ply among the wheat,
   Then trundle home the sheaves,
And there 's a rustling of the feet
   Thro' early-fallen leaves ;
Entice her where the orchard glows
   With apples plump and tart,
And tell her plain the thing she knows,
   And ask her for her heart.
For Autumn is the season, boy,
   To gather what we sow ;
If you be bold, she won't be coy,
   Nor ever say you no,
               Say no,
   Nor ever say you no.

When woodmen clear the coppice lands,
   And arch the hornbeam drive,
And stamp their feet, and chafe their hands,
   To keep their blood alive ;
Then lead her where, where vows are heard,
   The church-bells peal and swing,
And, as the parson speaks the word,
   Then on her clap the ring.
For Winter is a cheerless time
   To live and lie alone ;
But what to him is snow or rime
   Who calls his love his own,
               His own,
   Who calls his love his own ?

419. *Love's Trinity*

SOUL, heart, and body, we thus singly name,
  Are not in love divisible and distinct,
    But each with each inseparably link'd.
  One is not honour, and the other shame,
But burn as closely fused as fuel, heat, and flame.

They do not love who give the body and keep
  The heart ungiven; nor they who yield the soul,
    And guard the body. Love doth give the whole;
  Its range being high as heaven, as ocean deep,
Wide as the realms of air or planet's curving sweep.

THOMAS ASHE

1836-1889

420. *Meet we no Angels, Pansie?*

CAME, on a Sabbath noon, my sweet,
  In white, to find her lover;
The grass grew proud beneath her feet,
  The green elm-leaves above her :—
    Meet we no angels, Pansie?

She said, 'We meet no angels now';
  And soft lights stream'd upon her;
And with white hand she touch'd a bough;
  She did it that great honour :—
    What! meet no angels, Pansie?

O sweet brown hat, brown hair, brown eyes,
  Down-dropp'd brown eyes, so tender!
Then what said I ?—gallant replies
  Seem flattery, and offend her :—
    But—meet no angels, Pansie?

421.   *The City Clerk*

'TIS strange how my head runs on! 'tis a puzzle to
     understand
Such fancies stirring in me, for a whiff of hay in the
     Strand!

I see the old farmhouse, and garden wall, and the bees;
I see the mowers stretch'd, with their bottles, under the
     trees;

I hear the little brook a-ripple down in the dell;
I hear the old-folk croon—'Our son, he is doing well!'

O yes, I am doing well; but I'd be again, for a day,
A simple farmer's lad, among the girls in the hay.

422.   *A Machine Hand*

MY little milliner has slipp'd
     The doctors, with their drugs and ways:
Her years were only twenty-two,
     Though long enough her working-days.

At eight she went, through wet or snow,
     Nor dallied for the sun to shine;
And walk'd an hour to work, and home
     Content if she was in by nine.

She had a little gloomy room,
     Up stair on stair, within the roof;
Where hung her pictures on the wall,
     Wherever it was weather-proof.

She

She held her head erect and proud,
　　Nor ask'd of man or woman aid ;
And struggled, till the last ; and died
　　But of the parish pit afraid.

Jennie, lie still ! The hair you loved
　　You wraps, unclipp'd, if you but knew !
We by a quiet graveyard wall,
　　For love and pity, buried you !

THOMAS BAILEY ALDRICH

1836-1907

423.　　　*Prescience*

THE new moon hung in the sky,
　　The sun was low in the west,
And my betroth'd and I
　　In the churchyard paused to rest—
　　　Happy maiden and lover,
　　　Dreaming the old dream over :
The light winds wander'd by,
　　And robins chirp'd from the nest.

And lo ! in the meadow-sweet
　　Was the grave of a little child,
With a crumbling stone at the feet,
　　And the ivy running wild—
　　　Tangled ivy and clover
　　　Folding it over and over :
Close to my sweetheart's feet
　　Was the little mound up-piled.

566

Stricken with nameless fears
    She shrank and clung to me;
And her eyes were fill'd with tears
    For a sorrow I did not see :
        Lightly the winds were blowing,
        Softly her tears were flowing—
    Tears for the unknown years,
        And a sorrow that was to be !

THEODORE WATTS-DUNTON

b. 1836

424.   *Coleridge*

I SEE thee pine like her in golden story
    Who, in her prison, woke and saw, one day,
    The gates thrown open—saw the sunbeams play,
With only a web 'tween her and summer's glory ;
Who, when that web—so frail, so transitory,
    It broke before her breath—had fallen away,
    Saw other webs and others rise for aye,
Which kept her prisoned till her hair was hoary.
Those songs half-sung that yet were all divine—
    That woke Romance, the queen, to reign afresh—
Had been but preludes from that lyre of thine,
    Could thy rare spirit's wings have pierced the mesh
    Spun by the wizard who compels the flesh,
But lets the poet see how heav'n can shine.

425.   *Mother Carey's Chicken*

I CANNOT brook thy gaze, belovèd bird ;
    That sorrow is more than human in thine eye ;
Too deeply, brother, is my spirit stirr'd
    To see thee here, beneath the landsmen's sky,

567   Coop'd

Coop'd in a cage with food thou canst not eat,
Thy ' snow-flake ' soil'd, and soil'd those conquering feet
That walk'd the billows, while thy ' *sweet-sweet-sweet* '
    Proclaim'd the tempest nigh.

Bird whom I welcomed while the sailors cursed,
    Friend whom I bless'd wherever keels may roam,
Prince of my childish dreams, whom mermaids nursed
    In purple of billows—silver of ocean-foam,
Abash'd I stand before the mighty grief
That quells all other : Sorrow's King and Chief,
Who rides the wind and holds the sea in fief,
    Then finds a cage for home !

From out thy jail thou seest yon heath and woods,
    But canst thou hear the birds or smell the flowers ?
Ah, no ! those rain-drops twinkling on the buds
    Bring only visions of the salt sea-showers.
' The sea ! ' the linnets pipe from hedge and heath ;
' The sea ! ' the honeysuckles whisper and breathe,
And tumbling waves, where those wild-roses wreathe,
    Murmur from inland bowers.

These winds so soft to others—how they burn !
    The mavis sings with gurgle and ripple and plash,
To thee yon swallow seems a wheeling tern ;
    And when the rain recalls the briny lash,
Old Ocean's kiss we love—oh, when thy sight
Is mocked with Ocean's horses—manes of white,
The long and shadowy flanks, the shoulders bright—
    Bright as the lightning's flash—

When all these scents of heather and brier and whin,
  All kindly breaths of land-shrub, flower, and vine,
Recall the sea-scents, till thy feather'd skin
  Tingles in answer to a dream of brine—
When thou, remembering there thy royal birth,
Dost see between the bars a world of dearth,
Is there a grief—a grief on all the earth—
  So heavy and dark as thine ?

But I can buy thy freedom—I (thank God !),
  Who loved thee more than albatross or gull—
Loved thee, and loved the waves thy footsteps trod—
  Dream'd of thee when, becalm'd, we lay a-hull—
'Tis I, thy friend, who once, a child of six,
To find where Mother Carey fed her chicks,
Climb'd up the boat and then with bramble sticks
  Tried all in vain to scull—

Thy friend who shared thy Paradise of Storm—
  The little dreamer of the cliffs and coves,
Who knew thy mother, saw her shadowy form
  Behind the cloudy bastions where she moves,
And heard her call : ' Come ! for the welkin thickens,
And tempests mutter and the lightning quickens ! '
Then, starting from his dream, would find the chickens
  Were daws or blue rock-doves—

Thy friend who owned another Paradise,
  Of calmer air, a floating isle of fruit,
Where sang the Nereids on a breeze of spice,
  While Triton, from afar, would sound salute :
There wast thou winging, though the skies were calm ;
For marvellous strains, as of the morning's shalm,
Were struck by ripples round that isle of palm
  Whose shores were Ocean's lute.

And

And now to see thee here, my king, my king,
  Far-glittering memories mirror'd in those eyes,
As if there shone within each iris-ring
  An orbèd world—ocean and hills and skies !—
Those black wings ruffled whose triumphant sweep
Conquer'd in sport !—yea, up the glimmering steep
Of highest billow, down the deepest deep,
      Sported with victories !—

To see thee here !—a coil of wilted weeds
  Beneath those feet that danced on diamond spray,
Rider of sportive Ocean's reinless steeds—
  Winner in Mother Carey's Sabbath-fray
When, stung by magic of the Witch's chant,
  They rise, each foamy-crested combatant—
They rise and fall and leap and foam and gallop and pant
  Till albatross, sea-swallow, and cormorant
      Must flee like doves away !

And shalt thou ride no more where thou hast ridden,
  And feast no more in hyaline halls and caves,
Master of Mother Carey's secrets hidden,
  Master and monarch of the wind and waves,
Who never, save in stress of angriest blast,
Ask'd ship for shelter—never till at last
The foam-flakes hurled against the sloping mast
      Slash'd thee like whirling glaives ?

Right home to fields no seamew ever kenn'd,
  Where scarce the great sea-wanderer fares with thee,
I come to take thee—nay, 'tis I, thy friend !
  Ah, tremble not—I come to set thee free ;
I come to tear this cage from off this wall,
And take thee hence to that fierce festival
Where billows march and winds are musical,
      Hymning the Victor-Sea !

•   •   •   •   •   •   •

Yea, lift thine eyes to mine. Dost know me now ?
  Thou'rt free ! thou'rt free ! Ah, surely a bird can
    smile !
Dost know me, Petrel ? Dost remember how
  I fed thee in the wake for many a mile,
Whilst thou wouldst pat the waves, then, rising, take
The morsel up and wheel about the wake ?
Thou'rt free, thou'rt free, but for thine own dear sake
    I keep thee caged awhile.

Away to sea ! no matter where the coast :
  The road that turns for home turns never wrong ;
Where waves run high my bird will not be lost :
  His home I know : 'tis where the winds are strong—
Where, on a throne of billows, rolling hoary
And green and blue and splash'd with sunny glory,
Far, far from shore—from farthest promontory—
Prophetic Nature bares the secret of the story
    That holds the spheres in song !

ALGERNON CHARLES SWINBURNE

1837-1909

426.   *Chorus from 'Atalanta'*

BEFORE the beginning of years
    There came to the making of man
Time, with a gift of tears ;
  Grief, with a glass that ran ;
Pleasure, with pain for leaven ;
  Summer, with flowers that fell ;
Remembrance fallen from heaven,
  And madness risen from hell ;
Strength without hands to smite ;
  Love that endures for a breath ;
Night, the shadow of light,
  And life, the shadow of death.

And

And the high gods took in hand
   Fire, and the falling of tears,
And a measure of sliding sand
   From under the feet of the years ;
And froth and drift of the sea ;
   And dust of the labouring earth ;
And bodies of things to be
   In the houses of death and of birth ;
And wrought with weeping and laughter,
   And fashion'd with loathing and love,
With life before and after
   And death beneath and above,
For a day and a night and a morrow,
   That his strength might endure for a span
With travail and heavy sorrow,
   The holy spirit of man.

From the winds of the north and the south
   They gather'd as unto strife ;
They breathed upon his mouth,
   They fill'd his body with life ;
Eyesight and speech they wrought
   For the veils of the soul therein,
A time for labour and thought,
   A time to serve and to sin ;
They gave him light in his ways,
   And love, and a space for delight,
And beauty and length of days,
   And night, and sleep in the night.
His speech is a burning fire ;
   With his lips he travaileth ;
In his heart is a blind desire,
   In his eyes foreknowledge of death ;

He weaves, and is clothed with derision ;
    Sows, and he shall not reap ;
His life is a watch or a vision
    Between a sleep and a sleep.

427.   *The Death of Meleager*

MELEAGER

LET your hands meet
    Round the weight of my head ;
Lift ye my feet
    As the feet of the dead ;
For the flesh of my body is molten, the limbs of it molten
    as lead.

CHORUS

O thy luminous face,
    Thine imperious eyes !
O the grief, O the grace,
    As of day when it dies !
Who is this bending over thee, lord, with tears and
    suppression of sighs ?

MELEAGER

Is a bride so fair ?
    Is a maid so meek ?
With unchapleted hair,
    With unfilleted cheek,
Atalanta, the pure among women, whose name is as
    blessing to speak.

ATALANTA

I would that with feet
    Unsandall'd, unshod,
Overbold, overfleet,
    I had swum not nor trod
From Arcadia to Calydon northward, a blast of the envy
    of God.

                Unto

ALGERNON CHARLES SWINBURNE

Unto each man his fate ;
Unto each as he saith
In whose fingers the weight
Of the world is as breath ;
Yet I would that in clamour of battle mine hands had
laid hold upon death.

CHORUS

Not with cleaving of shields
And their clash in thine ear,
When the lord of fought fields
Breaketh spearshaft from spear,
Thou art broken, our lord, thou art broken, with travail
and labour and fear.

MELEAGER

Would God he had found me
Beneath fresh boughs !
Would God he had bound me
Unawares in mine house,
With light in mine eyes, and songs in my lips, and a crown
on my brows !

CHORUS

Whence art thou sent from us ?
Whither thy goal ?
How art thou rent from us,
Thou that wert whole,
As with severing of eyelids and eyes, as with sundering
of body and soul !

MELEAGER

My heart is within me
As an ash in the fire ;

Whosoever hath seen me,
    Without lute, without lyre,
Shall sing of me grievous things, even things that were
    ill to desire.

CHORUS

Who shall raise thee
    From the house of the dead ?
Or what man praise thee
    That thy praise may be said ?
Alas thy beauty ! alas thy body ! alas thine head !

MELEAGER

But thou, O mother,
    The dreamer of dreams,
Wilt thou bring forth another
    To feel the sun's beams
When I move among shadows a shadow, and wail by
    impassable streams ?

ŒNEUS

What thing wilt thou leave me
    Now this thing is done ?
A man wilt thou give me,
    A son for my son,
For the light of mine eyes, the desire of my life, the
    desirable one ?

CHORUS

Thou wert glad above others,
    Yea, fair beyond word ;
Thou wert glad among mothers ;
    For each man that heard
Of thee, praise there was added unto thee, as wings to
    the feet of a bird.

Who

ALGERNON CHARLES SWINBURNE

ŒNEUS

Who shall give back
Thy face of old years
With travail made black,
Grown grey among fears,
Mother of sorrow, mother of cursing, mother of tears ?

MELEAGER

Though thou art as fire
Fed with fuel in vain,
My delight, my desire,
Is more chaste than the rain,
More pure than the dewfall, more holy than stars are
that live without stain.

ATALANTA

I would that as water
My life's blood had thawn,
Or as winter's wan daughter
Leaves lowland and lawn
Spring-stricken, or ever mine eyes had beheld thee made
dark in thy dawn.

CHORUS

When thou dravest the men
Of the chosen of Thrace,
None turn'd him again
Nor endured he thy face
Clothed round with the blush of the battle, with light
from a terrible place.

ŒNEUS

Thou shouldst die as he dies
For whom none sheddeth tears ;

576

ALGERNON CHARLES SWINBURNE

Filling thine eyes
And fulfilling thine ears
With the brilliance of battle, the bloom and the beauty,
the splendour of spears.

CHORUS

In the ears of the world
It is sung, it is told,
And the light thereof hurl'd
And the noise thereof roll'd
From the Acroceraunian snow to the ford of the fleece
of gold.

MELEAGER

Would God ye could carry me
Forth of all these ;
Heap sand and bury me
By the Chersonese,
Where the thundering Bosphorus answers the thunder of
Pontic seas.

OENEUS

Dost thou mock at our praise
And the singing begun,
And the men of strange days
Praising my son
In the folds of the hills of home, high places of Calydon ?

MELEAGER

For the dead man no home is ;
Ah, better to be
What the flower of the foam is
In fields of the sea,
That the sea-waves might be as my raiment, the gulf-
stream a garment for me !

ALGERNON CHARLES SWINBURNE

Who shall seek thee and bring
   And restore thee thy day,
When the dove dipt her wing
   And the oars won their way
Where the narrowing Symplegades whiten'd the straits
   of Propontis with spray ?

MELEAGER

Will ye crown me my tomb
   Or exalt me my name,
Now my spirits consume,
   Now my flesh is a flame ?
Let the sea slake it once, and men speak of me sleeping
   to praise me or shame.

CHORUS

Turn back now, turn thee,
   As who turns him to wake ;
Though the life in thee burn thee,
   Couldst thou bathe it and slake
Where the sea-ridge of Helle hangs heavier, and east
   upon west waters break ?

MELEAGER

Would the winds blow me back,
   Or the waves hurl me home ?
Ah, to touch in the track
   Where the pine learnt to roam
Cold girdles and crowns of the sea-gods, cool blossoms
   of water and foam !

CHORUS

The gods may release
   That they made fast :

Thy soul shall have ease
In thy limbs at the last ;
But what shall they give thee for life, sweet life that is
overpast ?

MELEAGER

Not the life of men's veins,
Not of flesh that conceives ;
But the grace that remains,
The fair beauty that cleaves
To the life of the rains in the grasses, the life of the
dews on the leaves.

CHORUS

Thou wert helmsman and chief ;
Wilt thou turn in an hour,
Thy limbs to the leaf,
Thy face to the flower,
Thy blood to the water, thy soul to the gods who divide
and devour ?

MELEAGER

The years are hungry,
They wail all their days ;
The gods wax angry
And weary of praise ;
And who shall bridle their lips ? and who shall straiten
their ways ?

CHORUS

The gods guard over us
With sword and with rod ;
Weaving shadow to cover us,
Heaping the sod,
That law may fulfil herself wholly, to darken man's face
before God.

428.   *Hymn to Proserpine*

(AFTER THE PROCLAMATION IN ROME OF THE
CHRISTIAN FAITH)

Vicisti, Galilaee.

I HAVE lived long enough, having seen one thing, that
love hath an end ;
Goddess and maiden and queen, be near me now and
befriend.
Thou art more than the day or the morrow, the seasons
that laugh or that weep ;
For these give joy and sorrow ; but thou, Proserpina,
sleep.
Sweet is the treading of wine, and sweet the feet of the
dove ;
But a goodlier gift is thine than foam of the grapes or love.
Yea, is not even Apollo, with hair and harpstring of gold,
A bitter God to follow, a beautiful God to behold ?
I am sick of singing : the bays burn deep and chafe :
I am fain
To rest a little from praise and grievous pleasure and pain.
For the Gods we know not of, who give us our daily
breath,
We know they are cruel as love or life, and lovely as death.
O Gods dethroned and deceased, cast forth, wiped out
in a day !
From your wrath is the world released, redeem'd from
your chains, men say.
New Gods are crown'd in the city ; their flowers have
broken your rods ;
They are merciful, clothed with pity, the young com-
passionate Gods.

But for me their new device is barren, the days are bare ;
Things long past over suffice, and men forgotten that
  were.
Time and the Gods are at strife ; ye dwell in the midst
  thereof,
Draining a little life from the barren breasts of love.
I say to you, cease, take rest ; yea, I say to you all, be
  at peace,
Till the bitter milk of her breast and the barren bosom
  shall cease.
Wilt thou yet take all, Galilean ? but these thou shalt
  not take,
The laurel, the palms and the paean, the breasts of the
  nymphs in the brake ;
Breasts more soft than a dove's, that tremble with
  tenderer breath ;
And all the wings of the Loves, and all the joy before
  death ;
All the feet of the hours that sound as a single lyre,
Dropp'd and deep in the flowers, with strings that flicker
  like fire.
More than these wilt thou give, things fairer than all
  these things ?
Nay, for a little we live, and life hath mutable wings.
A little while and we die ; shall life not thrive as it may ?
For no man under the sky lives twice, outliving his day.
And grief is a grievous thing, and a man hath enough of
  his tears :
Why should he labour, and bring fresh grief to blacken
  his years ?
Thou hast conquer'd, O pale Galilean ; the world has
  grown grey from thy breath ;
We have drunken of things Lethean, and fed on the
  fullness of death.

Laurel

Laurel is green for a season, and love is sweet for a day ;
But love grows bitter with treason, and laurel outlives
    not May.
Sleep, shall we sleep after all ? for the world is not sweet
    in the end ;
For the old faiths loosen and fall, the new years ruin and
    rend.
Fate is a sea without shore, and the soul is a rock that
    abides ;
But her ears are vex'd with the roar and her face with
    the foam of the tides.
O lips that the live blood faints in, the leavings of racks
    and rods !
O ghastly glories of saints, dead limbs of gibbeted Gods !
Though all men abase them before you in spirit, and all
    knees bend,
I kneel not, neither adore you, but standing, look to the
    end.
All delicate days and pleasant, all spirits and sorrows are
    cast
Far out with the foam of the present that sweeps to the
    surf of the past :
Where beyond the extreme sea-wall, and between the
    remote sea-gates,
Waste water washes, and tall ships founder, and deep
    death waits :
Where, mighty with deepening sides, clad about with the
    seas as with wings,
And impell'd of invisible tides, and fulfill'd of unspeakable
    things,
White-eyed and poisonous-finn'd, shark-tooth'd and
    serpentine-curl'd,
Rolls, under the whitening wind of the future, the wave
    of the world.

The depths stand naked in sunder behind it, the storms
    flee away ;
In the hollow before it the thunder is taken and snared
    as a prey ;
In its sides is the north-wind bound ; and its salt is of
    all men's tears ;
With light of ruin, and sound of changes, and pulse of
    years :
With travail of day after day, and with trouble of hour
    upon hour ;
And bitter as blood is the spray ; and the crests are as
    fangs that devour :
And its vapour and storm of its steam as the sighing of
    spirits to be ;
And its noise as the noise in a dream ; and its depth as
    the roots of the sea :
And the height of its heads as the height of the utmost
    stars of the air :
And the ends of the earth at the might thereof tremble,
    and time is made bare.
Will ye bridle the deep sea with reins, will ye chasten
    the high sea with rods ?
Will ye take her to chain her with chains, who is older
    than all ye Gods ?
All ye as a wind shall go by, as a fire shall ye pass and
    be past ;
Ye are Gods, and behold, ye shall die, and the waves be
    upon you at last.
In the darkness of time, in the deeps of the years, in the
    changes of things,
Ye shall sleep as a slain man sleeps, and the world shall
    forget you for kings.
Though the feet of thine high priests tread where thy
    lords and our forefathers trod,

            Though

Though these that were Gods are dead, and thou being
   dead art a God,
Though before thee the throned Cytherean be fallen,
   and hidden her head,
Yet thy kingdom shall pass, Galilean, thy dead shall go
   down to thee dead.
Of the maiden thy mother men sing as a goddess with
   grace clad around ;
Thou art throned where another was king ; where another
   was queen she is crown'd.
Yea, once we had sight of another : but now she is queen,
   say these.
Not as thine, not as thine was our mother, a blossom of
   flowering seas,
Clothed round with the world's desire as with raiment,
   and fair as the foam,
And fleeter than kindled fire, and a goddess, and mother
   of Rome.
For thine came pale and a maiden, and sister to sorrow ;
   but ours,
Her deep hair heavily laden with odour and colour of
   flowers,
White rose of the rose-white water, a silver splendour,
   a flame,
Bent down unto us that besought her, and earth grew
   sweet with her name.
For thine came weeping, a slave among slaves, and
   rejected ; but she
Came flush'd from the full-flush'd wave, and imperial,
   her foot on the sea.
And the wonderful waters knew her, the winds and the
   viewless ways,
And the roses grew rosier, and bluer the sea-blue stream
   of the bays.

Ye are fallen, our lords, by what token ? we wist that
ye should not fall.

Ye were all so fair that are broken ; and one more fair
than ye all.

But I turn to her still, having seen she shall surely abide
in the end ;

Goddess and maiden and queen, be near me now and
befriend.

O daughter of earth, of my mother, her crown and
blossom of birth,

I am also, I also, thy brother ; I go as I came unto
earth.

In the night where thine eyes are as moons are in heaven,
the night where thou art,

Where the silence is more than all tunes, where sleep
overflows from the heart,

Where the poppies are sweet as the rose in our world, and
the red rose is white,

And the wind falls faint as it blows with the fume of the
flowers of the night,

And the murmur of spirits that sleep in the shadow of
Gods from afar

Grows dim in thine ears and deep as the deep dim soul
of a star,

In the sweet low light of thy face, under heavens untrod
by the sun,

Let my soul with their souls find place, and forget what
is done and undone.

Thou art more than the Gods who number the days of
our temporal breath ;

For these give labour and slumber ; but thou, Proserpina,
death.

Therefore now at thy feet I abide for a season in silence.
I know

I shall

I shall die as my fathers died, and sleep as they sleep; even so.

For the glass of the years is brittle wherein we gaze for a span;

A little soul for a little bears up this corpse which is man.

So long I endure, no longer; and laugh not again, neither weep.

For there is no God found stronger than death; and death is a sleep.

429.   *A Match*

IF love were what the rose is,
   And I were like the leaf,
Our lives would grow together
In sad or singing weather,
Blown fields or flowerful closes,
   Green pleasure or grey grief;
If love were what the rose is,
   And I were like the leaf.

If I were what the words are,
   And love were like the tune,
With double sound and single
Delight our lips would mingle,
With kisses glad as birds are
   That get sweet rain at noon;
If I were what the words are,
   And love were like the tune.

If you were life, my darling,
　　And I your love were death,
We'd shine and snow together
Ere March made sweet the weather
With daffodil and starling
　　And hours of fruitful breath ;
If you were life, my darling,
　　And I your love were death.

If you were thrall to sorrow,
　　And I were page to joy,
We'd play for lives and seasons
With loving looks and treasons
And tears of night and morrow
　　And laughs of maid and boy ;
If you were thrall to sorrow,
　　And I were page to joy.

If you were April's lady,
　　And I were lord in May,
We'd throw with leaves for hours
And draw for days with flowers,
Till day like night were shady
　　And night were bright like day ;
If you were April's lady,
　　And I were lord in May.

If you were queen of pleasure,
　　And I were king of pain,
We'd hunt down love together,
Pluck out his flying-feather,
And teach his feet a measure,
　　And find his mouth a rein ;
If you were queen of pleasure,
　　And I were king of pain.

430.   *A Leave-taking*

LET us go hence, my songs ; she will not hear.
    Let us go hence together without fear ;
Keep silence now, for singing-time is over,
And over all old things and all things dear.
She loves not you nor me as all we love her.
Yea, though we sang as angels in her ear,
            She would not hear.

Let us rise up and part ; she will not know.
Let us go seaward as the great winds go,
Full of blown sand and foam ; what help is here ?
There is no help, for all these things are so,
And all the world is bitter as a tear.
And how these things are, though ye strove to show,
            She would not know.

Let us go home and hence ; she will not weep.
We gave love many dreams and days to keep,
Flowers without scent, and fruits that would not grow,
Saying ' If thou wilt, thrust in thy sickle and reap.'
All is reap'd now ; no grass is left to mow ;
And we that sow'd, though all we fell on sleep,
            She would not weep.

Let us go hence and rest ; she will not love.
She shall not hear us if we sing hereof,
Nor see love's ways, how sore they are and steep.
Come hence, let be, lie still ; it is enough.
Love is a barren sea, bitter and deep ;
And though she saw all heaven in flower above,
            She would not love.

Let us give up, go down ; she will not care.
Though all the stars made gold of all the air,
And the sea moving saw before it move
One moon-flower making all the foam-flowers fair ;
Though all those waves went over us, and drove
Deep down the stifling lips and drowning hair,
      She would not care.

Let us go hence, go hence ; she will not see.
Sing all once more together ; surely she,
She too, remembering days and words that were,
Will turn a little toward us, sighing ; but we,
We are hence, we are gone, as though we had not been
      there.
Nay, and though all men seeing had pity on me,
      She would not see.

431.   *Before the Mirror*

(VERSES WRITTEN UNDER A PICTURE)

I

WHITE rose in red rose-garden
    Is not so white ;
Snowdrops that plead for pardon
    And pine for fright
Because the hard East blows
Over their maiden rows
    Grow not as this face grows from pale to bright.

      Behind

Behind the veil, forbidden,
  Shut up from sight,
Love, is there sorrow hidden,
  Is there delight ?
Is joy thy dower or grief,
White rose of weary leaf,
   Late rose whose life is brief, whose loves are light ?

Soft snows that hard winds harden
  Till each flake bite,
Fill all the flowerless garden
  Whose flowers took flight
Long since, when summer ceased,
And men rose up from feast,
   And warm west wind grew east, and warm day night.

II

' Come snow, come wind or thunder
  High up in air,
I watch my face, and wonder
  At my bright hair ;
Nought else exalts or grieves
The rose at heart, that heaves
   With love of her own leaves and lips that pair.

' She knows not loves that kiss'd her
  She knows not where.
Art thou the ghost, my sister,
  White sister there,
Am I the ghost, who knows ?
My hand, a fallen rose,
   Lies snow-white on white snows, and takes no care.

' I cannot see what pleasures
　　Or what pains were ;
What pale new loves and treasures
　　New years will bear ;
What beam will fall, what shower,
What grief or joy for dower ;
　　But one thing knows the flower ; the flower is fair.'

III

Glad, but not flush'd with gladness,
　　Since joys go by ;
Sad, but not bent with sadness,
　　Since sorrows die ;
Deep in the gleaming glass
She sees all past things pass,
　　And all sweet life that was lie down and lie.

There glowing ghosts of flowers
　　Draw down, draw nigh ;
And wings of swift spent hours
　　Take flight and fly ;
She sees by formless gleams,
She hears across cold streams,
　　Dead mouths of many dreams that sing and sigh.

Face fallen and white throat lifted,
　　With sleepless eye
She sees old loves that drifted,
　　She knew not why,
Old loves and faded fears
Float down a stream that hears
　　The flowing of all men's tears beneath the sky.

432.   *Hesperia*

OUT of the golden remote wild west where the sea
    without shore is,
  Full of the sunset, and sad, if at all, with the fullness
    of joy,
As a wind sets in with the autumn that blows from the
    region of stories,
  Blows with a perfume of songs and of memories
    beloved from a boy,
Blows from the capes of the past oversea to the bays of
    the present,
  Fill'd as with shadow of sound with the pulse of
    invisible feet,
Far out to the shallows and straits of the future, by
    rough ways or pleasant,
  Is it thither the wind's wings beat ? is it hither to me,
    O my sweet ?
For thee, in the stream of the deep tide-wind blowing
    in with the water,
  Thee I behold as a bird borne in with the wind from
    the west,
Straight from the sunset, across white waves whence rose
    as a daughter
  Venus thy mother, in years when the world was a water
    at rest.
Out of the distance of dreams, as a dream that abides
    after slumber,
  Stray'd from the fugitive flock of the night, when the
    moon overhead
Wanes in the wan waste heights of the heaven, and stars
    without number
  Die without sound, and are spent like lamps that are
    burnt by the dead,

Comes back to me, stays by me, lulls me with touch of
    forgotten caresses,
  One warm dream clad about with a fire as of life that
    endures ;
The delight of thy face, and the sound of thy feet, and
    the wind of thy tresses,
  And all of a man that regrets, and all of a maid that
    allures.
But thy bosom is warm for my face and profound as
    a manifold flower,
  Thy silence as music, thy voice as an odour that fades
    in a flame ;
Not a dream, not a dream is the kiss of thy mouth, and
    the bountiful hour
  That makes me forget what was sin, and would make
    me forget were it shame.
Thine eyes that are quiet, thine hands that are tender,
    thy lips that are loving,
  Comfort and cool me as dew in the dawn of a moon
    like a dream ;
And my heart yearns baffled and blind, moved vainly
    toward thee, and moving
  As the refluent seaweed moves in the languid exuberant
    stream,
Fair as a rose is on earth, as a rose under water in prison,
  That stretches and swings to the slow passionate pulse
    of the sea,
Closed up from the air and the sun, but alive, as a ghost
    rearisen,
  Pale as the love that revives as a ghost rearisen in me.
From the bountiful infinite west, from the happy
    memorial places
  Full of the stately repose and the lordly delight of the
    dead,

          Where

Where the fortunate islands are lit with the light of
    ineffable faces,
  And the sound of a sea without wind is about them,
    and sunset is red,
Come back to redeem and release me from love that
    recalls and represses,
  That cleaves to my flesh as a flame, till the serpent has
    eaten his fill ;
From the bitter delights of the dark, and the feverish,
    the furtive caresses
  That murder the youth in a man or ever his heart
    have its will.
Thy lips cannot laugh and thine eyes cannot weep ; thou
    art pale as a rose is,
  Paler and sweeter than leaves that cover the blush of
    the bud ;
And the heart of the flower is compassion, and pity the
    core it encloses,
  Pity, not love, that is born of the breath and decays
    with the blood.
As the cross that a wild nun clasps till the edge of it
    bruises her bosom,
  So love wounds as we grasp it, and blackens and burns
    as a flame ;
I have loved overmuch in my life ; when the live bud
    bursts with the blossom,
  Bitter as ashes or tears is the fruit, and the wine thereof
    shame.
As a heart that its anguish divides is the green bud cloven
    asunder ;
  As the blood of a man self-slain is the flush of the
    leaves that allure ;
And the perfume as poison and wine to the brain, a
    delight and a wonder ;

And the thorns are too sharp for a boy, too slight for
a man, to endure.
Too soon did I love it, and lost love's rose; and I cared
not for glory's:
Only the blossoms of sleep and of pleasure were mix'd
in my hair.
Was it myrtle or poppy thy garland was woven with,
O my Dolores?
Was it pallor of slumber, or blush as of blood, that
I found in thee fair?
For desire is a respite from love, and the flesh not the
heart is her fuel;
She was sweet to me once, who am fled and escaped
from the rage of her reign;
Who behold as of old time at hand as I turn, with her
mouth growing cruel,
And flush'd as with wine with the blood of her lovers,
Our Lady of Pain.
Low down where the thicket is thicker with thorns than
with leaves in the summer,
In the brake is a gleaming of eyes and a hissing of
tongues that I knew;
And the lithe long throats of her snakes reach round her,
their mouths overcome her,
And her lips grow cool with their foam, made moist
as a desert with dew.
With the thirst and the hunger of lust though her
beautiful lips be so bitter,
With the cold foul foam of the snakes they soften and
redden and smile;
And her fierce mouth sweetens, her eyes wax wide and
her eyelashes glitter,
And she laughs with a savour of blood in her face, and
a savour of guile.

                                            She

She laughs, and her hands reach hither, her hair blows
    hither and hisses,
    As a low-lit flame in a wind, back-blown till it shudder
        and leap ;
Let her lips not again lay hold on my soul, nor her
    poisonous kisses,
    To consume it alive and divide from thy bosom, Our
        Lady of Sleep.
Ah daughter of sunset and slumber ! if now it return into
    prison,
    Who shall redeem it anew ? but we, if thou wilt, let
        us fly ;
Let us take to us, now that the white skies thrill with
    a moon unarisen,
    Swift horses of fear or of love, take flight and depart
        and not die.
They are swifter than dreams, they are stronger than
    death ; there is none that hath ridden,
    None that shall ride in the dim strange ways of his life
        as we ride ;
By the meadows of memory, the highlands of hope, and
    the shore that is hidden,
    Where life breaks loud and unseen, a sonorous invisible
        tide ;
By the sands where sorrow has trodden, the salt pools
    bitter and sterile,
    By the thundering reef and the low sea-wall and the
        channel of years,
Our wild steeds press on the night, strain hard through
    pleasure and peril,
    Labour and listen and pant not or pause for the peril
        that nears ;
And the sound of them trampling the way cleaves night
    as an arrow asunder,

And slow by the sand-hill and swift by the down with
    its glimpses of grass,
Sudden and steady the music, as eight hoofs trample and
    thunder,
    Rings in the ear of the low blind wind of the night
      as we pass ;
Shrill shrieks in our faces the blind bland air that was
    mute as a maiden,
    Stung into storm by the speed of our passage, and deaf
      where we past ;
And our spirits too burn as we bound, thine holy but
    mine heavy-laden,
    As we burn with the fire of our flight ; ah love ! shall
      we win at the last ?

433.   *A Forsaken Garden*

IN a coign of the cliff between lowland and highland,
    At the sea-down's edge between windward and lee,
Wall'd round with rocks as an inland island,
    The ghost of a garden fronts the sea.
A girdle of brushwood and thorn encloses
    The steep square slope of the blossomless bed
Where the weeds that grew green from the graves of its
      roses
      Now lie dead.

The fields fall southward, abrupt and broken,
    To the low last edge of the long lone land.
If a step should sound or a word be spoken,
    Would a ghost not rise at the strange guest's hand ?
So long have the grey bare walks lain guestless,
    Through branches and briars if a man make way,
He shall find no life but the sea-wind's, restless
      Night and day.

          The

ALGERNON CHARLES SWINBURNE

The dense hard passage is blind and stifled
   That crawls by a track none turn to climb
To the strait waste place that the years have rifled
   Of all but the thorns that are touch'd not of time.
The thorns he spares when the rose is taken ;
   The rocks are left when he wastes the plain.
The wind that wanders, the weeds wind-shaken,
      These remain.

Not a flower to be press'd of the foot that falls not ;
   As the heart of a dead man the seed-plots are dry ;
From the thicket of thorns whence the nightingale calls
      not,
   Could she call, there were never a rose to reply.
Over the meadows that blossom and wither
   Rings but the note of a sea-bird's song ;
Only the sun and the rain come hither
      All year long.

The sun burns sere and the rain dishevels
   One gaunt bleak blossom of scentless breath.
Only the wind here hovers and revels
   In a round where life seems barren as death.
Here there was laughing of old, there was weeping,
   Haply, of lovers none ever will know,
Whose eyes went seaward a hundred sleeping
      Years ago.

Heart handfast in heart as they stood, ' Look thither,'
   Did he whisper ? ' look forth from the flowers to the
      sea ;
For the foam-flowers endure when the rose-blossoms
      wither,
   And men that love lightly may die—but we ? '

And the same wind sang and the same waves whiten'd,
   And or ever the garden's last petals were shed,
In the lips that had whisper'd, the eyes that had lighten'd,
      Love was dead.

Or they loved their life through, and then went whither?
   And were one to the end—but what end who knows?
Love deep as the sea as a rose must wither,
   As the rose-red seaweed that mocks the rose.
Shall the dead take thought for the dead to love them?
   What love was ever as deep as a grave?
They are loveless now as the grass above them
      Or the wave.

All are at one now, roses and lovers,
   Not known of the cliffs and the fields and the sea.
Not a breath of the time that has been hovers
   In the air now soft with a summer to be.
Not a breath shall there sweeten the seasons hereafter
   Of the flowers or the lovers that laugh now or weep,
When as they that are free now of weeping and laughter
      We shall sleep.

Here death may deal not again for ever;
   Here change may come not till all change end.
From the graves they have made they shall rise up never,
   Who have left nought living to ravage and rend.
Earth, stones, and thorns of the wild ground growing,
   While the sun and the rain live, these shall be;
Till a last wind's breath upon all these blowing
      Roll the sea.

Till the slow sea rise and the sheer cliff crumble,
   Till terrace and meadow the deep gulfs drink,

      Till

Till the strength of the waves of the high tides humble
   The fields that lessen, the rocks that shrink,
Here now in his triumph where all things falter,
   Stretch'd out on the spoils that his own hand spread,
As a god self-slain on his own strange altar,
        Death lies dead.

434.   *To Victor Hugo*

I N the fair days when God
    By man as godlike trod,
And each alike was Greek, alike was free,
   God's lightning spared, they said,
   Alone the happier head
Whose laurels screen'd it ; fruitless grace for thee,
   To whom the high gods gave of right
Their thunders and their laurels and their light.

   Sunbeams and bays before
   Our master's servants wore,
For these Apollo left in all men's lands ;
   But far from these ere now
   And watch'd with jealous brow
Lay the blind lightnings shut between God's hands,
   And only loosed on slaves and kings
The terror of the tempest of their wings.

   Born in those younger years
   That shone with storms of spears
And shook in the wind blown from a dead world's pyre,
   When by her back-blown hair
   Napoleon caught the fair
And fierce Republic with her feet of fire,
   And stay'd with iron words and hands
Her flight, and freedom in a thousand lands :

ALGERNON CHARLES SWINBURNE

Thou sawest the tides of things
    Close over heads of kings,
And thine hand felt the thunder, and to thee
    Laurels and lightnings were
    As sunbeams and soft air
Mix'd each in other, or as mist with sea
    Mix'd, or as memory with desire,
Or the lute's pulses with the louder lyre.

For thee man's spirit stood
    Disrobed of flesh and blood,
And bare the heart of the most secret hours ;
    And to thine hand more tame
    Than birds in winter came
High hopes and unknown flying forms of powers,
    And from thy table fed, and sang
Till with the tune men's ears took fire and rang.

Even all men's eyes and ears
    With fiery sound and tears
Wax'd hot, and cheeks caught flame and eyelid light,
    At those high songs of thine
    That stung the sense like wine,
Or fell more soft than dew or snow by night,
    Or wail'd as in some flooded cave
Sobs the strong broken spirit of a wave.

But we, our Master, we
    Whose hearts uplift to thee,
Ache with the pulse of thy remember'd song,
    We ask not nor await
    From the clench'd hands of fate,
As thou, remission of the world's old wrong ;
    Respite we ask not, nor release ;
Freedom a man may have, he shall not peace.

         Though

Though thy most fiery hope
 Storm heaven, to set wide ope
The all-sought-for gate whence God or Chance debars
 All feet of men, all eyes—
 The old night resumes her skies,
Her hollow hiding-place of clouds and stars,
 Where nought save these is sure in sight ;
And, paven with death, our days are roof'd with night.

 One thing we can ; to be
 Awhile, as men may, free ;
But not by hope or pleasure the most stern
 Goddess, most awful-eyed,
 Sits, but on either side
Sit sorrow and the wrath of hearts that burn,
 Sad faith that cannot hope or fear,
And memory grey with many a flowerless year.

 Not that in stranger's wise
 I lift not loving eyes
To the fair foster-mother France, that gave
 Beyond the pale fleet foam
 Help to my sires and home,
Whose great sweet breast could shelter those and save
 Whom from her nursing breasts and hands
Their land cast forth of old on gentler lands.

 Not without thoughts that ache
 For theirs and for thy sake,
I, born of exiles, hail thy banish'd head ;
 I whose young song took flight
 Toward the great heat and light
On me a child from thy far splendour shed,
 From thine high place of soul and song,
Which, fallen on eyes yet feeble, made them strong.

Ah, not with lessening love
For memories born hereof,
I look to that sweet mother-land, and see
The old fields and fair full streams,
And skies, but fled like dreams
The feet of freedom and the thought of thee;
And all between the skies and graves
The mirth of mockers and the shame of slaves.

She, kill'd with noisome air,
Even she! and still so fair,
Who said ' Let there be freedom,' and there was
Freedom; and as a lance
The fiery eyes of France
Touch'd the world's sleep, and as a sleep made pass
Forth of men's heavier ears and eyes
Smitten with fire and thunder from new skies.

Are they men's friends indeed
Who watch them weep and bleed?
Because thou hast loved us, shall the gods love thee?
Thou, first of men and friend,
Seest thou, even thou, the end?
Thou knowest what hath been, knowest thou what shall be?
Evils may pass and hopes endure;
But fate is dim, and all the gods obscure.

O nursed in airs apart,
O poet highest of heart,
Hast thou seen time, who hast seen so many things?
Are not the years more wise,
More sad than keenest eyes,
The years with soundless feet and sounding wings?
Passing we hear them not, but past
The clamour of them thrills us, and their blast.

Thou

ALGERNON CHARLES SWINBURNE

Thou art chief of us, and lord ;
 Thy song is as a sword
Keen-edged and scented in the blade from flowers ;
 Thou art lord and king ; but we
 Lift younger eyes, and see
Less of high hope, less light on wandering hours :
 Hours that have borne men down so long,
Seen the right fail, and watch'd uplift the wrong.

 But thine imperial soul,
 As years and ruins roll
To the same end, and all things and all dreams
 With the same wreck and roar
 Drift on the dim same shore,
Still in the bitter foam and brackish streams
 Tracks the fresh water-spring to be
And sudden sweeter fountains in the sea.

 As once the high God bound
 With many a rivet round
Man's saviour, and with iron nail'd him through,
 At the wild end of things,
 Where even his own bird's wings
Flagg'd, whence the sea shone like a drop of dew,
 From Caucasus beheld below
Past fathoms of unfathomable snow ;

 So the strong God, the chance
 Central of circumstance,
Still shows him exile who will not be slave ;
 All thy great fame and thee
 Girt by the dim strait sea
With multitudinous walls of wandering wave ;
 Shows us our greatest from his throne,
Fate-stricken, and rejected of his own.

Yea, he is strong, thou say'st,
A mystery many-faced,
The wild beasts know him and the wild birds flee;
The blind night sees him, death
Shrinks beaten at his breath,
And his right hand is heavy on the sea:
We know he hath made us, and is king;
We know not if he care for anything.

Thus much, no more, we know;
He bade what is be so,
Bade light be and bade night be, one by one;
Bade hope and fear, bade ill
And good redeem and kill,
Till all men be aweary of the sun
And his world burn in its own flame
And bear no witness longer of his name.

Yet though all this be thus,
Be those men praised of us
Who have loved and wrought and sorrow'd and not sinn'd
For fame or fear or gold,
Nor wax'd for winter cold,
Nor changed for changes of the worldly wind;
Praised above men of men be these,
Till this one world and work we know shall cease.

Yea, one thing more than this,
We know that one thing is,
The splendour of a spirit without blame,
That not the labouring years
Blind-born, nor any fears,
Nor men nor any gods can tire or tame;
But purer power with fiery breath
Fills, and exalts above the gulfs of death.

Praised

Praised above men be thou,
Whose laurel-laden brow,
Made for the morning, droops not in the night;
Praised and beloved, that none
Of all thy great things done
Flies higher than thy most equal spirit's flight;
Praised, that nor doubt nor hope could bend
Earth's loftiest head, found upright to the end.

435.   *Super Flumina Babylonis*

BY the waters of Babylon we sat down and wept,
        Remembering thee,
That for ages of agony hast endured, and slept,
        And wouldst not see.

By the waters of Babylon we stood up and sang,
        Considering thee,
That a blast of deliverance in the darkness rang,
        To set thee free.

And with trumpets and thunderings and with morning
            song
        Came up the light;
And thy spirit uplifted thee to forget thy wrong
        As day doth night.

And thy sons were dejected not any more, as then
        When thou wast shamed;
When thy lovers went heavily without heart, as men
        Whose life was maim'd.

In the desolate distances, with a great desire,
    For thy love's sake,
With our hearts going back to thee, they were fill'd with
    fire,
    Were nigh to break.

It was said to us : ' Verily ye are great of heart,
    But ye shall bend ;
Ye are bondmen and bondwomen, to be scourged and
    smart,
    To toil and tend.

And with harrows men harrow'd us, and subdued with
    spears,
    And crush'd with shame ;
And the summer and winter was, and the length of years,
    And no change came.

By the rivers of Italy, by the sacred streams,
    By town, by tower,
There was feasting with revelling, there was sleep with
    dreams,
    Until thine hour.

And they slept and they rioted on their rose-hung beds,
    With mouths on flame,
And with love-locks vine-chapleted, and with rose-
    crown'd heads
    And robes of shame.

And they knew not their forefathers, nor the hills and
    streams
    And words of power,
Nor the gods that were good to them, but with songs
    and dreams
    Fill'd up their hour.

        By

By the rivers of Italy, by the dry streams' beds,
    When thy time came,
There was casting of crowns from them, from their young
      men's heads,
    The crowns of shame.

By the horn of Eridanus, by the Tiber mouth,
    As thy day rose,
They arose up and girded them to the north and south,
    By seas, by snows.

As a water in January the frost confines,
    Thy kings bound thee ;
As a water in April is, in the new-blown vines,
    Thy sons made free.

And thy lovers that look'd for thee, and that mourn'd
      from far,
    For thy sake dead,
We rejoiced in the light of thee, in the signal star
    Above thine head.

In thy grief had we follow'd thee, in thy passion loved,
    Loved in thy loss ;
In thy shame we stood fast to thee, with thy pangs were
      moved,
    Clung to thy cross.

By the hillside of Calvary we beheld thy blood,
    Thy blood-red tears,
As a mother's in bitterness, an unebbing flood,
    Years upon years.

And the north was Gethsemane, without leaf or bloom,
  A garden seal'd ;
And the south was Aceldama, for a sanguine fume
  Hid all the field.

By the stone of the sepulchre we return'd to weep,
  From far, from prison ;
And the guards by it keeping it we beheld asleep,
  But thou wast risen.

And an angel's similitude by the unseal'd grave,
  And by the stone :
And the voice was angelical, to whose words God gave
  Strength like his own.

' Lo, the graveclothes of Italy that are folded up
  In the grave's gloom !
And the guards as men wrought upon with a charmèd cup,
  By the open tomb.

' And her body most beautiful, and her shining head,
  These are not here ;
For your mother, for Italy, is not surely dead :
  Have ye no fear.

' As of old time she spake to you, and you hardly heard,
  Hardly took heed,
So now also she saith to you, yet another word,
  Who is risen indeed.

' By my saying she saith to you, in your ears she saith,
  Who hear these things,
Put no trust in men's royalties, nor in great men's breath,
  Nor words of kings.

' For the life of them vanishes and is no more seen,
      Nor no more known ;
Nor shall any remember him if a crown hath been,
      Or where a throne.

' Unto each man his handiwork, unto each his crown,
      The just Fate gives ;
Whoso takes the world's life on him and his own lays
      down,
      He, dying so, lives.

' Whoso bears the whole heaviness of the wrong'd world's
      weight
      And puts it by,
It is well with him suffering, though he face man's fate ;
      How should he die ?

' Seeing death has no part in him any more, no power
      Upon his head ;
He has bought his eternity with a little hour,
      And is not dead.

' For an hour if ye look for him, he is no more found,
      For one hour's space ;
Then ye lift up your eyes to him and behold him crown'd,
      A deathless face.

' On the mountains of memory, by the world's well-
      springs,
      In all men's eyes,
Where the light of the life of him is on all past things,
      Death only dies.

'Not the light that was quench'd for us, nor the deeds
 that were,
  Nor the ancient days,
Nor the sorrows not sorrowful, nor the face most fair
  Of perfect praise.'

So the angel of Italy's resurrection said,
  So yet he saith ;
So the son of her suffering, that from breasts nigh dead
  Drew life, not death.

That the pavement of Golgotha should be white as snow,
  Not red, but white ;
That the waters of Babylon should no longer flow,
  And men see light.

436.   *A Jacobite's Exile*

1746

THE weary day rins down and dies,
  The weary night wears through :
And never an hour is fair wi' flower,
  And never a flower wi' dew.

I would the day were night for me,
  I would the night were day :
For then would I stand in my ain fair land,
  As now in dreams I may.

O lordly flow the Loire and Seine,
  And loud the dark Durance :
But bonnier shine the braes of Tyne
  Than a' the fields of France ;
And the waves of Till that speak sae still
  Gleam goodlier where they glance.

ALGERNON CHARLES SWINBURNE

O weel were they that fell fighting
   On dark Drumossie's day :
They keep their hame ayont the faem,
   And we die far away.

O sound they sleep, and saft, and deep,
   But night and day wake we ;
And ever between the sea-banks green
   Sounds loud the sundering sea.

And ill we sleep, sae sair we weep,
   But sweet and fast sleep they ;
And the mool that haps them roun' and laps them
   Is e'en their country's clay ;
But the land we tread that are not dead
   Is strange as night by day.

Strange as night in a strange man's sight,
   Though fair as dawn it be :
For what is here that a stranger's cheer
   Should yet wax blithe to see ?

The hills stand steep, the dells lie deep,
   The fields are green and gold :
The hill-streams sing, and the hill-sides ring,
   As ours at home of old.

But hills and flowers are nane of ours,
   And ours are oversea :
And the kind strange land whereon we stand,
   It wotsna what were we
Or ever we came, wi' scathe and shame,
   To try what end might be.

Scathe, and shame, and a waefu' name,
    And a weary time and strange,
Have they that seeing a weird for dreeing
    Can die, and cannot change.

Shame and scorn may we thole that mourn,
    Though sair be they to dree :
But ill may we bide the thoughts we hide,
    Mair keen than wind and sea.

Ill may we thole the night's watches,
    And ill the weary day :
And the dreams that keep the gates of sleep,
    A waefu' gift gie they ;
For the sangs they sing us, the sights they bring us,
    The morn blaws all away.

On Aikenshaw the sun blinks braw,
    The burn rins blithe and fain :
There 's nought wi' me I wadna gie
    To look thereon again.

On Keilder-side the wind blaws wide ;
    There sounds nae hunting-horn
That rings sae sweet as the winds that beat
    Round banks where Tyne is born.

The Wansbeck sings with all her springs,
    The bents and braes give ear ;
But the wood that rings wi' the sang she sings
    I may not see nor hear ;
For far and far thae blithe burns are,
    And strange is a' thing near.

The

The light there lightens, the day there brightens,
　　The loud wind there lives free :
Nae light comes nigh me or wind blaws by me
　　That I wad hear or see.

But O gin I were there again,
　　Afar ayont the faem,
Cauld and dead in the sweet saft bed
　　That haps my sires at hame !

We'll see nae mair the sea-banks fair,
　　And the sweet grey gleaming sky,
And the lordly strand of Northumberland,
　　And the goodly towers thereby :
And none shall know but the winds that blow
　　The graves wherein we lie.

437.　　　　　*Child's Song*

WHAT is gold worth, say,
　　Worth for work or play,
Worth to keep or pay,
Hide or throw away,
　　　Hope about or fear ?
What is love worth, pray ?
　　　Worth a tear ?

Golden on the mould
Lie the dead leaves roll'd
Of the wet woods old,
Yellow leaves and cold,
　　　Woods without a dove ;
Gold is worth but gold ;
　　　Love 's worth love.

614

WILLIAM DEAN HOWELLS

b. 1837

438.   *Earliest Spring*

TOSSING his mane of snows in wildest eddies and
     tangles,
   Lion-like March cometh in, hoarse, with tempestuous
     breath,
Through all the moaning chimneys, and 'thwart all the
     hollows and angles
   Round the shuddering house, threating of winter and
     death.

But in my heart I feel the life of the wood and the meadow
   Thrilling the pulses that own kindred with fibres that
     lift
Bud and blade to the sunward, within the inscrutable
     shadow,
   Deep in the oak's chill core, under the gathering drift.

Nay, to earth's life in mine some prescience, or dream,
     or desire
   (How shall I name it aright?) comes for a moment and
     goes—
Rapture of life ineffable, perfect—as if in the brier,
   Leafless there by my door, trembled a sense of the rose.

DAVID GRAY

1838-1861

439. *My Epitaph*

BELOW lies one whose name was traced in sand :
He died, not knowing what it was to live :
Died, while the first sweet consciousness of manhood
To maiden thoughts electrified his soul,
Faint heatings in the calyx of the rose.

Bewilder'd reader, pass without a sigh
In a proud sorrow ! There is life with God
In other kingdom of a sweeter air.
In Eden every flower is blown : Amen.

DOUGLAS AINSLIE

b. 1838

Two Songs from the Sanskrit

440. *i. Apprehension*

BEFORE that my loved one
Has come within sight,
Run quickly and tell him :
' She 's angry to-night,
Your darling '—run quickly,
For ah ! if I see
That ill-behaved dear one,
I know how 'twill be :
My face will grow smiling,
Though struggling with tears—
He is so beguiling,
That dearest of dears.

616

441.   ## ii. The Archer

THE Archer, the Archer!
   Though formless, alive;
His bow is of blossoms,
   His arrows but five.
So mobile the mask and
   So formless his mind:
How then can he harm me,
   The Archer that's blind?
But the pain that I suffer
   All doubting removes,
And the truth of this nonsense
   'Tis loving that proves.

BRET HARTE

1839-1902

442.   ## What the Bullet Sang

O JOY of creation,
      To be!
O rapture, to fly
      And be free!
Be the battle lost or won,
Though its smoke shall hide the sun,
I shall find my love—the one
      Born for me!

I shall know him where he stands
      All alone,
With the power in his hands
      Not o'erthrown;

I

I shall know him by his face,
By his godlike front and grace,
I shall hold him for a space
    All my own !

It is he—O my love !
    So bold !
It is I—all thy love
    Foretold !
It is I—O love, what bliss !
Dost thou answer to my kiss ?
O sweetheart ! what is this
    Lieth there so cold ?

HERMAN CHARLES MERIVALE

b. 1839

443.   *Aetate xix*

NINETEEN ! of years a pleasant number ;
    And it were well
If on his post old Time would slumber
    For Isabel :

If he would leave her, fair and girlish,
    Untouch'd of him,
Forgetting once his fashions churlish
    Just for a whim !

But no, not he ; ashore, aboard ship,
    Sleep we, or wake,
He lays aside his right of lordship
    For no man's sake ;

But all untiring girds his loins up
    For great and small ;
And as a miser sums his coins up,
    Still counts us all.

As jealous as a nine-days' lover,
    He will not spare,
'Spite of the wealth his presses cover,
    One silver hair ;

But writes his wrinkles far and near in
    Life's every page,
With ink invisible, made clear in
    The fire of age.

Child ! while the treacherous flame yet shines not
    On thy smooth brow,
Where even Envy's eye divines not
    That writing now,

In this brief homily I read you
    There should be found
Some wholesome moral, that might lead you
    To look around,

And think how swift, as sunlight passes
    Into the shade,
The pretty picture in your glass is
    Foredoomed to fade.

But, 'faith, the birthday genius quarrels
    With moral rhyme,
And I was never good at morals
    At any time ;

While

While with ill omens to alarm you
   'Twere vain to try ;
To show how little mine should harm you,
   Your mother 's by !

And what can Time hurt me, I pray, with,
   If he insures
Such friends to laugh regrets away with
   As you—and yours ?

JOHN TODHUNTER

b. 1839

444.   *Song*

BRING from the craggy haunts of birch and pine,
   Thou wild wind, bring
Keen forest odours from that realm of thine,
   Upon thy wing !

O wind, O mighty, melancholy wind,
   Blow through me, blow !
Thou blowest forgotten things into my mind,
   From long ago.

445.   *The Black Knight*

A BEATEN and a baffled man,
   My life drags lamely day by day,
Too young to die, too old to plan,
   In failure grey.

The knights ride east, the knights ride west,
For ladyes' tokens blithe of cheer,
Each bound upon some gallant quest ;
   While I rust here.

446. *Maureen*

O, YOU plant the pain in my heart with your wistful
  eyes,
   Girl of my choice, Maureen !
Will you drive me mad for the kisses your shy, sweet
  mouth denies,
   Maureen ?

Like a walking ghost I am, and no words to woo,
   White rose of the West, Maureen :
For it 's pale you are, and the fear that 's on you is over
  me too,
   Maureen !

Sure it 's one complaint that 's on us, asthore, this day,
   Bride of my dreams, Maureen :
The smart of the bee that stung us his honey must cure,
  they say,
   Maureen !

I'll coax the light to your eyes, and the rose to your face,
   Mavourneen, my own Maureen !
When I feel the warmth of your breast, and your nest is
  my arm's embrace,
   Maureen !

O where was the King o' the World that day ?—only me,
   My one true love, Maureen !
And you the Queen with me there, and your throne in
  my heart, machree,
   Maureen !

447.   *Aghadoe*

THERE 's a glade in Aghadoe, Aghadoe, Aghadoe,
    There 's a green and silent glade in Aghadoe,
Where we met, my love and I, Love's fair planet in the
        sky,
    O'er that sweet and silent glade in Aghadoe.

There 's a glen in Aghadoe, Aghadoe, Aghadoe,
    There 's a deep and secret glen in Aghadoe,
Where I hid from the eyes of the red-coats and their
        spies,
    That year the trouble came to Aghadoe.

O, my curse on one black heart in Aghadoe, Ahgadoe,
    On Shaun Dhu, my mother's son in Aghadoe!
When your throat fries in hell's drouth, salt the flame be
        in your mouth,
    For the treachery you did in Aghadoe!

For they track'd me to that glen in Aghadoe, Aghadoe,
    When the price was on his head in Aghadoe:
O'er the mountain, through the wood, as I stole to him
        with food,
    Where in hiding lone he lay in Aghadoe.

But they never took him living in Aghadoe, Aghadoe;
    With the bullets in his heart in Aghadoe,
There he lay, the head, my breast keeps the warmth of
        where 'twould rest,
    Gone, to win the traitor's gold, from Aghadoe!

JOHN TODHUNTER

I walk'd to Mallow town from Aghadoe, Aghadoe,
  Brought his head from the gaol's gate to Aghadoe ;
Then I cover'd him with fern, and I piled on him the
    cairn,
  Like an Irish King he sleeps in Aghadoe.

O, to creep into that cairn in Aghadoe, Aghadoe !
  There to rest upon his breast in Aghadoe !
Sure your dog for you could die with no truer heart than I,
  Your own love, cold on your cairn in Aghadoe.

JOHN ADDINGTON SYMONDS
1840-1893

448. *Le Jeune Homme Caressant Sa Chimère*

FOR AN INTAGLIO

A BOY of eighteen years mid myrtle-boughs
    Lying love-languid on a morn of May,
Watch'd half-asleep his goats insatiate browse
  Thin shoots of thyme and lentisk, by the spray
  Of biting sea-winds bitter made and grey :
Therewith when shadows fell, his waking thought
Of love into a wondrous dream was wrought.

A woman lay beside him,—so it seem'd ;
  For on her marble shoulders, like a mist
Irradiate with tawny moonrise, gleam'd
  Thick silken tresses ; her white woman's wrist,
  Glittering with snaky gold and amethyst,
Upheld a dainty chin ; and there beneath,
Her twin breasts shone like pinks that lilies wreathe.

What

What colour were her eyes I cannot tell ;
 For as he gazed thereon, at times they darted
Dun rays like water in a dusky well ;
 Then turn'd to topaz : then like rubies smarted
 With smouldering flames of passion tiger-hearted ;
Then 'neath blue-veinèd lids swam soft and tender
With pleadings and shy timorous surrender.

Thus far a woman : but the breath that lifted
 Her panting breast with long melodious sighs,
Stirr'd o'er her neck and hair broad wings that sifted
 The perfumes of meridian Paradise ;
 Dusk were they, furr'd like velvet, gemm'd with eyes
Of such dull lustre as in isles afar
Night-flying moths spread to the summer star.

Music these pinions made—a sound and surge
 Of pines innumerous near lisping waves—
Rustling of reeds and rushes on the verge
 Of level lakes and naiad-haunted caves—
 Drown'd whispers of a wandering stream that laves
Deep alder-boughs and tracts of ferny grass
Border'd with azure-bell'd campanulas.

Potent they were : for never since her birth
 With feet of woman this fair siren press'd
Sleek meadow swards or stony ways of earth ;
 But 'neath the silken marvel of her breast,
 Display'd in sinuous length of coil and crest,
Glitter'd a serpent's tail, fold over fold,
In massy labyrinths of languor roll'd.

JOHN ADDINGTON SYMONDS

Ah, me ! what fascination ! what faint stars
   Of emerald and opal, with the shine
Of rubies intermingled, and dim bars
   Of twisting turquoise and pale coralline !
   What rings and rounds ! what thin streaks sapphirine
Freckled that gleaming glory, like the bed
Of Eden streams with gems enamellèd !

There lurk'd no loathing, no soul-freezing fear,
   But luxury and love these coils between :
Faint grew the boy ; the siren fill'd his ear
   With singing sweet as when the village-green
   Re-echoes to the tinkling tambourine,
And feet of girls aglow with laughter glance
In myriad mazy errors of the dance.

How long he dallied with delusive joy
   I know not ; but thereafter never more
The peace of passionless slumber soothed the boy ;
   For he was stricken to the very core
   With sickness of desire exceeding sore,
And through the radiance of his eyes there shone
Consuming fire too fierce to gaze upon.

He, ere he died—and they whom lips divine
   Have touch'd, fade flower-like and cease to be—
Bade Charicles on agate carve a sign
   Of his strange slumber : therefore can we see
   Here in the ruddy gem's transparency
The boy, the myrtle boughs, the triple spell
Of moth and snake and white witch terrible.

449.   Κοινὰ τὰ τῶν φίλων

G IVE freely to the friend thou hast ;
   Unto thyself thou givest :
On barren soil thou canst not cast,
   For by his life thou livest.

Nay, this alone doth trouble me—
   That I should still be giving
Through him unto myself, when he
   Is love within me living.

I fain would give to him alone,
   Nor let him guess the giver ;
Like dews that drop on hills unknown,
   To feed a lordly river.

450.   *Farewell*

I T is buried and done with,
   The love that we knew :
Those cobwebs we spun with
   Are beaded with dew.

I loved thee ; I leave thee :
   To love thee was pain :
I dare not believe thee
   To love thee again.

Like spectres unshriven
   Are the years that I lost ;
To thee they were given
   Without count of cost.

626

I cannot revive them
　　By penance or prayer ;
Hell's tempest must drive them
　　Thro' turbulent air.

Farewell, and forget me :
　　For I too am free
From the shame that beset me,
　　The sorrow of thee.

AUGUSTA WEBSTER

1840-1894

451.　　　　*Seeds*

SEEDS with wings, between earth and sky
　　Fluttering, flying ;
　Seeds of a lily with blood-red core
　Breathing of myrrh and of giroflore :
Where winds drop them, there must they lie,
　　Living or dying.

Some to the garden, some to the wall,
　　Fluttering, falling,
　Some to the river, some to earth :
　Those that reach the right soil get birth :
None of the rest have lived at all.
　　Whose voice is calling ?—

' Here is soil for wing'd seeds that near,
　　Fluttering, fearing,
　Where they shall root and burgeon and spread.
　Lacking the heart-room the Song lies dead :
Half is the Song that reaches the ear,
　　Half is the hearing.

THOMAS HARDY

b. 1840

452.   *The Darkling Thrush*

I LEANT upon a coppice gate
   When Frost was spectre-gray,
And Winter's dregs made desolate
   The weakening eye of day.
The tangled bine-stems scored the sky
   Like strings of broken lyres,
And all mankind that haunted nigh
   Had sought their household fires.

The land's sharp features seem'd to be
   The Century's corpse outleant,
His crypt the cloudy canopy,
   The wind his death-lament.
The ancient pulse of germ and birth
   Was shrunken hard and dry,
And every spirit upon earth
   Seem'd fervourless as I.

At once a voice arose among
   The bleak twigs overhead
In a full-hearted evensong
   Of joy illimited ;
An aged thrush, frail, gaunt, and small,
   In blast-beruffled plume,
Had chosen thus to fling his soul
   Upon the growing gloom.

So little cause for carollings
    Of such ecstatic sound
Was written on terrestrial things
    Afar or nigh around,
That I could think there trembled through
    His happy good-night air
Some blessèd Hope, whereof he knew
    And I was unaware.

453.   *She, to Him*

i

WHEN you shall see me in the toils of Time,
    My lauded beauties carried off from me,
My eyes no longer stars as in their prime,
My name forgot of Maiden Fair and Free ;

When in your being heart concedes to mind,
And judgement, though you scarce its process know,
Recalls the excellences I once enshrined,
And you are irk'd that they have wither'd so ;

Remembering mine the loss is, not the blame,
That Sportsman Time but rears his brood to kill,
Knowing me in my soul the very same—
One who would die to spare you touch of ill !—
Will you not grant to old affection's claim
The hand of friendship down Life's sunless hill ?

ii

PERHAPS, long hence, when I have pass'd away,
    Some other's feature, accent, thought like mine,
Will carry you back to what I used to say,
And bring some memory of your love's decline.

629   Then

Then you may pause awhile and think, ' Poor jade ! '
And yield a sigh to me—as ample due,
Not as the tittle of a debt unpaid
To one who could resign her all to you—

And thus reflecting, you will never see
That your thin thought, in two small words convey'd,
Was no such fleeting phantom-thought to me,
But the Whole Life wherein my part was play'd ;
And you amid its fitful masquerade
A Thought—as I in yours but seem to be.

454   ' *I need not go* '

I NEED not go
   Through sleet and snow
To where I know
She waits for me ;
She will tarry me there
Till I find it fair,
And have time to spare
From company.

When I've overgot
The world somewhat,
When things cost not
Such stress and strain,
Is soon enough
By cypress sough
To tell my Love
I am come again.

And if some day,
When none cries nay,
I still delay
To seek her side,
(Though ample measure
Of fitting leisure
Await my pleasure)
She will not chide.

What—not upbraid me
That I delay'd me,
Nor ask what stay'd me
So long ? Ah, no !—
New cares may claim me.
New loves inflame me,
She will not blame me,
But suffer it so.

455.   *Friends Beyond*

WILLIAM DEWY, Tranter Reuben, Farmer
        Ledlow late at plough,
    Robert's kin, and John's, and Ned's,
And the Squire, and Lady Susan, lie in Mellstock
        churchyard now !

'Gone,' I call them, gone for good, that group of
        local hearts and heads ;
    Yet at mothy curfew-tide,
And at midnight when the noon-heat breathes it
        back from walls and leads,

631   They've

They've a way of whispering to me—fellow-wight
    who yet abide—
    In the muted, measured note
Of a ripple under archways, or a lone cave's stillicide :

' We have triumph'd : this achievement turns the
    bane to antidote,
    Unsuccesses to success,
Many thought-worn eves and morrows to a morrow
    free of thought.

' No more need we corn and clothing, feel of old
    terrestrial stress ;
    Chill detraction stirs no sigh ;
Fear of death has even bygone us : death gave all
    that we possess.'

W. D.—' Ye mid burn the old bass-viol that set I such
    value by.'
Squire.—' You may hold the manse in fee,
    You may wed my spouse, may let my children's
    memory of me die.'

Lady.—' You may have my rich brocades, my laces ; take
    each household key ;
    Ransack coffer, desk, bureau ;
Quiz the few poor treasures hid there, con the letters
    kept by me.'

Far.—' Ye mid zell my favourite heifer, ye mid let the
    charlock grow,
    Foul the grinterns, give up thrift.'
Wife.—' If ye break my best blue china, children, I shan't
    care or ho.'

All.—'We've no wish to hear the tidings, how the people's
        fortunes shift ;
    What your daily doings are ;
Who are wedded, born, divided ; if your lives beat
        slow or swift.

' Curious not the least are we if our intents you make
        or mar,
    If you quire to our old tune,
If the City stage still passes, if the weirs still roar
        afar.'

—Thus, with very gods' composure, freed those
        crosses late and soon
    Which, in life, the Trine allow
(Why, none witteth), and ignoring all that haps
        beneath the moon,

William Dewy, Tranter Reuben, Farmer Ledlow late
        at plough,
    Robert's kin, and John's, and Ned's,
And the Squire, and Lady Susan, murmur mildly to
        me now.

WILFRID SCAWEN BLUNT
b. 1840

456.   *Song*

O FLY not, Pleasure, pleasant-hearted Pleasure ;
    Fold me thy wings, I prithee, yet and stay :
  For my heart no measure
  Knows, nor other treasure
To buy a garland for my love to-day.

        And

And thou, too, Sorrow, tender-hearted Sorrow,
  Thou gray-eyed mourner, fly not yet away :
      For I fain would borrow
      Thy sad weeds to-morrow,
  To make a mourning for love's yesterday.

The voice of Pity, Time's divine dear Pity,
  Moved me to tears : I dared not say them nay,
      But pass'd forth from the city,
      Making thus my ditty
  Of fair love lost for ever and a day.

457.   *The Desolate City*

DARK to me is the earth.   Dark to me are the heavens.
    Where is she that I loved, the woman with eyes like
    stars ?
Desolate are the streets.   Desolate is the city.
    A city taken by storm, where none are left but the slain.

Sadly I rose at dawn, undid the latch of my shutters,
    Thinking to let in light, but I only let in love.
Birds in the boughs were awake ; I listen'd to their
    chaunting ;
    Each one sang to his love ; only I was alone.

This, I said in my heart, is the hour of life and of pleasure.
    Now each creature on earth has his joy, and lives in the
    sun,
Each in another's eyes finds light, the light of compassion,
    This is the moment of pity, this is the moment of love.

Speak, O desolate city ! Speak, O silence in sadness !
  Where is she that I loved in my strength, that spoke
    to my soul ?
Where are those passionate eyes that appeal'd to my eyes
    in passion ?
  Where is the mouth that kiss'd me, the breast I laid
    to my own ?

Speak, thou soul of my soul, for rage in my heart is kindled.
  Tell me, where didst thou flee in the day of destruction
    and fear ?
See, my arms still enfold thee, enfolding thus all heaven,
  See, my desire is fulfill'd in thee, for it fills the earth.

Thus in my grief I lamented. Then turn'd I from the
  window,
  Turn'd to the stair, and the open door, and the empty
    street,
Crying aloud in my grief, for there was none to chide me,
  None to mock my weakness, none to behold my tears.

Groping I went, as blind. I sought her house, my
  belovèd's.
  There I stopp'd at the silent door, and listen'd and
    tried the latch.
Love, I cried, dost thou slumber ? This is no hour for
  slumber,
  This is the hour of love, and love I bring in my hand.

I knew the house, with its windows barr'd, and its leafless
  fig-tree,
  Climbing round by the doorstep, the only one in the
    street ;

I

I knew where my hope had climb'd to its goal and there
    encircled
    All that those desolate walls once held, my belovèd's
      heart.

There in my grief she consoled me. She loved me when
    I loved not.
    She put her hand in my hand, and set her lips to my
      lips.
She told me all her pain and show'd me all her trouble.
    I, like a fool, scarce heard, hardly return'd her kiss.

Love, thy eyes were like torches. They changed as I
    beheld them.
    Love, thy lips were like gems, the seal thou sett'st on
      my life.
Love, if I loved not then, behold this hour thy vengeance ;
    This is the fruit of thy love and thee, the unwise grown
      wise.

Weeping strangled my voice. I call'd out, but none
    answer'd ;
    Blindly the windows gazed back at me, dumbly the
      door ;
She whom I love, who loved me, look'd not on my
    yearning,
    Gave me no more her hands to kiss, show'd me no more
      her soul.

Therefore the earth is dark to me, the sunlight blackness,
    Therefore I go in tears and alone, by night and day ;
Therefore I find no love in heaven, no light, no beauty,
    A heaven taken by storm, where none are left but the
      slain !

458.   *With Esther*

HE who has once been happy is for aye
    Out of destruction's reach. His fortune then
Holds nothing secret ; and Eternity,
    Which is a mystery to other men,
Has like a woman given him its joy.
    Time is his conquest. Life, if it should fret,
Has paid him tribute. He can bear to die,
    He who has once been happy ! When I set
The world before me and survey its range,
    Its mean ambitions, its scant fantasies,
The shreds of pleasure which for lack of change
    Men wrap around them and call happiness,
The poor delights which are the tale and sum
Of the world's courage in its martyrdom ;

When I hear laughter from a tavern door,
    When I see crowds agape and in the rain
Watching on tiptoe and with stifled roar
    To see a rocket fired or a bull slain,
When misers handle gold, when orators
    Touch strong men's hearts with glory till they weep,
When cities deck their streets for barren wars
    Which have laid waste their youth, and when I keep
Calmly the count of my own life and see
    On what poor stuff my manhood's dreams were fed
Till I too learn'd what dole of vanity
    Will serve a human soul for daily bread,
—Then I remember that I once was young
And lived with Esther the world's gods among.

459. *To Manon, Comparing her to a Falcon*

BRAVE as a falcon and as merciless,
 With bright eyes watching still the world, thy prey,
I saw thee pass in thy lone majesty,
Untamed, unmated, high above the press.
The dull crowd gazed at thee.   It could not guess
The secret of thy proud aërial way,
Or read in thy mute face the soul which lay
A prisoner there in chains of tenderness.
Lo, thou art captured.   In my hand to-day
I hold thee, and awhile thou deignest to be
Pleased with my jesses.   I would fain beguile
My foolish heart to think thou lovest me.   See,
I dare not love thee quite.   A little while
And thou shalt sail back heavenwards.   Woe is me !

460.   *St. Valentine's Day*

TO-DAY, all day, I rode upon the down,
 With hounds and horsemen, a brave company,
On this side in its glory lay the sea,
On that the Sussex weald, a sea of brown.
The wind was light, and brightly the sun shone,
And still we gallop'd on from gorse to gorse :
And once, when check'd, a thrush sang, and my horse
Prick'd his quick ears as to a sound unknown.
 I knew the Spring was come.   I knew it even
Better than all by this, that through my chase
In bush and stone and hill and sea and heaven
I seem'd to see and follow still your face.
Your face my quarry was.   For it I rode,
My horse a thing of wings, myself a god.

461.   *Gibraltar*

SEVEN weeks of sea, and twice seven days of storm
    Upon the huge Atlantic, and once more
We ride into still water and the calm
Of a sweet evening, screen'd by either shore
Of Spain and Barbary.   Our toils are o'er,
Our exile is accomplish'd.   Once again
We look on Europe, mistress as of yore
Of the fair earth and of the hearts of men.
    Ay, this is the famed rock which Hercules
And Goth and Moor bequeath'd us.   At this door
England stands sentry.   God ! to hear the shrill
Sweet treble of her fifes upon the breeze,
And at the summons of the rock gun's roar
To see her red coats marching from the hill !

462.   *Written at Florence*

O WORLD, in very truth thou art too young ;
    When wilt thou learn to wear the garb of age ?
World, with thy covering of yellow flowers,
Hast thou forgot what generations sprung
Out of thy loins and loved thee and are gone ?
Hast thou no place in all their heritage
Where thou dost only weep, that I may come
Nor fear the mockery of thy yellow flowers ?
    O world, in very truth thou art too young.
The heroic wealth of passionate emprize
Built thee fair cities for thy naked plains :
How hast thou set thy summer growth among
The broken stones which were their palaces !
Hast thou forgot the darkness where *he* lies
Who made thee beautiful, or have thy bees
Found out his grave to build their honeycombs ?

O world, in very truth thou art too young :
They gave thee love who measured out thy skies,
And, when they found for thee another star,
Who made a festival and straightway hung
The jewel on thy neck.   O merry world,
Hast thou forgot the glory of those eyes
Which first look'd love in thine ?   Thou hast not furl'd
One banner of thy bridal car for them.
　O world, in very truth thou art too young.
There was a voice which sang about thy spring,
Till winter froze the sweetness of his lips,
And lo, the worms had hardly left his tongue
Before thy nightingales were come again.
O world, what courage hast thou thus to sing ?
Say, has thy merriment no secret pain,
No sudden weariness that thou art young ?

463.　　　　　*The Old Squire*

I LIKE the hunting of the hare
　　Better than that of the fox ;
I like the joyous morning air,
　　And the crowing of the cocks.

I like the calm of the early fields,
　　The ducks asleep by the lake,
The quiet hour which Nature yields,
　　Before mankind is awake.

I like the pheasants and feeding things
　　Of the unsuspicious morn ;
I like the flap of the wood-pigeon's wings
　　As she rises from the corn.

WILFRID SCAWEN BLUNT

I like the blackbird's shriek, and his rush
　　From the turnips as I pass by,
And the partridge hiding her head in a bush
　　For her young ones cannot fly.

I like these things, and I like to ride
　　When all the world is in bed,
To the top of the hill where the sky grows wide,
　　And where the sun grows red.

The beagles at my horse heels trot
　　In silence after me ;
There 's Ruby, Roger, Diamond, Dot,
　　Old Slut and Margery,—

A score of names well used, and dear,
　　The names my childhood knew ;
The horn, with which I rouse their cheer,
　　Is the horn my father blew.

I like the hunting of the hare
　　Better than that of the fox ;
The new world still is all less fair
　　Than the old world it mocks.

I covet not a wider range
　　Than these dear manors give ;
I take my pleasures without change,
　　And as I lived I live.

I leave my neighbours to their thought ;
　　My choice it is, and pride,
On my own lands to find my sport,
　　In my own fields to ride.

WILFRID SCAWEN BLUNT

The hare herself no better loves
    The field where she was bred,
Than I the habit of these groves,
    My own inherited.

I know my quarries every one,
    The meuse where she sits low ;
The road she chose to-day was run
    A hundred years ago.

The lags, the gills, the forest ways,
    The hedgerows one and all,
These are the kingdoms of my chase,
    And bounded by my wall ;

Nor has the world a better thing,
    Though one should search it round,
Than thus to live one's own sole king,
    Upon one's own sole ground.

I like the hunting of the hare ;
    It brings me, day by day,
The memory of old days as fair,
    With dead men past away.

To these, as homeward still I ply
    And pass the churchyard gate
Where all are laid as I must lie,
    I stop and raise my hat.

I like the hunting of the hare ;
    New sports I hold in scorn.
I like to be as my fathers were,
    In the days e'er I was born.

AUSTIN DOBSON

464.   *A Garden Song*

HERE in this sequester'd close
    Bloom the hyacinth and rose,
Here beside the modest stock
Flaunts the flaring hollyhock ;
Here, without a pang, one sees
Ranks, conditions, and degrees.

All the seasons run their race
In this quiet resting-place ;
Peach and apricot and fig
Here will ripen and grow big ;
Here is store and overplus,—
More had not Alcinous !

Here, in alleys cool and green,
Far ahead the thrush is seen ;
Here along the southern wall
Keeps the bee his festival ;
All is quiet else—afar
Sounds of toil and turmoil are.

Here be shadows large and long ;
Here be spaces meet for song ;
Grant, O garden-god, that I,
Now that none profane is nigh,—
Now that mood and moment please,—
Find the fair Pierides !

643

465. *A Fancy from Fontenelle*

' De mémoires de Rose on n'a point vu mourir le Jardinier.'

THE Rose in the garden slipp'd her bud,
  And she laugh'd in the pride of her youthful blood,
As she thought of the Gardener standing by—
' He is old,—so old ! And he soon must die ! '

The full Rose wax'd in the warm June air,
And she spread and spread till her heart lay bare ;
And she laugh'd once more as she heard his tread—
' He is older now ! He will soon be dead ! '

But the breeze of the morning blew, and found
That the leaves of the blown Rose strew'd the ground ;
And he came at noon, that Gardener old,
And he raked them softly under the mould.

And I wove the thing to a random rhyme,
For the Rose is Beauty, the Gardener Time.

466. *' Good Night, Babette !'*

' Si vieillesse pouvait !—'

SCENE.—*A small neat Room. In a high Voltaire Chair sits
a white-haired old Gentleman.*

MONSIEUR VIEUXBOIS   BABETTE

M. VIEUXBOIS (*turning querulously*)

DAY of my life ! Where *can* she get ?
  BABETTE ! I say ! BABETTE !—BABETTE ! !

BABETTE (*entering hurriedly*)

Coming, M'sieu ! If M'sieu speaks
So loud he won't be well for weeks !

M. VIEUXBOIS

Where have you been ?

BABETTE

     Why, M'sieu knows :—
April ! . . . Ville-d'Avray ! . . . Ma'am'selle ROSE !

M. VIEUXBOIS

Ah ! I am old,—and I forget.
Was the place growing green, BABETTE ?

BABETTE

But of a greenness !—yes, M'sieu !
And then the sky so blue !—so blue !
And when I dropped my *immortelle*,
How the birds sang !
   (*Lifting her apron to her eyes*)
     This poor Ma'am'selle !

M. VIEUXBOIS

You're a good girl, BABETTE, but she,—
She was an Angel, verily.
Sometimes I think I see her yet
Stand smiling by the cabinet ;
And once, I know, she peep'd and laugh'd
Betwixt the curtains . . .
     Where 's the draught ?
   (*She gives him a cup*)
Now I shall sleep, I think, BABETTE ;—
Sing me your Norman *chansonnette*.

Once

AUSTIN DOBSON

BABETTE (*sings*)

'*Once at the Angelus*
(Ere I was dead),
Angels all glorious
Came to my Bed ;—
Angels in blue and white
Crown'd on the Head.'

M. VIEUXBOIS (*drowsily*)

' She was an Angel ' . . . ' Once she laugh'd ' . . .
What, was I dreaming ?

Where 's the draught ?

BABETTE (*showing the empty cup*)

The draught, M'sieu ?

M. VIEUXBOIS

How I forget !
I am so old ! But sing, BABETTE !

BABETTE (*sings*)

'*One was the Friend I left*
Stark in the Snow ;
One was the Wife that died
Long,—long ago ;
One was the Love I lost . . .
How could she know ? '

M. VIEUXBOIS (*murmuring*)

Ah, PAUL ! . . . old PAUL ! . . . EULALIE too !
And ROSE ! . . . And O ! ' the sky so blue ! '

BABETTE (*sings*)
 ' *One had my Mother's eyes,*
   Wistful and mild ;
  One had my Father's face ;
   One was a Child :
  All of them bent to me,—
   Bent down and smiled ! '

(He is asleep !)

      M. VIEUXBOIS (*almost inaudibly*)
      How I forget !
I am so old ! . . . Good night, BABETTE !

467.   A Ballad to Queen Elizabeth

OF THE SPANISH ARMADA

KING PHILIP had vaunted his claims ;
   He had sworn for a year he would sack us ;
With an army of heathenish names
   He was coming to fagot and stack us ;
   Like the thieves of the sea he would track us,
And shatter our ships on the main ;
   But we had bold Neptune to back us,—
And where are the galleons of Spain ?

His carackes were christen'd of dames
   To the kirtles whereof he would tack us ;
With his saints and his gilded stern-frames,
   He had thought like an egg-shell to crack us :
   Now Howard may get to his Flaccus,
And Drake to his Devon again,
   And Hawkins bowl rubbers to Bacchus,—
For where are the galleons of Spain ?

Let

Let his Majesty hang to St. James
    The axe that he whetted to hack us ;
He must play at some lustier games
    Or at sea he can hope to out-thwack us ;
    To his mines of Peru he would pack us
To tug at his bullet and chain ;
    Alas that his Greatness should lack us !—
But where are the galleons of Spain ?

Envoy

GLORIANA !—the Don may attack us
Whenever his stomach be fain ;
    He must reach us before he can rack us, . . .
And where are the galleons of Spain ?

468. *On a Fan that belonged to the*
      Marquise de Pompadour

CHICKEN-SKIN, delicate, white,
    Painted by Carlo Vanloo,
Loves in a riot of light,
    Roses and vaporous blue ;
    Hark to the dainty *frou-frou !*
Picture above if you can,
    Eyes that could melt as the dew,—
This was the Pompadour's fan !

See how they rise at the sight,
    Thronging the *Œil de Bœuf* through,
Courtiers as butterflies bright,
    Beauties that Fragonard drew,

Talon-rouge, falbala, queue,
    Cardinal, Duke,—to a man,
    Eager to sigh or to sue,—
This was the Pompadour's fan !

Ah ! but things more than polite
    Hung on this toy, *voyez vous !*
Matters of state and of might,
    Things that great ministers do ;
    Things that, maybe, overthrew
Those in whose brains they began ;
    Here was the sign and the cue,—
This was the Pompadour's fan !

Envoy

Where are the secrets it knew ?
    Weavings of plot and of plan ?
—But where is the Pompadour, too ?
    This was the Pompadour's *Fan !*

469.   *In After Days*

IN after days when grasses high
   O'er-top the stone where I shall lie,
   Though ill or well the world adjust
   My slender claim to honour'd dust,
I shall not question nor reply.

I shall not see the morning sky ;
I shall not hear the night-wind sigh ;
   I shall be mute, as all men must
     In after days !

But

But yet, now living, fain would I
That some one then should testify,
    Saying—' He held his pen in trust
    To Art, not serving shame or lust.'
Will none ?—Then let my memory die
    In after days !

WILLIAM COSMO MONKHOUSE

1840-1901

470.   *In Arcady*

IN yon hollow Damon lies,
    Lost in slumber deep.
(Hush, hush, ye shepherd girls,
    Break not his sleep.)

Phyllis passes tiptoe by ;
    Whither is she hieing ?
(Peep, peep, ye shepherd girls,
    He for her is dying.)

Now she pauses, now she bends,
    Ah, she kiss'd him purely.
(Look away, ye shepherd girls,
    Frown, frown demurely.)

See he clips her in his arms,
    She who was the proudest.
(Laugh, laugh, ye shepherd girls,
    Laugh, laugh your loudest.)

471. *From 'A Dead March'*

PLAY me a march lowtoned and slow—a march for
    a silent tread,
Fit for the wandering feet of one who dreams of the
    silent dead,
Lonely, between the bones below and the souls that are
    overhead.

Here for awhile they smiled and sang, alive in the inter-
    space ;
Here with the grass beneath the foot, and the stars above
    the face,
Now are their feet beneath the grass, and whither has
    flown their grace ?

Who shall assure us whence they come or tell us the way
    they go ?
Verily, life with them was joy, and now they have left
    us, woe ;
Once they were not, and now they are not, and this is
    the sum we know. . . .

Why do we mourn the days that go—for the same sun
    shines each day,
Ever a spring her primrose hath, and ever a May her
    may—
Sweet as the rose that died last year, is the rose that is
    born to-day.

Do we not too return, we men, as ever the round earth
    whirls ?
Never a head is dimm'd with gray, but another is sunn'd
    with curls,
She was a girl and he was a boy, but yet there are boys
    and girls.

Ah,

Ah, but alas for the smile of smiles that never but one
　　face wore!
Ah for the voice that has flown away like a bird to an
　　unseen shore!
Ah for the face—the flower of flowers—that blossoms on
　　earth no more!

472.　　　　*The Night Express*

WITH three great snorts of strength,
　　　Stretching my mighty length,
Like some long dragon stirring in his sleep,
　　Out from the glare of gas
　　Into the night I pass,
And plunge alone into the silence deep.

　　Little I know or care
　　What be the load I bear,
Why thus compell'd, I seek not to divine;
　　At man's command I stir,
　　I, his stern messenger!
Does he his duty well as I do mine?

　　Straight on my silent road,
　　Flank'd by no man's abode,
No foe I parley with, no friend I greet;
　　On like a bolt I fly
　　Under the starry sky,
Scorning the current of the sluggish street.

　　Onward from South to North,
　　Onward from Thames to Forth,
On—like a comet—on, unceasingly;
　　Faster and faster yet
　　On—where far boughs of jet
Stretch their wild woof against the pearly sky.

WILLIAM COSMO MONKHOUSE

Faster and faster still—
Dive I through rock and hill,
Starting the echoes with my shrill alarms;
Swiftly I curve and bend;
While, like an eager friend,
The distance runs to clasp me in its arms.

Ne'er from my path I swerve
Rattling around a curve
Not vainly trusting to my trusty bars;
On through the hollow night,
While, or to left or right,
A city glistens like a clump of stars.

On through the night I steer;
Never a sound I hear
Save the strong beating of my steady stroke—
Save when the circling owl
Hoots, or the screaming fowl
Rise from the marshes like a sudden smoke.

Now o'er a gulf I go:
Dark is the depth below,
Smites the slant beam the shoulder of the height—
Now through a lane of trees—
Past sleeping villages,
Their white walls whiter in the silver light.

Be the night foul or fair,
Little I reck or care,
Bandy with storms, and with the tempests jest;
Little I care or know
What winds may rage or blow,
But charge the whirlwind with a dauntless breast.

Now

WILLIAM COSMO MONKHOUSE

Now through the level plain,
While, like a mighty mane,
Stretches my endless breath in cloudy miles;
Now o'er a dull lagoon,
While the broad beamèd moon
Lights up its sadness into sickly smiles.

O, 'tis a race sublime!
I, neck and neck with Time,—
I, with my thews of iron and heart of fire,—
Run without pause for breath,
While all the earth beneath
Shakes with the shocks of my tremendous ire!

On—till the race be won;
On—till the coming sun
Blinds moon and stars with his excessive light;
On—till the earth be green,
And the first lark be seen
Shaking away with songs the dews of night.

Sudden my speed I slack—
Sudden all force I lack—
Without a struggle yield I up my breath;
Numb'd are my thews of steel,
Wearily rolls each wheel,
My heart cools slowly to the sleep of death.

Why for so brief a length
Dower'd with such mighty strength?
Man is my God—I seek not to divine:
At his command I stir,
I, his stern messenger ;—
Does he his duty well as I do mine?

SARAH WILLIAMS

1841-1868

473.   *Youth and Maidenhood*

LIKE a drop of water is my heart
      Laid upon her soft and rosy palm,
Turn'd whichever way her hand doth turn,
      Trembling in an ecstasy of calm.

Like a broken rose-leaf is my heart,
      Held within her close and burning clasp,
Breathing only dying sweetness out,
      Withering beneath the fatal grasp.

Like a vapoury cloudlet is my heart,
      Growing into beauty near the sun,
Gaining rainbow hues in her embrace,
      Melting into tears when it is done.

Like mine own dear harp is this my heart,
      Dumb without the hand that sweeps its strings ;
Tho' the hand be careless or be cruel,
      When it comes my heart breaks forth and sings.

HENRY CLARENCE KENDALL

1841-1882

474.   *September in Australia*

GREY winter hath gone like a wearisome guest,
    And, behold, for repayment,
September comes in with the wind of the west,
    And the spring in her raiment !
The ways of the frost have been fill'd of the flowers,
    While the forest discovers
Wild wings, with the halo of hyaline hours,
    And the music of lovers.

September, the maid with the swift, silver feet,
    She glides, and she graces
The valleys of coolness, the slopes of the heat,
    With her blossomy traces.
Sweet month, with a mouth that is made of a rose,
    She lightens and lingers
In spots where the harp of the evening glows,
    Attuned by her fingers.

The stream from its home in the hollow hill slips
    In a darling old fashion ;
And the day goeth down with a song on its lips
    Whose key-note is passion.
Far out in the fierce, bitter front of the sea
    I stand, and remember
Dead things that were brothers and sisters of thee,
    Resplendent September.

The west, when it blows at the fall of the noon,
    And beats on the beaches,

Is fill'd with a tender and tremulous tune
    That touches and teaches ;
The stories of Youth, of the burden of Time,
    And the death of devotion,
Come back with the wind, and are themes of the rhyme
    In the waves of the ocean.

We, having a secret to others unknown
    In the cool mountain mosses,
May whisper together, September, alone
    Of our loves and our losses.
One word for her beauty, and one for the grace
    She gave to the hours ;
And then we may kiss her, and suffer her face
    To sleep with the flowers.

High places that knew of the gold and the white
    On the forehead of morning,
Now darken and quake, and the steps of the Night
    Are heavy with warning !
Her voice in the distance is lofty and loud,
    Thro' its echoing gorges ;
She hath hidden her eyes in a mantle of cloud,
    And her feet in the surges !

On the top of the hills, on the turreted cones—
    Chief temples of thunder—
The gale, like a ghost in the middle watch moans,
    Gliding over and under.
The sea, flying white through the rack and the rain,
    Leapeth wild to the forelands ;
And the plover, whose cry is like passion with pain,
    Complains in the moorlands.

O, season

O, season of changes, of shadow and shine,
　　September the splendid !
My song hath no music to mingle with thine,
　　And its burden is ended ;
But thou, being born of the winds and the sun,
　　By mountain, by river,
May lighten and listen, and loiter and run,
　　With thy voices for ever.

475.　　　　　　　　*Mooni*

HE that is by Mooni now
　　Sees the water-sapphires gleaming
Where the River Spirit, dreaming,
Sleeps by fall and fountain streaming
　　Under lute of leaf and bough !—
Hears what stamp of Storm with stress is,
Psalms from unseen wildernesses
Deep amongst far hill-recesses—
　　He that is by Mooni now.

Yea, for him by Mooni's marge
Sings the yellow-hair'd September,
With the face the gods remember,
When the ridge is burnt to ember,
　　And the dumb sea chains the barge !
Where the mount like molten brass is,
Down beneath fern-feather'd passes
Noonday dew in cool green grasses
　　Gleams on him by Mooni's marge.

Who that dwells by Mooni yet,
Feels in flowerful forest arches
Smiting wings and breath that parches
Where strong Summer's path of march is,
　　And the suns in thunder set !

HENRY CLARENCE KENDALL

Housed beneath the gracious kirtle
Of the shadowy water-myrtle—
Winds may kiss with heat and hurtle,
   He is safe by Mooni yet !

Days there were when he who sings
(Dumb so long through passion's losses)
Stood where Mooni's water crosses
Shining tracks of green-hair'd mosses,
   Like a soul with radiant wings :
Then the psalm the wind rehearses—
Then the song the stream disperses—
Lent a beauty to his verses,
   Who to-night of Mooni sings.

Ah, the theme—the sad, gray theme !
Certain days are not above me,
Certain hearts have ceased to love me,
Certain fancies fail to move me,
   Like the effluent morning dream.
Head whereon the white is stealing,
Heart whose hurts are past all healing,
Where is now the first, pure feeling ?
   Ah, the theme—the sad, gray theme !

   .   .   .

Still to be by Mooni cool—
Where the water-blossoms glister,
And by gleaming vale and vista
Sits the English April's sister,
   Soft and sweet and wonderful !
Just to rest beneath the burning
Outer world—its sneers and spurning ;
Ah, my heart—my heart is yearning
   Still to be by Mooni cool !

MATHILDE BLIND

476. *Hymn to Horus*

HAIL, God revived in glory !
    The night is over and done ;
Far mountains wrinkled and hoary,
Fair cities great in story,
    Flash in the rising sun.

The young-eyed Day uncloses
    Curtains of filmy lawn,
And blossoming like roses
The Wilderness reposes
    Beneath the Rose of Dawn.

Hail, golden House of Horus,
    Lap of heav'n's holiest God !
From lotus-banks before us
Birds in ecstatic chorus
    Fly, singing, from the sod.

Up, up, into the shining
    Translucent morning sky,
No longer dull and pining,
With drooping wings declining,
    The storks and eagles fly.

The Nile amid his rushes
    Reflects thy risen disk ;
A light of gladness gushes
Thro' kindling halls, and flushes
    Each flaming Obelisk.

660

Vast temples catch thy splendour ;
　Vistas of columns shine
Celestial, with a tender
Rose-bloom on every slender
　Papyrus-pillar'd shrine.

In manifold disguises
　And under many names,
Thrice-holy son of Isis,
We worship him who rises
　A Child-god fledged in flames.

Hail, sacred Hawk, who winging
　Crossest the heavenly sea !
With harp-playing, with singing,
With linen robes white-clinging,
　We come, fair God, to thee.

Thou, whom our soul espouses,
　When weary of the way,
Enter our golden houses,
And with thy mystic spouses
　Rest from the long, long way !

477　　*Dare Quam Accipere*

AH ! yesterday was dark and drear,
　My heart was deadly sore ;
Without thy love it seem'd, my Dear,
　That I could live no more.

And yet I laugh and sing to-day ;
　Care or care not for me,
Thou canst not take the love away
　Wherewith I worship thee.

　　　　　　　　And

And if to-morrow, Dear, I live,
    My heart I shall not break :
For still I hold it that to give
    Is sweeter than to take.

478.   *The Dead*

THE dead abide with us. Though stark and cold
    Earth seem to grip them, they are with us still :
They have forged our chains of being for good or ill,
And their invisible hands these hands yet hold.
Our perishable bodies are the mould
    In which their strong imperishable will—
    Mortality's deep yearning to fulfil—
Hath grown incorporate through dim time untold.
    Vibrations infinite of life in death,
    As a star's travelling light survives its star !
    So may we hold our lives that, when we are
        The fate of those who then will draw this breath,
    They shall not drag us to their judgment bar
        And curse the heritage that we bequeath.

ROBERT BUCHANAN
1841-1901

479.   *The Faëry Reaper*

'TIS on Eilanowen,
    There 's laughter nightly !
For the Fays are sowing
    Their golden grain :
It springs by moonlight
    So stilly and brightly,
And it drinks no sunlight,
    Or silver rain ;—

ROBERT BUCHANAN

Tho' the shoots upcreeping
   No man may see,
When men are reaping
   It reapt must be ;
But to reap it rightly,
   With sickle keen,
They must lead there nightly
   A pure colleen !

Yes, pure completely
   Must be that maiden.
Just feeling sweetly
    Her love's first dream.
Should one steal thither
   With evil laden,
The crop would wither
    In the pale moon's beam !
For midnights seven,
   While all men sleep,
'Neath the silent heaven
   The maid must reap ;
And the sweeter and whiter
   Of soul is she,
The better and brighter
   Will that harvest be !

. . . In Lough Bawn's bosom
   The isle is lying,
Like a bright green blossom
    On a maiden's breast—
There the water-eagle
   O'erhead is flying,
And beneath the sea-gull
    Doth build its nest.

And

And across the water
  A farm gleams fair,
And the farmer's daughter
  Dwelt lonely there :—
And on Eilanowen
  She'd sit and sing,
When the Fays were sowing
  Their seeds in spring,

She could not hear them,
  Nor see them peeping ;
Tho' she wander'd near them
  The spring-tide thro',
When the grouse was crowing,
  The trout was leaping,
And with hare-bells blowing
  The banks were blue.
But not by moonlight
  She dared to stay,
Only by sunlight
  She went that way.
And on Eilanowen
  They walk'd each night,
Her footprints sowing
  With lilies white !

When the sun above her
  Was brightly blazing,
She'd bare (God love her!)
  Each round white limb.
Unseen, unnoted,
  Save fay-folk gazing,
Dark hair'd, white throated,
  She'd strip to swim !

Out yonder blushing
  A space she'd stand,
Then falter flushing
  Across the strand,—
Till the bright still water
  Would sparkle sweet,
As it kiss'd and caught her
  From neck to feet !

There, sparkling round her
  With fond caresses,
It clasp'd her, crown'd her,
  My maiden fair !
Then, brighter glowing
  From its crystal kisses,
The bright drops flowing
  From her dripping hair,
Outleaping, running
  Beneath the sky,
The bright light sunning
  Her limbs, she'd fly,—
And 'mid tinkling laughter
  Of elfin bowers,
The Fays ran after
  With leaves and flowers !

Could the Fays behold her,
  Nor long to gain her ?
From foot to shoulder
  None pure as she !
They cried ' God keep her,
  No sorrow stain her !
The Faëry Reaper
  In troth she'll be ! ' . . .

With

With stalks of amber
  And silvern ears,
From earth's dark chamber
  The grain appears.
'Tis harvest weather!
  The moon swims high :
And they flock together
  With elfin cry!

Now long and truly
  I'd loved that maiden ;
And served her duly
    With kiss and sign ;
And that same season
  My soul love-laden
Had found new reason
    To wish her mine.
For her cheek grew paler,
  Her laughter less,
And what might ail her
  I could not guess.
Each harvest morrow
  We kissing met,
And with weary sorrow
  Her eyes seem'd wet.

' Oh, speak, *Mavourneen*,
  What ails ye nightly ?
For sure each morning
  'Tis sad ye seem ! '
Her eyes not weeping
  Looked on me brightly :—
' Each night when sleeping
  I dream a Dream.

ROBERT BUCHANAN

'Tis on Eilanowen
  I seem to be,
And bright grain growing
  I surely see ;
A golden sickle
  My fingers keep,
And my slow tears trickle
  On what I reap !

' The moon is gleaming,
  The faëries gather,
Like glow-worms gleaming,
   Their eyes flash quick ;
I try while reaping
  To name ' Our Father ! '
But round me leaping
   They pinch and prick—
On the stalks of amber,
  On the silvern ears,
They cling, they clamber,
  Till day appears !
And here I'm waking
  In bed, once more,
My bones all aching,
  My heart full sore ! '

I kiss'd her, crying
  ' God bless your reaping !
For sure no sighing
  Can set you free.
They'll bless your wedding
  Who vex your sleeping ;
So do their bidding,
   Ma cushla chree !

But

But O, remember!
　Your fate is cast,
And ere December
　Hath fairly past,
The Faëry Reaper
　Must be a Bride,
Or a sad cold sleeper
　On the green hill-side!

' Sure wedding 's better
　Than dying sadly ! '
She smiled, and set her
　Soft hand in mine.
For three nights after
　She labour'd gladly,
'Mid fairy laughter,
　And did not pine ;
And when the seven
　Long nights were run,
Full well 'neath Heaven
　That work was done :
Their sheaves were slanted,
　Their harvest made,
And no more they wanted
　A mortal's aid.

'Tis on Eilanowen
　There 's laughter nightly,
When the Fays are sowing
　Their golden grain !
God bless that laughter
　That grain blow brightly !
For luck came after
　My Mary's pain.

And when sweet Mary
   Was wed to me,
Sure the folk of faëry
   Were there to see :—
The white board spreading,
   Unheard, unseen,
They blest the wedding
   Of a pure colleen !

480. *The Pilgrim and the Herdboy*

Pilgrim :

LITTLE Herdboy, sitting there,
   With the sunshine on thy hair,
And thy flocks so white and still
Spilt around thee on the hill,
Tell me true, in thy sweet speech,
Of the City I would reach.

'Tis a City of God's Light
Most imperishably bright,
And its gates are golden all,—
And at dawn and evenfall
They grow ruby-bright and blest
To the east and to the west.

Here, among the hills it lies,
Like a lamb with lustrous eyes
Lying at the Shepherd's feet ;
And the breath of it is sweet,
As it rises from the sward
To the nostrils of the Lord !

Little Herdboy, tell me right,
Hast thou seen it from thy height ?
For it lieth up this way,
And at dawn or death of day
Thou hast surely seen it shine
With the light that is divine ?

The little Herdboy :

Where the buttercups so sweet
Dust with gold my naked feet,
Where the grass grows green and long,
Sit I here and sing my song,
And the brown bird cries ' Cuckoo '
Under skies for ever blue !

Now and then, while I sing loud,
Flits a little fleecy cloud,
And uplooking I behold
How it turns to rain of gold,
Falling lightly, while around
Comes the stir of its soft sound !

Bright above and dim below
Is the many-colour'd Bow ;
'Tis the only light I mark,
Till the mountain-tops grow dark,
And uplooking I espy
Shining glowworms in the sky ;

Then I hear the runlet's call,
And the voice o' the waterfall
Growing louder, and 'tis cold
As I guide my flocks to fold ;
But no City, great or small,
Have I ever seen at all !

481. *Judas Iscariot*

’TWAS the soul of Judas Iscariot,
    Strange, and sad, and tall,
Stood all alone at dead of night
    Before a lighted hall.

And the wold was white with snow,
    And his foot-marks black and damp,
And the ghost of the silvern Moon arose,
    Holding her yellow lamp.

And the icicles were on the eaves,
    And the walls were deep with white,
And the shadows of the guests within
    Pass’d on the window light.

The shadows of the wedding guests
    Did strangely come and go,
And the body of Judas Iscariot
    Lay stretch’d along the snow.

The body of Judas Iscariot
    Lay stretched along the snow ;
’Twas the soul of Judas Iscariot
    Ran swiftly to and fro.

To and fro, and up and down,
    He ran so swiftly there,
As round and round the frozen Pole
    Glideth the lean white bear.

. . . ’Twas the Bridegroom sat at the table-head,
    And the lights burnt bright and clear—
‘ Oh, who is that,’ the Bridegroom said,
    ‘ Whose weary feet I hear ? ’

’Twas

'Twas one looked from the lighted hall,
    And answer'd soft and slow,
' It is a wolf runs up and down
    With a black track in the snow.'

The Bridegroom in his robe of white
    Sat at the table-head—
' Oh, who is that who moans without ? '
    The blessèd Bridegroom said.

'Twas one look'd from the lighted hall,
    And answer'd fierce and low,
' 'Tis the soul of Judas Iscariot
    Gliding to and fro.'

'Twas the soul of Judas Iscariot
    Did hush itself and stand,
And saw the Bridegroom at the door
    With a light in his hand.

The Bridegroom stood in the open door,
    And he was clad in white,
And far within the Lord's Supper
    Was spread so broad and bright.

The Bridegroom shaded his eyes and look'd,
    And his face was bright to see—
' What dost thou here at the Lord's Supper
    With thy body's sins ? ' said he.

'Twas the soul of Judas Iscariot
    Stood black, and sad, and bare—
' I have wander'd many nights and days ;
    There is no light elsewhere.'

'Twas the wedding guests cried out within,
   And their eyes were fierce and bright—
' Scourge the soul of Judas Iscariot
   Away into the night ! '

The Bridegroom stood in the open door,
   And he waved hands still and slow,
And the third time that he waved his hands
   The air was thick with snow.

And of every flake of falling snow,
   Before it touch'd the ground,
There came a dove, and a thousand doves
   Made sweet sound.

'Twas the body of Judas Iscariot
   Floated away full fleet,
And the wings of the doves that bare it off
   Were like its winding-sheet.

'Twas the Bridegroom stood at the open door,
   And beckon'd, smiling sweet ;
'Twas the soul of Judas Iscariot
   Stole in, and fell at his feet.

' The Holy Supper is spread within,
   And the many candles shine,
And I have waited long for thee
   Before I pour'd the wine ! '

The supper wine is pour'd at last,
   The lights burn bright and fair,
Iscariot washes the Bridegroom's feet,
   And dries them with his hair.

482.   *Rococo*

STRAIGHT and swift the swallows fly
    To the sojourn of the sun ;
All the golden year is done,
All the flower-time flitted by ;
Thro' the boughs the witch-winds sigh ;
But heart's summer is begun ;
Life and love at last are one ;
Love-lights glitter in the sky.
Summer days were soon outrun
With the setting of the sun ;
Love's delight is never done.
Let the turn-coat roses die ;
We are lovers, Love and I ;
In Love's lips my roses lie.

483. *Of Three Damsels in a Meadow*

ABOUT a well-spring, in a little mead,
    Of tender grasses full and flow'rets fair,
  There sat three youngling angels as it were
Their loves recounting ; and for each, indeed,
Her sweet face shaded, 'gainst the noonday need,
  A spray of green, that bound her golden hair ;
  Whilst, in and out by turns, a frolic air
The two clear colours blended at its heed.

And one, after a little, thus heard I
  Say to her mates, ' Lo, if by chance there lit
The lovers of each one of us hereby,
  Should we flee hence for fear or quiet sit ? '
Whereto the twain made answer, ' Who should fly
  From such a fortune sure were scant of wit.'

ARTHUR GRAY BUTLER

1831-1909

484. *Edith and Harold*

I KNOW it will not ease the smart ;
  I know it will increase the pain ;
'Tis torture to a wounded heart ;
  Yet, O ! to see him once again.

Tho' other lips be press'd to his,
  And other arms about him twine,
And tho' another reign in bliss
  In that true heart that once was mine ;

Yet, O ! I cry it in my grief,
  I cry it blindly in my pain,
I know it will not bring relief,
  Yet O ! to see him once again.

485. *Two Long Vacations : Grasmere*

SEVEN we were, and two are gone :
  Two ! What are those remaining ?
Ghosts of the Past, with cloud o'ercast,
  Cloud that is always raining !

Ah me ! Last year, when I came back,
  Like faithful hound returning
For old sake's sake to each loved track,
  With heart and memory burning ;

There

ARTHUR GRAY BUTLER

There was the knoll, there was the road,
  There was our humble dwelling;
There o'er the Raise of Dunmail showed
  The shoulder of Helvellyn;

And there the great heights black with cloud,
  Whence flow'd the white stream under;
And glens with echoing torrent loud,
  And cataracts' distant thunder;

And seven men's eyes looked dimly out
  Beneath our old house rafter;
And seven men's forms crept round about
  With peals of ghostly laughter;

And sad yews dripp'd on the mossy stone;
  And fuchsia and rose grew rank;
And the woodbine wept as the rain pour'd on;
  And ferns spread over the bank;

And trees o'ergrown shut out the light
  Of Easedale's cascade falling;
And hearing, after-born of sight,
  No longer heard it calling.

And no one cared : save only there
  Where flowers make silence sweet,
By pilgrims worn, that rocky stair!
  Look up! It is Wordsworth's seat.

Where glass'd in those far-reaching eyes
  He read all nature plain;
And saw more things in earth and skies
  Than will ever be seen again.

There found he wealth, to others dearth,
    And peace, from a world's wild din ;
And, would we know the soul of earth,
    He bade us look within.

All else is changed. Yet rain may pour,
    Weeds spread, and all grow rotten ;
But something lives from days of yore,
    Still fresh, still unforgotten :

The lamp of truth we lit in youth,
    The dreams of life's young morning :
In that dark hour I found their power
    Still in the embers burning.

O vows, I cried, so oft denied,
    And you resolves forsaken,
Befriend me still ! A new-born will
    Trusts in you newly taken.

But, how to live, O, tell me, friend,
    In age still wisdom gaining ?
The clouds descend ; ah, bid them blend
    With fires of youth remaining !

GEORGE HOOKHAM

b. 1842

486.   *Chamonix*

VOICE of the river running through Chamonix,
    Long had I heard it, running through Chamonix,
With ears that heard not rivers and rivulets
Close to me running, calling or whispering,
For the voice of the river running through Chamonix.

        To-day

To-day I hear it with ears that dream not :
Even as I listen 'tis Arve no longer,
But the voice of the mountain, the voice of Mónt-Blanc.
    Mountain of mountains, Europe's mystery,
Brow of Minos calm and terrible,
Brow of Minos giving judgement,
Calm and white and smooth and terrible.
    The voice of Mónt-Blanc :—' They struggle upwards,
Reaching up, the other mountains,
Up and up they strain around me,
Up with horn and peak and needle,
Storm'd round by hurricane, splinter'd by lightning,
Split by the deadly assiduous ice-wedge,
The riving, rending, cleaving crystal,
The diamond fang no rock can mollify,
That loosens block and crumbles surface,
Till the mountain-tops bow and bend and thunder,
Or, atom by atom drawn down, to the valleys,
Are the sands of Time's hour-glass and steal with the
        centuries,
And ever I watch them sharpening and dwindling,
Changing in aeons as clouds in minutes.
    Ages and ages, millions of ages
Ago, I sign'd to the snow to cover me ;
Drew my soft snow-armour about me ;
Struck a league with the ice for ever ;
Made my friend of the foe of the mountains.
    Therefore I change not : sword of sunlight,
Arrow of moonlight, reach me never ;
I change not ever : calm my forehead,
Smooth my brow as the brow of ocean ;
Therefore as ocean I change not and change not,
Till heaven above or earth change beneath me.'

GEORGE HOOKHAM

(Not the iron, the steel, the adamant,
Not the rock or whatever is harder,
Not these are strong to face eternity,
But the soft, soft snow and the fleeting water.
 Not iron will, steel-temper of intellect
Shall endure and dominate saved humanity,
But weakest forms and gentlest essences,
Looks of kindness, touches of tenderness,
And the soft, soft fall of loving syllables.)

 The voice of Mónt-Blanc :—' Of those the atomies,
Mites and motes and specks of mortality,
That crawl up snow and writhe up precipice,
Intruding life on my lifeless solitudes—
Some I accept to kiss my forehead,
Some I let fall from knee or shoulder—
Footslip or spit of stone or avalanche,
They are quiet at last and life ceases to cumber me ;
Or wandering the snow-field in darkness and doubting,
Will sapp'd and joint and sinew melting,
They despair of the way and will wait for the morning ;
And they breathe the drowsy breath of the ice-wind,—
And long-forgotten dreams entangle them,
And far-off long-lost scenes bewilder them,
Field and hedge-row, wood and watercourse—
And they pace and tramp and circle a little,
Then sleep a little, then sleep for ever.
 Lo, I deliver a Minos judgement :
I am death ; life never had part or lot in me.'

Voice of the river running through Chamonix,
Mountain that usest the voice of the river,
Through life I have heard you, in death I shall hear.

FREDERIC WILLIAM HENRY MYERS

1843-1901

487.   *From 'Teneriffe'*

ATLANTID islands, phantom-fair,
    Throned on the solitary seas,
Immersed in amethystine air,
    Haunt of Hesperides !
Farewell ! I leave Madeira thus
Drowned in a sunset glorious,
The Holy Harbour fading far
Beneath a blaze of cinnabar.

Then all is twilight ; pile on pile
    The scattered flocks of cloudland close,
An alabaster wall, erewhile
    Much redder than the rose !—
Falls like a sleep on souls forspent
Majestic Night's abandonment ;
Wakes like a waking life afar
Hung o'er the sea one eastern star.

O Nature's glory, Nature's youth,
    Perfected sempiternal whole !
And is the World's in very truth
    An impercipient Soul ?
Or doth that Spirit, past our ken,
Live a profounder life than men,
Awaits our passing days, and thus
In secret places calls to us ?

O fear not thou, whate'er befall
   Thy transient individual breath ;—
Behold, thou knowest not at all
   What kind of thing is Death :
And here indeed might Death be fair,
If Death be dying into air,—
If souls evanish'd mix with thee,
Illumined Heaven, eternal Sea.

488.   *Evanescence*

I SAW, I saw the lovely child
   I watch'd her by the way,
I learnt her gestures sweet and wild,
   Her loving eyes and gay.

Her name ?—I heard not, nay, nor care ;
   Enough it was for me
To find her innocently fair
   And delicately free.

O cease and go ere dreams be done,
   Nor trace the angel's birth,
Nor find the Paradisal one
   A blossom of the earth !

Thus is it with our subtlest joys,—
   How quick the soul's alarm !
How lightly deed or word destroys
   That evanescent charm !

It comes unbidden, comes unbought,
   Unfetter'd flees away ;
His swiftest and his sweetest thought
   Can never poet say.

1843–1905

489.   *A May Song*

A LITTLE while my love and I,
    Before the mowing of the hay,
Twined daisy-chains and cowslip-balls,
And caroll'd glees and madrigals,
    Before the hay, beneath the may,
My love (who loved me then) and I.

For long years now my love and I
    Tread sever'd paths to varied ends ;
We sometimes meet, and sometimes say
The trivial things of every day,
    And meet as comrades, meet as friends,
My love (who loved me once) and I.

But never more my love and I
    Will wander forth, as once, together,
Or sing the songs we used to sing
    In spring-time, in the cloudless weather :
Some chord is mute that used to ring,
    Some word forgot we used to say
    Amongst the may, before the hay,
My love (who loves me not) and I.

490. *Afterwards*

I KNOW that these poor rags of womanhood—
 This oaten pipe whereon the wild winds play'd
  Making sad music,—tatter'd and outfray'd,
Cast off, play'd out—can hold no more of good,
 Of love or song, or sense of sun and shade.

What homely neighbours elbow me (hard by
 'Neath the black yews) I know I shall not know,
  Nor take account of changing winds that blow
Shifting the golden arrow, set on high
 On the gray spire, nor mark who come and go.

Yet would I lie in some familiar place,
 Nor share my rest with uncongenial dead,—
  Somewhere, may be, where friendly feet will tread,—
As if from out some little chink of space
 Mine eyes might see them tripping overhead.

And tho' too sweet to deck a sepulchre
 Seem twinkling daisy-buds and meadow grass ;
  And so would more than serve me, lest they pass
Who fain would know what woman rested there,
 What her demeanour or her story was,—

For there I would that on a sculptured stone
 (Fenced round with iron-work to keep secure)
  Should sleep a form with folded palms demure,
In aspect like the dreamer that was gone,
 With these words carved, ' *I hoped, but was not sure.*'

EDWARD DOWDEN

Renunciants

SEEMS not our breathing light ?
   Sound not our voices free ?
Bid to Life's festal bright
   No gladder guests there be.

Ah stranger, lay aside
   Cold prudence !   I divine
The secret you would hide,
   And you conjecture mine.

You too have temperate eyes,
   Have put your heart to school,
Are proved.   I recognize
   A brother of the rule.

I knew it by your lip,
   A something when you smiled,
Which meant ' close scholarship,
   A master of the guild '.

Well, and how good is life !
   Good to be born, have breath,
The calms good, and the strife,
   Good life, and perfect death.

Come, for the dancers wheel,
   Join we the pleasant din
—Comrade, it serves to feel
   The sackcloth next the skin.

492.   *In the Cathedral Close*

IN the Dean's porch a nest of clay
    With five small tenants may be seen;
Five solemn faces, each as wise
    As if its owner were a Dean;

Five downy fledglings in a row,
    Pack'd close, as in the antique pew
The school-girls are whose foreheads clear
    At the *Venite* shine on you.

Day after day the swallows sit
    With scarce a stir, with scarce a sound,
But dreaming and digesting much
    They grow thus wise and soft and round:

They watch the Canons come to dine,
    And hear, the mullion-bars across,
Over the fragrant fruit and wine
    Deep talk of rood-screen and reredos.

Her hands with field-flowers drench'd, a child
    Leaps past in wind-blown dress and hair,
The swallows turn their heads askew—
    Five judges deem that she is fair.

Prelusive touches sound within,
    Straightway they recognize the sign,
And, blandly nodding, they approve
    The minuet of Rubinstein.

They mark the cousins' schoolboy talk,
    (Male birds flown wide from minster bell),
And blink at each broad term of art,
    Binomial or bicycle.

Ah !

EDWARD DOWDEN

Ah ! downy young ones, soft and warm,
　　Doth such a stillness mask from sight
Such swiftness ?　can such peace conceal
　　Passion and ecstasy of flight ?

Yet somewhere 'mid your Eastern suns,
　　Under a white Greek architrave
At morn, or when the shaft of fire
　　Lies large upon the Indian wave,

A sense of something dear gone by
　　Will stir, strange longings thrill the heart
For a small world embower'd and close,
　　Of which ye sometime were a part.

The dew-drench'd flowers, the child's glad eyes
　　Your joy unhuman shall control,
And in your wings a light and wind
　　Shall move from the Maestro's soul.

ARTHUR WILLIAM EDGAR O'SHAUGHNESSY

1844-1881

493.　　　　　　　*Ode*

WE are the music-makers,
　　And we are the dreamers of dreams,
Wandering by lone sea-breakers,
　　And sitting by desolate streams ;
World-losers and world-forsakers,
　　On whom the pale moon gleams :
Yet we are the movers and shakers
　　Of the world for ever, it seems.

With wonderful deathless ditties
We build up the world's great cities,
   And out of a fabulous story
   We fashion an empire's glory :
One man with a dream, at pleasure,
   Shall go forth and conquer a crown ;
And three with a new song's measure
   Can trample an empire down.

We, in the ages lying
   In the buried past of the earth,
Built Nineveh with our sighing,
   And Babel itself with our mirth ;
And o'erthrew them with prophesying
   To the old of the new world's worth ;
For each age is a dream that is dying,
   Or one that is coming to birth.

494.   *Song*

I MADE another garden, yea,
   For my new Love :
I left the dead rose where it lay
   And set the new above.
Why did my Summer not begin ?
   Why did my heart not haste ?
My old Love came and walk'd therein,
   And laid the garden waste.

She enter'd with her weary smile,
   Just as of old ;
She look'd around a little while
   And shiver'd with the cold :
Her passing touch was death to all,
   Her passing look a blight ;

         She

> She made the white rose-petals fall,
>   And turn'd the red rose white.

> Her pale robe clinging to the grass
>   Seem'd like a snake
> That bit the grass and ground, alas!
>   And a sad trail did make.
> She went up slowly to the gate,
>   And then, just as of yore,
> She turn'd back at the last to wait
>   And say farewell once more.

495.   *The Fountain of Tears*

IF you go over desert and mountain,
  Far into the country of Sorrow,
  To-day and to-night and to-morrow,
And maybe for months and for years;
  You shall come with a heart that is bursting
  For trouble and toiling and thirsting,
You shall certainly come to the fountain
At length,—to the Fountain of Tears.

Very peaceful the place is, and solely
  For piteous lamenting and sighing,
  And those who come living or dying
Alike from their hopes and their fears;
  Full of cypress-like shadows the place is
  And statues that cover their faces:
But out of the gloom springs the holy
And beautiful Fountain of Tears.

And it flows and it flows with a motion
  So gentle and lovely and listless,
  And murmurs a tune so resistless
To him who hath suffer'd and hears—
688

You shall surely—without a word spoken,
   Kneel down there and know your heart broken,
   And yield to the long-curb'd emotion
That day by the Fountain of Tears.

For it grows and it grows, as though leaping
   Up higher the more one is thinking ;
   And ever its tunes go on sinking
More poignantly into the ears :
   Yea, so blessèd and good seems that fountain,
   Reach'd after dry desert and mountain,
You shall fall down at length in your weeping
And bathe your sad face in the tears.

Then alas ! while you lie there a season
   And sob between living and dying,
   And give up the land you were trying
To find 'mid your hopes and your fears ;
   —O the world shall come up and pass o'er you,
   Strong men shall not stay to care for you,
Nor wonder indeed for what reason
Your way should seem harder than theirs.

But perhaps, while you lie, never lifting
   Your cheek from the wet leaves it presses,
   Nor caring to raise your wet tresses
And look how the cold world appears—
   O perhaps the mere silences round you—
   All things in that place Grief hath found you—
Yea, e'en to the clouds o'er you drifting,
May soothe you somewhat through your tears.

You may feel, when a falling leaf brushes
   Your face, as though some one had kiss'd you ;
   Or think at least some one who miss'd you
Had sent you a thought,—if that cheers ;

Or,

Or a bird's little song, faint and broken,
  May pass for a tender word spoken :
—Enough, while around you there rushes
That life-drowning torrent of tears.

And the tears shall flow faster and faster,
  Brim over and baffle resistance,
  And roll down blear'd roads to each distance
Of past desolation and years ;
  Till they cover the place of each sorrow,
  And leave you no past and no morrow :
For what man is able to master
And stem the great Fountain of Tears ?

But the floods and the tears meet and gather ;
  The sound of them all grows like thunder :
  —O into what bosom, I wonder,
Is pour'd the whole sorrow of years ?
  For Eternity only seems keeping
  Account of the great human weeping :
May God, then, the Maker and Father—
May He find a place for the tears !

496.   *Doom*

IN either mood, to bless or curse
  God bringeth forth the breath of man ;
No angel sire, no woman nurse
  Shall change the work that God began.

One spirit shall be like a star,
  He shall delight to honour one :
Another spirit he shall mar :
  None shall undo what God hath done.

GERARD MANLEY HOPKINS

497. *The Starlight Night*

LOOK at the stars ! look, look up at the skies !
   O look at all the fire-folk sitting in the air !
  The bright boroughs, the quivering citadels there !
The dim woods quick with diamond wells ; the elf-eyes !
The grey lawns cold where quaking gold-dew lies !
  Wind-beat white-beam ; airy abeles all on flare !
  Flake-doves sent floating out at a farmyard scare !—
Ah well ! it is a purchase and a prize.

Buy then ! Bid then !—What ?—Prayer, patience, alms,
   vows.—
Look, look ! a May-mess, like on orchard boughs ;
  Look ! March-bloom, like on meal'd-with-yellow
   sallows.—
These are indeed the barn : within-doors house
The shocks. This piece-bright paling hides the Spouse
  Christ, and the mother of Christ and all his hallows.

JOHN BOYLE O'REILLY

498. *A White Rose*

THE red rose whispers of passion,
   And the white rose breathes of love ;
O, the red rose is a falcon,
   And the white rose is a dove.

But I send you a cream-white rosebud
   With a flush on its petal tips ;
For the love that is purest and sweetest
   Has a kiss of desire on the lips.

691

JOHN BOYLE O'REILLY

499. *Experience*

THE world was made when a man was born,
He must taste for himself the forbidden springs ;
He can never take warning from old-fashion'd things ;
He must fight as a boy, he must drink as a youth,
He must kiss, he must love, he must swear to the truth
Of the friend of his soul ; he must laugh to scorn
The hints of deceit in a woman's eyes—
They are clear as the wells of Paradise.

And so he goes on till the world grows old,
Till his tongue has grown cautious, his heart has grown
    cold,
Till the smile leaves his mouth, till the ring leaves his
    laugh,
And he shirks the bright headache you ask him to quaff.
He grows formal with men, and with women polite,
And distrustful of both when they're out of his sight.
Then he eats for his palate and drinks for his head,
And loves for his pleasure,—and 'tis time he was dead.

ANDREW LANG

1844-1912

500. *Heliodore*

POUR wine, and cry, again, again, again,
        To Heliodore !
And mingle the sweet word ye call in vain
        With that ye pour :
And bring to me her wreath of yesterday
        That 's dark with myrrh ;
Hesternae Rosae, ah, my friends, but they
        Remember her.

Lo ! the kind roses, loved of lovers, weep,
    As who repine ;
For if on any breast they see her sleep,
    It is not mine.

501.   *The Odyssey*

AS one that for a weary space has lain
    Lull'd by the song of Circe and her wine
In gardens near the pale of Proserpine,
Where that Æean isle forgets the main,
And only the low lutes of love complain,
    And only shadows of wan lovers pine—
As such an one were glad to know the brine
Salt on his lips, and the large air again,—
So gladly, from the songs of modern speech
    Men turn, and see the stars, and feel the free
        Shrill wind beyond the close of heavy flowers,
        And through the music of the languid hours
They hear like Ocean on the western beach
    The surge and thunder of the Odyssey.

502.   *Almae Matres*

            (*St. Andrews* 1862—*Oxford* 1865)

ST. ANDREWS by the Northern Sea,
    A haunted town it is to me !
A little city, worn and gray,
    The gray North Ocean girds it round,
And o'er the rocks, and up the bay,
    The long sea-rollers surge and sound.

                    693   And

And still the thin and biting spray
  Drives down the melancholy street,
And still endure, and still decay,
  Towers that the salt winds vainly beat.
Ghost-like and shadowy they stand
Clear mirror'd in the wet sea-sand.

O, ruin'd chapel, long ago
  We loiter'd idly where the tall
Fresh-budded mountain-ashes blow
  Within thy desecrated wall :
The tough roots broke the tomb below,
  The April birds sang clamorous,
We did not dream, we could not know
  How soon the Fates would sunder us !

O, broken minster, looking forth
  Beyond the bay, above the town,
O, winter of the kindly North,
  O, college of the scarlet gown,
And shining sands beside the sea,
  And stretch of links beyond the sand,
Once more I watch you, and to me
  It is as if I touch'd his hand !
And therefore art thou yet more dear,
  O, little city, gray and sere,
Though shrunken from thine ancient pride,
  And lonely by thy lonely sea,
Than these fair halls on Isis' side,
  Where Youth an hour came back to me.

A land of waters green and clear,
  Of willows and of poplars tall,
And in the Spring-time of the year,
  The white may breaking over all,
694

And Pleasure quick to come at call ;
    And summer rides by marsh and wold,
And Autumn with her crimson pall
    About the towers of Magdalen roll'd :
And strange enchantments from the past,
    And memories of the friends of old,
And strong Tradition, binding fast
    The flying terms with bands of gold,—
All these hath Oxford : all are dear,
    But dearer far the little town,
The drifting surf, the wintry year,
    The college of the scarlet gown,
St. Andrews by the Northern Sea,
That is a haunted town to me !

503.   *Twilight on Tweed*

THREE crests against the saffron sky,
    Beyond the purple plain,
The kind remember'd melody
    Of Tweed once more again.

Wan water from the border hills,
    Dear voice from the old years,
Thy distant music lulls and stills,
    And moves to quiet tears.

Like a loved ghost thy fabled flood
    Fleets through the dusky land ;
Where Scott, come home to die, has stood,
    My feet returning stand.

A mist of memory broods and floats,
    The Border waters flow ;
The air is full of ballad notes,
    Borne out of long ago.

Old

Old songs that sung themselves to me,
  Sweet through a boy's day-dream,
While trout below the blossom'd tree
  Flash'd in the golden stream.

        .   .   .   .   .   .

Twilight, and Tweed, and Eildon Hill,
  Fair and too fair you be ;
You tell me that the voice is still
  That should have welcomed me.

ERNEST MYERS

b. 1844

504.   *Fiorentina*

O SURELY surely life is fair,
    And surely surely hearts are true ;
Be witness, balm of April air,
    And boundless depth of midnight blue.

The trouble of an hour ago,
    That seem'd to gather round our way,
Is vanish'd as the last-year snow
    That hid the hills of Fesole.

And softly still the moonlight falls,
    O love, and makes for thee and me
An Eden 'mid the bay-leaf walls,
    The fragrant bowers of Boboli.

How gently o'er our spirits move
    The golden hours we fear'd would die !
The very flame that threaten'd Love
    Has lent us light to see him by.

696

505.   *Achilles*

ATHWART the sunrise of our western day
 The form of great Achilles, high and clear,
Stands forth in arms, wielding the Pelian spear.
The sanguine tides of that immortal fray,
Swept on by Gods, around him surge and sway,
  Wherethrough the helms of many a warrior peer,
  Strong men and swift, their tossing plumes uprear.
But stronger, swifter, goodlier he than they,
More awful, more divine. Yet mark anigh;
  Some fiery pang hath rent his soul within,
    Some hovering shade his brows encompasseth.
What gifts hath Fate for all his chivalry?
  Even such as hearts heroic oftenest win;
    Honour, a friend, anguish, untimely death.

ROBERT BRIDGES

b. 1844

506. *Awake, my heart, to be loved*

AWAKE, my heart, to be loved, awake, awake!
 The darkness silvers away, the morn doth break,
It leaps in the sky: unrisen lustres slake
The o'ertaken moon.   Awake, O heart, awake!

She too that loveth awaketh and hopes for thee;
Her eyes already have sped the shades that flee,
Already they watch the path thy feet shall take:
Awake, O heart, to be loved, awake, awake!

And if thou tarry from her,—if this could be,—
She cometh herself, O heart, to be loved, to thee;
For thee would unashamèd herself forsake:
Awake to be loved, my heart, awake, awake!

Awake,

Awake, the land is scattered with light, and see,
Uncanopied sleep is flying from field and tree :
And blossoming boughs of April in laughter shake ;
Awake, O heart, to be loved, awake, awake !

Lo all things wake and tarry and look for thee :
She looketh and saith, ' O sun, now bring him to me.
Come more adored, O adored, for his coming's sake,
And awake my heart to be loved : awake, awake ! '

507.   *Spirits*

ANGEL spirits of sleep,
   White-robed, with silver hair,
In your meadows fair,
Where the willows weep,
And the sad moonbeam
On the gliding stream
Writes her scatter'd dream :

   Angel spirits of sleep,
Dancing to the weir
In the hollow roar
Of its waters deep ;
Know ye how men say
That ye haunt no more
Isle and grassy shore
With your moonlit play ;
That ye dance not here,
White-robed spirits of sleep,
All the summer night
Threading dances light ?

698

508.   *A Passer-By*

WHITHER, O splendid ship, thy white sails crowd-
        ing,
  Leaning across the bosom of the urgent West,
That fearest nor sea rising, nor sky clouding,
  Whither away, fair rover, and what thy quest?
  Ah! soon, when Winter has all our vales opprest,
When skies are cold and misty, and hail is hurling,
  Wilt thou glide on the blue Pacific, or rest
In a summer haven asleep, thy white sails furling.

I there before thee, in the country that well thou knowest,
  Already arrived am inhaling the odorous air:
I watch thee enter unerringly where thou goest,
  And anchor queen of the strange shipping there,
  Thy sails for awnings spread, thy masts bare;
Nor is aught from the foaming reef to the snow-capp'd,
        grandest
  Peak, that is over the feathery palms more fair
Than thou, so upright, so stately, and still thou standest.

And yet, O splendid ship, unhail'd and nameless,
  I know not if, aiming a fancy, I rightly divine
That thou hast a purpose joyful, a courage blameless,
  Thy port assured in a happier land than mine.
  But for all I have given thee, beauty enough is thine,
As thou, aslant with trim tackle and shrouding,
  From the proud nostril curve of a prow's line
In the offing scatterest foam, thy white sails crowding.

509. *Elegy: On a Lady, whom Grief*
  for the Death of her Betrothed killed

ASSEMBLE, all ye maidens, at the door,
  And all ye loves, assemble ; far and wide
Proclaim the bridal, that proclaim'd before
Has been deferr'd to this late eventide :
    For on this night the bride,
    The days of her betrothal over,
  Leaves the parental hearth for evermore ;
To-night the bride goes forth to meet her lover.

Reach down the wedding vesture, that has lain
Yet all unvisited, the silken gown :
Bring out the bracelets, and the golden chain
Her dearer friends provided : sere and brown
    Bring out the festal crown,
    And set it on her forehead lightly :
  Though it be wither'd, twine no wreath again ;
This only is the crown she can wear rightly.

Cloke her in ermine, for the night is cold,
And wrap her warmly, for the night is long,
In pious hands the flaming torches hold,
While her attendants, chosen from among
    Her faithful virgin throng,
    May lay her in her cedar litter,
  Decking her coverlet with sprigs of gold,
Roses, and lilies white that best befit her.

Sound flute and tabor, that the bridal be
Not without music, nor with these alone ;

But let the viol lead the melody,
With lesser intervals, and plaintive moan
      Of sinking semitone ;
    And, all in choir, the virgin voices
  Rest not from singing in skill'd harmony
The song that aye the bridegroom's ear rejoices.

Let the priests go before, array'd in white,
And let the dark-stoled minstrels follow slow,
Next they that bear her, honour'd on this night,
And then the maidens, in a double row,
      Each singing soft and low,
    And each on high a torch upstaying :
  Unto her lover lead her forth with light,
With music, and with singing, and with praying.

'Twas at this sheltering hour he nightly came,
And found her trusty window open wide,
And knew the signal of the timorous flame,
That long the restless curtain would not hide
      Her form that stood beside ;
    As scarce she dared to be delighted,
  Listening to that sweet tale, that is no shame
To faithful lovers, that their hearts have plighted.

But now for many days the dewy grass
Has shown no markings of his feet at morn :
And watching she has seen no shadow pass
The moonlit walk, and heard no music borne
      Upon her ear forlorn.
    In vain has she looked out to greet him ;
  He has not come, he will not come, alas !
So let us bear her out where she must meet him.

Now

Now to the river bank the priests are come :
The bark is ready to receive its freight :
Let some prepare her place therein, and some
Embark the litter with its slender weight :
　　The rest stand by in state,
　　　And sing her a safe passage over ;
　While she is oar'd across to her new home,
Into the arms of her expectant lover.

And thou, O lover, that art on the watch,
Where, on the banks of the forgetful streams,
The pale indifferent ghosts wander, and snatch
The sweeter moments of their broken dreams,—
　　Thou, when the torchlight gleams,
　　　When thou shalt see the slow procession,
　And when thine ears the fitful music catch,
Rejoice, for thou art near to thy possession.

510.　　　　　　　　*Pater Filio*

S ENSE with keenest edge unusèd,
　　Yet unsteel'd by scathing fire ;
Lovely feet as yet unbruisèd
　　On the ways of dark desire ;
Sweetest hope that lookest smiling
O'er the wilderness defiling !

Why such beauty, to be blighted
　　By the swarm of foul destruction ?
Why such innocence delighted,
　　When sin stalks to thy seduction ?
All the litanies e'er chaunted
Shall not keep thy faith undaunted.

I have pray'd the sainted Morning
    To unclasp her hands to hold thee ;
From resignful Eve's adorning
    Stol'n a robe of peace to enfold thee ·
With all charms of man's contriving
Arm'd thee for thy lonely striving.

Me too once unthinking Nature,
    —Whence Love's timeless mockery took me,—
Fashion'd so divine a creature,
    Yea, and like a beast forsook me.
I forgave, but tell the measure
Of her crime in thee, my treasure.

511.   *Weep not To-day*

WEEP not to-day : why should this sadness be ?
    Learn in present fears
    To o'ermaster those tears
That unhinder'd conquer thee.

Think on thy past valour, thy future praise :
    Up, sad heart, nor faint
    In ungracious complaint,
Or a prayer for better days.

Daily thy life shortens, the grave's dark peace
    Draweth surely nigh,
    When good-night is good-bye ;
For the sleeping shall not cease.

Fight, to be found fighting : nor far away
    Deem, nor strange thy doom.
    Like this sorrow 'twill come,
And the day will be to-day.

512. *Founder's Day*

A Secular Ode on the Ninth Jubilee of
Eton College

CHRIST and his Mother, heavenly maid,
Mary, in whose fair name was laid
Eton's corner, bless our youth
With Truth, and Purity, mother of truth !

O ye, 'neath breezy skies of June,
By silver Thames's lulling tune,
In shade of willow or oak, who try
The golden gates of poesy ;

Or on the tabled sward all day
Match your strength in England's play,
Scholars of Henry, giving grace
To toil and force in game or race ;

Exceed the prayer and keep the fame
Of him, the sorrowful king, who came
Here in his realm a realm to found,
Where he might stand for ever crown'd.

Or whether with naked bodies flashing
Ye plunge in the lashing weir ; or dashing
The oars of cedar skiffs, ye strain
Round the rushes and home again ;—

Or what pursuit soe'er it be
That makes your mingled presence free,
When by the school gate 'neath the limes
Ye muster, waiting the lazy chimes ;

May Peace, that conquereth sin and death,
Temper for you her sword of faith ;
Crown with honour the loving eyes,
And touch with mirth the mouth of the wise.

Here is eternal spring : for you
The very stars of heaven are new ;
And aged Fame again is born,
Fresh as a peeping flower of morn.

For you shall Shakespeare's scene unroll,
Mozart shall steal your ravish'd soul,
Homer his bardic hymn rehearse,
Virgil recite his maiden verse.

Now learn, love, have, do, be the best ;
Each in one thing excel the rest :
Strive ; and hold fast this truth of heaven—
To him that hath shall more be given.

Slow on your dial the shadows creep,
So many hours for food and sleep,
So many hours till study tire,
So many hours for heart's desire.

These suns and moons shall memory save,
Mirrors bright for her magic cave ;
Wherein may steadfast eyes behold
A self that groweth never old.

O in such prime enjoy your lot,
And when ye leave regret it not ;
With wishing gifts in festal state
Pass ye the angel-sworded gate.

Then to the world let shine your light,
Children in play be lions in fight,
And match with red immortal deeds
The victory that made ring the meads :

Or by firm wisdom save your land
From giddy head and grasping hand :
IMPROVE THE BEST ; so shall your sons
Better what ye have better'd once.

Send them here to the court of grace
Bearing your name to fill your place :
Ye in their time shall live again
The happy dream of Henry's reign :

And on his day your steps be bent
Where, saint and king, crown'd with content,
He biddeth a prayer to bless his youth
With Truth, and Purity, mother of Truth.

513.   *Nightingales*

BEAUTIFUL must be the mountains whence ye
come,
And bright in the fruitful valleys the streams, where-
from
           Ye learn your song :
Where are those starry woods ?   O might I wander there,
Among the flowers, which in that heavenly air
           Bloom the year long !

Nay, barren are those mountains and spent the streams:
Our song is the voice of desire, that haunts our dreams,
           A throe of the heart,

706

ROBERT BRIDGES

Whose pining visions dim, forbidden hopes profound,
  No dying cadence nor long sigh can sound,
      For all our art.

  Alone, aloud in the raptured ear of men
  We pour our dark nocturnal secret ; and then,
      As night is withdrawn
From these sweet-springing meads and bursting boughs
    of May,
  Dream, while the innumerable choir of day
      Welcome the dawn.

SAMUEL WADDINGTON

b. 1844

514. *The Inn of Care*

AT Nebra, by the Unstrut,—
  So travellers declare,—
There stands an ancient tavern,
It is the ' Inn of Care '.
To all the world 'tis open ;
It sets a goodly fare ;
And every soul is welcome
That deigns to sojourn there.

The landlord with his helpers,
(He is a stalwart host,)
To please his guest still labours
With ' bouilli ' and with ' roast ' ;—
And ho ! he laughs so roundly,
He laughs, and loves to boast
That he who bears the beaker
May live to share the ' toast '

707

Lucus

SAMUEL WADDINGTON

Lucus a non lucendo—
Thus named might seem the inn,
So careless is its laughter,
So loud its merry din ;
Yet ere to doubt its title
You do, in sooth, begin,
Go, watch the pallid faces
Approach and pass within.

To Nebra, by the Unstrut,
May all the world repair,
And meet a hearty welcome,
And share a goodly fare ;
The world ! 'tis worn and weary—
'Tis tired of gilt and glare !
The inn ! 'tis named full wisely,
It is the ' Inn of Care '.

515. ## *Morning*

NOW o'er the topmost pine,
   The distant pine-clad peak,
There dawns a golden streak
Of light, an orient line :—
Phoebus, the light is thine,
   Thine is the glory,—seek
   Each dale and dewy creek,
And in full splendour shine !

Thy steeds now chafe and fret
   To scour the dusky plain :
   Speed forth with flashing rein,
Speed o'er the land,—and yet,
   Ah ! linger in this lane,
Kissing each violet.

708

SAMUEL WADDINGTON

516.   *Soul and Body*

WHERE wert thou, Soul, ere yet my body born
  Became thy dwelling place? Didst thou on earth,
Or in the clouds, await this body's birth?
Or by what chance upon that winter's morn
Didst thou this body find, a babe forlorn?
  Didst thou in sorrow enter, or in mirth?
  Or for a jest, perchance, to try its worth
Thou tookest flesh, ne'er from it to be torn?

Nay, Soul, I will not mock thee; well I know
  Thou wert not on the earth, nor in the sky;
For with my body's growth thou too didst grow;
  But with that body's death wilt thou too die?
I know not, and thou canst not tell me, so
  In doubt we'll go together—thou and I.

EMILY HENRIETTA HICKEY

b. 1845

517.   *Song*

BELOVÈD, it is morn!
  A redder berry on the thorn,
  A deeper yellow on the corn,
For this good day new-born:
      Pray, Sweet, for me
      That I may be
      Faithful to God and thee.

Belovèd, it is day!
  And lovers work, as children play,
  With heart and brain untired alway:

709   Dear

Dear love, look up and pray.
　　Pray, Sweet, for me
　　That I may be
　　Faithful to God and thee.

Belovèd, it is night!
　　Thy heart and mine are full of light,
　　Thy spirit shineth clear and white,—
God keep thee in his sight!
　　Pray, Sweet, for me
　　That I may be
　　Faithful to God and thee.

WALTER CRANE

b. 1845

518. *A Seat for Three: written on a Settle*

A SEAT for three, where host and guest
　　May side-by-side pass toast or jest;
And be their number two or three,
　　With elbow-room and liberty,
What need to wander east or west?

A book for thought, a nook for rest,
And, meet for fasting or for fest,
　　In fair and equal parts to be
　　A seat for three.

Then give you pleasant company,
For youth or elder shady tree;
　　A roof for council or sequest,
　　A corner in a homely nest;
Free, equal, and fraternally,
　　A seat for three.

710

EUGENE LEE-HAMILTON

1845-1907

519.   *Song*

UNDER the Winter, dear,
   Summer's note lieth :
If it be sweet to hear,
   Song never dieth.

Soon in the forest, love,
   Breezes shall bear it ;
There, in the bough above,
   Lo, thou shalt hear it.

520.   *Fairy Godmothers*

I THINK the fairies to my christening came ;
   But they were wicked sprites and envious elves,
   Who brought me gall, as bitter as themselves,
In tiny tankards wrought with fairy flame.
They wish'd me love of books—each little dame—
   With power to read no book upon my shelves ;
   Fair limbs for numbness ; Dead-Sea fruits by twelves,
And every bitter blessing you can name.

But one good elf there was, and she let fall
   A single drop of Poesy's wine of gold
In every little tankard full of gall.
   So, year by year, as woes and pains grow old,
The little golden drop is in them all ;
   But bitterer is the cup than can be told.

711

521. *Lost Years*

MY boyhood went : it went where went the trace
   Left by the pony's hoofs upon the sand ;
  It went where went the stream sought rod in hand ;
It went where went the ice on the pond's face.
Then went my youth : it went where Dawn doth chase
   The ballroom's lights away with pearly wand ;
  It went where went the echoes of the band ;
It went where go the nights that steal Day's place.

And now my manhood goes where goes the song
   Of captive birds, the cry of crippled things ;
    It goes where goes the day that unused dies.
The cage is narrow and the bars are strong
   In which my restless spirit beats its wings ;
    And round me stretch unfathomable skies.

522. *To My Tortoise* ΑΝΑΓΚΗ

SAY it were true that thou outliv'st us all,
   O footstool once of Venus ; come, renew
   Thy tale of old Greek isles, where thy youth grew
In myrtle shadow, near her temple wall ;
Or tell me how the eagle let thee fall
   Upon the Greek bard's head from heaven's blue,
   And Apathy killed Song. And is it true
That thy domed shell would bear a huge stone ball ?

O Tortoise, Tortoise, there are weights, alack !
   Heavier than stone, and viewless as the air,
    Which none have ever tried upon thy back ;
Which, ever and anon, we men must bear—
   Weights which would make thy solid cover crack
    And how we bear them, let those ask who care !

EUGENE LEE-HAMILTON

523.   *Elfin Skates*

i

THEY wheel'd me up the snow-clear'd garden way,
    And left me where the dazzling heaps were thrown ;
And as I mused on winter sports once known,
Up came a tiny man to where I lay.
He was six inches high ; his beard was grey
    As silver frost ; his coat and cap were brown,
    Of mouse's fur ; while two wee skates hung down
From his wee belt, and gleam'd in winter's ray.

He clamber'd up my couch, and eyed me long.
    'Show me thy skates,' said I ; 'for once, alas !
        I too could skate.   What pixie mayst thou be ? '
'I am the king', he answered, 'of the throng
    Called Winter Elves.   We live in roots, and pass
        The summer months asleep.   Frost sets us free.'

ii

'WE find by moonlight little pools of ice,
    Just one yard wide,' the imp of winter said ;
    'And skate all night, while mortals are in bed,
In tiny circles of our elf device ;
And when it snows we harness forest mice
    To wee bark sleighs, with lightest fibrous thread,
    And scour the woods ; or play all night instead
With snowballs large as peas, well patted thrice.

But is it true, as I have heard them say,
    That thou canst share in winter games no more,
        But liest motionless, year in, year out?
That must be hard.   To-day I cannot stay,
    But I'll return each year, when all is hoar,
        And tell thee when the skaters are about.'

713

524. *The Death of Puck*

i

I FEAR that Puck is dead,—it is so long
  Since men last saw him ;—dead with all the rest
  Of that sweet elfin crew that made their nest
In hollow nuts, where hazels sing their song ;
Dead and for ever, like the antique throng
    The elves replaced : the Dryad that you guess'd
    Behind the leaves ; the Naiad weed-bedress'd ;
The leaf-ear'd Faun that loved to lead you wrong.

Tell me, thou hopping Robin, hast thou met
  A little man, no bigger than thyself,
Whom they call Puck, where woodland bells are wet ?
  Tell me, thou Wood-Mouse, hast thou seen an elf
Whom they call Puck, and is he seated yet,
    Capp'd with a snail-shell, on his mushroom shelf ?

ii

THE Robin gave three hops, and chirp'd, and said :
  ' Yes, I knew Puck, and loved him ; though I trow
  He mimick'd oft my whistle, chuckling low ;
Yes, I knew cousin Puck ; but he is dead.
We found him lying on his mushroom bed—
    The Wren and I,—half cover'd up with snow,
    As we were hopping where the berries grow.
We think he died of cold. Ay, Puck is fled.'

And then the Wood-Mouse said : ' We made the Mole
  Dig him a little grave beneath the moss,
And four big Dormice placed him in the hole.
  The Squirrel made with sticks a little cross ;
Puck was a Christian elf, and had a soul ;
    And all we velvet jackets mourn his loss.'

714

525. *Idle Charon*

THE shores of Styx are lone for evermore,
   And not one shadowy form upon the steep
  Looms through the dusk, as far as eyes can sweep,
To call the ferry over as of yore ;
But tintless rushes, all about the shore,
   Have hemm'd the old boat in, where, lock'd in sleep,
   Hoar-bearded Charon lies ; while pale weeds creep
With tightening grasp all round the unused oar.

For in the world of Life strange rumours run
  That now the Soul departs not with the breath,
But that the Body and the Soul are one ;
  And in the loved one's mouth, now, after death,
The widow puts no obol, nor the son,
  To pay the ferry in the world beneath.

526. *What the Sonnet is*

FOURTEEN small broider'd berries on the hem
  Of Circe's mantle, each of magic gold ;
  Fourteen of lone Calypso's tears that roll'd
Into the sea, for pearls to come to them ;
Fourteen clear signs of omen in the gem
  With which Medea human fate foretold ;
  Fourteen small drops, which Faustus, growing old,
Craved of the Fiend, to water Life's dry stem.

It is the pure white diamond Dante brought
  To Beatrice ; the sapphire Laura wore
When Petrarch cut it sparkling out of thought ;
  The ruby Shakespeare hew'd from his heart's core ;
The dark deep emerald that Rossetti wrought
  For his own soul, to wear for evermore.

715

527.   *Wood-Song*

WHEN we are gone, love,
    Gone as the breeze,
Woods will be sweet, love,
    Even as these.

Sunflecks will dance, love,
    Even as now,
Here on the moss, love,
    Under the bough.

Others unborn, love,
    Maybe will sit
Here in the wood, love,
    Leafily lit ;

Hearking as now, love,
    Treble of birds ;
Breathing as we, love,
    Wondering words.

Others will sigh, love,
    Even as we :
' Only a day, love,'
    Murmurs the bee.

THE HON. EMILY LAWLESS

528. *Dirge of the Munster Forest.* 1581

BRING out the hemlock ! bring the funeral yew !
  The faithful ivy that doth all enfold ;
Heap high the rocks, the patient brown earth strew,
And cover them against the numbing cold.
Marshal my retinue of bird and beast,
Wren, titmouse, robin, birds of every hue ;
Let none keep back, no, not the very least,
Nor fox, nor deer, nor tiny nibbling crew,
Only bid one of all my forest clan
Keep far from us on this our funeral day.
On the grey wolf I lay my sovereign ban,
The great grey wolf who scrapes the earth away,
Lest, with hook'd claw and furious hunger, he
Lay bare my dead for gloating foes to see—
Lay bare my dead, who died, and died for me.

For I must shortly die as they have died,
And lo ! my doom stands yoked and link'd with theirs ;
The axe is sharpen'd to cut down my pride :
I pass, I die, and leave no natural heirs.
Soon shall my sylvan coronals be cast ;
My hidden sanctuaries, my secret ways,
Naked must stand to the rebellious blast ;
No Spring shall quicken what this Autumn slays.
Therefore, while still I keep my russet crown,
I summon all my lieges to the feast.
Hither, ye flutterers ! black, or pied, or brown ;
Hither, ye furr'd ones ! Hither every beast !

Only

Only to one of all my forest clan
I cry, ' Avaunt ! Our mourning revels flee ! '
On the grey wolf I lay my sovereign ban,
The great grey wolf with scraping claws, lest he
Lay bare my dead for gloating foes to see—
Lay bare my dead, who died, and died for me.

JAMES LOGIE ROBERTSON

(HUGH HALIBURTON)

b. 1846

529.   *Spring on the Ochils*

FRA whaur in fragrant wuds ye bide
    Secure fra winter care,
Come, gentle Spring, to Ochilside
    And Ochil valleys fair.
For sweet as ony pagan spring
    Are Devon's watters clear ;
And life wad be a lovely thing
    Gif ye were only here.

She comes ! the waffin' o' her wings
    Wi' music fills the air ;
An' wintry thochts o' men an' things
    Vex human hearts nae mair.
On Devon banks wi' me she strays,
    Her poet for the while,
And Ochil brooks and Ochil braes
    Grow classic in her smile !

GEORGE BARLOW

b. 1847

530.   *The Soul*

THE Soul shall burst her fetters
    At last, and shall be
As the stars, as the wind, as the night,
    As the sun, as the sea.

The Soul shall struggle and stand
    In the end swift and free
As the stars, as the wind, as the night,
    As the sun, as the sea.

The Soul shall be crown'd and calm,
    Eyes fearless—and she
Shall be queen of the wind and the night,
    Stars, sun, and the sea.

531.   *Spiritual Passion*

I FEEL towards God just as a woman might
    Who hears her lord praised by the adoring crowd :
    Who hears them hymn his strength with paean loud—
His glory in thought or speech, his force in fight.
She knows him better.   Thro' the silent night
    She has watch'd his face beneath keen sorrow bow'd ;
Him she has cherish'd with embraces white ;
    She has kiss'd the lips that seem to men so proud.

She cannot fear : she loves.   She can but smile
    That men should dread like some disastrous wand
His sceptre wielded o'er the people, while
    She knows the sea-deep love that lies beyond.
She trusts her lord without one thought of guile,
    Knowing her union holier and more fond.

532. *The Dead Child*

BUT yesterday she played with childish things,
With toys and painted fruit.
To-day she may be speeding on bright wings
Beyond the stars ! We ask. The stars are mute.

But yesterday her doll was all in all ;
She laughed and was content.
To-day she will not answer, if we call :
She dropp'd no toys to show the road she went.

But yesterday she smiled and ranged with art
Her playthings on the bed.
To-day and yesterday are leagues apart !
She will not smile to-day, for she is dead.

WILLIAM ERNEST HENLEY

1849-1903

533. *Collige Rosas*

O GATHER me the rose, the rose,
While yet in flower we find it,
For summer smiles, but summer goes,
And winter waits behind it.

For with the dream foregone, foregone,
The deed forborne for ever,
The worm Regret will canker on,
And time will turn him never.

So were it well to love, my love,
    And cheat of any laughter
The fate beneath us and above,
    The dark before and after.

The myrtle and the rose, the rose,
    The sunshine and the swallow,
The dream that comes, the wish that goes,
    The memories that follow !

534.   *On the Way to Kew*

ON the way to Kew,
    By the river old and gray,
Where in the Long Ago
We laugh'd and loiter'd so,
I met a ghost to-day,
A ghost that told of you—
A ghost of low replies
And sweet inscrutable eyes
      Coming up from Richmond
As you used to do.

By the river old and gray,
The enchanted Long Ago
Murmur'd and smiled anew.
On the way to Kew,
March had the laugh of May,
The bare boughs look'd aglow,
And old immortal words
Sang in my breast like birds,
      Coming up from Richmond
As I used with you.

With

With the life of Long Ago
Lived my thought of you.
By the river old and gray
Flowing his appointed way
As I watch'd I knew
What is so good to know :
Not in vain, not in vain,
I shall look for you again
      Coming up from Richmond
On the way to Kew.

535.   *Invictus*

OUT of the night that covers me,
    Black as the pit from pole to pole,
I thank whatever gods may be
    For my unconquerable soul.

In the fell clutch of circumstance
    I have not winced nor cried aloud :
Under the bludgeonings of chance
    My head is bloody, but unbow'd.

Beyond this place of wrath and tears
    Looms but the Horror of the shade,
And yet the menace of the years
    Finds and shall find me unafraid.

It matters not how strait the gate,
    How charged with punishments the scroll,
I am the master of my fate :
    I am the captain of my soul.

WILLIAM ERNEST HENLEY

536.   *England, my England*

WHAT have I done for you,
    England, my England ?
What is there I would not do,
    England, my own ?
With your glorious eyes austere,
As the Lord were walking near,
Whispering terrible things and dear
    As the Song on your bugles blown,
        England—
Round the world on your bugles blown !

Where shall the watchful sun,
    England, my England,
Match the master-work you've done,
    England, my own ?
When shall he rejoice agen
Such a breed of mighty men
As come forward, one to ten,
    To the Song on your bugles blown,
        England—
    Down the years on your bugles blown ?

Ever the faith endures,
    England, my England :—
' Take and break us : we are yours,
    England, my own !
Life is good, and joy runs high
Between English earth and sky :
Death is death ; but we shall die
    To the Song on your bugles blown,
        England—
    To the stars on your bugles blown ! '

They

They call you proud and hard,
   England, my England :
You with worlds to watch and ward,
   England, my own !
You whose mail'd hand keeps the keys
Of such teeming destinies,
You could know nor dread nor ease
   Were the Song on your bugles blown,
     England,
   Round the Pit on your bugles blown !

Mother of Ships whose might,
   England, my England,
Is the fierce old Sea's delight,
   England, my own,
Chosen daughter of the Lord,
Spouse-in-Chief of the ancient Sword,
There 's the menace of the Word
   In the Song on your bugles blown,
     England—
   Out of heaven on your bugles blown !

537.   *Margaritae Sorori*

A LATE lark twitters from the quiet skies
   And from the west,
Where the sun, his day's work ended,
Lingers as in content,
There falls on the old, gray city
An influence luminous and serene,
A shining peace.

724

The smoke ascends
In a rosy-and-golden haze.   The spires
Shine and are changed.   In the valley
Shadows rise.   The lark sings on.   The sun,
Closing his benediction,
Sinks, and the darkening air
Thrills with a sense of the triumphing night—
Night with her train of stars
And her great gift of sleep.

So be my passing !
My task accomplish'd and the long day done,
My wages taken, and in my heart
Some late lark singing,
Let me be gather'd to the quiet west,
The sundown splendid and serene,
Death.

EDMUND GOSSE

b. 1849

538.   *Lying in the Grass*

BETWEEN two golden tufts of summer grass
   I see the world through hot air as through glass,
And by my face sweet lights and colours pass.

Before me, dark against the fading sky,
I watch three mowers mowing, as I lie :
With brawny arms they sweep in harmony.

Brown English faces by the sun burnt red,
Rich glowing colour on bare throat and head,
My heart would leap to watch them, were I dead !

725   And

And in my strong young living as I lie,
I seem to move with them in harmony,—
A fourth is mowing, and that fourth am I.

The music of the scythes that glide and leap,
The young men whistling as their great arms sweep,
And all the perfume and sweet sense of sleep,

The weary butterflies that droop their wings,
The dreamy nightingale that hardly sings,
And all the lassitude of happy things,

Is mingling with the warm and pulsing blood
That gushes through my veins a languid flood,
And feeds my spirit as the sap a bud.

Behind the mowers, on the amber air,
A dark-green beech-wood rises, still and fair,
A white path winding up it like a stair.

And see that girl, with pitcher on her head,
And clean white apron on her gown of red,—
Her even-song of love is but half-said :

She waits the youngest mower.   Now he goes ;
Her cheeks are redder than the wild blush-rose :
They climb up where the deepest shadows close.

But though they pass, and vanish, I am there.
I watch his rough hands meet beneath her hair,
Their broken speech sounds sweet to me like prayer.

Ah ! now the rosy children come to play,
And romp and struggle with the new-mown hay ;
Their clear high voices sound from far away.

They know so little why the world is sad,
They dig themselves warm graves and yet are glad ;
Their muffled screams and laughter make me mad !

I long to go and play among them there ;
Unseen, like wind, to take them by the hair,
And gently make their rosy cheeks more fair.

The happy children ! full of frank surprise,
And sudden whims and innocent ecstasies ;
What godhead sparkles from their liquid eyes !

No wonder round those urns of mingled clays
That Tuscan potters fashion'd in old days,
And colour'd like the torrid earth ablaze,

We find the little gods and loves portray'd,
Through ancient forests wandering undismay'd,
And fluting hymns of pleasure unafraid.

They knew, as I do now, what keen delight,
A strong man feels to watch the tender flight
Of little children playing in his sight ;

What pure sweet pleasure, and what sacred love,
Comes drifting down upon us from above,
In watching how their limbs and features move.

I do not hunger for a well-stored mind,
I only wish to live my life, and find
My heart in unison with all mankind.

My life is like the single dewy star
That trembles on the horizon's primrose-bar,—
A microcosm where all things living are.

And

And if, among the noiseless grasses, Death
Should come behind and take away my breath,
I should not rise as one who sorroweth ;

For I should pass ; but all the world would be
Full of desire and young delight and glee,
And why should men be sad through loss of me ?

The light is flying ; in the silver-blue
The young moon shines from her bright window through :
The mowers are all gone, and I go too.

539. *The Charcoal-Burner*

HE lives within the hollow wood,
    From one clear dell he seldom ranges ;
His daily toil in solitude
    Revolves, but never changes.

A still old man, with grizzled beard,
    Grey eye, bent shape, and smoke-tann'd features,
His quiet footstep is not fear'd
    By shyest woodland creatures.

I love to watch the pale blue spire
    His scented labour builds above it ;
I track the woodland by his fire,
    And, seen afar, I love it.

It seems among the serious trees
    The emblem of a living pleasure,
It animates the silences
    As with a tuneful measure.

And dream not that such humdrum ways
    Fold naught of nature's charm around him ;
The mystery of soundless days
    Hath sought for him and found him.

He hides within his simple brain
    An instinct innocent and holy,
The music of a wood-bird's strain,—
    Not blithe, nor melancholy,

But hung upon the calm content
    Of wholesome leaf and bough and blossom—
An unecstatic ravishment
    Born in a rustic bosom.

He knows the moods of forest things,
    He feels, in his own speechless fashion,
For helpless forms of fur and wings
    A mild paternal passion.

Within his horny hand he holds
    The warm brood of the ruddy squirrel ;
Their bushy mother storms and scolds,
    But knows no sense of peril.

The dormouse shares his crumb of cheese,
    His homeward trudge the rabbits follow ;
He finds, in angles of the trees,
    The cup-nest of the swallow.

And through this sympathy, perchance,
    The beating heart of life he reaches
Far more than we who idly dance
    An hour beneath the beeches.

729   Our

Our science and our empty pride,
 Our busy dream of introspection,
To God seem vain and poor beside
 This dumb, sincere reflection.

Yet he will die unsought, unknown,
 A nameless head-stone stand above him,
And the vast woodland, vague and lone,
 Be all that 's left to love him.

540.   *Revelation*

UNTO the silver night
  She brought with her pale hand
The topaz lanthorn-light,
And darted splendour o'er the land ;
  Around her in a band,
Ringstraked and pied, the great soft moths came flying,
 And flapping with their mad wings, fann'd
The flickering flame, ascending, falling, dying.

 Behind the thorny pink
  Close wall of blossom'd may,
 I gazed thro' one green chink
And saw no more than thousands may,—
  Saw sweetness, tender and gay,—
Saw full rose lips as rounded as the cherry,
 Saw braided locks more dark than bay,
And flashing eyes decorous, pure, and merry.

730

With food for furry friends
 She pass'd, her lamp and she,
Till eaves and gable-ends
Hid all that saffron sheen from me :
 Around my rosy tree
Once more the silver-starry night was shining,
 With depths of heaven, dewy and free,
And crystals of a carven moon declining.

 Alas ! for him who dwells
  In frigid air of thought,
 When warmer light dispels
The frozen calm his spirit sought ;
  By life too lately taught
He sees the ecstatic Human from him stealing ;
 Reels from the joy experience brought,
And dares not clutch what Love was half revealing.

541.   *Epithalamium*

HIGH in the organ-loft with lilied hair,
 Love plied the pedals with his snowy foot,
 Pouring forth music like the scent of fruit,
And stirring all the incense-laden air ;
We knelt before the altar's gold rail, where
 The priest stood robed, with chalice and palm-shoot,
 With music-men who bore citole and lute
Behind us, and the attendant virgins fair.

And so our red aurora flash'd to gold,
 Our dawn to sudden sun ; and all the while
The high-voiced children trebled clear and cold,
 The censer-boys went swinging down the aisle,
And far above, with fingers strong and sure,
Love closed our lives' triumphant overture.

731

1850-1887

542.   *The Rose and the Wind*

Dawn

The Rose.

WHEN, think you, comes the Wind,
    The Wind that kisses me and is so kind ?
Lo, how the Lily sleeps ! her sleep is light ;
Would I were like the Lily, pale and white !
Will the Wind come?

The Beech.

Perchance for you too soon.

The Rose.

If not, how could I live until the noon?
What, think you, Beech-tree, makes the Wind delay ?
Why comes he not at breaking of the day ?

The Beech.

Hush, child, and, like the Lily, go to sleep.

The Rose.

You know I cannot.

The Beech.

        Nay, then, do not weep.
        (*After a pause.*)
Your lover comes : be happy now, O Rose !
He softly through my bending branches goes.
Soon he shall come, and you shall feel his kiss.

The Rose.

Already my flush'd heart grows faint with bliss ;
Love, I have long'd for you through all the night.

732

PHILIP BOURKE MARSTON

The Wind.
And I to kiss your petals warm and bright.

The Rose.
Laugh round me, Love, and kiss me ; it is well.
Nay, have no fear, the Lily will not tell.

Morning
The Rose.
'Twas dawn when first you came ; and now the sun
Shines brightly and the dews of dawn are done.
'Tis well you take me so in your embrace ;
But lay me back again into my place,
For I am worn, perhaps with bliss extreme.

The Wind.
Nay, you must wake, Love, from this childish dream.

The Rose.
'Tis you, Love, who seem changed ; your laugh is loud,
And 'neath your stormy kiss my head is bow'd.
O Love, O Wind, a space will you not spare ?

The Wind.
Not while your petals are so soft and fair.

The Rose.
My buds are blind with leaves, they cannot see,—
O Love, O Wind, will you not pity me ?

Evening
The Beech.
O Wind, a word with you before you pass ;
What did you to the Rose that on the grass
Broken she lies and pale, who loved you so ?

The Wind.
Roses must live and love, and winds must blow.

543. *The Old Churchyard at Bonchurch*

THE churchyard leans to the sea with its dead,—
It leans to the sea with its dead so long.
Do they hear, I wonder, the first bird's song,
When the winter's anger is all but fled ;
The high, sweet voice of the west wind,
The fall of the warm, soft rain,
When the second month of the year
Puts heart in the earth again?

Do they hear, through the glad April weather,
The green grasses waving above them?
Do they think there are none left to love them,
They have lain for so long there, together?
Do they hear the note of the cuckoo,
The cry of gulls on the wing,
The laughter of winds and waters,
The feet of the dancing Spring ?

Do they feel the old land slipping seaward,—
The old land, with its hills and its graves,—
As they gradually slide to the waves,
With the wind blowing past them to leeward?
Do they know of the change that awaits them,—
The sepulchre vast and strange?
Do they long for the days to go over,
And bring that miraculous change?

Or love they their night with no moonlight,
With no starlight, no dawn to its gloom?
Do they sigh : ' 'Neath the snow, or the bloom
Of the wild things that wave from our night,

PHILIP BOURKE MARSTON

We are warm, through winter and summer
We hear the winds rave, and we say,—
" The storm-wind blows over our heads,
But we, here, are out of its way " ' ?

Do they mumble low, one to another,
With a sense that the waters that thunder
Shall ingather them all, draw them under,—
' Ah, how long to our moving, my brother?
How long shall we quietly rest here,
In graves of darkness and ease?
The waves, even now, may be on us,
To draw us down under the seas! '

Do they think 'twill be cold when the waters
That they love not, that neither can love them?
Shall eternally thunder above them?
Have they dread of the sea's shining daughters,
That people the bright sea-regions
And play with the young sea-kings?
Have they dread of their cold embraces,
And dread of all strange sea-things?

But their dread or their joy,—it is bootless:
They shall pass from the breast of their mother,
They shall lie low, dead brother by brother,
In a place that is radiant and fruitless:
And the folk that sail over their heads
In violent weather
Shall come down to them, haply, and all
They shall lie there, together.

1850-1894

544.   *Romance*

I WILL make you brooches and toys for your delight
  Of bird-song at morning and star-shine at night.
I will make a palace fit for you and me,
Of green days in forests and blue days at sea.

I will make my kitchen, and you shall keep your room,
Where white flows the river and bright blows the broom,
And you shall wash your linen and keep your body white
In rainfall at morning and dewfall at night.

And this shall be for music when no one else is near,
The fine song for singing, the rare song to hear!
That only I remember, that only you admire,
Of the broad road that stretches and the roadside fire.

545.   *Alcaics: to H. F. B.*

BRAVE lads in olden musical centuries
  Sang, night by night, adorable choruses,
    Sat late by alehouse doors in April
    Chaunting in joy as the moon was rising.

Moon-seen and merry, under the trellises,
Flush-faced they play'd with old polysyllables
    Spring scents inspired, old wine diluted:
    Love and Apollo were there to chorus.

Now these, the songs, remain to eternity,
Those, only those, the bountiful choristers
    Gone—those are gone, those unremember'd
    Sleep and are silent in earth for ever.

So man himself appears and evanishes,
So smiles and goes ; as wanderers halting at
   Some green-embower'd house, play their music,
   Play and are gone on the windy highway.

Yet dwells the strain enshrined in the memory
Long after they departed eternally,
   Forth-faring tow'rd far mountain summits,
   Cities of men or the sounding Ocean.

Youth sang the song in years immemorial :
Brave chanticleer, he sang and was beautiful ;
   Bird-haunted green tree-tops in springtime
   Heard, and were pleased by the voice of singing.

Youth goes and leaves behind him a prodigy—
Songs sent by thee afar from Venetian
   Sea-grey lagunes, sea-paven highways,
   Dear to me here in my Alpine exile.

546.   *In the Highlands*

IN the highlands, in the country places,
   Where the old plain men have rosy faces,
     And the young fair maidens
       Quiet eyes ;
Where essential silence chills and blesses,
And for ever in the hill-recesses
     Her more lovely music
       Broods and dies—

O to mount again where erst I haunted ;
Where the old red hills are bird-enchanted,
     And the low green meadows
       Bright with sward ;

And when even dies, the million-tinted,
And the night has come, and planets glinted,
    Lo, the valley hollow
      Lamp-bestarr'd !

O to dream, O to awake and wander
There, and with delight to take and render,
    Through the trance of silence,
      Quiet breath !
Lo ! for there, among the flowers and grasses,
Only the mightier movement sounds and passes ;
    Only winds and rivers,
      Life and death.

547. *Christmas at Sea*

THE sheets were frozen hard, and they cut the naked
    hand ;
The decks were like a slide, where a seaman scarce could
    stand,
The wind was a nor'-wester, blowing squally off the sea ;
And cliffs and spouting breakers were the only things a-lee.

They heard the surf a-roaring before the break of day ;
But 'twas only with the peep of light we saw how ill we lay.
We tumbled every hand on deck instanter, with a shout,
And we gave her the maintops'l, and stood by to go about.

All day we tack'd and tack'd between the South Head
    and the North ;
All day we haul'd the frozen sheets, and got no further
    forth ;
All day as cold as charity, in bitter pain and dread,
For very life and nature we tack'd from head to head.

We gave the South a wider berth, for there the tide-race
    roar'd ;
But every tack we made we brought the North Head close
    aboard ;
So 's we saw the cliffs and houses, and the breakers running
    high,
And the coastguard in his garden, with his glass against
    his eye.

The frost was on the village roofs as white as ocean foam;
The good red fires were burning bright in every 'longshore
    home ;
The windows sparkled clear, and the chimneys volley'd
    out ;
And I vow we sniff'd the victuals as the vessel went about.

The bells upon the church were rung with a mighty jovial
    cheer ;
For it 's just that I should tell you how (of all days in the
    year)
This day of our adversity was blessèd Christmas morn,
And the house above the coastguard's was the house where
    I was born.

O well I saw the pleasant room, the pleasant faces there,
My mother's silver spectacles, my father's silver hair ;
And well I saw the firelight, like a flight of homely elves
Go dancing round the china-plates that stand upon the
    shelves !

And well I knew the talk they had, the talk that was of me,
Of the shadow on the household and the son that went
    to sea ;
And O the wicked fool I seem'd, in every kind of way,
To be here and hauling frozen ropes on blessèd Christmas
    Day.

               They

They lit the high sea-light, and the dark began to fall.
'All hands to loose topgallant sails !' I heard the captain
    call.
' By the Lord, she'll never stand it,' our first mate Jackson
    cried.
. . . ' It 's the one way or the other, Mr. Jackson,' he
    replied.

She stagger'd to her bearings, but the sails were new and
    good,
And the ship smelt up to windward just as though she
    understood.
As the winter's day was ending, in the entry of the night,
We clear'd the weary headland, and pass'd below the
    light.

And they heaved a mighty breath, every soul on board
    but me,
As they saw her nose again pointing handsome out to sea ;
But all that I could think of, in the darkness and the cold,
Was just that I was leaving home and my folks were
    growing old.

548.   *Wishes*

GO, little book, and wish to all
    Flowers in the garden, meat in the hall,
A bin of wine, a spice of wit,
A house with lawns enclosing it,
A living river by the door,
A nightingale in the sycamore.

ROBERT LOUIS STEVENSON

549. *Requiem*

UNDER the wide and starry sky
  Dig the grave and let me lie :
Glad did I live and gladly die,
  And I laid me down with a will.

This be the verse you grave for me :
Here he lies where he long'd to be ;
Home is the sailor, home from sea,
  And the hunter home from the hill.

BERTRAM DOBELL

b. 1842

550. *Microcosm*

HIS home a speck in a vast Universe,
  He a mere atom on that tiny speck,
Victim of countless evils that coerce
  And force him onward on a pathless track :
And yet a being made to dominate
  O'er all things else by mind's controlling power :
Spoilt favourite at once and sport of fate,
  Football of fortune, time's consummate flower !

To him alone did Nature's self impart
  A spark of her divinest energy,
With power to create a world of Art,
  And intellect to solve all mystery :
So great and yet so little ! blest and curst—
Nature's most noble offspring—yet her worst !

741

b. 1850

551. *The Old Parish Church, Whitby*

WE climb'd the steep where headless Edwin lies—
  The king who struck for Christ, and striking fell ;
Beyond the harbour, toll'd the beacon bell ;
Saint Mary's peal sent down her glad replies ;
So entered we the Church : white galleries,
    Cross-stanchions, frequent stairs, dissembled well
    A ship's mid-hold,—we almost felt the swell
Beneath, and caught o'erhead the sailors' cries.

But as we heard the congregational sound,
    And reasonable voice of common prayer
        And common praise, new wind was in our sails—
Heart called to heart, beyond the horizon's bound
    With Christ we steer'd, through angel-haunted air,
        A ship that meets all storms, rides out all gales.

WALTER HERRIES POLLOCK

b. 1850

552. *A Conquest*

I FOUND him openly wearing her token ;
  I knew that her troth could never be broken ;
I laid my hand on the hilt of my sword,
He did the same, and he spoke no word ;
He faced me with his villainy ;
He laugh'd, and said, ' She gave it me.'
We search'd for seconds, they soon were found ;
They measured our swords ; they measured the ground :
They held to the deadly work too fast ;
They thought to gain our place at last.
We fought in the sheen of a wintry wood,
The fair white snow was red with his blood ;
But his was the victory, for, as he died,
He swore by the rood that he had not lied.

553.   *Song*

THERE's one great bunch of stars in heaven
    That shines so sturdily,
Where good Saint Peter's sinewy hand
    Holds up the dull gold-wroughten key.

There's eke a little twinkling gem
    As green as beryl-blue can be,
The lowest bead the Blessèd Virgin
    Shakes a-telling her rosary.

There's one that flashes flames and fire,
    No doubt the mighty rubicel
That sparkles from the centre point
    I' the buckler of stout Raphael.

And also there's a little star—
    So white, a virgin's it must be ;—
Perhaps the lamp my love in heaven
    Hangs out to light the way for me.

554.   *A Violinist*

THE lark above our heads doth know
    A heaven we see not here below ;
She sees it, and for joy she sings ;
Then falls with ineffectual wings.

Ah, soaring soul ! faint not nor tire !
Each heaven attain'd reveals a higher.
Thy thought is of thy failure ; we
List raptured, and thank God for thee.

FRANCIS WILLIAM BOURDILLON

555. *The Night has a Thousand Eyes*

THE night has a thousand eyes,
    And the day but one;
Yet the light of the bright world dies
    With the dying sun.

The mind has a thousand eyes,
    And the heart but one;
Yet the light of a whole life dies
    When love is done.

FRANCIS BURDETT MONEY-COUTTS

b. 1852

556. *The Dream*

HAIL, bright morning beam!
    Now my task retaking,
I indite the dream
    God for me is making.

We may draw our theme,
    Management, and measure
Out of Earth; the dream
    Comes of God's good pleasure.

557. *From 'A Little Sequence'*

i

NO wonder you so oft have wept;
    For I was born unblest:
Yet wounded creature never crept
    To you but found a rest;

744

To you the patient hound's mild eyes
  Are turn'd in perfect trust,
And into yours, with sure surmise,
  The baby's hand is thrust ;

The little birds make you their friend,
  The flowers in your sweet hand
Arrange themselves, and graceful bend,
  As if they understand.

And when these die,—the household pet,—
  The babe (though not your own),—
Yes, or the very flowers,—you fret
  To fly where they have flown.

ii

FORGIVE !
  And tell me that sweet tale,
How you and I one day may live
  In some diviner vale.

In some diviner vale, dear child,
  Than this in which we lie
And watch the monstrous mountains piled
  And clouded into sky.

Yet even there, far out of reach
  Are peaks we cannot scale,
For God has something still to teach
  In that diviner vale.

745

558.   *Any Father to Any Son*

FOR thee a crown of thorns I wear,
    And thought imperative constrains
My labouring heart for thee to bear
    The travail of a woman's pains ;

For with intolerable preságe
    Of all the amazements of thy life,
The pits of ancient woe I gauge,
    The vast impediments of strife ;

Or else in dreadful dreaming cast,
    I see thy form before me fly,
By prescience never overpast
    Nor fleetest foot that love can ply.

Still as thy shadow must I run,
    When all the shadows fall behind,
And in the rich seductive sun
    Thou to the darker bars art blind.

559.   *Empires*

HOW dare we deem that in this age
    The end of all the ages lurks ?
That God is printing the last page
    Of the last volume of his Works ?

Have we not canted of the mills
    Of God, how very slow they grind ?
Why should we fancy on our hills
    Their sails are sped by earthly wind ?

Persia and Egypt, Greece and Rome,
 And vaster dynasties before,
Now faded in Time's monochrome,
 In what do we surpass their lore ?

Some things they knew that we know not ;
 Some things we know by them unknown ;
But the axles of their wheels were hot
 With the same frenzies as our own.

560. *Mors, Morituri Te Salutamus*

I HATE thee, Death !
 Not that I fear thee,—more than mortal sprite
 Fears the dark entrance, whence no man returns ;
For who would not resign his scanty breath,
Unreal joy, and troublesome delight,
 To marble coffer or sepulchral urn's
   Inviolate keeping ?
 To quench the smouldering lamp, that feebly burns
  Within this chamber, to procure sweet sleeping,
 Is not a madman's act.   And yet I hate thee,
  Swift breaker of life's poor illusion,
  Stern ender of love's fond confusion,
 And with rebellion in my heart await thee.

Like mariners we sail, of fate unwist,
 With orders seal'd and only to be read
When home has faded in the morning mist
 And simple faith and innocence are fled !

Oft we neglect them, being much dismay'd
  By phantoms and weird wonders
   That haunt the deep,
  By voices, winds, and thunders,

Old

Old mariners that cannot pray nor weep,
  And faces of drown'd souls that cannot sleep !
Or else our crew is mutinous, array'd
Against us, and the mandate is delay'd.

But when the forces that rebell'd
Are satisfied or quell'd ;
When sails are trimm'd to catch the merry wind,
And billows dance before and foam behind ;
Free, free at last from tumult and distraction
Of pleasure beckon'd and of pain repell'd,—
Free from ourselves and disciplined for action,—
We break the seal of destiny, to find
The bourne or venture for our cruise design'd,
Then, at that very moment, hark ! a cry
  On deck ; and then a silence, as of breath
Held. In the offing, low against the sky,
  Hoves thy black flag ! . . . Therefore I hate thee, Death !

561.   *Two Epitaphs*

i. On a Fair Woman

IN this green chest is laid away
  The fairest frock she ever wore ;
It clothed her both by night and day,
  And none shall wear it evermore.

ii. On a Wife

ONCE I learnt in wilful hour
  How to vex him ; still I keep,
Now unwilfully, my power :
  Every day he comes to weep.

748

THOMAS HERBERT WARREN
PRESIDENT OF MAGDALEN COLLEGE

b. 1853

562. *May-day on Magdalen Tower*

WRITTEN FOR MR. HOLMAN HUNT'S PICTURE

MORN of the year, of day and May the prime!
How fitly do we scale the steep dark stair!
Into the brightness of the matin air,
To praise with chanted hymn and echoing chime,
Dear Lord of Light, Thy lowlihead sublime
That stoop'd erewhile our life's frail weed to wear!
Sun, cloud, and hill, all things Thou framest so fair,
With us are glad and gay, greeting the time.

The college of the lily leaves her sleep;
The grey tower rocks and trembles into sound,
Dawn-smitten Memnon of a happier hour;
Through faint-hued fields the silver waters creep;
Day grows, birds pipe, and robed anew and crown'd,
Green Spring trips forth to set the world aflower.

563. *Lines for a Sundial*

Meditatur Homo.

DAWNE TO DARKE
GRADE BY GRADE
SHADOWES MARKE.

Monet Solarium.

SHADOWE HARKE
WHAT YS SAYDE!

Monitio.

THYNGES DIVRNALLE
BIN A SHADE
OF ETERNALLE.

749

ANNIE MATHESON

564.   *A Song of Handicrafts*

The Weaver

SUNLIGHT from the sky's own heart,
　　Flax unfolded to receive :
Out of sky and flax and art,
　　Lovely raiment I achieve—
Earth a part and heaven a part,
　　God in all, for Whom I weave !

The Carpenter

Deep into the wood I hew,
　　A message fell from the sun's lip ;
Fire and strength it downward drew
　　For the faggot and the ship :
God's own, in the forest, grew
　　Timber that I hew and chip.

The Mason

Out of clay or living rock
　　I will make my brick or stone :
At the door of God I knock,
　　Builder whose command I own,
Who can birth and death unlock,
　　And in dust can find a throne.

750

ANNIE MATHESON

Chorus

Mighty Craftsman ! craftsmen, we,
    Feel Thy spirit in our hands :
All the worlds are full of Thee—
    Wake our eyes and break our bands—
Servants, and for ever free,
    Sons, and heirs of all thy lands !

565.   *Love's Cosmopolitan*

(A SONNET DEDICATED TO LONDON'S CATHEDRAL OF
SAINT PAUL THE TENTMAKER)

APOSTLE, citizen, and artisan !
    About thy vast cathedral, through the street
Is hurrying tramp of multitudinous feet ;
But far within, for many a homeless man
Thy shrine is home, where, for a passing span,
    Cool silence stills the heart's tumultuous beat :
    Before the altar he may rest and eat
Who has not broken bread since day began.

Thou who didst glory in the uplifted cross
    Whereby ascended Love, self-sacrificed,
        Draws all men near, and heart to heart a few,
Thou who didst count the world for love but loss,
    Hail, chosen servant of the risen Christ,
        Ambassador of God, great-hearted Jew !

751

WILLIAM JAMES DAWSON

b. 1854

566. *Deliverance*

IN that sore hour around thy bed there stood
　A silent guard of shadows, each equipp'd
With dart or arrow aim'd against thy life.
Thy breath came slowly all that awful night ;
Outside I heard the wind and earth at strife,
And on the window's ledge incessant dripp'd
The pitiless rain.　At last I left thy room,
And passing out, upon its threshold's edge
Who should I meet but Death !　A wan clear light
Fell from his fathomless eyes, his brow was gloom,
His rustling raiment seem'd to sigh like sedge
When the salt marsh-winds wail and beat thereon.
He paused, he turn'd ;　and while I stood and wept,
Behold a crimson signal waved and shone
On the door's lintel, even such an one
As he obey'd in Egypt, and I knew
Death heard some higher summons, and withdrew :
When I return'd, like a tired child you slept.

OLIVER MADOX BROWN

1855-1874

567. *Laura's Song*

ALAS !　who knows or cares, my love,
　If our love live or die,—
If thou thy frailty, sweet, should prove,
　Or my soul thine deny ?
Yet, merging sorrow in delight,
Love's dream disputes our devious night.

None know, sweet love, nor care a thought
    For our heart's vague desire,
Nor if our longing come to nought,
    Or burn in aimless fire ;
Let them alone, we'll waste no sighs :
Cling closer, love, and close thine eyes !

FANNY PARNELL

1855–1883

568.   *After Death*

SHALL mine eyes behold thy glory, O my country ?
    Shall mine eyes behold thy glory ?
Or shall the darkness close around them, ere the sun-
    blaze break at last upon thy story ?

When the nations ope for thee their queenly circle, as
    a new sweet sister hail thee,
Shall these lips be seal'd in callous death and silence, that
    have known but to bewail thee ?

Shall the ear be deaf that only loved thy praises, when
    all men their tribute bring thee ?
Shall the mouth be clay that sang thee in thy squalor,
    when all poets' mouths shall sing thee ?

Ah ! the harpings and the salvoes and the shouting of
    thy exiled sons returning !
I should hear tho' dead and moulder'd, and the grave-
    damps should not chill my bosom's burning.

Ah ! the tramp of feet victorious ! I should hear them
    'mid the shamrocks and the mosses,
And my heart would toss within the shroud and quiver
    as a captive dreamer tosses.

753   I should

I should turn and rend the cere-clothes round me, giant
    sinews I should borrow—
Crying, ' O my brothers, I have also loved her in her
    loneliness and sorrow !

' Let me join with you the jubilant procession ; let me
    chant with you her story ;
Then contented I shall go back to the shamrocks, now
    mine eyes have seen her glory ! '

EDWARD CRACROFT LEFROY

1855–1891

Echoes from Theocritus

569. *i. A Summer Day in Old Sicily*

GODS, what a sun ! I think the world 's aglow.
  This garment irks me. Phoebus, it is hot !
'Twere sad if Glycera should find me shot
By flame-tipp'd arrows from the Archer's bow.
  Perchance he envies me,—the villain ! O
For one tree's shadow or a cliff-side grot !
Where shall I shelter that he slay me not ?
In what cool air or element ?—I know.

The sea shall save me from the sweltering land :
    Far out I'll wade, till creeping up and up,
      The cold green water quenches every limb.
Then to the jealous god with lifted hand
    I'll pour libation from a rosy cup,
      And leap, and dive, and see the tunnies swim.

570.   *ii. Ageanax*

DEAR voyager, a lucky star be thine,
    To Mytilenè sailing over sea,
Or foul or fair the constellations shine,
    Or east or west the wind-blown billows flee.
May halcyon-birds that hover o'er the brine
    Diffuse abroad their own tranquillity,
Till ocean stretches stilly as the wine
    In this deep cup which now we drain to thee.

From lip to lip the merry circle through
    We pass the tankard and repeat thy name ;
And having pledged thee once, we pledge anew,
    Lest in thy friends' neglect thou suffer shame.
God-speed to ship, good health to pious crew,
    Peace by the way, and port of noble fame !

571.   *iii. The Flute of Daphnis*

I AM the flute of Daphnis. On this wall
    He nail'd his tribute to the great god Pan,
What time he grew from boyhood, shapely, tall,
    And felt the first deep ardours of a man.
    Through adult veins more swift the song-tide ran,—
A vernal stream whose swollen torrents call
    For instant ease in utterance. Then began
That course of triumph reverenced by all.

Him the gods loved, and more than other men
    Blessed with the flower of beauty, and endow'd
His soul of music with the strength of ten.
    Now on a festal day I see the crowd
Look fondly at my resting-place, and when
    I think whose lips have press'd me, I am proud.

572.   *iv. The Epitaph of Eusthenes*

A BARD is buried here, not strong, but sweet;
    A Teacher too, not great, but gently wise;
This modest stone (the burghers thought it meet)
    May tell the world where so much virtue lies.
His happy skill it was in mart and street
    To scan men's faces with a true surmise,
Follow the spirit to its inmost seat,
    And read the soul reflected in the eyes.

No part had he in catholic renown,
    Which none but god-inspirèd poets share;
Not his to trail the philosophic gown,
    That only sages of the School may wear;
But his at least to fill an alien town
    With friends, who make his tomb their loving care.

573.   *A Cricket Bowler*

T WO minutes' rest till the next man goes in!
    The tired arms lie with every sinew slack
On the mown grass.   Unbent the supple back,
And elbows apt to make the leather spin
Up the slow bat and round the unwary shin,—
    In knavish hands a most unkindly knack;
    But no guile shelters under this boy's black
Crisp hair, frank eyes, and honest English skin.

Two minutes only.   Conscious of a name,
    The new man plants his weapon with profound
        Long-practised skill that no mere trick may scare.
Not loth, the rested lad resumes the game:
    The flung ball takes one madding tortuous bound,
        And the mid-stump three somersaults in air.

EDWARD CRACROFT LEFROY

On a Spring-board

THE light falls gently from the dormer-panes,
   And sleeps upon the water sleeping too,—
Such water as the fond Boeotian knew
When in the liquid fount he view'd the stains
Of his own love-looks.   What sweet idlesse reigns
   From gleam to gleam, and makes the soul in view
   Of long'd-for bliss a longer path pursue,
And still be hoping while she still refrains ?

Now see me work a deed exceeding rash !
There sinks my pocket-wealth of hoarded cash
   Through the green floor.   So did the Samian king,
   Blest overmuch, engulph the fateful ring ;
   But here are no fat fish to bolt and bring
My treasure back from limbo, therefore—splash !

OSCAR WILDE

1856-1900

Requiescat

TREAD lightly, she is near
   Under the snow,
Speak gently, she can hear
   The daisies grow.

All her bright golden hair
   Tarnished with rust,
She that was young and fair
   Fallen to dust.

Lily-like

Lily-like, white as snow,
      She hardly knew
She was a woman, so
      Sweetly she grew.

Coffin board, heavy stone,
      Lie on her breast,
I vex my heart alone,
      SHE is at rest.

Peace, peace, she cannot hear
      Lyre or sonnet,
All my life's buried here,
      Heap earth upon it.

WILLIAM SHARP

1856-1902

576. *On a Nightingale in April*

THE yellow moon is a dancing phantom
      Down secret ways of the flowing shade ;
And the waveless stream has a murmuring whisper
      Where the alders wade.

Not a breath, not a sigh, save the slow stream's whisper :
      Only the moon is a dancing blade
That leads a host of the Crescent warriors
      To a phantom raid.

Out of the lands of Faerie a summons,
      A long strange cry that thrills thro' the glade :—
The grey-green glooms of the elm are stirring,
      Newly afraid.

758

Last heard, white music, under the olives
  Where once Theocritus sang and play'd—
Thy Thracian song is the old new wonder—
    O moon-white maid !

577.   *Shule, Agrah !*

HIS face was glad as dawn to me,
  His breath was sweet as dusk to me,
His eyes were burning flames to me,
    Shule, shule, shule, agrah !

The broad noon-day was night to me,
The full-moon night was dark to me,
The stars whirl'd and the poles span
The hour that God took him far from me.

Perhaps he dreams in heaven now,
Perhaps he doth in worship bow,
A white flame round his foam-white brow,
    Shule, shule, shule, agrah !

I laugh to think of him like this,
Who once found all his joy and bliss
Against my heart, against my kiss,
    Shule, shule, shule, agrah !

Star of my joy, art still the same
Now thou hast gotten a new name ?
Pulse of my heart, my Blood, my Flame,
    Shule, shule, shule, agrah !

DOUGLAS BROOK WHEELTON SLADEN

b. 1856

578. *Under the Wattle*

'WHY should not Wattle do
    For Mistletoe ? '
Ask'd one—they were but two—
    Where wattles grow.

He was her lover, too,
    Who urged her so—
' Why should not Wattle do
    For Mistletoe ? '

A rose-cheek rosier grew ;
    Rose-lips breathed low—
' Since it is here—and You—
    I hardly know
Why Wattle should not do.'

MARGARET L. WOODS

b. 1856

579. *March Thoughts from England*

O THAT I were lying under the olives,
    Lying alone among the anemones !
Shell-colour'd blossoms they bloom there and scarlet,
Far under stretches of silver woodland,
Flame in the delicate shade of the olives.

O that I were lying under the olives !
Grey grows the thyme on the shadowless headland,
The long low headland, where white in the sunshine
The rocks run seaward.   It seems suspended
Lone in an infinite gulf of azure.

MARGARET L. WOODS

There, were I lying under the olives,
Might I behold come following seaward,
Clear brown shapes in a world of sunshine,
A russet shepherd, his sheep too, russet.
Watch them wander the long grey headland
Out to the edge of the burning azure.
O that I were lying under the olives !
So should I see the far-off cities
Glittering low by the purple water,
Gleaming high on the purple mountain ;
See where the road goes winding southward.
It passes the valleys of almond blossom,
Curves round the crag o'er the steep-hanging orchards,
Where almond and peach are aflush 'mid the olives—
Hardly the amethyst sea shines through them—
Over it cypress on solemn cypress
Lead to the lonely pilgrimage places.

O that I were dreaming under the olives
Hearing alone on the sun-steeped headland
A crystalline wave, almost inaudible,
Steal round the shore ; and thin, far off,
The shepherd's music ! So did it sound
In fields Sicilian : Theocritus heard it,
Moschus and Bion piped it at noontide.

O that I were listening under the olives !
So should I hear behind in the woodland
The peasants talking. Either a woman,
A wrinkled grandame, stands in the sunshine,
Stirs the brown soil in an acre of violets—
Large odorous violets—and answers slowly
A child's swift babble ; or else at noon
The labourers come. They rest in the shadow,
Eating their dinner of herbs, and are merry.

Soft

Soft speech Provençal under the olives !
Like a queen's raiment from days long perish'd,
Breathing aromas of old unremember'd
Perfumes and shining in dust-cover'd places
With sudden hints of forgotten splendour—
So on the lips of the peasant his language,
His only now, the tongue of the peasant.

Would I were listening under the olives !
So should I see in an airy pageant
A proud chivalrous pomp sweep by me ;
Hear in high courts the joyous ladies
Devising of Love in a world of lovers ;
Hear the song of the Lion-hearted,
A deep-voiced song—and O ! perchance,
Ghostly and strange and sweet to madness,
Rudel sing the Lady of Tripoli.

580.   *The Mariners*

THE mariners sleep by the sea.
   The wild wind comes up from the sea,
It wails round the tower, and it blows through the grasses,
It scatters the sand o'er the graves where it passes
And the sound and the scent of the sea.

The white waves beat up from the shore,
They beat on the church by the shore,
They rush round the grave-stones aslant to the leeward,
And the wall and the mariners' graves lying seaward,
That are bank'd with the stones from the shore.

For the huge sea comes up in the storm,
Like a beast from the lair of the storm,
To claim with its ravenous leap and to mingle
The mariners' bones with the surf and the shingle
That it rolls round the shore in the storm.

There is nothing beyond but the sky,
But the sea and the slow-moving sky,
Where a cloud from the grey lifts the gleam of its edges,
Where the foam flashes white from the shouldering ridges,
As they crowd on the uttermost sky.

The mariners sleep by the sea.
Far away there 's a shrine by the sea ;
The pale women climb up the path to it slowly,
To pray to Our Lady of Storms ere they wholly
Despair of their men from the sea.

The children at play on the sand,
Where once from the shell-broider'd sand
They would watch for the sails coming in from far places,
Are forgetting the ships and forgetting the faces
Lying here, lying hid in the sand.

When at night there 's a seething of surf,
The grandames look out o'er the surf,
They reckon their dead and their long years of sadness,
And they shake their lean fists at the sea and its madness,
And curse the white fangs of the surf.

But the mariners sleep by the sea.
They hear not the sound of the sea,
Nor the hum from the church where the psalm is uplifted,
Nor the crying of birds that above them are drifted.
The mariners sleep by the sea.

MARGARET L. WOODS

581. *Genius Loci*

PEACE, Shepherd, peace ! What boots it singing on ?
    Since long ago grace-giving Phœbus died,
  And all the train that loved the stream-bright side
Of the poetic mount with him are gone
Beyond the shores of Styx and Acheron,
    In unexplorèd realms of night to hide.
    The clouds that strew their shadows far and wide
Are all of Heaven that visits Helicon.

Yet here, where never muse or god did haunt,
    Still may some nameless power of Nature stray,
Pleased with the reedy stream's continual chant
    And purple pomp of these broad fields in May.
The shepherds meet him where he herds the kine,
And careless pass him by whose is the gift divine.

JOHN DAVIDSON

1857-1909

582. *Song*

THE boat is chafing at our long delay,
    And we must leave too soon
The spicy sea-pinks and the inborne spray,
    The tawny sands, the moon.

Keep us, O Thetis, in our western flight !
    Watch from thy pearly throne
Our vessel, plunging deeper into night
    To reach a land unknown.

764

JOHN DAVIDSON

Holiday

LITHE and listen, gentlemen :
    Other knight of sword or pen
Shall not, while the planets shine,
Spend a holiday like mine.

Fate and I, we play'd at dice :
    Thrice I won and lost the main ;
Thrice I died the death, and thrice
    By my will I lived again.

First a woman broke my heart
    As a careless woman can,
Ere the aureoles depart
    From the woman and the man.

Dead of love, I found a tomb
    Anywhere : beneath, above,
Worms nor stars transpierced the gloom
    Of the sepulchre of love.

Wine-cups were the charnel-lights ;
    Festal songs, the funeral dole ;
Joyful ladies, gallant knights,
    Comrades of my buried soul.

Tired to death of lying dead
    In a common sepulchre,
On an Easter morn I sped
    Upward where the world 's astir.

Soon

Soon I gather'd wealth and friends,
  Donn'd the livery of the hour,
And atoning diverse ends
  Bridged the gulf to place and power.

All the brilliances of Hell
  Crush'd by me, with honey'd breath
Fawn'd upon me till I fell,
  By pretenders done to death.

Buried in an outland tract,
  Long I rotted in the mould,
Though the virgin woodland lack'd
  Nothing of the age of gold.

Roses spiced the dews and damps,
  Nightly falling of decay ;
Dawn and sunset lit the lamps
  Where entomb'd I deeply lay.

My companions of the grave
  Were the flowers, the growing grass ;
Larks intoned a morning stave ;
  Nightingales a midnight mass.

But at me, effete and dead,
  Did my spirit gibe and scoff :
Then the gravecloth from my head
  And my shroud—I shook them off.

Drawing strength and subtle craft
  Out of ruin's husk and core,
Through the earth I ran a shaft
  Upward to the light once more.

JOHN DAVIDSON

Soon I made me wealth and friends,
  Donn'd the livery of the age ;
And atoning many ends,
  Reign'd as sovereign, priest, and mage.

But my pomp and towering state,
  Puissance and supreme device,
Crumbled on the cast of Fate—
  Fate, that plays with loaded dice.

I whose arms had harried Hell
  Naked faced a heavenly host :
Carved with countless wounds I fell,
  Sadly yielding up the ghost.

In a burning mountain thrown
  (Titans such a tomb attain),
Many a grisly age had flown
  Ere I rose and lived again.

Parch'd and charr'd I lay ; my cries
  Shook and rent the mountain-side ;
Lustres, decades, centuries
  Fled while daily there I died.

But my essence and intent
  Ripen'd in the smelting fire ;
Flame became my element,
  Agony my soul's desire.

Twenty centuries of Pain
  Mightier than Love or Art,
Woke the meaning in my brain
  And the purpose of my heart.

Straightway

Straightway then aloft I swam
　　Through the mountain's sulphurous sty :
Not eternal death could damn
　　Such a hardy soul as I.

From the mountain's burning crest
　　Like a god I come again,
And with an immortal zest
　　Challenge Fate to throw the main.

584.　　　　　　*The Merchantman*

The Markethaunters

NOW, while our money is piping hot
　　From the mint of our toil that coins the sheaves,
Merchantman, merchantman, what have you got
　　In your tabernacle hung with leaves ?
　　　　　What have you got ?
　　　　　The sun rides high ;
　　　　　Our money is hot ;
　　　　　We must buy, buy, buy !

The Merchantman

I come from the elfin king's demesne
　　With chrysolite, hyacinth, tourmaline ;
I have emeralds here of living green ;
　　I have rubies, each like a cup of wine ;
And diamonds, diamonds that never have been
　　Outshone by eyes the most divine !

The Markethaunters

Jewellery ?—Baubles ; bad for the soul ;
　　Desire of the heart and lust of the eye !

Diamonds, indeed ! We wanted coal.
  What else do you sell ? Come, sound your cry !
      Our money is hot ;
        The night draws nigh ;
      What have you got
        That we want to buy?

The Merchantman

I have here enshrined the soul of the rose
  Exhaled in the land of the daystar's birth ;
I have casks whose golden staves enclose
  Eternal youth, eternal mirth ;
And cordials that bring repose,
  And the tranquil night, and the end of the earth.

The Markethaunters

Rapture of wine ? But it never pays :
  We must keep our common-sense alert.
Raisins are healthier, medicine says—
  Raisins and almonds for dessert.
      But we want to buy ;
        For our money is hot,
      And age draws nigh :
        What else have you got ?

The Merchantman

I have lamps that gild the lustre of noon ;
  Shadowy arrows that pierce the brain ;
Dulcimers strung with beams of the moon ;
  Psalteries fashion'd of pleasure and pain ;
A song and a sword and a haunting tune
  That may never be offer'd the world again.

JOHN DAVIDSON

The Markethaunters

Dulcimers ! psalteries ! Whom do you mock ?
    Arrows and songs ?   We have axes to grind !
Shut up your booth and your mouldering stock,
    For we never shall deal.—Come away ; let us find
        What the others have got !
            We must buy, buy, buy ;
            For our money is hot,
            And death draws nigh.

585.   *In Romney Marsh*

AS I went down to Dymchurch Wall,
    I heard the South sing o'er the land ;
I saw the yellow sunlight fall
    On knolls where Norman churches stand.

And ringing shrilly, taut and lithe,
    Within the wind a core of sound,
The wire from Romney town to Hythe
    Alone its airy journey wound.

A veil of purple vapour flowed
    And trail'd its fringe along the Straits ;
The upper air like sapphire glow'd ;
    And roses fill'd Heaven's central gates.

Masts in the offing wagg'd their tops ;
    The swinging waves peal'd on the shore ;
The saffron beach, all diamond drops
    And beads of surge, prolong'd the roar.

770

JOHN DAVIDSON

As I came up from Dymchurch Wall,
  I saw above the Downs' low crest
The crimson brands of sunset fall,
  Flicker and fade from out the west.

Night sank: like flakes of silver fire
  The stars in one great shower came down;
Shrill blew the wind; and shrill the wire
  Rang out from Hythe to Romney town.

The darkly shining salt sea drops
  Streamed as the waves clashed on the shore;
The beach, with all its organ stops
  Pealing again, prolong'd the roar.

586.   *A Runnable Stag*

WHEN the pods went pop on the broom, green
      broom,
  And apples began to be golden-skinn'd,
We harbour'd a stag in the Priory coomb,
  And we feather'd his trail up-wind, up-wind,
  We feather'd his trail up-wind—
    A stag of warrant, a stag, a stag,
    A runnable stag, a kingly crop,
    Brow, bay and tray and three on top,
    A stag, a runnable stag.

Then the huntsman's horn rang yap, yap yap,
  And ' Forwards ' we heard the harbourer shout;
But 'twas only a brocket that broke a gap
  In the beechen underwood, driven out,
  From the underwood antler'd out

By

By warrant and might of the stag, the stag,
　The runnable stag, whose lordly mind
　Was bent on sleep, though beam'd and tined
　He stood, a runnable stag.

So we tufted the covert till afternoon
　With Tinkerman's Pup and Bell-of-the-North ;
And hunters were sulky and hounds out of tune
　Before we tufted the right stag forth,
　Before we tufted him forth,
　　The stag of warrant, the wily stag,
　　The runnable stag with his kingly crop,
　　Brow, bay and tray and three on top,
　　The royal and runnable stag.

It was Bell-of-the-North and Tinkerman's Pup
　That stuck to the scent till the copse was drawn.
' Tally ho ! tally ho ! ' and the hunt was up,
　The tufters whipp'd and the pack laid on,
　The resolute pack laid on,
　　And the stag of warrant away at last,
　　The runnable stag, the same, the same,
　　His hoofs on fire, his horns like flame,
　　A stag, a runnable stag.

' Let your gelding be : if you check or chide
　He stumbles at once and you're out of the hunt ;
For three hundred gentlemen, able to ride,
　On hunters accustom'd to bear the brunt,
　Accustom'd to bear the brunt,
　　Are after the runnable stag, the stag,
　　The runnable stag with his kingly crop.
　　Brow, bay and tray and three on top,
　　The right, the runnable stag.'

JOHN DAVIDSON

By perilous paths in coomb and dell,
   The heather, the rocks, and the river-bed,
The pace grew hot, for the scent lay well,
   And a runnable stag goes right ahead.
   The quarry went right ahead—
      Ahead, ahead, and fast and far ;
      His antler'd crest, his cloven hoof,
      Brow, bay and tray and three aloof,
      The stag, the runnable stag.

For a matter of twenty miles and more,
   By the densest hedge and the highest wall,
Through herds of bullocks he baffled the lore
   Of harbourer, huntsman, hounds and all,
   Of harbourer, hounds and all—
      The stag of warrant, the wily stag,
      For twenty miles, and five and five,
      He ran, and he never was caught alive,
      This stag, this runnable stag.

When he turn'd at bay in the leafy gloom,
   In the emerald gloom where the brook ran deep
He heard in the distance the rollers boom,
   And he saw in a vision of peaceful sleep
   In a wonderful vision of sleep,
      A stag of warrant, a stag, a stag,
      A runnable stag in a jewell'd bed,
      Under the sheltering ocean dead,
      A stag, a runnable stag.

So a fateful hope lit up his eye,
   And he open'd his nostrils wide again,
And he toss'd his branching antlers high
   As he headed the hunt down the Charlock glen,
   As he raced down the echoing glen—

For

For five miles more, the stag, the stag,
For twenty miles, and five and five,
Not to be caught now, dead or alive,
The stag, the runnable stag.

Three hundred gentlemen, able to ride,
    Three hundred horses as gallant and free,
Beheld him escape on the evening tide,
    Far out till he sank in the Severn Sea,
    Till he sank in the depths of the sea—
        The stag, the buoyant stag, the stag
        That slept at last in a jewell'd bed
        Under the sheltering ocean spread,
        The stag, the runnable stag.

T. W. ROLLESTON
b. 1857

587.   The Dead at Clonmacnois

FROM THE IRISH OF ANGUS O'GILLAN

IN a quiet water'd land, a land of roses,
    Stands Saint Kieran's city fair ;
And the warriors of Erin in their famous generations
    Slumber there.

There beneath the dewy hillside sleep the noblest
    Of the clan of Conn,
Each below his stone with name in branching Ogham
    And the sacred knot thereon.

There they laid to rest the seven Kings of Tara,
    There the sons of Cairbrè sleep—
Battle-banners of the Gael that in Kieran's plain of crosses
    Now their final hosting keep.

And in Clonmacnois they laid the men of Teffia,
    And right many a lord of Breagh ;
Deep the sod above Clan Creidè and Clan Conaill,
    Kind in hall and fierce in fray.

Many and many a son of Conn the Hundred-Fighter
    In the red earth lies at rest ;
Many a blue eye of Clan Colman the turf covers,
    Many a swan-white breast.

AGNES MARY FRANCES DUCLAUX
(ROBINSON-DARMESTETER)

b. 1857

588.   *Le Roi est Mort*

AND shall I weep that Love 's no more,
    And magnify his reign ?
Sure never mortal man before
    Would have his grief again.
Farewell the long-continued ache,
The days a-dream, the nights awake,
I will rejoice and merry make,
    And never more complain.

King Love is dead and gone for aye,
    Who ruled with might and main,
For with a bitter word one day,
    I found my tyrant slain :
And he in Heathenesse was bred,
Nor ever was baptized, 'tis said,
Nor is of any creed, and dead
    Can never rise again.

775

589.   *Cockayne Country*

NEAR where yonder evening star
    Makes a glory in the air,
Lies a land dream-found and far
    Where it is light alway.
There those lovely ghosts repair
    Who in Sleep's enchantment are,
In Cockayne dwell all things fair—
    (But it is far away.)

Through the gates—a goodly sight—
    Troops of men and maidens come,
There shut out from Heaven at night
    Belated angels stray ;
Down those wide-arch'd groves they roam
    Through a land of great delight,
Dreaming they are safe at home—
    (But it is far away.)

There the leaves of all the trees
    Written are with a running rhyme,
There all poets live at peace,
    And lovers are true, they say.
Earth in that unwinter'd clime
    Like a star incarnate sees
The glory of her future time.—
    (But it is far away.)

Hard to find as it is far !
    Dark nights shroud its brilliance rare,
Crouching round the cloudy bar
    Under the wings of day.
But if thither ye will fare,
    Love and Death the pilots are,—
Might either one convey me there !
    (But it is far away.)

590.   *Celia's Home-Coming*

MAIDENS, kilt your skirts and go
    Down the stormy garden-ways.
Pluck the last sweet pinks that blow,
    Gather roses, gather bays,
Since our Celia comes to-day,
That has been so long away.

Crowd her chamber with your sweets—
    Not a flower but grows for her !
Make her bed with linen sheets
    That have lain in lavender :
Light a fire before she come,
Lest she find us chill at home.

Ah, what joy when Celia stands
    By the leaping blaze at last,
Stooping low to warm her hands
    All benumbèd with the blast,
While we hide her cloak away,
To assure us she shall stay !

Cyder bring and cowslip wine,
    Fruits and flavours from the East,
Pears and pippins too, and fine
    Saffron loaves to make a feast ;
China dishes, silver cups,
For the board where Celia sups !

Then, when all the feasting 's done,
    She shall draw us round the blaze,
Laugh, and tell us every one
    Of her far triumphant days—
Celia, out of doors a star,
By the hearth a holier Lar !

AGNES MARY FRANCES DUCLAUX

591. *Retrospect*

HERE beside my Paris fire, I sit alone and ponder
    All my life of long ago that lies so far asunder ;
' Here, how came I thence ? ' I say, and greater grows
    the wonder
As I recall the farms and fields and placid hamlets yonder.

. . . See, the meadow-sweet is white against the water-
    courses,
Marshy lands are kingcup-gay and bright with streams
    and sources,
Dew-bespangled shines the hill where half-abloom the
    gorse is ;
And all the northern fallows steam beneath the ploughing
    horses.

There 's the red-brick-chimney'd house, the ivied haunt
    of swallows,
All its garden up and down and full of hills and hollows ;
Past the lawn, the sunken fence whose brink the laurel
    follows ;
And then the knee-deep pasture where the herd for ever
    wallows !

So they've clipp'd the lilac bush : a thousand thousand
    pities !
'Twas the blue old-fashion'd sort that never grows in
    cities.
There we little children play'd and chaunted aimless
    ditties,
While oft th' old grandsire looked at us and smiled his
    Nunc Dimittis !

778

Green, O green with ancient peace, and full of sap and
    sunny,
Lusty fields of Warwickshire, O land of milk and honey,
Might I live to pluck again a spike of agrimony,
A silver tormentilla leaf or ladysmock upon ye !

Patience !—for I keep at heart your pure and perfect
    seeming,
I can see you wide awake as clearly as in dreaming,
Softer, with an inner light, and dearer, to my deeming,
Than when beside your brooks at noon I watch'd the
    sallows gleaming !

MAY PROBYN

592.   *'Is it Nothing to You'*

WE were playing on the green together,
    My sweetheart and I—
O ! so heedless in the gay June weather
    When the word went forth that we must die.
O ! so merrily the balls of amber
    And of ivory toss'd we to the sky,
While the word went forth in the King's chamber
    That we both must die.

O ! so idly straying thro' the pleasaunce
    Pluck'd we here and there
Fruit and bud, while in the royal presence
    The King's son was casting from his hair

    Glory

Glory of the wreathen gold that crown'd it,
  And, ungirdling all his garments fair,
Flinging by the jewell'd clasp that bound it,
  With his feet made bare.

Down the myrtled stairway of the palace,
  Ashes on his head,
Came he, thro' the rose and citron alleys,
  In rough sark of sackcloth habited,
And in the hempen halter—O ! we jested
  Lightly, and we laugh'd as he was led
To the torture, while the bloom we breasted
  Where the grapes grew red.

O ! so sweet the birds, when he was dying,
  Piped to her and me—
Is no room this glad June day for sighing—
  He is dead, and she and I go free !
When the sun shall set on all our pleasure
  We will mourn him—What, so you decree
We are heartless ? Nay, but in what measure
  Do you more than we ?

593.   *Christmas Carol*

LACKING samite and sable,
    Lacking silver and gold,
The Prince Jesus in the poor stable
  Slept, and was three hours old.

As doves by the fair water,
  Mary, not touch'd of sin,
Sat by Him,—the King's daughter,
  All glorious within.

A lily without one stain, a
  Star where no spot hath room.
Ave, gratia plena—
  Virgo Virginum!

Clad not in pearl-sewn vesture,
  Clad not in cramoisie,
She hath hush'd, she hath cradled to rest, her
  God the first time on her knee.

Where is one to adore Him?
  The ox hath dumbly confess'd,
With the ass, meek kneeling before Him,
  Et homo factus est.

Not throned on ivory or cedar,
  Not crown'd with a Queen's crown,
At her breast it is Mary shall feed her
  Maker, from Heaven come down.

The trees in Paradise blossom
  Sudden, and its bells chime—
She giveth Him, held to her bosom,
  Her immaculate milk the first time.

The night with wings of angels
  Was alight, and its snow-pack'd ways
Sweet made (say the Evangels)
  With the noise of their virelays.

Quem vidistis, pastores?
  Why go ye feet unshod?
Wot ye within yon door is
  Mary, the Mother of God?

No

No smoke of spice is ascending
  There—no roses are piled—
But, choicer than all balms blending
  There Mary hath kiss'd her child.

Dilectus meus mihi
  Et ego Illi—cold
Small cheek against her cheek, He
  Sleepeth, three hours old.

WILLIAM WATSON

b. 1858

594. *Song*

APRIL, April,
  Laugh thy girlish laughter;
Then, the moment after,
Weep thy girlish tears!
April, that mine ears
Like a lover greetest,
If I tell thee, sweetest,
All my hopes and fears,
April, April,
Laugh thy golden laughter
But, the moment after,
Weep thy golden tears!

595. *Ode in May*

LET me go forth, and share
  The overflowing Sun
  With one wise friend, or one
Better than wise, being fair,

WILLIAM WATSON

Where the pewit wheels and dips
  On heights of bracken and ling,
And Earth, unto her leaflet tips,
  Tingles with the Spring.

What is so sweet and dear
  As a prosperous morn in May,
  The confident prime of the day,
And the dauntless youth of the year,
When nothing that asks for bliss,
  Asking aright, is denied,
And half of the world a bridegroom is,
  And half of the world a bride ?

The Song of Mingling flows,
  Grave, ceremonial, pure,
  As once, from lips that endure,
The cosmic descant rose,
When the temporal lord of life,
  Going his golden way,
Had taken a wondrous maid to wife
  That long had said him nay.

For of old the Sun, our sire,
  Came wooing the mother of men,
  Earth, that was virginal then,
Vestal fire to his fire.
Silent her bosom and coy,
  But the strong god sued and press'd ;
And born of their starry nuptial joy
  Are all that drink of her breast.

And the triumph of him that begot,
  And the travail of her that bore,
  Behold they are evermore
As warp and weft in our lot.

We

We are children of splendour and flame,
    Of shuddering, also, and tears.
Magnificent out of the dust we came,
    And abject from the Spheres.

O bright irresistible lord !
    We are fruit of Earth's womb, each one,
    And fruit of thy loins, O Sun,
Whence first was the seed outpour'd.
To thee as our Father we bow,
    Forbidden thy Father to see,
Who is older and greater than thou, as thou
    Art greater and older than we.

Thou art but as a word of his speech ;
    Thou art but as a wave of his hand ;
    Thou art brief as a glitter of sand
'Twixt tide and tide on his beach;
Thou art less than a spark of his fire,
    Or a moment's mood of his soul :
Thou art lost in the notes on the lips of his choir
    That chant the chant of the Whole.

596.   *Autumn*

THOU burden of all songs the earth hath sung,
    Thou retrospect in Time's averted eyes,
    Thou metaphor of everything that dies,
That dies ill-starr'd, or dies beloved and young
    And therefore blest and wise—
O be less beautiful, or be less brief,
    Thou tragic splendour, strange and full of fear !
    In vain her pageant shall the summer rear ?
At thy mute signal, leaf by golden leaf,
    Crumbles the gorgeous year.

WILLIAM WATSON

Ah, ghostly as remembered mirth, the tale
  Of summer's bloom, the legend of the spring!
  And thou, too, flutterest an impatient wing,
Thou presence yet more fugitive and frail,
  Thou most unbodied thing,
Whose very being is his going hence.
  And passage and departure all thy theme,
  Whose life doth still a splendid dying seem,
And thou, at height of thy magnificence,
  A figment and a dream.

Still'd is the virgin rapture that was June,
  And cold is August's panting heart of fire;
  And in the storm-dismantled forest choir,
For thine own elegy thy winds attune
  Their wild and wizard lyre.
And poignant grows the charm of thy decay,
  The pathos of thy beauty and the sting,
  Thou parable of greatness vanishing!
For me, thy woods of gold and skies of grey
  With speech fantastic ring.

For me, to dreams resign'd, there come and go,
  'Twixt mountains draped and hooded night and morn,
  Elusive notes in wandering wafture borne
From undiscoverable lips that blow
  An immaterial horn;
And spectral seem thy winter-boding trees,
  Thy ruinous bowers and drifted foliage wet;
  O Past and Future in sad bridal met,
O voice of everything that perishes,
  And soul of all regret!

597.   *Vita Nuova*

LONG hath she slept, forgetful of delight :
    At last, at last, the enchanted princess, Earth,
Claim'd with a kiss by Spring the adventurer,
In slumber knows the destined lips, and thrilled
Through all the deeps of her unageing heart
With passionate necessity of joy,
Wakens, and yields her loveliness to love.

    O ancient streams, O far-descended woods
Full of the fluttering of melodious souls ;
O hills and valleys that adorn yourselves
In solemn jubilation ; winds and clouds,
Ocean and land in stormy nuptials clasp'd,
And all exuberant creatures that acclaim
The Earth's divine renewal : lo, I too
With yours would mingle somewhat of glad song.
I too have come through wintry terrors,—yea,
Through tempest and through cataclysm of soul
Have come, and am deliver'd. Me the Spring,
Me also, dimly with new life hath touch'd,
And with regenerate hope, the salt of life ;
And I would dedicate these thankful tears
To whatsoever Power beneficent,
Veil'd though his countenance, undivulged his thought,
Hath led me from the haunted darkness forth
Into the gracious air and vernal morn,
And suffers me to know my spirit a note
Of this great chorus, one with bird and stream
And voiceful mountain,—nay, a string, how jarr'd
And all but broken ! of that lyre of life

Whereon himself, the master harp-player,
Resolving all its mortal dissonance
To one immortal and most perfect strain,
Harps without pause, building with song the world.

598.   *The Great Misgiving*

' NOT ours,' say some, ' the thought of death to dread;
        Asking no heaven, we fear no fabled hell :
Life is a feast, and we have banqueted—
    Shall not the worms as well ?

' The after-silence, when the feast is o'er,
    And void the places where the minstrels stood,
Differs in nought from what hath been before,
    And is nor ill nor good.'

Ah, but the Apparition—the dumb sign—
    The beckoning finger bidding me forgo
The fellowship, the converse, and the wine,
    The songs, the festal glow !

And ah, to know not, while with friends I sit,
    And while the purple joy is pass'd about,
Whether 'tis ampler day divinelier lit
    Or homeless night without ;

And whether, stepping forth, my soul shall see
    New prospects, or fall sheer—a blinded thing !
There is, O grave, thy hourly victory,
    And there, O death, thy sting.

ROBERT OFFLEY ASHBURTON CREWE-MILNES, MARQUESS OF CREWE

b. 1858

599.   *Seven Years*

To join the ages they have gone,
      Those seven years,—
Receding as the months roll on ;
Yet very oft my fancy hears
Your voice,—'twas music to my ears
      Those seven years.

Scant the shadow and high the sun
      Those seven years ;
Can hearts be one, then ours were one,
One for laughter and one for tears,
Knit together in hopes and fears,
      Those seven years.

How, perchance, do they seem to you,
      Those seven years,
Spirit-free in the wider blue ?
When Time in Eternity disappears,
What if all you have learn'd but the more endears
      Those seven years ?

SIR JAMES RENNELL RODD

600.   *A Roman Mirror*

THEY found it in her hollow marble bed,
     There where the numberless dead cities sleep,
   They found it lying where the spade struck deep
A broken mirror by a maiden dead :

These things—the beads she wore about her throat
     Alternate blue and amber all untied,
     A lamp to light her way, and on one side
The toll men pay to that strange ferry-boat.

No trace to-day of what in her was fair !
     Only the record of long years grown green
     Upon the mirror's lustreless dead sheen,
Grown dim at last, when all else wither'd there.

Dead, broken, lustreless ! It keeps for me
     One picture of that immemorial land ;
     For oft as I have held thee in my hand
The dull bronze brightens, and I dream to see

A fair face gazing in thee wondering-wise,
     And o'er one marble shoulder all the while
     Strange lips that whisper till her own lips smile,
And all the mirror laughs about her eyes.

SIR JAMES RENNELL RODD

It was well thought to set thee there, so she
    Might smooth the windy ripples of her hair
    And knot their tangled waywardness, or ere
She stood before the Queen Persephone.

And still, it may be, where the dead folk rest
    She holds a shadowy mirror to her eyes,
    And looks upon the changelessness and sighs
And sets the dead-land-lilies in her breast.

FRANCIS THOMPSON

1859–1907

601.   *Daisy*

WHERE the thistle lifts a purple crown
    Six foot out of the turf,
And the harebell shakes on the windy hill—
    O the breath of the distant surf !—

The hills look over on the South,
    And southward dreams the sea ;
And, with the sea-breeze hand in hand,
    Came innocence and she.

Where 'mid the gorse the raspberry
    Red for the gatherer springs,
Two children did we stray and talk
    Wise, idle, childish things.

FRANCIS THOMPSON

She listen'd with big-lipp'd surprise,
    Breast-deep 'mid flower and spine :
Her skin was like a grape, whose veins
    Run snow instead of wine.

She knew not those sweet words she spake,
    Nor knew her own sweet way ;
But there 's never a bird, so sweet a song
    Throng'd in whose throat that day !

O, there were flowers in Storrington
    On the turf and on the spray ;
But the sweetest flower on Sussex hills
    Was the Daisy-flower that day !

Her beauty smooth'd earth's furrow'd face !
    She gave me tokens three :—
A look, a word of her winsome mouth,
    And a wild raspberry.

A berry red, a guileless look,
    A still word,—strings of sand !
And yet they made my wild, wild heart
    Fly down to her little hand.

For, standing artless as the air,
    And candid as the skies,
She took the berries with her hand,
    And the love with her sweet eyes.

The fairest things have fleetest end :
    Their scent survives their close,
But the rose's scent is bitterness
    To him that loved the rose !

         She

She looked a little wistfully,
    Then went her sunshine way :—
The sea's eye had a mist on it,
    And the leaves fell from the day.

She went her unremembering way,
    She went, and left in me
The pang of all the partings gone,
    And partings yet to be.

She left me marvelling why my soul
    Was sad that she was glad ;
At all the sadness in the sweet,
    The sweetness in the sad.

Still, still I seem'd to see her, still
    Look up with soft replies,
And take the berries with her hand,
    And the love with her lovely eyes.

Nothing begins, and nothing ends,
    That is not paid with moan ;
For we are born in other's pain,
    And perish in our own.

602.   *The Mistress of Vision*

SECRET was the garden ;
    Set i' the pathless awe
Where no star its breath can draw.
    Life, that is its warden,
Sits behind the fosse of death.   Mine eyes saw not, and
        I saw.

It was a mazeful wonder ;
Thrice three times it was enwall'd
With an emerald—
Sealèd so asunder.
All its birds in middle air hung a-dream, their music
      thrall'd.

The Lady of fair weeping,
At the garden's core,
Sang a song of sweet and sore
And the after-sleeping ;
In the land of Luthany, and the tracts of Elenore.

With sweet-pang'd singing
Sang she through a dream-night's day ;
That the bowers might stay,
Birds bate their winging,
Nor the wall of emerald float in wreathèd haze away.

The lily kept its gleaming,
In her tears (divine conservers !)
Washèd with sad art ;
And the flowers of dreaming
Palèd not their fervours,
For her blood flow'd through their nervures ;
And the roses were most red, for she dipt them in her
      heart.

There was never moon,
Save the white sufficing woman :
Light most heavenly-human—
Like the unseen form of sound,
Sensed invisibly in tune,—

        With

With a sun-derivèd stole
Did inaureole
All her lovely body round ;
Lovelily her lucid body with that light was interstrewn.

The sun which lit that garden wholly,
Low and vibrant visible,
Temper'd glory woke ;
And it seemèd solely
Like a silver thurible
Solemnly swung, slowly,
Fuming clouds of golden fire for a cloud of incense-smoke.

But woe 's me, and woe 's me,
For the secrets of her eyes !
In my visions fearfully
They are ever shown to be
As fringèd pools, whereof each lies
Pallid-dark beneath the skies
Of a night that is
But one blear necropolis.
And her eyes a little tremble, in the wind of her own sighs.

Many changes rise on
Their phantasmal mysteries.
They grow to an horizon
Where earth and heaven meet ;
And like a wing that dies on
The vague twilight-verges,
Many a sinking dream doth fleet
Lessening down their secrecies.
And, as dusk with day converges,
Their orbs are troublously
Over-gloom'd and over-glow'd with hope and fear of
things to be.

There is a peak on Himalay,
And on the peak undeluged snow,
And on the snow not eagles stray ;
There if your strong feet could go,—
Looking over tow'rd Cathay
From the never-deluged snow—
Farthest ken might not survey
Where the peoples underground dwell whom antique
fables know.

East, ah, east of Himalay,
Dwell the nations underground ;
Hiding from the shock of Day,
For the sun's uprising-sound :
Dare not issue from the ground
At the tumults of the Day,
So fearfully the sun doth sound
Clanging up beyond Cathay ;
For the great earthquaking sunrise rolling up beyond
Cathay.

Lend me, O lend me
The terrors of that sound,
That its music may attend me,
Wrap my chant in thunders round ;
While I tell the ancient secrets in that Lady's singing
found.

On Ararat there grew a vine,
When Asia from her bathing rose ;
Our first sailor made a twine
Thereof for his prefiguring brows.
Canst divine
Where, upon our dusty earth, of that vine a cluster grows?

On

FRANCIS THOMPSON

On Golgotha there grew a thorn
Round the long-prefigured Brows.
Mourn, O mourn !
For the vine have we the spine ?   Is this all the Heaven
        allows ?

On Calvary was shook a spear ;
Press the point into thy heart—
Joy and fear !
All the spines upon the thorn into curling tendrils start.

O dismay !
I, a wingless mortal, sporting
With the tresses of the sun ?
I, that dare my hand to lay
On the thunder in its snorting ?
Ere begun,
Falls my singed song down the sky, even the old Icarian
        way.

From the fall precipitant
These dim snatches of her chant
Only have remainèd mine ;—
That from spear and thorn alone
May be grown
For the front of saint or singer any divinizing twine.

Her song said that no springing
Paradise but evermore
Hangeth on a singing
That has chords of weeping,
And that sings the after-sleeping
To souls which wake too sore.

' But woe the singer, woe ! ' she said ; ' beyond the dead
　　　his singing-lore,
　　　　All its art of sweet and sore
　　　　He learns, in Elenore ! '

　　　　Where is the land of Luthany,
　　　　Where is the tract of Elenore ?
　　　　I am bound therefor.

　　　　' Pierce thy heart to find the key ;
　　　　With thee take
　　　　Only what none else would keep ;
　　　　Learn to dream when thou dost wake,
　　　　Learn to wake when thou dost sleep.
　　　　Learn to water joy with tears,
　　　　Learn from fears to vanquish fears ;
　　　　To hope, for thou dar'st not despair,
　　　　Exult, for that thou dar'st not grieve ;
　　　　Plough thou the rock until it bear ;
　　　　Know, for thou else couldst not believe ;
　　　　Lose, that the lost thou may'st receive ;
　　　　Die, for none other way canst live.
　　　　When earth and heaven lay down their veil,
　　　　And that apocalypse turns thee pale ;
　　　　When thy seeing blindeth thee
　　　　To what thy fellow-mortals see ;
　　　　When their sight to thee is sightless ;
　　　　Their living, death ; their light, most lightless ;
　　　　Search no more—
Pass the gates of Luthany, tread the region Elenore.'

　　　　Where is the land of Luthany,
　　　　And where the region Elenore ?
　　　　I do faint therefor.

　　　　　　　　' When

' When to the new eyes of thee
All things by immortal power,
Near or far,
Hiddenly
To each other linkèd are,
That thou canst not stir a flower
Without troubling of a star ;
When thy song is shield and mirror
To the fair snake-curlèd Pain,
Where thou dar'st affront her terror
That on her thou may'st attain
Perséan conquest ; seek no more,
O seek no more !
Pass the gates of Luthany, tread the region Elenore.'

So sang she, so wept she,
Through a dream-night's day ;
And with her magic singing kept she—
Mystical in music—
That garden of enchanting
In visionary May ;
Swayless for my spirit's haunting,
Thrice-threefold wall'd with emerald from our mortal
        mornings grey.

And as a necromancer
Raises from the rose-ash
The ghost of the rose ;
My heart so made answer
To her voice's silver plash,—
Stirr'd in reddening flash,
And from out its mortal ruins the purpureal phantom
        blows.

Her tears made dulcet fretting,
Her voice had no word,
More than thunder or the bird.
Yet, unforgetting,
The ravish'd soul her meanings knew. Mine ears heard
    not, and I heard.

When she shall unwind
All those wiles she wound about me,
Tears shall break from out me,
That I cannot find
Music in the holy poets to my wistful want, I doubt me!

603. *From the Night of Forebeing*

AN ODE AFTER EASTER

CAST wide the folding doorways of the East,
  For now is light increased !
And the wind-besom'd chambers of the air,
See they be garnish'd fair ;
And look the ways exhale some precious odours,
And set ye all about wild-breathing spice,
Most fit for Paradise.
Now is no time for sober gravity,
Season enough has Nature to be wise ;
But now discinct, with raiment glittering free,
Shake she the ringing rafters of the skies
With festal footing and bold joyance sweet,
And let the earth be drunken and carouse !
For lo, into her house
Spring is come home with her world-wandering feet,
And all things are made young with young desires ;
And all for her is light increased

In

In yellow stars and yellow daffodils,
And East to West, and West to East,
Fling answering welcome-fires,
By dawn and day-fall, on the jocund hills
And ye, wing'd minstrels of her fair meinie,
Being newly coated in glad livery,
Upon her steps attend,
And round her treading dance and without end
Reel your shrill lutany.
What popular breath her coming does out-tell
The garrulous leaves among !
What little noises stir and pass
From blade to blade along the voluble grass !
O Nature, never-done
Ungaped-at Pentecostal miracle,
We hear thee, each man in his proper tongue
Break, elemental children, break ye loose
From the strict frosty rule
Of grey-beard Winter's school.
Vault, O young winds, vault in your tricksome courses
Upon the snowy steeds that reinless use
In coerule pampas of the heaven to run ;
Foal'd of the white sea-horses,
Wash'd in the lambent waters of the sun.
Let even the slug-abed snail upon the thorn
Put forth a conscious horn !
Mine elemental co-mates, joy each one ;
And ah, my foster-brethren, seem not sad—
No, seem not sad,
That my strange heart and I should be so little glad.
Suffer me at your leafy feast
To sit apart, a somewhat alien guest,
And watch your mirth,
Unsharing in the liberal laugh of earth ;

Yet with a sympathy,
Begot of wholly sad and half-sweet memory—
The little sweetness making grief complete ;
Faint wind of wings from hours that distant beat,
When I, I too,
Was once, O wild companions, as are you,
Ran with such wilful feet.

A higher and a solemn voice
I heard through your gay-hearted noise ;
A solemn meaning and a stiller voice
Sounds to me from far days when I too shall rejoice,
Nor more be with your jollity at strife.
Hark to the *Jubilate* of the bird
For them that found the dying way to life !
And they have heard,
And quicken to the great precursive word ;
Green spray showers lightly down the cascade of the larch ;
The graves are riven,
And the Sun comes with power amid the clouds of heaven!
Before his way
Went forth the trumpet of the March ;
Before his way, before his way
Dances the pennon of the May !
O earth, unchilded, widow'd Earth, so long
Lifting in patient pine and ivy-tree
Mournful belief and steadfast prophecy,
Behold how all things are made true !
Behold your bridegroom cometh in to you,
Exceeding glad and strong.
Raise up your eyes, O raise your eyes abroad !
No more shall you sit sole and vidual,
Searching, in servile pall,
Upon the hieratic night the star-seal'd sense of all :

Rejoice, O barren, and look forth abroad !
Your children gather'd back to your embrace
See with a mother's face.
Look up, O mortals, and the portent heed ;
In very deed,
Wash'd with new fire to their irradiant birth,
Reintegrated are the heavens and earth !
From sky to sod,
The world's unfolded blossom smells of God.

And thou up-floatest, warm, and newly-bathed,
Earth, through delicious air,
And with thine own apparent beauties swathed,
Wringing the waters from thine arborous hair ;
That all men's hearts, which do behold and see,
Grow weak with their exceeding much desire,
And turn to thee on fire,
Enamour'd with their utter wish of thee,
Anadyomene !
What vine-outquickening life all creatures sup,
Feel, for the air within its sapphire cup
How it does leap, and twinkle headily !
Feel, for Earth's bosom pants, and heaves her scarfing sea ;
And round and round in bacchanal rout reel the swift
        spheres intemperably !

My little-worlded self ! the shadows pass
In this thy sister-world, as in a glass,
Of all processions that revolve in thee :
Not only of cyclic Man
Thou here discern'st the plan,
Not only of cyclic Man, but of the cyclic Me.
Not solely of Mortality's great years
The reflex just appears,

But thine own bosom's year, still circling round
In ample and in ampler gyre
Toward the far completion, wherewith crown'd,
Love unconsumed shall chant in his own furnace-fire.
How many trampled and deciduous joys
Enrich thy soul for joys deciduous still,
Before the distance shall fulfil
Cyclic unrest with solemn equipoise !
Happiness is the shadow of things past,
Which fools still take for that which is to be !
And not all foolishly :
For all the past, read true, is prophecy,
And all the firsts are hauntings of some Last,
And all the springs are flash-lights of one Spring.
Then leaf, and flower, and fall-less fruit
Shall hang together on the unyellowing bough ;
And silence shall be Music mute
For her surchargèd heart.   Hush thou !
These things are far too sure that thou should'st dream
Thereof, lest they appear as things that seem.

Shade within shade ! for deeper in the glass
Now other imaged meanings pass ;
And as the man, the poet there is read.
Winter with me, alack !
Winter on every hand I find :
Soul, brain, and pulses dead ;
The mind no further by the warm sense fed,
The soul weak-stirring in the arid mind . . .

Giver of spring,
And song, and every young new thing !
Thou only seëst in me, so stripp'd and bare,
The lyric secret waiting to be born,

The

The patient term allow'd
Before it stretch and flutteringly unfold
Its rumpled webs of amethyst-freak'd, diaphanous gold.
And what hard task abstracts me from delight,
Filling with hopeless hope and dear despair
The still-born day and parchèd fields of night,
That my old way of song, no longer fair,
For lack of serene care,
Is grown a stony and a weed-choked plot,
Thou only know'st aright,
Thou only know'st, for I know not.
How many songs must die that this may live !
And shall this most rash hope and fugitive,
Fulfill'd with beauty and with might
In days whose feet are rumorous on the air,
Make me forget to grieve
For songs which might have been, nor ever were ?

Stern the denial, the travail slow,
The struggling wall will scantly grow :
And though with that dread rite of sacrifice
Ordain'd for during edifice,
How long, how long ago !
Into that wall which will not thrive
I build myself alive,
Ah, who shall tell me will the wall uprise ?
Thou wilt not tell me, who dost only know !
Yet still in mind I keep,
He which observes the wind shall hardly sow,
He which regards the clouds shall hardly reap.
Thine ancient way ! I give,
Nor wit if I receive ;
Risk all, who all would gain : and blindly. Be it so.

Nature, enough ! within thy glass
Too many and too stern the shadows pass.
In this delighted season, flaming
For thy resurrection-feast,
Ah, more I think the long ensepulture cold,
Than stony winter roll'd
From the unseal'd mouth of the holy East ;
The snowdrop's saintly stoles less heed
Than the snow-cloister'd penance of the seed.
'Tis the weak flesh reclaiming
Against the ordinance
Which yet for just the accepting spirit scans.
Earth waits, and patient heaven,
Self-bonded God doth wait
Thrice-promulgated bans
Of his fair nuptial-date.
And power is man's,
With that great word of ' wait ',
To still the sea of tears,
And shake the iron heart of Fate.
In that one word is strong
An else, alas, much-mortal song ;
With sight to pass the frontier of all spheres,
And voice which does my sight such wrong.

Not without fortitude I wait
The dark majestical ensuit
Of destiny, nor peevish rate
Calm-knowledged Fate.
I, that no part have in the time's bragg'd way,
And its loud bruit ;
I, in this house so rifted, marr'd,
So ill to live in, hard to leave ;
I, so star-weary, over-warr'd,

That

That have no joy in this your day—
Rather foul fume englutting, that of day
Confounds all ray—
But only stand aside and grieve ;
I yet have sight beyond the smoke,
And kiss the god's feet, though they wreak
Upon me stroke and again stroke ;
And this my seeing is not weak.
The Woman I behold, whose vision seek
All eyes and know not ; t'ward whom climb
The steps o' the world, and beats all wing of rhyme,
And knows not ; 'twixt the sun and moon
Her inexpressible front enstarr'd
Tempers the wrangling spheres to tune ;
Their divergent harmonies
Concluded in the concord of her eyes,
And vestal dances of her glad regard.
I see, which fretteth with surmise
Much heads grown unsagacious-grey,
The slow aim of wise-hearted Time,
Which folded cycles within cycles cloak :
We pass, we pass, we pass ; this does not pass away,
But holds the furrowing earth still harness'd to its yoke.
The stars still write their golden purposes
On heaven's high palimpsest, and no man sees,
Nor any therein Daniel ; I do hear
From the revolving year
A voice which cries :
' All dies ;
Lo, how all dies ! O seer,
And all things too arise :
All dies, and all is born ;
But each resurgent morn, behold, more near the Perfect
    Morn.'

Firm is the man, and set beyond the cast
Of Fortune's game, and the iniquitous hour,
Whose falcon soul sits fast,
And not intends her high sagacious tour
Or ere the quarry sighted ; who looks past
To slow much sweet from little instant sour.
And in the first does always see the last.

604.   '*Ex Ore Infantium*'

LITTLE Jesus, wast Thou shy
Once, and just so small as I ?
And what did it feel like to be
Out of Heaven, and just like me ?
Didst Thou sometimes think of *there*,
And ask where all the angels were ?
I should think that I would cry
For my house all made of sky ;
I would look about the air,
And wonder where my angels were ;
And at waking 'twould distress me—
Not an angel there to dress me !

Hadst Thou ever any toys,
Like us little girls and boys ?
And didst Thou play in Heaven with all
The angels that were not too tall,
With stars for marbles ? Did the things
Play *Can you see me?* through their wings ?
And did thy Mother let Thee spoil
Thy robes, with playing on *our* soil ?

How

How nice to have them always new
In Heaven, because 'twas quite clean blue !

Didst Thou kneel at night to pray,
And didst Thou join thy hands, this way ?
And did they tire sometimes, being young,
And make the prayer seem very long ?
And dost Thou like it best, that we
Should join our hands to pray to Thee ?
I used to think, before I knew,
The prayer not said unless we do.
And did thy Mother at the night
Kiss Thee, and fold the clothes in right ?
And didst Thou feel quite good in bed,
Kiss'd, and sweet, and thy prayers said ?

Thou canst not have forgotten all
That it feels like to be small :
And Thou know'st I cannot pray
To Thee in my father's way—
When Thou wast so little, say,
Couldst Thou talk thy Father's way ?—
So, a little Child, come down
And hear a child's tongue like thy own ;
Take me by the hand and walk,
And listen to my baby-talk.
To thy Father show my prayer
(He will look, Thou art so fair),
And say : ' O Father, I, thy Son,
Bring the prayer of a little one.'

And He will smile, that children's tongue
Has not changed since Thou wast young !

HENRY CHARLES BEECHING

b. 1859

605.   *Prayers*

GOD who created me
    Nimble and light of limb,
In three elements free,
    To run, to ride, to swim :
Not when the sense is dim,
    But now from the heart of joy,
I would remember Him :
    Take the thanks of a boy.

Jesu, King and Lord,
    Whose are my foes to fight,
Gird me with thy sword
    Swift and sharp and bright.
Thee would I serve if I might ;
    And conquer if I can,
From day-dawn till night,
    Take the strength of a man.

Spirit of Love and Truth,
    Breathing in grosser clay,
The light and flame of youth,
    Delight of men in the fray,
Wisdom in strength's decay ;
    From pain, strife, wrong to be free,
This best gift I pray,
    Take my spirit to Thee.

606.   *Going down Hill on a Bicycle*

A Boy's Song

WITH lifted feet, hands still,
   I am poised, and down the hill
Dart, with heedful mind ;
The air goes by in a wind.

Swifter and yet more swift,
Till the heart with a mighty lift
Makes the lungs laugh, the throat cry :—
' O bird, see ; see, bird, I fly !

' Is this, is this your joy ?
O bird, then I, though a boy,
For a golden moment share
Your feathery life in air ! '

Say, heart, is there aught like this
In a world that is full of bliss ?
'Tis more than skating, bound
Steel-shod to the level ground.

Speed slackens now, I float
Awhile in my airy boat ;
Till, when the wheels scarce crawl,
My feet to the treadles fall.

Alas, that the longest hill
Must end in a vale ; but still,
Who climbs with toil, wheresoe'er,
Shall find wings waiting there.

810

607.   *The Blackbird*

DEAREST, these household cares remit ;
   And while the sky is blue to-day,
Here in this sunny shelter sit,
   To list the blackbird's lay.

Is all so rare, romantic boy ?
   Is love so new and strange, that thou
Must with that wild and shrilling joy
   Thrill the yet wintry bough ?

Ah, now 'tis softer grown, more sweet,—
   ' I come, I come, O love, O my love,'—
And he is fluttering to her feet
   In yonder purple grove.

Now hark ! all summer swells the note
   And dreams of mellow ripeness make
So ripe, so rich his warbling throat
   For spouse and children's sake.

Lover and prophet, see ! the flower
   Of cherry is hardly white, and figs
Are leafless, and thy nuptial bower
   A cage of rattling twigs.

Yet faith is evidence, and hope
   Substance, and love sufficient fire ;
And Art in these finds ampler scope
   Than in fulfill'd desire.

So play thy Pan's pipe, happy Faun,
   Till some May night with moonshine pale,
Thou pin'st, to hear by wood or lawn
   Apollo's nightingale.

608.   *Accidia*

THERE breathes a sense of Spring in the boon air :
      The woods are amber, purple, misty red,
   Primrose and violet rouse them from their bed,
Their skiey homes the patient rooks repair ;
Everywhere hope is rife, joy everywhere ;
   But I, thy heart, lie yet unquickenèd,
      And bleating lambs and larks that sing o'erhead
Charm not away my sluggish cold despair.

Peace, peace, fond heart ; thy spring-tide is not this ;
   Thy sap of joy mounted, though flowers were sere,
      That day, though leaves fell thick before the West.
Nor grudge nor envy thou a natural bliss.
   Birds keep their season, thou through all the year
      May'st sing thy song, soar skyward, make thy nest.

609.   *Knowledge after Death*

SICCINE *separat amara mors ?*
      Is death so bitter ? Can it shut us fast
   Off from ourselves, that future from this past,
When time compels us through those narrow doors ?
Must we supplanted by ourselves in the course,
   Changelings, become as they who know at last
      A river's secret, never having cast
One guess, or known one doubt, about its source ?

Is it so bitter ? Does not knowledge here
   Forget her gradual growth, and how each day
      Seals up the sum of each world-conscious soul ?
So tho' our ghosts forget us, waste no tear ;
   We, being ourselves, would gladly be as they,
      And we, being they, are still ourselves made whole.

b. 1859

610. *Diana*

THIS new Diana makes weak men her prey,
  And, making captive, still would fain pursue,
And still would keep, and still would drive away,—
      So day by day
  Hate, hunt, do murder, and yet love them too
        Ah, dear Diana !

'Twere well, poor fools, to shun her cruel spear,
  More fatal far than that which slew of old ;
Her spear is wit that she so brings to bear,
      Then laughs to hear
  When it has struck, and one more heart runs cold :
        Ah, dear Diana !

Be wise, O fools, and shun her cruel eyes,
  Which when you see you straight must love, to death.
This new Diana has such sorceries,
      Who loves her, dies—
  And dying cries still with his latest breath—
        Ah, dear Diana !

611. *An Autobiography*

WALES England wed ; so I was bred. 'Twas merry
  London gave me breath.
  I dreamt of love, and fame : I strove. But Ireland
    taught me love was best :
  And Irish eyes, and London cries, and streams of Wales
    may tell the rest.
What more than these I ask'd of Life I am content to
    have from Death.

1861-1889

612.   *A London Plane-Tree*

GREEN is the plane-tree in the square,
    The other trees are brown ;
They droop and pine for country air ;
    The plane-tree loves the town.

Here from my garret-pane I mark
    The plane-tree bud and blow,
Shed her recuperative bark,
    And spread her shade below.

Among her branches, in and out,
    The city breezes play ;
The dull fog wraps her round about ;
    Above, the smoke curls grey.

Others the country take for choice,
    And hold the town in scorn ;
But she has listen'd to the voice
    On city breezes borne.

613.   *New Love, New Life*

i

SHE, who so long has lain
    Stone-stiff with folded wings,
Within my heart again
    The brown bird wakes and sings.

814

Brown nightingale, whose strain
   Is heard by day, by night,
She sings of joy and pain,
   Of sorrow and delight.

ii

'Tis true,—in other days
   Have I unbarr'd the door ;
He knows the walks and ways—
   Love has been here before.

Love blest and love accurst
   Was here in days long past ;
This time is not the first,
   But this time is the last.

614. *London Poets*

THEY trod the streets and squares where now I tread,
   With weary hearts, a little while ago ;
  When, thin and grey, the melancholy snow
Clung to the leafless branches overhead ;
Or when the smoke-veil'd sky grew stormy-red
   In autumn ; with a re-arisen woe
   Wrestled, what time the passionate spring-winds blow ;
And paced scorch'd stones in summer. They are dead.

The sorrow of their souls to them did seem
   As real as mine to me, as permanent.
To-day—it is the shadow of a dream,
   The half-forgotten breath of breezes spent.
So shall another soothe his woe supreme—
   No more he comes, who this way came and went.

1861-1907

615.   *Blue and White*

BLUE is Our Lady's colour,
    White is Our Lord's.
To-morrow I will wear a knot
    Of blue and white cords,
That you may see it, where you ride
    Among the flashing swords.

     .   .   .   .

O banner, white and sunny blue,
    With prayer I wove thee !
For love the white, for faith the heavenly hue,
And both for him, so tender-true,
    Him that doth love me !

616.   *Our Lady*

MOTHER of God ! no lady thou :
    Common woman of common earth
Our Lady ladies call thee now,
    But Christ was never of gentle birth ;
    A common man of the common earth.

For God's ways are not as our ways.
    The noblest lady in the land
Would have given up half her days,
    Would have cut off her right hand,
    To bear the child that was God of the land.

Never a lady did He choose,
    Only a maid of low degree,
So humble she might not refuse
    The carpenter of Galilee :
    A daughter of the people, she.

Out she sang the song of her heart.
   Never a lady so had sung.
She knew no letters, had no art;
   To all mankind, in woman's tongue,
   Hath Israelitish Mary sung.

And still for men to come she sings,
   Nor shall her singing pass away.
' *He hath fillèd the hungry with good things* '—
   Oh, listen, lords and ladies gay !—
   ' *And the rich He hath sent empty away.*'

617.   *A Huguenot*

O a gallant set were they,
   , As they charged on us that day,
A thousand riding like one !
Their trumpets crying,
And their white plumes flying,
And their sabres flashing in the sun.

O, a sorry lot were we,
As we stood beside the sea,
Each man for himself as he stood !
We were scatter'd and lonely—
A little force only
Of the good men fighting for the good.

But I never loved more
On sea or on shore
The ringing of my own true blade.
Like lightning it quiver'd,
And the hard helms shiver'd,
As I sang, ' None maketh me afraid ! '

817

618. *Punctilio*

O LET me be in loving nice,
  Dainty, fine, and o'er precise,
That I may charm my charmèd dear
As tho' I felt a secret fear
To lose what never can be lost,—
Her faith who still delights me most !
So shall I be more than true,
Ever in my ageing new.
So dull habit shall not be
Wrongly call'd Fidelity.

619. *Unwelcome*

WE were young, we were merry, we were very very
      wise,
    And the door stood open at our feast,
When there pass'd us a woman with the West in her eyes,
    And a man with his back to the East.

O, still grew the hearts that were beating so fast,
    The loudest voice was still.
The jest died away on our lips as they pass'd,
    And the rays of July struck chill.

The cups of red wine turn'd pale on the board,
    The white bread black as soot.
The hound forgot the hand of her lord,
    She fell down at his foot.

Low let me lie, where the dead dog lies,
    Ere I sit me down again at a feast,
When there passes a woman with the West in her eyes,
    And a man with his back to the East.

620.   *Mortal Combat*

IT is because you were my friend,
    I fought you as the devil fights.
Whatever fortune God may send,
    For once I set the world to rights.

And that was when I thrust you down,
    And stabb'd you twice and twice again,
Because you dared take off your crown,
    And be a man like other men.

621.   *Gone*

ABOUT the little chambers of my heart
    Friends have been coming—going—many a year.
        The doors stand open there.
Some, lightly stepping, enter ; some depart.

Freely they come and freely go, at will.
The walls give back their laughter ; all day long
        They fill the house with song.
One door alone is shut, one chamber still.

622.   *The King*

IT was but the lightest word of the King,
    When he was neither merry nor sad ;
It was but a very little thing,
    Yet it made his servant glad.

He gave a look as it befell,
    Between a smile and a smother'd sigh.
Whether he meant it, who can tell ?
    But the man went out to die.

BLISS CARMAN

b. 1861

623.   *The Joys of the Road*

NOW the joys of the road are chiefly these :
A crimson touch on the hard-wood trees ;

A vagrant's morning wide and blue,
In early fall, when the wind walks, too ;

A shadowy highway cool and brown,
Alluring up and enticing down

From rippled water to dappled swamp,
From purple glory to scarlet pomp ;

The outward eye, the quiet will,
And the striding heart from hill to hill ;

The tempter apple over the fence ;
The cobweb bloom on the yellow quince ;

The palish asters along the wood,—
A lyric touch of the solitude ;

An open hand, an easy shoe,
And a hope to make the day go through,—

Another to sleep with, and a third
To wake me up at the voice of a bird ;

A scrap of gossip at the ferry ;
A comrade neither glum nor merry,

Who never defers and never demands,
But, smiling, takes the world in his hands,—

Seeing it good when God first saw
And gave it the weight of his will for law.

And O the joy that is never won,
But follows and follows the journeying sun,

By marsh and tide, by meadow and stream,
A will-o'-the-wind, a light-o'-dream,

The racy smell of the forest loam,
When the stealthy, sad-heart leaves go home ;

The broad gold wake of the afternoon ;
The silent fleck of the cold new moon ;

The sound of the hollow sea's release
From stormy tumult to starry peace ;

With only another league to wend ;
And two brown arms at the journey's end !

These are the joys of the open road—
For him who travels without a load.

624.   *In the House of Idiedaily*

*O but life went gaily, gaily,
, In the house of Idiedaily !*

There were always throats to sing
Down the river-banks with spring,

When the stir of heart's desire
Set the sapling's heart on fire.

Bob-o-lincolns in the meadows,
Leisure in the purple shadows,

Till the poppies without number
Bow'd their heads in crimson slumber,

And

And the twilight came to cover
Every unreluctant lover.

Not a night but some brown maiden
Better'd all the dusk she stray'd in,

While the roses in her hair
Bankrupted oblivion there.

O, but life went gaily, gaily,
In the house of Idiedaily !

But this hostelry, The Barrow,
With its chambers, bare and narrow,

Mean, ill-window'd, damp, and wormy,
Where the silence makes you squirmy,

And the guests are never seen to,
Is a vile place, a mere lean-to,

Not a traveller speaks well of ;
Even worse than I heard tell of,

Mouldy, ramshackle, and foul—
What a dwelling for a soul !

O, but life went gaily, gaily,
In the house of Idiedaily !

There the hearth was always warm
From the slander of the storm.

There your comrade was your neighbour,
Living on to-morrow's labour.

And the board was always steaming,
Though Sir Ringlets might be dreaming.

Not a plate but scoff'd at porridge,
Not a cup but floated borage.

There were always jugs of sherry
Waiting for the makers merry,

And the dark Burgundian wine
That would make a fool divine.

O, but life went gaily, gaily,
In the house of Idiedaily !

625.   *A Northern Vigil*

HERE by the grey north sea,
    In the wintry heart of the wild,
Comes the old dream of thee,
Guendolen, mistress and child.

The heart of the forest grieves
In the drift against my door ;
A voice is under the eaves,
A footfall on the floor.

Threshold, mirror, and hall,
Vacant and strangely aware,
Wait for their soul's recall
With the dumb expectant air.

Here when the smouldering west
Burns down into the sea,
I take no heed of rest
And keep the watch for thee.

I sit

BLISS CARMAN

I sit by the fire and hear
The restless wind go by,
On the long dirge and drear,
Under the low bleak sky.

When day puts out to sea
And night makes in for land,
There is no lock for thee,
Each door awaits thy hand !

When night goes over the hill
And dawn comes down the dale,
It 's O for the wild sweet will
That shall no more prevail !

When the zenith moon is round,
And snow-wraiths gather and run,
And there is set no bound
To love beneath the sun,

O wayward will, come near
The old mad wilful way,
The soft mouth at my ear
With words too sweet to say !

Come, for the night is cold,
The ghostly moonlight fills
Hollow and rift and fold
Of the eerie Ardise hills !

The windows of my room
Are dark with bitter frost,
The stillness aches with doom
Of something loved and lost.

BLISS CARMAN

Outside, the great blue star
Burns in the ghostland pale,
Where giant Algebar
Holds on the endless trail.

Come, for the years are long
And silence keeps the door,
Where shapes with the shadows throng
The firelit chamber floor.

Come, for thy kiss was warm,
With the red embers' glare
Across thy folding arm
And dark tumultuous hair !

And though thy coming rouse
The sleep-cry of no bird,
The keepers of the house
Shall tremble at thy word.

Come, for the soul is free !
In all the vast dreamland
There is no lock for thee,
Each door awaits thy hand.

Ah, not in dreams at all,
Fleering, perishing, dim,
But thy old self, supple and tall,
Mistress and child of whim !

The proud imperious guise,
Impetuous and serene,
The sad mysterious eyes,
And dignity of mien !

Yea,

Yea, wilt thou not return,
When the late hill-winds veer,
And the bright hill-flowers burn
With the reviving year ?

When April comes, and the sea
Sparkles as if it smiled,
Will they restore to me
My dark Love, empress and child ?

The curtains seem to part ;
A sound is on the stair,
As if at the last . . . I start ;
Only the wind is there.

Lo, now far on the hills
The crimson fumes uncurl'd,
Where the caldron mantles and spills
Another dawn on the world !

626.   *Why*

FOR a name unknown,
   Whose fame unblown
Sleeps in the hills
   For ever and aye ;

For her who hears
The stir of the years
Go by on the wind
   By night and day ;

And heeds no thing
Of the needs of spring,
Of autumn's wonder
   Or winter's chill ;

BLISS CARMAN

For one who sees
The great sun freeze,
As he wanders a-cold
    From hill to hill ;

And all her heart
Is a woven part
Of the flurry and drift
    Of whirling snow ;

For the sake of two
Sad eyes and true,
And the old, old love
    So long ago.

DOUGLAS HYDE

b. 1861

627.   *My Grief on the Sea*

FROM THE IRISH

MY grief on the sea,
    How the waves of it roll !
For they heave between me
    And the love of my soul !

Abandon'd, forsaken,
    To grief and to care,
Will the sea ever waken
    Relief from despair ?

My grief and my trouble !
    Would he and I were
In the province of Leinster,
    Or County of Clare !

Were

Were I and my darling—
    O heart-bitter wound !—
On board of the ship
    For America bound.

On a green bed of rushes
    All last night I lay,
And I flung it abroad
    With the heat of the day.

And my Love came behind me,
    He came from the South ;
His breast to my bosom,
    His mouth to my mouth.

628.   *The Cooleen*

A HONEY mist on a day of frost in a dark oak wood,
    And love for thee in my heart in me, thou bright
        white and good ;
Thy slender form, soft and warm, thy red lips apart,
Thou hast found me, and hast bound me, and put grief
    in my heart.

In fair-green and market men mark thee, bright, young
    and merry,
Tho' thou hurt them like foes with the rose of thy blush
    of the berry :
Her cheeks are a poppy, her eye it is Cupid's helper,
But each foolish man dreams that its beams for himself are.

Whoe'er saw the Cooleen in a cool dewy meadow
On a morning in summer in sunshine and shadow ;
All the young men go wild for her, my childeen, my
    treasure,
But now let them go mope, they've no hope to possess her.

DOUGLAS HYDE

Let us roam, O my darling, afar thro' the mountains,
Drink milk of the goat, wine and bulcaun in fountains ;
With music and play every day from my lyre,
And leave to come rest on my breast when you tire.

MAURICE HEWLETT

b. 1861

629.   *Rosa Nascosa*

MORE than those
    Enfranchised beauties her perfection shows,
Like a concealèd rose,
But to the thickets where she lieth close.

These libertines
Encompass her with hardy-visaged spines ;
She frets not nor repines,
But does their bidding meekly, and resigns

Herself to be
Their bond-servant, who shall be more than free
Having a liberty
There where her soul can fear no enemy.

There she doth find
All broad dominion and a heaven all kind,
In her unravisht mind
Whereto her brute possessioners are blind.

Possession goes
No deeper than the surface ; there are mines
Far down, whose sacred fee
And golden hold no trammelling can bind.

KATHARINE TYNAN HINKSON

630.   *Of an Orchard*

GOOD is an Orchard, the Saint saith,
   To meditate on life and death,
With a cool well, a hive of bees,
A hermit's grot below the trees.

Good is an Orchard : very good,
Though one should wear no monkish hood ;
Right good when Spring awakes her flute,
And good in yellowing time of fruit :

Very good in the grass to lie
And see the network 'gainst the sky,
A living lace of blue and green
And boughs that let the gold between.

The bees are types of souls that dwell
With honey in a quiet cell ;
The ripe fruit figures goldenly
The soul's perfection in God's eye.

Prayer and praise in a country home
Honey and fruit : a man might come
Fed on such meats to walk abroad
And in his Orchard talk with God.

631.   *Sheep and Lambs*

ALL in the April morning,
    April airs were abroad ;
The sheep with their little lambs
    Pass'd me by on the road.

The sheep with their little lambs
    Pass'd me by on the road ;
All in an April evening
    I thought on the Lamb of God.

The lambs were weary, and crying
    With a weak human cry,
I thought on the Lamb of God
    Going meekly to die.

Up in the blue, blue mountains
    Dewy pastures are sweet :
Rest for the little bodies,
    Rest for the little feet.

But for the Lamb of God
    Up on the hill-top green,
Only a cross of shame
    Two stark crosses between.

All in the April evening,
    April airs were abroad ;
I saw the sheep with their lambs,
    And thought on the Lamb of God.

632.   *A Prayer*

NOW wilt me take for Jesus' sake,
    Nor cast me out at all ;
I shall not fear the foe awake,
    Saved by thy City wall ;
But in the night without affright
    Shall hear him steal without,
Who may not scale thy wall of might,
    Thy bastion, nor redoubt.

Full well I know that to the foe
    Wilt yield me not for aye,
Unless mine own hand should undo
    The gates that are my stay—
My folly and pride should open wide
    Thy doors and set me free
'Mid tigers striped and panthers pied
    Far from thy liberty.

Unless by debt myself I set
    Outside thy loving ken,
And yield myself by weight of debt
    Unto my fellow-men ;
Deal with my guilt Thou as Thou wilt,
    And ' Hold ! ' I shall not cry,
So I be thine in storm and shine,
    Thine only till I die.

MATILDA BETHAM EDWARDS

633. *A Valentine*

WHAT shall I send my love to-day,
  When all the woods attune to love,
  And I would show the lark and dove
That I can love as well as they ? . . .

I'll send a kiss, for that would be
  The quickest sent, the lightest borne ;
  And well I know to-morrow morn
She'll send it back again to me.

Go, happy winds ! ah, do not stay
  Enamour'd of my lady's cheek,
  But hasten home, and I'll bespeak
Your services another day !

634. *The Pansy and the Prayer-Book*

FOLLOWING across the moors a sound of bells,
  We found a church, the smallest that could be,
  Hid in a tamarisk-grove beside the sea,
And graves of shipwreck'd men set round with shells.
We enter'd when the prayers were almost done :
  The little children nodded on their knees,
  The preacher's voice was drown'd in hum of bees
That danced about the lectern in the sun.

Awhile we knelt I let a pansy glide
  Between her sweet grave face and open book,
  And whisper'd as she turn'd with chiding look—
'Heaven has not will'd, dear heart, that aught divide
Love pure as ours, nor blames if thought of me
Come like this flower between thy God and thee.'

LOUISE IMOGEN GUINEY

635.   *In Leinster*

I TRY to knead and spin, but my life is low the while.
  O, I long to be alone and walk abroad a mile !
Yet if I walk alone, and think of naught at all,
Why from me that 's young should the wild tears fall ?

The shower-stricken earth, the earth-colour'd streams,
They breathe on me awake and moan to me in dreams ;
And yonder ivy fondling the broke castle-wall,
It pulls upon my heart till the wild tears fall.

The cabin door looks down a furze-lighted hill,
And far as Leighlin Cross the fields are green and still ;
But once I hear the blackbird in Leighlin hedges call,
The foolishness is on me, and the wild tears fall.

636.   *Carol*

VINES branching stilly
    Shade the open door
In the house of Sion's lily
    Cleanly and poor.
O, brighter than wild laurel
    The Babe bounds in her hand !
The King, who for apparel
    Hath but a swaddling band,
Who sees her heavenlier smiling than
    Stars in his command.

834

Soon mystic changes
   Part Him from her breast :
Yet there awhile He ranges
   Gardens of rest,
Yea, she the first to ponder
   Our ransom and recall,
Awhile may rock Him under
   Her young curls' fall,
Against that only tender
   Love loyal heart of all !

What shall inure Him
   Unto the deadly dream
When the tetrarch shall abjure Him,
   The thief blaspheme ?
And Scribe and Soldier jostle
   About the shameful Tree,
When even the Apostle
   Demands to touch and see ?
But she hath kiss'd her Flower
   Where the wounds are to be.

637.   *Tryste Noel*

THE Ox he openeth wide the Doore,
  And from the Snowe he calls her inne ;
And he hath seen her smile therefore,
     Our Ladye without sinne.
     Now soone from Sleepe
     A Starre shall leap,
And soone arrive both King and Hinde ;
      Amen, Amen ;
But O the Place co'd I but finde !

         The

The Ox hath husht his Voyce and bent
Trewe eye of Pitty ore the Mow ;
And on his lovelie Neck, forspent
  The Blessèd lays her Browe.
  Around her feet
  Full warme and sweete
His bowerie Breath doth meeklie dwell ;
   Amen, Amen ;
But sore am I with Vaine Travel !

The Ox is host in Juda's stall,
And Host of more than onely one ;
For close she gathereth withal
  Our Lorde, her little Sonne.
  Glad Hinde and King
  Their Gyfte may bring,
But wo'd to-night my Teares were there ;
   Amen, Amen ;
Between her Bosome and His hayre !

ALICE MEYNELL

638.   *The Shepherdess*

SHE walks—the lady of my delight—
 A shepherdess of sheep.
Her flocks are thoughts. She keeps them white ;
 She guards them from the steep ;
She feeds them on the fragrant height,
 And folds them in for sleep.

She roams maternal hills and bright,
    Dark valleys safe and deep.
Into that tender breast at night
    The chastest stars may peep.
She walks—the lady of my delight—
    A shepherdess of sheep.

She holds her little thoughts in sight,
    Though gay they run and leap.
She is so circumspect and right;
    She has her soul to keep.
She walks—the lady of my delight—
    A shepherdess of sheep.

639.   *Renouncement*

I MUST not think of thee; and, tired yet strong,
I shun the thought that lurks in all delight—
    The thought of thee—and in the blue heaven's height,
And in the dearest passage of a song.

Oh, just beyond the fairest thoughts that throng
    This breast, the thought of thee waits hidden yet bright;
    But it must never, never come in sight;
I must stop short of thee the whole day long.

But when sleep comes to close each difficult day,
    When night gives pause to the long watch I keep,
    And all my bonds I needs must loose apart,
Must doff my will as raiment laid away,—
    With the first dream that comes with the first sleep
    I run, I run, I am gather'd to thy heart.

640.　*The Two Poets*

WHOSE is the speech
　　That moves the voices of this lonely beech ?
Out of the long west did this wild wind come—
Oh strong and silent ! And the tree was dumb,
　　　　Ready and dumb, until
The dumb gale struck it on the darken'd hill.

　　　　Two memories,
Two powers, two promises, two silences
Closed in this cry, closed in these thousand leaves
Articulate.　This sudden hour retrieves
　　　　The purpose of the past,
Separate, apart—embraced, embraced at last.

　　　　' Whose is the word ?
Is it I that spake ? Is it thou ? Is it I that heard ? '
' Thine earth was solitary, yet I found thee ! '
' Thy sky was pathless, but I caught, I bound thee,
　　　　Thou visitant divine.'
' O thou my Voice, the word was thine.'　' Was thine.'

641.　*At Night*

HOME, home from the horizon far and clear,
　　Hither the soft wings sweep ;
Flocks of the memories of the day draw near
　　　　The dovecote doors of sleep.

O, which are they that come through sweetest light
　　　　Of all these homing birds ?
Which with the straightest and the swiftest flight ?
　　　　Your words to me, your words !

HENRY NEWBOLT

b. 1862

642.   *Drake's Drum*

DRAKE he's in his hammock an' a thousand mile
     away,
     (Capten, art tha sleepin' there below ?)
Slung atween the round shot in Nombre Dios Bay,
     An' dreamin' arl the time o' Plymouth Hoe.
Yarnder lumes the Island, yarnder lie the ships,
     Wi' sailor lads a-dancin' heel-an'-toe,
An' the shore-lights flashin', an' the night-tide dashin',
     He sees et arl so plainly as he saw et long ago.

Drake he was a Devon man, an' ruled the Devon seas,
     (Capten, art tha sleepin' there below ?),
Rovin' tho' his death fell, he went wi' heart at ease,
     An' dreamin' arl the time o' Plymouth Hoe.
' Take my drum to England, hang et by the shore,
     Strike et when your powder 's runnin' low ;
If the Dons sight Devon, I'll quit the port o' Heaven,
     An' drum them up the Channel as we drumm'd them
         long ago.'

Drake he's in his hammock till the great Armadas come,
     (Capten, art tha sleepin' there below ?),
Slung atween the round shot, listenin' for the drum,
     An' dreamin' arl the time o' Plymouth Hoe.
Call him on the deep sea, call him up the Sound,
     Call him when ye sail to meet the foe ;
Where the old trade 's plyin' an' the old flag flyin'
     They shall find him ware an' wakin', as they found him
         long ago !

643.   *He fell among Thieves*

' YE have robb'd,' said he, ' ye have slaughter'd and
      made an end,
  Take your ill-got plunder, and bury the dead :
What will ye more of your guest and sometime friend ? '
  ' Blood for our blood,' they said.

He laugh'd : ' If one may settle the score for five,
  I am ready ; but let the reckoning stand till day :
I have loved the sunlight as dearly as any alive.'
  ' You shall die at dawn,' said they.

He flung his empty revolver down the slope,
  He climb'd alone to the Eastward edge of the trees ;
All night long in a dream untroubled of hope
  He brooded, clasping his knees.

He did not hear the monotonous roar that fills
  The ravine where the Yassin river sullenly flows ;
He did not see the starlight on the Laspur hills,
  Or the far Afghan snows.

He saw the April noon on his books aglow,
  The wistaria trailing in at the window wide ;
He heard his father's voice from the terrace below
  Calling him down to ride.

He saw the gray little church across the park,
  The mounds that hid the loved and honour'd **dead** ;
The Norman arch, the chancel softly dark,
  The brasses black and red.

He saw the School Close, sunny and green,
    The runner beside him, the stand by the parapet wall,
The distant tape, and the crowd roaring between,
    His own name over all.

He saw the dark wainscot and timber'd roof,
    The long tables, and the faces merry and keen,
The College Eight and their trainer dining aloof,
    The Dons on the daïs serene.

He watch'd the liner's stem ploughing the foam,
    He felt her trembling speed and the thrash of her screw ;
He heard the passengers' voices talking of home,
    He saw the flag she flew.

And now it was dawn. He rose strong on his feet,
    And strode to his ruin'd camp below the wood ;
He drank the breath of the morning cool and sweet,
    His murderers round him stood.

Light on the Laspur hills was broadening fast,
    The blood-red snow-peaks chill'd to a dazzling white ;
He turn'd, and saw the golden circle at last,
    Cut by the Eastern height.

' O glorious Life, Who dwellest in earth and sun,
    I have lived, I praise and adore Thee.'
                A sword swept.
Over the pass the voices one by one
    Faded, and the hill slept.

644.   *Commemoration*

I SAT by the granite pillar, and sunlight fell
    Where the sunlight fell of old,
And the hour was the hour my heart remember'd well,
    And the sermon roll'd and roll'd
As it used to roll when the place was still unhaunted,
And the strangest tale in the world was still untold.

And I knew that of all this rushing of urgent sound
    That I so clearly heard,
The green young forest of saplings cluster'd round
    Was heeding not one word:
Their heads were bow'd in a still serried patience
Such as an angel's breath could never have stirr'd.

For some were already away to the hazardous pitch,
    Or lining the parapet wall,
And some were in glorious battle, or great and rich,
    Or throned in a college hall:
And among the rest was one like my own young phantom,
Dreaming for ever beyond my utmost call.

' O Youth,' the preacher was crying, ' deem not thou
    Thy life is thine alone;
Thou bearest the will of the ages, seeing how
    They built thee bone by bone,
And within thy blood the Great Age sleeps sepulchred
Till thou and thine shall roll away the stone.

' Therefore the days are coming when thou shalt burn
    With passion whitely hot;
Rest shall be rest no more; thy feet shall spurn

All that thy hand hath got ;
And One that is stronger shall gird thee, and lead thee
    swiftly
Whither, O heart of Youth, thou wouldest not.'

And the School pass'd ; and I saw the living and dead
    Set in their seats again,
And I long'd to hear them speak of the word that was said,
    But I knew that I long'd in vain.
And they stretch'd forth their hands, and the wind of the
    spirit took them
Lightly as drifted leaves on an endless plain.

645.   *Clifton Chapel*

THIS is the Chapel : here, my son,
    Your father thought the thoughts of youth,
And heard the words that one by one
    The touch of Life has turn'd to truth.
Here in a day that is not far
    You too may speak with noble ghosts,
Of manhood and the vows of war
    You made before the Lord of Hosts.

To set the Cause above renown,
    To love the game beyond the prize,
To honour, while you strike him down,
    The foe that comes with fearless eyes :
To count the life of battle good,
    And dear the land that gave you birth,
And dearer yet the brotherhood
    That binds the brave of all the earth.—

My

HENRY NEWBOLT

My son, the oath is yours : the end
   Is His, Who built the world of strife,
Who gave His children Pain for friend,
   And Death for surest hope of life.
To-day and here the fight 's begun,
   Of the great fellowship you're free ;
Henceforth the School and you are one,
   And what You are, the race shall be.

God send you fortune : yet be sure,
   Among the lights that gleam and pass,
You'll live to follow none more pure
   Than that which glows on yonder brass :
' *Qui procul hinc,*' the legend 's writ,—
   The frontier-grave is far away—
' *Qui ante diem periit :*
   Sed miles, sed pro patria.'

ARTHUR CHRISTOPHER BENSON

b. 1862

646.   *Prelude*

HUSH'D is each busy shout :
   The reverent people wait,
To see the sacred pomp stream out
   Beside the temple-gate.

The bull with garlands hung,
   Stern priests in vesture grim :
With rolling voices swiftly sung
   Peals out the jocund hymn.

In front, behind, beside,
   Beneath the chiming towers,
Pass boys that fling the censer wide,
   And striplings scattering flowers.

Victim or minister
I dare not claim to be,
But in the concourse and the stir,
There shall be room for me.

The victim feels the stroke :
The priests are bow'd in prayer :—
I feed the porch with fragrant smoke,
Strew roses on the stair.

647. *Lord Vyet*

WHAT, must my lord be gone ?
Command his horse, and call
The servants, one and all.
' Nay, nay, I go alone.'

My Lord, I shall unfold
Thy cloak of sables rare
To shield thee from the air :
' Nay, nay, I must be cold.'

At least thy leech I'll tell
Some drowsy draught to make,
Less thou should toss awake.
' Nay, nay, I shall sleep well.'

My lady keeps her bower :—
I hear the lute delight
The dark and frozen night,
High up within the tower.

Wilt thou that she descend ?
Thy son is in the hall,
Tossing his golden ball,
Shall he my lord attend ?

' Nay,

' Nay, sirs, unbar the door,
    The broken lute shall fall ;
    My son will leave his ball
To tarnish on the floor.'

Yon bell to triumph rings !
    To greet thee, monarchs wait
    Beside their palace gate.
' Yes, I shall sleep with kings.'

My lord will soon alight
    With some rich prince, his friend,
    Who shall his ease attend.
' I shall lodge low to-night.'

My lord hath lodging nigh ?
    ' Yes, yes, I go not far,—
    And yet the furthest star
Is not so far as I.'

648.   *The Phoenix*

I

BY feathers green, across Casbeen
    The pilgrims track the Phoenix flown,
By gems he strew'd in waste and wood,
    And jewell'd plumes at random thrown.

Till wandering far, by moon and star,
    They stand beside the fruitful pyre,
Where breaking bright with sanguine light
    The impulsive bird forgets his sire.

Those ashes shine like ruby wine,
    Like bag of Tyrian murex spilt,
The claw, the jowl of the flying fowl
    Are with the glorious anguish gilt.

So rare the light, so rich the sight,
  Those pilgrim men, on profit bent,
Drop hands and eyes and merchandise,
  And are with gazing most content.

649.   *Amen*

RETURN, sad sister, Faith;
  Dim, unsubstantial wraith!
Return, thy votary saith
    He needs thee now:
Thou wert serenely fair!
But some diviner air
Gleams on thy silver'd hair,
    And crowns thy brow;

Thou wilt return, and I
Shall rather sing than sigh,
In that great company
    Of souls forlorn:
One with all hearts that break
For some belovèd's sake,
The hopeless hearts, that ache
    And dare not mourn.

Wherefore, since pain and pride
Must sleep unsatisfied,—
Because Thy heart is wide,
    And dim our ken,—
To that vast prayer that rolls
Beyond the frozen poles,
With all desirous souls
    I cry, Amen.

b. 1862

650.   *The Country Faith*

HERE in the country's heart
    Where the grass is green,
Life is the same sweet life
As it e'er hath been.

Trust in a God still lives,
And the bell at morn
Floats with a thought of God
O'er the rising corn.

God comes down in the rain,
And the crop grows tall—
This is the country faith,
And the best of all.

651.   *The Shaded Pool*

A LAUGHING knot of village maids
    Goes gaily tripping to the brook,
For water-nymphs they mean to be,
And seek some still, secluded nook.
Here Laura goes, my own delight,
And Colin's love, the madcap Jane,
And half a score of goddesses
Trip over daisies in the plain :
Already now they loose their hair
And peep from out the tangled gold,
Or speed the flying foot to reach
The brook that's only summer-cold ;
The lovely locks stream out behind
The shepherdesses on the wing,
And Laura's is the wealth I love,
And Laura's is the gold I sing.

848

A-row upon the bank they pant,
And all unlace the country shoe ;
Their fingers tug the garter-knots
To loose the hose of varied hue.
The flashing knee at last appears,
The lower curves of youth and grace.
Whereat the maidens' eyes do scan
The mazy thickets of the place.
But who 's to see besides the thrush
Upon the wild crab-apple tree ?
Within his branchy haunt he sits—
A very Peeping Tom is he !
Now music bubbles in his throat,
And now he pipes the scene in song—
The virgins slipping from their robes,
The cheated stockings lean and long,
The swift-descending petticoat,
The breasts that heave because they ran,
The rounded arms, the brilliant limbs,
The pretty necklaces of tan.
Did ever amorous god in Greece,
In search of some young mouth to kiss,
By any river chance upon
A sylvan scene as bright as this ?
But though each maid is pure and fair,
For one alone my heart I bring,
And Laura's is the shape I love,
And Laura's is the snow I sing.

And now upon the brook's green brink,
A milk-white bevy, lo, they stand,
Half shy, half frighten'd, reaching back
The beauty of a poising hand !
How musical their little screams

849   When

When ripples kiss their shrinking feet !
And then the brook embraces all
Till gold and white and water meet !
Within the streamlet's soft cool arms
Delight and love and gracefulness
Sport till a horde of tiny waves
Swamps all the beds of floating cress :
And on his shining face are seen
Great yellow lilies drifting down
Beyond the ringing apple-tree,
Beyond the empty homespun gown.
Did ever Orpheus with his lute,
When making melody of old,
E'er find a stream in Attica
So ripely full of pink and gold ?
At last they climb the sloping bank
And shake upon the thirsty soil
A treasury of diamond-drops
Not gain'd by aught of grimy toil.
Again the garters clasp the hose,
Again the polish'd knee is hid,
Again the breathless babble tells
What Colin said, what Colin did.
In grace upon the grass they lie
And spread their tresses to the sun,
And rival, musical as they,
The blackbird's alto shake and run.
Did ever Love, on hunting bent,
Come idly humming through the hay,
And, to his sudden joyfulness,
Find fairer game at close of day ?
Though every maid 's a lily-rose,
And meet to sway a sceptred king,
Yet Laura's is the face I love,
And Laura's are the lips I sing.

EDEN PHILLPOTTS

b. 1862

652.   *Man's Days*

A SUDDEN wakin', a sudden weepin',
   A li'l suckin', a li'l sleepin' ;
A cheel's full joys an' a cheel's short sorrows,
Wi' a power o' faith in gert to-morrows.

Young blood red-hot an' the love of a maid,
One glorious day as'll never fade ;
Some shadows, some sunshine, some triumphs, some tears,
And a gatherin' weight o' the flyin' years.

Then old man's talk o' the days behind 'e,
Your darter's youngest darter to mind 'e ;
A li'l dreamin', a li'l dyin' :
A li'l lew corner o' airth to lie in.

SIR GILBERT PARKER

b. 1862

653.   *Reunited*

WHEN you and I have play'd the little hour,
   Have seen the tall subaltern Life to Death
  Yield up his sword ; and, smiling, draw the breath,
The first long breath of freedom ; when the flower
Of Recompense hath flutter'd to our feet,
  As to an actor's ; and, the curtain down,
  We turn to face each other all alone—
Alone, we two, who never yet did meet,
Alone, and absolute, and free : O then,
  O then, most dear, how shall be told the tale ?
Clasp'd hands, press'd lips, and so clasp'd hands again ;
  No words. But as the proud wind fills the sail,
    My love to yours shall reach, then one deep moan
    Of joy, and then our infinite Alone.

ROSAMUND MARRIOTT WATSON

654.   *A South Coast Idyll*

BENEATH these sun-warm'd pines among the
 heather,
A white goat, bleating, strains his hempen tether,
  A purple stain dreams on the broad blue plain,
The waters and the west wind sing together.

The soft grey lichen creeps o'er ridge and hollow,
Where swift and sudden skims the slim sea swallow;
  The hid cicalas play their viols all the day,
Merry of heart, although they may not follow.

Beyond yon slope, out-wearied with his reaping,
With vine-bound brows, young Daphnis lies a-sleeping;
  Stolen from the sea on feet of ivory,
The white nymphs whisper, through the pine stems
    peeping.

We hear their steps, yet turn to seek them never,
Nor scale the sunny slope in fond endeavour;
  It may not be, too swiftly would they flee
Our world-stain'd gaze and come no more for ever.

Pan, Pan is piping in the noontide golden,
Let us lie still, as in a dream enfolden,
  Hear by the sea the airs of Arcady,
And feel the wind of tresses unbeholden.

ROSAMUND MARRIOTT WATSON

655.   *The Farm on the Links*

GREY o'er the pallid links, haggard and forsaken,
    Still the old roof-tree hangs rotting overhead,
Still the black windows stare sullenly to seaward,
    Still the blank doorway gapes, open to the dead.

What is it cries with the crying of the curlews ?
    What comes apace on those fearful, stealthy feet,
Back from the chill sea-deeps, gliding o'er the sand-dunes,
    Home to the old home, once again to meet ?

What is to say as they gather round the hearth-stone,
    Flameless and dull as the feuds and fears of old ?
Laughing and fleering still, menacing and mocking,
    Sadder than death itself, harsher than the cold.

Woe for the ruin'd hearth, black with dule and evil,
    Woe for the wrong and the hate too deep to die !
Woe for the deeds of the dreary days past over,
    Woe for the grief of the gloomy days gone by !

Where do they come from ? furtive and despairing,
    Where are they bound for ? those that gather there,
Slow, with the sea-wind sobbing through the chambers,
    Soft, with the salt mist stealing up the stair ?

Names that are nameless now, names of dread and
        loathing,
    Bann'd and forbidden yet, dark with spot and stain :
Only the old house watches and remembers,
    Only the old home welcomes them again.

ROSAMUND MARRIOTT WATSON

656.   *The Last Fairy*

UNDER the yellow moon, when the young men and
    maidens pass in the lanes,
Outcast I flit, looking down through the leaves of the
    elm-trees,
Peering out over the fields as their voices grow fainter ;
Furtive and lone
Sometimes I steal through the green rushes down by the
    river,
Hearing shrill laughter and song while the rosy-limb'd
    bathers
Gleam in the dusk.
Seen, they would pass me disdainful, or stone me un-
    witting ;
No room is left in their hearts for my kinsfolk or me.
Fain would I, too, fading out like a moth in the twilight,
Follow my kin,
Whither I know not, and ever I seek but I find not—
Whither I know not, nor knoweth the wandering swallow ;
' Where are they, where ? '
Oft-times I cry ; but I hearken in vain for their footsteps,
Always in vain.

High in a last year's nest, in the boughs of the pine-tree,
Musing I sit, looking up to the deeps of the sky,
Clasping my knees as I watch there and wonder, forsaken ;
Ever the hollow sky
Voiceless and vast, and the golden moon silently sailing,
Look on my pain and they care not,
There is none that remembers :
Only the nightingale knows me—she knows and remem-
    bers—
Deep in the dusk of the thicket she sorrows for me.

854

Yet, on the wings of the wind sweeping over the uplands,
Fitfully borne,
Murmuring echoes remember'd—the ghosts of old voices
Faint as a dream, and uncertain as cloud-shadow'd sun-
    light,
Fall on mine ear.
Whence do they call me ? From golden-dew'd valleys
    forgotten ?
Or from the strongholds of eld, where red banners of
    sunset
Flame o'er the sea ?
Or from anear, on the dim airy slopes of the dawn-world,
Over light-flowering meads between daybreak and sun-
    rise
Level and grey ?
Truly I know not, but steadfast and longing I listen,
Straining mine ears for the lilt of their tinkling laughter
Sweeter than sheep-bells at even ;—I watch and I hearken.
O for the summons to sound !—for the pipes plaining
    shrilly,
Calling me home !

SIR ARTHUR QUILLER-COUCH

b. 1863

657. *Upon New Year's Eve*

N OW winds of winter glue
    Their tears upon the thorn,
And earth has voices few,
    And those forlorn.

And 'tis our solemn night
    When maidens sand the porch
And play at *Jack's Alight*
    With burning torch,

855

Or

Or cards, or *Kiss i' the Ring*—
   While ashen faggots blaze,
And late wassailers sing
   In miry ways.

Then, dear my wife, be blithe
   To bid the New Year hail
And welcome—plough, drill, scythe,
   And jolly flail.

For though the snows he'll shake
   Of winter from his head,
To settle, flake by flake,
   On ours instead ;

Yet we be wreathèd green
   Beyond his blight or chill,
Who kiss'd at seventeen,
   And worship still.

We know not what he'll bring ;
   But this we know to-night—
He doth prepare the Spring
   For our delight.

With birds he'll comfort us,
   With blossoms, balms, and bees,
With brooks, and odorous
   Wild breath o' the breeze.

Come then, O festal prime !
   With sweets thy bosom fill
And dance it, dripping thyme,
   On Lantick hill.

West wind awake ! and comb
　　Our garden blade from blade—
We, in our little home,
　　Sit unafraid.

658. *Upon Eckington Bridge, River Avon*

O PASTORAL heart of England ! like a psalm
　　Of green days telling with a quiet beat—
O wave into the sunset flowing calm !
　　O tirèd lark descending on the wheat !
Lies it all peace beyond that western fold
　　Where now the lingering shepherd sees his star
Rise upon Malvern ? Paints an Age of Gold
　　　Yon cloud with prophecies of linkèd ease—
　　　Lulling this Land, with hills drawn up like knees,
　　To drowse beside her implements of war ?

Man shall outlast his battles. They have swept
　　Avon from Naseby Field to Severn Ham ;
And Evesham's dedicated stones have stepp'd
　　Down to the dust with Montfort's oriflamme.
Nor the red tear nor the reflected tower
　　Abides ; but yet these eloquent grooves remain,
Worn in the sandstone parapet hour by hour
　　　By labouring bargemen where they shifted ropes.
　　　E'en so shall man turn back from violent hopes
　　To Adam's cheer, and toil with spade again.

Ay, and his mother Nature, to whose lap
　　Like a repentant child at length he hies,
Not in the whirlwind or the thunder-clap
　　Proclaims her more tremendous mysteries :

　　　　　　　　　　　　　　　But

But when in winter's grave, bereft of light,
   With still, small voice divinelier whispering
  —Lifting the green head of the aconite,
    Feeding with sap of hope the hazel-shoot—
  She feels God's finger active at the root,
Turns in her sleep, and murmurs of the Spring.

659.   *Alma Mater*

K NOW you her secret none can utter ?
   —Hers of the Book, the tripled Crown ?
Still on the spire the pigeons flutter ;
  Still by the gateway haunts the gown ;
Still on the street from corbel and gutter,
  Faces of stone look down.

Faces of stone, and other faces—
  Some from library windows wan
Forth on her gardens, her green spaces,
  Peer and turn to their books anon.
Hence, my Muse, from the green oases
  Gather the tent, begone !

Nay, should she by the pavement linger
  Under the rooms where once she play'd,
Who from the feast would rise and fling her
  One poor *sou* for her serenade ?
One poor laugh for the antic finger
  Thrumming a lute-string fray'd ?

Once, my dear,—but the world was young, then—
  Magdalen elms and Trinity limes—

Lissom the blades and the backs that swung then,
   Eight good men in the good old times—
Careless we, and the chorus flung then
   Under St. Mary's chimes !

Reins lay loose and the ways led random—
   Christ Church meadow and Iffley track—
' Idleness horrid and dogcart ' (tandem)—
   Aylesbury grind and Bicester pack—
Pleasant our lines, and faith ! we scann'd 'em ;
   Having that artless knack.

Come, old limmer, the times grow colder :
   Leaves of the creeper redden and fall.
Was it a hand then clapp'd my shoulder ?
   —Only the wind by the chapel wall.
Dead leaves drift on the lute : so . . . fold her
   Under the faded shawl.

Never we wince, though none deplore us,
   We, who go reaping that we sow'd ;
Cities at cock-crow wake before us—
   Hey, for the lilt of the London road !
One look back and a rousing chorus !
   Never a palinode !

Still on her spire the pigeons hover ;
   Still by her gateway haunts the gown.
Ah, but her secret ?   You, young lover,
   Drumming her old ones forth from town,
Know you the secret none discover ?
   Tell it—when *you* go down.

Yet

Yet if at length you seek her, prove her,
   Lean to her whispers never so nigh ;
Yet if at last not less her lover
   You in your hansom leave the High ;
Down from her towers a ray shall hover,
   Touch you—a passer-by !

STEPHEN PHILLIPS

b. 1864

660.   *The Apparition*

MY dead Love came to me, and said :
   'God gives me one hour's rest
To spend upon the earth with thee :
   How shall we spend it best ?

'Why, as of old,' I said, and so
   We quarrell'd as of old.
But when I turn'd to make my peace
   That one short hour was told.

NEIL MUNRO

b. 1864

661.   *The Heather*

IF I were King of France, that noble fine land,
   And the gold was elbow deep within my chests,
And my castles lay in scores along the wine-land
   With towers as high as where the eagle nests ;
If harpers sweet, and swordsmen stout and vaunting,
   My history sang, my stainless tartan wore,
Was not my fortune poor, with one thing wanting,—
   The heather at my door.

My galleys might be sailing every ocean,
Robbing the isles, and sacking hold and keep,
My chevaliers go prancing at my notion,
To bring me back of cattle, horse and sheep ;
Fond arms be round my neck, the young heart's tether,
And true love-kisses all the night might fill,
But oh ! *mochree*, if I had not the heather,
  Before me on the hill !

A hunter's fare is all I would be craving,
A shepherd's plaiding and a beggar's pay,
If I might earn them where the heather, waving,
Gave fragrance to the day.
The stars might see me, homeless one and weary,
Without a roof to fend me from the dew,
And still content, I'd find a bedding cheery
  Where'er the heather grew !

HERBERT TRENCH

662.   *A Charge*

b. 1865

IF thou hast squander'd years to grave a gem
 Commission'd by thy absent Lord, and while
  'Tis incomplete,
Others would bribe thy needy skill to them—
 Dismiss them to the street !

Should'st thou at last discover Beauty's grove,
 At last be panting on the fragrant verge,
  But in the track,
Drunk with divine possession, thou meet Love—
 Turn at her bidding back.

     When

When round thy ship in tempest Hell appears,
    And every spectre mutters up more dire
        To snatch control
And loose to madness thy deep-kennell'd Fears—
    Then to the helm, O Soul !

Last ; if upon the cold green-mantling sea
    Thou cling, alone with Truth, to the last spar,
        Both castaway,
And one must perish—let it not be he
    Whom thou art sworn to obey !

663. *Come, let us make Love deathless*

COME, let us make love deathless, thou and I,
    Seeing that our footing on the Earth is brief—
Seeing that her multitudes sweep out to die
    Mocking at all that passes their belief.
For standard of our love not theirs we take :
        If we go hence to-day,
Fill the high cup that is so soon to break
        With richer wine than they !

Ay, since beyond these walls no heavens there be,
    Joy to revive or wasted youth repair,
I'll not bedim the lovely flame in thee,
    Nor sully the sad splendour that we wear.
Great be the love, if with the lover dies
        Our greatness past recall,
And nobler for the fading of those eyes
        The world seen once for all.

664. *She comes not when Noon is on the Roses*

SHE comes not when Noon is on the roses—
    Too bright is Day.
She comes not to the Soul till it reposes
    From work and play.

But when Night is on the hills, and the great Voices
    Roll in from Sea,
By starlight and by candlelight and dreamlight
    She comes to me.

WILLIAM BUTLER YEATS

b. 1865

665. *Where My Books go*

ALL the words that I utter,
    And all the words that I write,
Must spread out their wings untiring,
    And never rest in their flight,
Till they come where your sad, sad heart is,
    And sing to you in the night,
Beyond where the waters are moving,
    Storm-darken'd or starry bright.

666. *The Rose of the World*

WHO dream'd that beauty passes like a dream ?
    For these red lips, with all their mournful pride,
Mournful that no new wonder may betide,
Troy pass'd away in one high funeral gleam,
And Usna's children died.

We

We and the labouring world are passing by :
Amid men's souls, that waver and give place
Like the pale waters in their wintry race
Under the passing stars, foam of the sky,
Lives on this lonely face.

Bow down, archangels, in your dim abode :
Before you were, or any hearts to beat,
Weary and kind one linger'd by His seat ;
He made the world to be a grassy road
Before her wandering feet.

667. *The Rose of Peace*

IF Michael, leader of God's host
   When Heaven and Hell are met,
Look'd down on you from Heaven's door-post
He would his deeds forget.

Brooding no more upon God's wars
In his Divine homestead,
He would go weave out of the stars
A chaplet for your head.

And all folk seeing him bow down,
And white stars tell your praise,
Would come at last to God's great town,
Led on by gentle ways ;

And God would bid his warfare cease.
Saying all things were well ;
And softly make a rosy peace,
A peace of Heaven with Hell.

668. *Aedh wishes for the Cloths of Heaven*

HAD I the heavens' embroider'd cloths,
　　Enwrought with golden and silver light,
The blue and the dim and the dark cloths
Of night and light and the half light,
I would spread the cloths under your feet:
But I, being poor, have only my dreams;
I have spread my dreams under your feet;
Tread softly because you tread on my dreams.

669. *Down by the Salley Gardens*

DOWN by the salley gardens my love and I did meet;
　　She pass'd the salley gardens with little snow-white
　　　feet.
She bid me take love easy, as the leaves grow on the tree;
But I, being young and foolish, with her would not agree.

In a field by the river my love and I did stand,
And on my leaning shoulder she laid her snow-white hand.
She bid me take life easy, as the grass grows on the weirs;
But I was young and foolish, and now am full of tears.

670. *The Cap and Bells*

A JESTER walk'd in the garden:
　　The garden had fallen still;
He bade his soul rise upward
And stand on her window-sill.

It

It rose in a straight blue garment,
When owls began to call :
It had grown wise-tongued by thinking
Of a quiet and light footfall ;

But the young queen would not listen :
She rose in her pale night gown ;
She drew in the heavy casement
And push'd the latches down.

He bade his heart go to her,
When the owls call'd out no more :
In a red and quivering garment
It sang to her through the door.

It had grown sweet-tongued by dreaming
Of a flutter of flower-like hair ;
But she took up her fan from the table
And waved it off on the air.

' I have cap and bells,' he ponder'd,
' I will send them to her and die ' ;
And when the morning whiten'd
He left them where she went by.

She laid them upon her bosom,
Under a cloud of her hair,
And her red lips sang them a love song,
Till stars grew out of the air.

She open'd her door and her window,
And the heart and the soul came through,
To her right hand came the red one,
To her left hand came the blue.

They set up a noise like crickets,
A chattering wise and sweet,
And her hair was a folded flower,
And the quiet of love in her feet.

671.   *The Fiddler of Dooney*

WHEN I play on my fiddle in Dooney
Folk dance like a wave of the sea :
My cousin is priest in Kilvarnet,
My brother in Moharabuiee.

I pass'd my brother and cousin :
They read in their books of prayers ;
I read in my book of songs
I bought at the Sligo fair.

When we come at the end of time,
To Peter sitting in state,
He will smile on the three old spirits,
But call me first through the gate ;

For the good are always the merry,
Save by an evil chance ;
And the merry love the fiddle,
And the merry love to dance :

And when the folk there spy me,
They will all come up to me,
With ' Here is the fiddler of Dooney ! '
And dance like a wave of the sea.

672.   *When You are Old*

WHEN you are old and gray and full of sleep
   And, nodding by the fire, take down this book,
   And slowly read, and dream of the soft look
Your eyes had once, and of their shadows deep ;

How many loved your moments of glad grace,
   And loved your beauty with love false or true ;
   But one man loved the pilgrim soul in you,
And loved the sorrows of your changing face.

And bending down beside the glowing bars,
   Murmur, a little sadly, how love fled
   And paced upon the mountains overhead,
And hid his face amid a crowd of stars.

673.   *The Lake Isle of Innisfree*

I WILL arise and go now, and go to Innisfree,
   And a small cabin build there, of clay and wattles
     made ;
Nine bean rows will I have there, a hive for the honey bee,
   And live alone in the bee-loud glade.

And I shall have some peace there, for peace comes
     dropping slow,
Dropping from the veils of the morning to where the
     cricket sings ;
There midnight 's all a glimmer, and noon a purple glow,
   And evening full of the linnet's wings.

I will arise and go now, for always night and day
I hear lake water lapping with low sounds by the shore ;
While I stand on the roadway, or on the pavements gray,
   I hear it in the deep heart's core.

RUDYARD KIPLING

674.   *A Dedication*

MY new-cut ashlar takes the light
    Where crimson-blank the windows flare ;
By my own work, before the night,
    Great Overseer, I make my prayer.

If there be good in that I wrought,
    Thy hand compell'd it, Master, Thine ;
Where I have fail'd to meet Thy thought
    I know, through Thee, the blame is mine.

One instant's toil to Thee denied
    Stands all Eternity's offence ;
Of that I did with Thee to guide
    To Thee, through Thee, be excellence.

Who, lest all thought of Eden fade,
    Bring'st Eden to the craftsman's brain,
Godlike to muse o'er his own trade
    And manlike stand with God again.

The depth and dream of my desire,
    The bitter paths wherein I stray,
Thou knowest Who hast made the Fire,
    Thou knowest Who hast made the Clay.

One stone the more swings to her place
    In that dread Temple of Thy worth—
It is enough that through Thy grace
    I saw naught common on Thy earth.

Take

Take not that vision from my ken ;
O, whatsoe'er may spoil or speed,
Help me to need no aid from men,
That I may help such men as need !

675. *The Last Chantey*

THUS said The Lord in the Vault above the Cherubim,
Calling to the Angels and the Souls in their degree :
'Lo ! Earth has pass'd away
On the smoke of Judgment Day.
That Our word may be establish'd shall We gather up
the sea ? '

Loud sang the souls of the jolly, jolly mariners :
'Plague upon the hurricane that made us furl and flee !
But the war is done between us,
In the deep the Lord hath seen us—
Our bones we'll leave the barracout', and God may
sink the sea ! '

Then said the soul of Judas that betrayéd Him :
'Lord, hast Thou forgotten thy covenant with me ?
How once a year I go
To cool me on the floe ?
And Ye take my day of mercy if Ye take away the sea ! '

Then said the soul of the Angel of the Off-shore Wind :
(He that bits the thunder when the bull-mouth'd
breakers flee) :
'I have watch and ward to keep
O'er thy wonders on the deep,
And Ye take mine honour from me if Ye take away
the sea ! '

Loud sang the souls of the jolly, jolly mariners :
  ' Nay, but we were angry, and a hasty folk are we !
    If we work'd the ship together
    Till she founder'd in foul weather,
  Are we babes that we should clamour for a vengeance
    on the sea ? '

Then said the souls of the slaves that men threw over-
    board :
  ' Kennell'd in the picaroon a weary band were we ;
    But thy arm was strong to save,
    And it touch'd us on the wave,
  And we drowsed the long tides idle till thy Trumpets
    tore the sea.'

Then cried the soul of the stout Apostle Paul to God :
  ' Once we frapp'd a ship, and she labour'd woundily.
    There were fourteen score of these,
    And they bless'd Thee on their knees,
  When they learn'd thy Grace and Glory under Malta
    by the sea ! '

Loud sang the souls of the jolly, jolly mariners,
  Plucking at their harps, and they pluck'd unhandily :
    ' Our thumbs are rough and tarr'd,
    And the tune is something hard—
  May we lift a Deepsea Chantey such as seamen use at
    sea ? '

Then said the souls of the gentlemen-adventurers—
  Fetter'd wrist to bar all for red iniquity :
    ' Ho, we revel in our chains
    O'er the sorrow that was Spain's ;
  Heave or sink it, leave or drink it, we were masters of
    the sea ! '

Up

Up spake the soul of a gray Gothavn 'speckshioner—
    (He that led the flinching in the fleets of fair Dundee) :
      ' O, the ice-blink white and near,
      And the bowhead breaching clear !
    Will Ye whelm them all for wantonness that wallow in
      the sea ? '

Loud sang the souls of the jolly, jolly mariners,
    Crying : ' Under Heaven, here is neither lead nor lea !
      Must we sing for evermore
      On the windless, glassy floor ?
    Take back your golden fiddles and we'll beat to open
      sea ! '

Then stoop'd the Lord, and He call'd the good sea up
    to Him,
    And 'stablish'd his borders unto all eternity,
      That such as have no pleasure
      For to praise the Lord by measure,
    They may enter into galleons and serve Him on the sea.

Sun, wind, and cloud shall fail not from the face of it,
    Stinging, ringing spindrift, nor the fulmar flying free ;
      And the ships shall go abroad
      To the Glory of the Lord
    Who heard the silly sailor-folk and gave them back their
      sea !

676.   **The Flowers**

    *B*UY *my English posies !*
      Kent and Surrey May—
Violets of the Undercliff
    Wet with Channel spray ;

Cowslips from a Devon combe—
  Midland furze afire—
Buy my English posies
  And I'll sell your heart's desire !

Buy my English posies !
  You that scorn the May,
Won't you greet a friend from home
  Half the world away ?
Green against the draggled drift,
  Faint and frail and first—
Buy my Northern blood-root
  And I'll know where you were nursed :
Robin down the logging-road whistles, ' Come to me ! '
Spring has found the maple-grove, the sap is running
  free ;
All the winds of Canada call the ploughing-rain.
Take the flower and turn the hour, and kiss your love
  again !

Buy my English posies !
  Here 's to match your need—
Buy a tuft of royal heath,
  Buy a bunch of weed
White as sand of Muysenberg
  Spun before the gale—
Buy my heath and lilies
  And I'll tell you whence you hail !
Under hot Constantia broad the vineyards lie—
Throned and thorn'd the aching berg props the speckless
  sky—
Slow below the Wynberg firs trails the tilted wain—
Take the flower and turn the hour, and kiss your love
  again !

Buy

Buy my English posies !
   You that will not turn—
Buy my hot-wood clematis,
   Buy a frond o' fern
Gather'd where the Erskine leaps
   Down the road to Lorne—
Buy my Christmas creeper
   And I'll say where you were born !
West away from Melbourne dust holidays begin—
They that mock at Paradise woo at Cora Lynn—
Through the great South Otway gums sings the great
   South Main—
Take the flower and turn the hour, and kiss your love
   again !

Buy my English posies !
   Here 's your choice unsold !
Buy a blood-red myrtle-bloom,
   Buy the kowhai's gold
Flung for gift on Taupo's face,
   Sign that spring is come—
Buy my clinging myrtle
   And I'll give you back your home !
Broom behind the windy town ; pollen o' the pine—
Bell-bird in the leafy deep where the *ratas* twine—
Fern above the saddle-bow, flax upon the plain—
Take the flower and turn the hour, and kiss your love
   again !

Buy my English posies !
   Ye that have your own
Buy them for a brother's sake
   Overseas, alone.

Weed ye trample underfoot
   Floods his heart abrim—
Bird ye never heeded,
    O, she calls his dead to him!
Far and far our homes are set round the Seven Seas;
Woe for us if we forget, we that hold by these!
Unto each his mother-beach, bloom and bird and land—
Masters of the Seven Seas, O, love and understand!

677.   The Way Through the Woods

THEY shut the road through the woods
   Seventy years ago.
Weather and rain have undone it again,
   And now you would never know
There was once a path through the woods
   Before they planted the trees:
It is underneath the coppice and heath,
   And the thin anemones.
   Only the keeper sees
That, where the ring-dove broods
   And the badgers roll at ease,
There was once a road through the woods.

Yet, if you enter the woods
   Of a summer evening late,
When the night-air cools on the trout-ring'd pools
   Where the otter whistles his mate
(They fear not men in the woods
   Because they see so few),
You will hear the beat of a horse's feet
   And the swish of a skirt in the dew,

Steadily cantering through
The misty solitudes,
　　As though they perfectly knew
The old lost road through the woods . . .
But there is no road through the woods.

678.   *L' Envoi*

THERE 's a whisper down the field where the year
　　has shot her yield
And the ricks stand grey to the sun,
Singing :—' Over then, come over, for the bee has quit
　　the clover
And your English summer 's done.'
　　You have heard the beat of the off-shore wind
　　And the thresh of the deep-sea rain ;
　　You have heard the song—how long ! how long !
　　Pull out on the trail again !

Ha' done with the Tents of Shem, dear lass,
We've seen the seasons through,
And it 's time to turn on the old trail, our own trail, the
　　out trail,
Pull out, pull out, on the Long Trail—the trail that is
　　always new.

It 's North you may run to the rime-ring'd sun,
　　Or South to the blind Horn's hate ;
Or East all the way into Mississippi Bay,
　　Or West to the Golden Gate ;

Where the blindest bluffs hold good, dear lass,
And the wildest tales are true,
And the men bulk big on the old trail, our own trail, the
out trail,
And life runs large on the Long Trail—the trail that is
always new.

The days are sick and cold, and the skies are gray and old,
And the twice-breathed airs blow damp ;
And I'd sell my tirèd soul for the bucking beam-sea roll
Of a black Bilbao tramp ;
With her load-line over her hatch, dear lass,
And a drunken Dago crew,
And her nose held down on the old trail, our own trail,
the out trail,
From Cadiz Bar on the Long Trail—the trail that is
always new.

There be triple ways to take, of the eagle or the snake,
Or the way of a man with a maid ;
But the sweetest way to me is a ship's upon the sea
In the heel of the North-East Trade.
Can you hear the crash on her bows, dear lass,
And the drum of the racing screw,
As she ships it green on the old trail, our own trail, the
out trail,
As she lifts and 'scends on the Long Trail—the trail that
is always new ?

See the shaking funnels roar, with the Peter at the fore,
And the fenders grind and heave,
And the derricks clack and grate, as the tackle hooks the
crate,
And the fall-rope whines through the sheave ;

It

It 's ' Gang-plank up and in,' dear lass,
It 's ' Hawsers warp her through ! '
And it 's ' All clear aft ' on the old trail, our own trail,
    the out trail,
We're backing down on the Long Trail—the trail that is
    always new.

O the mutter overside, when the port-fog holds us
    tied,
  And the sirens hoot their dread !
When foot by foot we creep o'er the hueless viewless
    deep
  To the sob of the questing lead !
It 's down by the Lower Hope, dear lass,
With the Gunfleet Sands in view,
Till the Mouse swings green on the old trail, our own
    trail, the out trail,
And the Gull Light lifts on the Long Trail—the trail
    that is always new.

O the blazing tropic night, when the wake 's a welt of
    light
  That holds the hot sky tame,
And the steady fore-foot snores through the planet-
    powder'd floors
  Where the scared whale flukes in flame !
Her plates are scarr'd by the sun, dear lass,
And her ropes are taut with the dew,
For we're booming down on the old trail, our own trail,
    the out trail,
We're sagging south on the Long Trail—the trail that is
    always new.

Then home, get her home, where the drunken rollers
  comb,
  And the shouting seas drive by,
And the engines stamp and ring, and the wet bows reel
  and swing,
  And the Southern Cross rides high !
Yes, the old lost stars wheel back, dear lass,
That blaze in the velvet blue.
They're all old friends on the old trail, our own trail,
  the out trail,
They're God's own guides on the Long Trail—the trail
  that is always new.

Fly forward, O my heart, from the Foreland to the
  Start—
  We're steaming all too slow,
And it 's twenty thousand mile to our little lazy isle
  Where the trumpet-orchids blow !
You have heard the call of the off-shore wind
And the voice of the deep-sea rain ;
You have heard the song—how long ! how long !
  Pull out on the trail again !

The Lord knows what we may find, dear lass,
And the deuce knows what we may do—
But we're back once more on the old trail, our own trail,
  the out trail,
We're down, hull down on the Long Trail—the trail that is
  always new.

679.   *Recessional*

June 22, 1897.

GOD of our fathers, known of old—
   Lord of our far-flung battle-line—
Beneath whose awful Hand we hold
   Dominion over palm and pine—
Lord God of Hosts, be with us yet,
Lest we forget, lest we forget !

The tumult and the shouting dies—
   The captains and the kings depart—
Still stands Thine ancient sacrifice,
   An humble and a contrite heart.
Lord God of Hosts, be with us yet,
Lest we forget, lest we forget !

Far-call'd our navies melt away—
   On dune and headland sinks the fire—
Lo, all our pomp of yesterday
   Is one with Nineveh and Tyre !
Judge of the Nations, spare us yet,
Lest we forget, lest we forget !

If, drunk with sight of power, we loose
   Wild tongues that have not Thee in awe—
Such boasting as the Gentiles use
   Or lesser breeds without the Law—
Lord God of Hosts, be with us yet,
Lest we forget, lest we forget !

For heathen heart that puts her trust
   In reeking tube and iron shard—
All valiant dust that builds on dust,
   And guarding calls not Thee to guard—
For frantic boast and foolish word,
Thy Mercy on Thy People, Lord !

b. 1865

680.   *Rain on the Down*

NIGHT, and the down by the sea,
    And the veil of rain on the down;
And she came through the mist and the rain to me
From the safe warm lights of the town.

The rain shone in her hair,
    And her face gleam'd in the rain;
And only the night and the rain were there
As she came to me out of the rain.

681.   *Emmy*

EMMY'S exquisite youth and her virginal air,
    Eyes and teeth in the flash of a musical smile,
Come to me out of the past, and I see her there
As I saw her once for a while.

Emmy's laughter rings in my ears, as bright,
Fresh and sweet as the voice of a mountain brook,
And still I hear her telling us tales that night,
Out of Boccaccio's book.

There, in the midst of the villainous dancing-hall,
Leaning across the table, over the beer,
While the music madden'd the whirling skirts of the ball,
As the midnight hour drew near,

There with the women, haggard, painted and old,
One fresh bud in a garland wither'd and stale,
She, with her innocent voice and her clear eyes, told
Tale after shameless tale.

And

And ever the witching smile, to her face beguiled,
Paused and broaden'd, and broke in a ripple of fun,
And the soul of a child look'd out of the eyes of a child,
Or ever the tale was done.

O my child, who wrong'd you first, and began
First the dance of death that you dance so well ?
Soul for soul : and I think the soul of a man
Shall answer for yours in hell.

682.   *The Shadow*

WHEN I am walking sadly or triumphantly,
    With eyes that brood upon the smould'ring thought
        of you,
    And long desire and brief delight leap up anew,
Why is it that the eyes of all men turn to me ?

There 's pity in the eyes of women as they turn,
    And in the eyes of men self-pity, fear, desire :
    As those who see the far-off shadow of a fire
Gaze earnestly, and wonder if their roof-trees burn.

683.   *Credo*

EACH, in himself, his hour to be and cease
    Endures alone, but who of men shall dare,
    Sole with himself, his single burden bear,
All the long day until the night's release ?
Yet ere night falls, and the last shadows close,
    This labour of himself is each man's lot ;
    All he has gain'd of earth shall be forgot,
Himself he leaves behind him when he goes.

If he has any valiancy within,
  If he has made his life his very own,
  If he has loved or labour'd, and has known
A strenuous virtue, or a strenuous sin ;
Then, being dead, his life was not all vain,
  For he has saved what most desire to lose,
  And he has chosen what the few must choose,
Since life, once lived, shall not return again.
For of our time we lose so large a part
  In serious trifles, and so oft let slip
  The wine of every moment, at the lip
Its moment, and the moment of the heart.
We are awake so little on the earth,
  And we shall sleep so long, and rise so late,
  If there is any knocking at that gate
Which is the gate of death, the gate of birth.

RICHARD LE GALLIENNE

b. 1866

684.   *Song*

S HE 's somewhere in the sunlight strong,
  Her tears are in the falling rain,
She calls me in the wind's soft song,
  And with the flowers she comes again.

Yon bird is but her messenger,
  The moon is but her silver car.
Yea ! sun and moon are sent by her,
  And every wistful waiting star.

685.   *All Sung*

WHAT shall I sing when all is sung
    And every tale is told,
And in the world is nothing young
    That was not long since old ?

Why should I fret unwilling ears
    With old things sung anew
While voices from the old dead year
    Still go on singing too ?

A dead man singing of his maid
    Makes all my rhymes in vain,
Yet his poor lips must fade and fade,
    And mine shall sing again.

Why should I strive thro' weary moons
    To make my music true ?
Only the dead men know the tunes
    The live world dances to.

686.   *The Second Crucifixion*

LOUD mockers in the roaring street
    Say Christ is crucified again :
Twice pierced His gospel-bearing feet,
    Twice broken His great heart in vain.

I hear, and to myself I smile,
For Christ talks with me all the while.

884

RICHARD LE GALLIENNE

No angel now to roll the stone
 From off His unawaking sleep,
In vain shall Mary watch alone,
 In vain the soldiers vigil keep.

Yet while they deem my Lord is dead
My eyes are on His shining head.

Ah ! never more shall Mary hear
 That voice exceeding sweet and low
Within the garden calling clear :
 Her Lord is gone, and she must go.

Yet all the while my Lord I meet
In every London lane and street.

Poor Lazarus shall wait in vain,
 And Bartimæus still go blind ;
The healing hem shall ne'er again
 Be touch'd by suffering humankind.

Yet all the while I see them rest,
The poor and outcast, on His breast.

No more unto the stubborn heart
 With gentle knocking shall He plead,
No more the mystic pity start,
 For Christ twice dead is dead indeed.

So in the street I hear men say :
Yet Christ is with me all the day.

ERNEST DOWSON

1867-1900

687.   Non Sum Qualis Eram Bonae
Sub Regno Cynarae

LAST night, ah, yesternight, betwixt her lips and mine
    There fell thy shadow, Cynara ! thy breath was shed
Upon my soul between the kisses and the wine ;
And I was desolate and sick of an old passion,
    Yea, I was desolate and bow'd my head :
I have been faithful to thee, Cynara ! in my fashion.

All night upon mine heart I felt her warm heart beat,
Night-long within mine arms in love and sleep she lay ;
Surely the kisses of her bought red mouth were sweet ;
But I was desolate and sick of an old passion,
    When I awoke and found the dawn was gray :
I have been faithful to thee, Cynara ! in my fashion.

I have forgot much, Cynara ! gone with the wind,
Flung roses, roses, riotously with the throng,
Dancing, to put thy pale lost lilies out of mind ;
But I was desolate and sick of an old passion,
    Yea, all the time, because the dance was long :
I have been faithful to thee, Cynara ! in my fashion.

I cried for madder music and for stronger wine,
But when the feast is finish'd and the lamps expire,
Then falls thy shadow, Cynara ! the night is thine ;
And I am desolate and sick of an old passion,
    Yea, hungry for the lips of my desire :
I have been faithful to thee, Cynara ! in my fashion.

LIONEL JOHNSON

1867-1902

688.   *Winchester*

TO the fairest !
            Then to thee
Consecrate and bounden be,
Winchester ! this verse of mine.
Ah, that loveliness of thine !
To have lived enchaunted years
Free from sorrows, free from fears,
Where thy Tower's great shadow falls
Over those proud buttress'd walls ;
Whence a purpling glory pours
From high heaven's inheritors,
Throned within the arching stone !
To have wander'd, hush'd, alone,
Gently round thy fair, fern-grown
Chauntry of the Lilies, lying
Where the soft night winds go sighing
Round thy Cloisters, in moonlight
Branching dark, or touch'd with white :
Round old, chill aisles, where moon-smitten
Blanches the *Orate*, written
Under each worn old-world face
Graven on Death's holy place !

To the noblest !
                None but thee.
Blest our living eyes, that see
Half a thousand years fulfill'd
Of that age, which Wykeham will'd
Thee to win ; yet all unworn,
As upon that first March morn,

When

LIONEL JOHNSON

When thine honour'd city saw
Thy young beauty without flaw,
Born within her water-flowing
Ancient hollows, by wind-blowing
Hills enfolded evermore.
Thee, that lord of splendid lore,
Orient from old Hellas' shore,
Grocyn, had to mother : thee,
Monumental majesty
Of most high philosophy
Honours, in thy wizard Browne :
Tender Otway's dear renown,
Mover of a perfect pity,
Victim of the iron city,
Thine to cherish is : and thee,
Laureate of Liberty ;
Harper of the Highland faith,
Elf, and faëry, and wan wraith ;
Chaunting softly, chaunting slowly.
Minstrel of all melancholy ;
Master of all melody,
Made to cling round memory ;
Passion's poet, Evening's voice,
Collins glorified. Rejoice,
Mother ! in thy sons : for all
Love thine immemorial
Name, august and musical.
Not least he, who left thy side,
For his sire's, thine earlier pride.
Arnold : whom we mourn to-day,
Prince of song, and gone away
To his brothers of the bay :
Thine the love of all his years ;
His be now thy praising tears.

LIONEL JOHNSON

To the dearest !
   Ah, to thee !
Hast thou not in all to me
Mother, more than mother, been ?
Well t'ward thee may Mary Queen
Bend her with a mother's mien ;
Who so rarely dost express
An inspiring tenderness,
Woven with thy sterner strain,
Prelude of the world's true pain.
But two years, and still my feet
Found thy very stones more sweet
Than the richest fields elsewhere :
Two years, and thy sacred air
Still pour'd balm upon me, when
Nearer drew the world of men ;
When the passions, one by one,
All sprang upward to the sun ;
Two years have I lived, still thine :
Lost, thy presence ! gone, that shrine,
Where six years, what years ! were mine.
Music is the thought of thee ;
Fragrance all thy memory.
Those thy rugged Chambers old,
In their gloom and rudeness, hold
Dear remembrances of gold.
Some first blossoming of flowers
Made delight of all the hours ;
Greatness, beauty, all things fair
Made the spirit of thine air :
Old years live with thee ; thy sons
Walk with high companions.
Then, the natural joy of earth,
Joy of very health and birth !

     Hills

LIONEL JOHNSON

Hills, upon a summer noon :
Water Meads, on eves of June :
Chamber Court, beneath the moon :
Days of spring, on Twyford Down,
Or when autumn woods grew brown,
As they look'd when here came Keats,
Chaunting of autumnal sweets ;
Through this city of old haunts,
Murmuring immortal chaunts ;
As when Pope, art's earlier king,
Here, a child, did nought but sing,
Sang, a child, by nature's rule,
Round the trees of Twyford School :
Hours of sun beside Meads' Wall,
Ere the May began to fall ;
Watching the rooks rise and soar,
High from lime and sycamore :
Wanderings by old-world ways,
Walks and streets of ancient days ;
Closes, churches, arches, halls,
Vanish'd men's memorials.
There was beauty, there was grace,
Each place was an holy place :
There the kindly fates allow'd
Me too room ; and made me proud
(Prouder name I have not wist !)
With the name of Wykehamist.
These thy joys, and more than these :
Ah, to watch beneath thy trees,
Through long twilights linden-scented,
Sunsets, lingering, lamented,
In the purple west ; prevented,
Ere they fell, by evening star !
Ah, long nights of Winter ! far

Leaps and roars the faggot fire ;
Ruddy smoke rolls higher, higher,
Broken through by flame's desire ;
Circling faces glow, all eyes
Take the light ; deep radiance flies,
Merrily flushing overhead
Names of brothers, long since fled,
And fresh clusters in their stead,
Jubilant round fierce forest flame.
Friendship too must make her claim :
But what songs, what memories end,
When they tell of friend on friend ?
And for them I thank thy name.

Love alone of gifts, no shame
Lessens, and I love thee : yet
Sound it but of echoes, let
This my maiden music be
Of the love I bear to thee,
Witness and interpreter,
Mother mine : loved Winchester !

689.   *Oxford*

OVER, the four long years ! And now there rings
   One voice of freedom and regret : *Farewell !*
Now old remembrance sorrows, and now sings :
But song from sorrow, now, I cannot tell.

City of weather'd cloister and worn court ;
Grey city of strong towers and clustering spires :
Where art's fresh loveliness would first resort ;
Where lingering art kindled her latest fires !

Where

LIONEL JOHNSON

Where on all hands, wondrous with ancient grace,
Grace touch'd with age, rise works of goodliest men :
Next Wykeham's art obtain their splendid place
The zeal of Inigo, the strength of Wren.

Where at each coign of every antique street,
A memory hath taken root in stone :
There, Raleigh shone ; there, toil'd Franciscan feet ;
There, Johnson flinch'd not, but endured alone.

There, Shelley dream'd his white Platonic dreams ;
There, classic Landor throve on Roman thought ;
There, Addison pursued his quiet themes ;
There, smiled Erasmus, and there, Colet taught.

And there, O memory more sweet than all !
Lived he, whose eyes keep yet our passing light ;
Whose crystal lips Athenian speech recall ;
Who wears Rome's purple with least pride, most right.

That is the Oxford strong to charm us yet :
Eternal in her beauty and her past.
What, though her soul be vex'd ?   She can forget
Cares of an hour : only the great things last.

Only the gracious air, only the charm,
And ancient might of true humanities,
These nor assault of man, nor time, can harm :
Not these, nor Oxford with her memories.

Together have we walk'd with willing feet
Gardens of plenteous trees, bowering soft lawn ;
Hills whither Arnold wander'd ; and all sweet
June meadows, from the troubling world withdrawn;

LIONEL JOHNSON

Chapels of cedarn fragrance, and rich gloom
Pour'd from empurpled panes on either hand ;
Cool pavements, carved with legends of the tomb ;
Grave haunts, where we might dream, and understand.

Over, the four long years ! And unknown powers
Call to us, going forth upon our way :
Ah ! Turn we, and look back upon the towers
That rose above our lives, and cheer'd the day.

Proud and serene, against the sky they gleam :
Proud and secure, upon the earth they stand.
Our city hath the air of a pure dream,
And hers indeed is a Hesperian land.

Think of her so ! The wonderful, the fair,
The immemorial, and the ever young :
The city sweet with our forefathers' care :
The city where the Muses all have sung.

Ill times may be ; she hath no thought of time :
She reigns beside the waters yet in pride.
Rude voices cry : but in her ears the chime
Of full sad bells brings back her old springtide.

Like to a queen in pride of place, she wears
The splendour of a crown in Radcliffe's dome.
Well fare she—well ! As perfect beauty fares,
And those high places that are beauty's home.

690. *By the Statue of King Charles*
at Charing Cross

SOMBRE and rich, the skies,
  Great glooms, and starry plains;
Gently the night wind sighs;
Else a vast silence reigns.

The splendid silence clings
Around me: and around
The saddest of all Kings,
Crown'd, and again discrown'd.

Comely and calm, he rides
Hard by his own Whitehall.
Only the night wind glides:
No crowds, nor rebels, brawl.

Gone, too, his Court: and yet,
The stars his courtiers are:
Stars in their stations set;
And every wandering star.

Alone he rides, alone,
The fair and fatal King:
Dark night is all his own,
That strange and solemn thing.

Which are more full of fate:
The stars; or those sad eyes?
Which are more still and great:
Those brows, or the dark skies?

LIONEL JOHNSON

Although his whole heart yearn
In passionate tragedy,
Never was face so stern
With sweet austerity.

Vanquish'd in life, his death
By beauty made amends :
The passing of his breath
Won his defeated ends.

Brief life, and hapless ? Nay :
Through death, life grew sublime.
Speak after sentence ? Yea :
And to the end of time.

Armour'd he rides, his head
Bare to the stars of doom ;
He triumphs now, the dead,
Beholding London's gloom.

Our wearier spirit faints,
Vex'd in the world's employ :
His soul was of the saints ;
And art to him was joy.

King, tried in fires of woe !
Men hunger for thy grace :
And through the night I go,
Loving thy mournful face.

Yet, when the city sleeps,
When all the cries are still,
The stars and heavenly deeps
Work out a perfect will.

LIONEL JOHNSON

691.   *Cadgwith*

MY windows open to the autumn night,
   In vain I watch'd for sleep to visit me;
How should sleep dull mine ears, and dim my sight,
Who saw the stars, and listen'd to the sea?

Ah, how the City of our God is fair!
If, without sea, and starless though it be,
For joy of the majestic beauty there,
Men shall not miss the stars, nor mourn the sea.

GEORGE WILLIAM RUSSELL ('A. E.')

b. 1867

692.   *The Man to the Angel*

I HAVE wept a million tears;
   Pure and proud one, where are thine?
What the gain tho' all thy years
   In unbroken beauty shine?

All your beauty cannot win
   Truth we learn in pain and sighs:
You can never enter in
   To the circle of the wise.

They are but the slaves of light
   Who have never known the gloom,
And between the dark and light
   Will'd in freedom their own doom.

Think not, in your pureness there,
   That our pain but follows sin;
There are fires for those who dare
   Seek the throne of might to win.

Pure one, from your pride refrain :
Dark and lost amid the strife,
I am myriad years of pain
Nearer to the fount of life.

When defiance fierce is thrown
At the God to whom you bow,
Rest the lips of the Unknown
Tenderest upon my brow.

693. *By the Margin of the Great Deep*

WHEN the breath of twilight blows to flame the
misty skies,
All its vaporous sapphire, violet glow and silver gleam,
With their magic flood me through the gateway of the
eyes ;
I am one with the twilight's dream.

When the trees and skies and fields are one in dusky mood,
Every heart of man is rapt within the mother's breast :
Full of peace and sleep and dreams in the vasty quietude,
I am one with their hearts at rest.

From our immemorial joys of hearth and home and love
Stray'd away along the margin of the unknown tide,
All its reach of soundless calm can thrill me far above
Word or touch from the lips beside.

Aye, and deep and deep and deeper let me drink and draw
From the olden fountain more than light or peace or
dream,
Such primaeval being as o'erfills the heart with awe
Growing one with its silent stream.

694. *A Farewell*

ONLY in my deep heart I love you, sweetest heart.
　　Many another vesture hath the soul, I pray
Call me not forth from this.　If from the light I part
　　Only with clay I cling unto the clay.

And ah ! my bright companion, you and I must go
　　Our ways, unfolding lonely glories, not our own,
Not from each other gather'd, but an inward glow
　　Breathed by the Lone One to the seeker lone.

If for the heart's own sake we break the heart, we may,
　　When the last ruby drop dissolves in diamond light,
Meet in a deeper vesture in another day ;
　　Until that dawn, dear heart, good-night, good-night !

695. *A Memory of Earth*

IN the wet dusk silver-sweet,
　　Down the violet-scented ways,
As I moved with quiet feet
　　I was met by mighty days.

On the hedge the hanging dew
　　Glass'd the eve and stars and skies ;
While I gazed a madness grew
　　Into thunder'd battle-cries.

Where the hawthorn glimmer'd white,
　　Flashed the spear and fell the stroke,
Ah, what faces pale and bright
　　Where the dazzling battle broke !

There a hero-hearted queen
   With young beauty lit the van.
Gone ! the darkness flow'd between
   All the ancient wars of man.

While I paced the valley's gloom,
   Where the rabbits patter'd near,
Shone a temple and a tomb
   With a legend carven clear :

Time put by a myriad fates
   That her day might dawn in glory :
Death made wide a million gates
   So to close her tragic story.

LAURENCE HOUSMAN

b. 1867

696.   *The Settlers*

HOW green the earth, how blue the sky,
   How pleasant all the days that pass,
Here where the British settlers lie
   Beneath their cloaks of grass !

Here ancient peace resumes her round,
   And rich from toil stand hill and plain ;
Men reap and store ; but they sleep sound,
   The men who sow'd the grain.

Hard to the plough their hands they put,
   And wheresoe'er the soil had need
The furrow drave, and underfoot
   They sow'd themselves for seed.

Ah !

LAURENCE HOUSMAN

Ah ! not like him whose hand made yield
　The brazen kine with fiery breath,
And over all the Colchian field
　Strew'd far the seeds of death ;

Till, as day sank, awoke to war
　The seedlings of the dragon's teeth,
And death ran multiplied once more
　Across the hideous heath.

But rich in flocks be all these farms,
　And fruitful be the fields which hide
Brave eyes that loved the light, and arms
　That never clasp'd a bride !

O willing hearts turn'd quick to clay,
　Glad lovers holding death in scorn,
Out of the lives ye cast away
　The coming race is born.

DORA SIGERSON SHORTER

697.　　　*Ireland*

'TWAS the dream of a God,
　And the mould of His hand,
That you shook 'neath His stroke,
That you trembled and broke
　To this beautiful land.

Here He loosed from His hold
　A brown tumult of wings,
Till the wind on the sea
Bore the strange melody
　Of an island that sings.

900

He made you all fair,
　　You in purple and gold,
You in silver and green,
Till no eye that has seen
　　Without love can behold.

I have left you behind
　　In the path of the past,
With the white breath of flowers,
With the best of God's hours,
　　I have left you at last.

698.　　　*A Bird from the West*

AT the grey dawn, amongst the falling leaves,
　　A little bird outside my window swung,
High on a topmost branch he trill'd his song,
　　And ' Ireland ! Ireland ! Ireland ! ' ever sung.

' Take me,' I cried, ' back to my island home ;
　　Sweet bird, my soul shall ride between thy wings ' ;
For my lone spirit wide his pinions spread,
　　And home and home and home he ever sings.

We linger'd over Ulster stern and wild.
　　I call'd : ' Arise ! doth none remember me ? '
One turnèd in the darkness murmuring,
　　' How loud upon the breakers sobs the sea ! '

We rested over Connaught—whispering said :
　　' Awake, awake, and welcome ! I am here.'
One woke and shiver'd at the morning grey ;
　　' The trees, I never heard them sigh so drear.'

901　　　　　　　　　　　　We

We flew low over Munster.   Long I wept :
   ' You used to love me, love me once again ! '
They spoke from out the shadows wondering ;
   ' You'd think of tears, so bitter falls the rain.'

Long over Leinster linger'd we.   ' Good-bye !
   My best beloved, good-bye for evermore.'
Sleepless they toss'd and whisper'd to the dawn ;
   ' So sad a wind was never heard before.'

Was it a dream I dreamt ?   For yet there swings
   In the grey morn a bird upon the bough,
And ' Ireland ! Ireland ! Ireland ! ' ever sings.
   O, fair the breaking day in Ireland now !

699.　　　*The Gypsies' Road*

I SHALL go on the gypsies' road,
   The road that has no ending ;
For the sedge is brown on the lone lake side,
   The wild geese eastward tending.

I shall go as the unfetter'd wave,
   From shore to shore, forgetting
The grief that lies 'neath a roof-tree's shade,
   The years that bring regretting.

No law shall dare my wandering stay,
   No man my acres measure ;
The world was made for the gypsies' feet,
   The winding road for pleasure.

And I shall drift as the pale leaf stray'd,
   Whither the wild wind listed,
I shall sleep in the dark of the hedge,
   'Neath rose and thorn entwisted.

This was a call in the heart of the night,
  A whispering dream's dear treasure :
' The world was made for the nomads' feet,
  The winding road for pleasure.'

I stole at dawn from my roof-tree's shade,
  And the cares that it did cover ;
I flew to the heart of the fierce north wind,
  As a maid will greet her lover.

But a thousand hands did draw me back
  And bid me to their tending ;
I may not go on the gypsies' road—
  The road that has no ending.

MOIRA O'NEILL

700.   *A Broken Song*

*W*HERE *am I from ?* From the green hills of Erin.
  Have I no song then ? My songs are all sung.
What o' my love ? 'Tis alone I am farin',
Old grows my heart, an' my voice yet is young.

If she was tall ? Like a king's own daughter.
If she was fair ? Like a mornin' o' May.
When she'd come laughin' 'twas the runnin' wather,
When she'd come blushin' 'twas the break o' day.

Where did she dwell ? Where one'st I had my dwellin'.
Who loved her best ? There 's no one now will know.
Where is she gone ? Och, why would I be tellin' !
Where she is gone there I can never go.

903

701.   *The Fairy Lough*

LOUGHAREEMA ! Loughareema
  Lies so high among the heather ;
A little lough, a dark lough,
  The wather 's black an' deep.
Ould herons go a-fishin' there,
  An' seagulls all together
Float roun' the one green island
  On the fairy lough asleep.

Loughareema ! Loughareema !
  When the sun goes down at seven,
When the hills are dark an' *airy*,
  'Tis a curlew whistles sweet !
Then somethin' rustles all the reeds
  That stand so thick and even ;
A little wave runs up the shore
  An' flees as if on feet.

Loughareema ! Loughareema !
  Stars come out, an' stars are hidin' ;
The wather whispers on the stones,
  The flittherin' moths are free.
One'st before the mornin' light
  The Horsemen will come ridin'
Roun' and roun' the fairy lough,
  An' no one there to see !

HENRY DAWSON LOWRY

702. *Holiday*

LAST night God barr'd the portals of the East,
    And half-asleep I heard the sudden rain,
Most welcome, petulant at my window-pane :
And knew sweet Spring, Hell's prisoner, was released.

To-day the North-West comes across the hills,
Kindly but cold, and in the splendid bay
White are the waves, and white the flying spray,
More white the clouds wherewith the vast sky fills.

Sudden, the rain ! more swift, more icy cold
Than even hail : then, quick, the hearty sun !
And all day long, until the day is done,
Dance the gay daffodils in smocks of gold.

JANE BARLOW

703. *Christmas Rede*

FULL clear and bright this Christmas night range
    fields of Heaven fire-sown ;
But beam from star fled ne'er so far as mine Heart's Light
    hath flown
Since kindest eyes beneath yon skies fell dark and left me
    lone.

Ah, Mary blest ! on kingly quest wise men had miss'd
    their way,
But evermore they saw before a star of soothfast ray,
And follow'd, till its lamp stood still where He who lit
    it lay.

905   Such

Such light to friend their search had end, now mine doth
but begin,
Yet, mother sweet, may wand'ring feet anigh thy Mansion
win,
Above that roof no star for proof need shine to guide
them in.

If kindest eyes in olden wise smile soft to bid me learn
That Love, the flower of Earth's dim hour, hath found
a bower eterne
Shall burn rose-red while stars be sped ; tho' stars dropt
dead would burn.

LAURENCE BINYON

b. 1869

704.   *Invocation to Youth*

COME then, as ever, like the wind at morning !
   Joyous, O Youth, in the agèd world renew
Freshness to feel the eternities around it,
   Rain, stars and clouds, light and the sacred dew.
      The strong sun shines above thee :
      That strength, that radiance bring !
      If Winter come to Winter,
      When shall men hope for Spring ?

705. *The Little Dancers : a London Vision*

LONELY, save for a few faint stars, the sky
   Dreams ; and lonely, below, the little street
Into its gloom retires, secluded and shy.
Scarcely the dumb roar enters this soft retreat ;

And all is dark, save where come flooding rays
From a tavern window : there, to the brisk measure
Of an organ that down in an alley merrily plays,
Two children, all alone and no one by,
Holding their tatter'd frocks, through an airy maze
Of motion, lightly threaded with nimble feet,
Dance sedately : face to face they gaze,
Their eyes shining, grave with a perfect pleasure.

706.   *The Statues*

TARRY a moment, happy feet,
    That to the sound of laughter glide !
O glad ones of the evening street,
Behold what forms are at your side !

You conquerors of the toilsome day
Pass by with laughter, labour done ;
But these within their durance stay ;
Their travail sleeps not with the sun.

They, like dim statues without end,
Their patient attitudes maintain ;
Your triumphing bright course attend,
But from your eager ways abstain.

Now, if you chafe in secret thought,
A moment turn from light distress,
And see how Fate on these hath wrought,
Who yet so deeply acquiesce.

Behold

Behold them, stricken, silent, weak,
The maim'd, the mute, the halt, the blind,
Condemn'd in hopeless hope to seek
The thing which they shall never find.

They haunt the shadows of your ways
In masks of perishable mould :
Their souls a changing flesh arrays,
But they are changeless from of old.

Their lips repeat an empty call,
But silence wraps their thoughts around.
On them, like snow, the ages fall ;
Time muffles all this transient sound.

When Shalmaneser pitch'd his tent
By Tigris, and his flag unfurl'd,
And forth his summons proudly sent
Into the new unconquer'd world ;

Or when with spears Cambyses rode
Through Memphis and her bending slaves,
Or first the Tyrian gazed abroad
Upon the bright vast outer waves ;

When sages, star-instructed men,
To the young glory of Babylon
Foreknew no ending ; even then
Innumerable years had flown

Since first the chisel in her hand
Necessity, the sculptor, took,
And in her spacious meaning plann'd
These forms, and that eternal look ;

LAURENCE BINYON

These foreheads, moulded from afar,
These soft, unfathomable eyes,
Gazing from darkness, like a star ;
These lips, whose grief is to be wise.

As from the mountain marble rude
The growing statue rises fair,
She from immortal patience hew'd
The limbs of ever-young despair.

There is no bliss so new and dear,
It hath not them far-off allured.
All things that we have yet to fear
They have already long endured.

Nor is there any sorrow more
Than hath ere now befallen these,
Whose gaze is as an opening door
On wild interminable seas.

O Youth, run fast upon thy feet,
With full joy haste thee to be fill'd,
And out of moments brief and sweet
Thou shalt a power for ages build.

Does thy heart falter ?   Here, then, seek
What strength is in thy kind !   With pain
Immortal bow'd, these mortals weak
Gentle and unsubdued remain.

707.   *Amasis*

I

'O KING AMASIS, hail !
        News from thy friend, the King Polycrates !
My oars have never rested on the seas
From Samos, nor on land my horse's hoofs,
Till I might tell my tale.'
Sais, the sacred city, bask'd her roofs
And gardens whispering in the western light ;
Men throng'd abroad to taste the coming cool of night :
Only the palace closed
Unechoing courts, where by the lake reposed,
Wide-eyed, the enthronèd shapes of Memphian deities ;
And King Amasis in the cloister'd shade,
That guards them, of a giant colonnade,
Paced musing ; there he ponder'd mysteries
That are the veils of truth ;
For mid those gods of grave, ignoring smile
Large auguries he spell'd,
Forgot the spears, the tumults of his youth,
And strangled Apries, and the redden'd Nile.
Now turning, he beheld,
Half in a golden shadow and half touch'd with flame,
The white-robed stranger from the Grecian isle,
And heard pronounced his name.

II

' Welcome from Samos, friend !
Good news, I think, thou bearest in thy mien,'
The king spoke welcoming with voice serene.
' How is it with Polycrates, thy lord ?
Peace on his name attend !

Would he were here in Egypt, and his sword
Could sheathe, and we at god-like ease discourse
Of counsel no ignoble needs enforce,
And take august regale
Of wisdom from the Powers whose purpose cannot fail.
I, too, O man of Samos, bred to war,
Pass'd youth, pass'd manhood, in a life of blood ;
But many victories bring the heart no certain good.
Would that he too might tease his fate no more,
And I might see his face
In presence of my land's ancestral Powers,—
See, from their countenance, what a grandeur beams !
Thou know'st I love thy race ;
Bright wits ye have, skill in adventurous schemes ;
But deeper life is ours :
Fed by these springs, your strength might bless the
    world.   But lo !
The light begins to fade from the high towers.
Thy errand let me know.'

III

' Thus saith Polycrates :
The counsel which thou wrotest me is well ;
For, seeing how full crops my granaries swell,
How all winds waft me to prosperity,
How I gain all with ease,
And my raised banner pledges victory,
Thou didst advise me cast away what most
Brought pleasure to my eyes and seem'd of rarest cost.
And after heavy thought
I chose the ring which Theodorus wrought,
My famous emerald, where young Phaëthon
Shoots headlong with pale limbs through glowing air,
While green waves from beneath toss white drops to his
    hair.

911   A long

A long time, very loth, I gazed thereon ;
For this cause, thought I, men most envy me ;
I took a ship, and fifty beating oars
Bore me far out to sea :
I stood upon the poop—but wherefore tell
What now is rumour'd round all Asian shores ?
Say only I did well,
Who the world's envy treasured yet in deep waves drown'd.
Homeward I came, and mourn'd within my doors
Three days, nor solace found.'

IV

Amasis without word
Listens, dark-brow'd : the Samian speaks anew :
' Let not the king this thing so deeply rue ;
Truly the gem was of imperial price,
Nay even, men averr'd,
Coveted more than wealthy satrapies,
Nor twenty talents could its loss redeem :
Yet hear ! the Gods are more benignant than men dream.
Thus saith my lord : The moon
Not once had waned, when as I sat at noon
Within my palace court above the Lydian bay,
They led before me with much wondering noise
A fisherman ; between two staggering boys
Slung heavily a fish he brought, that day
Caught in his bursting net,
A royal fish for royal destiny !
I marvell'd ; but amaze broke deeper yet
To recognise Heaven's hand,
When from its cloven belly (surely high
In that large grace I stand)
Dazzled my eyes with light, my heart with joy, the ring
Restored !—Why rendest thou thy robe, and why
Lamentest thou, O king ? '

V

' O lamentable news ! '
Amasis cried ; ' now have the Gods indeed
Doom on thy head, Polycrates, decreed !
I fear'd already, when I heard thy joy
Must need stoop down to choose
For sacrifice, loss of a shining toy,
Searching the suburbs only of content,
Not thy heart's home : what God this blindness on thee
    sent ?
Gone was thy ring ; yet how
Was thy soul clear'd, or thou more greatly thou ?
Were vain things vainer, or the dear more dear ?
Hast thou, bent gazing o'er thy child asleep,
Thoughts springing, tender as new leaves ? Deep, deep,
Deep as thy inmost hope, as thy most sacred fear,
Thou shouldst have sought the pain
That changes earth's wide aspect in an hour,
Heaved by abysmal throes !
Ah, then our pleasant refuges are vain ;
Yet, thrill'd, the soul assembles all her power,
And clear'd by peril glows,
Seeing immortal hosts array'd upon her side !
Blind man, the scornful Gods thy offering slight :
My fears are certified.'

VI

Swift are the thoughts of fear.
But Fate at will rides swifter far ; and lo !
Even as Amasis bows to boded woe,
Even as his robe, with a sad cry, he rends,
The accomplishment is here.
The sun that from the Egyptian plain descends,

Blessing

Blessing with holier shade
Those strange gods dreaming throned by the vast colon-
nade,
Burns o'er the northern sea,
Firing the peak of Asian Mycale,
Firing a cross raised on the mountain side !
Polycrates the Fortunate hangs there :
The false Oroetes hath him in a snare ;
Now with his quivering limbs his soul is crucified ;
And in his last hour first
He tastes the extremity of loss ; he burns
With ecstasy of thirst ;
Nought recks he even of his dearest now,
Moaning for breath ; no pity he discerns
On the dark Persian's brow.
Grave on his milk-white horse, in silks of Sidon shawl'd,
The Satrap smiles, and on his finger turns
The all-envied emerald.

708.   *Day's End*

WHEN I am weary, throng'd with the cares of the
vain day
That tease as harsh winds tease the unresting autumn
boughs,
I still my mind at evening and put all else away
But the image of my Love, where all my hopes I house.

The thoughts of her fall gently as the gentleness of snow
That after storm makes smoothness in the ways that are
rough ;
White with a hush of beauty over my heart they grow
To the peace of which my heart can never hold enough.

T STURGE MOORE

709. Sent from Egypt with a Fair Robe of Tissue to a Sicilian Vinedresser.

B.C. 276

PUT out to sea, if wine thou wouldest make
   Such as is made in Cos : when open boat
May safely launch, advice of pilots take ;
And find the deepest bottom, most remote
From all encroachment of the crumbling shore,
Where no fresh stream tempers the rich salt wave,
Forcing rash sweetness on sage ocean's brine ;
As youthful shepherds pour
Their first love forth to Battos gnarl'd and grave,
Fooling shrewd age to bless some fond design.

Not after storm ! but when, for a long spell,
No white-maned horse has raced across the blue,
Put from the beach ! lest troubled be the well—
Less pure thy draught than from such depth were due.
Fast close thy largest jars, prepared and clean !
Next weight each buoyant womb down through the flood,
Far down ! when, with a cord the lid remove,
And it will fill unseen,
Swift as a heart Love smites sucks back the blood :—
This bubbles, deeper born than sighs, shall prove.

If thy bow'd shoulders ache, as thou dost haul—
Those groan who climb with rich ore from the mine ;
Labour untold round Ilion girt a wall ;
A god toil'd that Achilles' arms might shine ;

Think

Think of these things and double knit thy will!
Then, should the sun be hot on thy return,
Cover thy jars with piles of bladder weed,
Dripping, and fragrant still
From sea-wolds where it grows like bracken-fern:
A grapnel dragg'd will soon supply thy need.

Home to a tun convey thy precious freight!
Wherein, for thirty days, it should abide,
Closed, yet not quite closed from the air, and wait
While, through dim stillness, slowly doth subside
Thick sediment. The humour of a day,
Which has defeated youth and health and joy,
Down, through a dreamless sleep, will settle thus,
Till riseth maiden gay,
Set free from all glooms past—or else a boy
Once more a school-friend worthy Troilus.

Yet to such cool wood tank some dream might dip:
Vision of Aphrodite sunk to sleep,
Or of some sailor let down from a ship,
Young, dead, and lovely, while across the deep
Through the calm night his hoarse-voiced comrades
    chaunt—
So far at sea, they cannot reach the land
To lay him perfect in the warm brown earth.
Pray that such dreams there haunt!
While, through damp darkness, where thy tun doth stand,
Cold salamanders sidle round its girth.

Gently draw off the clear and tomb it yet,
For other twenty days, in cedarn casks!
Where through trance, surely, prophecy will set;
As, dedicated to light temple-tasks,

916

The young priest dreams the unknown mystery.
Through Ariadne, knelt disconsolate
In the sea's marge, so well'd back warmth which throbb'd
With nuptial promise : she
Turn'd ; and, half-choked through dewy glens, some great,
Some magic drone of revel coming sobb'd.

Of glorious fruit, indeed, must be thy choice !
Such as has fully ripen'd on the branch,
Such as due rain, then sunshine, made rejoice,
Which, pulp'd and colour'd, now deep bloom doth blanch !
Clusters like odes for victors in the games,
Strophe on strophe globed, pure nectar all !
Spread such to dry ! if Helios grant thee grace,
Exposed unto his flames
Two days, or, if not, three, or, should rain fall,
Stretch them on hurdles in the house four days !

Grapes are not sharded chestnuts, which the tree
Lets fall to burst them on the ground, where red
Rolls forth the fruit, from white-lined wards set free,
And all undamaged glows 'mid husks it shed ;
Nay, they are soft and should be singly stripp'd
From off the bunch, by maiden's dainty hand,
Then dropp'd through the cool silent depth to sink
(Coy, as herself hath slipp'd,
Bathing, from shelves in caves along the strand)
Till round each dark grape water barely wink ;

Since some nine measures of sea-water fill
A butt of fifty, ere the plump fruit peep,
Like sombre dolphin shoals when nights are still,
Which penn'd in Proteus' wizard circle sleep,

And

And 'twixt them glinting curves of silver glance
If Zephyr, dimpling dark calm, counts them o'er.
Let soak thy fruit for two days thus, then tread!
While bare-legg'd bumpkins dance,
Bright from thy bursting press arch'd spouts shall pour,
And gurgling torrents towards thy vats run red.

Meanwhile the maidens, each with wooden rake,
Drag back the skins and laugh at aprons splash'd;
Or youths rest, boasting how their brown arms ache,
So fast their shovels for so long have flash'd,
Baffling their comrades' legs with mounting heaps.
Treble their labour! still the happier they,
Who, at this genial task, wear out long hours,
Till vast night round them creeps,
When soon the torch-light dance whirls them away;
For gods, who love wine, double all their powers.

Iacchus is the always grateful god!
His vineyards are more fair than gardens far;
Hanging, like those of Babylon, they nod
O'er each Ionian cliff and hill-side scar!
While Cypris lends him saltness, depth, and peace;
The brown earth yields him sap for richest green;
And he has borrow'd laughter from the sky;
Wildness from winds; and bees
Bring honey.—Then choose casks which thou hast seen
Are leakless, very wholesome, and quite dry!

That Coan wine the very finest is,
I do assure thee, who have travell'd much
And learn'd to judge of diverse vintages.
Faint not before the toil! this wine is such

T. STURGE MOORE

As tempteth princes launch long pirate barks ;—
From which may Zeus protect Sicilian bays,
And, ere long, me safe home from Egypt bring,
Letting no black-sail'd sharks
Scent this king's gifts, for whom I sweeten praise
With those same songs thou didst to Chloë sing !

I wrote them 'neath the vine-cloak'd elm, for thee.
Recall those nights ! our couches were a load
Of scented lentisk ; upward, tree by tree,
Thy father's orchard sloped, and past us flow'd
A stream sluiced for his vineyards ; when, above,
The apples fell, they on to us were roll'd,
But kept us not awake,—O Laco, own
How thou didst rave of love !
Now art thou staid, thy son is three years old ;
But I, who made thee love-songs, live alone.

Muse thou at dawn o'er thy yet slumbering wife !—
Not chary of her best was Nature there,
Who, though a third of her full gift of life
Was spent, still added beauties still more rare ;
What calm slow days, what holy sleep at night,
Evolved her for long twilight trystings fraught
With panic blushes and tip-toe surmise :
And then, what mystic might—
All, with a crowning boon, through travail brought !
Consider this and give thy best likewise !

Ungrateful be not ! Laco, ne'er be that !
Well worth thy while to make such wine 'twould be :
I see thy red face 'neath thy broad straw hat,
I see thy house, thy vineyards, Sicily !—

Thou

Thou dost demur, good, but too easy, friend :
Come put those doubts away ! thou hast strong lads,
Brave wenches ; on the steep beach lolls thy ship,
Where vine-clad slopes descend,
Sheltering our bay, that headlong rillet glads,
Like a stripp'd child fain in the sea to dip.

710.   *A Duet*

' FLOWERS nodding gaily, scent in air,
    Flowers posied, flowers for the hair,
Sleepy flowers, flowers bold to stare——'
        ' O pick me some ! '

' Shells with lip, or tooth, or bleeding gum,
Tell-tale shells, and shells that whisper *Come*,
Shells that stammer, blush, and yet are dumb——'
        ' O let me hear.'

' Eyes so black they draw one trembling near,
Brown eyes, caverns flooded with a tear,
Cloudless eyes, blue eyes so windy clear——'
        ' O look at me ! '

' Kisses sadly blown across the sea,
Darkling kisses, kisses fair and free,
Bob-a-cherry kisses 'neath a tree——'
        ' O give me one ! '

Thus sang a king and queen in Babylon.

ARTHUR SHEARLY CRIPPS

b. 1869

711. ‘ *Les Belles Roses Sans Mercie* ’

A.D. 1465

‘O pity, pity, gentle heaven, pity!
.   .   .   .   .   .
Wither one rose, and let the other flourish!
If you contend, a thousand lives must wither!’
King Henry VI, Part III, Act ii, Sc. 5.

HEIGH ! brother mine, art a-waking or a-sleeping ?
    Mind’st that merry moon of roses a many summers
    fled ?
Mind’st thou the green and the dancing and the leaping ?
Mind’st thou the haycocks and the moon above them
    creeping ?
Mind’st thou how soft were the pillows of our heaping ?
Mind’st thou our dole when the merry day was sped ?
I do mind how every night
Thou would’st pull me roses white,
Ancient sign of our proud line, argent rose on verdant
    bough !

Heigh ! sweetheart mine, art a-waking or a-sleeping ?
See’st again the roses that blossom’d long ago ?
See’st again the garden with its paths so still and shady ?
See’st again the dew lie as beads for night’s white lady ?
See’st thou aught else but the blue eyne of thy maidie ?
See’st thou their brimming in their pity of thy woe ?
Sweet, I see thee offer up
Roses red as wine in cup,
Such befit (thou say’st it) golden head and lily brow !

921   Heigh

Heigh ho ! ye twain, that should wake in lieu of sleeping !
Rue ye that rose-time when the roses all were reft ?
Ruest thou, sweet heart, that the favour red thou worest?
Ruest thou, my brother, that the badge of snow thou
    borest ?
Rue ye that noon when the fight flash'd thro' the forest ?
Rue ye the maid's tears so life-long lonely left ?
Rose of white, and rose of red,
That did each one claim her dead,
Twining be at amity round about my window now !

HILAIRE BELLOC

b. 1870

712.   *The South Country*

WHEN I am living in the Midlands
    That are sodden and unkind,
I light my lamp in the evening :
    My work is left behind ;
And the great hills of the South Country
    Come back into my mind.

The great hills of the South Country
    They stand along the sea ;
And it's there walking in the high woods
    That I could wish to be,
And the men that were boys when I was a boy
    Walking along with me.

The men that live in North England
    I saw them for a day :

Their hearts are set upon the waste fells,
   Their skies are fast and grey ;
From their castle-walls a man may see
   The mountains far away.

The men that live in West England
   They see the Severn strong,
A-rolling on rough water brown
   Light aspen leaves along.
They have the secret of the Rocks,
   And the oldest kind of song.

But the men that live in the South Country
   Are the kindest and most wise,
They get their laughter from the loud surf,
   And the faith in their happy eyes
Comes surely from our Sister the Spring
   When over the sea she flies ;
The violets suddenly bloom at her feet,
   She blesses us with surprise.

I never get between the pines
   But I smell the Sussex air ;
Nor I never come on a belt of sand
   But my home is there.
And along the sky the line of the Downs
   So noble and so bare.

A lost thing could I never find,
   Nor a broken thing mend :
And I fear I shall be all alone
   When I get towards the end.
Who will there be to comfort me
   Or who will be my friend ?

I will

I will gather and carefully make my friends
    Of the men of the Sussex Weald,
They watch the stars from silent folds,
    They stiffly plough the field.
By them and the God of the South Country
    My poor soul shall be heal'd.

If I ever become a rich man,
    Or if ever I grow to be old,
I will build a house with deep thatch
    To shelter me from the cold,
And there shall the Sussex songs be sung
    And the story of Sussex told.

I will hold my house in the high wood
    Within a walk of the sea,
And the men that were boys when I was a boy
    Shall sit and drink with me.

713.   *Song*

INVITING THE INFLUENCE OF A YOUNG LADY UPON
THE OPENING YEAR

YOU wear the morning like your dress
    And are with mastery crown'd ;
When as you walk your loveliness
Goes shining all around :
Upon your secret, smiling way
Such new contents were found,
The Dancing Loves made holiday
On that delightful ground.

924

Then summon April forth, and send
Commandment through the flowers ;
About our woods your grace extend,
A queen of careless hours.
For O ! not Vera veil'd in rain,
Nor Dian's sacred Ring,
With all her royal nymphs in train
Could so lead on the Spring.

714.   *The Night*

MOST Holy Night, that still dost keep
   The keys of all the doors of sleep,
To me when my tired eyelids close
      Give thou repose.

And let the far lament of them
That chaunt the dead day's requiem
Make in my ears, who wakeful lie,
      Soft lullaby.

Let them that guard the hornèd Moon
By my bedside their memories croon.
So shall I have new dreams and blest
      In my brief rest.

Fold thy great wings about my face,
Hide day-dawn from my resting-place,
And cheat me with thy false delight,
      Most Holy Night.

b. 1870

715.   *Impression de Nuit: London*

SEE what a mass of gems the city wears
   Upon her broad live bosom ! row on row
Rubies and emeralds and amethysts glow.
See ! that huge circle, like a necklace, stares
With thousands of bold eyes to heaven, and dares
   The golden stars to dim the lamps below,
   And in the mirror of the mire I know
The moon has left her image unawares.

That 's the great town at night : I see her breasts,
   Prick'd out with lamps they stand like huge black towers,
   I think they move ! I hear her panting breath.
And that 's her head where the tiara rests.
   And in her brain, through lanes as dark as death,
   Men creep like thoughts . . . The lamps are like pale
     flowers.

716.   *To Olive*

I HAVE been profligate of happiness
   And reckless of the world's hostility,
   The blessèd part has not been given to me
Gladly to suffer fools, I do confess
I have enticed and merited distress,
   By this, that I have never bow'd the knee
   Before the shrine of wise Hypocrisy,
Nor worn self-righteous anger like a dress.

Yet write you this, sweet one, when I am dead :
   ' Love like a lamp sway'd over all his days
   And all his life was like a lamp-lit chamber,
Where is no nook, no chink unvisited
   By the soft affluence of golden rays,
   And all the room is bathed in liquid amber.'

926

LORD ALFRED DOUGLAS

717.   *The Green River*

I KNOW a green grass path that leaves the field,
  And like a running river, winds along
  Into a leafy wood where is no throng
Of birds at noon-day, and no soft throats yield
Their music to the moon. The place is seal'd,
  An unclaim'd sovereignty of voiceless song,
  And all the unravish'd silences belong
To some sweet singer lost or unreveal'd.

So is my soul become a silent place.
  Oh may I wake from this uneasy night
    To find a voice of music manifold.
Let it be shape of sorrow with wan face,
  Or Love that swoons on sleep, or else delight
    That is as wide-eyed as a marigold.

PERCY ADDLESHAW (HEMINGWAY)

b. 1870

718.   *The Happy Wanderer*

HE is the happy wanderer who goes
  Singing upon his way, with eyes awake
  To every scene, with ears alert to take
The sweetness of all sounds, who loves and knows
The secrets of the highway, holds the rose
  Is fairer for the wounds the briars make ;
  He welcomes rain that he his thirst may slake,
The sun because it dries his dripping clothes :

Treasures experience beyond all store,
  Careless if pain or pleasure he shall win,
So that his knowledge widen more and more :
  Ready each hour to worship or to sin,
Until tired, wise, content, he halts before
  The sign o' The Grave, a cool and quiet inn.

JOHN M. SYNGE

1871-1909

719.   *On an Island*

YOU'VE pluck'd a curlew, drawn a hen,
   Wash'd the shirts of seven men,
You've stuff'd my pillow, stretch'd the sheet,
And fill'd the pan to wash your feet,
You've coop'd the pullets, wound the clock,
And rinsed the young men's drinking crock ;
And now we'll dance to jigs and reels,
Nail'd boots chasing girls' naked heels,
Until your father'll start to snore,
And Jude, now you're married, will stretch on the floor.

720.   *A Question*

I ASK'D if I got sick and died, would you
   With my black funeral go walking too,
If you'd stand close to hear them talk or pray
While I'm let down in that steep bank of clay.

And, No, you said, for if you saw a crew
Of living idiots pressing round that new
Oak coffin—they alive, I dead beneath
That board—you'd rave and rend them with your teeth.

JOHN SWINNERTON PHILLIMORE

721.   *In a Meadow*

THIS is the place
　　Where far from the unholy populace
The daughter of Philosophy and Sleep
　　　Her court doth keep,
Sweet Contemplation.   To her service bound
　　　Hover around
The little amiable summer airs,
　　　Her courtiers.

　　　The deep black soil
Makes mute her palace-floors with thick trefoil ;
The grasses sagely nodding overhead
　　　Curtain her bed ;
And lest the feet of strangers overpass
　　　Her walls of grass,
Gravely a little river goes his rounds
　　　To beat the bounds.

　　　—No bustling flood
To make a tumult in her neighbourhood,
But such a stream as knows to go and come
　　　Discreetly dumb.
Therein are chambers tapestried with weeds
　　　And screen'd with reeds ;
For roof the waterlily-leaves serene
　　　Spread tiles of green.

　　　The sun's large eye
Falls soberly upon me where I lie ;
For delicate webs of immaterial haze
　　　Refine his rays.

1346   H h   929   The

The air is full of music none knows what,
    Or half-forgot ;
The living echo of dead voices fills
    The unseen hills.

    I hear the song
Of cuckoo answering cuckoo all day long ;
And know not if it be my inward sprite
    For my delight
Making remember'd poetry appear
    As sound in the ear :
Like a salt savour poignant in the breeze
    From distant seas.

    Dreams without sleep,
And sleep too clear for dreaming and too deep ;
And Quiet very large and manifold
    About me roll'd ;
Satiety, that momentary flower,
    Stretch'd to an hour :
These are her gifts which all mankind may use,
    And all refuse.

WALTER DE LA MARE

b. 1873

722.   *An Epitaph*

HERE lies a most beautiful lady,
    Light of step and heart was she :
I think she was the most beautiful lady
    That ever was in the West Country.
But beauty vanishes ; beauty passes ;
    However rare, rare it be ;
And when I crumble who shall remember
    This lady of the West Country ?

WALTER DE LA MARE

723.   *The Listeners*

' IS there anybody there ? ' said the Traveller,
   Knocking on the moonlit door ;
And his horse in the silence champ'd the grasses
   Of the forest's ferny floor :
And a bird flew up out of the turret,
   Above the Traveller's head :
And he smote upon the door again a second time ;
   ' Is there anybody there ? ' he said.
But no one descended to the Traveller ;
   No head from the leaf-fringed sill
Lean'd over and look'd into his grey eyes,
   Where he stood perplex'd and still.
But only a host of phantom listeners
   That dwelt in the lone house then
Stood listening in the quiet of the moonlight
   To that voice from the world of men :
Stood thronging the faint moonbeams on the dark stair,
   That goes down to the empty hall,
Hearkening in an air stirr'd and shaken
   By the lonely Traveller's call.
And he felt in his heart their strangeness,
   Their stillness answering his cry,
While his horse moved, cropping the dark turf,
   'Neath the starr'd and leafy sky ;
For he suddenly smote on the door, even
   Louder, and lifted his head :—
' Tell them I came, and no one answer'd,
   That I kept my word,' he said.
Never the least stir made the listeners,
   Though every word he spake
Fell echoing through the shadowiness of the still house
   From the one man left awake :

Ay,

Ay, they heard his foot upon the stirrup,
  And the sound of iron on stone,
And how the silence surged softly backward,
  When the plunging hoofs were gone.

HAROLD MONRO

b. 1879

724. *The Wind*

So wayward is the wind to-night
  'Twill send the planets tumbling down ;
And all the waving trees are dight
  In gauzes wafted from the moon.

Faint streaky wisps of roaming cloud
  Are swiftly from the mountains swirl'd ;
The wind is like a floating shroud
  Wound light about the shivering world.

I think I see a little star
  Entangled in a knotty tree,
As trembling fishes captured are
  In nets from the eternal sea.

There seems a bevy in the air
  Of spirits from the sparkling skies :
There seems a maiden with her hair
  All tumbled in my blinded eyes.

O, how they whisper, how conspire,
  And shrill to one another call !
I fear that, if they cannot tire,
  The moon, her shining self, will fall.

Blow ! Scatter even if you will
   Like spray the stars about mine eyes !
Wind, overturn the goblet, spill
   On me the everlasting skies !

725. *At a Country Dance in Provence*

COMRADES, when the air is sweet,
   It is fair, in stately measure,
With a sound of gliding feet,
It is fair and very meet
To be join'd in pleasure.
Listen to the rhythmic beat :
Let us mingle, move and sway
Solemnly as at some rite
Of a festive mystic god,
While the sunlight holds the day.
Comrades, is it not delight
To be govern'd by the rod
Of the music, and to go
Moving, moving, moving slow ?
Very stately are your ways,
Stately—and the southern glow
Of the sun is in your eyes :
Under lids inclining low
All the light of harvest days,
And the gleam of summer skies
Tenderly reflected lies.
May I not be one of you
Even for this little space ?
Humbly I am fain to sue
That our arms may interlace.
I am otherwise I know ;
Many books have made me sad :

Yet

Yet indeed your stately slow
Motion and its rhythmic flow
Drive me, drive me, drive me mad.
Must I now, as always, gaze
Patiently from far away
At the pageant of the days ?—
Only let me live to-day !
For your hair is ebon black,
And your eyes celestial blue ;
For your measure is so true,
Slowly forward, slowly back—
I would fain be one of you.
Comrades, comrades !—but the sound
Of the music with a start
Ceases, and you pass me by.
Slowly from the dancing-ground
To the tavern you depart.
All the earth is silent grown
After so much joy, and I
Suddenly am quite alone
With the beating of my heart.

ALFRED NOYES

726.   *The World's May-Queen*

WHEN Spring comes back to England
And crowns her brows with May,
Round the merry moonlit world
She goes the greenwood way :
She throws a rose to Italy,
A fleur-de-lys to France ;
But round her regal morris-ring
The seas of England dance.

When Spring comes back to England
   And dons her robe of green,
There's many a nation garlanded,
   But England is the Queen;
She's Queen, she's Queen of all the world
   Beneath the laughing sky,
For the nations go a-Maying
   When they hear the New Year cry—

'Come over the water to England,
   My old love, my new love,
Come over the water to England
   In showers of flowery rain;
Come over the water to England,
   April, my true love,
And tell the heart of England
   The Spring is here again!'

727.   *Our Lady of the Sea*

QUEEN VENUS wander'd away with a cry,—
   N'oserez-vous, mon bel ami?—
For the purple wound in Adon's thigh;
   Je vous en prie, pity me;
With a bitter farewell from sky to sky,
   And a moan, a moan from sea to sea;
N'oserez-vous, mon bel, mon bel,
   N'oserez-vous, mon bel ami?

The soft Aegean heard her sigh,—
   N'oserez-vous, mon bel ami?—
Heard the Spartan hills reply
   Je vous en prie, pity me;

935   Spain

Spain was aware of her drawing nigh
　　Foot-gilt from the blossoms of Italy ;
N'oserez-vous, mon bel, mon bel,
　　N'oserez-vous, mon bel ami ?

In France they heard her voice go by,—
　　N'oserez-vous, mon bel ami ?—
And on the May-wind droop and die,
　　Je vous en prie, pity me ;
Your maidens choose their loves, but I—
　　White as I came from the foam-white sea,
N'oserez-vous, mon bel, mon bel,
　　N'oserez-vous, mon bel ami ?

The warm red-meal-wing'd butterfly,—
　　N'oserez-vous, mon bel ami ?—
Beat on her breast in the golden rye,—
　　Je vous en prie, pity me ;
Stain'd her breast with a dusty dye
　　Red as the print of a kiss might be !
N'oserez-vous, mon bel, mon bel,
　　N'oserez-vous, mon bel ami ?

Is there no land, afar or nigh,—
　　N'oserez-vous, mon bel ami ?—
But dreads the kiss o' the sea ?　Ah, why—
　　Je vous en prie, pity me !—
Why will ye cling to the loves that die ?
　　Is earth all Adon to my plea ?
N'oserez-vous, mon bel, mon bel,
　　N'oserez-vous, mon bel ami ?

Under the warm blue summer sky,—
　　N'oserez-vous, mon bel ami ?—

With outstretch'd arms and a low long sigh,—
   Je vous en prie, pity me !—
Over the Channel they saw her fly
   To the white-cliff'd island that crowns the sea—
N'oserez-vous, mon bel, mon bel,
   N'oserez-vous, mon bel ami ?

England laugh'd as her queen drew nigh,—
   N'oserez-vous, mon bel ami ?—
To the white-wall'd cottages gleaming high ;
   Je vous en prie, pity me !
They drew her in with a joyful cry
   To the hearth where she sits with a babe on her knee,
She has turn'd her moan to a lullaby,
   She is nursing a son to the kings of the sea—-
N'oserez-vous, mon bel, mon bel,
   N'oserez-vous, mon bel ami ?

728.   *A Japanese Love-Song*

THE young moon is white,
   But the willows are blue :
Your small lips are red,
   But the great clouds are gray :
The waves are so many
   That whisper to you ;
But my love is only
   One flight of spray.

The bright drops are many,
   The dark wave is one :
The dark wave subsides,
   And the bright sea remains !

        And

And wherever, O singing
    Maid, you may run,
You are one with the world
    For all your pains.

Tho' the great skies are dark,
    And your small feet are white,
Tho' your wide eyes are blue
    And the closed poppies red,
Tho' the kisses are many
    That colour the night,
They are linkèd like pearls
    On one golden thread.

Were the gray clouds not made
    For the red of your mouth ;
The ages for flight
    Of the butterfly years ;
The sweet of the peach
    For the pale lips of drouth,
The sunlight of smiles
    For the shadow of tears ?

Love, Love is the thread
    That has pierced them with bliss !
All their hues are but notes
    In one world-wide tune :
Lips, willows and waves,
    We are one as we kiss,
And your face and the flowers
    Faint away in the moon.

938

729. *On the Death of Francis Thompson*

HOW grandly glow the bays
   Purpureally enwound
With those rich thorns, the brows
   How infinitely crown'd
That now thro' Death's dark house
   Have pass'd with royal gaze :
Purpureally enwound
   How grandly glow the bays !

Sweet, sweet and three-fold sweet,
   Pulsing with three-fold pain,
Where the lark fails of flight
   Soar'd the celestial strain ;
Beyond the sapphire height
   Flew the gold-wingèd feet
Beautiful, pierced with pain,
   Sweet, sweet and three-fold sweet ;

And where *Is not* and *Is*
   Are wed in one sweet name,
And the world's rootless vine
   With dew of stars aflame
Laughs, from those deep divine
   Impossibilities,
Our reason all to shame—
   This cannot be, but is ;

Into the Vast, the Deep
   Beyond all mortal sight,
The Nothingness that conceived
   The worlds of day and night,

The

The Nothingness that heaved
  Pure sides in virgin sleep,
Brought out of darkness, light ;
  And man from out the Deep.

Into that Mystery
  Let not thine hand be thrust :
Nothingness is a world
  Thy science well may trust . . .
But lo, a leaf unfurl'd,
  Nay, a cry mocking thee
From the first grain of dust—
  I am, yet cannot be !

Adventuring unafraid
  Into that last deep shrine,
Must not the child-heart see
  Its deepest symbol shine—
The world's Birth-mystery,
  Whereto the suns are shade ?
Lo, the white breast divine—
  The Holy Mother-maid !

How miss that Sacrifice,
  That cross of Yea and Nay,
That paradox of heaven
  Whose palms point either way,
Thro' each a nail being driven
  That the arms outspan the skies
And our earth-dust this day
  Out-sweeten Paradise !

We part the seamless robe,
  Our wisdom would divide
940

The raiment of the King,
  Our spear is in His side,
Even while the angels sing
  Around our perishing globe,
And Death re-knits in pride
  The seamless purple robe . . .

And grandly glow the bays
  Purpureally enwound
With those rich thorns, the brows
  How infinitely crown'd
That now thro' Death's dark house
  Have pass'd with royal gaze :
Purpureally crown'd
  How grandly glow the bays !

730.   *Creation*

IN the beginning, there was nought
  But heaven, one Majesty of Light,
Beyond all speech, beyond all thought,
  Beyond all depth, beyond all height,
Consummate heaven, the first and last,
  Enfolding in its perfect prime
No future rushing to the past,
  But one rapt Now, that knew not Space or Time.

Formless it was, being gold on gold,
  And void—but with that complete Life
Where music could no wings unfold
  Till lo, God smote the strings of strife !
' Myself unto Myself am Throne,
  Myself unto Myself am Thrall !
I that am All am all alone,'
  He said, ' Yea, I have nothing, having all.'

941   And

And, gathering round His mount of bliss
   The angel-squadrons of His will,
He said, ' One battle yet there is
   To win, one vision to fulfil !
Since heaven where'er I gaze expands,
   And power that knows no strife or cry,
Weakness shall bind and pierce my hands
   And make a world for Me wherein to die.

All might, all vastness and all glory
   Being mine, I must descend and make
Out of my heart a song, a story
   Of little hearts that burn and break ;
Out of my passion without end
   I will make little azure seas,
And into small sad fields descend
   And make green grass, white daisies, rustling trees.'

Then shrank His angels, knowing He thrust
   His arms out East and West and gave
For every little dream of dust
   Part of his Life as to a grave !
' *Enough, O Father, for thy words*
   Have pierced thy hands ! ' But low and sweet,
He said ' Sunsets and streams and birds,
   And drifting clouds ! '—The purple stain'd his feet.—

' Enough ! ' His angels moan'd in fear,
   ' *Father, thy words have pierced thy side !* '
He whisper'd ' Roses shall grow there,
   And there must be a hawthorn-tide,
And ferns, dewy at dawn,' and still
   They moan'd—*Enough, the red drops bleed !*
' And,' sweet and low, ' on every hill,'
   He said, ' I will have flocks and lambs to lead.'

His angels bow'd their heads beneath
    Their wings till that great pang was gone :
Pour not thy soul out unto Death !
    They moan'd, and still his Love flow'd on,
' There shall be small white wings to stray
    From bliss to bliss, from bloom to bloom,
And blue flowers in the wheat ; and—' ' *Stay !*
    Speak not,' they cried, ' *the word that seals thy tomb !* '

He spake—' I have thought of a little child
    That I will have there to embark
On small adventures in the wild,
    And front slight perils in the dark ;
And I will hide from him and lure
    His laughing eyes with suns and moons,
And rainbows that shall not endure ;
    And—when he is weary sing him drowsy tunes.'

His angels fell before Him weeping,
    ' *Enough ! Tempt not the Gates of Hell !* '
He said ' His soul is in his keeping
    That we may love each other well,
And lest the dark too much affright him,
    I will strew countless little stars
Across his childish skies to light him
    That he may wage in peace his mimic wars

And oft forget Me as he plays
    With swords and childish merchandise,
Or with his elfin balance weighs,
    Or with his foot-rule metes, the skies ;
Or builds his castles by the deep,
    Or tunnels through the rocks, and then—
Turn to Me as he falls asleep,
    And, in his dreams, feel for My hand again.

And

And when he is older he shall be
　My friend and walk here at My side ;
Or—when he wills—grow young with Me,
　And, to that happy world where once we died
Descending through the calm blue weather,
　Buy life once more with our immortal breath,
And wander through the little fields together,
　And taste of Love and Death.'

RACHEL ANNAND TAYLOR

731.　　*The Knights to Chrysola*

WE crazed for you, aspired and fell for you ;
　　Over us trod Desire, with feet of fire.
Ah ! the sad stories we would tell for you,
　　Full of dark nights and sighing
　　While—you were dying,
　　　　Chrysola !

Roundels and all rich rimes we rang for you ;
　How from the plangent lyre pled our Desire !
But the musicians vainly sang for you ;—
　　Through the dear music, crying
　　That—you were dying,
　　　　Chrysola !

High on the golden throne love wrought for you
　With eyes enthrall'd of rest, tired of our best ;
You sat unheeding while we fought for you
　　Glaive unto glaive replying ;
　　For—you were dying,
　　　　Chrysola !

944

Frenzied from out the jousts we came to you;
  'Can we love more, Dream-fast? Crown, then, at
    last.'
But love and hate were one dim flame to you;
    Strange things you smiled us—dying,
      O! You were dying,
          Chrysola!

Great spoils of frankincense we burn'd for you,
  Round your death-chamber proud—then cursed aloud
Christian or Pagan god that yearn'd for you,
    Till you were undenying.—
      O Dream undying,
          Chrysola!

732.   *The Joys of Art*

AS a dancer dancing in a shower of roses before her King
                    (A dreamer dark, the King)
Throws back her head like a wind-loved flower, and makes
    her cymbals ring
                    (O'er her lit eyes they ring);
As a fair white dancer strange of heart, and crown'd and
    shod with gold,
My soul exults before the Art, the magian Art of old.

733.   *Non Nobis*

NOT unto us, O Lord,
    Not unto us the rapture of the day,
The peace of night, or love's divine surprise,
High heart, high speech, high deeds 'mid honouring eyes ;
For at Thy word
All these are taken away.

Not unto us, O Lord :
To us thou givest the scorn, the scourge, the scar,
The ache of life, the loneliness of death,
The insufferable sufficiency of breath ;
And with Thy sword
Thou piercest very far.

Not unto us, O Lord :
Nay, Lord, but unto her be all things given—
May light and life and earth and sky be blasted—
But let not all that wealth of loss be wasted :
Let Hell afford
The pavement of her Heaven !

CHARLES GRANVILLE

734.   *Traveller's Hope*

LAY me to rest in some fair spot
    Where sound of waters near,
And songs of sailors in their ships
    Shall reach my waiting ear :

946

Where I shall catch the Captain's call:
  ' All hands again to sea ! '
When swift embarking, I may fare
    To founts of life to be ;

Fare to the dream'd-of lands that lie
    Beyond the Port of Death ;
Fare to the Dawn of whose glad realms
    God sometimes whispereth ;

With hope of flowers that lift their heads
    After the night is past,
And joy of sailors in their ships
    When home 's in sight at last.

H. C. COMPTON MACKENZIE

735.   *A Song of Parting*

MY dear, the time has come to say
    Farewell to London town,
Farewell to each familiar street,
    The room where we look'd down
Upon the people going by,
    The river flowing fast :
The innumerable shine of lamps,
    The bridges and—our past.

Our past of London days and nights,
    When every night we dream'd
Of Love and Art and Happiness,
    And every day it seem'd,

Ah !

H. C. COMPTON MACKENZIE

Ah! little room, you held my life,
　　In you I found my all;
A white hand on the mantelpiece,
　　A shadow on the wall.

My dear, what dinners we have had,
　　What cigarettes and wine
In faded corners of Soho,
　　Your fingers touching mine!
And now the time has come to say
　　Farewell to London town;
The prologue of our play is done,
　　So ring the curtain down.

There lies a crowded life ahead
　　In field and sleepy lane,
A fairer picture than we saw
　　Framed in our window-pane.
There'll be the stars on summer nights,
　　The white moon thro' the trees,
Moths, and the song of nightingales
　　To float along the breeze.

And in the morning we shall see
　　The swallows in the sun,
And hear the cuckoo on the hill
　　Welcome a day begun.
And life will open with the rose
　　For me, sweet, and for you,
And on our life and on the rose
　　How soft the falling dew!

So let us take this tranquil path,
　　But drop a parting tear
For town, whose greatest gift to us
　　Was to be lovers here.

736. *The Lilies of the Field*

To F. L. U.

THY soul is not enchanted by the moon ;
No influential comet draws thy mind
To steeps intolerable where all behind
Is dark, and many ruin'd stars are strewn.
But thou, contented, canst enthrall the tune
That haunts each wood and every singing wind ;
Thou, fortunate philosopher, canst find
The dreams of Earth in every drowsy noon.

Match not thy soul against the seraphim :
They are no more than moths blown to and fro
About the tempest of the eternal Will.
Rest undismay'd in field and forest dim
And, childlike, on some morning thou shalt know
The certain faith of a March daffodil.

FRANCES CORNFORD

737. *Autumn Morning at Cambridge*

I RAN out in the morning when the air was clean and
new,
And all the grass was glittering and grey with autumn
dew ;
I ran out to the apple-tree and pull'd an apple down,
And all the bells were ringing in the grey old town.

Down in the town off the bridges and the grass
They are sweeping up the leaves to let the people pass,—
Sweeping up the old leaves, golden-reds and browns,
Whilst the men go to lecture with the wind in their
gowns.

EDWARD WILLIAM THOMSON

738. *Aspiration*

MY friend conceived the soul hereafter dwells
　　In any heaven the inmost heart desires,
The heart, which craves delight, at pain rebels,
And balks, or obeys the soul till life expires.

He deem'd that all the eternal Force contrives
Is wrought to revigorate its own control,
And that its alchemy some strength derives
From every tested and unflagging soul.

He deem'd a spirit which avails to guide
A human heart, gives proof of energy
To be received in That which never bides,
But ever toils for what can never be—

A perfect All—toward which the Eternal strives
To urge for ever every atom's range,
The Ideal, which never unto Form arrives,
Because new concept emanates from change.

He deem'd the inmost heart is what aligns
Man's aspiration, noble or impure,
And that immortal Tolerance assigns
Each soul what Aspiration would secure.

And if it choose what highest souls would rue—
Some endless round of mortal joys inane—
Such fate befits what souls could not subdue
The heart's poor shrinking from the chrism of pain.

.　.　.　.　.　.　.　.　.

EDWARD WILLIAM THOMSON

My friend review'd, nigh death, how staunch the soul
Had waged in him a conflict, never done,
To rule the dual self that fought control,
Spirit and flesh inextricably one.

His passionless judgement ponder'd well the past,
Patient, relentless, ere he spoke sincere,—
' Through all the strife my soul prevail'd at last,
It rules my inmost heart's desire here ;

' My Will craves not some paradise of zest
Where mortal joys eternally renew,
Nor blank nirvana, nor elysian rest,
Nor palaced pomp to bombast fancy true ;

' It yearns no whit to swell some choiring strain
In endless amplitudes of useless praise ;
It dares to aspire to share the immortal pain
Of toil in moulding Form from phase to phase.

' To me, of old, such fate some terror bore,
But now great gladness in my spirit glows,
While death clings round me friendlier than before,
To loose the soul that mounts beyond repose.'

.   .   .   .

Yet, at the end, from seeming death he stirr'd
As one whose sleep is broke by sudden shine,
And whisper'd *Christ*, as if the soul had heard
Tidings of some exceeding sweet design.

739. *The Red-Haired Man's Wife*

I HAVE taken that vow—
 And you were my friend
But yesterday—now
 All that 's at an end,
And you are my husband, and claim me, and I must
  depend.

Yesterday I was free,
 Now you, as I stand,
Walk over to me
 And take hold of my hand.
You look at my lips, your eyes are too bold, your smile
  is too bland.

My old name is lost,
 My distinction of race :
Now the line has been cross'd,
 Must I step to your pace ?
Must I walk as you list, and obey, and smile up in your
  face ?

All the white and the red
 Of my cheeks you have won ;
All the hair of my head,
 And my feet, tho' they run,
Are yours, and you own me and end me just as I begun.

JAMES STEPHENS

Must I bow when you speak,
  Be silent and hear,
Inclining my cheek
  And incredulous ear
To your voice, and command, and behest, hold your
    lightest wish dear ?

I am woman, but still
  Am alive, and can feel
Every intimate thrill
  That is woe or is weal.
I, aloof, and divided, apart, standing far, can I kneel ?

O, if kneeling were right,
  I should kneel nor be sad,
And abase in your sight
  All the pride that I had,
I should come to you, hold to you, cling to you, call to
    you, glad.

If not, I shall know,
  I shall surely find out,
And your world will throw
  In disaster and rout ;
I am woman and glory and beauty, I mystery, terror, and
    doubt.

I am separate still,
  I am I and not you :
And my mind and my will,
  As in secret they grew,
Still are secret, unreach'd and untouch'd and not subject
    to you.

953

740.

Hate

MY enemy came nigh,
And I
Stared fiercely in his face.
My lips went writhing back in a grimace,
And stern I watch'd him with a narrow eye.
Then, as I turn'd away, my enemy,
That bitter heart and savage, said to me :
' Some day, when this is past,
When all the arrows that we have are cast,
We may ask one another why we hate,
And fail to find a story to relate.
It may seem to us then a mystery
That we could hate each other.'

                 Thus said he,
And did not turn away,
Waiting to hear what I might have to say,
But I fled quickly, fearing if I stay'd
I might have kiss'd him as I would a maid.

741.

The Watcher

AROSE for a young head,
A ring for a bride,
Joy for the homestead
Clean and wide—
    Who 's that waiting
    In the rain outside ?

A heart for an old friend,
A hand for the new :
Love can to earth lend
Heaven's hue—
    Who 's that standing
    In the silver dew ?

A smile for the parting,
A tear as they go,
God's sweethearting
Ends just so—
 Who's that watching
 Where the black winds blow?

He who is waiting
In the rain outside,
He who is standing
Where the dew drops wide,
He who is watching
In the wind must ride
 (Tho' the pale hands cling)
 With the rose
 And the ring
 And the bride,
  Must ride
With the red of the rose,
And the gold of the ring,
And the lips and the hair of the bride.

RICHARD MIDDLETON

742. *Pagan Epitaph*

SERVANT of the eternal Must
 I lie here, here let me lie,
In the ashes and the dust,
 Dreaming, dreaming pleasantly.
When I lived I sought no wings,
 Schemed no heaven, plann'd no hell,
But, content with little things,
 Made an earth, and it was well.

      Song

Song and laughter, food and wine,
　　Roses, roses red and white,
And a star or two to shine
　　On my dewy world at night.
Lord, what more could I desire ?
　　With my little heart of clay
I have lit no eternal fire
　　To burn my dreams on Judgement Day !

Well I loved, but they who knew
　　What my laughing heart could be,
What my singing lips could do,
　　Lie a-dreaming here with me.
I can feel their finger-tips
　　Stroke the darkness from my face,
And the music of their lips
　　Fills my pleasant resting-place
In the ashes and the dust,
　　Where I wonder as I lie,
Servant of the eternal Must,
　　Dreaming, dreaming pleasantly.

743.　　　　*Any Lover, Any Lass*

WHY are her eyes so bright, so bright,
　　Why do her lips control
The kisses of a summer night,
　　When I would love her soul ?

God set her brave eyes wide apart
　　And painted them with fire ;
They stir the ashes of my heart
　　To embers of desire.

956

Her lips so tenderly are wrought
  In so divine a shape,
That I am servant to my thought
  And can no wise escape.

Her body is a flower, her hair
  About her neck doth play ;
I find her colours everywhere,
  They are the pride of day.

Her little hands are soft, and when
  I see her fingers move
I know in very truth that men
  Have died for less than love.

Ah, dear, live, lovely thing ! my eyes
  Have sought her like a prayer ;
It is my better self that cries
  ' Would she were not so fair ! '

Would I might forfeit ecstasy
  And find a calmer place,
Where I might undesirous see
  Her too desirèd face :

Nor find her eyes so bright, so bright,
  Nor hear her lips unroll
Dream after dream the lifelong night,
  When I would love her soul.

744.　　　*On a Dead Child*

MAN proposes, God in His time disposes,
  And so I wander'd up to where you lay,
A little rose among the little roses,
  And no more dead than they.

It

It seem'd your childish feet were tired of straying,
　　You did not greet me from your flower-strewn bed,
Yet still I knew that you were only playing—
　　Playing at being dead.

I might have thought that you were really sleeping,
　　So quiet lay your eyelids to the sky,
So still your hair, but surely you were peeping ;
　　And so I did not cry.

God knows, and in His proper time disposes,
　　And so I smiled and gently called your name,
Added my rose to your sweet heap of roses,
　　And left you to your game.

JOHN MASEFIELD

745.　　　　　　*Cargoes*

QUINQUIREME of Nineveh from distant Ophir
　　Rowing home to haven in sunny Palestine,
With a cargo of ivory,
And apes and peacocks,
Sandalwood, cedarwood, and sweet white wine.

Stately Spanish galleon coming from the Isthmus,
Dipping through the Tropics by the palm-green shores,
With a cargo of diamonds,
Emeralds, amethysts,
Topazes, and cinnamon, and gold moidores.

Dirty British coaster with a salt-caked smoke-stack,
Butting through the Channel in the mad March days,
With a cargo of Tyne coal,
Road-rails, pig-lead,
Firewood, iron-ware, and cheap tin trays.

746. *Sea Fever*

I MUST go down to the seas again, to the lonely sea
  and the sky,
And all I ask is a tall ship and a star to steer her by;
And the wheel's kick and the wind's song and the white
  sail's shaking,
And a grey mist on the sea's face, and a grey dawn
  breaking.

I must go down to the seas again, for the call of the
  running tide
Is a wild call and a clear call that may not be denied;
And all I ask is a windy day with the white clouds flying,
And the flung spray and the blown spume, and the sea-
  gulls crying.

I must go down to the seas again, to the vagrant gypsy life,
To the gull's way and the whale's way where the wind's
  like a whetted knife;
And all I ask is a merry yarn from a laughing fellow-rover,
And quiet sleep and a sweet dream when the long trick's
  over.

747. *To his Mother, C. L. M.*

IN the dark womb where I began
  My mother's life made me a man.
Through all the months of human birth
Her beauty fed my common earth.
I cannot see, nor breathe, nor stir,
But through the death of some of her.

Down in the darkness of the grave
She cannot see the life she gave.

For

For all her love, she cannot tell
Whether I use it ill or well,
Nor knock at dusty doors to find
Her beauty dusty in the mind.

If the grave's gates could be undone,
She would not know her little son,
I am so grown.   If we should meet,
She would pass by me in the street,
Unless my soul's face let her see
My sense of what she did for me.

What have I done to keep in mind
My debt to her and womankind ?
What woman's happier life repays
Her for those months of wretched days ?
For all my mouthless body leech'd
Ere Birth's releasing hell was reach'd ?

What have I done, or tried, or said
In thanks to that dear woman dead ?
Men triumph over women still,
Men trample women's rights at will,
And man's lust roves the world untamed.

.   .   .   .

O grave, keep shut lest I be shamed !

WILFRID THORLEY

748.   *Buttercups*

THERE must be fairy miners
    Just underneath the mould,
Such wondrous quaint designers
    Who live in caves of gold.

They take the shining metals,
　　And beat them into shreds ;
And mould them into petals,
　　To make the flowers' heads.

Sometimes they melt the flowers,
　　To tiny seeds like pearls,
And store them up in bowers
　　For little boys and girls.

And still a tiny fan turns
　　Above a forge of gold ;
To keep with fairy lanterns,
　　The world from growing old.

749.　　　　*Chant for Reapers*

WHY do you hide, O dryads ! when we seek
　　Your healing hands in solace ?
Who shall soften like you the places rough ?
Who shall hasten the harvest ?

Why do you fly, O dryads ! when we pray
　　For laden boughs and blossom ?
Who shall quicken like you the sapling trees ?
Who shall ripen the orchards ?

Bare in the wind the branches wave and break,
　　The hazel nuts are hollow.
Who shall garner the wheat if you be gone ?
Who shall sharpen his sickle ?

Wine have we spilt, O dryads ! on our knees
　　Have made you our oblation.
Who shall save us from dearth if you be fled ?
Who shall comfort and kindle ?

Sadly we delve the furrows, string the vine
    Whose flimsy burden topples.
Downward tumble the woods if you be dumb,
Stript of honey and garland.

Why do you hide, O dryads ! when we call,
    With pleading hands up-lifted ?
Smile and bless us again that all be well ;
Smile again on your children.

JAMES ELROY FLECKER

750.   *Rioupéroux*

HIGH and solemn mountains guard Rioupéroux
    —Small untidy village where the river drives a mill—
Frail as wood anemones, white and frail were you,
And drooping a little, like the slender daffodil.

O I will go to France again, and tramp the valley through,
And I will change these gentle clothes for clog and
    corduroy,
And work with the mill-hands of black Rioupéroux,
And walk with you, and talk with you, like any other boy.

751.   *War Song of the Saracens*

WE are they who come faster than fate : we are they
    who ride early or late :
We storm at your ivory gate : Pale Kings of the Sunset,
    beware !
Not on silk nor in samet we lie, not in curtain'd solemnity
    die

Among women who chatter and cry, and children who
    mumble a prayer.
But we sleep by the ropes of the camp, and we rise with
    a shout, and we tramp
With the sun or the moon for a lamp, and the spray of
    the wind in our hair.

From the lands where the elephants are, to the forts of
    Merou and Balghar,
Our steel we have brought and our star to shine on the
    ruins of Rûm.
We have marched from the Indus to Spain, and by God
    we will go there again ;
We have stood on the shore of the plain where the Waters
    of Destiny boom.

A mart of destruction we made at Jalula where men were
    afraid,
For death was a difficult trade, and the sword was a broker
    of doom ;
And the Spear was a Desert Physician who cured not
    a few of ambition,
And drave not a few to perdition with medicine bitter
    and strong :
And the shield was a grief to the fool and as bright as
    a desolate pool,
And as straight as the rock of Stamboul when their
    cavalry thunder'd along :
For the coward was drown'd with the brave when our
    battle sheer'd up like a wave,
And the dead to the desert we gave, and the glory to
    God in our song.

SIDNEY ROYSE LYSAGHT

752.   *First Pathways*

WHERE were the pathways that your childhood
      knew ?—
   In mountain glens ? or by the ocean strands ?
   Or where, beyond the ripening harvest lands,
The distant hills were blue ?

Where evening sunlight threw a golden haze
   Over a mellow city's walls and towers ?
   Or where the fields and lanes were bright with flowers,
In quiet woodland ways ?

And whether here or there, or east or west,
   That place you dwelt in first was holy ground ;
   Its shelter was the kindest you have found,
Its pathways were the best.

And even in the city's smoke and mire
   I doubt not that a golden light was shed
   On those first paths, and that they also led
To lands of heart's desire.

And where the children in dark alleys penn'd,
   Heard the caged lark sing of the April hills,
   Or where they damm'd the muddy gutter rills,
Or made a dog their friend ;

Or where they gather'd, dancing hand in hand,
   About the organ man, for them, too, lay
   Beyond the dismal alley's entrance way,
The gates of wonderland.

For 'tis my faith that Earth's first words are sweet
   To all her children,—never a rebuff ;
    And that we only saw, where ways were rough,
The flowers about our feet.

RUPERT BROOKE

753.   *Dust*

WHEN the white flame in us is gone,
    And we that lost the world's delight
Stiffen in darkness, left alone
    To crumble in our separate night ;

When your swift hair is quiet in death,
    And through the lips corruption thrust
Has still'd the labour of my breath—
    When we are dust, when we are dust !—

Not dead, not undesirous yet,
    Still sentient, still unsatisfied,
We'll ride the air, and shine, and flit,
    Around the places where we died,

And dance as dust before the sun,
    And light of foot and unconfined,
Hurry from road to road, and run
    About the errands of the wind.

And every mote, on earth or air,
    Will speed and gleam, down later days,
And like a secret pilgrim fare
    By eager and invisible ways,

Nor ever rest, nor ever lie,
    Till, beyond thinking, out of view,
One mote of all the dust that 's I
    Shall meet one atom that was you.

Then in some garden hush'd from wind,
    Warm in a sunset's afterglow,
The lovers in the flowers will find
    A sweet and strange unquiet grow

Upon the peace ; and, past desiring,
    So high a beauty in the air,
And such a light, and such a quiring,
    And such a radiant ecstasy there,

They'll know not if it 's fire, or dew,
    Or out of earth, or in the height,
Singing, or flame, or scent, or hue,
    Or two that pass, in light, to light,

Out of the garden, higher, higher. . . .
    But in that instant they shall learn
The shattering ecstasy of our fire,
    And the weak passionless hearts will burn

And faint in that amazing glow,
    Until the darkness close above ;
And they will know—poor fools, they'll know !—
    One moment, what it is to love.

754.   *The One Before the Last*

I DREAMT I was in love again
    With the One Before the Last,
And smiled to greet the pleasant pain
    Of that innocent young past.

But I jump'd to feel how sharp had been
   The pain when it did live,
How the faded dreams of Nineteen-ten
   Were Hell in Nineteen-five.

The boy's woe was as keen and clear,
   The boy's love just as true,
And the One Before the Last, my dear,
   Hurt quite as much as you.

.   .   .   .   .   .

Sickly I ponder'd how the lover
   Wrongs the unanswering tomb,
And sentimentalizes over
   What earn'd a better doom.

Gently he tombs the poor dim last time,
   Strews pinkish dust above,
And sighs, ' The dear dead boyish pastime ;
   But *this*—ah, God !—is Love ! '

—Better oblivion hide dead true loves,
   Better the night enfold,
Than men, to eke the praise of new loves,
   Should lie about the old !

.   .   .   .   .   .

Oh ! bitter thoughts I had in plenty.
   But here 's the worst of it—
I shall forget, in Nineteen-twenty,
   You ever hurt a bit !

755.   *Second Best*

HERE in the dark, O heart;
    Alone with the enduring Earth, and Night,
And Silence, and the warm strange smell of clover;
Clear-vision'd, though it break you; far apart
From the dead best, the dear and old delight;
Throw down your dreams of immortality,
O faithful, O foolish lover!
Here's peace for you, and surety; here the one
Wisdom—the truth!—' All day the good glad sun
Showers love and labour on you, wine and song;
The greenwood laughs, the wind blows, all day long
Till night.'   And night ends all things.
                                    Then shall be
No lamp relumed in heaven, no voices crying,
Or changing lights, or dreams and forms that hover!
(And, heart, for all your sighing,
That gladness and those tears are over, over. . . .)

And has the truth brought no new hope at all,
Heart, that you're weeping yet for Paradise?
Do they still whisper, the old weary cries?
' *'Mid youth and song, feasting and carnival,*
Through laughter, through the roses, as of old
Comes Death, on shadowy and relentless feet,
Death, unappeasable by prayer or gold;
Death is the end, the end! '
Proud, then, clear-eyed and laughing, go to greet
Death as a friend!

Exile of immortality, strongly wise,
Strain through the dark with undesirous eyes

RUPERT BROOKE

To what may lie beyond it. Sets your star,
O heart, for ever ? Yet, behind the night,
Waits for the great unborn, somewhere afar,
Some white tremendous daybreak. And the light,
Returning, shall give back the golden hours,
Ocean a windless level, Earth a lawn
Spacious and full of sunlit dancing-places,
And laughter, and music, and, among the flowers,
The gay child-hearts of men, and the child-faces,
O heart, in the great dawn !

THE HON. MAURICE BARING

756. *ΛΕΙΡΙΟΕΣΣΑ ΚΑΛΥΞ*

SHE listen'd to the music of the spheres ;
  We thought she did not hear our happy strings ;
    Stars diadem'd her hair in misty rings,
And all too late we knew those stars were tears.
Without she was a temple of pure snow,
    Within were piteous flames of sacrifice ;
    And underneath the dazzling mask of ice
A heart of swiftest fire was dying slow.

She in herself, as lonely lilies fold
Stiff silver petals over secret gold,
    Shielded her passion and remain'd afar
From pity. Cast red roses on the pyre !
She that was snow shall rise to Heaven as fire
    In the still glory of the morning star.

WILLIAM H. DAVIES

757. *Songs of Joy*

SING out, my Soul, thy songs of joy;
  Such as a happy bird will sing
Beneath a Rainbow's lovely arch
  In early spring.

Think not of Death in thy young days;
  —Why shouldst thou that grim tyrant fear?
And fear him not when thou art old,
  And he is near.

Strive not for gold, for greedy fools
  Measure themselves by poor men never;
Their standard, still being richer men,
  Makes them poor ever.

Train up thy mind to feel content;
  What matters then how low thy store?
What we enjoy, and not possess,
  Makes rich or poor.

Fill'd with sweet thought, then happy I
  Take not my state from others' eyes;
What 's in my mind—not on my flesh
  Or theirs—I prize.

Sing, happy Soul, thy songs of joy;
  Such as a Brook sings in the wood,
That all night has been strengthen'd by
  Heaven's purer flood.

758. *Truly Great*

MY walls outside must have some flowers,
   My walls within must have some books;
A house that's small; a garden large,
   And in it leafy nooks:

A little gold that's sure each week;
   That comes not from my living kind,
But from a dead man in his grave,
   Who cannot change his mind:

A lovely wife, and gentle too;
   Contented that no eyes but mine
Can see her many charms, nor voice
   To call her beauty fine:

Where she would in that stone cage live,
   A self-made prisoner, with me;
While many a wild bird sang around,
   On gate, on bush, on tree:

And she sometimes to answer them,
   In her far sweeter voice than all;
Till birds, that loved to look on leaves,
   Will doat on a stone wall.

—With this small house, this garden large,
   This little gold, this lovely mate,
With health in body, peace at heart—
   Show me a man more great.

759.   *Money*

WHEN I had money, money, O !
     I knew no joy till I went poor ;
For many a false man as a friend
     Came knocking all day at my door.

Then felt I like a child that holds
     A trumpet that he must not blow
Because a man is dead ; I dared
     Not speak to let this false world know.

Much have I thought of life, and seen
     How poor men's hearts are ever light ;
And how their wives do hum like bees
     About their work from morn till night.

So, when I hear these poor ones laugh,
     And see the rich ones coldly frown—
Poor men, think I, need not go up
     So much as rich men should come down.

When I had money, money, O !
     My many friends proved all untrue ;
But now I have no money, O !
     My friends are real, though very few.

760.   *In May*

YES, I will spend the livelong day
     With Nature in this month of May ;
And sit beneath the trees, and share
My bread with birds whose homes are there ;
While cows lie down to eat, and sheep
Stand to their necks in grass so deep ;

While birds do sing with all their might,
As though they felt the earth in flight.
This is the hour I dream'd of, when
I sat surrounded by poor men ;
And thought of how the Arab sat
Alone at evening, gazing at
The stars that bubbled in clear skies ;
And of young dreamers, when their eyes
Enjoy'd methought a precious boon
In the adventures of the Moon
Whose light, behind the Clouds' dark bars,
Search'd for her stolen flocks of stars.
When I, hemm'd in by wrecks of men,
Thought of some lonely cottage then,
Full of sweet books ; and miles of sea,
With passing ships, in front of me ;
And having, on the other hand,
A flowery, green, bird-singing land.

761.   *Leisure*

WHAT is this life if, full of care,
    We have no time to stand and stare ?—

No time to stand beneath the boughs
And stare as long as sheep or cows :

No time to see, when woods we pass,
Where squirrels hide their nuts in grass :

No time to see, in broad daylight,
Streams full of stars, like skies at night :

No time to turn at Beauty's glance,
And watch her feet, how they can dance :

No

No time to wait till her mouth can
Enrich that smile her eyes began ?

A poor life this if, full of care,
We have no time to stand and stare.

762.   *The Elements*

N O house of stone
      Was built for me ;
When the Sun shines—
      I am a bee.

No sooner comes
      The Rain so warm,
I come to light—
      I am a worm.

When the Winds blow,
      I do not strip,
But set my sails—
      I am a ship.

When Lightning comes,
      It plays with me
And I with it—
      I am a tree.

When drown'd men rise
      At Thunder's word,
Sings Nightingale—
      I am a bird.

WILFRID WILSON GIBSON

763.   *Song*

IF once I could gather in song
  A flower from my garden of dreams—
    The dew from its petals unshaken,
    When starry and bright they awaken—
All men to the wonder would throng.

Though ever at dawning I go
By the marge of the life-giving streams
    That, shadow'd by blossoms upspringing,
    Remember the hills in their singing,
The fells of their birth in their flow;

Or early or late though I fare
To gather my garden of dreams
    For the barren, forsaken and lonely,
    I bring from the shadow-world only
Pale blossoms that perish in air.

764.   *Flannan Isle*

'THOUGH three men dwell on Flannan Isle
  To keep the lamp alight,
As we steer'd under the lee, we caught
No glimmer through the night.'

A passing ship at dawn had brought
The news; and quickly we set sail,
To find out what strange thing might ail
The keepers of the deep-sea light.

The

WILFRID WILSON GIBSON

The winter day broke blue and bright,
With glancing sun and glancing spray,
As o'er the swell our boat made way,
As gallant as a gull in flight.

But, as we near'd the lonely Isle ;
And look'd up at the naked height ;
And saw the lighthouse towering white,
With blinded lantern, that all night
Had never shot a spark
Of comfort through the dark,
So ghostly in the cold sunlight
It seem'd, that we were struck the while
With wonder all too dread for words.

And, as into the tiny creek
We stole beneath the hanging crag,
We saw three queer, black, ugly birds—
Too big, by far, in my belief,
For guillemot or shag—
Like seamen sitting bolt-upright
Upon a half-tide reef :
But, as we near'd, they plunged from sight,
Without a sound, or spurt of white.

And still too mazed to speak,
We landed ; and made fast the boat ;
And climb'd the track in single file,
Each wishing he was safe afloat,
On any sea, however far,
So it be far from Flannan Isle :
And still we seem'd to climb, and climb,
As though we'd lost all count of time,

And so must climb for evermore.
Yet, all too soon, we reached the door—
The black, sun-blister'd lighthouse-door,
That gaped for us ajar.

As, on the threshold, for a spell,
We paused, we seem'd to breathe the smell
Of limewash and of tar,
Familiar as our daily breath,
As though 'twere some strange scent of death :
And so, yet wondering, side by side,
We stood a moment, still tongue-tied :
And each with black foreboding eyed
The door, ere we should fling it wide,
To leave the sunlight for the gloom :
Till, plucking courage up, at last,
Hard on each other's heels we pass'd
Into the living-room.

Yet, as we crowded through the door,
We only saw a table, spread
For dinner, meat and cheese and bread ;
But all untouch'd ; and no one there :
As though, when they sat down to eat,
Ere they could even taste,
Alarm had come ; and they in haste
Had risen and left the bread and meat :
For at the table-head a chair
Lay tumbled on the floor.

We listen'd ; but we only heard
The feeble cheeping of a bird
That starved upon its perch :
And, listening still, without a word,
We set about our hopeless search.

We

WILFRID WILSON GIBSON

We hunted high, we hunted low ;
And soon ransack'd the empty house ;
Then o'er the Island, to and fro,
We ranged, to listen and to look
In every cranny, cleft or nook
That might have hid a bird or mouse :
But, though we search'd from shore to shore,
We found no sign in any place :
And soon again stood face to face
Before the gaping door :
And stole into the room once more
As frighten'd children steal.

Aye : though we hunted high and low,
And hunted everywhere,
Of the three men's fate we found no trace
Of any kind in any place,
But a door ajar, and an untouch'd meal,
And an overtoppled chair.

And, as we listen'd in the gloom
Of that forsaken living-room—
A chill clutch on our breath—
We thought how ill-chance came to all
Who kept the Flannan Light :
And how the rock had been the death
Of many a likely lad :
How six had come to a sudden end,
And three had gone stark mad :
And one whom we'd all known as friend
Had leapt from the lantern one still night,
And fallen dead by the lighthouse wall :
And long we thought
On the three we sought,
And of what might yet befall.

Like curs, a glance has brought to heel,
We listen'd, flinching there :
And look'd, and look'd, on the untouch'd meal,
And the overtoppled chair.

We seem'd to stand for an endless while,
Though still no word was said,
Three men alive on Flannan Isle,
Who thought, on three men dead.

ALICE FURLONG

765.   *My Share of the World*

I AM jealous : I am true :
Sick at heart for love of you,
    O my share of the world !
I am cold, O, cold as stone
To all men save you alone.

Seven times slower creeps the day
When your face is far away,
    O my share of the world !
Seven times darker falls the night
When you gladden not my sight.

Measureless my joy and pride
Would you choose me for your bride,
    O my share of the world !
For your face is my delight,
Morn and even, noon and night.

979   To

ALICE FURLONG

To the dance and to the wake
Still I go but for your sake,
  O my share of the world !
Just to see your face awhile,
Meet your eyes and win your smile.

And the gay word on my lip
Never lets my secret slip
  To my share of the world !
Light my feet trip over the green—
But my heart cries in the keen !

My poor mother sighs anew
When my looks go after you,
  O my share of the world !
And my father's brow grows black
When you smile and turn your back.

I would part with wealth and ease,
I would go beyond the seas,
  For my share of the world !
I would leave my hearth and home
If he only whisper'd ' Come ! '

Houseless under sun and dew,
I would beg my bread with you,
  O my share of the world !
Houseless in the snow and storm,
Your heart's love would keep me warm.

I would pray and I would crave
To be with you in the grave,
  O my share of the world !
I would go through fire and flood,
I would give up all but God
  For my share of the world !

766.   *The Woods are Still*

THE woods are still that were so gay at primrose-
    springing,
Through the dry woods the brown field-fares are winging,
And I alone of love, of love am singing.

I sing of love to the haggard palmer-worm,
Of love 'mid the crumpled oak-leaves that once were firm,
Laughing, I sing of love at the summer's term.

Of love, on a path where the snake's cast skin is lying,
Blue feathers on the floor, and no cuckoo flying ;
I sing to the echo of my own voice crying.

767.   *Renewal*

AS the young phoenix, duteous to his sire,
    Lifts in his beak the creature he has been,
   And, lifting o'er the corse broad vans for screen,
Bears it to solitudes, erects a pyre,
And, soon as it is wasted by the fire,
   Grids with disdainful claw the ashes clean ;
   Then spreading unencumber'd wings serene
Mounts to the aether with renew'd desire :

So joyously I lift myself above
   The life I buried in hot flames to-day.
    The flames themselves are dead : and I can range
Alone through the untarnish'd sky I love,
   And I trust myself, as from the grave I may,
    To the enchanting miracles of change.

JAMES JOYCE

768. *Song*

O, IT was out by Donnycarney,
    When the bat flew from tree to tree,
My love and I did walk together;
    And sweet were the words she said to me!

Along with us the summer wind
    Went murmuring—O, happily!—
But softer than the breath of summer
    Was the kiss she gave to me.

EZRA POUND

769. *Portrait*

NOW would I weave her portrait out of all dim
    splendour.
Of Provence and far halls of memory,
Lo, there come echoes, faint diversity
Of blended bells at even's end, or
As the distant seas should send her
The tribute of their trembling, ceaselessly
Resonant.   Out of all dreams that be,
Say, shall I bid the deepest dreams attend her?

Nay! For I have seen the purplest shadows stand
Alway with reverent cheer that look'd on her,
Silence himself is grown her worshipper
And ever doth attend her in that land
Wherein she reigneth, wherefore let there stir
Naught but the softest voices, praising her.

EZRA POUND

Ballad for Gloom

FOR God, our God, is a gallant foe
That playeth behind the veil.

I have loved my God as a child at heart
That seeketh deep bosoms for rest,
I have loved my God as maid to man,
But lo, this thing is best :

To love your God as a gallant foe
                    that plays behind the veil,
To meet your God as the night winds meet
                    beyond Arcturus' pale.

I have play'd with God for a woman,
I have staked with my God for truth,
I have lost to my God as a man, clear eyed,
        His dice be not of ruth.

For I am made as a naked blade,
        But hear ye this thing in sooth :

Who loseth to God as man to man
        Shall win at the turn of the game.
I have drawn my blade where the lightnings meet,
        But the ending is the same :
Who loseth to God as the sword blades lose
        Shall win at the end of the game.

For God, our God, is a gallant foe
                    that playeth behind the veil,
Whom God deigns not to overthrow
                    Hath need of triple mail.

983

GORDON BOTTOMLEY

771.   *To Iron-Founders and Others*

WHEN you destroy a blade of grass
    You poison England at her roots:
Remember no man's foot can pass
Where evermore no green life shoots.

You force the birds to wing too high
Where your unnatural vapours creep:
Surely the living rocks shall die
When birds no rightful distance keep.

You have brought down the firmament
And yet no heaven is more near;
You shape huge deeds without event,
And half-made men believe and fear.

Your worship is your furnaces,
Which, like old idols, lost obscenes,
Have molten bowels; your vision is
Machines for making more machines.

O, you are busied in the night,
Preparing destinies of rust;
Iron misused must turn to blight
And dwindle to a tetter'd crust.

The grass, forerunner of life, has gone,
But plants that spring in ruins and shards
Attend until your dream is done:
I have seen hemlock in your yards.

The generations of the worm
Know not your loads piled on their soil ;
Their knotted ganglions shall wax firm
Till your strong flagstones heave and toil.

When the old hollow'd earth is crack'd,
And when, to grasp more power and feasts,
Its ores are emptied, wasted, lack'd,
The middens of your burning beasts

Shall be raked over till they yield
Last priceless slags for fashionings high,
Ploughs to wake grass in every field,
Chisels men's hands to magnify.

LADY MARGARET SACKVILLE

772. *The Apple*

EVE, smiling, pluck'd the apple, then
Laugh'd, sigh'd—and tasted it again :
' Strange such a pleasant, juicy thing
On a forbidden tree should spring ! '

But had she seen with clearer eyes,
Or had the serpent been less wise,
She'd scarce have shown such little wit
As to let Adam taste of it !

ELINOR SWEETMAN

773. *The Orchard by the Shore: a Pastoral*

COLIN

HOW look'd your love, sweet Shepherd, yestereven,
   When under apple-boughs ye stole a tryst,
While Hesper held the glowing gates of heaven
   Ere colder stars besprent its amethyst ?
Ah ! happy one, how look'd those lids ye kiss'd,
   And seem'd her blush of half its rose bereaven
By wan green glimmer and by meadow mist,
   From grassy floor, with leaves enshadow'd o'er,
Dim filtering through the seven-score trees and seven
   Of the orchard by the shore ?

SHEPHERD

Colin, the grass was grey and wet the sod
   O'er which I heard her velvet footfall come ;
But heaven, where yet no pallid crescent rode
   Flower'd in fire behind the bloomless plum ;
There stirr'd no wing nor wind, the wood was dumb,
   Only blown roses shook their leaves abroad
On stems more tender than an infant's thumb—
   Soft leaves, soft hued, and curl'd like Cupid's lip ;
And each dim tree shed sweetness over me,
   From honey-dews that breathless boughs let slip
In the orchard by the sea.

ELINOR SWEETMAN

COLIN

Yea, Shepherd, I have seen how blossoms fold,
    And waded deep, where deep an orchard grows ;
But what of her whose sweet ye leave untold,
    Whose step fell softer than a south-wind blows ?
What of her beauty ?—saw ye not unroll'd
    O'er little ears and throat a twine of gold ?
And wore her lip the blown or budded rose ?
    O did she reach through balmy pear and peach
White arms for greeting—did ye heaven hold
    In the orchard by the beach ?

SHEPHERD

Nay, Colin, but I heard through walls of laurel
    A tide impassion'd brimming silent spaces,
Guess'd its soft weight, and knew its hoarded coral
    Given and withdrawn to shyer farther places ;
Methought each wave shook loose in long embraces
    Wild trees and tangle over shells auroral,
And never wave but held all heaven's faces,
    And seem'd to sweep a mirror'd moon asleep,
To break and blanch among the wet wood-sorrel,
    In the orchard by the deep.

COLIN

O Shepherd, leave to speak of ocean-brede,
    And crescents gliding o'er the cold sea-floor ;
All men may watch a risen tide recede,
    And scarlet secrets of the deep explore.
Were not your nymph's fair face and footstep more
    Than foam and flake within a garden weed ?
More sweet than hymning seas her sweet love-lore ?
    Her hair, her hand, more soft than feathers fann'd
From sleeping doves, by small winds newly freed
    In the orchard by the strand ?

O dull

ELINOR SWEETMAN

O dull of soul and senseless ! get thee gone !
   What though the lyre of him who loves be strung
To deep of heaven and deep of sea—alone
   The deep of love is evermore unsung !
Such music lieth hush upon the tongue.
   No, by the gods ! not thou, nor any one
Shall force these stammering lips to do it wrong,
   Nor babble o'er from common door to door
What I, by favour of my gods, have known
   In the orchard by the shore !

GEORGE SANTAYANA

774. *The Rustic at the Play*

OUR youth is like a rustic at the play
   That cries aloud in simple-hearted fear,
Curses the villain, shudders at the fray,
   And weeps before the maiden's wreathèd bier.

Yet once familiar with the changing show,
   He starts no longer at a brandished knife ;
But, his heart chasten'd at the sight of woe,
   Ponders the mirror'd sorrows of his life.

So tutor'd too, I watch the moving art
   Of all this magic and impassion'd pain
That tells the story of the human heart
   In a false instance, such as poets feign.

I smile, and keep within the parchment furl'd
That prompts the passions of this strutting world.

ERNEST RADFORD

775.

Quiet

TIRED brain, there is a place of rest
    On the broad bosom of the land
Where quiet will reward the quest.
    The dinning of the iron hand
Will be unheard ; ah ! there shall we
    Have with the noise of tumbling rills,
And with the music of the sea,
    The quiet that my dream fulfils
Of Quiet, aching tho' it be.

JOHN DRINKWATER

776.

A Prayer

LORD, not for light in darkness do we pray,
    Not that the veil be lifted from our eyes,
Nor that the slow ascension of our day
        Be otherwise.

Not for a clearer vision of the things
Whereof the fashioning shall make us great,
Not for the remission of the peril and stings
        Of time and fate.

Not for a fuller knowledge of the end
Whereto we travel, bruised yet unafraid,
Nor that the little healing that we lend
        Shall be repaid.

Not

Not these, O Lord.   We would not break the bars
Thy wisdom sets about us ; we shall climb
Unfetter'd to the secrets of the stars
       In Thy good time.

We do not crave the high perception swift
When to refrain were well, and when fulfil,
Nor yet the understanding strong to sift
       The good from ill.

Not these, O Lord.   For these Thou hast reveal'd,
We know the golden season when to reap
The heavy-fruited treasure of the field,
       The hour to sleep.

Not these.   We know the hemlock from the rose,
The pure from stain'd, the noble from the base,
The tranquil holy light of truth that glows
       On Pity's face.

We know the paths wherein our feet should press,
Across our hearts are written Thy decrees :
Yet now, O Lord, be merciful to bless
       With more than these.

Grant us the will to fashion as we feel,
Grant us the strength to labour as we know,
Grant us the purpose, ribb'd and edged with steel,
       To strike the blow.

Knowledge we ask not—knowledge Thou hast lent,
But, Lord, the will—there lies our bitter need,
Give us to build above the deep intent
       The deed, the deed.

777.   *Hymn to Love*

WE are thine, O Love, being in thee and made of thee,
     As thóu, Lóve, were the déep thought
And we the speech of the thought ; yea, spoken are we,
       Thy fires of thought out-spoken :

But burn'd not through us thy imagining
     Like fiérce móod in a sóng cáught,
We were as clamour'd words a fool may fling,
       Loose words, of meaning broken.

For what more like the brainless speech of a fool,—
     The lives travelling dark fears,
And as a boy throws pebbles in a pool
       Thrown down abysmal places ?

Hazardous are the stars, yet is our birth
     And our journeying time theirs ;
As words of air, life makes of starry earth
       Sweet soul-delighted faces ;

As voices are we in the worldly wind ;
     The great wind of the world's fate
Is turned, as air to a shapen sound, to mind
       And marvellous desires.

But not in the world as voices storm-shatter'd,
     Not borne down by the wind's weight ;
The rushing time rings with our splendid word
       Like darkness fill'd with fires.

           For

For Love doth use us for a sound of song,
 And Love's meaning our life wields,
Making our souls like syllables to throng
  His tunes of exultation.

Down the blind speed of a fatal world we fly,
 As rain blown along earth's fields ;
Yet are we god-desiring liturgy,
  Sung joys of adoration ;

Yea, made of chance and all a labouring strife,
 We go charged with a strong flame ;
For as a language Love hath seized on life
  His burning heart to story.

Yea, Love, we are thine, the liturgy of thee,
 Thy thought's golden and glad name,
The mortal conscience of immortal glee,
  Love's zeal in Love's own glory.

778.   *Epilogue*

WHAT shall we do for Love these days ?
 How shall we make an altar-blaze
To smite the horny eyes of men
With the renown of our Heaven,
And to the unbelievers prove
Our service to our dear god, Love ?
What torches shall we lift above
The crowd that pushes through the mire,
To amaze the dark heads with strange fire ?
I should think I were much to blame,
If never I held some fragrant flame

LASCELLES ABERCROMBIE

Above the noises of the world,
And openly 'mid men's hurrying stares,
Worshipt before the sacred fears
That are like flashing curtains furl'd
Across the presence of our Lord Love.

Nay, would that I could fill the gaze
Of the whole earth with some great praise
Made in a marvel for men's eyes,
Some tower of glittering masonries,
Therein such a spirit flourishing
Men should see what my heart can sing :
All that Love hath done to me
Built into stone, a visible glee ;
Marble carried to gleaming height
As moved aloft by inward delight ;
Not as with toil of chisels hewn,
But seeming poised in a mighty tune.
For of all those who have been known
To lodge with our kind host, the sun,
I envy one for just one thing :

In Cordova of the Moors
There dwelt a passion-minded King,
Who set great bands of marble-hewers
To fashion his heart's thanksgiving
In a tall palace, shapen so
All the wondering world might know
The joy he had of his Moorish lass.
His love, that brighter and larger was
Than the starry places, into firm stone
He sent, as if the stone were glass
Fired and into beauty blown.

Solemn

LASCELLES ABERCROMBIE

Solemn and invented gravely
In its bulk the fabric stood,
Even as Love, that trusteth bravely
In its own exceeding good
To be better than the waste
Of time's devices ; grandly spaced,
Seriously the fabric stood.
But over it all a pleasure went
Of carven delicate ornament,
Wreathing up like ravishment,
Mentioning in sculptures twined
The blitheness Love hath in his mind ;
And like delighted senses were
The windows, and the columns there
Made the following sight to ache
As the heart that did them make.
Well I can see that shining song
Flowering there, the upward throng
Of porches, pillars and window'd walls,
Spires like piercing panpipe calls,
Up to the roof's snow-cloud flight ;
All glancing in the Spanish light
White as water of arctic tides,
Save an amber dazzle on sunny sides.
You had said, the radiant sheen
Of that palace might have been
A young god's fantasy, ere he came
His serious worlds and suns to frame ;
Such an immortal passion
Quiver'd among the slim hewn stone.
And in the nights it seem'd a jar
Cut in the substance of a star,
Wherein a wine, that will be pour'd
Some time for feasting Heaven, was stored.

But within this fretted shell,
The wonder of Love made visible,
The King a private gentle mood
There placed, of pleasant quietude.
For right amidst there was a court,
Where always muskèd silences
Listen'd to water and to trees ;
And herbage of all fragrant sort,—
Lavender, lad's-love, rosemary,
Basil, tansy, centaury,—
Was the grass of that orchard, hid
Love's amazements all amid.
Jarring the air with rumour cool,
Small fountains play'd into a pool
With sound as soft as the barley's hiss
When its beard just sprouting is ;
Whence a young stream, that trod on moss,
Prettily rimpled the court across.
And in the pool's clear idleness,
Moving like dreams through happiness,
Shoals of small bright fishes were ;
In and out weed-thickets bent
Perch and carp, and sauntering went
With mounching jaws and eyes a-stare ;
Or on a lotus leaf would crawl
A brinded loach to bask and sprawl,
Tasting the warm sun ere it dipt
Into the water ; but quick as fear
Back his shining brown head slipt
To crouch on the gravel of his lair,
Where the cool'd sunbeams broke in wrack,
Spilt shatter'd gold about his back.

So within that green-veil'd air,

Within

Within that white-wall'd quiet, where
Innocent water thought aloud,—
Childish prattle that must make
The wise sunlight with laughter shake
On the leafage overbow'd,—
Often the King and his love-lass
Let the delicious hours pass.
All the outer world could see
Graved and sawn amazingly
Their love's delighted riotise,
Fixt in marble for all men's eyes;
But only these twain could abide
In the cool peace that withinside
Thrilling desire and passion dwelt;
They only knew the still meaning spelt
By Love's flaming script, which is
God's word written in ecstasies.

  And where is now that palace gone,
All the magical skill'd stone,
All the dreaming towers wrought
By Love as if no more than thought
The unresisting marble was?
How could such a wonder pass?
Ah, it was but built in vain
Against the stupid horns of Rome,
That pusht down into the common loam
The loveliness that shone in Spain.
But we have raised it up again!
A loftier palace, fairer far,
Is ours, and one that fears no war.
Safe in marvellous walls we are;
Wondering sense like builded fires,
High amazement of desires,

Delight and certainty of love,
Closing around, roofing above
Our unapproacht and perfect hour
Within the splendours of love's power.

779.   *Ceremonial Ode Intended for*
            a University

WHEN from Eternity were separate
        The curdled element
And gathered forces, and the world began,—
The Spirit that was shut and darkly blent
Within this being, did the whole distress
With a blind hanker after spaciousness.
Into its wrestle, strictly tied up in Fate
And closely natured, came like an open'd grate
        At last the Mind of Man,
Letting the sky in, and a faculty
To light the cell with lost Eternity.

So commerce with the Infinite was regain'd :
        For upward grew Man's ken
And trode with founded footsteps the grievous fen
Where other life festering and prone remain'd.
With knowledge painfully quarried and hewn fair,
Platforms of lore, and many a hanging stair
Of strong imagination Man has raised
His Wisdom like the watch-towers of a town ;
        That he, though fasten'd down
In law, be with its cruelty not amazed,
But be of outer vastness greatly aware.

This

LASCELLES ABERCROMBIE

This, then, is yours : to build exultingly
    High, and yet more high,
The knowledgeable towers above base wars
And sinful surges reaching up to lay
Dishonouring hands upon your work, and drag
From their uprightness your desires to lag
Among low places with a common gait.
That so Man's mind, not conquer'd by his clay,
    May sit above his fate,
Inhabiting the purpose of the stars,
And trade with his Eternity.

INDEX OF AUTHORS

The references are to the numbers of the poems.

999

INDEX OF AUTHORS

INDEX OF AUTHORS

INDEX OF AUTHORS

INDEX OF AUTHORS

INDEX OF FIRST LINES

INDEX OF FIRST LINES

INDEX OF FIRST LINES

INDEX OF FIRST LINES

INDEX OF FIRST LINES

INDEX OF FIRST LINES

INDEX OF FIRST LINES

INDEX OF FIRST LINES

INDEX OF FIRST LINES

INDEX OF FIRST LINES

INDEX OF FIRST LINES

INDEX OF FIRST LINES

INDEX OF FIRST LINES

INDEX OF FIRST LINES

INDEX OF FIRST LINES

INDEX OF FIRST LINES

INDEX OF FIRST LINES

INDEX OF FIRST LINES

INDEX OF FIRST LINES

PRINTED IN GREAT BRITAIN
AT THE UNIVERSITY PRESS, OXFORD
BY VIVIAN RIDLER
PRINTER TO THE UNIVERSITY